Microsoft Teams Administration Cookbook

Quick Solutions for Administrators in the Modern Workplace

Fabrizio Volpe

Beijing • Boston • Farnham • Sebastopol • Tokyo

Microsoft Teams Administration Cookbook
by Fabrizio Volpe

Published by O'Reilly Media, Inc., 1005 Gravenstein Highway North, Sebastopol, CA 95472.

O'Reilly books may be purchased for educational, business, or sales promotional use. Online editions are also available for most titles (*http://oreilly.com*). For more information, contact our corporate/institutional sales department: 800-998-9938 or *corporate@oreilly.com*.

Acquisitions Editor: Andy Kwan
Development Editor: Corbin Collins
Production Editor: Clare Laylock
Copyeditor: Nicole Taché
Proofreader: Rachel Head
Indexer: nSight, Inc.
Interior Designer: David Futato
Cover Designer: Karen Montgomery
Illustrator: Kate Dullea

September 2023: First Edition

Revision History for the First Edition
2023-08-22: First Release

See *http://oreilly.com/catalog/errata.csp?isbn=9781098133047* for release details.

978-1-098-13304-7

[LSI]

This book is dedicated to my son Federico.
I am always proud of you, and I love the person you are.
I look forward to seeing how you will chart your own path in life.

Table of Contents

Preface

When Microsoft Teams was launched in 2017, the reaction was mixed. Some were optimistic about the new solution; others were busy comparing it to competitors that looked to be ahead of Teams in a specific market. Users' experience with some previous cloud offerings from Microsoft, such as Skype for Business Online, had created some preconceptions (often not positive ones).

Since then, Teams has come a long way in the right direction, covering a lot of ground in a short time, adding features and flexibility, and improving the experience for both users and administrators.

Teams now has a strong position as one of the leading collaboration and communication platforms for businesses and organizations. It is also a welcome "single pane of glass," providing a centralized and unified interface for users to access and manage various collaboration and communication features, all within a single application.

The range of hardware and software dedicated to Teams has evolved, and now anyone who wants to use the product has a wide variety of solutions that integrate with Microsoft 365 services. Even AI is being gradually added as a new ingredient to Teams, and we will surely see plenty of exciting news in the coming months.

Who Should Use This Book

I've tried to capture as much as possible of the current landscape of Teams in this book, ensuring that it provides a comprehensive overview of the information and recipes relevant for a Teams administrator (and, more generally, for all Microsoft 365 administrators who have Teams on their list of competencies).

As an administrator, you play a vital role in managing and optimizing the Teams environment for your organization. The recipes in this book are in a handy format to help you quickly understand and use the features you will manage and deploy.

People who are involved in managing projects that include Teams and adoption experts who are helping companies to adopt a Modern Workplace approach (aimed to optimize collaboration, flexibility, and innovation) can benefit from this book too.

How to Use This Book

I don't assume that the reader has a deep understanding of Microsoft 365 or Teams. If you have some previous experience as an administrator in one of the various Microsoft 365 products (like Teams, Exchange Online, SharePoint Online, and so on), and if you've had some exposure to PowerShell, you will start from a better position when reading some of the recipes. But I do try to explain all the steps without taking anything as a given.

All recipes developed for this book were tested on a demo tenant, with a user having Global Admin permissions. I suggest readers try the contents of the book with a similar arrangement (for example, you should be able to use a demo tenant using the Microsoft 365 Developer Program (*https://oreil.ly/t-yiA*)). As exciting as it is to work with real-world scenarios, testing the recipes and trying to apply them directly to production is not the best approach, due to the risk of errors or mismatches between the results you expect and the results you will achieve. As a more sensible approach, starting with a demo tenant will work better for your mental well-being, sparing you a lot of stress.

In July 2023, Microsoft started the process of renaming all the Azure Active Directory–related services to match with the Entra products family. Some of the changes (that we have already applied to the text) include:

- Azure AD → Microsoft Entra ID
- Azure AD tenant → Microsoft Entra tenant
- Azure AD account → Microsoft Entra account
- Azure AD joined → Microsoft Entra joined
- Azure AD Conditional Access → Microsoft Entra Conditional Access

For more details, see Microsoft's July 2023 announcement (*https://oreil.ly/WWwbn*).

Conventions Used in This Book

The following typographical conventions are used in this book:

Italic
: Indicates new terms, URLs, email addresses, filenames, and file extensions.

`Constant width`
: Used for program listings, as well as within paragraphs to refer to program elements such as variable or function names, databases, data types, environment variables, statements, and keywords.

`Constant width bold`
: Shows commands or other text that should be typed literally by the user.

`Constant width italic`
: Shows text that should be replaced with user-supplied values or by values determined by context.

This element signifies a tip or suggestion.

This element signifies a general note.

This icon indicates a warning or caution.

O'Reilly Online Learning

For almost 40 years, *O'Reilly* (*http://oreilly.com*) has provided technology and business training, knowledge, and insight to help companies succeed.

Our unique network of experts and innovators share their knowledge and expertise through books, articles, conferences, and our online learning platform. O'Reilly's online learning platform gives you on-demand access to live training courses, in-depth learning paths, interactive coding environments, and a vast collection of text and video from O'Reilly and 200+ other publishers. For more information, please visit *http://oreilly.com*.

How to Contact Us

Please address comments and questions concerning this book to the publisher:

O'Reilly Media, Inc.
1005 Gravenstein Highway North
Sebastopol, CA 95472
800-889-8969 (in the United States or Canada)
707-829-7019 (international or local)
707-829-0104 (fax)
support@oreilly.com
https://www.oreilly.com/about/contact.html

We have a web page for this book, where we list errata, examples, and any additional information. You can access this page at *https://oreil.ly/MicrosoftTeamsAdmin*.

For news and information about our books and courses, visit *https://oreilly.com*.

Find us on LinkedIn: *https://linkedin.com/company/oreilly-media*

Follow us on Twitter: *https://twitter.com/oreillymedia*

Watch us on YouTube: *https://youtube.com/oreillymedia*

Acknowledgments

Writing a book is always a demanding experience, even if you have done it before, as I have. While I was writing this book, plenty of events happened to me, both work and personal, so completing this work wasn't something I ever took for granted. I am grateful to my family and to my loved ones for supporting me over so many months with unwavering trust, even when I was not feeling optimistic.

Now, let's talk about the people who helped me in transforming what was just an idea into reality. I will start with Randy Chapman (who contributed Chapter 9 on Teams Meeting Rooms) and Lesley Crook (contributor of the Viva appendix). Their input on these topics, as well-known experts, brings additional value to readers, and I really appreciate their contributions and their availability to be involved with this cookbook.

The quality of this book has been vastly improved by the technical reviews of John A. Cook, Paul Dredge, Amanda Sterner, and Luca Vitali. Without their contribution and expertise, the book would have gaps and inaccuracies. I want to give special recognition to John's work, because he tested and checked every single step and detail, giving me plenty of opportunities to improve the text.

A heartfelt thank you to the O'Reilly team (including Andy Kwan, Corbin Collins, and Clare Laylock). Andy was responsible for putting the whole mechanism into motion and managing the early steps, while Corbin had the unenviable job of dealing with me for more than one year. To both of you, thank you again.

I hope all of you are as proud as I am of the result we have here.

CHAPTER 1
Users and Teams Management

If you use Microsoft Teams, you may have heard this phrase a few times: *Teams is the hub for your teamwork*. That's usually meant to point out the different features and functions that Teams provides to make collaboration as easy and effective as possible. In the context of this book, that phrase reinforces the idea that Teams administration and management incorporate functionalities that used to be in separated silos. Teams is deeply integrated in the Microsoft 365 platform to deliver a seamless user experience.

The logical consequence of this integration is that managing users, groups, and teams often involves administrative tasks that are not specific to Teams. The Teams Admin Center (TAC) and the Teams PowerShell module won't be the only tools you will use to manage Teams.

Throughout the book, I will use *Teams* (with a capital *T*) when I refer to the app and platform, and *teams* (with a lowercase *t*) when talking about grouping people and giving them a channel to work together.

The TAC lets you manage many aspects of Teams within the browser. Policies can be created within the TAC, assigned to users, updated, and removed. The downside, however, is that the TAC does not provide detailed feedback, information, or error handling—especially when performing batch updates. PowerShell provides more details (regular PowerShell error handling and code) and is the best choice to manage multiple tenants or to leverage functions from Microsoft 365 and Microsoft Entra ID at the same time.

With regard to user and team management in Teams, this chapter will introduce some activities that are typically required on an almost daily basis, such as assessing what kinds of licenses you have and what those licenses enable in terms of features and access to different products.

When managing your tenant, there is also a considerable amount of work required to keep Teams manageable and compliant with company standards, including managing the lifecycle of teams and channels. Compliance involves tools that span Microsoft 365. We'll discuss some of the required activities in this chapter, and we'll explore compliance in more detail in Chapter 16.

Finally, one more aspect to consider in the administration of Teams is the interaction with external users accessing your Teams environment from other companies. They are not your users, strictly speaking, but they impact compliance and security, among other things. Chapter 11 explores this topic in detail.

1.1 Reporting the Assigned Office 365 License

Problem

You want to generate a report with a list of available and in-use licenses.

Solution

You will use the Microsoft Graph PowerShell SDK for this solution.

If you have not installed the Graph PowerShell SDK, the Discussion section of this recipe gives you additional information and resources. The solution has been tested with Microsoft.Graph module version 1.21.0. You can check the installed version of the module (if any) using the following command:

```
Get-InstalledModule
```

As a first step, you must identify the required scopes (permissions) for the specific service you want to access. In this solution, the `Get-MgSubscribedSku` command is used to get the list of commercial subscriptions that an organization has acquired:

```
Find-MgGraphCommand -Command Get-MgSubscribedSku | Select -First 1 `
-ExpandProperty Permissions
```

Figure 1-1 shows the output.

```
          Find-MgGraphCommand -command Get-MgSubscribedSku | Select -F
irst 1 -ExpandProperty Permissions

Name                           IsAdmin Description
----                           ------- -----------
Directory.Read.All             True    Read directory data
Directory.ReadWrite.All        True    Read and write directory data
Organization.Read.All          True    Read organization information
Organization.ReadWrite.All     True    Read and write organization infor...
```

Figure 1-1. Permissions required for the `Get-MgSubscribedSku` command

For `Get-MgSubscribedSku`, the required permissions are `Directory.Read.All`, `Directory.ReadWrite.All`, `Organization.Read.All`, and `Organization.ReadWrite.All`.

Graph users must sign in using the `Connect-MgGraph` command, and they must explicitly specify the permissions required for the API they are accessing when issuing the command. `Find-MgGraphCommand` will help you understand which permissions to ask for when you invoke the `Connect-MgGraph` command.

If a user fails to include required permissions when issuing the `Connect-MgGraph` command, and those permissions have not already been granted to the application or to the user, then subsequent commands that access the APIs authorized via those permissions will fail.

The next step is connecting the Graph PowerShell SDK with the correct scope. There could be a multi-factor authentication (MFA) prompt and a request to assign Microsoft Graph PowerShell permissions, depending on your tenant configuration. A successful connection will display the message "Welcome to Microsoft Graph!"

You can assign the scope by running the following command:

```
Connect-MgGraph -Scopes "Directory.Read.All","Directory.ReadWrite.All", `
"Organization.Read.All", "Organization.ReadWrite.All"
```

When you use the `Connect-MgGraph` cmdlet (a small, lightweight command used in PowerShell), the last tenant you signed into during a session will be used by default. If you want to force a specific tenant, the `-TenantId` parameter is required, as in the following example:

```
Connect-MgGraph -TenantId "eab48e2f-746a-4346-bf7f-xxxxxxxxx"
```

To see all the SKUs for a company, use the following command:

```
Get-MgSubscribedSku | select ConsumedUnits,SkuId,SkuPartNumber
```

Figure 1-2 shows the output.

```
Teams_Cookbook>  Get-MgsubscribedSku | select ConsumedUnits,SkuId,SkuPar
tnumber

ConsumedUnits SkuId                                SkuPartNumber
------------- -----                                -------------
            3 f30db892-07e9-47e9-837c-80727f46fd3d FLOW_FREE
            4 0dab259f-bf13-4952-b7f8-7db8f131b28d MCOPSTN1
            3 440eaaa8-b3e0-484b-a8be-62870b9ba70a PHONESYSTEM_VIRTU...
            1 710779e8-3d4a-4c88-adb9-386c958d1fdf TEAMS_EXPLORATORY
           19 184efa21-98c3-4e5d-95ab-d07053a96e67 INFORMATION_PROTE...
```

Figure 1-2. Output including available licensing plans for your organization

SKU stands for stock-keeping unit, but Microsoft uses it to define a specific business product that it sells.

Within each license type, there are also service plans (apps) provided by the license. To enable or disable a service plan, you need to use the `ServicePlanId`. You can view the service plans, included in an SKU, using the following commands:

```
$license = Get-MgSubscribedSku
$license[0].ServicePlans
```

Figure 1-3 shows the `ServicePlanId` view, after running the previous commands.

```
Teams_Cookbook>> $license = Get-MgSubscribedSku
Teams_Cookbook>  $license[0].Serviceplans

AppliesTo ProvisioningStatus ServicePlanId                        ServicePl
                                                                  anName
--------- ------------------ -------------                        ---------
Company   Success            113feb6c-3fe4-4440-bddc-54d774bf0318 EXCHAN...
User      Success            17ab22cd-a0b3-4536-910a-cb6eb12696c0 DYN365...
User      Success            50e68c76-46c6-4674-81f9-75456511b170 FLOW_P...
```

Figure 1-3. Service plans included in the product that corresponds to the first SKU

To visualize a list of assigned SKUs for a single user (for example, *AllanD@M365x01033383.onmicrosoft.com*), use the following command:

```
Get-MgUserLicenseDetail -UserId AllanD@M365x01033383.onmicrosoft.com | fl
```

The `Get-*` cmdlets return objects, which can contain properties that are arrays of values. When you use the pipe symbol (`|`) to forward those objects to the `Format-List` cmdlet, PowerShell only shows you the first four, by default.

Since the results that you see in the previous command are truncated, you can use the `FormatEnumerationLimit` variable to tell PowerShell how many occurrences to include in the formatted output. If you set the variable to -1, PowerShell displays all occurrences (as in the following command):

```
$FormatEnumerationLimit=-1
```

Discussion

If you work with the Graph PowerShell SDK often, it makes sense to have a script to automate the scope assignment for the commands you use most frequently. The following script is just an example; you can save it in a PowerShell script (PS1 file) to execute whenever you need to use the Graph PowerShell SDK:

```
Select-MgProfile -Name "beta"
$scopes = @(
"AuditLog.Read.All",
"Directory.Read.All",
"Directory.ReadWrite.All",
"Group.ReadWrite.All",
"GroupMember.ReadWrite.All",
"Organization.Read.All",
"Organization.ReadWrite.All",
"TeamsApp.ReadWrite.All",
"TeamsAppInstallation.ReadWriteForTeam",
"TeamsAppInstallation.ReadWriteSelfForTeam",
"TeamSettings.ReadWrite.All",
"TeamsTab.ReadWrite.All",
"TeamMember.ReadWrite.All",
"User.Read.All"
)
Connect-MgGraph -Scopes $scopes -TenantId "eab48e2f-746a-4346-bf7f-xxxxxxxxx"
```

You can save this script in a file called *GraphConnect.ps1* and use it in every solution that requires connectivity to Graph.

Microsoft provides services from its cloud (such as Azure and Microsoft 365) based on the licenses that are purchased and assigned to a user. One of the routine activities for Microsoft 365 and Teams administrators is assigning and removing Microsoft licenses, especially because companies prefer to acquire (and pay for) as few licenses as possible and reusing existing ones is a common practice.

In the past, different Microsoft resources—Azure Active Directory (AD) (now Entra ID), Exchange Online (EXO), etc.—had different sets of APIs and were considered to be different endpoints. Microsoft is moving to a different approach, with the goal to connect everything. This new approach is based on Graph exposing REST APIs and client libraries to consume and manage all the different Microsoft cloud services.

Microsoft Graph offers access to:

- Microsoft 365 core services
- Enterprise Mobility + Security services
- Windows services
- Dynamics 365 Business Central services

The basic way to use Graph is via HTTP using *https://graph.microsoft.com*. It is possible to access the Graph REST APIs using an SDK, available in different languages, to simplify building applications that access Graph. One of the supported languages is PowerShell.

The Graph PowerShell SDK is a collection of PowerShell modules that contain commands for calling the Graph service, and it's the one that we are going to use for our recipes.

To install and import the Graph SDK in Windows PowerShell, run the following commands:

```
Install-Module Microsoft.Graph -Scope CurrentUser
Import-Module Microsoft.Graph
```

The import command may produce the following error:

```
Import-Module: Function "XYZ" cannot be created because function capacity 4096 `
has been exceeded for this scope.
```

If that happens, use the following commands to increase the function count and the variable count, and run the `Import-Module` command again:

```
$MaximumFunctionCount = 8192
$MaximumVariableCount = 8192
```

The `-Scope CurrentUser` parameter in PowerShell specifies the current user environment as the target scope for a particular command. When this parameter is specified, the command will only operate on the user environment variables, registry settings, and other elements that are specific to the current user, as opposed to the system-wide environment. This is particularly useful when you do not have full administrative rights on the machine you are using. Throughout the book, the `-Scope` parameter will usually be omitted. The decision of whether to include it or not will depend on the level of access you have to the machine you are using and whether you intend to make changes on a machine-wide or user-specific level.

Prerequisites and additional details about the Graph PowerShell SDK installation are detailed in the Microsoft article "Get started with the Microsoft Graph PowerShell SDK" (*https://oreil.ly/KdP3y*).

Microsoft licensing evolves with the solutions offered in Microsoft 365. Paired with the basic license (for example, an E3 or an E5), there are add-ons that may be required to access specific features, like Public Switched Telephone Network (PSTN) calling or conditional access. A clear understanding of what is included in each plan, what is required to deliver the necessary functionalities, and what you already have is extremely important.

The official Microsoft documentation (*https://oreil.ly/qnaWH*) provides a list of product names and service plans for licensing. The M365Maps website (*https://oreil.ly/MOXJH*) is also a useful (unofficial) guide to the different Microsoft licenses. You can use it as a starting point if you need an overview of the different options.

The information available from the `Get-MgSubscribedSku` command includes the following:

`AccountObjectId`
: The unique ID of the account this SKU belongs to

`AccountSkuId`
: The unique string ID of the account/SKU combination

`ActiveUnits`
: The number of active licenses

`ConsumedUnits`
: The number of licenses consumed

`ServiceStatus`
: The provisioning status of individual services belonging to this SKU

`SkuId`
: The unique ID for the SKU

`SkuPartNumber`
: The part number of this SKU

`SubscriptionIds`
: A list of all subscriptions associated with this SKU (for the purposes of assigning licenses, all subscriptions with the same SKU will be grouped into a single license pool)

`SuspendedUnits`
: The number of suspended licenses (these licenses are not available for assignment)

1.2 Allocating and Removing User Licenses

Problem

You want to assign and remove Office 365 licenses for a Microsoft 365 group.

Solution

In this recipe, you will assign or remove Office 365 E5 licenses to/from a Microsoft 365 group named "Users with Teams Voice."

You can leverage the `SkuPartNumber` information gathered with the cmdlets used in the previous recipe to define which licenses to assign or remove. The license you want to add is `ENTERPRISEPREMIUM`. The license you want to remove is `VISIOCLIENT`.

You must first connect to the Graph PowerShell SDK module:

```
.\GraphConnect.ps1
```

The license information needs to be saved in variables:

```
$ENTERPRISEPREMIUM = Get-MgSubscribedSku -All | where SkuPartNumber -eq `
        "ENTERPRISEPREMIUM"

$VISIOCLIENT = Get-MgSubscribedSku -All | where SkuPartNumber -eq "VISIOCLIENT"
```

A quick check of one of the variables (for example, `$VISIOCLIENT`) will show the information is correctly stored (see Figure 1-4).

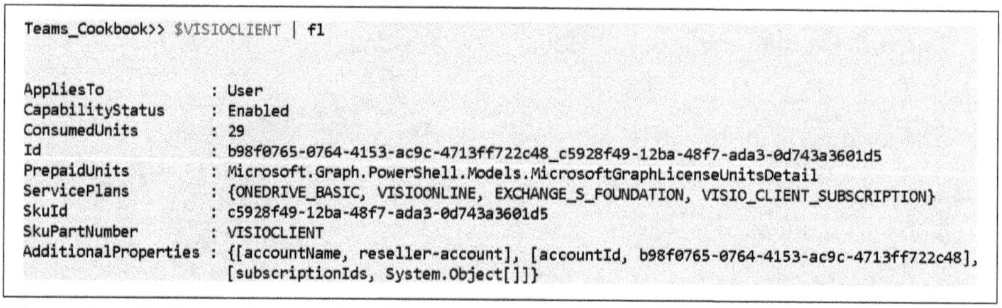

```
Teams_Cookbook>> $VISIOCLIENT | fl


AppliesTo            : User
CapabilityStatus     : Enabled
ConsumedUnits        : 29
Id                   : b98f0765-0764-4153-ac9c-4713ff722c48_c5928f49-12ba-48f7-ada3-0d743a3601d5
PrepaidUnits         : Microsoft.Graph.PowerShell.Models.MicrosoftGraphLicenseUnitsDetail
ServicePlans         : {ONEDRIVE_BASIC, VISIOONLINE, EXCHANGE_S_FOUNDATION, VISIO_CLIENT_SUBSCRIPTION}
SkuId                : c5928f49-12ba-48f7-ada3-0d743a3601d5
SkuPartNumber        : VISIOCLIENT
AdditionalProperties : {[accountName, reseller-account], [accountId, b98f0765-0764-4153-ac9c-4713ff722c48],
                       [subscriptionIds, System.Object[]]}
```

Figure 1-4. Gathering license details

You now need to find the `GroupId` for the group "Users with Teams Voice." The following command searches for the group using a filter (`DisplayName` starting with "Users with Teams Voice") and puts the results in a variable:

```
$Group = Get-MgGroup -Filter "DisplayName eq 'Users with Teams Voice'" `
        -CountVariable CountVar -Top 1 -Sort "DisplayName" -ConsistencyLevel `
        eventual
```

The `GroupId` makes it possible to create a list of the group members. In our case, the parameter we're interested in is the user's email address:

```
Get-MgGroupMember -GroupId $Group.Id | select AdditionalProperties | `
foreach {get-mguser -userid $_.AdditionalProperties.mail}
```

In the previous command, I'm assuming that the user principal name (UPN) and email address are the same. If this is not the case, you must edit the command to match your tenant's naming standard for users.

You can assign a license to all the users in the group with the following command:

```
Get-MgGroupMember -GroupId $Group.Id | select AdditionalProperties | `
foreach {Set-MgUserLicense -UserId $_.AdditionalProperties.mail `
-AddLicenses @{SkuId = $ENTERPRISEPREMIUM.SkuId} -RemoveLicenses @()}
```

You can use the following command to quickly check that the licenses have been assigned:

```
Get-MgGroupMember -GroupId $Group.Id | select AdditionalProperties | foreach `
{Get-MgUserLicenseDetail -UserId $_.AdditionalProperties.mail}
```

The output will look like Figure 1-5.

```
Teams_Cookbook>> Get-MgGroupMember -GroupId $Group.Id | select Additional
Properties | foreach { Get-MgUserLicenseDetail -UserId $_.AdditionalPrope
rties.mail}

Id                                          SkuId
--                                          -----
1nNX3swGWUu3CmPpBrTFT-h5B3FKPYhMrbk4bJWNH98 710779e8-3d4a-4c88-adb9-3...
1nNX3swGWUu3CmPpBrTFTyH6ThjDmF1OlavQcFOpbmc 184efa21-98c3-4e5d-95ab-d...
1nNX3swGWUu3CmPpBrTFT5K4DfPpB-lHg3yAcn9G_T0 f30db892-07e9-47e9-837c-8...
1nNX3swGWUu3CmPpBrTFT-h5B3FKPYhMrbk4bJWNH98 710779e8-3d4a-4c88-adb9-3...
1nNX3swGWUu3CmPpBrTFTyH6ThjDmF1OlavQcFOpbmc 184efa21-98c3-4e5d-95ab-d...
1nNX3swGWUu3CmPpBrTFT58lqw0Tv1JJt_h9uPExso0 0dab259f-bf13-4952-b7f8-7...
1nNX3swGWUu3CmPpBrTFTyH6ThjDmF1OlavQcFOpbmc 184efa21-98c3-4e5d-95ab-d...
1nNX3swGWUu3CmPpBrTFT5K4DfPpB-lHg3yAcn9G_T0 f30db892-07e9-47e9-837c-8...
1nNX3swGWUu3CmPpBrTFTyH6ThjDmF1OlavQcFOpbmc 184efa21-98c3-4e5d-95ab-d...
1nNX3swGWUu3CmPpBrTFTyH6ThjDmF1OlavQcFOpbmc 184efa21-98c3-4e5d-95ab-d...
```

Figure 1-5. Licenses applied to a user group

In a similar way, you can remove licenses:

```
Get-MgGroupMember -GroupId $Group.Id | select AdditionalProperties | foreach `
{Set-MgUserLicense -UserId $_.AdditionalProperties.mail -AddLicenses @() `
-RemoveLicenses $VISIOCLIENT.SkuId}
```

Discussion

Managing licenses and applications based on the joiners, movers, and leavers (JML) process within a company is a task that happens on an almost daily basis. To streamline this process and reduce the risk of errors, you can make use of user groups and PowerShell.

Entra ID is the underlying infrastructure that supports identity management for all Microsoft cloud services. Entra ID stores information about license assignment states for users and automatically manages license modifications when group membership changes. Some key takeaways about this problem's solution are as follows:

- Licenses can be assigned to any security group in Entra ID.
- You can disable one or more service plans inside a specific SKU.
- All Microsoft cloud services that require user-level licensing are supported.
- Users who receive licenses from different groups they are members of will get all the products and services assigned to these different groups.

1.3 Scripting the Creation of Teams

Problem

You want to standardize and streamline the tasks related to teams and channels.

Solution

Create a new team with the following parameters:

- `DisplayName`: "Teams Cookbook"
- `Description`: "Teams Cookbook Information Sharing"
- `Visibility`: Public
- `Owner`: *admin@M365x01033383.onmicrosoft.com*

Then, disable Giphy usage, add a channel, and add members to the team using the "Users with Teams Voice" user group.

Giphy is a third-party source. Its content is not controlled by Microsoft, and there is a risk that inappropriate content may appear. Animated GIFs also add complexity to message compliance controls.

Let's start by connecting to Teams:

```
Import-Module MicrosoftTeams
Connect-MicrosoftTeams
```

The following command will create the team with the required parameters:

```
New-Team -DisplayName "Teams Cookbook" -Description `
"Teams Cookbook Information Sharing" -Visibility Public -Owner `
admin@M365x01033383.onmicrosoft.com
```

You can check the results with the following commands:

```
$team = Get-Team -DisplayName "Teams Cookbook"
$team | fl
```

The output is shown in Figure 1-6.

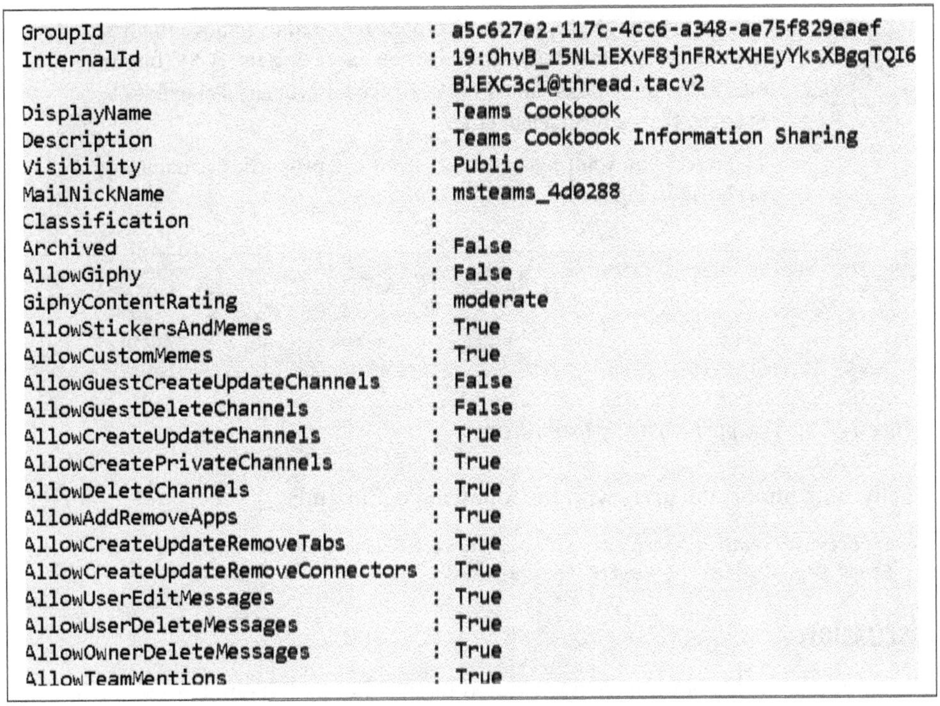

```
GroupId                             : a5c627e2-117c-4cc6-a348-ae75f829eaef
InternalId                          : 19:OhvB_15NLlEXvF8jnFRxtXHEyYksXBgqTQI6
                                      BlEXC3c1@thread.tacv2
DisplayName                         : Teams Cookbook
Description                         : Teams Cookbook Information Sharing
Visibility                          : Public
MailNickName                        : msteams_4d0288
Classification                      :
Archived                            : False
AllowGiphy                          : False
GiphyContentRating                  : moderate
AllowStickersAndMemes               : True
AllowCustomMemes                    : True
AllowGuestCreateUpdateChannels      : False
AllowGuestDeleteChannels            : False
AllowCreateUpdateChannels           : True
AllowCreatePrivateChannels          : True
AllowDeleteChannels                 : True
AllowAddRemoveApps                  : True
AllowCreateUpdateRemoveTabs         : True
AllowCreateUpdateRemoveConnectors   : True
AllowUserEditMessages               : True
AllowUserDeleteMessages             : True
AllowOwnerDeleteMessages            : True
AllowTeamMentions                   : True
```

Figure 1-6. Checking the new team created with PowerShell

Next, disable Giphy usage inside the channel:

```
Set-Team -GroupId $team.GroupId -AllowGiphy $false
```

And add a channel to the team:

```
New-TeamChannel -DisplayName "Teams Cookbook Private Channel" `
-GroupId $team.GroupId -MembershipType Private
```

Connect to the Graph PowerShell SDK and get the `GroupId` using a variable, as in Solution 1.2:

```
.\GraphConnect.ps1

$Group = Get-MgGroup -Filter "startswith(displayName, `
        'Users with Teams Voice')" -CountVariable CountVar -Top 1 -Sort `
        "displayName" -ConsistencyLevel eventual
```

Then list the group members and export the UPN in a comma-separated values (CSV) file:

```
Get-MgGroupMember -GroupId $Group.Id | select AdditionalProperties | foreach `
{Get-MgUser -UserId $_.AdditionalProperties.mail} | Export-Csv `
c:\temp\users.csv -notypeinformation
```

The parameter `-NoTypeInformation` is required to remove the first line that is automatically created when exporting to a CSV file. In our case, that looks like `#TYPE Microsoft.Graph.PowerShell.Models.MicrosoftGraphUser1`.

The result you want instead must show the properties as columns, as shown in Figure 1-7.

LicenseAssignmentStates	LicenseDetails	Mail	MailFolders	MailNickname
		Rexrcll@contoso.com		Rexrcll
		AdeleV@contoso.com		AdeleV
		MarkTJ@contoso.com		MarkTJ

Figure 1-7. CSV export correctly formatted

Finally, bulk import the users with the following command:

```
Import-Csv -Path c:\temp\users.csv | foreach {Add-TeamUser -GroupId `
$team.GroupId -User $_.UserPrincipalName}
```

Discussion

The solutions in this book have been tested using Microsoft Teams PowerShell module version 4.9.3.

You could also use Graph to create a team, using the `New-MgTeam` command. The basic format of the command requires a `Template` and a `DisplayName`. The IDs of the different templates are available inside the TAC (on the Teams tab, under "Team templates," as you can see in Figure 1-8).

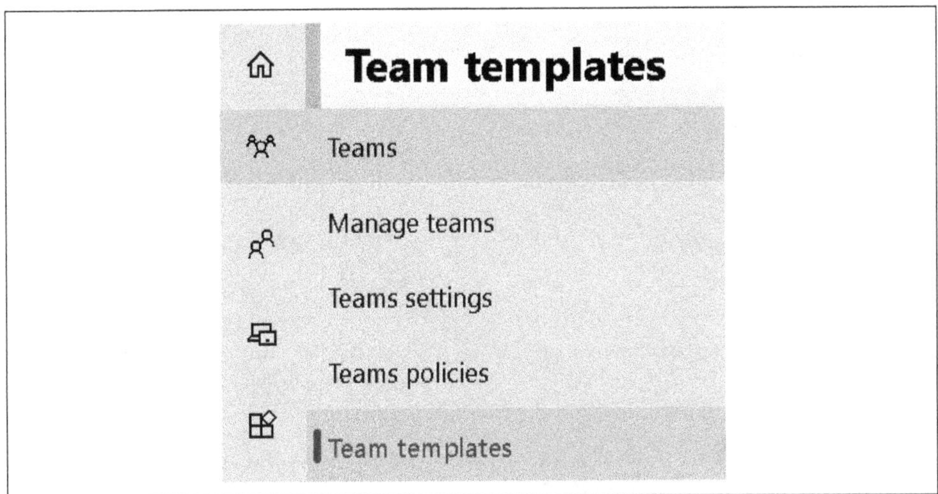

Figure 1-8. Team templates listed in the TAC

Each template has a template ID that is visible in the details of the template. For example, Incident Response has the following template ID:

```
com.microsoft.teams.template.CoordinateIncidentResponse
```

So to create a new team called "Incident Response Team" using the Incident Response template, you could use the following command (in a PS1 file):

```
Using Namespace Microsoft.Graph.PowerShell.Models
[MicrosoftGraphTeam1]@{
Template = [MicrosoftGraphTeamsTemplate]@{
Id = 'com.microsoft.teams.template.CoordinateIncidentResponse'
}
DisplayName = "Incident Response Team"
Description = "Incident Response Team"
} | New-MgTeam
```

1.4 Teams: Creating a Team with Dynamic Membership

Problem

You want to assign membership to a team using a dynamic Microsoft 365 group.

Solution

You can create a team that uses an Entra ID group with dynamic membership to define its own members list. The Discussion section of this recipe talks more about dynamic membership groups. Focusing on the Teams administration part of the solution, you must first log in to a Teams client with your administrative account and select "Join or create a team," and then select "Create a team." Click "From a group or team," as shown in Figure 1-9.

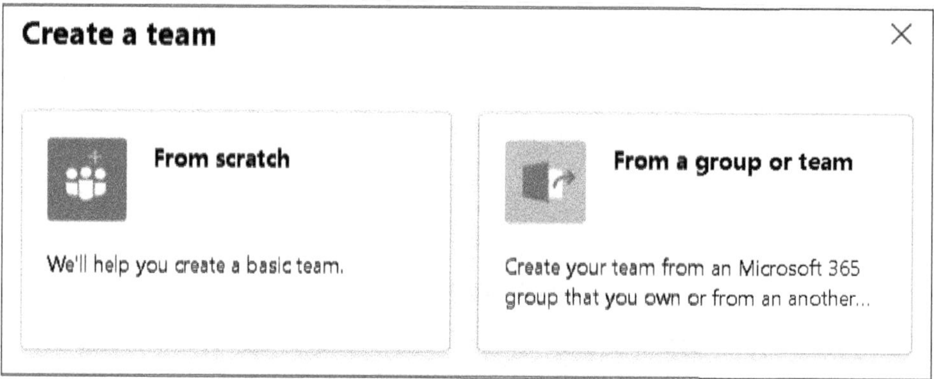

Create a team
From scratch
We'll help you create a basic team.
From a group or team
Create your team from an Microsoft 365 group that you own or from an another...

Figure 1-9. Creating a team from a group

Then, choose "Microsoft 365 group," as shown in Figure 1-10.

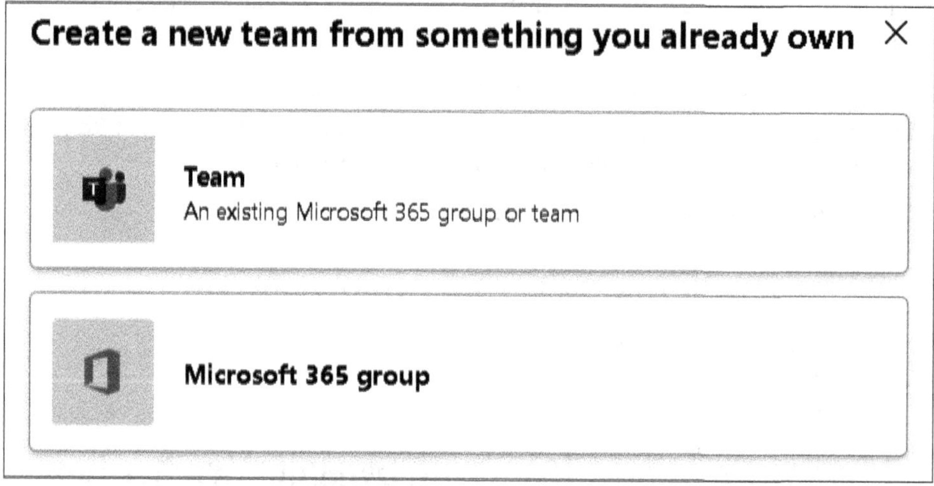

Figure 1-10. Using a Microsoft 365 Group

In our example, the group is called "DynamicGroupTeams" (Figure 1-11).

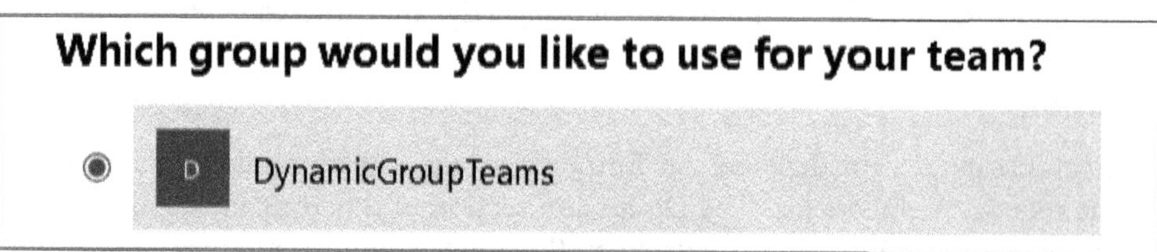

Which group would you like to use for your team?
D
DynamicGroupTeams

Figure 1-11. Selecting the dynamic membership group

Discussion

Microsoft Teams supports teams associated with Microsoft 365 groups with dynamic membership. *Dynamic membership* for Microsoft 365 groups means that the list of the users included in the group (and, as a consequence, in the team) will be created and updated based on one or more rules that check for certain user attributes in Entra ID. Users are automatically added to or removed from the correct groups as user attributes change or as users join and leave the tenant.

Let's quickly define a group with dynamic membership. Our query filters users that have street addresses containing "205" and a state equal to "WA."

First, sign in to the Microsoft Entra admin center (*https://oreil.ly/z2kuq*) with an account that has a role as Global Administrator, Intune Administrator, or User Administrator in the organization.

Search for and select Groups, as shown in Figure 1-12.

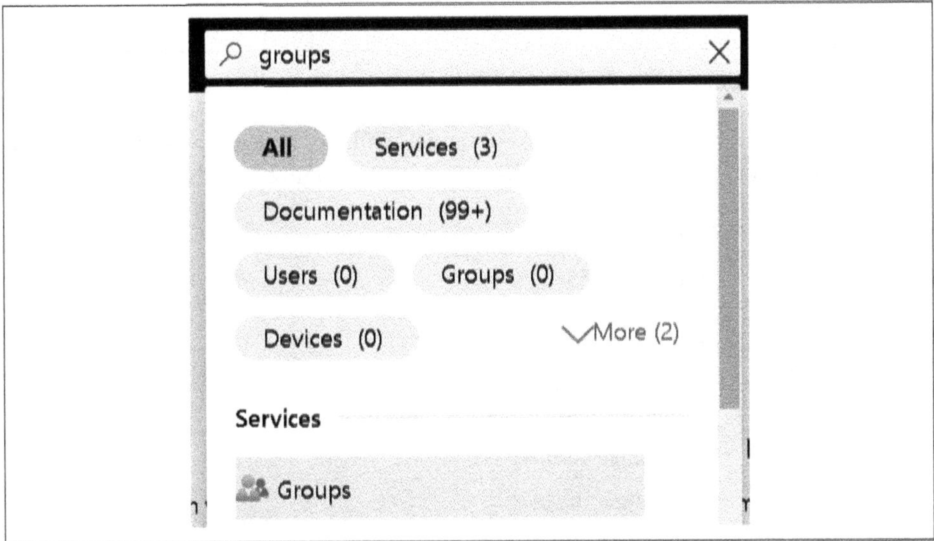

Figure 1-12. Opening the groups management screen in Entra ID

Select "All groups," and then click "New group," as shown in Figure 1-13.

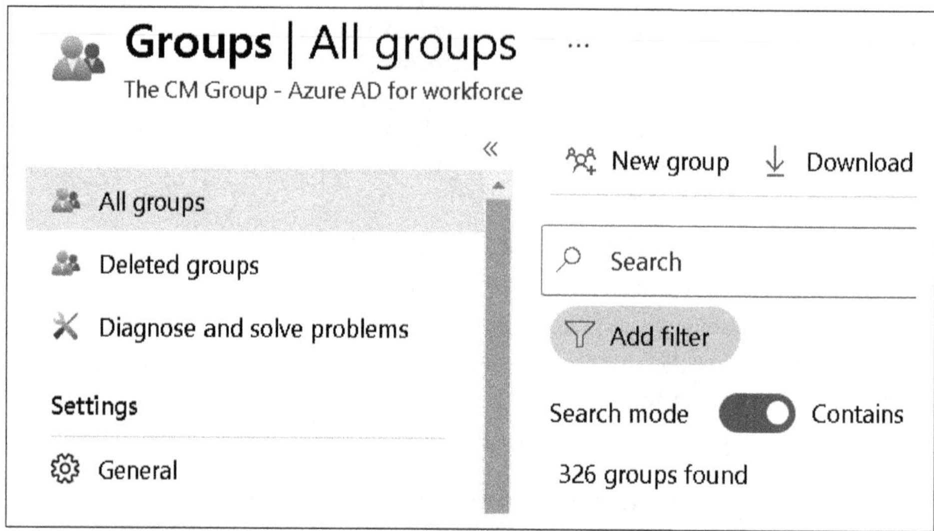

Figure 1-13. Defining a new group in Entra ID

After you select "New group," "Group name" will be DynamicGroupTeams and "Membership type" will be Dynamic User, as shown in Figure 1-14.

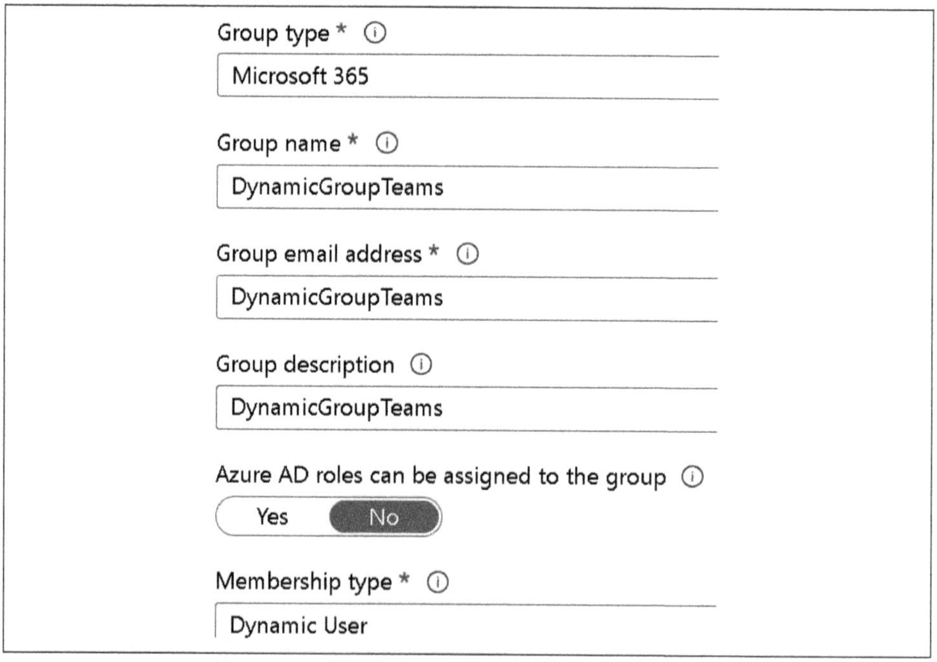

Figure 1-14. Parameters for the dynamic membership group

At the bottom, click "Add dynamic query."

As Figure 1-15 shows, our query will be `(user.streetAddress -contains "205") and (user.state -eq "WA")`.

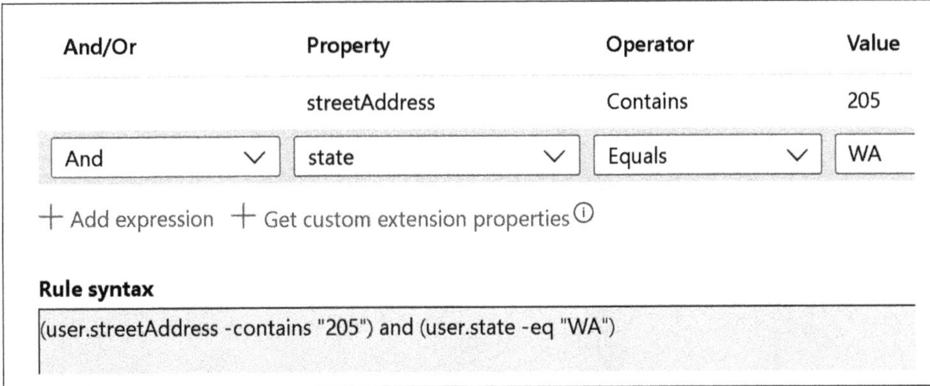

Figure 1-15. Defining the dynamic membership rule

Select Validate Rules to test the query on a few users, as shown in Figure 1-16.

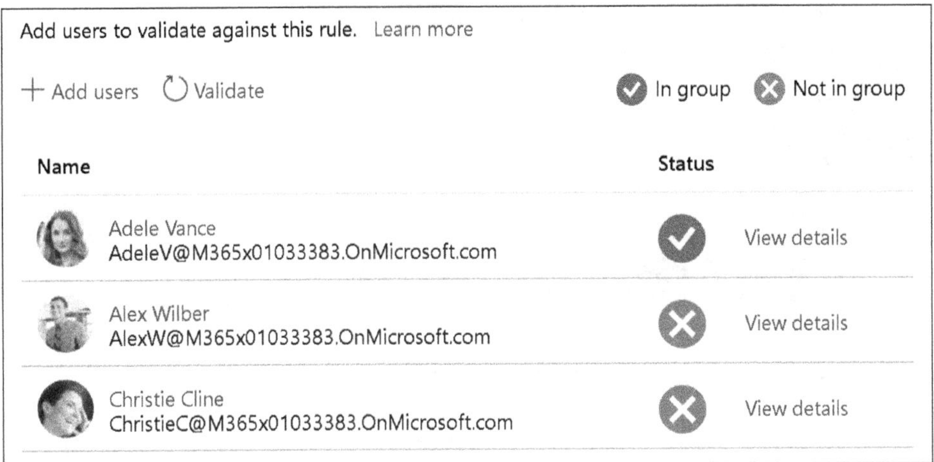

Figure 1-16. Testing the dynamic membership query

Save the query and select Create. For a team with dynamic membership, the capability to add members manually will not be available. Figure 1-17 shows the limited number of options you have for teams with dynamic membership.

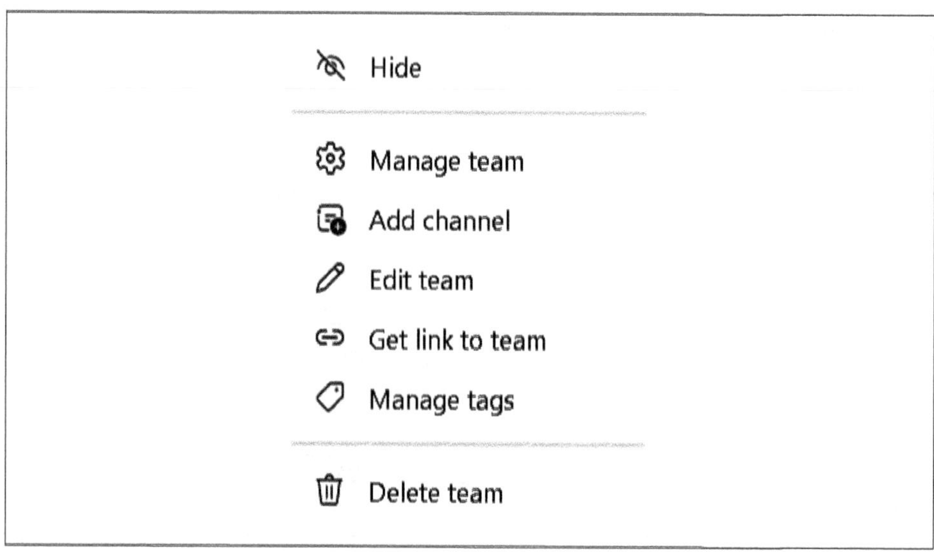

Figure 1-17. Options available for a team with dynamic membership

When you open the Members tab (see Figure 1-18), you will see a disclaimer that the membership settings prevent you from adding or removing members.

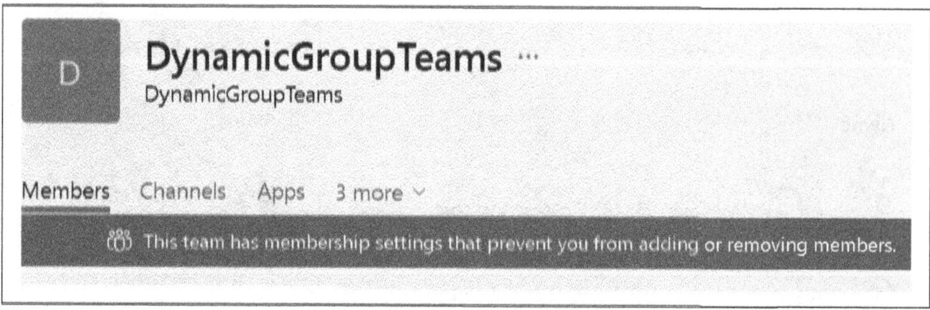

Figure 1-18. Dynamic membership banner on the Members tab

Owners will not be able to add or remove users as members of the team, since members are defined by dynamic membership rules.

The Graph PowerShell SDK offers a command that you can use to create a dynamic Microsoft 365 group: New-MgGroup. For example, if you want to create a new dynamic group called "Dynamic_Group_Created_with_Graph" with the same membership rules that we used earlier, you can use the following command:

```
New-MgGroup -DisplayName "Dynamic_Group_Created_with_Graph" `
-Description "Dynamic Group Created with Graph" `
-MailEnabled:$True -SecurityEnabled:$True -MailNickname `
DynamicGroupGraph -GroupTypes "DynamicMembership", "Unified" `
-MembershipRule "(user.streetAddress -contains ""205"") and `
(user.state -eq ""WA"")" -MembershipRuleProcessingState "On"
```

1.5 Managing Apps in Teams and Channels

Problem

You want to generate a report about the apps installed in a specific team.

Solution

You want to list all the apps installed in a specific team (Sales and Marketing) and gather some additional information about them.

The TAC has tools to manage the permissions related to app installation. However, we cannot see which apps are installed in a specific team. The Teams module for PowerShell does not have a cmdlet to return information about the installed apps, so the best solution is to use the Graph PowerShell SDK.

First, connect to Teams with the usual command:

```
Connect-MicrosoftTeams
```

Then get the team's `GroupId` using the following command:

```
Get-Team -DisplayName "Sales and Marketing"
```

Figure 1-19 shows the output.

```
Teams_Cookbook>  get-team -DisplayName "Sales and Marketing"

GroupId                              DisplayName       Visibility  Arch
                                                                   ived
-------                              -----------       ----------  ----
e5ac9743-4586-426f-a36b-bbe4a72b5802 Sales and Marke... Public      F...
```

Figure 1-19. Gathering team information

Next, connect to the Graph PowerShell SDK module, retrieve the information, and save it in a variable (expanding the properties that we need):

```
.\GraphConnect.ps1

$app_info = Get-MgTeamInstalledApp  -TeamId `
e5ac9743-4586-426f-a36b-bbe4a72b5802 -ExpandProperty TeamsApp,TeamsAppDefinition
```

You can export the list of installed apps in a CSV file:

```
$app_info.TeamsApp | Export-Csv c:\temp\app_info.csv -NoTypeInformation
```

The result will look like Figure 1-20.

AppDefinitions	DisplayName	DistributionMethod	ExternalId	Id
	Activity	store		14d6962d-6eeb-4f48-8890-de55454bb136
	Calling	store		20c3440d-c67e-4420-9f80-0e50c39693df
	Teams	store		2a84919f-59d8-4441-a975-2a8c2643b741
	Saved	store		34b01851-c13d-4604-bb3b-5de1ecbf0288
	Chat	store		86fcd49b-61a2-4701-b771-54728cd291fb
	Search	store		a2da8768-95d5-419e-9441-3b539865b118
	Calendar	store		ef56c0de-36fc-4ef8-b417-3d82ba9d073c
	Power Automate A	store		00001016-de05-492e-9106-4828fc8a8687
	Milestones	store		040880f4-0c68-4c38-8821-d5efd2b6ddbe
	SharePoint Pages	store		0ae35b36-0fd7-422e-805b-d53af1579093
	OneNote	store		0d820ecd-def2-4297-adad-78056cde7c78
	Excel	store		1c256a65-83a6-4b5c-9ccf-78f8afb6f1e8
	Power BI	store		1c4340de-2a85-40e5-8eb0-4f295368978b
	Lists	store		26bc2873-6023-480c-a11b-76b66605ce8c

Figure 1-20. Installed apps in a team

Additional information about the apps is available if we export the app definitions using a command like this one:

```
$app_info.TeamsAppDefinition | Export-Csv c:\temp\TeamsAppDefinition.csv `
-NoTypeInformation
```

We can see an example of an export in Figure 1-21.

AllowedInstallationScopes	Description	AzureAdAppId
	Activity app bar entry.	
	Calling app bar entry.	
	Teams app bar entry.	b55b276d-2b09-4ad2-8de5-f09cf24ffba9
	Saved messages view.	
	Chat app bar entry.	
	Search results view.	
	Meeting invites, updates and re	c9224372-5534-42cb-a48b-8db4f4a3892e
team,personal	Automate time-consuming and	7df0a125-d3be-4c96-aa54-591f83ff541c
team	Plan, track, and prioritize team's	9362bc14-3e81-4ef9-8b77-f1c40afe68e0
team	Add a SharePoint page from you	00000003-0000-0ff1-ce00-000000000000
team,groupChat,personal	Use OneNote to collaborate on	2d4d3d8e-2be3-4bef-9f87-7875a61c29de
team,groupChat,personal	Organize your data in familiar s	1c256a65-83a6-4b5c-9ccf-78f8afb6f1e8

Figure 1-21. Installed apps in a team, including app descriptions

Discussion

The Graph PowerShell SDK is a collection of PowerShell modules that contain commands for calling the Graph service.

The Graph PowerShell SDK is organized into modules that contain related commands and functions. Each module focuses on a specific aspect of Microsoft 365 administration, such as users, groups, SharePoint, or Teams. Modularity allows administrators to load and use only the modules they need, ensuring a lighter and more customized user experience.

The Graph PowerShell SDK complies with Microsoft's security and compliance standards. Administrators can ensure that Microsoft 365 services are secure by using built-in security features and controls. PowerShell scripts and credentials can be secured with MFA, application permissions, and best practices. This helps administrators comply with organizational requirements and maintain a robust security posture.

1.6 Creating User Reports: Active Users and Channels

Problem

You want to export information about all the teams deployed in your organization.

Solution

The script you'll use exports the names of all the teams, as well as the following information for each team: team object ID, team owners, team member count, list of all the team members, number of channels in the team, channel names, SharePoint site, access type, and team guests.

Connect to Teams:

```
Connect-MicrosoftTeams
```

Connect to Exchange Online:

```
Connect-ExchangeOnline -UserPrincipalName admin@domain.com
```

Run the following script (save it in a PS1 file):

```
$AllTeamsInOrg = (Get-Team).GroupID
$TeamList = @()

Foreach ($Team in $AllTeamsInOrg)
{
        $TeamGUID = $Team.ToString()
        $TeamGroup = Get-UnifiedGroup -Identity $Team.ToString()
        $TeamName = (Get-Team | ?{$_.GroupID -eq $Team}).DisplayName
```

```
        $TeamOwner = (Get-TeamUser -GroupId $Team | ?{$_.Role -eq 'Owner'}).User
        $TeamMembers = (Get-TeamUser -GroupId $Team | ?{$_.Role -eq `
                'Member'}).User
        $TeamUserCount = ((Get-TeamUser -GroupId $Team).UserId).Count
        $TeamGuest = (Get-UnifiedGroupLinks -LinkType Members -Identity $Team `
        | ?{$_.Name -Match "#EXT#"}).Name
            if ($TeamGuest -eq $null)
            {
                $TeamGuest = "No Guests in Team"
            }
        $TeamChannels = (Get-TeamChannel -GroupId $Team).DisplayName
                $ChannelCount = (Get-TeamChannel -GroupId $Team).ID.Count
        $TeamList = $TeamList + [PSCustomObject]@{TeamName = $TeamName; `
                TeamObjectID = $TeamGUID; TeamOwners = $TeamOwner -join ', '; `
                TeamMemberCount = $TeamUserCount;TeamMembers = "$TeamMembers"; `
                NoOfChannels = $ChannelCount; ChannelNames = $TeamChannels `
                -join ', '; SharePointSite = $TeamGroup.SharePointSiteURL; `
                AccessType = $TeamGroup.AccessType; TeamGuests = $TeamGuest `
                -join ','}
}

$TeamList | Export-Csv c:\temp\TeamsDatav2.csv -NoTypeInformation
```

Discussion

Using the TAC to generate reports on channels in different teams, team members, team owners, and so on is complex. The Microsoft Teams PowerShell module can display and export the relevant information.

The original script (*https://oreil.ly/GoLDg*) for this solution was published on Microsoft's TechCommunity website. I have modified it slightly to export a list of all members in a team.

You can add any information you want to the export by simply adding a line with the property and an additional parameter to the `$TeamList` variable. For example, let's say you want to see whether a team is archived or not. You can add a line to the following script (I added it after line 9):

```
$TeamArchived = (Get-Team | ?{$_.GroupID -eq $Team}).Archived
```

Then, modify the `$TeamList` variable (the modification is in bold):

```
$TeamList = $TeamList + [PSCustomObject]@{TeamName = $TeamName; `
TeamArchived = $TeamArchived; TeamObjectID = $TeamGUID; `
TeamOwners = $TeamOwner -join ', '; TeamMemberCount = $TeamUserCount; `
TeamMembers = "$TeamMembers"; NoOfChannels = $ChannelCount; ChannelNames = `
$TeamChannels -join ', '; SharePointSite = $TeamGroup.SharePointSiteURL; `
AccessType = $TeamGroup.AccessType; TeamGuests = $TeamGuest -join ','
```

1.7 Reporting Teams User Policies

Problem

You need to verify that the right policies have been applied to your Teams users.

Solution

This script exports a report of all policies for all users who have accounts on Teams.

Start by connecting to Teams:

```
Connect-MicrosoftTeams
```

Then, run the following script (and save it in a PS1 file):

```
$TeamsUsers = Get-CsOnlineUser

$TeamsReport = @()

Foreach ($User in $TeamsUsers) {
    $Info = "" | Select "DisplayName","ObjectId","UserPrincipalName", `
        "SipAddress","Enabled","LineURI","WindowsEmailAddress", `
        "HostedVoiceMail","OnPremEnterpriseVoiceEnabled","OnPremLineURI", `
        "SipProxyAddress","OnlineDialinConferencingPolicy", `
        "TeamsUpgradeEffectiveMode","TeamsUpgradePolicy", `
        "HostingProvider","VoicePolicy","MeetingPolicy",`
        "TeamsMeetingPolicy","TeamsMessagingPolicy","TeamsAppSetupPolicy", `
        "TeamsCallingPolicy","VoicePolicySource","MeetingPolicySource", `
        "TeamsMeetingPolicySource","TeamsMessagingPolicySource", `
        "TeamsAppSetupPolicySource","TeamsCallingPolicySource"

    Write-Host "Querying policy information for" $User.DisplayName `
        -ForegroundColor Green

    $UserPolicies = Get-CsUserPolicyAssignment -Identity $User.SipAddress

    $Info.DisplayName = $User.DisplayName
    $Info.ObjectId = $User.ObjectId
    $Info.UserPrincipalName = $User.UserPrincipalName
    $Info.SipAddress = $User.SipAddress
    $Info.Enabled = $User.Enabled
    $Info.LineURI = $User.LineURI
    $Info.WindowsEmailAddress = $User.WindowsEmailAddress
    $Info.HostedVoiceMail = $User.HostedVoiceMail
    $Info.OnPremEnterpriseVoiceEnabled = $User.OnPremEnterpriseVoiceEnabled
    $Info.OnPremLineURI = $User.OnPremLineURI
    $Info.SipProxyAddress = $User.SipProxyAddress
    $Info.OnlineDialinConferencingPolicy = $User.OnlineDialinConferencingPolicy
    $Info.TeamsUpgradeEffectiveMode = $User.TeamsUpgradeEffectiveMode
    $Info.TeamsUpgradePolicy = $User.TeamsUpgradePolicy
    $Info.HostingProvider = $User.HostingProvider
```

```
    $Info.VoicePolicy = ($UserPolicies | Where-Object {$_.PolicyType -eq `
        "VoicePolicy"}).PolicyName
    $Info.VoicePolicy = (($UserPolicies | Where-Object {$_.PolicyType -eq `
        "VoicePolicy"}).PolicySource).AssignmentType
    $Info.MeetingPolicy = ($UserPolicies | Where-Object {$_.PolicyType -eq `
        "MeetingPolicy"}).PolicyName
    $Info.MeetingPolicySource = (($UserPolicies | Where-Object `
        {$_.PolicyType -eq "MeetingPolicy"}).PolicySource).AssignmentType
    $Info.TeamsMeetingPolicy = ($UserPolicies | Where-Object {$_.PolicyType `
        -eq "TeamsMeetingPolicy"}).PolicyName
    $Info.TeamsMeetingPolicySource = (($UserPolicies | Where-Object `
        {$_.PolicyType -eq "TeamsMeetingPolicy"}).PolicySource).AssignmentType
    $Info.TeamsMessagingPolicy = ($UserPolicies | Where-Object `
        {$_.PolicyType -eq "TeamsMessagingPolicy"}).PolicyName
    $Info.TeamsMessagingPolicySource = (($UserPolicies | Where-Object `
        {$_.PolicyType -eq "TeamsMessagingPolicy"}).PolicySource).AssignmentType
    $Info.TeamsAppSetupPolicy = ($UserPolicies | Where-Object `
        {$_.PolicyType -eq "TeamsAppSetupPolicy"}).PolicyName
    $Info.TeamsAppSetupPolicySource = (($UserPolicies | Where-Object `
        {$_.PolicyType -eq "TeamsAppSetupPolicy"}).PolicySource).AssignmentType
    $Info.TeamsCallingPolicy = ($UserPolicies | Where-Object {$_.PolicyType `
        -eq "TeamsCallingPolicy"}).PolicyName
    $Info.TeamsCallingPolicySource = (($UserPolicies | Where-Object `
        {$_.PolicyType -eq "TeamsCallingPolicy"}).PolicySource).AssignmentType

    $TeamsReport += $Info
    $Info = $null
    }

$TeamsReport | Export-Csv .\TeamsReport.csv -NoTypeInformation
```

Discussion

The basic script (which I have slightly modified) was published on the Microsoft TechCommunity website (*https://oreil.ly/KMM5I*). Removing one or more of the `$info.<parameter>` lines will give you a shorter report if you are focused on a specific group of policies.

1.8 Bulk Assignment of Teams User Policies

Problem

You need to deploy Teams user policies to your organization's users in batches.

Solution

Automating this kind of operation with PowerShell reduces administrative effort and risk of errors. We'll assign a Teams meeting policy (`RestrictedAnonymousNoRecording`) to an Entra ID group whose display name is "Design."

Connect to Teams:

```
Connect-MicrosoftTeams
```

Then connect to the Graph PowerShell SDK and run the following command to get the group information:

```
.\GraphConnect.ps1

$Group = Get-MgGroup -Filter "startswith(displayName, 'Design')"
```

Apply the Teams meeting policy to the group:

```
New-CsGroupPolicyAssignment -GroupId $group.id -PolicyType TeamsMeetingPolicy `
-PolicyName "RestrictedAnonymousNoRecording" -Rank 1
```

Check the result for policies assigned to the group:

```
Get-CsGroupPolicyAssignment -GroupId $group.id
```

Discussion

Assigning policies to Azure AD users and groups is a common task for whoever manages Teams administration. Using Azure AD groups reduces the required maintenance and the risk of assigning incorrect policies to a user. You can also execute this operation from the TAC, but it can be time-consuming.

Additionally, you can check which groups you have assigned a specific policy:

```
Get-CsGroupPolicyAssignment | Where-Object {$_.PolicyName -eq `
"RestrictedAnonymousNoRecording"}
```

You can also remove an assigned policy from a group:

```
Remove-CsGroupPolicyAssignment -PolicyType TeamsMeetingPolicy -GroupId $group.id
```

Group policy assignment supports all policy types used in Teams except:

- Teams App Permission Policy
- Teams Network Roaming Policy
- Teams Emergency Call Routing Policy
- Teams Voice Applications Policy
- Teams Upgrade Policy

1.9 Summary

This chapter provided insight into the various tools and methods that can be used to simplify the daily administration and management of Microsoft Teams. These tools include PowerShell, the Graph PowerShell SDK, and various administrative panels. The scripts and steps discussed in various scenarios are versatile and can be easily adapted or reused to fulfill other administrative needs. In the next chapter, the focus shifts to the security of Teams, highlighting the essential tools and concepts that are necessary to ensure the safety and productivity of Teams users.

CHAPTER 2

Microsoft Teams Security

To understand Microsoft Teams security, let's begin by looking at the Cyber Kill Chain, also known as the Attack Chain or Kill Chain. Developed by Lockheed Martin, the Cyber Kill Chain is a framework that gives a high-level chronological view of the typical malicious intrusion activities popularly known as *hacking*.

The different phases of the Cyber Kill Chain include the following:

Reconnaissance
: The attacker researches their target, and searches for vulnerabilities.

Weaponization
: With a better understanding of the target, the attacker uses or creates attack tools.

Delivery
: The attack tools are introduced into the target environment.

Exploitation
: The tools are activated, enabling the next phase.

Installation
: Backdoors or other control solutions are installed.

Command and Control
: The attacker now has some degree of access toand control over the target environment.

Actions on Objective(s)
: The attacker can perform additional actions to obtain their objectives.

For each step of the Cyber Kill Chain, Microsoft has developed a solution that aims to break the attack sequence, or at least minimize the impact. Figure 2-1 shows a high-level view of the Cyber Kill Chain and Microsoft's defensive solutions for each phase.

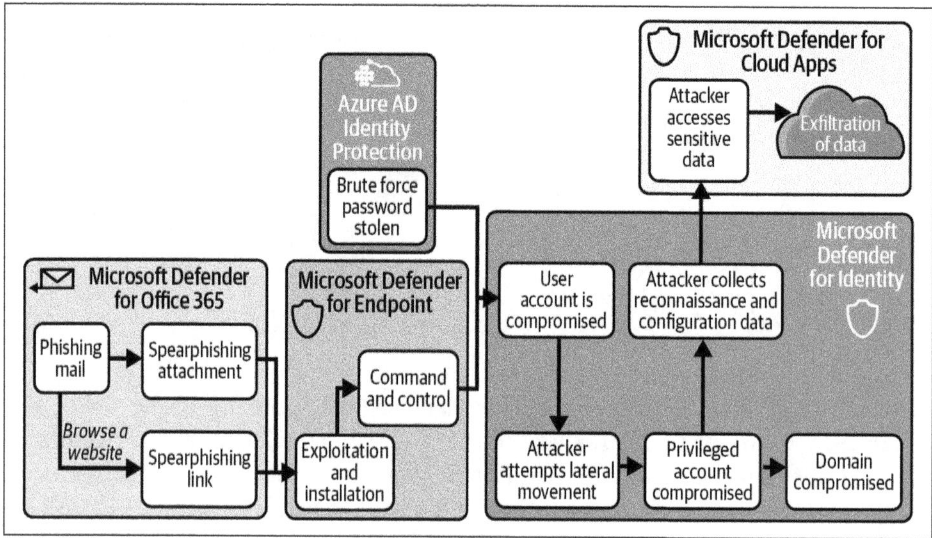

Figure 2-1. Microsoft defenses and the Cyber Kill Chain

Looking at the different stages of the Cyber Kill Chain, we can map Microsoft's various solutions for defense, including (but not limited to):

- Microsoft Defender
- Microsoft Sentinel
- Microsoft Defender for Identity
- Microsoft Defender for Cloud Apps

All of these solutions may be used with Microsoft Teams, and in this chapter, we will investigate the practical utility of a few of them.

There are many resources you can use to understand more about the Cyber Kill Chain and Microsoft Sentinel. I suggest starting with the Microsoft articles "Disrupting the kill chain" (*https://oreil.ly/9MWUX*) and "Advanced multistage attack detection in Microsoft Sentinel" (*https://oreil.ly/LSEb4*).

2.1 Getting Teams Security Insights and Logs with Sentinel

Problem

You want to enable Sentinel to provide insights specific to Microsoft Teams.

Solution

As reliable as your security product may be, it will not detect 100% of threats. To improve the effectiveness of your security (besides optimizing your configuration), you can provide your selected solution the security data specific to your organization.

For example, Microsoft Defender includes automation and incident handling, but to investigate an incident you need the additional capabilities included in Sentinel. With Sentinel, you can gain insights by gathering all security and information logs in a single dashboard.

First, initiate a connection to Exchange Online PowerShell (the dedicated administrative module for PowerShell):

```
Connect-ExchangeOnline
```

To enable Sentinel, you must gather Office 365 logs (also called *auditing*). The following command allows you to check whether the auditing for Office 365 is active:

```
Get-AdminAuditLogConfig | Fl UnifiedAuditLogIngestionEnabled
```

The expected result is as follows:

```
UnifiedAuditLogIngestionEnabled : True
```

If the audit is not enabled, execute the following command:

```
Set-AdminAuditLogConfig -UnifiedAuditLogIngestionEnabled $true
```

Now you must deploy the Office 365 activity log connector for Sentinel. This allows Sentinel to get details of operations executed inside Office 365, including access requests sent and changes to teams and channels. Figure 2-2 shows the Sentinel dashboard (*https://oreil.ly/kmpFE*).

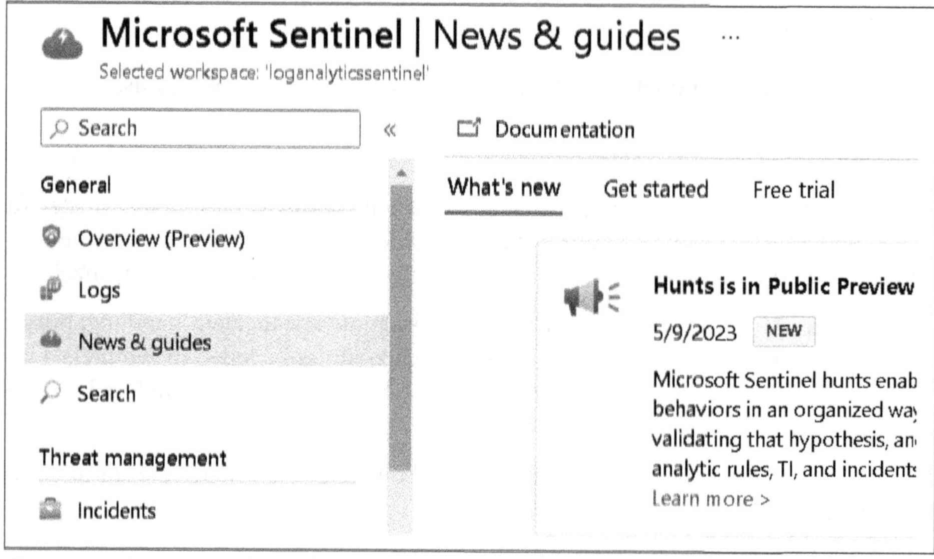

Figure 2-2. The Sentinel dashboard

If you do not have a Sentinel workspace deployed, you will see a "No Microsoft Sentinel workspaces to display" message. Click "Connect workspace" and create a Log Analytics workspace. Once you're back in the Sentinel dashboard, you will be able to add the workspace.

Click the Configuration menu (in the left pane) and select "Data connectors" to see a list of the available connectors. You can apply a filter to search "office 365," then select "Office 365" (as shown in Figure 2-3).

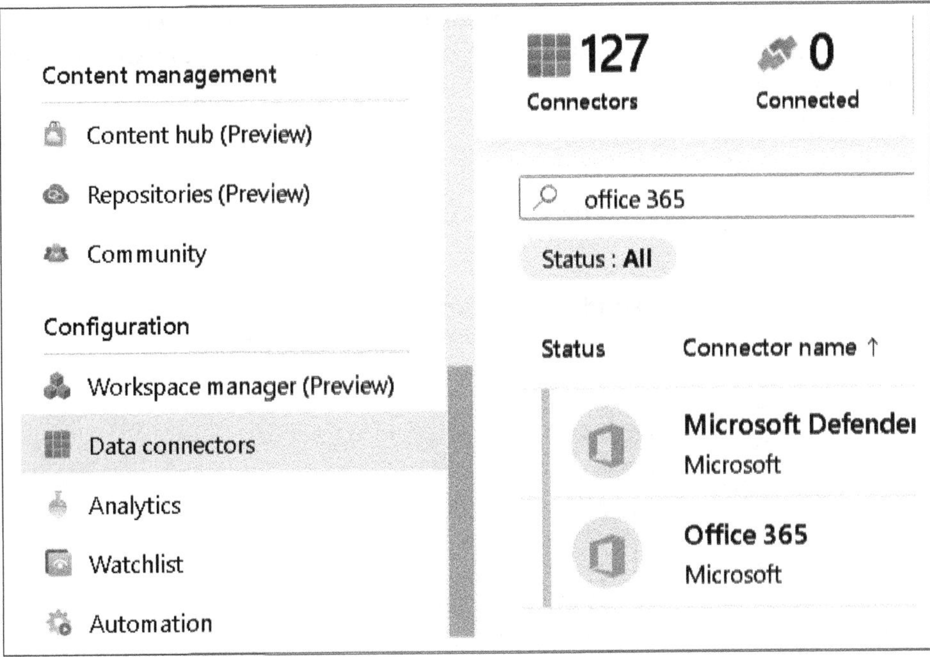

Figure 2-3. Selecting the Office 365 connector from the connector list in Sentinel

In the right pane, select "Open connector page." On the next page, opt to collect only the records for Teams and click Apply Changes, as shown in Figure 2-4.

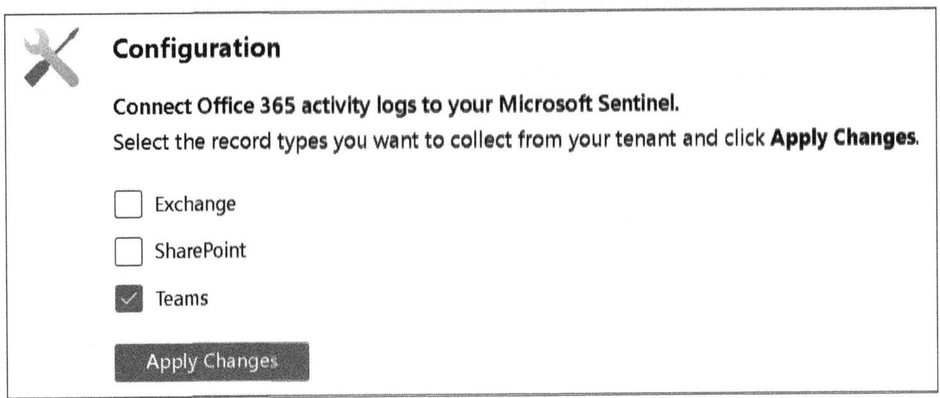

Configuration
Connect Office 365 activity logs to your Microsoft Sentinel.
Select the record types you want to collect from your tenant and click Apply Changes.
Exchange
SharePoint
Teams
Apply Changes

Figure 2-4. Connector settings for Teams

After a short time, Office 365 will be shown as connected (with a green indicator in the dashboard and in the list of connectors). In Figure 2-5, you can see an active Sentinel connector.

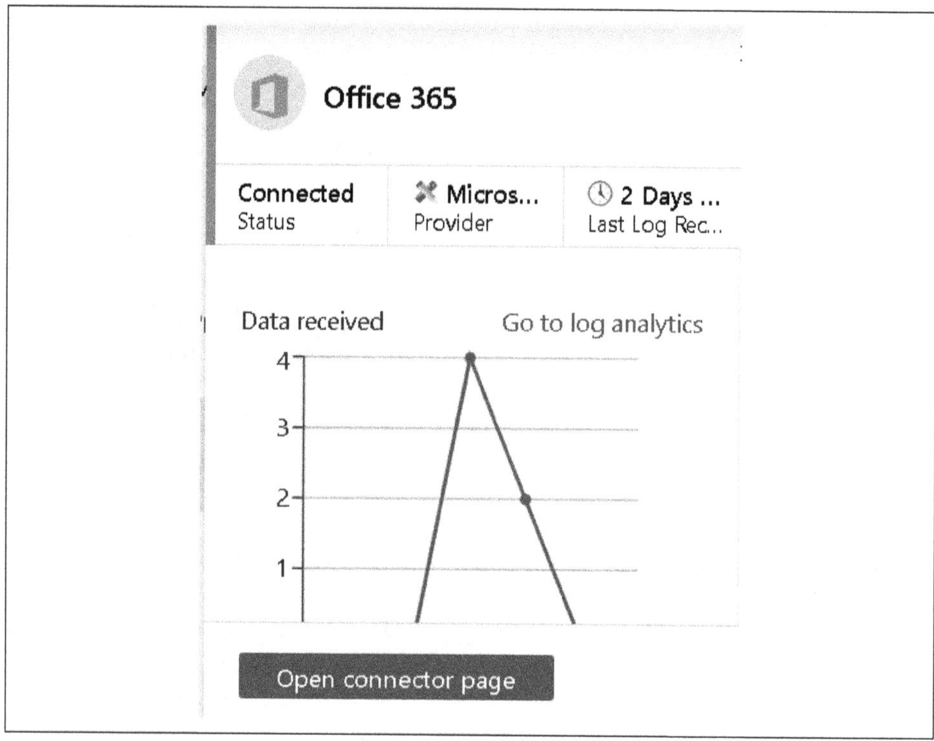

Figure 2-5. Sentinel actively connected to Office 365

Now you can open the Sentinel logs and apply some filters to see if the Teams activities are correctly captured (see Figure 2-6).

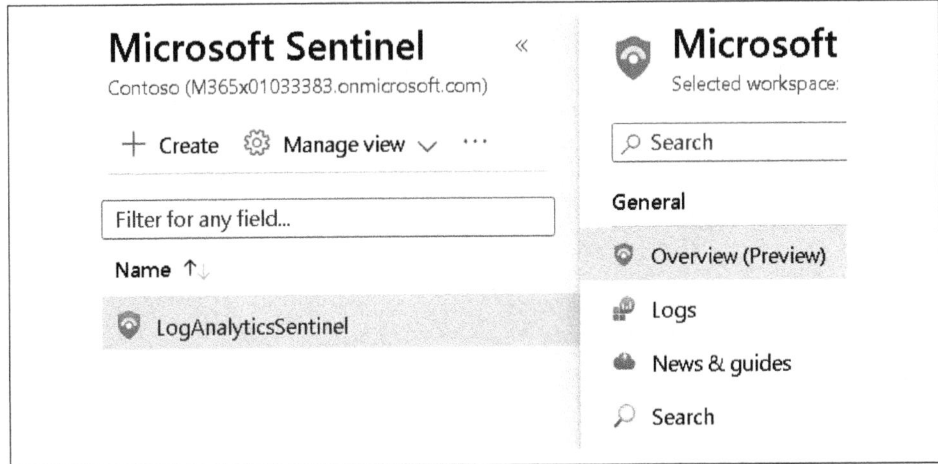

Figure 2-6. Opening the logs in Sentinel

Various filters are useful when you want to see a specific workload or a specific type of activity. An easy filter to apply is the following:

```
OfficeActivity
| where RecordType contains "Teams"
```

Figure 2-7 shows the filtered log.

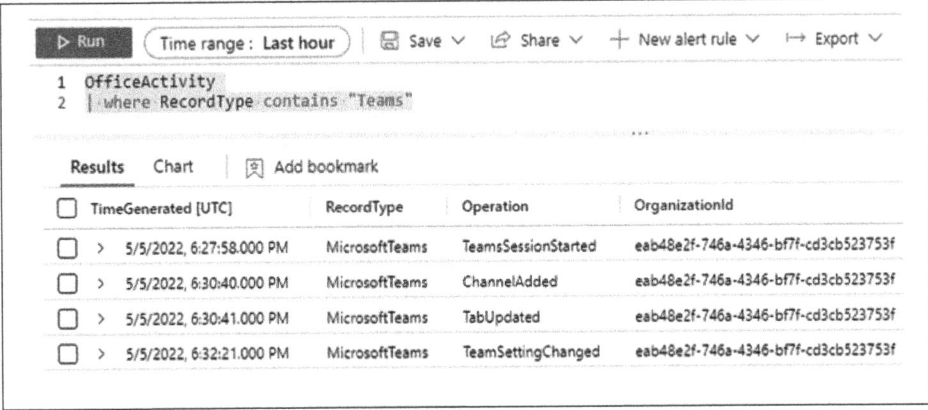

Figure 2-7. Filtering logs containing "Teams" as a keyword

As an alternative example, try the following query, filtering based on the workload name:

```
OfficeActivity
| where OfficeWorkload contains "Teams"
```

Discussion

Sentinel provides workbooks that are meant to make the reading and analysis of its logs easier. The Teams workbook created by the Azure Sentinel Community, for example, is intended to identify the activities on Teams (Figure 2-8).

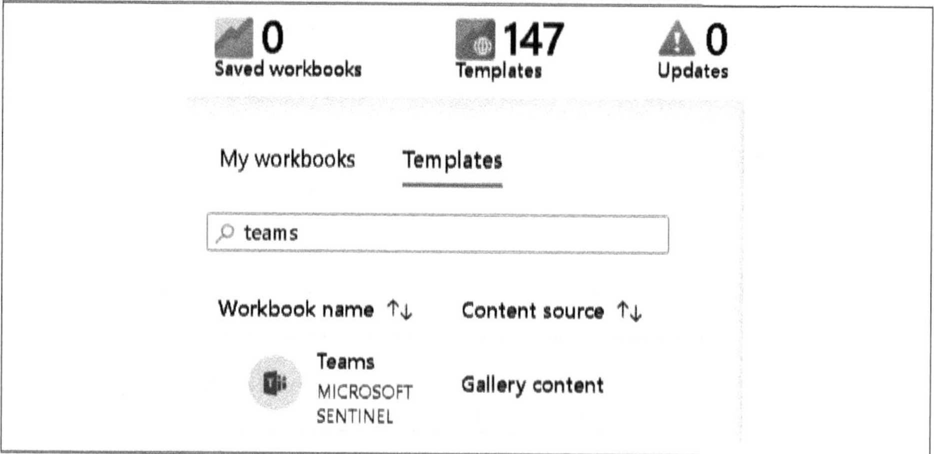

Figure 2-8. Microsoft Teams workbook template

Clicking "View template" lets you analyze a preview of the workbook results in your tenant, as shown in Figure 2-9 (you must select a Subscription and Workplace).

There are a number of prerequisites to using Sentinel, including an active Azure subscription and a running Log Analytics workspace deployed in Azure. The cost of the solution is proportional to the quantity of logs you are going to process.

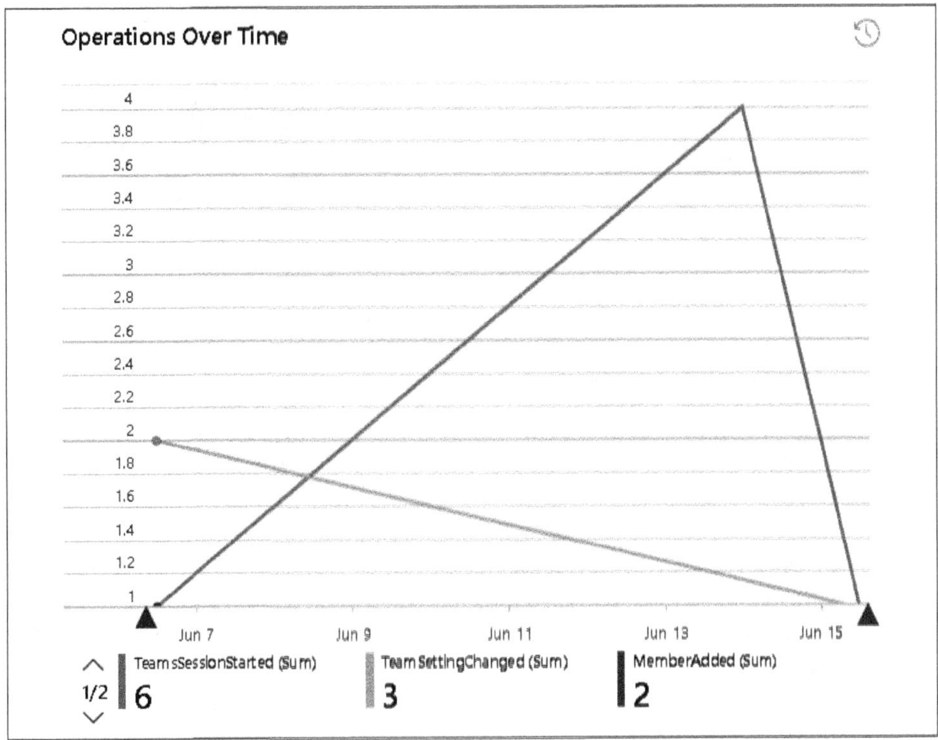

Figure 2-9. The "View template" screen

2.2 Limiting Administrator Rights Allocation with Azure AD Privileged Identity Management

Problem

You want to enforce just-in-time access to critical Teams roles using Privileged Identity Management (PIM).

Solution

Azure AD PIM (*https://oreil.ly/jVyol*) is available in the Microsoft Entra admin center (Figure 2-10).

Manage access
Users with excessive access are vulnerable in the event of account compromise. Ensure your organization manages to least privilege by periodically reviewing, renewing, or extending access to resources.
Manage
Activate just in time
Reduce the potential for lateral movement in the event of account compromise by eliminating persistent access to privileged roles and resources. Enforce just in time access to critical roles with PIM.
Activate

Figure 2-10. PIM dashboard in Entra admin portal

Once in the admin center, select "Azure AD roles," then Roles. You will edit the Teams Communications Administrator role so that no user has the role without an expiration date. Open the role, go to Settings, and then click Edit (in Figure 2-11 we are editing a role).

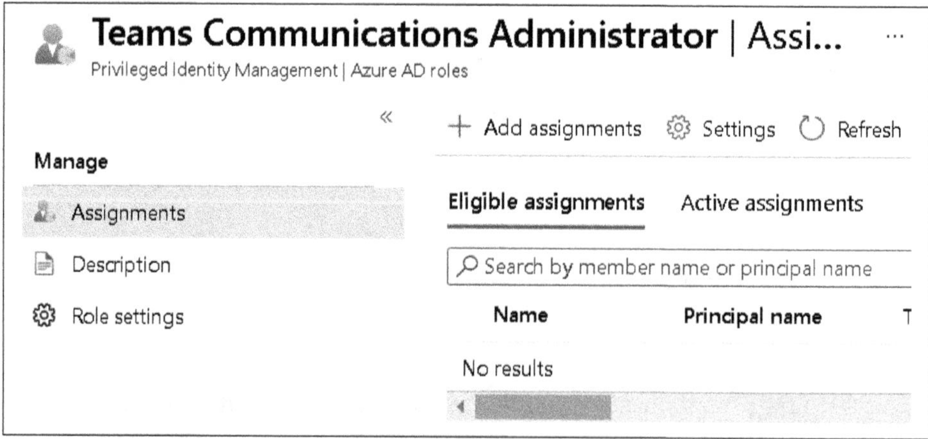

Figure 2-11. Editing a role

We want to establish an approver to accept or refuse requests for this role. In this solution, the approver is the user MOD Administrator. We can establish the approver by clicking on the Settings gear icon and then selecting Edit (the first tab displayed is Activation, as shown in Figure 2-12).

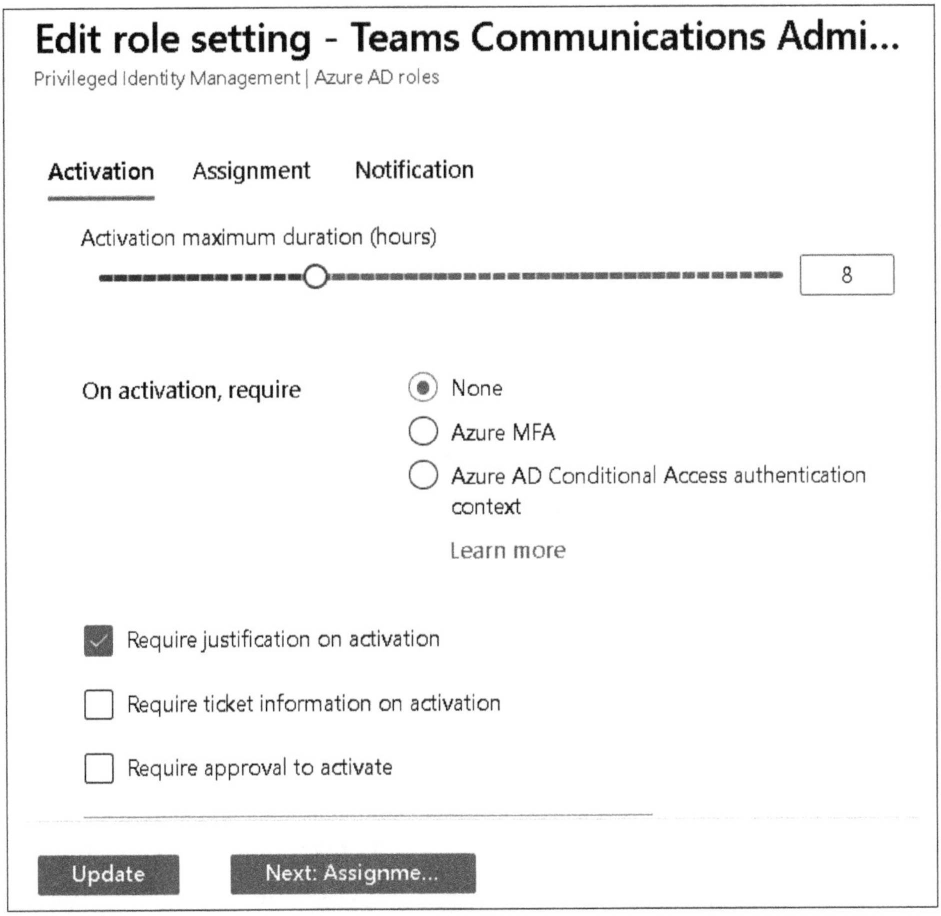

Edit role setting - Teams Communications Admi...
Privileged Identity Management | Azure AD roles
Activation Assignment Notification
Activation maximum duration (hours)
8
On activation, require
None
Azure MFA
Azure AD Conditional Access authentication context
Learn more
Require justification on activation
Require ticket information on activation
Require approval to activate
Update
Next: Assignme...

Figure 2-12. Defining an approver

The parameters you want to change are on the Assignment tab. You want to force an expiration for eligible or active roles (Figure 2-13).

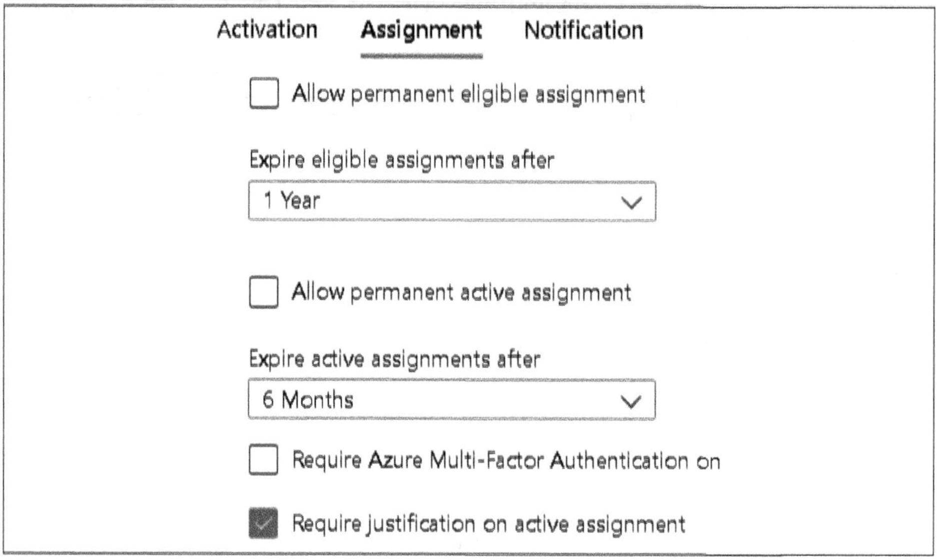

Activation Assignment Notification

Allow permanent eligible assignment

Expire eligible assignments after

1 Year

Allow permanent active assignment

Expire active assignments after

6 Months

Require Azure Multi-Factor Authentication on

Require justification on active assignment

Figure 2-13. Putting time limits on the role

Click Update, then go back to the PIM dashboard and select "Azure AD roles" > Roles. Select the Teams Communications Administrator role and click "Add assignment" (see Figure 2-14 for the assignment screen).

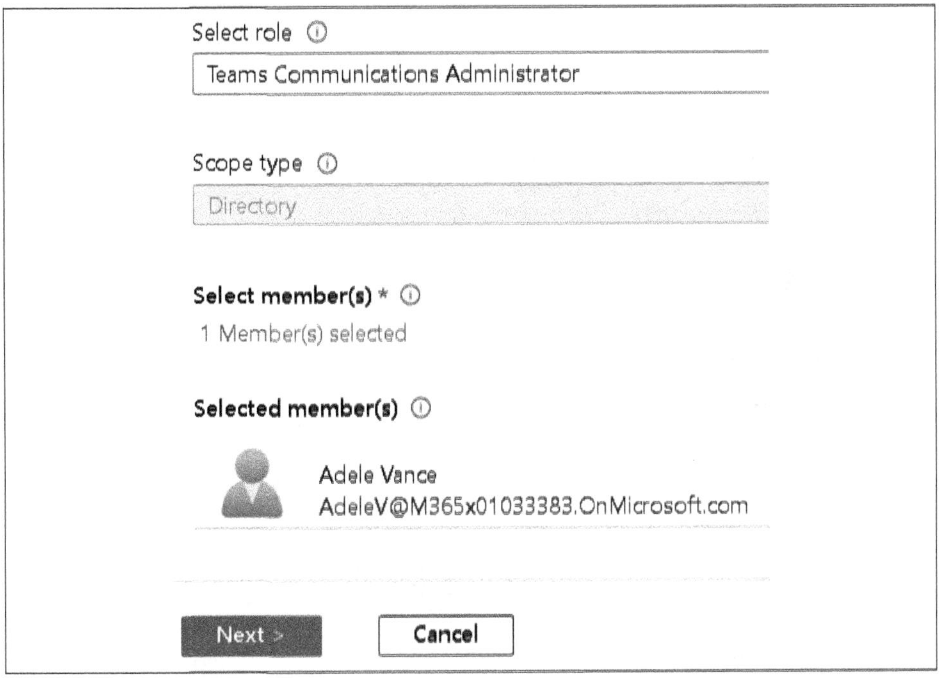

Select role

Teams Communications Administrator

Scope type

Directory

Select member(s) *

1 Member(s) selected

Selected member(s)

Adele Vance
AdeleV@M365x01033383.OnMicrosoft.com

Next >

Cancel

Figure 2-14. Assigning a role to a user

On the Setting tab (see Figure 2-15), you will see the role is now an eligible one with an expiration.

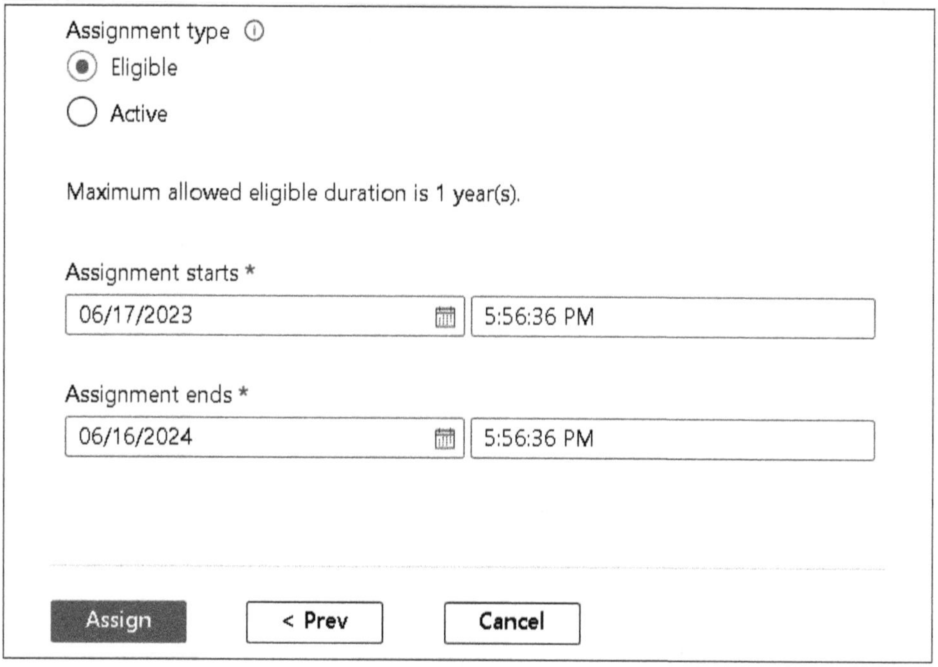

Assignment type ⓘ

(●) Eligible

( ) Active

Maximum allowed eligible duration is 1 year(s).

Assignment starts *

06/17/2023 | 5:56:36 PM

Assignment ends *

06/16/2024 | 5:56:36 PM

Assign | < Prev | Cancel

Figure 2-15. Eligible role with time limitations

Click Assign. Now, if you open the Azure portal for administrator Adele Vance and navigate to PIM, you will see an eligible role that the user can activate (see Figure 2-16).

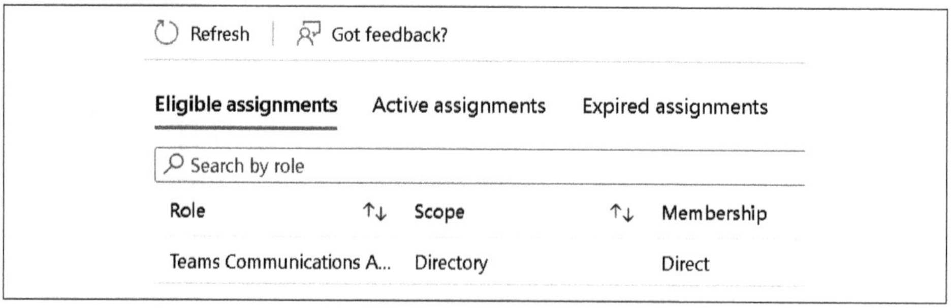

Refresh | Got feedback?

Eligible assignments | Active assignments | Expired assignments

Search by role

Role ↑↓	Scope ↑↓	Membership
Teams Communications A...	Directory	Direct

Figure 2-16. Eligible role available for the selected user

The user will be required to add a justification for the activation request, as shown in Figure 2-17.

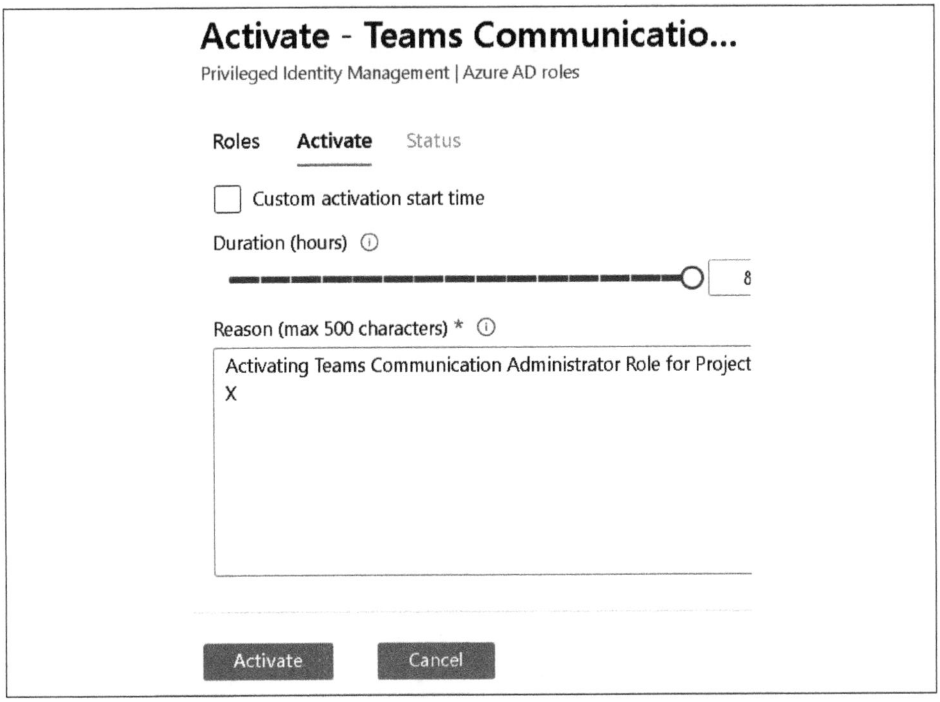

Figure 2-17. Just-in-time permissions request

User Adele will receive a notification about her pending request. The MOD Administrator (shown in Figure 2-18) will have a pending request to be approved. Approving assigns the role and starts the timers for the expiration.

Figure 2-18. MOD Administrator managing pending requests

Discussion

Organizations often have two opposing requirements:

- Minimize the number of people with access to critical configuration and information.
- Allow some users to carry out privileged operations in Microsoft 365.

Just-in-time privileged access to Azure and Azure AD, granted using Azure AD PIM, limits the duration of additional permissions, monitors the usage of those permissions, and reduces the potential for lateral movement (in the event of account compromise) by eliminating an administrator's persistent access to privileged roles and resources.

Having an activation and expiration process like the one described here would make the creation of custom roles (permissions tailored for a specific job with an expiration) even more useful. However, at the time of writing, the process to create custom roles is still extremely limited and does not allow you to apply a portion of the permissions required to perform many administrative tasks.

The licensing for PIM has two different levels:

- There is no specific license required for the users who set up PIM, configure policies, receive alerts, and set up access reviews.
- To perform any of the remaining tasks, a Microsoft Entra ID P2 license is required.

2.3 Blocking Malicious Links in Teams: Safe Links

Problem

You want to block malicious content in Teams.

Solution

As part of securing the user experience in Teams, phishing attacks and malicious URLs are risks being considered. Safe Links in Microsoft Defender for Office 365 scans URLs at the time of click to ensure that users are protected.

Safe Links checks the URL before opening the website. A URL can be blocked, considered malicious, or considered safe. In the first two scenarios, a notification is sent to the user to explain why the link was not opened. If the URL goes to a downloadable file, the file is checked in real time before the user can access it.

Safe Links is managed via the "Threat policies" screen. To access this screen, log in to the Security portal (*https://oreil.ly/1srdN*) and select "Email & collaboration" > "Policies & rules" > "Threat policies" (Figure 2-19).

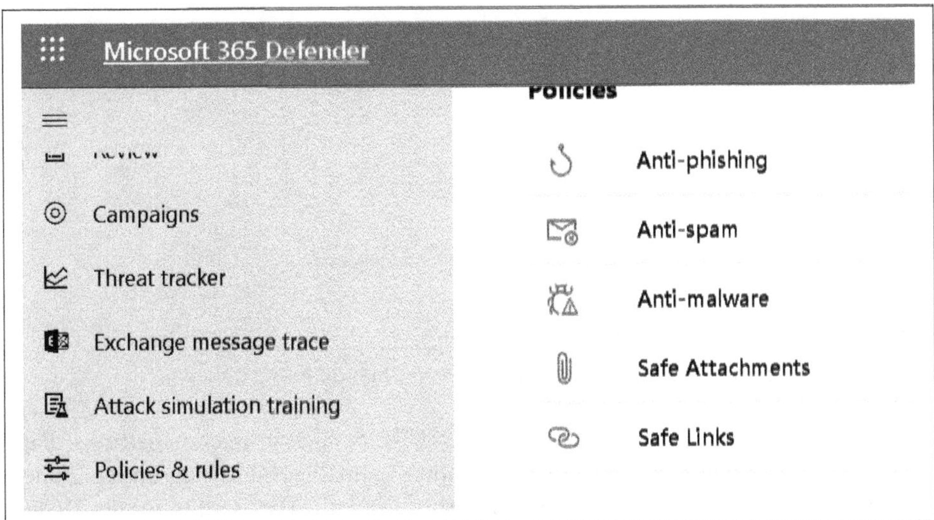

Figure 2-19. Threat policies in Microsoft Defender

Click Safe Links to access the related dashboard (see Figure 2-20).

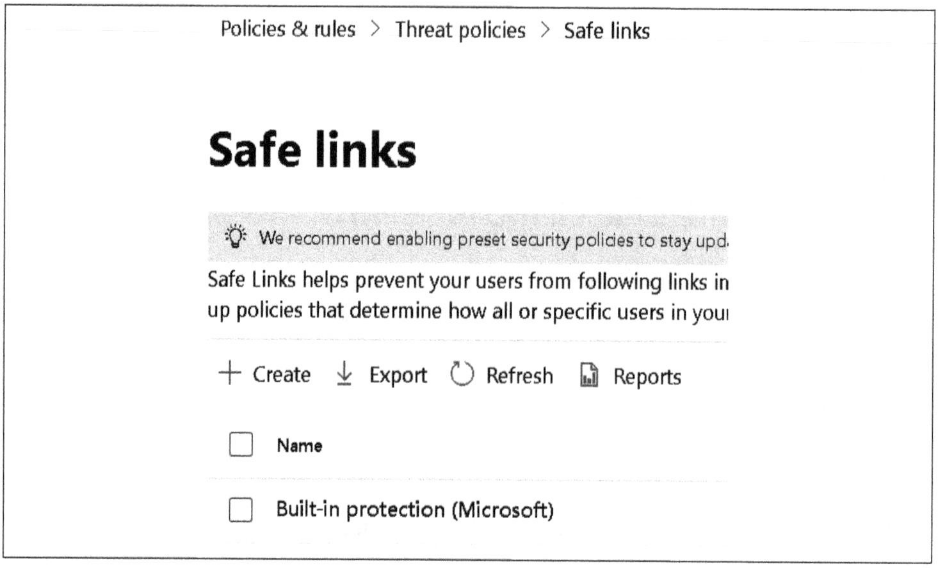

Figure 2-20. Safe Links management interface

Create a new policy, specifically for Teams. Select Create and add a name and description for your policy. Add Users, Groups or Domains as required. In this solution, we'll add the Legal Team (Figure 2-21).

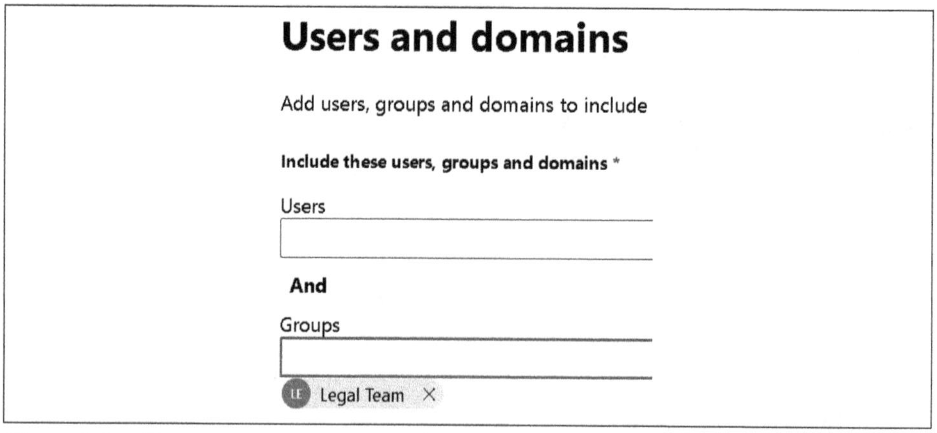

Figure 2-21. Choosing users, groups, or domains to include in the policy

Only a few of the Safe Links options on the "URL & click protection settings" page (Figure 2-22) are relevant to Teams. You'll want to enable the setting under "Action for potentially malicious URLs in Microsoft Teams." The setting under "Click protection settings," which is enabled by default, should stay that way, since tracking user clicks is a valuable practice from an auditing point of view.

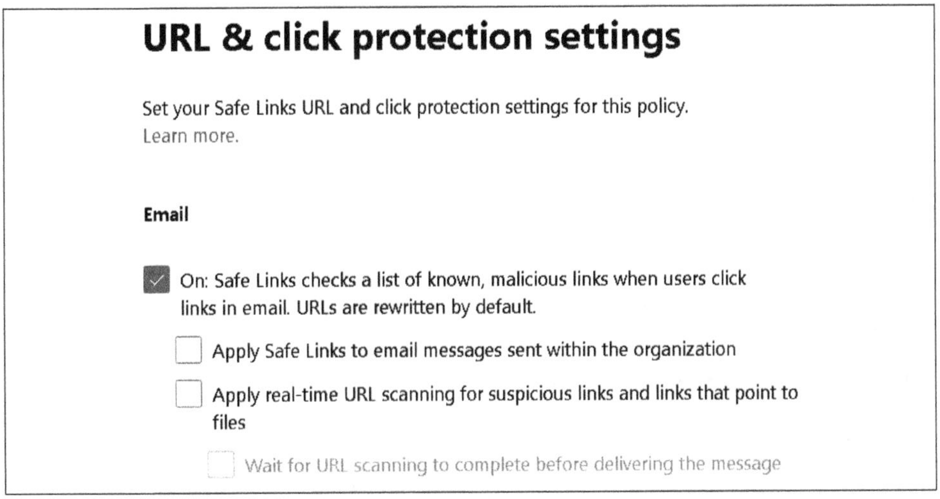

URL & click protection settings

Set your Safe Links URL and click protection settings for this policy.
Learn more.

Email

- [x] On: Safe Links checks a list of known, malicious links when users click links in email. URLs are rewritten by default.
  - [ ] Apply Safe Links to email messages sent within the organization
  - [ ] Apply real-time URL scanning for suspicious links and links that point to files
    - [ ] Wait for URL scanning to complete before delivering the message

Figure 2-22. Safe Links options for Teams

Navigate through the screens that follow (unless you want to add custom notification text) to activate the policy. Users will now get an error notification if they try to access malicious or blocked URLs (Figure 2-23).

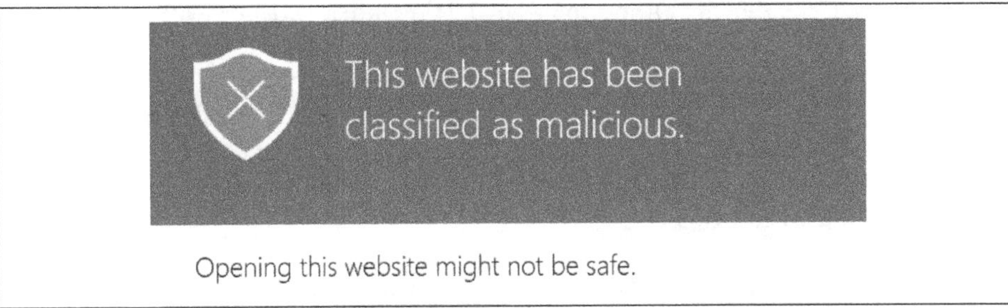

Figure 2-23. Malicious site notification for users

Discussion

URLs in Teams conversations, in group chats, and from channels are checked. When you opened the Safe Links page, you may have noticed the "Built-in protection" description. If you look at the settings for this specific policy (which is the one with the lowest priority) you will see the configuration in Figure 2-24.

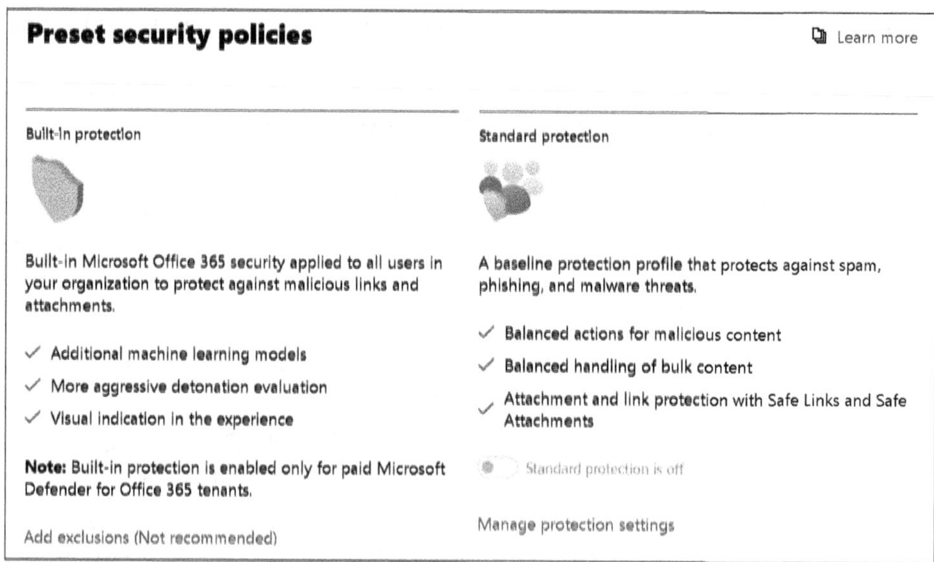

Preset security policies
Learn more
Built-in protection
Built-in Microsoft Office 365 security applied to all users in your organization to protect against malicious links and attachments.
Additional machine learning models
More aggressive detonation evaluation
Visual indication in the experience
Note: Built-in protection is enabled only for paid Microsoft Defender for Office 365 tenants.
Add exclusions (Not recommended)
Standard protection
A baseline protection profile that protects against spam, phishing, and malware threats.
Balanced actions for malicious content
Balanced handling of bulk content
Attachment and link protection with Safe Links and Safe Attachments
Standard protection is off
Manage protection settings

Figure 2-24. Microsoft's preset security policies

Microsoft Defender has two different plans, which include different features and require different licenses: Defender for Office 365 Plan 1 and Defender for Office 365 Plan 2.

- Microsoft Defender for Office 365 Plan 1 is included in Microsoft 365 Business Premium.
- Microsoft Defender for Office 365 Plan 2 is included in Office 365 E5, Office 365 A5, and Microsoft 365 E5.
- Microsoft Defender for Office 365 Plan 1 and Defender for Office 365 Plan 2 are also available as add-ons.

Safe Links is included in both Plans 1 and 2, as shown in Figure 2-25.

When you enable or disable Safe Links protection for Teams, it may take up to 24 hours for the change to take effect.

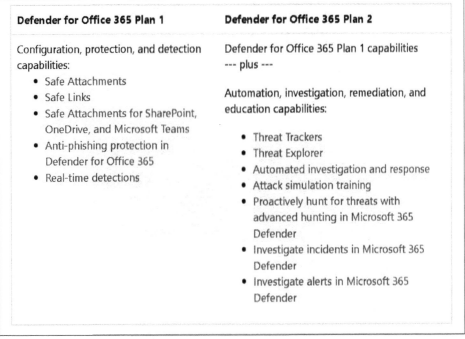

Defender for Office 365 Plan 1	Defender for Office 365 Plan 2
Configuration, protection, and detection capabilities: • Safe Attachments • Safe Links • Safe Attachments for SharePoint, OneDrive, and Microsoft Teams • Anti-phishing protection in Defender for Office 365 • Real-time detections	Defender for Office 365 Plan 1 capabilities --- plus --- Automation, investigation, remediation, and education capabilities: • Threat Trackers • Threat Explorer • Automated investigation and response • Attack simulation training • Proactively hunt for threats with advanced hunting in Microsoft 365 Defender • Investigate incidents in Microsoft 365 Defender • Investigate alerts in Microsoft 365 Defender

Figure 2-25. Comparing Defender for Office 365 Plan 1 and Plan 2

2.4 Blocking and Allowing Teams Apps with App Control

Problem

You want to block specific apps in your organization.

Solution

By default, Teams allows the installation of more than 1,000 apps. This may sound great for facilitating the work of your users and collaboration, but every security flaw in an app potentially exposes your organization, too. The TAC has dedicated tools to control the permissions on these apps. If the global (organization-wide) policy is quite broad, you can assign apps in Teams in a way that is relevant to the user role and requirement.

App management is performed inside the TAC. Open the TAC and navigate to "Teams apps" > "Manage apps." Figure 2-26 shows part of the "Manage apps" screen.

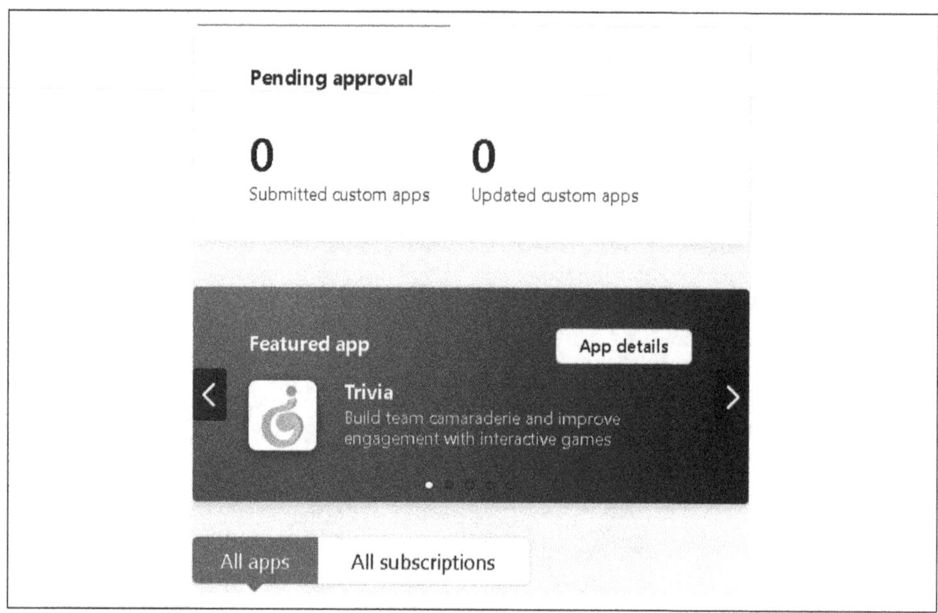

Figure 2-26. Teams app management

In this recipe, we want to allow MailChimp app installation only for the Contoso Marketing group. The first step is to navigate to "Permission policies" in the left pane and block the MailChimp app in the global policy (Figure 2-27).

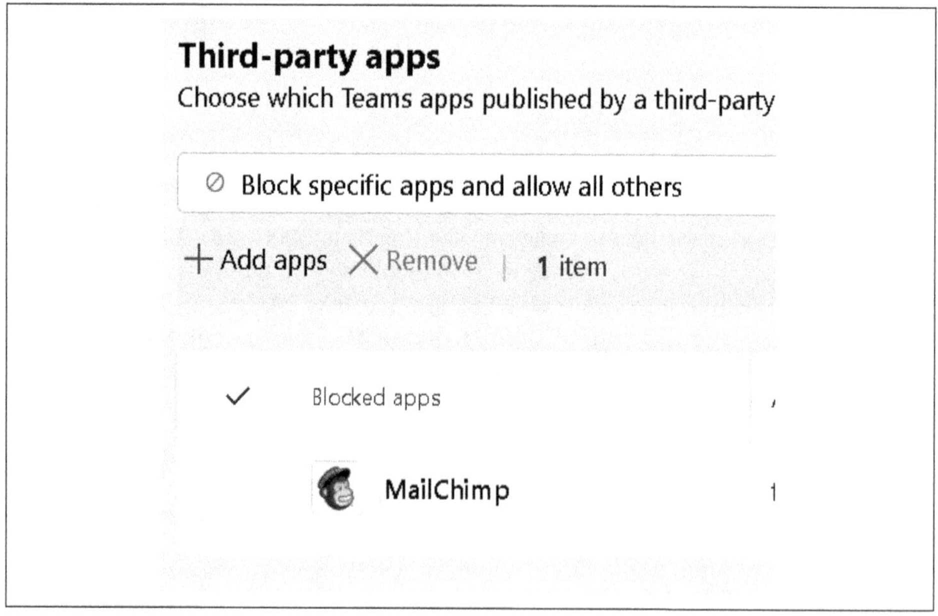

Figure 2-27. Blocking a third-party app

Save the policy. You must now define a second policy (let's call it *Allow MailChimp*) to allow the installation of the app.

Finally, you must apply the new policy to the Contoso Marketing group. As you saw in Chapter 1, you must first connect to Entra ID and gather the group information:

```
Connect-AzureAD
$Group = Get-AzureADGroup -SearchString "Contoso marketing"
```

You can now export the list of users in the group:

```
Get-AzureADGroupMember -ObjectId $Group.ObjectId | select UserPrincipalName `
| Export-Csv c:\temp\AppPolicyUsers.csv
```

Finally, apply the policy to all the users in the group:

```
Import-Csv -Path c:\temp\AppPolicyUsers.csv | foreach `
{Grant-CsTeamsAppPermissionPolicy -PolicyName "Allow MailChimp"}
```

Discussion

The TAC interface, at the time of writing, does not let you apply an app permission policy to a group of users.

Apps are divided into three macro categories:

First-party (Microsoft) apps
: Microsoft validates the basic functionality, usability, and security of its own apps.

Third-party apps
: These aren't controlled or owned by Microsoft and aren't governed by the Microsoft Online Subscription Agreement.

Custom apps
: Users can add a custom app (built specifically for your organization) to Teams by uploading an app package (called *sideloading*). Microsoft gives no warranty about the security or behavior of apps in this category.

2.5 Regulating Access to Teams with Conditional Access

Problem

You want to define access policies based on user, device, location, application, and session risk information.

Solution

The capability Microsoft 365 (and specifically Teams) offers to work from any device or location, and to collaborate easily with people external to the organization, brings plenty of positive benefits. However, you must also consider the risks of users connecting from their own devices and bypassing your security controls and compliance checks.

Microsoft 365 includes a solution called Conditional Access that defines access policies based on user, device, location, application, and even session risk information. This solution gives you more control as a Teams administrator.

To implement a Conditional Access policy, first open the Microsoft Entra admin center. Navigate to "All services" and search for Conditional Access (*https://oreil.ly/SenCc*). Click "New policy." The policy you define will be applied to a specific group (Legal Team, in our case). Figure 2-28 shows a user defining a new Conditional Access policy.

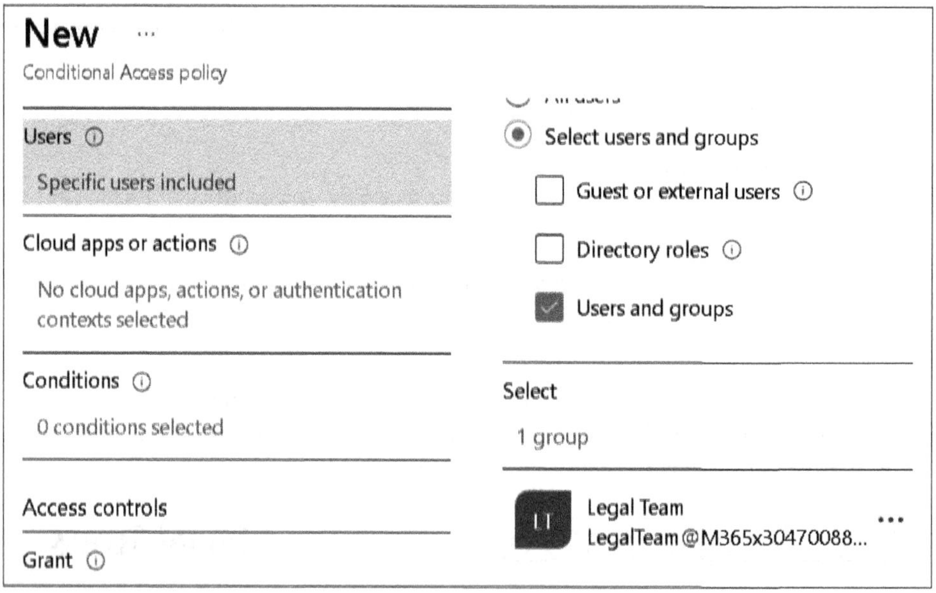

Figure 2-28. Defining a new Conditional Access policy

The Conditional Access policy will be applied only to the Teams app (shown in the "Cloud apps or actions" field in Figure 2-29).

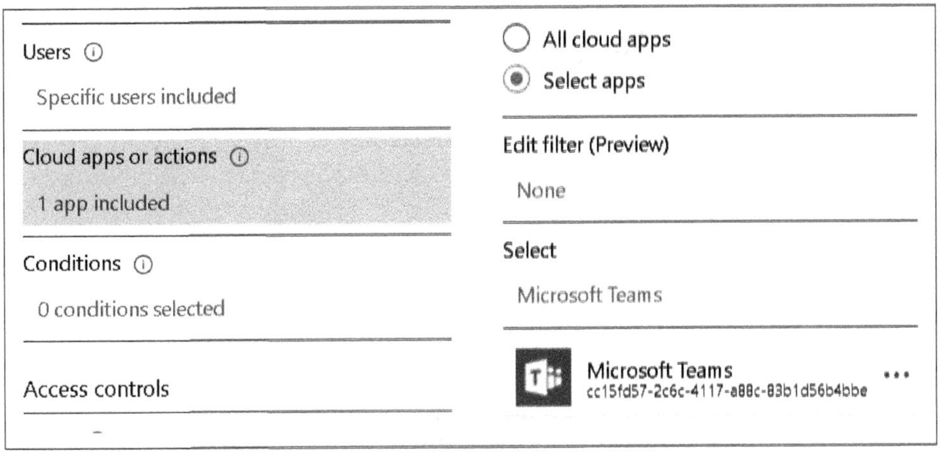

Figure 2-29. Applying the policy to the Teams app

In our scenario (see Figure 2-30), we are going to block users who are likely to have been compromised and any logins that present a high risk factor (on the Conditions screen).

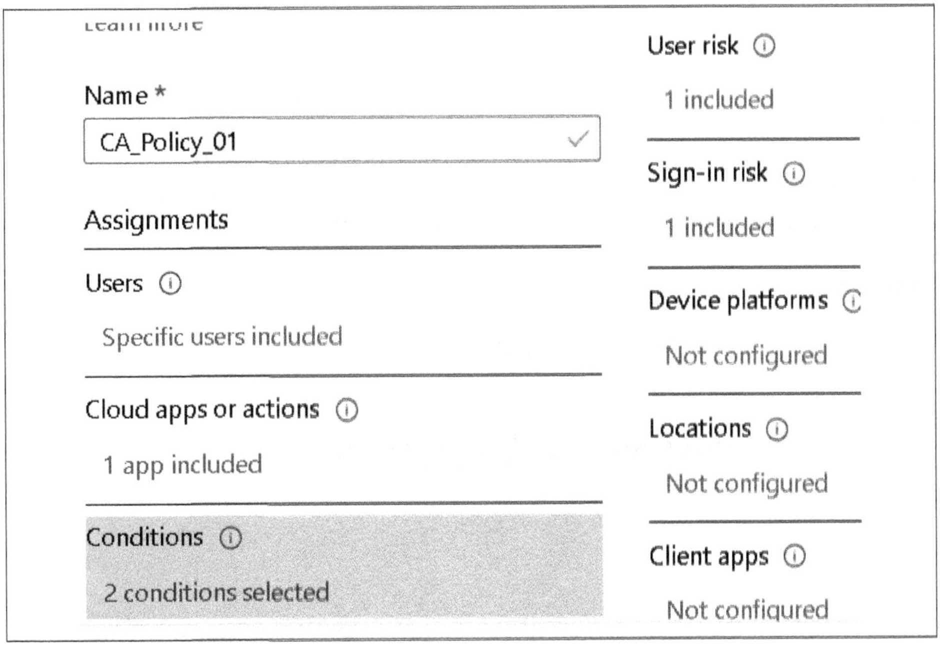

Figure 2-30. The policy will be activated by user risks and login risks

If one of the conditions (risks) is present, we will grant access only if multi-factor authentication (MFA) is used, as shown in Figure 2-31.

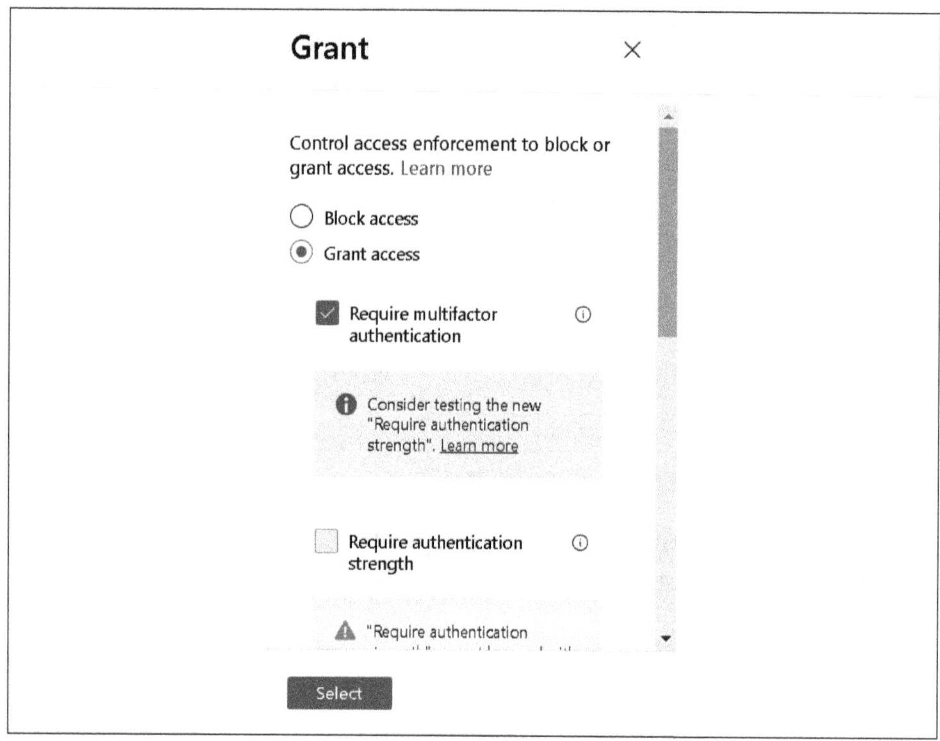

Figure 2-31. Requiring MFA for users signaled as a risk

The policy can be "Report-only" for the testing phase and be activated when you are confident it is not going to interfere with normal operations.

Discussion

This solution used risk factors to trigger other sign-in protections (MFA), instead of blocking access altogether.

2.6 Limiting the Domains Accepted for User Logins to Teams

Problem

You need to limit Teams access from the desktop app to a list of approved tenants.

Solution

One of the capabilities of Teams is to allow login to different tenants from the same client. When the user switches tenants, it exposes the rest of your deployment to risks because the policies and rules for another company may not be compliant with your requirements.

For managed devices running Windows (with Windows 7 as a minimum version), you can use Microsoft Endpoint Manager (MEM) policies to control the accounts that can be used in Teams. Users will only be allowed to sign in with accounts from Entra ID tenants that you specify.

First, open the Microsoft Endpoint Manager admin center (*https://oreil.ly/3Q4Cq*). Select Apps > "Policies for Office apps" (Figure 2-32).

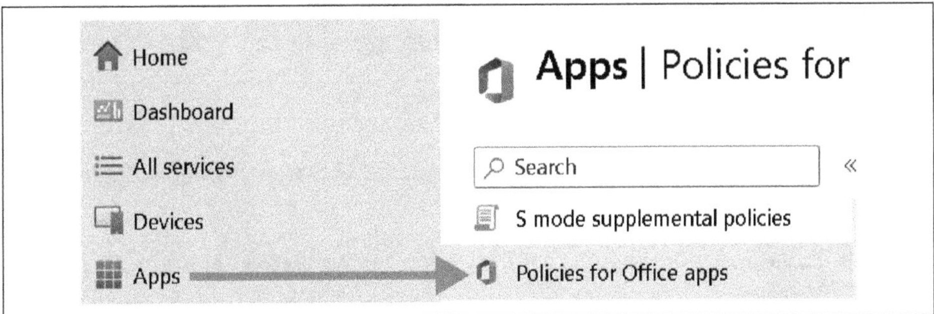

Figure 2-32. Policies inside the Microsoft Endpoint Manager admin center

Under "Policy configurations," select Create. Assign a name and description to the policy. In this solution, you will use "Restrict sign in to Teams to accounts in specific tenants" and "This policy setting allows you to control the accounts that can be used in Teams on managed devices running Windows."

Select the type for the policy and a group to apply it (in this solution, Sales and Marketing). To configure the policy configuration, go to the "Select policies" page, search for Teams, and select "Restrict sign in to Teams to accounts in specific tenants" (Figure 2-33).

Configure Settings
Select policy settings for this configuration
Total
2
Security Baseline
0
Accessibility Baseline
0
Configured
0
Policy
Platform
Restrict sign in to Teams to accounts in specific tenants
Prevent Microsoft Teams from starting automatically after installat...

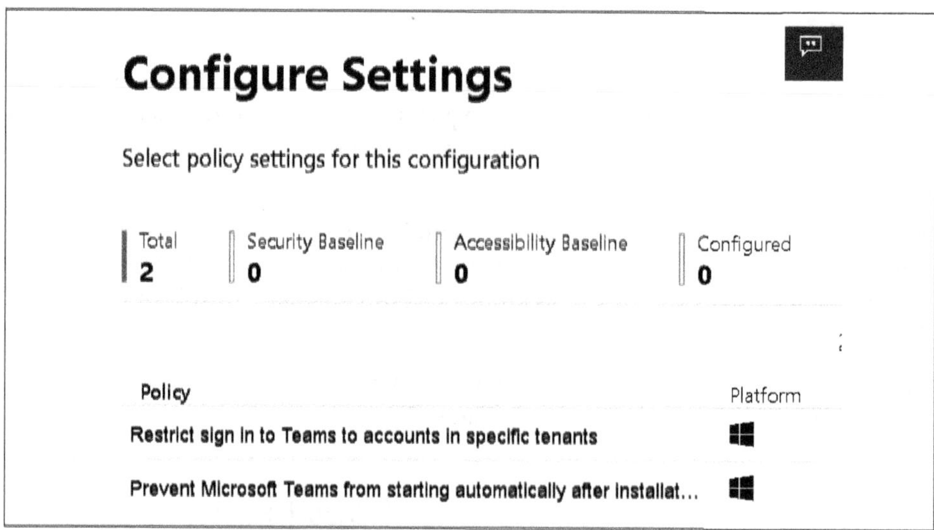

Figure 2-33. The available policies for Teams

Enable the policy and make a list of the domains you want to allow. Figure 2-34 shows an example of domain-based filtering.

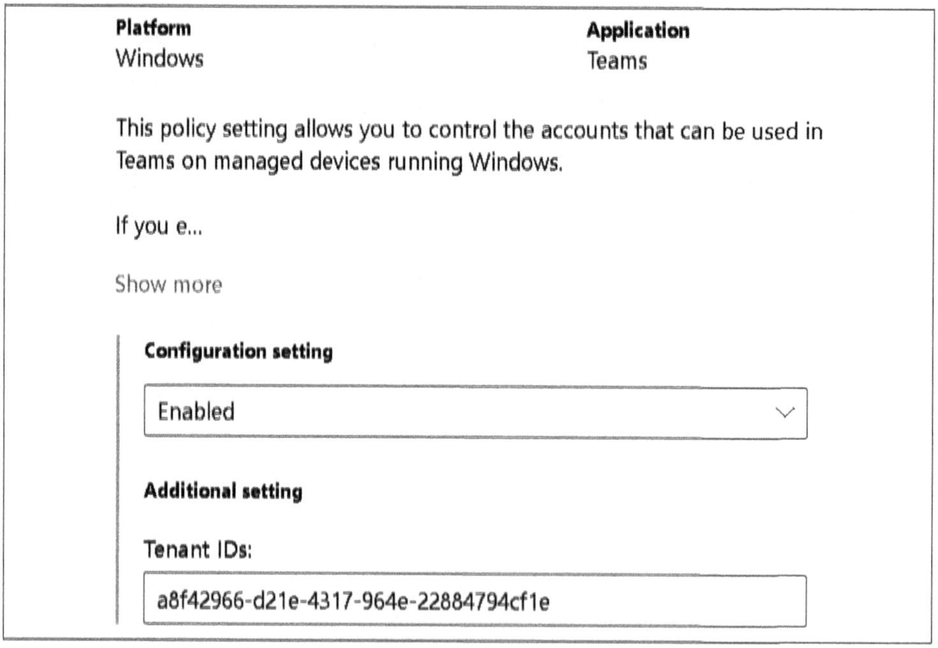

Platform
Windows
Application
Teams
This policy setting allows you to control the accounts that can be used in Teams on managed devices running Windows.
If you e...
Show more
Configuration setting
Enabled
Additional setting
Tenant IDs:
a8f42966-d21e-4317-964e-22884794cf1e

Figure 2-34. Creating a list of allowed domains

Discussion

For desktop devices not managed with MEM, you can use group policies to obtain the same result or apply a registry modification.

To use the Group Policy Objects (GPO) solution, install the Administrative Template files (ADMX/ADML) and Office Customization Tool for Microsoft 365 Apps for enterprise, Office 2019, and Office 2016 (*https://oreil.ly/O42_O*).

For mobile devices (iOS and Android), one possible solution is to push account configurations to Microsoft 365 accounts. For users enrolled in Microsoft Intune, you can deploy the account configuration settings using Intune in the Azure portal, as explained in the Microsoft article "How to restrict sign in on desktop devices" (*https://oreil.ly/x3vou*).

2.7 Summary

This chapter gave a high-level overview of the Cyber Kill Chain framework and introduced a series of tools that allow Teams administrators to break the attack sequence. We looked at some scenarios in which the correct configuration and usage of products inside the Microsoft 365 platform (like Microsoft Defender and Microsoft Sentinel) enhance the security of Teams and reduce risks for users. The recipes offered solutions to secure devices, apps, and links.

CHAPTER 3

Microsoft Teams Voice: Voice Users Deployment

Teams offers collaboration, communication, and productivity in one neat package. It's Microsoft's take on group chat, with an emphasis on team collaboration. As part of that team collaboration, users can share their calendars for meetings and more. However, as we'll see in this chapter, there are some limitations to the built-in calling features in Teams.

The good news is that it's possible to have a seamless experience using your organization's existing phone system and integrating it with Teams. Let's say you want to optimize your voice conversations by using just one application, instead of switching between different apps. There is more than one solution for this problem. Read on to understand the different voice options in Teams and how they can help you get the most out of your collaboration tool.

3.1 Selecting a PSTN Connectivity Option for Teams

Problem

You need to plan for the best Public Switched Telephone Network (PSTN) connectivity solution in order to deploy voice in Teams for your organization.

Solution

Microsoft offers multiple ways to connect Teams to the PSTN to make inbound and outbound calls. Each solution has its pros and cons, and you'll need to consider the best fit for your specific requirements. Some options for connecting Teams to the PSTN include:

Direct Routing
: You can deploy one or more Session Border Controllers (SBCs), or devices that will manage the connection between the PSTN (via a trunk to your telco) and Teams. A Teams Phone Standard license or Microsoft 365 Phone System license is required for each user you want to enable.

Calling Plans
: PSTN trunks are procured directly via Microsoft. For the uses, in addition to the Phone System licenses, a Calling Plan is required.

Operator Connect (and Operator Connect Mobile)
: You can buy the PSTN connectivity for Teams from a list of telcos in the Microsoft Operator Connect Program without the requirement to deploy your own SBC. User licensing is the same as for Direct Routing.

Quite often, connectivity to the PSTN inside an organization is based on a mix of these three solutions. The best approach depends on the requirements of each branch and office involved.

You could consider both Calling Plans and Operator Connect as a version of Direct Routing in which the SBCs and Session Initiation Protocol (SIP) trunks are fully managed by a third party, Microsoft, or the telco. You can deploy Direct Routing in every place in the world where there is a PSTN service (perhaps with an adapter on your SBC to bridge between the available legacy technologies and Teams). If you are looking at Calling Plans and Operator Connect, however, the first required check is the availability of the service:

Calling Plans
: Check country and region availability for Audio Conferencing and Calling Plans (*https://oreil.ly/yxM5V*), selecting the country that you are planning to serve with Calling Plans.

Operator Connect
: Check the Operator Directory (*https://oreil.ly/GL_6K*), selecting the country that you are planning to serve with Operator Connect.

If you are moving from a telco to Microsoft's Calling Plans or from one telco to another using Operator Connect and you want to keep the existing phone numbers, the new provider will conduct a process called *phone number porting*. It may take some time to complete this.

Operator Connect Mobile is the only option that supports integrating your mobile numbers with Teams, with a solution called Microsoft Teams Phone Mobile. If you need to integrate mobile phone numbers to be used as Teams PSTN numbers, this option is the only one you should consider.

Once you have verified which services are available, the next step is to verify the costs for PSTN calling. An agreement with a telco usually has the costs outlined by minutes and/or typologies (national, international, premium numbers, and so on). With Calling Plans, you can buy a fixed number of minutes for each user to be used monthly or a pay as you go for both domestic and international calling. Outgoing minutes are charged depending on the minutes used. There is no limit or charge for incoming calls. To see the different bundles and their costs, visit the Microsoft 365 Admin Portal (*https://oreil.ly/HPlpo*), click Marketplace and then search for Calling Plan.

With Direct Routing there is an additional cost to consider: the number of SIP channels provided by the telco inside your SIP trunk. We'll discuss this more later in the chapter.

The third step is dictated by the existing legacy devices in your organization. You might have analog or Digital Enhanced Cordless Telecommunications (DECT) devices that you are not able to remove (due to specific requirements). It's possible to integrate legacy devices using the SIP Gateway (for a limited number of supported devices and vendors) or an Analog Telephony Adapter (ATA). This creates a bridge between the existing hardware and the SBC that communicates with Teams (using Direct Routing, for example).

See Chapter 4 for more on analog devices, DECT, and legacy hardware integration.

Additional factors in your decision relate to the requirement for voice recording or call center services. We'll discuss voice recording and call centers with Teams later in this chapter. For this recipe, voice recording and call centers are not factors:

- There is currently no Microsoft solution for voice recording. Voice recording must be done by a certified third party and the available products are usually agnostic to the type of PSTN connectivity deployed.
- Microsoft has released a Digital Contact Center platform. Depending on the scenario, either the Microsoft solution or a third party's could be a better fit for your requirements. Again, the available solutions are usually agnostic to the type of PSTN connectivity deployed.

Based on the three steps we have discussed (availability check, cost exam, and legacy integration), you should be able to propose a design that delivers the required PSTN connectivity in Teams. The best option for PSTN connectivity is often a mix of the different possible deployment solutions, combining Direct Routing and/or Operator Connect or Calling Plans to provide the best result.

If you are migrating the users from an existing legacy Private Branch Exchange System (PBX), which is a private telephone network solution, and there is a requirement for coexistence, then the options you can use in your solution may be more limited. We'll discuss this in the following recipe.

Discussion

Calling Plans with pay-as-you-go and Microsoft Teams Phone Mobile are the latest additions to the list of available PSTN connectivity solutions.

Both have unique advantages and downsides. Pay-as-you-go, for example, could be the ideal solution to allocate a PSTN phone number to a meeting room, where the expectation is that more calls will be received than made. However, the same Calling Plan could be costly if applied to a standard user that makes more than a limited number of outgoing calls. Usually, in different offices and locations, you will deploy different PSTN connectivity options and mix them to get the best results. This kind of consideration is what you should look at during the second step of the Solution, when you are evaluating costs.

When you connect the PSTN to an SBC, the preferred technology (where available) is SIP. This is protocol enables Voice over IP (VoIP). Using SIP and VoIP, the PSTN connectivity is no longer based on physical cables and adapters but is delivered by the telco over the internet or using a dedicated network connection.

Each SIP connection between the telco and the SBC is called a *SIP trunk*. Inside one SIP trunk, many voice conversations can happen simultaneously. Each conversation will use what is called a *SIP channel*. The process is dynamic, so as soon as a voice call is over, the SIP channel is available for the next conversation. Telcos usually charge you for each SIP channel in the trunk. The decision you'll need to make, then, is how many SIP channels you need to be cost-effective and still deliver the required service (because if no SIP channel is available, the incoming or outgoing call is not going to happen).

If you have an existing PBX, look at the past months and years to get a good idea of how many simultaneous conversations happen. Then, size the SIP trunk accordingly. Otherwise, you will have to estimate a number. For a call center, the number of required SIP channels could be as high as one channel for every three active users. In a more common scenario, you can push the ratio to 1 channel for every 10 active users, and even up to 1:20 where the usage of the PSTN is low.

SIP trunks are defined via software, so it is possible to add or remove SIP channels if needed. That said, every change you make could impact your agreement with the telco and be costly (or not doable). It is critical that your plan be as accurate as possible, and be sure to include a SIP channel for contingency situations.

A single SBC could be (and usually is) used to connect different offices and locations to the PSTN using different providers. It is not unusual to have more than one SIP trunk connected to an SBC, with each trunk going to a different telco. In addition, a SIP trunk must go to Teams (Microsoft does not support any standard for PSTN connections other than SIP). A potential solution might look like the one shown in Figure 3-1.

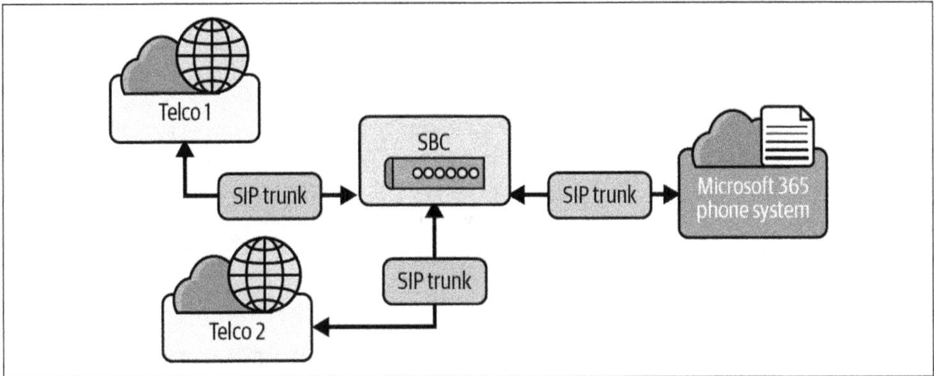

Figure 3-1. Direct Routing SBC with multiple SIP trunks

3.2 Migrating Voice from a Legacy PBX to Teams

Problem

You need to plan a solution to migrate your organization's users from a legacy PBX platform to Teams.

Solution

Phone calls, in recent decades, have moved from being the main communication tool to being just one of the many ways people can connect. In many scenarios, a PSTN call is not the ideal way to communicate when you consider instant messaging, email, and more. That said, some aspects of a business (especially when it comes to customer service and connecting with people outside the organization) still rely on traditional phone calls. Therefore, having to change an existing phone number or create a disruption during a migration from the legacy PBX to Teams is not an option.

There is no one-size-fits-all solution when talking about voice migrations, and some planning is usually required before implementing any solution.

The first step you must take is to understand whether the migration is going to be a big bang (moving all the existing phone numbers in a single day) or involve coexistence (a gradual migration of the legacy PBX to Teams). The latter is often the case.

In a coexistence scenario (and every time a user or device is left on the existing PBX), you will have to create a connection between Teams and the PBX (usually via a SIP trunk on the SBC). This connection is required to maintain internal communication between migrated users and users still on the legacy system.

The second step is planning the communication between the legacy system and Teams.

An alternative to connecting the legacy PBX with Teams is to route all the calls between users migrated to Teams and users on the PBX via the external PSTN, without any SIP trunk deployed internally. This solution adds complexity and costs, so I would advise against it unless you have a limited number of users on the PBX for a short time.

The third step is deciding whether your SBC is going to be upstream or downstream from the PSTN connection (with the legacy PBX going in the opposite direction). The schema in Figure 3-2 shows two possible configurations.

With an upstream configuration, the PSTN connectivity is moved from the PBX to the SBC. As a result, all incoming voice traffic going to Teams will move from the PSTN to the SBC and then to Teams. The voice calls for users still on the PBX will be routed there by the SBC. All the outgoing traffic (both from Teams and from the PBX) will be sent to the SBC and then to the PSTN. The configuration of the PBX must be changed accordingly.

In a downstream configuration, all incoming calls still go to the PBX and only the ones for users already migrated to Teams are sent to the SBC. For outgoing calls, all the voice traffic will be sent to the PBX and routed from there to the PSTN. This configuration requires a reduced number of changes to the PBX but limits the possible configuration of the SBC.

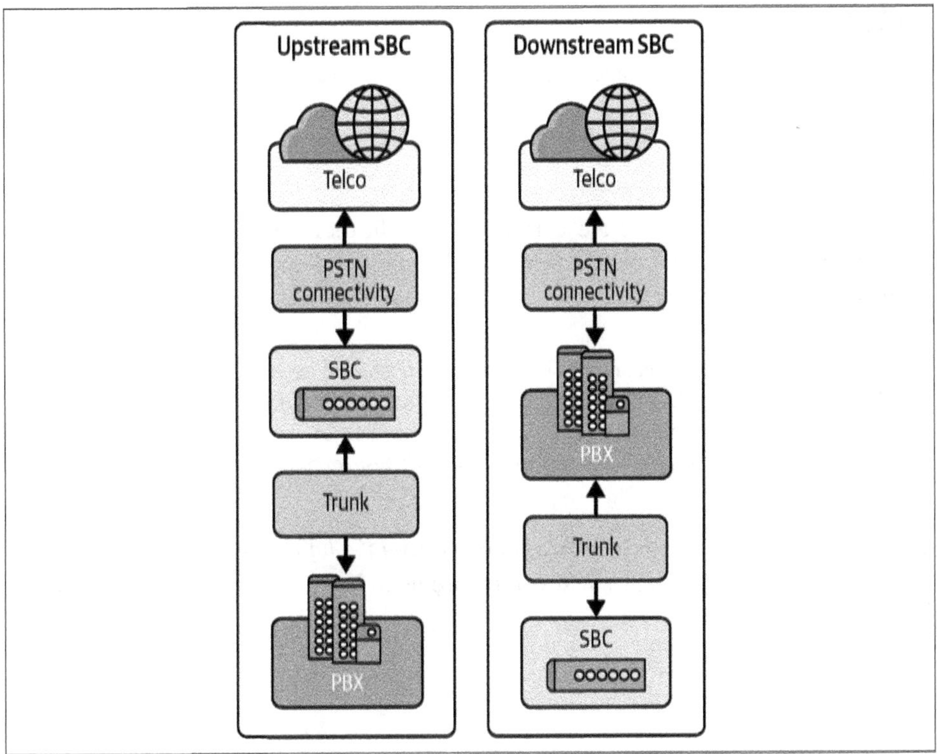

Figure 3-2. SBC with PSTN upstream and downstream

Discussion

The way in which you deploy the SIP trunk between the PBX and the SBC depends on the PBX vendor and on the type of SBC you are using. Some vendors have published documentation, but you may need to coordinate with the people in charge of the PBX to make the correct configuration.

For example, see the documentation: "Connecting Cisco Unified Communications Manager Ver. 12.0 with Microsoft Teams Direct Routing Enterprise Model Using AudioCodes Mediant SBC" (*https://oreil.ly/Rxmss*).

When enabling PSTN calling in Teams, as part of the user migration planning, it's important to consider the daily work of the users. Some examples include hunt groups, boss/admin delegations, and so on. Having some members of a hunt group on the legacy PBX and migrating others has consequences, like agent status not being updated between the two platforms, shared phone numbers remaining only on one of the voice platforms, and so on.

3.3 Deploying Voice Recording for Teams Users

Problem

Some of your Teams users have a requirement for recording voice calls, and you need to plan a solution.

Solution

In this solution, you will create a recording application (a bot) named *recording_bot@M365x01033383.onmicrosoft.com* in your tenant and apply a policy for automatic recording (`RecordingPolicy`) to the user *alland@M365x01033383.onmicrosoft.com*.

The voice recording solution you use should be compliant with the Microsoft Teams certification program. A list of certified partners is available in the article "Introduction to Teams policy-based recording for callings & meetings" (*https://oreil.ly/dQ6Wj*).

You'll use an `ApplicationId` of *2211e591-9355-4a5c-bd31-2ac89f7c5507*. In a real-world scenario, the `ApplicationId` will be provided by the producer of the recording solution.

Start by connecting to Teams:

```
Connect-MicrosoftTeams
```

The next step is to create the recording application (bot):

```
New-CsOnlineApplicationInstance -UserPrincipalName `
"recording_bot@M365x01033383.onmicrosoft.com" -DisplayName `
"RecordingBotInstance" -ApplicationId 2211e591-9355-4a5c-bd31-2ac89f7c5507

$Instance = Get-CsOnlineApplicationInstance -Identity `
recording_bot@M365x01033383.onmicrosoft.com

Sync-CsOnlineApplicationInstance -ObjectId $Instance.ObjectID
```

Next, define a Teams recording policy and associate it with the bot:

```
New-CsTeamsComplianceRecordingPolicy -Identity RecordingPolicy -Enabled $true `
-Description "Recording Policy"

Set-CsTeamsComplianceRecordingPolicy -Identity RecordingPolicy `
-ComplianceRecordingApplications @(New-CsTeamsComplianceRecordingApplication `
-Id $Instance.ObjectID -Parent RecordingPolicy `
-RequiredBeforeCallEstablishment $false -RequiredDuringCall $false `
-RequiredBeforeMeetingJoin $false -RequiredDuringMeeting $false)
```

PowerShell will output the result shown in Figure 3-3.

```
Identity                                              : Tag:RecordingPolicy
ComplianceRecordingApplications                       : {}
Enabled                                               : True
WarnUserOnRemoval                                     : True
DisableComplianceRecordingAudioNotificationForCalls : False
Description                                           : Recording Policy
RecordReroutedCalls                                   : False
```

Figure 3-3. Settings for the recording policy

Finally, apply the policy to the user:

```
Grant-CsTeamsComplianceRecordingPolicy -Identity `
"alland@M365x01033383.onmicrosoft.com" -PolicyName RecordingPolicy
```

Use the following command to quickly check the user settings:

```
Get-CsOnlineUser -Identity "alland@M365x01033383.onmicrosoft.com" | ft `
DisplayName,TeamsComplianceRecordingPolicy
```

Discussion

Some specific users, such as stockbrokers and traders, may be required to record and retain transactions that are made over the phone. Such recordings must remain intact for a certain period. Recording is used to capture and archive the transaction and provides both parties a proof of the transaction and agreement.

For on-prem PSTN solutions, the voice recorder is usually deployed alongside the PBX (or as part of the phone system). Moving users to Teams implies replacing the legacy voice recording system with a solution that is certified for Teams. In Teams, recording a call starts only if there is a recording policy matching the call. Therefore, it is mandatory to deploy policies that automatically start the recording every time it is required.

Teams supports different kinds of voice recording, which could be initiated by the user (Convenience recording) or by the organization (Organizational recording) or could be part of a feature in Teams like meeting transcription (Functional recording).

The relevant category for this solution is Organizational recording, which makes recording mandatory. Every time a user with an applied recording policy makes a call, the related bot is invited into the call. The recorder (the third-party recording solution) at that point can register the call, as you can see in Figure 3-4.

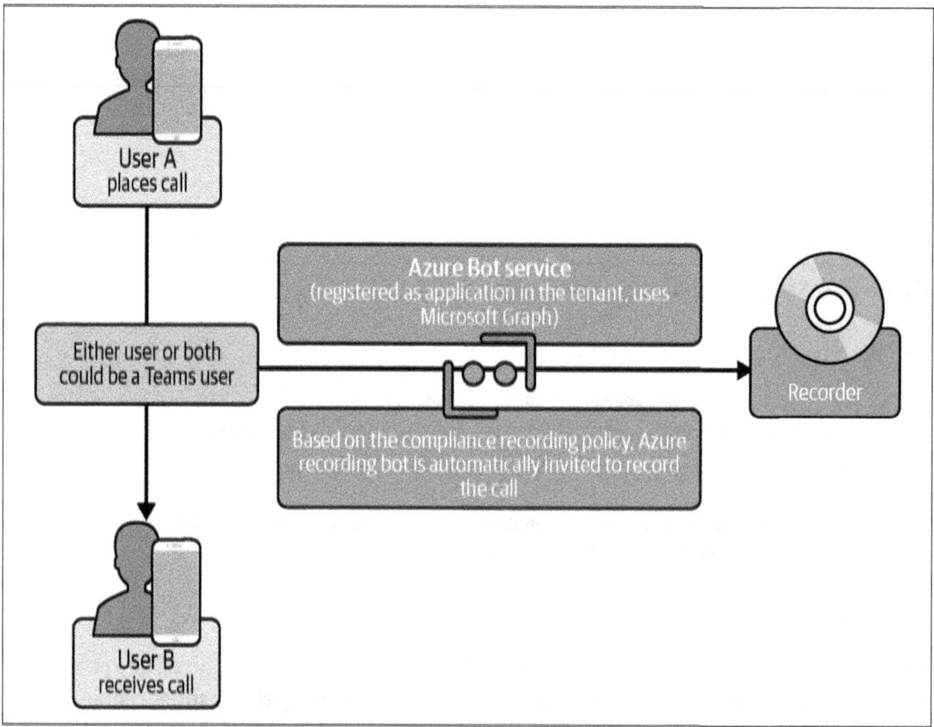
User A
places call
Either user or both
could be a Teams user
Azure Bot service
(registered as application in the tenant, uses
Microsoft Graph)
Based on the compliance recording policy, Azure
recording bot is automatically invited to record
the call
Recorder
User B
receives call

Figure 3-4. How the recording bot is added to a call

The whole mechanism is quite straightforward from a Teams point of view, but some additional configuration work is required on the recorder side. The recorder settings will determine who is recorded, when recordings are needed (for example, recording outgoing calls may not be required for compliance), what kind of access each user has to recordings (for example, users could require access to their recordings), who the administrator or auditor is for the voice recording, and so on.

How the recordings will be stored will also need to be decided—they could be stored in the cloud or on-prem, depending on legal requirements.

3.4 Creating Dial Plans

Problem

You must configure rules that convert phone numbers to a format that is acceptable for Teams Voice.

Solution

All the voice features in Teams are based on an international standard (called E.164 (*https://oreil.ly/RIvDw*)) that defines how phone numbers are formatted. A process called *normalization* must be applied to all the dialed phone numbers so that they are converted into E.164 standard format.

Normalization happens at the user level, where you apply the dial plans. A *dial plan* takes the number dialed by the user and (if the dialed pattern matches the rule) normalizes it. For example, if a user in London is dialing a local number, the number will automatically be prefixed by +44 for E.164 normalization (see Figure 3-5).

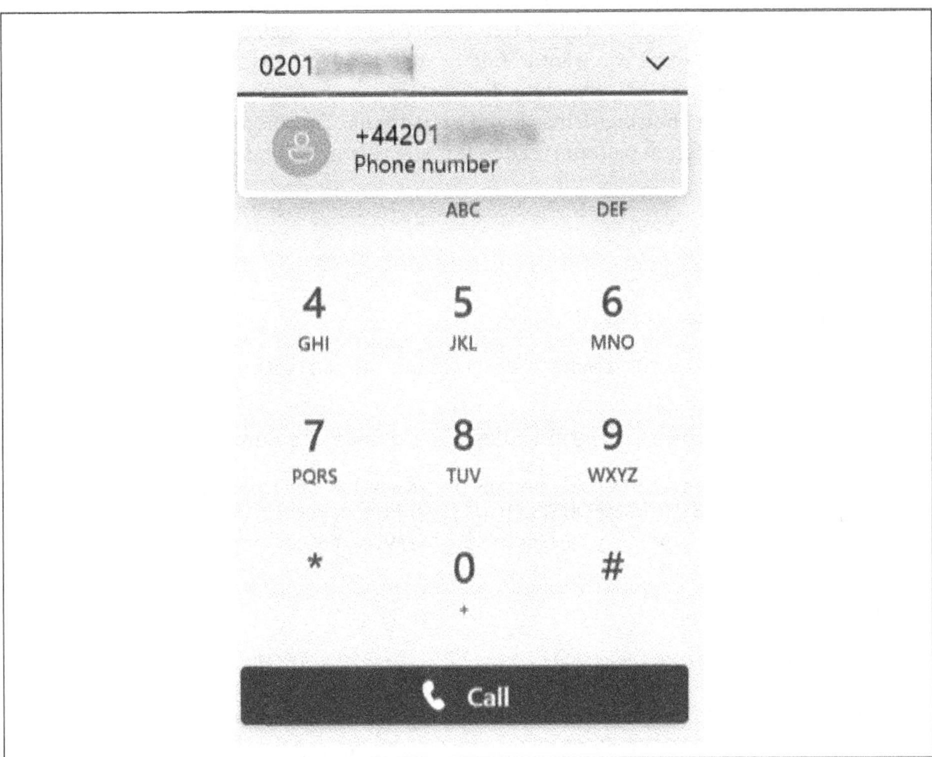

Figure 3-5. Normalization applied to a phone number dialed by a user

Each dial plan is usually tailored to a specific location (country, city, and so on) and must contain all the different options that the user could dial (there is a single dial plan applied to each user). In this solution, you will create a dial plan for a user located in London, including all the different options for phone numbers in the following categories:

- Service (starting with 999)
- Toll free (starting with 800)
- National
- Mobile (starting with 07)
- International
- Premium (for example, numbers starting with 09)

Normalization rules in Teams are written using *regular expressions* (regex). Regex allows you to specify rules that describe the desired text patterns you want to find or manipulate. It enables you to perform tasks like searching for specific words or phrases, replacing text, or splitting strings based on patterns. The Discussion explains the different patterns used in this solution in more detail.

Start by connecting to Teams:

```
Connect-MicrosoftTeams
```

The next step is to create a new dial plan:

```
New-CsTenantDialPlan "UK-London" -Description "Normalization rules for London, `
United Kingdom"
```

Let's start creating our normalization rules. First up, service numbers:

```
$UKService = New-CsVoiceNormalizationRule -Name 'UK-Service' -Parent UK-London `
-Pattern '^(1(47\d|70\d|800\d|1[68]\d{3}|\d\d)|999|[\*\#][\*\#\d]*\#)$' `
-Translation '$1' -InMemory -Description "Service number normalization for `
United Kingdom"
```

Then toll free numbers:

```
$UKTollFree = New-CsVoiceNormalizationRule -Name 'UK-TollFree' -Parent `
UK-London -Pattern '^0((80(0\d{6,7}|8\d{7}|01111)|500\d{6}))\d*$' `
-Translation '+44$1' -InMemory -Description "Toll Free number `
normalization for United Kingdom"
```

Followed by national, mobile, international, and premium numbers:

```
$UKNational = New-CsVoiceNormalizationRule -Name 'UK-National' -Parent `
UK-London -Pattern '^0((1[1-9]\d{7,8}|2[03489]\d{8}|3[0347]\d{8}|5[56]\d{8} `
|8((4[2-5]|70)\d{7}|45464\d)))\d*(\D+\d+)?$' -Translation '+44$1' -InMemory `
-Description "National number normalization for United Kingdom"

$UKMobile = New-CsVoiceNormalizationRule -Name 'UK-Mobile' -Parent `
UK-London -Pattern '^0((7([1-57-9]\d{8}|624\d{6})))$' -Translation '+44$1' `
-InMemory -Description "Mobile number normalization for United Kingdom"
```

```
$UKInternational = New-CsVoiceNormalizationRule -Name 'UK-International' `
-Parent UK-London -Pattern '^(?:\+|00)(1|7|2[07]|3[0-46]|39\d|4[013-9]|5[1-8]| `
6[0-6]|8[1246]|9[0-58]|2[1235689]\d|24[013-9]|242\d|3[578]\d|42\d|5[09]\d| `
6[789]\d|8[035789]\d|9[679]\d)(?:0)?(\d{5,14})(\D+\d+)?$' -Translation '+$1$2' `
-InMemory -Description "International number normalization for United Kingdom"

$UKPremium = New-CsVoiceNormalizationRule -Name 'UK-Premium' -Parent `
UK-London -Pattern '^0((9[018]\d|87[123]|70\d)\d{7})$' -Translation '+44$1' `
-InMemory -Description "Premium number normalization for United Kingdom"
```

The next step is to apply all the normalization rules to the dial plan:

```
Set-CsTenantDialPlan "UK-London" -NormalizationRules @{add=$UKService}
Set-CsTenantDialPlan "UK-London" -NormalizationRules @{add=$UKTollFree}
Set-CsTenantDialPlan "UK-London" -NormalizationRules @{add=$UKNational}
Set-CsTenantDialPlan "UK-London" -NormalizationRules @{add=$UKMobile}
Set-CsTenantDialPlan "UK-London" -NormalizationRules @{add=$UKInternational}
Set-CsTenantDialPlan "UK-London" -NormalizationRules @{add=$UKPremium}
```

Use the following command to see what normalization rules are applied in the UK-London dial plan:

```
(Get-CsTenantDialPlan -Identity "UK-London").NormalizationRules
```

Figure 3-6 shows the output.

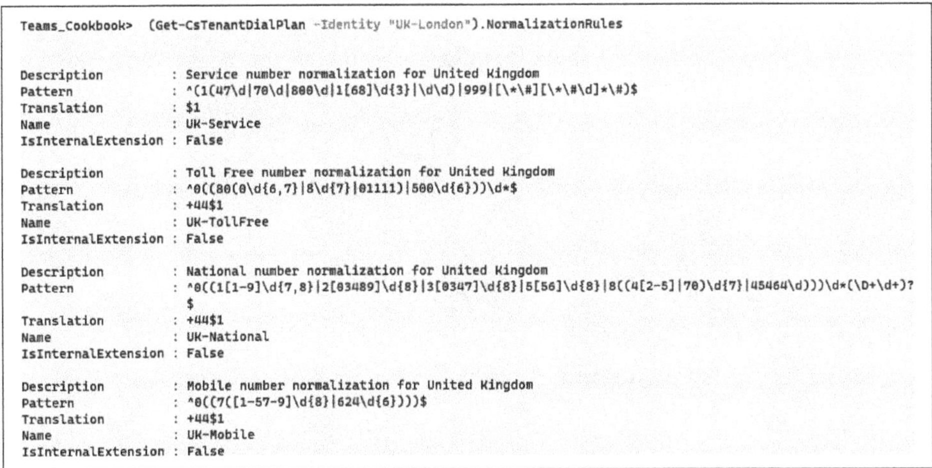

Figure 3-6. Normalization rules in the UK-London dial plan

You could also define an array and add all the normalization rules to it, using a script like this:

```
$NR = @()
    $NR += New-CsVoiceNormalizationRule -Name "Rule1"...
    $NR += New-CsVoiceNormalizationRule -Name "Rule2"...
```

Then, you can add `$NR` to the dial plan instead of the individual rules.

Discussion

It is possible to add the same normalization rules (and edit them) using the "Dial plans" tab in the TAC. Figure 3-7 shows one of the normalization rules we just created in the graphical interface.

Edit UK-National rule

Name

UK-National

Description

National number normalization for United Kingdom

Rule creation mode

Basic

Advanced

If condition Select from a template

The number dialed matches this regular expression

^0((1[1-9]\d{7,8}|2[03489]\d{8}|3[0347]\...

Figure 3-7. A normalization rule in the TAC

However, adding rules this way is time-consuming (especially if you need to create small variations of the same dial plan for different parts of the same country). Also, some tools that could help automate part of the process are based in PowerShell (my favorite is UCDialPlans (*https://oreil.ly/qjK3B*) by Ken Lasko).

When you need to remove a normalization rule, it's quite easy if you still have the rule saved in a variable. For example, let's say you want to remove the UK-Premium normalization rule. The command will be:

```
Set-CsTenantDialPlan "UK-London" -NormalizationRules @{remove=$UKPremium}
```

That said, if you need to remove or edit the rules a few hours or days later, using the TAC is more straightforward (Figure 3-8).

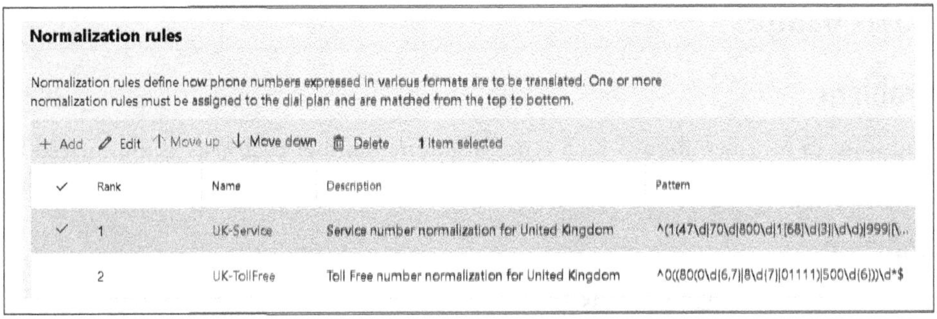

Normalization rules

Normalization rules define how phone numbers expressed in various formats are to be translated. One or more normalization rules must be assigned to the dial plan and are matched from the top to bottom.

+ Add Edit Move up Move down Delete 1 item selected

✓	Rank	Name	Description	Pattern
✓	1	UK-Service	Service number normalization for United Kingdom	^(1(47\d|70\d|800\d|1[68]\d|3|\d\d)|999|[\...
	2	UK-TollFree	Toll Free number normalization for United Kingdom	^0((80(0\d{6,7}|8\d{7}|01111)|500\d{6}))\d*$

Figure 3-8. Editing and deleting normalization rules in the TAC

If you are migrating from a legacy PBX, you may have to create normalization rules that are only to be used during the coexistence period, or preserve some dialing habit that the users had from the previous platform. For example, the PBX might have required a specific pattern before the phone number to identify an external call, and users might struggle if they cannot use that same pattern with Teams.

Finally, with regard to regex, let's take one of the strings we used before as an example:

```
'^0((7([1-57-9]\d{8}|624\d{6})))$'
```

A quick translation of this string would be:

- The pattern must start with 0 (`^0`), followed by either (| indicates "or"):
  - — 7, followed by a number between 1 and 5 or 7 and 9 (`1-57-9`) followed by any eight digits (`\d{8}`)
  - — 624, followed by any six digits (`\d{6}`)

Our normalization rule also contains an action. The E.164 international prefix for the United Kingdom (+44) will be added in front of the dialed number (`-Translation '+44$1'`).

A process like normalization is also applied to incoming calls because phone numbers presented by the PSTN may not be in the E.164 format and so may not be usable by Teams. Those rules are usually applied inside the SBC or by the telco (if you are using Calling Plans or Operator Connect).

3.5 Managing Voice Routing Policies, Voice Routes, and PSTN Usages

Problem

You want to set rules about which types of phone number each user is authorized to call.

Solution

Once users have a dial plan assigned, the next step is to evaluate whether they are allowed to call a specific phone number and where the call will be routed. Premium phone numbers, for example, have an additional cost, and they may be accessible only to a limited number of users. Each Teams user is assigned to a single Voice Routing Policy (VRP). Inside a VRP, there are one or more PSTN Usages that specify Voice Routes. Each Voice Route is a calling number matching pattern and its corresponding PSTN Gateway.

In this solution, you will define a VRP, PSTN Usages, and Voice Routes for the users based on the following parameters:

- Users are allowed to call service, toll free, national, and international numbers.
- Users are located in London.

Start by connecting to Teams:

```
Connect-MicrosoftTeams
```

To begin configuring the VRP, you must first create the PSTN Gateway (the SBC). The PSTN Gateway will be the next hop for outgoing and incoming calls. The details of the voice gateway are outside the scope of this book and may vary based on the vendor and selected configuration. For this solution, just know that the PSTN Gateway must have a public DNS record and a public Certificate Authority (CA) certificate applied.

The domain in which the PSTN Gateway is registered must be in the Microsoft 365 tenant and cannot be the *onmicrosoft.com* domain that is created by default. For the PowerShell commands, I will use my domain: *modern-workplace.uk*. The gateway's fully qualified domain name (FQDN) will be *PSTNgateway.modern-workplace.uk*.

The following command will add the PSTN Gateway and configure TCP port 5061 for the SIP communication:

```
New-CsOnlinePSTNGateway -Identity PSTNgateway.modern-workplace.uk -Enabled `
$true -SipSignalingPort 5061 -MaxConcurrentSessions 10
```

The output is shown in Figure 3-9.

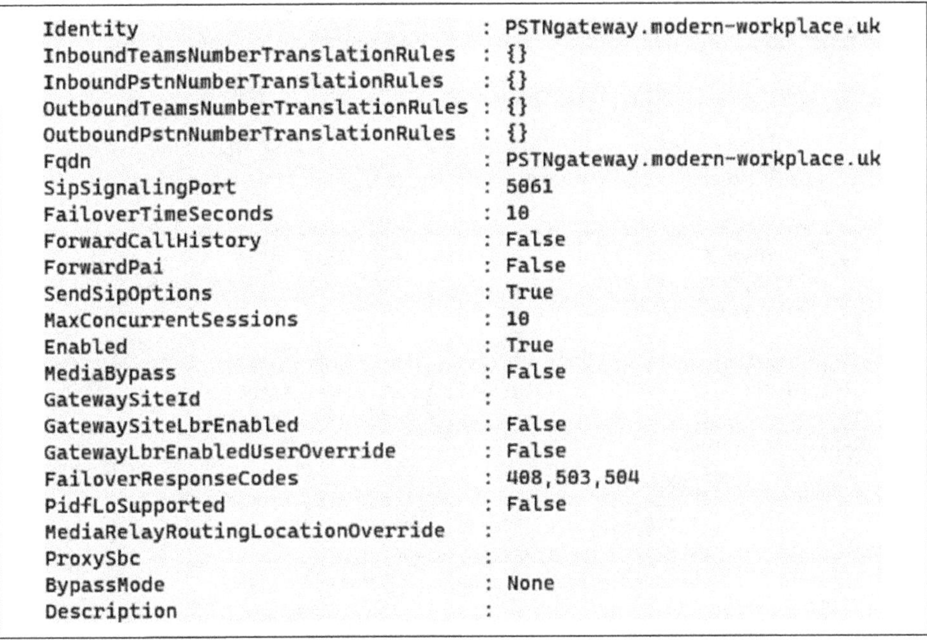

Identity : PSTNgateway.modern-workplace.uk
InboundTeamsNumberTranslationRules : {}
InboundPstnNumberTranslationRules : {}
OutboundTeamsNumberTranslationRules : {}
OutboundPstnNumberTranslationRules : {}
Fqdn : PSTNgateway.modern-workplace.uk
SipSignalingPort : 5061
FailoverTimeSeconds : 10
ForwardCallHistory : False
ForwardPai : False
SendSipOptions : True
MaxConcurrentSessions : 10
Enabled : True
MediaBypass : False
GatewaySiteId :
GatewaySiteLbrEnabled : False
GatewayLbrEnabledUserOverride : False
FailoverResponseCodes : 408,503,504
PidfLoSupported : False
MediaRelayRoutingLocationOverride :
ProxySbc :
BypassMode : None
Description :

Figure 3-9. Adding a PSTN Gateway

You may receive an error that looks like this:

```
New-CsOnlinePSTNGateway :  Cannot use the "PSTN Gateway FQDN" domain as it was `
not configured for this tenant
```

Even if your custom domain is correctly added to the Microsoft 365 tenant, you may see that the domain is missing from the list of SIP domains. You can check this by using the following command:

```
Get-CsTenant | fl TenantId,SipDomain
```

A quick solution is to (temporarily) assign a license, like an E3, to a user in the custom domain. Then, when the error is fixed, you can remove the license from the user.

Now you can create the necessary PSTN Usages in the global container:

```
Set-CsOnlinePstnUsage -Identity Global -Usage @{Add="UK-PSTNU-Service"}
Set-CsOnlinePstnUsage -Identity Global -Usage @{Add="UK-PSTNU-TollFree"}
Set-CsOnlinePstnUsage -Identity Global -Usage @{Add="UK-PSTNU-National"}
Set-CsOnlinePstnUsage -Identity Global -Usage @{Add="UK-PSTNU-Mobile"}
Set-CsOnlinePstnUsage -Identity Global -Usage @{Add="UK-PSTNU-International"}
Set-CsOnlinePstnUsage -Identity Global -Usage @{Add="UK-PSTNU-Premium"}
```

PSTN Usage policies are nothing more than labels. Inside each Voice Route, you will have the following:

- One or more PSTN Gateways
- A regex pattern to be matched for calls to be routed on that specific route
- The list of PSTN Usages that are allowed inside that Voice Route

You can now define a Voice Route for each pattern and Usage that matches your policies. In this solution, you can create a Voice Route that matches each Usage:

```
New-CsOnlineVoiceRoute -Identity "UK-VR-Service" -NumberPattern `
"^(1(47\d|70\d|800\d|1[68]\d{3}|\d\d)|999|[\*\#][\*\#\d]*\#)$" `
-OnlinePstnGatewayList PSTNgateway.modern-workplace.uk  -Priority 0 `
-OnlinePstnUsages "UK-PSTNU-Service"

New-CsOnlineVoiceRoute -Identity "UK-VR-TollFree" -NumberPattern `
"^0((80(0\d{6,7}|8\d{7}|01111)|500\d{6}))\d*$" -OnlinePstnGatewayList `
PSTNgateway.modern-workplace.uk  -Priority 1 -OnlinePstnUsages `
"UK-PSTNU-TollFree"

New-CsOnlineVoiceRoute -Identity "UK-VR-National" -NumberPattern `
"^0((1[1-9]\d{7,8}|2[03489]\d{8}|3[0347]\d{8}|5[56]\d{8}|8((4[2-5]|70)\d{7} `
|45464\d)))\d*(\D+\d+)?$" -OnlinePstnGatewayList `
PSTNgateway.modern-workplace.uk  -Priority 2 -OnlinePstnUsages `
"UK-PSTNU-National"

New-CsOnlineVoiceRoute -Identity "UK-VR-Mobile" -NumberPattern `
"^0((7([1-57-9]\d{8}|624\d{6})))$" -OnlinePstnGatewayList `
PSTNgateway.modern-workplace.uk  -Priority 3 -OnlinePstnUsages `
"UK-PSTNU-Mobile"

New-CsOnlineVoiceRoute -Identity "UK-VR-International" -NumberPattern `
"^(?:\+|00)(1|7|2[07]|3[0-46]|39\d|4[013-9]|5[1-8]|6[0-6]|8[1246]|9[0-58] `
|2[1235689]\d|24[013-9]|242\d|3[578]\d|42\d|5[09]\d|6[789]\d|8[035789]\d `
|9[679]\d)(?:0)?(\d{5,14})(\D+\d+)?$" -OnlinePstnGatewayList `
PSTNgateway.modern-workplace.uk  -Priority 4 -OnlinePstnUsages `
"UK-PSTNU-International"
```

Use the following command to quickly check the results:

```
Get-CsOnlineVoiceRoute | ft Identity,NumberPattern
```

You can now define the Voice Routing Policy with all the correct PSTN Usages:

```
New-CsOnlineVoiceRoutingPolicy -Identity UK-VRP-International -OnlinePstnUsages `
"UK-PSTNU-Service","UK-PSTNU-TollFree","UK-PSTNU-National","UK-PSTNU-Mobile", `
"UK-PSTNU-International"
```

The output is shown in Figure 3-10.

```
Identity          : Global
OnlinePstnUsages  : {}
Description       :
RouteType         : BYOT

Identity          : Tag:UK-VRP-International
OnlinePstnUsages  : {UK-PSTNU-Service, UK-PSTNU-TollFree,
                    UK-PSTNU-National, UK-PSTNU-Mobile...}
Description       :
RouteType         : BYOT
```

Figure 3-10. Voice Routing Policy with PSTN Usages listed

Discussion

In this scenario, Voice Routing Policies are applied to the users. The motivation to create different Voice Routes is that every time a pattern is matched, the user's Voice Routing Policy will be verified. If certain PSTN Usages are not in the policy, the user's call will be refused.

In this solution, you have applied a naming convention based on the nation name (UK in the example) and the type of voice setting deployed (PSTNU for PSTN Usages, VR for Voice Routes, and VRP for Voice Routing Policies). Even if it is not mandatory to use a specific naming standard, it is easier to debug and document your configuration if you apply one in a consistent way.

The Voice Routes you have defined are based on the same regex syntax used in the dial plans. This approach often makes sense because the logic for the normalization and the filter is similar. It is also doable to have a single Voice Route with a single PSTN Usage, though it depends on how much control the organization needs to have over the phone calls.

3.6 Enabling Enterprise Voice for Teams Users

Problem

You need to apply a configuration to each of the Teams users to enable them to make phone calls.

Solution

To enable PSTN calling for a user in Teams, use the following commands. This will enable Enterprise Voice and assign a Voice Routing Policy and a dial plan:

```
Set-CsPhoneNumberAssignment -Identity alland@m365x71772990.onmicrosoft.com `
-EnterpriseVoiceEnabled $true

Grant-CsOnlineVoiceRoutingPolicy -Identity `
alland@m365x71772990.onmicrosoft.com  -PolicyName "Tag:UK-VRP-International"

Grant-CsTenantDialPlan -Identity alland@m365x71772990.onmicrosoft.com `
-PolicyName "Tag:UK-London"
```

In the `set-CsPhoneNumberAssignment` command, you can also specify a phone number for the user. The command to do this is as follows:

```
Set-CsPhoneNumberAssignment -Identity alland@m365x71772990.onmicrosoft.com `
-PhoneNumber +44XXXXXXXXXX -PhoneNumberType DirectRouting
```

The `PhoneNumberType` parameter can be `CallingPlan`, `DirectRouting`, or `Operator Connect`.

To enable Teams PSTN calling in a batch, you could create a CSV file (for example, *w00.csv*) with the following columns: Identity, PhoneNumber, PSTNType, VRP, DialPlan. The command to do this is as follows:

```
$csv=import-csv w00.csv
foreach($c in $csv)
{Set-CsPhoneNumberAssignment -Identity $c.Identity -PhoneNumber $c.PhoneNumber `
-PhoneNumberType $c.PSTNType -EnterpriseVoiceEnabled $true
Grant-CsOnlineVoiceRoutingPolicy -Identity $c.Identity -PolicyName $c.VRP
Grant-CsTenantDialPlan -Identity $c.Identity -PolicyName $c.DialPlan
}
```

Discussion

Phone number management has been improved in the TAC, and the operations you have done here via PowerShell are now doable via the graphical interface as well. Bulk modifications and phone number assignments are still executed in an easier way using the commands we saw in the solution.

The Voice Routing Policy will limit which numbers the user is allowed to call. However, there is an additional policy (Calling Policy) that has an impact on the user experience. *Calling Policies* regulate things like the ability to make private calls, forward calls, or delegate your phone number. Three different default policies (Global, AllowCalling, and DisallowCalling) can address most standard scenarios. These three policies cannot be modified. You can see them in the Calling Policies tab of the TAC (Figure 3-11).

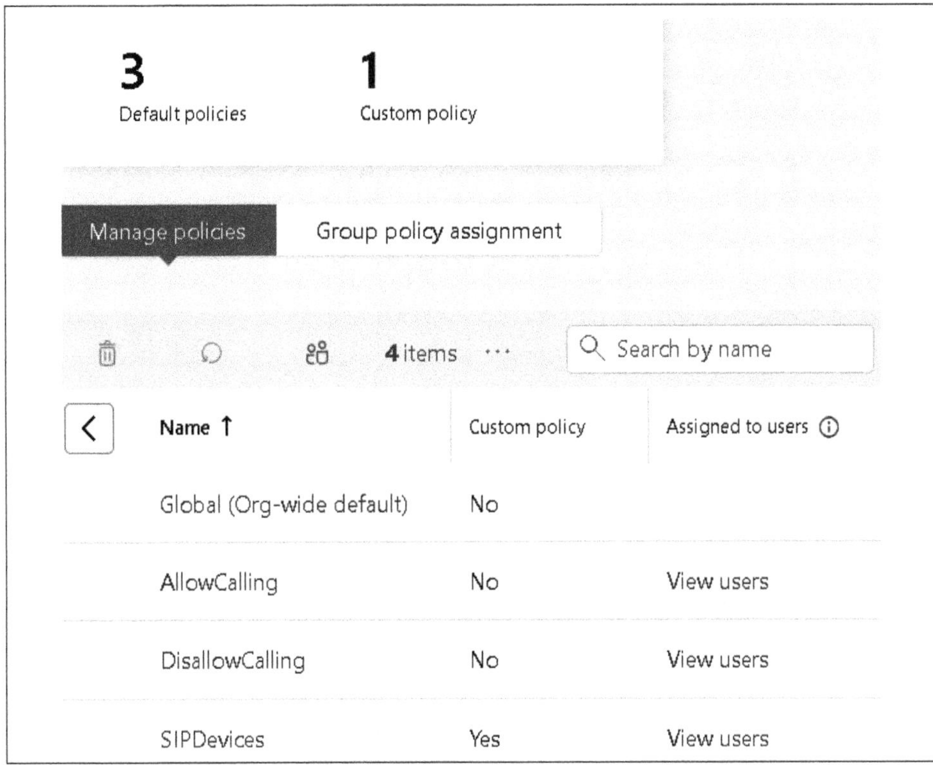

Figure 3-11. Default Calling Policies

If you need a custom Calling Policy, you must define a new one and assign it to the user.

3.7 Summary

This chapter introduced the fundamental configurations required to allow PSTN calling in your tenant, to migrate an existing voice platform, and to enable your Teams users to make PSTN calls. You have seen different ways to do these configurations, via PowerShell and the TAC.

Chapter 4 focuses on a specific aspect of Microsoft Teams Voice: analog devices, DECT, and legacy hardware integration.

CHAPTER 4

Analog Devices, DECT, and Legacy Hardware Integration with Teams Voice

As organizations undergo digital transformation, they must embrace new technologies. This can be a challenge. Many companies have older devices and applications that they don't want to get rid of. Legacy devices and services continue to be an important part of how businesses operate and how employees work. Operators of these legacy devices and services need to understand how to integrate with new technologies, such as Microsoft Teams, so that users can easily collaborate on tasks regardless of the devices they use or services they need.

In this chapter, you'll learn why integrating legacy hardware with new technologies is important, some ways to do integrations, and the pros and cons of integrating analog devices, Digital Enhanced Cordless Telecommunications (DECT) devices, and legacy hardware with Teams Phone System.

4.1 Connecting Analog Devices to Teams SIP Gateway

Problem

You want to enable legacy SIP phones to work with Teams.

Solution

Connect to Teams:

```
Connect-MicrosoftTeams
```

You need to assign at least one Calling Policy that has the `AllowSIPDevicesCalling` parameter set to `True`. You can check whether your policies have the right settings with the following command:

```
get-CsTeamsCallingPolicy | ft Identity,AllowSIPDevicesCalling
```

In this example, you will define a new policy called `SIPDevices` with `AllowSIPDevicesCalling` set to `$true`:

```
New-CsTeamsCallingPolicy -Identity SIPDevices -AllowSIPDevicesCalling $true
```

Running the `get-CsTeamsCallingPolicy` command again should show output like that shown in Figure 4-1.

```
Identity                                          AllowSIPDevicesCalling
--------                                          ----------------------
Global                                                             False
Tag:SIPDevices                                                      True
Tag:AllowCalling                                                   False
Tag:DisallowCalling                                                False
Tag:AllowCallingPreventTollBypass                                  False
Tag:AllowCallingPreventForwardingtoPhone                           False
```

Figure 4-1. Checking the `AllowSIPDevicesCalling` parameter

There are three different provisioning servers for the SIP Gateway, and they have to be configured manually or using Dynamic Host Configuration Protocol (DHCP) to the phones:

- EMEA (*http://emea.ipp.sdg.teams.microsoft.com*)
- Americas (*http://noam.ipp.sdg.teams.microsoft.com*)
- APAC (*http://apac.ipp.sdg.teams.microsoft.com*)

Depending on the phone manufacturer, the way you configure the provisioning server may vary. For example, if you're using a Microsoft DHCP server, for Yealink phones you'll need to edit option 66 in the relevant scope for SIP phones in the server admin tool (see Figure 4-2).

Different manufacturers may have additional parameters or a dedicated server to manage their SIP phones. Cisco, Poly, and AudioCodes phones will require an edit to option 160/161. Refer to the manufacturer's documentation to check if there are any additional steps required.

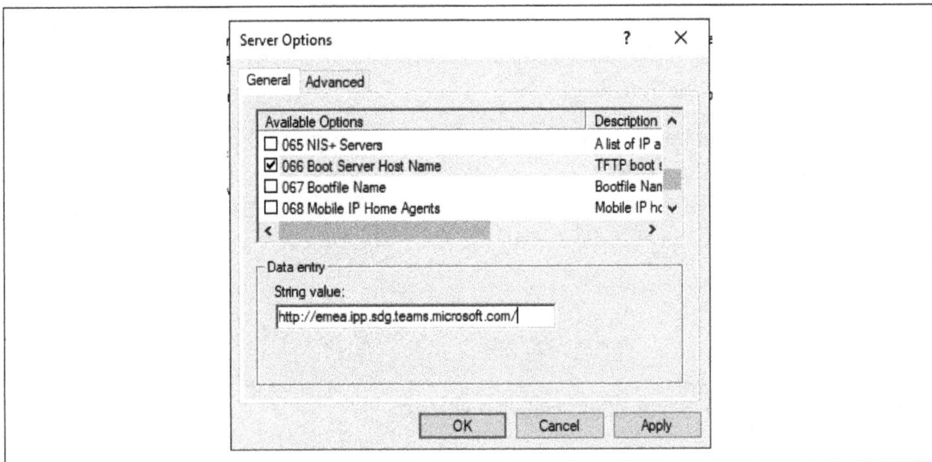

Figure 4-2. Setting option 66 for EMEA

The next step is to onboard the device, which is accomplished using the TAC ("Teams devices" > "SIP devices"). From the Actions menu, select "Provision devices." You will be sent to the Phones page. Click Add. The devices are onboarded using their MAC (Media Access Control) address. There are two options offered to do that, shown in Figure 4-3.

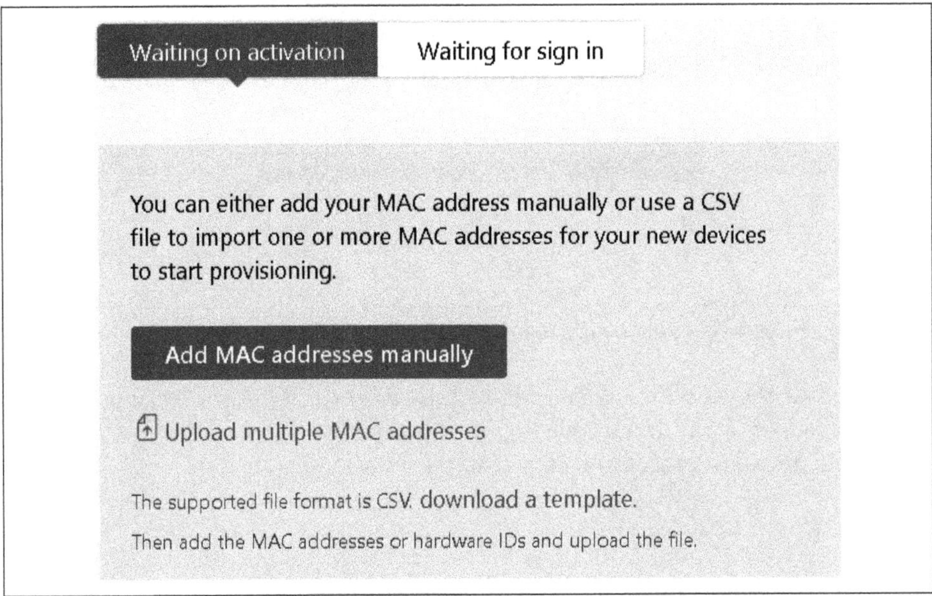

Figure 4-3. Provisioning phones in Teams

If you want to provision more than one device, you can download the CSV template and list all the phones' MAC addresses and their locations. The phones will be added to the "Waiting on activation" list.

The next step is to generate a verification code for the phone, by clicking "Generate verification code" (Figure 4-4).

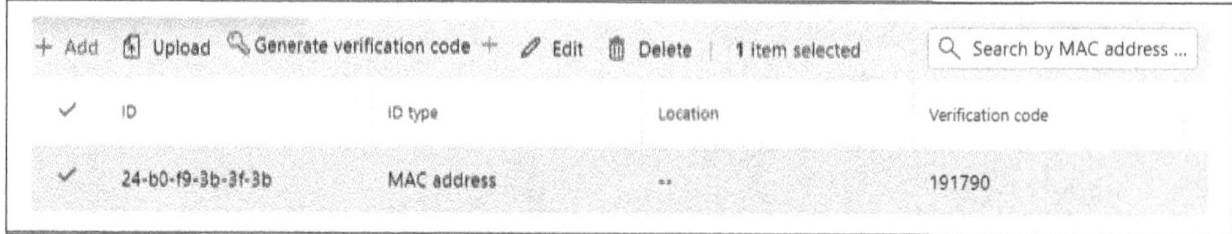

Figure 4-4. Phone with verification code generated

Then, on the device itself, go to Settings > "Provision device" and enter the verification code.

During this process, it is usually recommended to reset phones to their factory settings. Depending on the version of the firmware required by Microsoft, the phone could reboot more than once to upgrade its software.

At the end of the process a Teams logo will be shown on the device with a Sign In button. Proceed to the login page and copy the pair code (an example is shown in Figure 4-5).

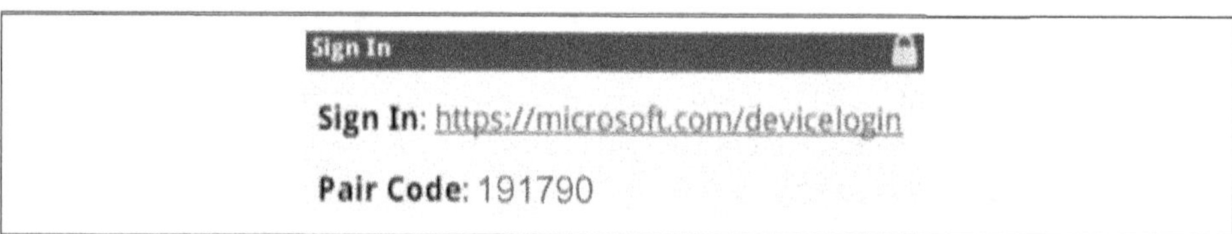

Figure 4-5. Phone displaying a pair code

The pair code shown on the screen will be used on the Microsoft Device Login page (*https://oreil.ly/mUeBB*). If the code is correctly added, a username and password are required to proceed. A successful connection is shown in Figure 4-6.

Microsoft

Teams SIP Gateway

You have signed in to the Teams SIP Gateway application on your device. You may now close this window.

Figure 4-6. Successful connection to the SIP Gateway

The account used for the Device Login page must have Enterprise Voice enabled.

The phone will reboot again, and at the end of the process you will have Teams firmware running on the device.

Discussion

Many organizations have legacy SIP phones (often referred to as *3PIP* phones). This kind of device looks like a standard desk phone but is connected to a VoIP system and grants some additional features. Desk phones that are native to Teams offer a better user experience compared to SIP phones, but there could be motivation (such as budget constraints) to keep the legacy devices after the PSTN platform has been migrated to Teams. As a way to enable legacy SIP phones to work with Teams Phone System, Microsoft proposes using the SIP Gateways, which allow core Teams calling functionalities on legacy phones.

The SIP Gateway is a viable solution *only* if you are using one of the devices listed under "Compatible devices" in the Microsoft article "Plan for SIP Gateway" (*https://oreil.ly/z71gt*).

There are some prerequisites to access the SIP Gateway, such as excluding any proxy server for the phones and setting the security (firewalls, Conditional Access, and so on) to allow the connection between the device and the SIP Gateway. All the required information is available in the Microsoft article "Configure SIP Gateway" (*https://oreil.ly/l6icf*).

In addition, the phones will require licensing, similar to the users, to enable Enterprise Voice. The licenses required are as follows:

- Teams Phone System (included in E5 or as an add-on to the existing license) or, for Common Area Phones (CAPs), a dedicated Shared Device license.
- PSTN enablement (with one of the options discussed in Chapter 3)

Cisco phones require a starting firmware called Multiplatform Phone (MPP) firmware. Even if a device is in the list of supported hardware, acquiring the MPP firmware is an additional requirement and may incur an additional cost.

Phones connected to the SIP Gateway support the following features:

- Inbound and outbound calls
- Call transfer
- Meeting dial-in and dial-out
- Device-based "do not disturb"
- Voicemail with message waiting indicator

As you can see from this list, some features that are available on a native Teams phone (such as calendar integration) are not included for devices connected to the SIP Gateway.

SIP Gateways must be considered the target solution for legacy (3PIP) phones. Microsoft is removing the Skype for Business Online infrastructure that provides support to 3PIP firmware. The end of life for 3PIP phones has been postponed more than once, but customers should change the firmware on 3PIP phones to SIP firmware and use them with Teams via the SIP Gateway.

4.2 Integrating Devices Not Supported by the SIP Gateway

Problem

You want to integrate a legacy analog device that is not supported by the SIP Gateway with Teams.

Solution

The analog device to be connected will have a phone number of +44 1632 96xxxx.

For this recipe, assume you have an SBC with three different SIP trunks providing the PSTN, Teams, and Analog Telephony Adapter (ATA) connectivity.

1. SIP trunk to Teams
2. SIP trunk to the PSTN
3. SIP trunk to the ATA

Figure 4-7 shows a high-level diagram of a possible ATA and SBC deployment for Teams.

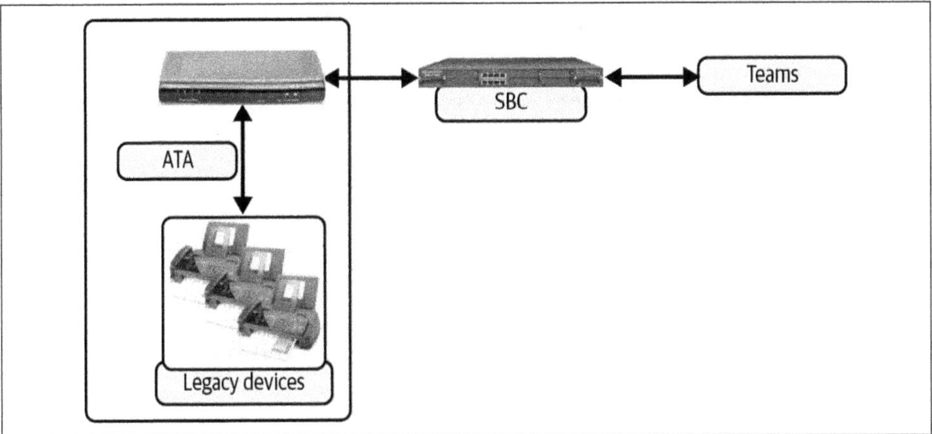

Figure 4-7. ATA and SBC connectivity

Configuring a SIP trunk is not part of this recipe. For this, refer to vendor manuals and documentation.

In this solution, I will use AudioCodes MediaPack analog media gateways as an example of device integration.

The first step is to patch the analogue device to a local ATA. You will be moving the telephone cable that was connecting the analog device to the PSTN over to the ATA. This assumes that the ATA is already connected to the network and reachable via an IP address.

The second step is to register the devices on the ATA. Log in to the ATA and choose "GW and IP to IP" > Hunt Group > EndPoint Phone Number (Figure 4-8).

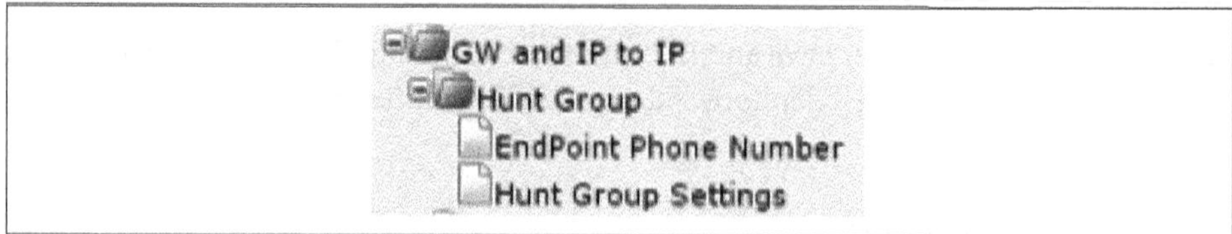

Figure 4-8. Configuration tabs in a MediaPack

There is a channel available for each Foreign Exchange Subscriber (FXS) port. You must input a phone number (for example, a three-digit extension) and a hunt group number for each connected analog device (Figure 4-9). In this solution, all the channels will be placed into hunt group 1.

Endpoint Phone Number Table

	Channel(s)	Phone Number
1	1	User1
2		
3		
4		
5		
6		

Figure 4-9. MediaPack endpoints

Now go to Hunt Group Settings. Here, you can register each device, as shown in Figure 4-10.

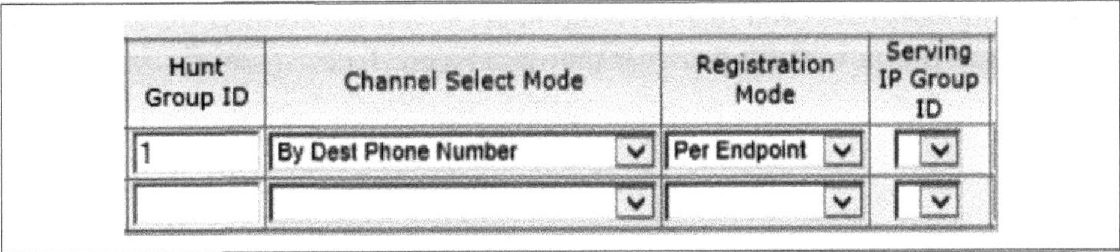

Figure 4-10. Registering the endpoints

Next, you need to create two different routes in the Routing folder (Figure 4-11). The first one is from the analog devices to the SBC ("Tel to IP Routing"). The second one is from the SBC to the analog devices ("IP to Hunt Group Routing").

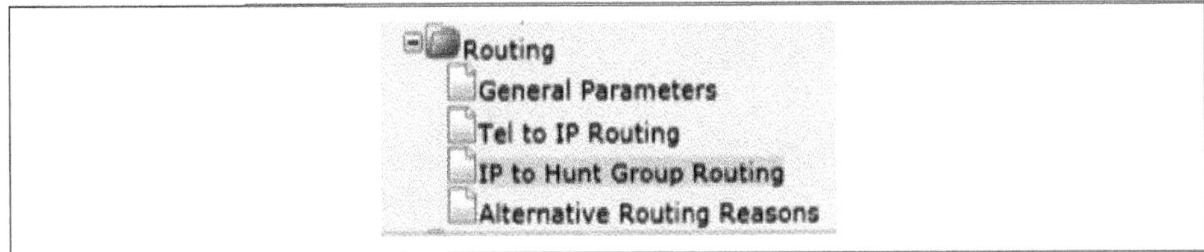

Figure 4-11. Routing menu

In the "Tel to IP Routing" path, you will set the source hunt group IP, the destination phone prefix, the source phone prefix, and the IP and port used to connect to your SBC.

In the "IP to Hunt Group Routing" path, you will set the destination phone prefix, the source phone prefix, the source IP address, and the destination hunt group IP.

In a basic configuration, you can use the following:

```
Tel to IP Routing:
Source hunt group IP = 1 (in our solution)
Destination phone prefix = *
Source phone prefix = *
IP and port used to connect to your SBC= IP and connection port for the SBC

IP to Hunt Group Routing:
Destination phone prefix = *
Source phone prefix = *
Source IP address = IP of the SBC
Destination hunt group IP = 1 (in our solution)
```

When the devices have been registered on the ATA, you will connect the ATA to the SBC using a SIP trunk. The topology is shown in Figure 4-12.

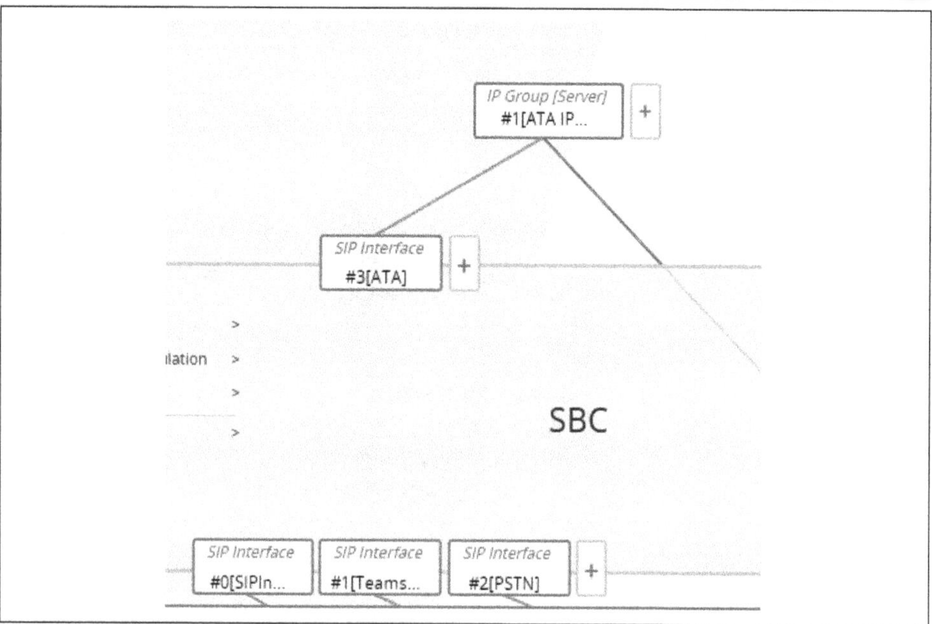

Figure 4-12. Topology of the SBC connections

Now, you need to create different voice routes:

- From the ATA to Teams
- From the ATA to the PSTN
- From Teams and the PSTN to the ATA

Voice routing can be configured using different parameters, like the calling number, the destination number, and so on. In your configuration, you'll use Alternative Routing. The calls outbound from the ATA will always try the Teams SIP trunk first. If an error code is received, the call will be routed to the PSTN SIP trunk. The two voice routes to be configured (in the "IP-to-IP Routing" path) are shown in Figures 4-13 and 4-14.

GENERAL
Index 0
Name ATA_To_Teams_Route
Alternative Route Options Route Row
MATCH
Source IP Group #1 [ATA IP] View
ACTION
Destination Type IP Group
Destination IP Group #2 [TEAMS IP] View
Destination SIP Interface -- View
Destination Address
Destination Port 0
Destination Transport Type

Figure 4-13. ATA to Teams

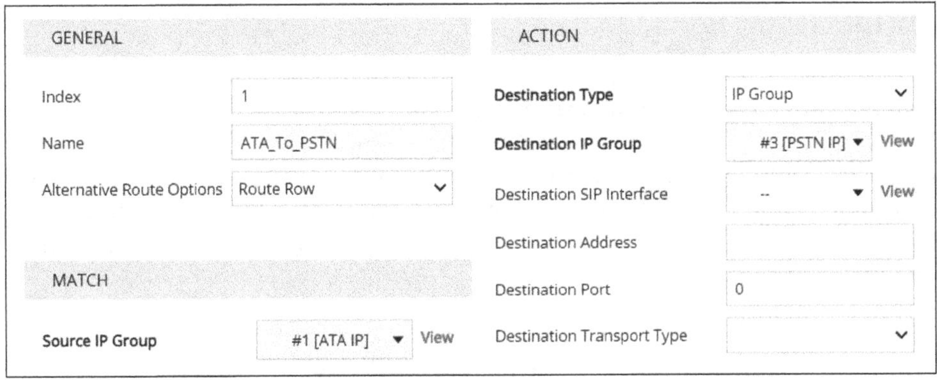

Figure 4-14. ATA to PSTN

Finally, a voice route is required from Teams and the PSTN inbound calls to the ATA, based on the destination number (Figure 4-15).

Figure 4-15. Configuring voice routes

Discussion

Devices like fax machines, elevator emergency phones, door openers, and doorbells that were part of the legacy phone system are not going to be supported by the SIP Gateway. The best solution for these devices is to replace them with a solution that is compatible with Teams (such as an elevator intercom connected to the mobile GSM network). However, in some scenarios, you may want to keep other legacy devices and integrate them with Teams Phone System. This recipe reviewed one option to achieve registration on the SBC.

The solution is based on the AudioCodes SBC and AudioCodes MediaPack ATA. The ATA is a device used to act as a bridge between a standard telephone and the rest of the network. The ATA will have one or more FXS ports used to physically connect the analog devices with a connector called an RJ11. (The standard Ethernet network cables have a different standard, called RJ45.)

Figure 4-16 shows an AudioCodes MediaPack ATA with eight FXS ports (depending on the model, FXS ports could be integrated or added as a module).

Figure 4-16. MP-118 with eight FXS ports

You can implement this solution and achieve the same result with any certified SBC with similar features.

As you saw in the solution, analog devices are not integrated with Teams as voice objects. Rather, they are managed as phone numbers, with a large part of the configuration depending on the ATA and the SBC. For this same reason, there is no management for analog devices in Teams, and fax machines are not going to be integrated with Exchange Online or similar. There are some workarounds to make the integration less complex, such as using a Resource Account (an object usable by the Teams clients) to receive and redirect the calls to the analog devices. We discuss Resource Accounts in more detail in Chapter 5.

The ATA device, which requires a physical connection to analog devices, is usually deployed on-prem. The SBC, on the other hand, can reside on-prem or in the cloud. In this type of configuration, it is important to consider that there will be some changes required to the corporate firewall to open the connectivity between the ATA and the SBC.

4.3 Joining DECT Devices to Teams Phone System

Problem

You want to connect Spectralink DECT phones to Teams.

Solution

The central piece of the Spectralink solution is the IP-DECT server. A firmware update is required on the server to add Microsoft Teams support.

An IP-DECT server can be a virtual or physical appliance. The number of supported handsets depends on the appliance used.

First, on the IP-DECT server, check the firmware level:

- Spectralink IP-DECT Server 200/400/6500 must have firmware version PCS22Aa or newer.
- Spectralink Virtual IP-DECT Server One must have firmware version PCS22Aa or newer.

Then, check the firmware on your handsets:

- Spectralink DECT Handsets 72x2, 75x2, 76x2, and 77x2 must have firmware PCS22Ab or newer.

Spectralink requires a license (a Microsoft Teams Interoperability license) for each handset. The licenses must be renewed annually. You must upload each license to the IP-DECT server.

To add the licenses:

1. Click Installation, and then click License.
2. Copy the provided license key from your email, paste it in the License field, and click Load (see Figure 4-17).
3. Reboot the server to activate the license.

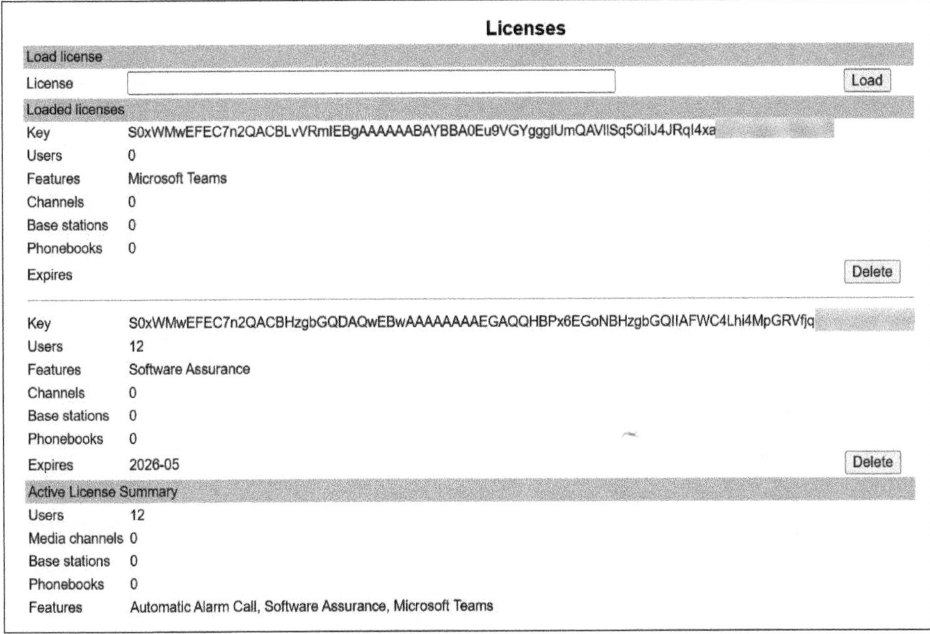

Figure 4-17. Loading licenses in an IP-DECT server

DECT telephony supports Generic Access Profile (GAP), a standard that enables devices from different manufacturers to communicate with each other. Before the Microsoft Teams Interoperability license requirement, it was possible to also connect other manufacturers' handsets to the IP-DECT server. However, after you apply this license, only a Spectralink handset will be accepted.

Now, you need to navigate to Configuration > Teams > Provisioning and use the following settings:

- *Method:* DHCP.
- *URL:* The Microsoft provisioning URL. This depends on the region, for the SIP Gateway.
- *Configuration sync time (hh:mm):* When to synchronize new configurations from the provisioning server.
- *Handset limit per account:* The number of handsets that are allowed to sign in to the same Teams account. This limit is set to 2 by default.

If the "Configuration sync time" field is left empty, then no synchronizations will be performed.

The configuration for a server located in EMEA should look like what is shown in Figure 4-18.

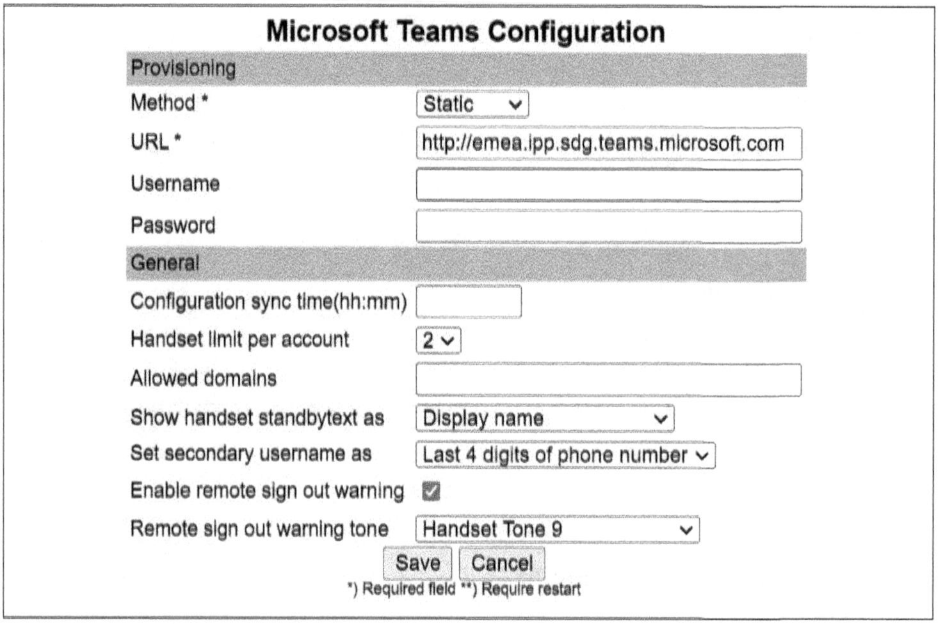

Microsoft Teams Configuration

Provisioning	
Method *	Static
URL *	http://emea.ipp.sdg.teams.microsoft.com
Username	
Password	
General	
Configuration sync time(hh:mm)	
Handset limit per account	2
Allowed domains	
Show handset standbytext as	Display name
Set secondary username as	Last 4 digits of phone number
Enable remote sign out warning	☑
Remote sign out warning tone	Handset Tone 9

Save Cancel

*) Required field **) Require restart

Figure 4-18. EMEA IP-DECT Teams server configuration

Additional settings will automatically change when the server is configured for Teams, including parameters in the General and Media sections of the SIP Configuration page, shown in Figure 4-19.

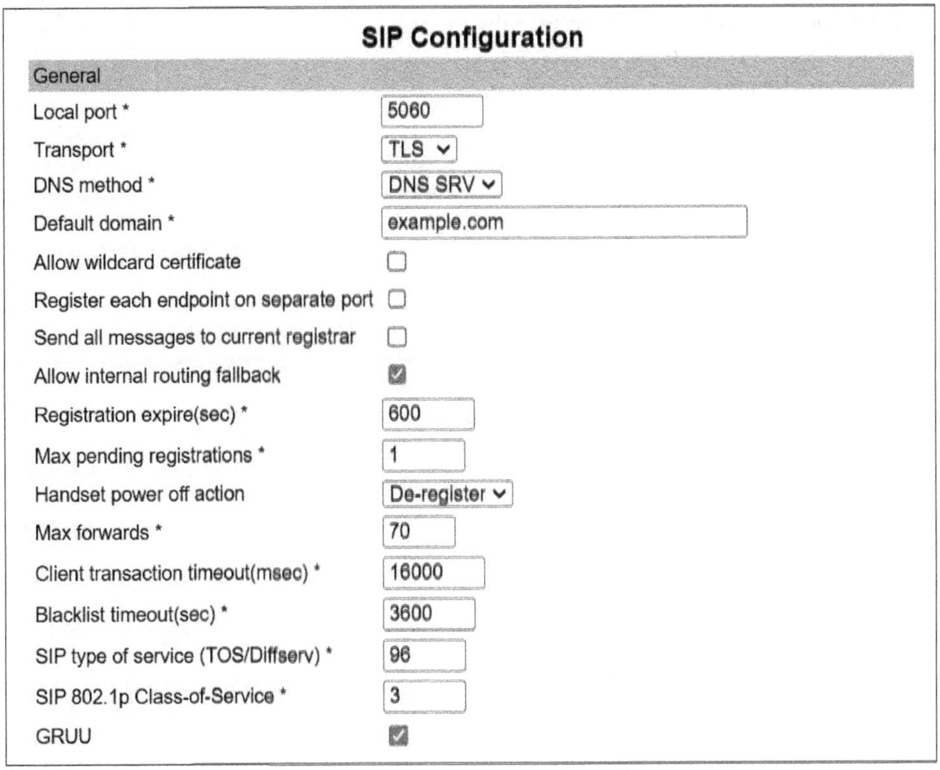

SIP Configuration

General	
Local port *	5060
Transport *	TLS
DNS method *	DNS SRV
Default domain *	example.com
Allow wildcard certificate	☐
Register each endpoint on separate port	☐
Send all messages to current registrar	☐
Allow internal routing fallback	☑
Registration expire(sec) *	600
Max pending registrations *	1
Handset power off action	De-register
Max forwards *	70
Client transaction timeout(msec) *	16000
Blacklist timeout(sec) *	3600
SIP type of service (TOS/Diffserv) *	96
SIP 802.1p Class-of-Service *	3
GRUU	☑

Figure 4-19. Some of the SIP configuration settings for Teams

The next step is onboarding the handsets. The server should show the screen in Figure 4-20.

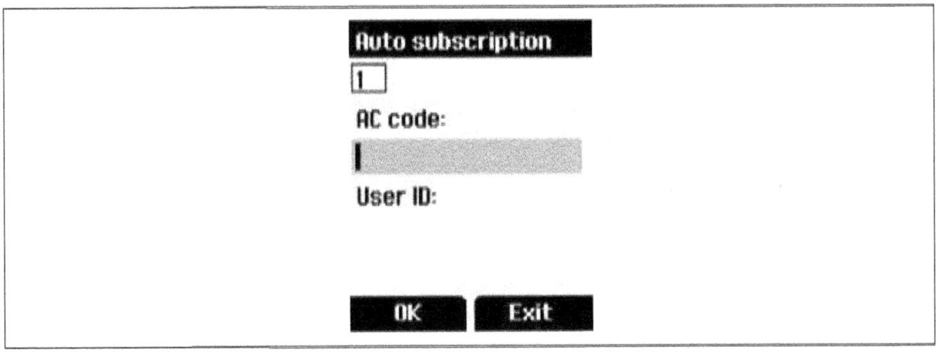

Auto subscription

1

AC code:

User ID:

OK Exit

Figure 4-20. Handset onboarding

You may need to input the AC code into the field. The AC code could be the last 4 digits of the ARI (shown on the General Status page of the server, as in Figure 4-21), or it may not be required at all.

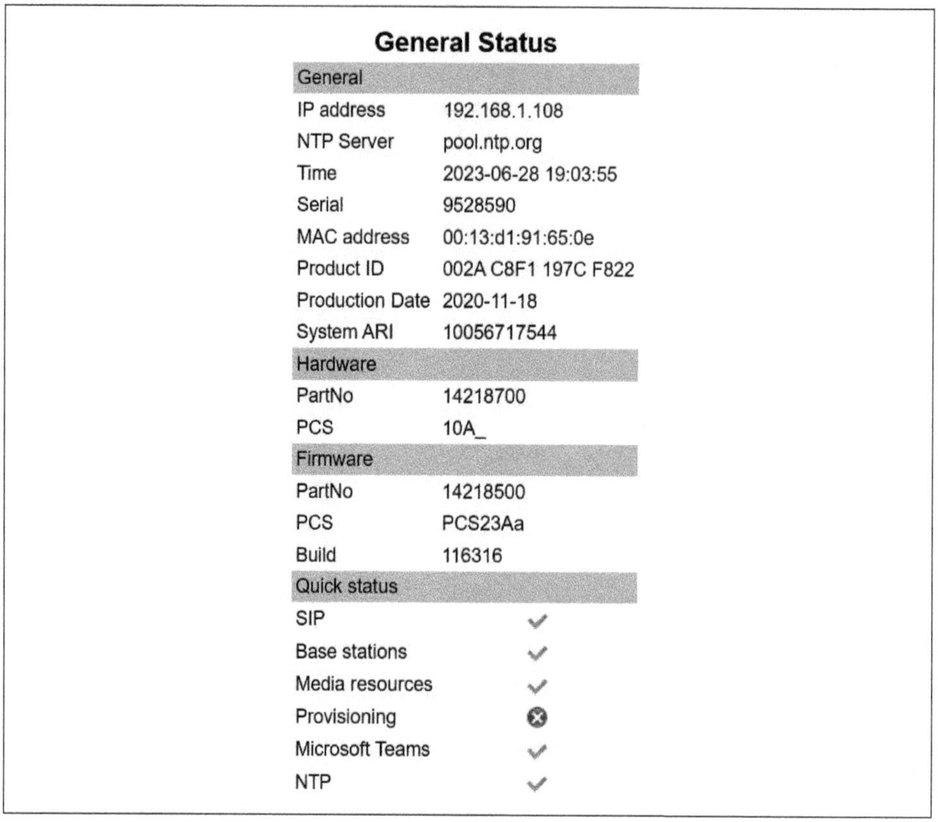

General Status

General	
IP address	192.168.1.108
NTP Server	pool.ntp.org
Time	2023-06-28 19:03:55
Serial	9528590
MAC address	00:13:d1:91:65:0e
Product ID	002A C8F1 197C F822
Production Date	2020-11-18
System ARI	10056717544
Hardware	
PartNo	14218700
PCS	10A_
Firmware	
PartNo	14218500
PCS	PCS23Aa
Build	116316
Quick status	
SIP	✓
Base stations	✓
Media resources	✓
Provisioning	✗
Microsoft Teams	✓
NTP	✓

Figure 4-21. Locating the ARI number for handset onboarding

The handset will reboot and load a new firmware. After that, a Teams option will be added to the menu (as shown in Figure 4-22).

Upon launching the Teams option, the onboarding process will start with the same steps as for other desk phones.

Figure 4-22. Microsoft Teams option added to handset menu

Discussion

So far, you have seen how to integrate analog devices with Teams. All the solutions you've seen apply to DECT phones, too, although DECT (as a technology) adds some complexity that you do not have with analog.

If you are using Ascom- or Poly-manufactured DECT devices, the registration process is not much different from what you have seen for other devices that are able to communicate with the SIP Gateway (assuming that all the prerequisites are met).

Considering that DECT adds some complexity to the deployment, and knowing that an organization could use WiFi-connected devices (like Android phones with the Teams client) instead of DECT, it is legit to question whether it is even worth deploying DECT devices. To compare the two solutions, it is important to understand that WiFi, when used for VoIP, has some specific issues, including quality of service (QoS), security, and roaming. DECT is more reliable (because it was designed for voice), more scalable (offering a higher number of devices per access point), and has security protocols embedded (reducing the need for external security solutions). On the other hand, DECT requires dedicated base stations and sometimes repeaters (devices that help to extend the range of cordless phones), which can make it an expensive solution. Leveraging an existing DECT infrastructure may make sense, but before deploying a completely new DECT system, a cost-benefit analysis is recommended.

A DECT system always contains two components: a base station (also called the *fixed part*) and at least one handset (usually a cordless phone, called the *portable part*). The base station forms the bridge between the telephone and internet connection and the handsets. Adding base stations enables you to cover a larger area. The base station continuously sends a "beacon signal" that synchronizes the handsets with the necessary information to allow them to connect and send data. When a DECT system connects to Teams, the way the VoIP is managed is different from with other voice platforms.

First, you need additional information about Teams phone calls. Each phone call consists of two components:

Signaling
: This does the work of establishing, maintaining, and tearing down the call.

Media
: This is the actual audio from the call.

Signaling establishes how the media flow will be managed. In a Teams communication, a large part of the network traffic is due to the media (where voice and video are transported). In comparison to other solutions discussed in this book, a DECT device behaves differently when connected to Teams, from a media transport point of view. Instead of communicating directly over TCP/IP, the handset will use the DECT protocol to connect to the base. From the base, the communication will go to the IP-DECT server (using TCP/IP) and finally to Teams. The server is a mandatory part of the communication.

4.4 Replacing Legacy Hardware

Problem

You need to provide advice about the best way to replace legacy hardware during a migration to Teams.

Solution

All the solutions we've discussed so far have been meant to leverage the hardware deployed with a legacy voice platform for Teams. However, in all the scenarios in which it is doable, the correct approach would be to *replace* the legacy devices with a solution that is certified to work with Teams. So, what replacements should you suggest?

First, make a list of the existing legacy devices. The categories you will usually see are as follows:

Fax machines

If having a physical fax machine is not a requirement, the easiest solution is to replace it with a fax server.

Desk phones

Microsoft has a list of desk phones & Teams displays (*https://oreil.ly/i8MG6*) that are certified for Teams. Managing and using certified devices with Teams provides the best user experience.

Analog phones/receptionist phones

For analog phones, a replacement with a certified device (as with desk phones) is usually the best option. Receptionist (attendant) phones, on the other hand, have a set of additional features that enable the operator to manage different calls at the same time. The solution for this specific usage is to deploy a soft client that enables the receptionist to work with Teams (like Landis Attendant Console or Luware Attendant Console for Microsoft Teams).

Door openers, intercoms, doorbells, elevator emergency phones

Some of the devices in this category are replaceable with a certified Teams device. Other hardware can be modified or replaced with devices that are able to connect to the GSM network. Avoiding the deployment of ATAs and analog adapters (as much as possible) reduces the complexity of the Teams Voice deployment.

Discussion

There are some additional considerations for the different scenarios discussed in this solution:

- There are some advantages to a fax server solution, including keeping all the documents in a digital format (instead of printing them), integrating the system with Teams and email, and removing the need for ATAs and SBC connections. There is no list of certified solutions for fax management and Teams, so you will need to evaluate the different vendors.
- It is not always possible to deliver a 1:1 replacement for an existing desk phone. The legacy device could have specific features that are not exactly mapped to Teams. Often, the solution is finding equivalent functionality using the features you have in Teams.
- To replace a receptionist phone where the number of features required is limited, a low-impact solution might involve deploying a phone with what is called a *sidecar*. This is an extension of the phone, attached to one side, that allows you to speed-dial internal and external phone numbers by pressing a single button. An example of a Teams phone with a sidecar is shown in Figure 4-23.

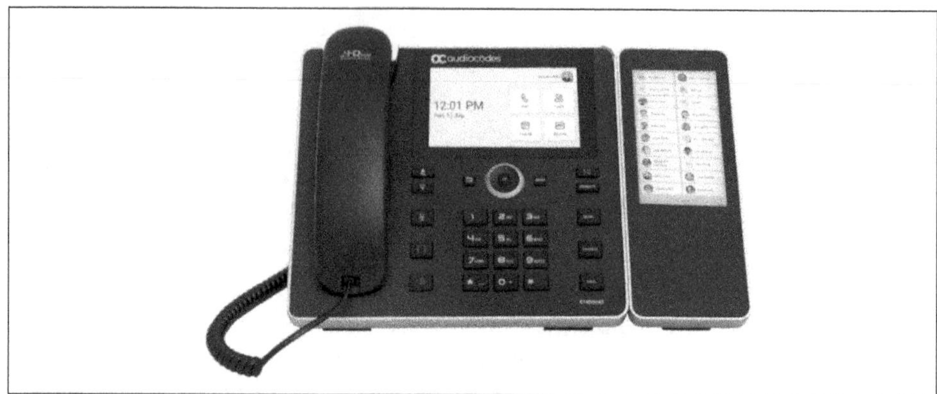

Figure 4-23. Teams phone (AudioCodes) with a sidecar

For more complex scenarios, receptionist software could be used on a standard workstation or on a Teams phone, depending on the specifics. A receptionist or attendant software solution improves the user interface in the Teams client. The emphasis is on quickly managing calls, automating tasks, and easily searching in a large number of contacts. Figure 4-24 shows an example.

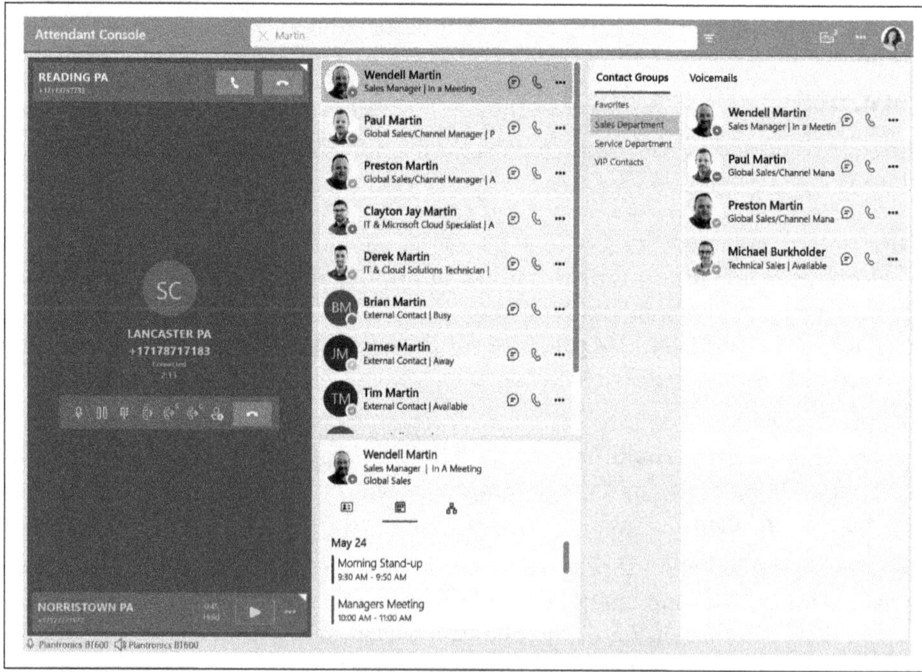

Figure 4-24. Receptionist/attendant console (Landis Technologies)

4.5 Summary

Despite the innate limitations of some of the integration scenarios between Teams and legacy, analog, and DECT devices, some organizations will still want to keep their existing hardware. This chapter introduced integration scenarios using the SIP Gateway or an SBC/ATA deployment. We also examined some ways to offer replacements for legacy devices. The next chapter focuses on Teams Voice advanced features, including Call Queues and Auto Attendants.

CHAPTER 5

Advanced Voice Features in Microsoft Teams

The increased adoption of Teams and the additional features related to voice that have been deployed in recent years have reduced the gap between Teams Phone System and legacy on-prem voice solutions. Influenced by the growing need to provide enterprise-class voice, Teams is now able to manage complex voice scenarios. The improvement in the number and quality of voice features in Teams has been particularly evident in areas like managing service (shared) phone numbers, agents, and phone number delegation.

The tools embedded in Teams allow for the management of customer services and similar systems. However, larger and more complex organizations may require an integrated call center solution. We will discuss this topic in more detail in Chapter 6.

To manage phone services and agents associated with PSTN numbers, the fundamental tools are Resource Accounts, Call Queues, and Auto Attendants. We'll explore these tools in this chapter.

5.1 Configuring and Managing Resource Accounts

Problem

You want to define a voice service for your organization connected to a phone number.

Solution

In this recipe, you will define a Resource Account (called Res-CQ-ServiceDesk) that will have a free license, a phone number assigned from a Calling Plan, and a Voice Routing Policy (VRP) called UK-VRP-International.

A license is required to enable the Resource Account (previously, a license was required only for Resource Accounts that needed Teams Phone System for receiving calls on a PSTN number and eventually enabling agents to make outgoing calls). You can use free Microsoft Teams Phone Resource Account licenses for this purpose. If you have never added these licenses to your tenant before, go to Marketplace and select "All products." Search for Microsoft Teams Phone Resource Account and then open Details. You can order Resource Account licenses at no cost here, as shown in Figure 5-1.

Figure 5-1. Ordering Microsoft Teams Phone Resource Account licenses

Click Buy and then Place Order.

Any organization that has at least one user license with Teams Phone System features has 25 Resource Account licenses available at no additional cost. Every additional 10 Phone System user licenses in your organization gives you 1 additional Resource Account license. So, for example, a company with 400 Phone System–enabled users has 65 (25 + 40) Resource Account licenses available. If you use all your free Resource Account licenses, you can buy more or apply a Phone System license.

Now, to create the new Resource Account, go to the TAC and select Voice > "Resource accounts." Click Add and fill in the required fields as shown in Figure 5-2.

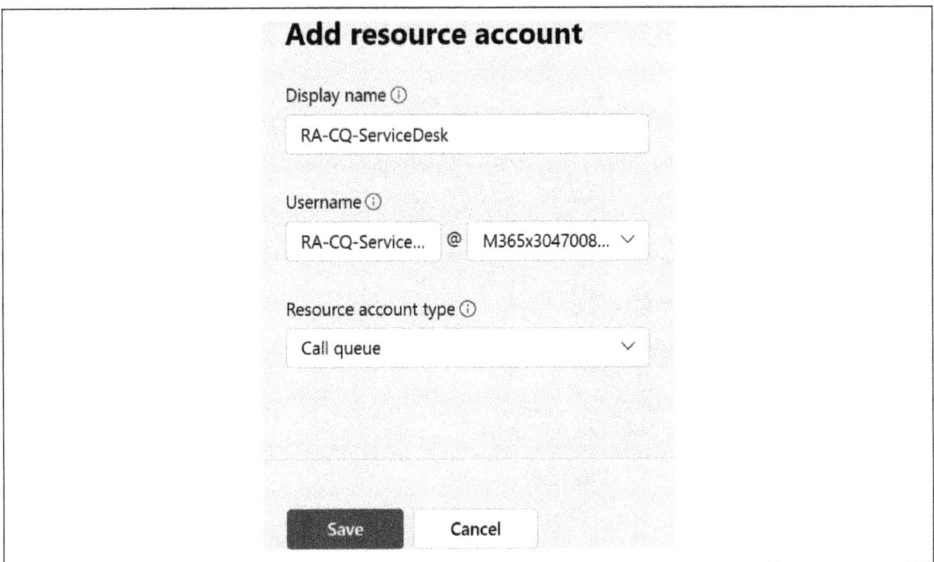

Figure 5-2. Creating a Resource Account

The Resource Account will be automatically assigned to the global VRP. From the "Resource accounts" screen in the TAC, it is possible to edit the display name, Resource Account type, and VRP. (It is not possible to assign a different VRP to an account when you first add it.) A VRP is necessary if the agents are going to make outgoing calls using the Resource Account phone number.

Select Edit and assign to the Resource Account the UK-VRP-International VRP. Select "Assign/unassign" and apply a phone number from any of the three types (Calling Plan, Operator Connect, or Direct Routing). In our solution, we will assign a phone number from a Calling Plan (as shown in Figure 5-3).

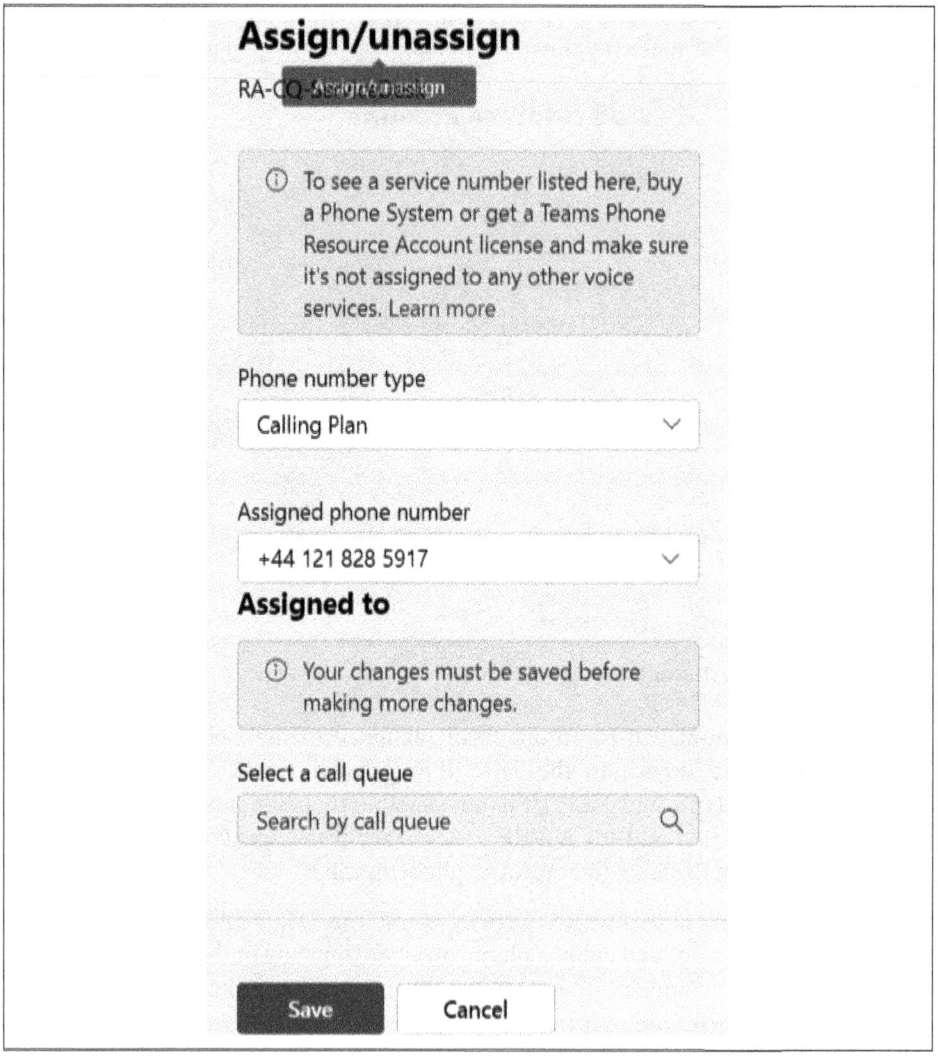

Figure 5-3. Assigning a phone number to a Resource Account

If you are going to use Calling Plans with your Resource Account, you have two different options for Call Queues and Auto Attendants. One of them is Toll (whoever calls the number pays the related cost), and the other one is Toll Free (see Figure 5-4).

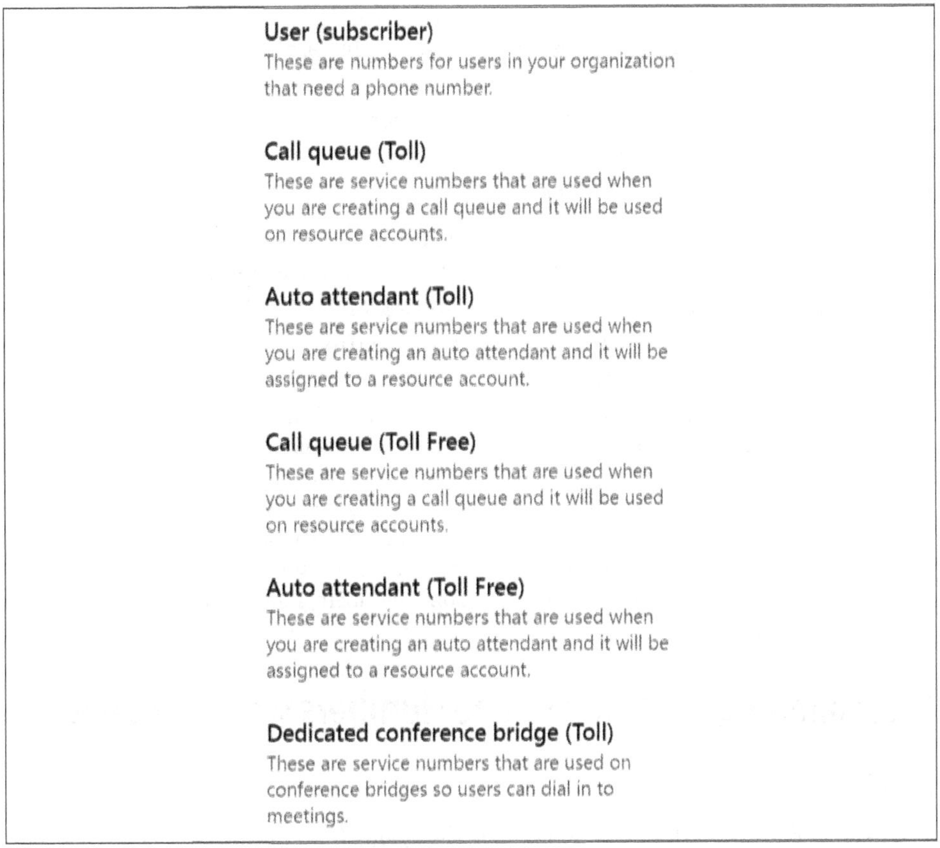

User (subscriber)
These are numbers for users in your organization that need a phone number.

Call queue (Toll)
These are service numbers that are used when you are creating a call queue and it will be used on resource accounts.

Auto attendant (Toll)
These are service numbers that are used when you are creating an auto attendant and it will be assigned to a resource account.

Call queue (Toll Free)
These are service numbers that are used when you are creating a call queue and it will be used on resource accounts.

Auto attendant (Toll Free)
These are service numbers that are used when you are creating an auto attendant and it will be assigned to a resource account.

Dedicated conference bridge (Toll)
These are service numbers that are used on conference bridges so users can dial in to meetings.

Figure 5-4. Service numbers in Calling Plans

Using toll free numbers requires your organization to pay a cost for the incoming calls (the cost is related to the Calling Plan you are using).

Discussion

A *Resource Account* is an account required to enable both Call Queues and Auto Attendants (you can define both, but without an associated Resource Account they will never be active). Resource Accounts can also be used with Teams Rooms on Windows, Teams Rooms on Android, Teams Rooms on Surface Hub, and hot-desking on Teams displays. If you need to assign a phone number to a Call Queue or to an Auto Attendant, the number will be the one connected to a Resource Account that you associate with the queue or attendant.

The Resource Account is not created as a standard user, but as an Application Instance. If you want to use PowerShell, the command will look like this:

```
New-CsOnlineApplicationInstance -UserPrincipalName `
resource_account@yourtenantname.com -ApplicationId "application_id_number" `
-DisplayName "Resource_Account"
```

Assigning policies and phone numbers is still performed with the commands you have already seen for standard users (like `Set-CsPhoneNumberAssignment`). The Resource Account is created with sign-in blocked.

The Microsoft application Auto Attendant has the `ApplicationId` *ce933385-9390-45d1-9512-c8d228074e07* and the Microsoft application Call Queue has the `ApplicationId` *11cd3e2e-fccb-42ad-ad00-878b93575e07*. Third-party applications available in a tenant will use other `ApplicationIds`.

Both for users and for Resource Accounts, it is possible to assign PSTN numbers that are classified as non-geographic (non-geo). A *non-geo* number is a telephone number associated with a country, but not any specific geographic location within that country. Non-geo numbers are an option for organizations that have a national reach and prefer not to be associated with a specific location. For example, in the United Kingdom, numbers starting with 03 are non-geo.

5.2 Managing Common Phone Numbers with Call Queues

Problem

You need to define a Call Queue to manage the agents for a phone service.

Solution

Teams Call Queues route incoming calls to multiple call *agents* (a list you define containing Microsoft 365 accounts that have Teams Voice enabled) in your organization. The way the calls are routed to the agents and the way the agents are included in the queue depends on the settings of the Call Queue. Call Queues provide the following:

- Language settings
- Greeting and hold music
- Selection of the agent group
- Routing methods to the agents
- Call overflow and call timeout management

It is possible to define different queues to provide services to callers in different languages.

As you can see, there is no option in the Call Queue to change actions based on calendar day or time of day, and there are no settings to give different options to the callers. Those settings are part of the Auto Attendant. Considering those limitations, service phone numbers are usually associated with Auto Attendants. A logical process to use, which minimizes the need to go back and forth multiple times into the same configurations, is as follows:

1. Procure as many phone numbers as required for the Resource Accounts.
2. Set the required VRPs if the existing ones are not a good fit.
3. Create the Resource Accounts and assign the licenses, phone numbers, and VRPs.
4. Define the required Call Queues.
5. Finally, set the Auto Attendants.

If you need to allow agents to make outgoing calls with a shared phone number, you must assign a PSTN number to the queue using a Resource Account. Outgoing calls can use the phone number of the Resource Account that enabled the call queue or the phone number of an additional Resource Account. The account used is selected in the "Assign calling ID" parameter of the call queue.

In this recipe, you will define a Call Queue (with an associated Resource Account) with the following settings:

- *Name:* CQ Service Desk Agents
- *Resource Account:* `ResCQ_Service_Desk` (note: the queue agents will use the Resource Account number for outgoing calls, too)
- *Language:* English (United Kingdom)
- *Greetings:* No greetings—hold music will be United Kingdom ring tone
- *Call Queue:* The Call Queue, for answering, will use the Service Desk Agents channel that is in the Service Desk team
- *Routing method:* Round robin
- *Presence-based routing:* On
- *Call agents can opt out of taking calls:* On

Any settings not listed here should be left on the defaults.

From the TAC, select Voice > "Call queues." Click Add, and set the options as shown in Figure 5-5.

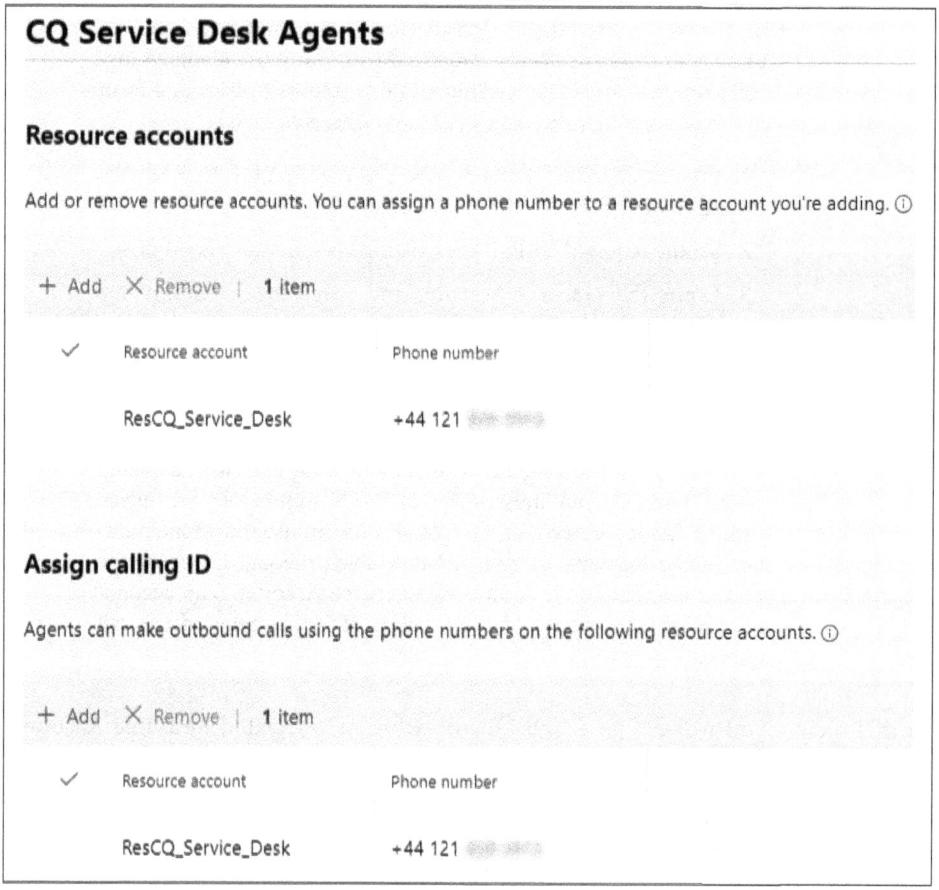

CQ Service Desk Agents

Resource accounts

Add or remove resource accounts. You can assign a phone number to a resource account you're adding. ⓘ

+ Add ✕ Remove | 1 item

✓	Resource account	Phone number
	ResCQ_Service_Desk	+44 121

Assign calling ID

Agents can make outbound calls using the phone numbers on the following resource accounts. ⓘ

+ Add ✕ Remove | 1 item

✓	Resource account	Phone number
	ResCQ_Service_Desk	+44 121

Figure 5-5. Call Queue settings

On the next page ("Greeting and music"), upload the file for hold music (Teams supports audio files in MP3, WAV, and WMA format, smaller than 5 MB). Click Next.

Often, an organization's preferred hold music is the local ring tone. The tones vary between countries, so I created a page (*https://oreil.ly/XOEzh*) where you can download the appropriate audio file for your country.

On the "Call answering" page, click "Add a channel" and select Service Desk > General. Click Next. Select "Round robin" as the routing method. The other options are already on by default. You can then click Submit—no further modification is required.

Discussion

For each Call Queue, you can decide whether the agents are automatically added when they log in to Teams. The control is in the Settings (Calls) menu of the Teams client, one for each Call Queue the user is an agent for. Every time a user is added to a queue, they get a notification in the Teams client (on the Activity tab).

The agent experience is different if you use a channel (also called a *voice-enabled channel*) or an Office 365 group (or a manual list of users) for call answering. If the agents are added using a channel, they will see an additional Calls tab in each voice-enabled channel that shows the received calls, the calls that were forwarded to voicemail, the status of the agents, and a dial pad. The Calls tab is shown in Figure 5-6.

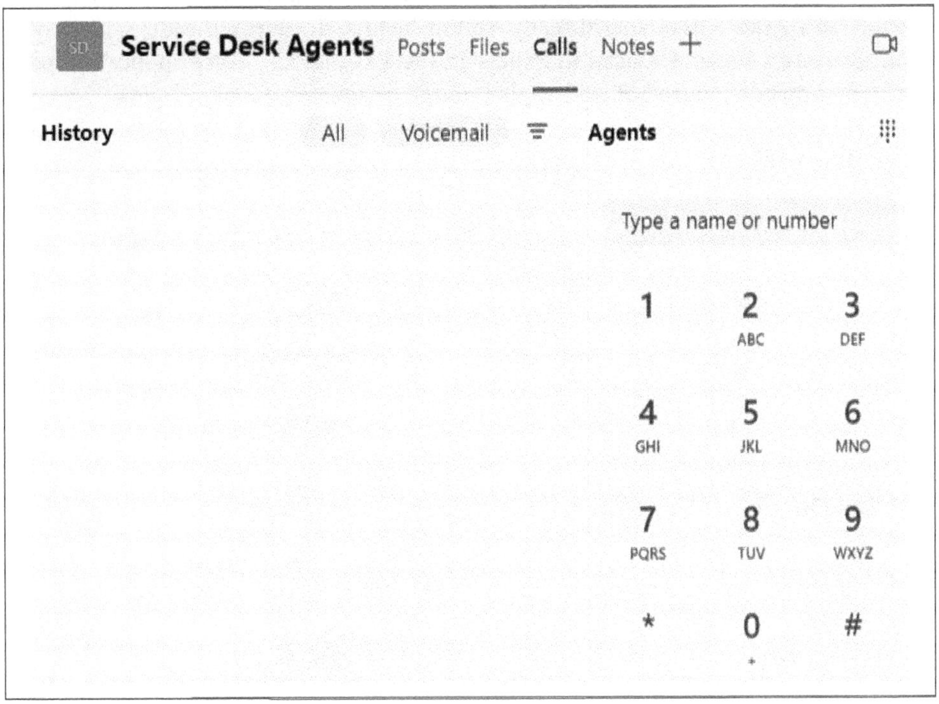

Figure 5-6. An agent's view of a voice-enabled channel

An agent in a voice-enabled channel can also change their status from the Calls tab, instead of going to the client settings. A moderator for Teams can change the status of the agents from the Calls tab too, without any access to the TAC. If the agent wants to make a call, they are offered a choice between their personal number and the Call Queue number (Figure 5-7).

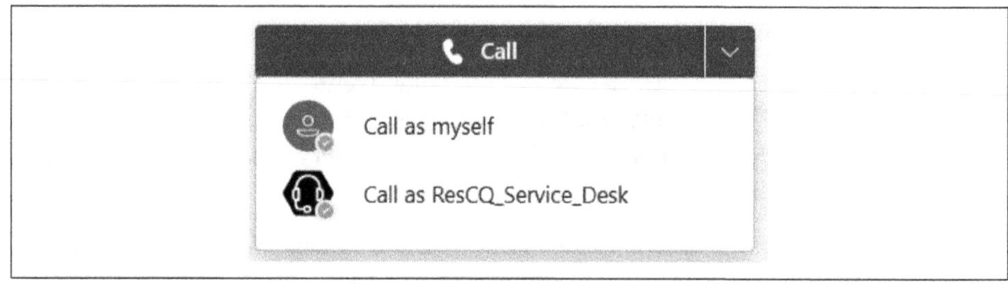

Figure 5-7. Drop-down menu for agent making a call

To make the management of Auto Attendants and Call Queues more flexible, you can authorize users to manage greetings and announcements for their respective Call Queues and Auto Attendants directly within Teams. To apply the delegation, you need to create a Voice Application Policy (in the TAC, select "Voice application policies"), as shown in Figure 5-8, and apply it to the designated users.

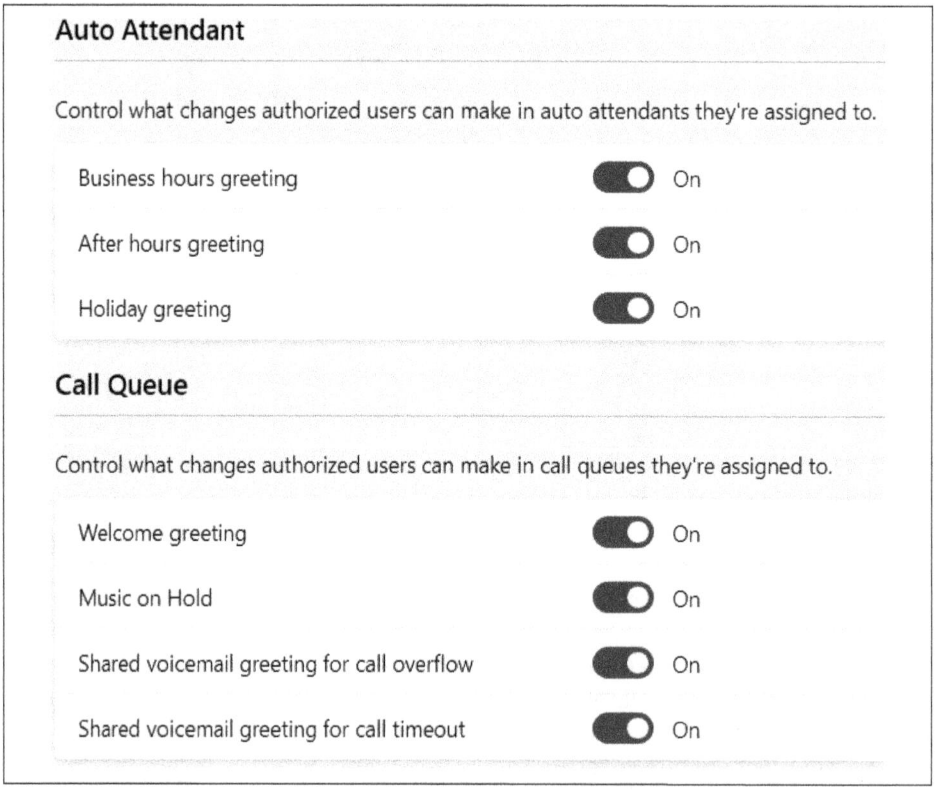

Auto Attendant

Control what changes authorized users can make in auto attendants they're assigned to.

Business hours greeting On

After hours greeting On

Holiday greeting On

Call Queue

Control what changes authorized users can make in call queues they're assigned to.

Welcome greeting On

Music on Hold On

Shared voicemail greeting for call overflow On

Shared voicemail greeting for call timeout On

Figure 5-8. Authorizing users to modify Auto Attendants and Call Queues

If you are using a voice-enabled channel, you can use the shared voicemail (that is automatically created) as a redirection destination for timed-out calls. Voicemail includes a transcript option. The voicemail is accessible from Outlook under Groups, inside the Service Desk folder (Figure 5-9).

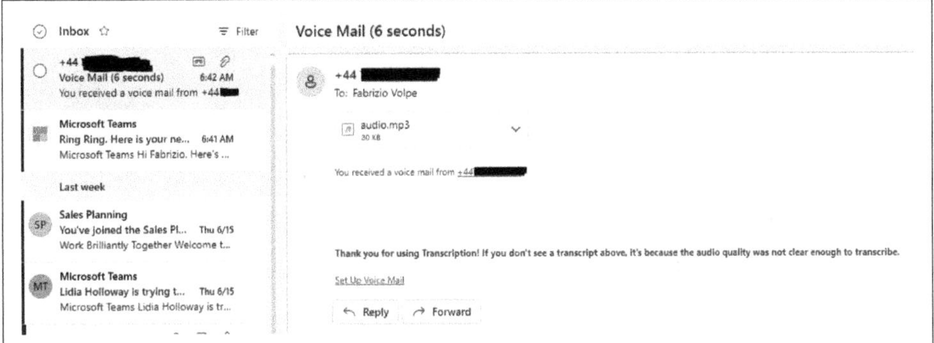

Figure 5-9. Voicemail for a voice-enabled channel (Service Desk)

In all the available solutions to add agents to the Call Queue, there is no way to see the missed calls that were not routed to a shared voicemail or the calls that were not routed to you.

If a member of the team is not Enterprise Voice-enabled in Teams, they will not see the Calls tab in the channel and they will not get any incoming calls. If you try to manually add a user with no Teams Phone System license (for example, Alex Wilber) to a Call Queue, you will receive the following message: "You are trying to link Alex Wilber but they aren't enterprise voice-enabled."

If you use a Microsoft 365 group instead of a channel, the agents will not have a common working area and each one of them will only be able to change their own status. The Office group voicemail will be accessible from Outlook, as you saw for voice-enabled channels.

5.3 Updating Holidays for Auto Attendants in Teams

Problem

You need to automate changing the holiday call settings for Auto Attendants.

Solution

Save the following script in a PS1 file (for example, *Get-PublicHolidaysUK.ps1*) and execute it:

```
Function Get-PublicHolidaysUK {
    Param([boolean]$IncludePast = $false)

    $URI = "https://www.gov.uk/bank-holidays.json"
    $Results = Invoke-RestMethod -Uri $URI -Method GET
    $HolidaysEW = $Results | Select-Object -ExpandProperty england-and-wales
    $FutureHolidaysEW =@()

    If ($IncludePast -eq $true)
    {
    Return $HolidaysEW.events
    } else {
    ForEach ($Hol in $HolidaysEW.events){
    If (([DateTime]$Hol.date) -gt $(Get-Date -Format yyyy-MM-dd))
    {
    $FutureHolidaysEW += $hol
    }
    }
    Return $FutureHolidaysEW
    }
    }

Connect-MicrosoftTeams

    $UKHols = Get-PublicHolidaysUK
    # Make new Schedule
    $tmpdtr = New-CsOnlineDateTimeRange -Start "01/01/2020 00:00" -Verbose
    $UKschedule = New-CsOnlineSchedule -Name "UK_Bank_Holidays" -FixedSchedule `
        -DateTimeRanges @($tmpdtr) -Verbose
    $UKschedule = Get-CsOnlineSchedule -Id $UKschedule.id
    Get-CsOnlineSchedule -Id $UKschedule.id
    Get-CsOnlineSchedule -Id $UKschedule.id | Select-Object -ExpandProperty `
        FixedSchedule

    ForEach ($Hol in $UKHols){
    $myDate = [datetime]::parseexact($Hol.date, 'yyyy-MM-dd', $null)
    $DateStart = $myDate.ToString('dd/MM/yyyy 00:00')
    $DateEnd = $myDate.ToString('dd/MM/yyyy 23:45')
    write-host $DateStart -ForegroundColor Green
    write-host $DateEnd -ForegroundColor red
    # Add a new Date Time Range ## supported formats: 'd/M/yyyy H:mm', `
    # 'd/M/yyyy'.
    $UKschedule.FixedSchedule.DateTimeRanges += New-CsOnlineDateTimeRange `
        -Start $DateStart -End $DateEnd
    Set-CsOnlineSchedule -Instance $UKschedule
    Start-Sleep 1
    }
```

To check your holiday schedule, you first need to use the command `Get-CsOnlineSchedule` to get the ID of the schedule (see the example in Figure 5-10).

```
Id                           : 50dbef95-603b-4921-b488-7a3dcdf79339
Name                         : UK_Bank_Holidays
Type                         : Fixed
WeeklyRecurrentSchedule      :
FixedSchedule                : Microsoft.Rtc.Management.Hosted.Online.Models.FixedSchedule
AssociatedConfigurationIds :
```

Figure 5-10. Checking holiday schedule information

To see details about the schedule, issue the following commands (note, in this PowerShell example the schedule ID is *55ce8afd-fef1-4c93-a0eb-e27a8538fd49*):

```
$sch = Get-CsOnlineSchedule -Id 55ce8afd-fef1-4c93-a0eb-e27a8538fd49
$sch.FixedSchedule
```

The output will look something like this:

```
DateTimeRanges : 01-01-2020 00:00 - 02-01-2020 00:00, 29-08-2022 00:00
                  - 29-08-2022 23:45, 26-12-2022 00:00 - 26-12-2022 23:45,
                 27-12-2022 00:00 - 27-12-2022 23:45, 02-01-2023 00:00
                 - 02-01-2023 23:45, 07-04-2023 00:00 - 07-04-2023 23:45,
                 10-04-2023 00:00 - 10-04-2023 23:45, 01-05-2023 00:00
                 - 01-05-2023 23:45, 29-05-2023 00:00 - 29-05-2023 23:45,
                 28-08-2023 00:00 - 28-08-2023 23:45, 25-12-2023 00:00
                 - 25-12-2023 23:45, 26-12-2023 00:00 - 26-12-2023 23:45
```

You can now apply the new holiday schedule where required, using the TAC or a script.

For this recipe, I have adapted a script originally found in the Reddit thread "Automatically Create Australian Public Holidays for Teams Calling Auto Attendants with PowerShell" (*https://oreil.ly/hs9Vw*).

Discussion

An Auto Attendant is used to route a call based on the options selected by a caller. The options could change based on time parameters (business hours, off hours, and holidays). You can create menu prompts by using text-to-speech or by uploading a recorded audio file, and you can also accept voice or dial pad inputs as answers to the menu options. You can also add an operator as a first step before engaging an Auto Attendant to manage incoming calls.

You can connect an Auto Attendant to a Call Queue or to another Auto Attendant, creating different call routes. For example, an Auto Attendant could be used to direct callers to additional Auto Attendants that support different languages. The call routing options of an Auto Attendant (menu options) can be presented using text-to-speech or an audio file. If your menu requires multiple languages, an audio file is the best option.

Auto Attendants are a good solution for switchboards and call center scenarios (especially when detailed monitoring of the number of calls and agent performance is not a requirement). Auto Attendants support a feature called Dial by Name or Extension where, using their voice or phone keypad, callers can specify the full or partial name or the extension of the person they would like to reach.

For Dial by Name:

- The Auto Attendant should have "Voice inputs" set to On in the General settings page.
- The call flow should go to a menu with no option keys associated and "Dial by name" selected as the directory search method (see Figure 5-11).

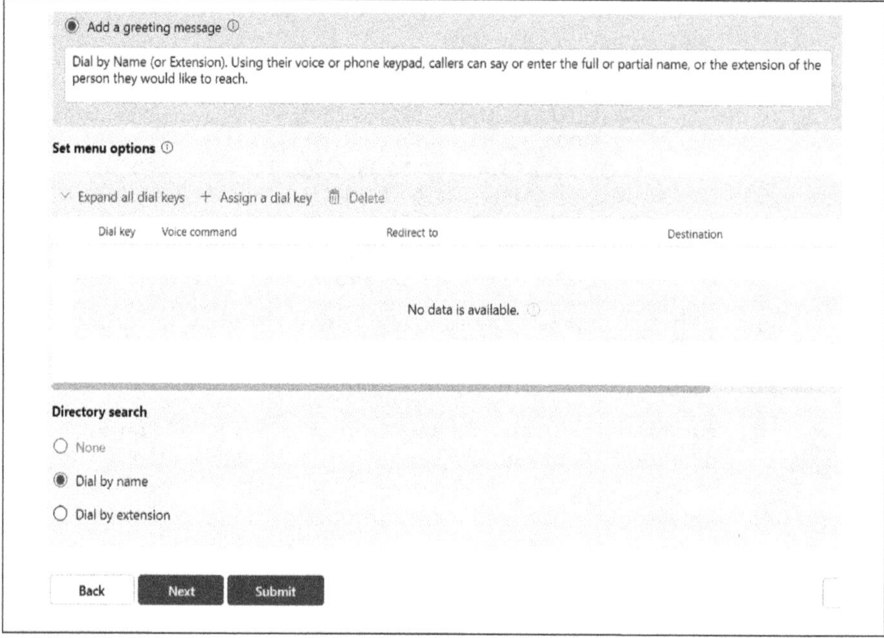

Figure 5-11. Configuring for Dial by Name

- The last step is to set the options in the "Dial scope" page. You can limit the scope of the search or exclude specific groups (Figure 5-12 shows the settings).

Dial scope
Set up the users or groups that will be listed and available in your organization's directory when a caller dials in to this auto attendant. When callers use Dial by name and search for a person, they'll be transferred to a user who has the Teams app installed. Learn more
Include
Select which users will be included and available in your organization's directory.
All online users
Custom user group
Exclude
Select which users or groups will be excluded from the organization's directory.
No one
Custom user group

Figure 5-12. Dial scope for Dial-by-Name directory search

Only online users that are Enterprise Voice–enabled (whether they have a phone number or not) are searchable. Also, input from the phone keypad is always enabled.

For Dial by Extension:

- You must enable extensions for your users. *Extensions* are short codes associated with a full phone number. The supported formats are as follows:
  - *+<phone number>;ext=<extension>*
  - *+<phone number>x<extension>*
  - *x<extension>*

For example, for a direct routing number with extension 1234, the phone number could be formatted as *+4411585XXXXX;ext=1234*. Both internal users and users calling the Auto Attendant can then connect to the desired person just using the extension digits.

As for Microsoft's MC487014, organizations that use extensions in their phone numbers have to adhere to some specific standards. For users with a unique phone number, removing the extension is the suggested solution.

For users with the same base number and different extensions, check that the calls are sent to Teams with the phone number formatted correctly, including the extension.

For more information, see "Microsoft Teams—What to Do Before March 2023 If You Use Phone Number Extensions (MC487014)" (*https://oreil.ly/J6nJ8*).

5.4 Delegating and Managing Call Groups

Problem

You must change the way phone calls are answered for a Teams user using an administrative account.

Solution

Enterprise Voice–enabled users can manage their incoming calls, redirecting them based on different parameters. Teams administrators can manipulate the same user settings using the TAC.

In the TAC, go to Users > "Manage users," select the desired user, and click the username. In the user settings, go to the Voice tab. The section you are interested in is called "Call answering rules."

As you can see in Figure 5-13, there are essentially three different options when a call is received:

- Forward the call, without ringing the local device.
- Enable another user or group to answer to the call.
- Route the call to a different destination after a wait time (the default is 20 seconds).

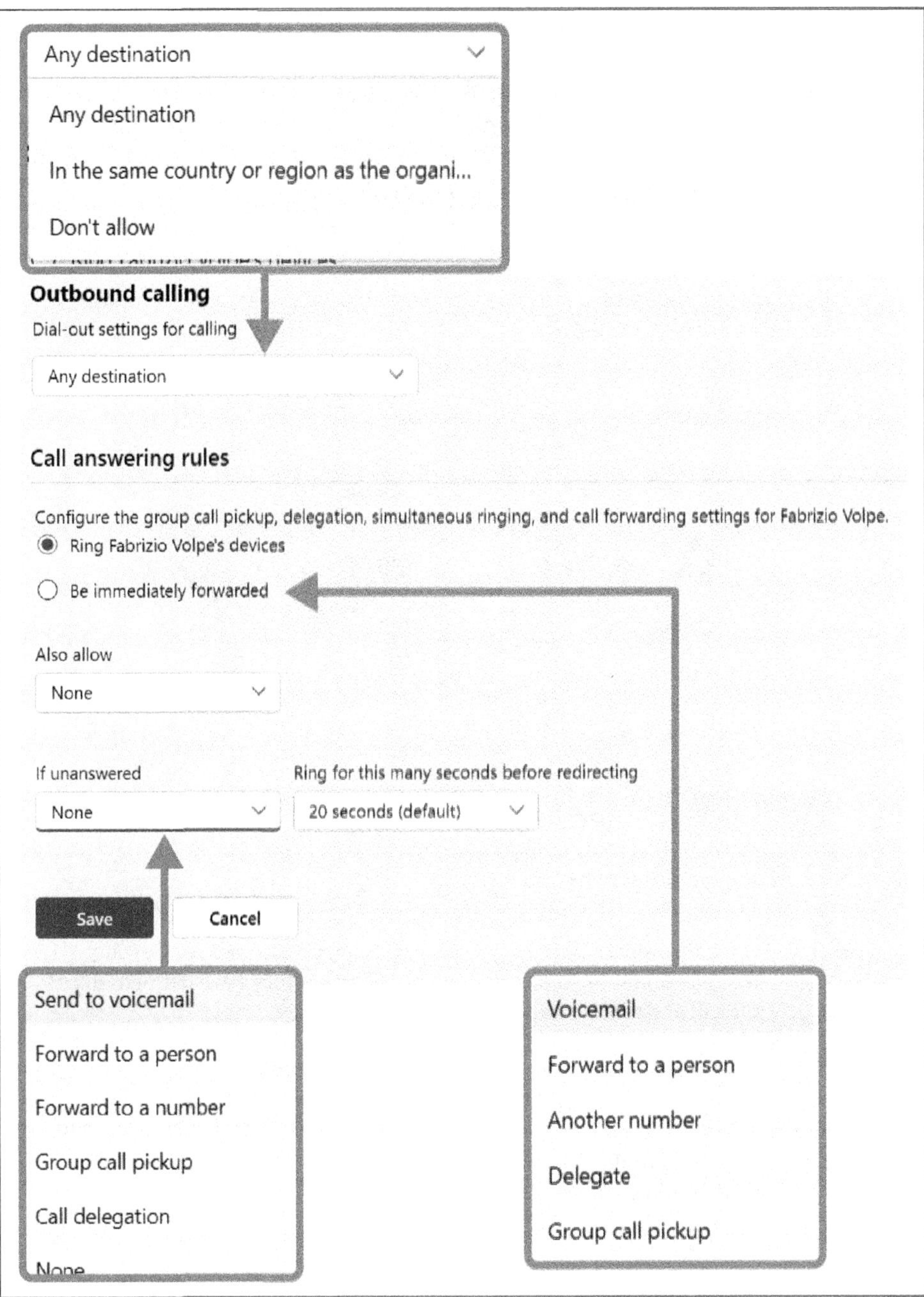
Any destination
Any destination
In the same country or region as the organi...
Don't allow
Outbound calling
Dial-out settings for calling
Any destination
Call answering rules
Configure the group call pickup, delegation, simultaneous ringing, and call forwarding settings for Fabrizio Volpe.
Ring Fabrizio Volpe's devices
Be immediately forwarded
Also allow
None
If unanswered
None
Ring for this many seconds before redirecting
20 seconds (default)
Save
Cancel
Send to voicemail
Forward to a person
Forward to a number
Group call pickup
Call delegation
Voicemail
Forward to a person
Another number
Delegate
Group call pickup

Figure 5-13. Call answering rules in the user's settings

"Group call pickup" and "Call delegation" enable the user to define some more complex call-routing scenarios. The group call pickup feature allows a user to create a group of voice-enabled users to whom calls that are not getting an answer are routed. As you can see in Figure 5-14, the "Manage call group" screen enables the definition of a group of users and the way their phones ring when a call arrives (all of them simultaneously or following the order of table rows).

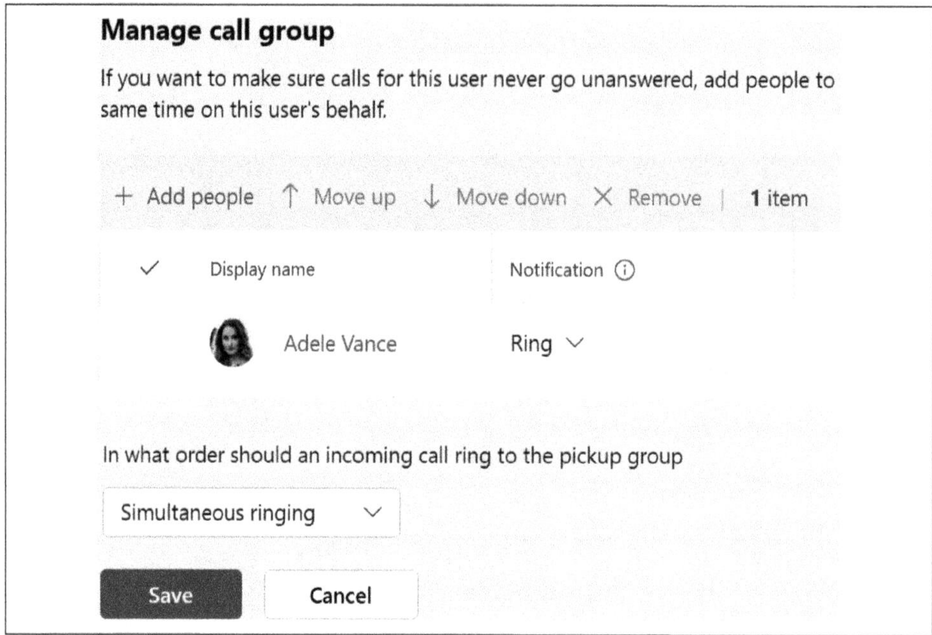

Figure 5-14. Managing call groups

If the incoming call is for a Call Queue, where the user is an agent, the call will not be redirected to the call group they have defined in the call answering rules.

Call delegation enables one user to receive or make calls on another user's behalf. You can change the settings on the "Call delegation" page (see Figure 5-15) and even allow the delegate to modify the same parameters.

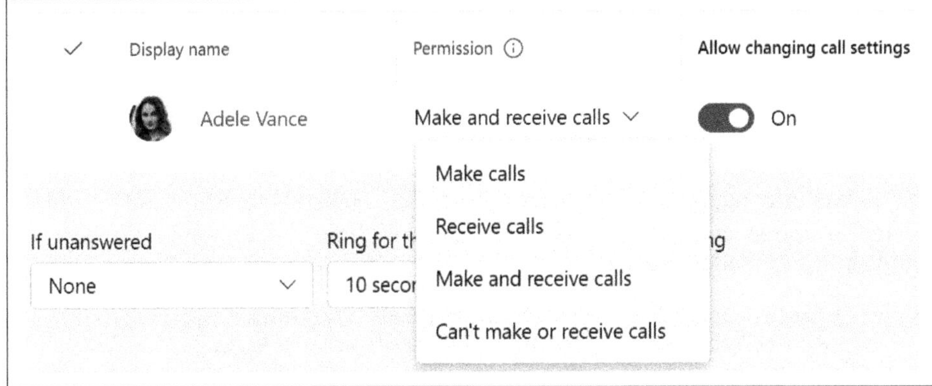

Figure 5-15. Call delegation permissions

The delegate will have shared lines in their Teams client, allowing them to make calls on behalf of the user that delegated the permission (as shown in Figure 5-16).

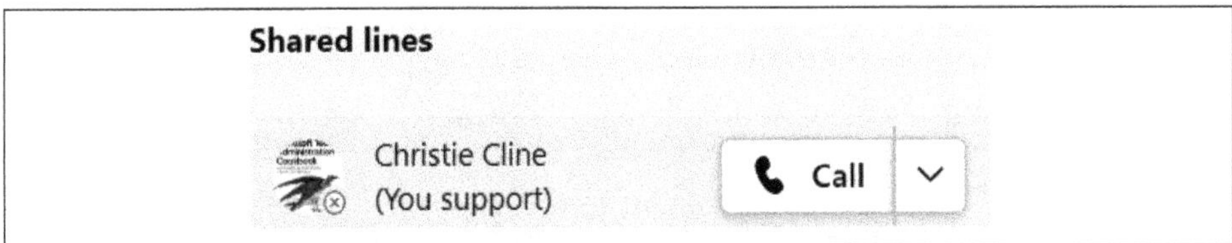

Figure 5-16. Making calls on behalf of another user with delegation

Inside the General section of the Teams client settings, there is a "Delegate settings" section. You can click "Manage delegates" from there and change the way the delegation is configured (Figure 5-17).

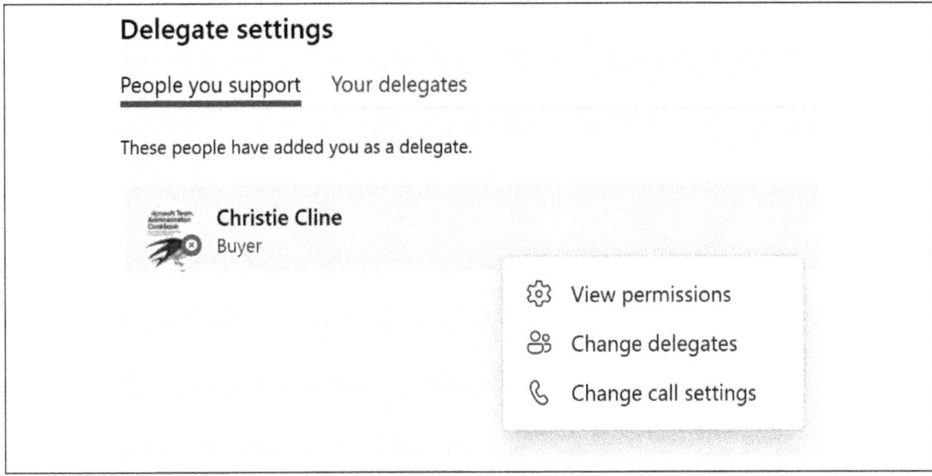

Figure 5-17. Changing your delegate settings

The simultaneous "ring a user" and "forward to a person" options let you use a Resource Account to route voice calls, so that the unanswered calls can be sent to an Auto Attendant or to a Call Queue (like a reception desk or switchboard).

Discussion

It is possible to manage the same settings using PowerShell. For example, if you wanted to immediately forward all calls for Adele Vance to a mobile number, you could use the following command:

```
Set-CsUserCallingSettings -Identity adelev@m365x71772990.onmicrosoft.com `
-IsForwardingEnabled $true -ForwardingType immediate -ForwardingTargetType `
singletarget -ForwardingTarget +447xxxxxxxxx
```

Another option is to forward the calls after 30 seconds if not answered:

```
Set-CsUserCallingSettings -Identity adelev@m365x71772990.onmicrosoft.com `
-IsUnansweredEnabled $true -UnansweredDelay 00:00:30 -UnansweredTargetType `
singleTarget -UnansweredTarget +447xxxxxxxxx
```

You must remove the immediate forwarding option (if enabled) before setting the options for managing unanswered calls. The quickest way to remove immediate forwarding is to use the following command:

```
Set-CsUserCallingSettings -Identity `
adelev@m365x71772990.onmicrosoft.com `
-IsForwardingEnabled $false
```

5.5 Enabling Call Park

Problem

You need to deploy call parking for your Teams users.

Solution

Open the TAC and go to Voice > "Call park policies." Click Add to create a new policy, called Call Parking Reception. It will use a range from 10 to 40 and time out after 300 seconds (see Figure 5-18).

Figure 5-18. Custom Call Park policy

Click Save. You can now assign the policy to a user. When the user receives a call, they can select Call Park. The call can be picked up using a short retrieval code, which is generated by Teams whenever a call is parked.

Discussion

Call Park allows users to place calls in a waiting area and retrieve them using a retrieval code. This enables a user to place a caller on hold while they are moving from one device to another, or to allow another person to pick up the call from the Call Park. When the user parks a call, Teams generates a retrieval code that is shown in the Teams client. Using the code, it is possible to unpark the call from the same or a different device.

The user that picks up the call must have a Teams Phone System license. The user that parks the call must also have a Call Park policy enabled.

Call Park can be enabled in two ways:

- Using the global Call Park policy
- Creating a Call Park policy to be assigned to the users

The Teams client has added, over time, new features related to voice that make it an effective replacement for existing legacy PBXs. For example, in addition to the features we have seen in the solutions so far, Teams users are able to perform a *consult transfer*. With this option, before transferring a call, the user can talk with the person who should receive the call to confirm whether the transfer is doable. The caller is placed on hold in the meantime.

It is also possible to add other people to a call. However, as soon as you add three or more people to a call, it will be converted into a meeting and you will see new options that were not available before.

5.6 Summary

In this chapter, we have seen some of the advanced voice features that make Teams a viable solution to replace existing phone systems. While a Microsoft solution does not always overlap perfectly with the legacy features, it typically allows similar functionalities. Using Call Queues and Auto Attendants, it is possible to create switchboard, reception, and call center solutions without the need to deploy third-party solutions (assuming advanced monitoring and management tools are not required for the solution you're designing). Chapter 6 will explore the integration that is possible with third-party call center solutions Dynamics and SharePoint.

CHAPTER 6

Microsoft Teams Integration

By integrating Teams with SharePoint, Exchange Online, and OneDrive, we can access to the features we use daily. The Microsoft Teams architecture shown in Figure 6-1 provides a clear picture of how deeply the integration goes.

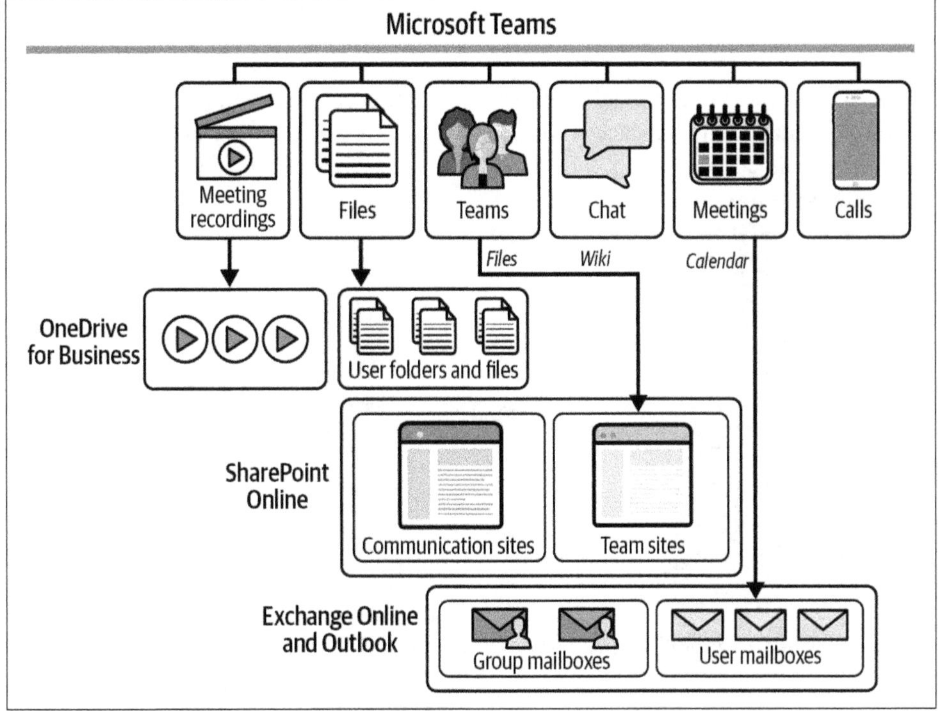

Figure 6-1. Microsoft Teams architecture overview

For example, real-time coauthoring, shared calendar, and document libraries in Teams are enabled by integrations with Microsoft 365. An additional integration (with third-party solutions) enables a contact center for customer service. Contact centers use various tools, including phone calls, notifications, and shared boards. Teams can provide the infrastructure for voice, chat, and teamwork (integrating a third-party product) for a contact center, or a full solution when used as part of the Microsoft Digital Contact Center Platform.

6.1 Integrating Contact Centers with Microsoft Teams

Problem

You need to integrate an external contact center solution with Teams.

Solution

We have already talked about Call Queues and Auto Attendants as a possible solution to contact center requirements. Native tools are useful to manage part of this scenario, but when more advanced analytics and tools are required there is a need for a third-party solution. It is possible to integrate third-party contact center solutions with Teams using three different models: Connect, Extend, and Power.

If you deploy a Connect model solution, the central point will be an SBC and Direct Routing to integrate the contact center with Teams' calling infrastructure. Figure 6-2 shows the basic configuration with the SIP trunks to the PSTN, Teams, and the contact center solution provider.

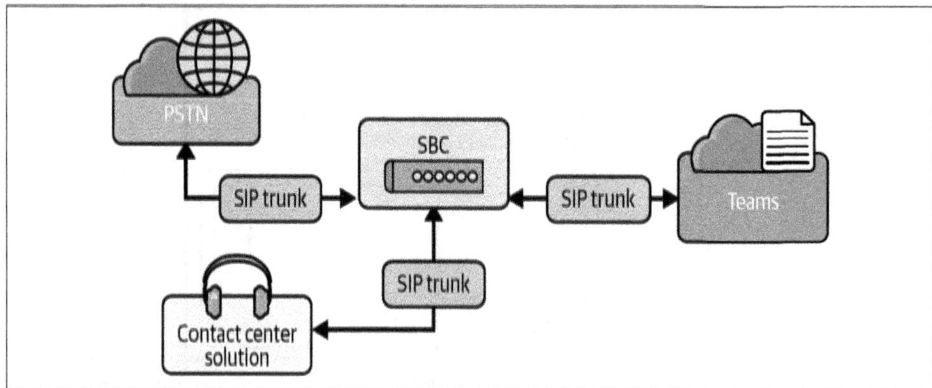

Figure 6-2. Connect model solution to integrate a third-party contact center solution

An incoming call to a phone number that is identified as a contact center number will be routed from the PSTN to the contact center. There, all the different features and workflows will be activated (skill-based routing, artificial intelligence, and so on, depending on the platform). A routing decision will be made based on the deployed configuration and the presence of the agents, which is detected using Microsoft Graph APIs.

If you deploy a solution based on the Extend model, which uses Microsoft Graph cloud communications APIs, the phone call stays inside your company's tenant. The deployment requires you to install an application instance that communicates with the solution provider, telling Teams what to do with phone calls. A typical installation will require the configuration of a calling bot and the installation of an app (usually via an app manifest), which will make the contact center app available to users. The app manifest usually requires tenant administrator permissions. In the TAC, go to "Teams apps" > "Manage apps," and select "Upload new app" (Figure 6-3).

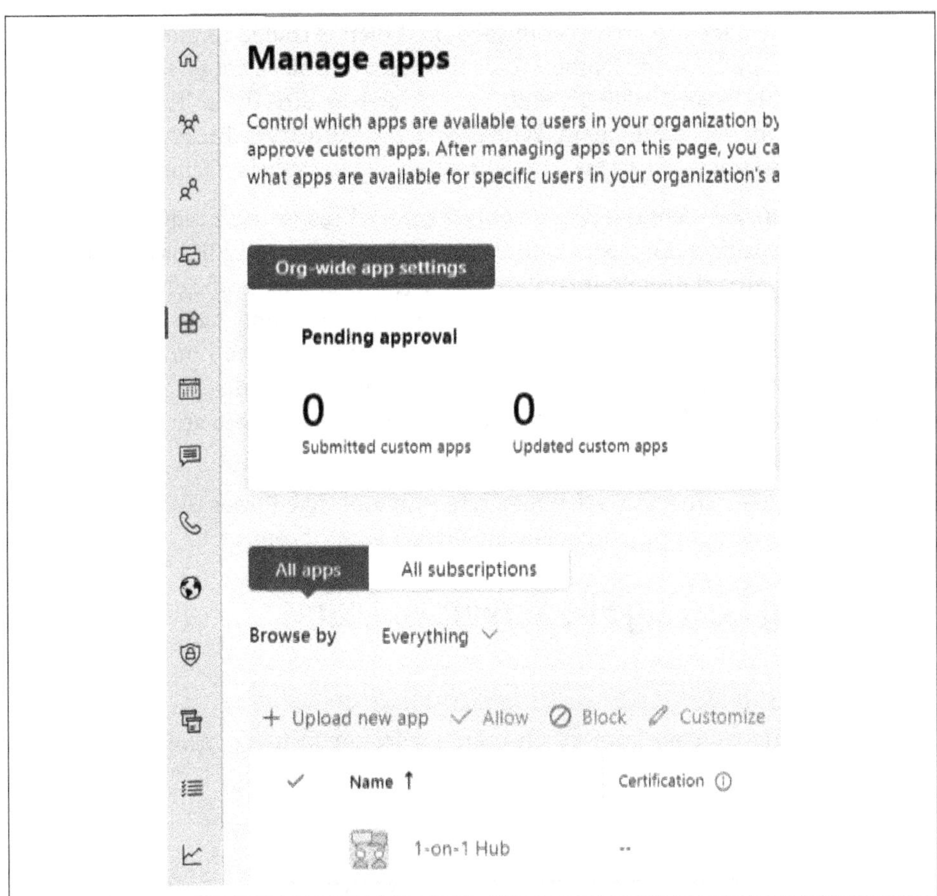

Figure 6-3. Managing an app in the TAC

You will be required to upload the custom app (using "Upload new app") by selecting a file in the TAC.

Finally, if you deploy a solution with the Power model, the Azure Communication Services (ACS) platform will route and manage calls, presenting the calls to agents in Teams. The Microsoft Digital Contact Center is an example of a platform that uses this approach.

Discussion

If you compare the three models, you can see how their different integrations with Teams change the results. With Connect, the contact center solution connects to Teams using SIP trunks. With Extend, the Teams app is expanded using the Graph cloud communication API. Finally, with Power, Teams functionalities are leveraged using the Teams SDK.

In the first model, the call arrives at the SBC and then is routed to the contact center solution. The contact center solution finds the best available agent in Teams and then sends the call to Teams. With Extend, the call arrives directly in Teams and stays inside the customer's Teams tenant. With Power, the call arrives directly in Teams and the call center solution can access all call functionality directly in Teams.

In this solution, we're considering a contact center because we need advanced features. To clarify what a third-party solution adds, let's start with skill-based routing. It is possible to define skills in our contact center (for example, proficiency with a specific language) and different levels of capability that our agents have in those skills. Every time you receive a call that requires a specific skill, you can route it to an agent that meets those requirements. If the preferred agent is busy, you can select an alternate agent, and so on. This ensures that, at any given moment, you are giving the best service to your customers.

The capability to create reports that integrate with tools like Power BI, for example, is another requirement for properly managing larger contact centers.

6.2 Moving Existing File Servers to Teams

Problem

You need to migrate data from an on-prem environment to Teams, OneDrive, and SharePoint.

Solution

You will need to have Global Administrator or OneDrive/SharePoint Administrator permissions in the Microsoft 365 tenant, as well as read access to any data you want to migrate. From the SharePoint administrator center, select Migration and click "Get started" under "File shares." The Migration Manager requires an agent to be installed on the on-prem file server. On the "Migrate your file shares content to Microsoft 365" page, click "Download agent" (Figure 6-4).

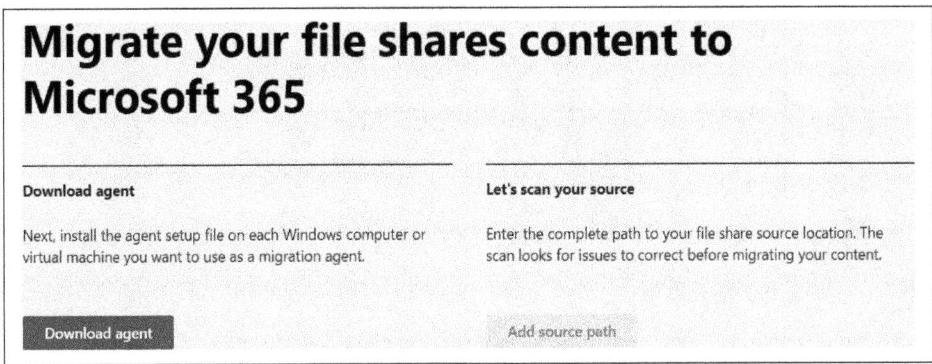

Migrate your file shares content to Microsoft 365
Download agent
Next, install the agent setup file on each Windows computer or virtual machine you want to use as a migration agent.
Download agent
Let's scan your source
Enter the complete path to your file share source location. The scan looks for issues to correct before migrating your content.
Add source path

Figure 6-4. Installing the Migration Manager agent on-prem

Next, run the setup script for the agent (*agentsetup.exe*) on the on-prem server. Click Next on the welcome screen. You will be required to input two different sets of credentials: SharePoint credentials and credentials of a Windows account with access to the file shares. Click Install when finished.

The next screen will show "Migration agent setup is complete." Type the path to the shared folder (in the *\\servername\folder* format), as shown in Figure 6-5. Click Test to verify that you have access to the folder, then click Close.

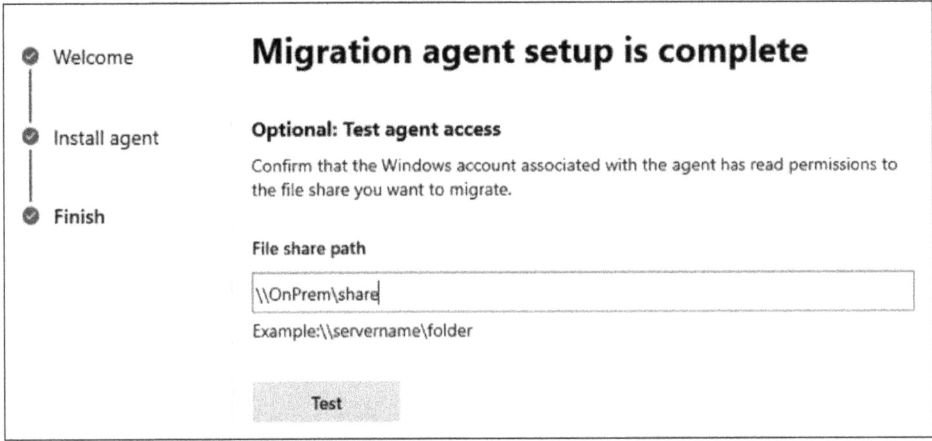

Figure 6-5. Selecting the data origination source for the migration

Back in the SharePoint administrator center, under "Let's scan your source," click "Add source path." Select "Specify a single source path" and type the path of the folder using the server FQDN. In the example shown in Figure 6-6, the FQDN of the server is OnPrem. Click Add.

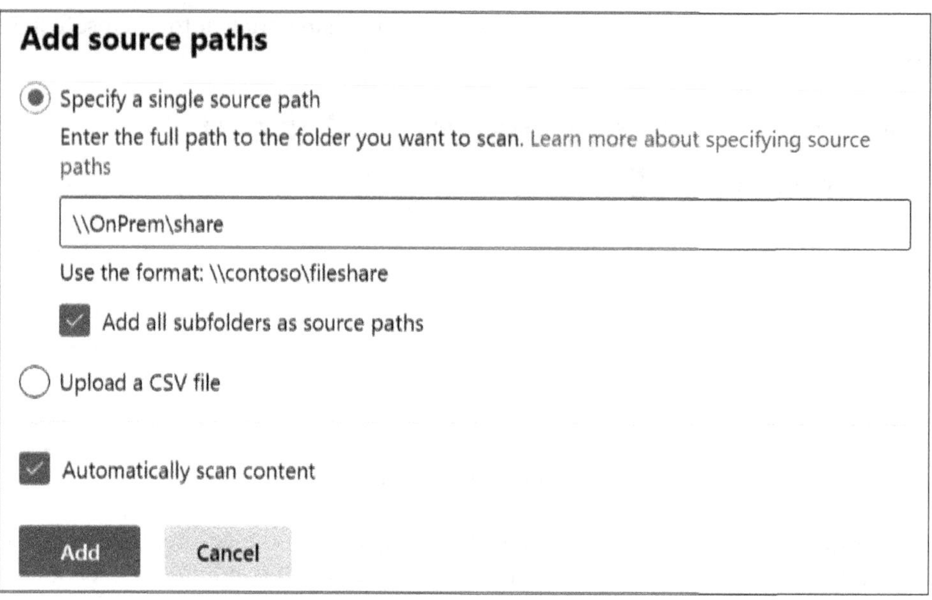

Figure 6-6. Adding a source path for the migration

The shared folder and its contents will be shown under Scans (as in Figure 6-7).

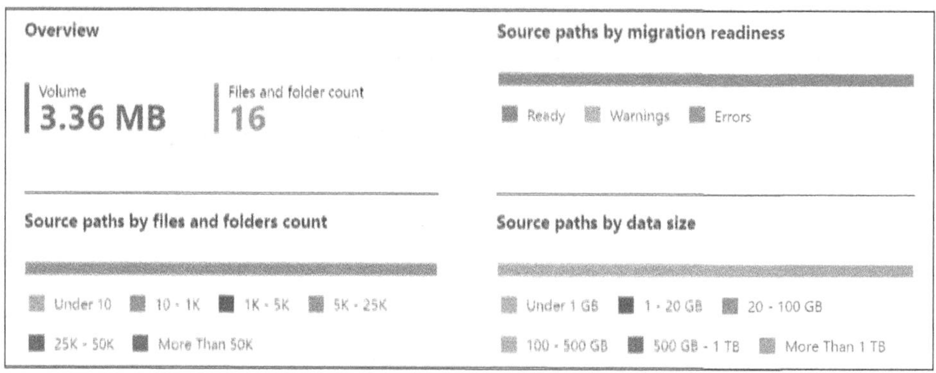

Figure 6-7. Source folders will be added under Scans

Next, click Migrations and select "Add task." Under Method, select "Single source and destination" and click Next. On the Source page, type the path of the source folder in the same format used before. Click Next. The possible destinations are OneDrive, SharePoint, and Teams. Select Teams and click Next.

You will be required to select a team and a channel (Figure 6-8). Click Next.

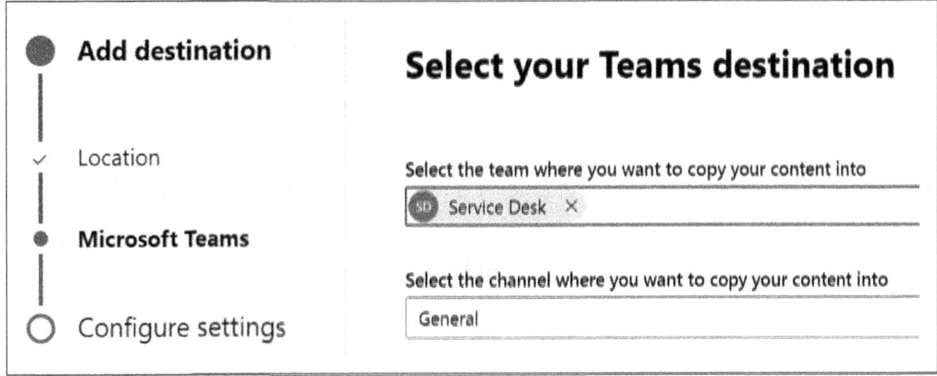

Figure 6-8. Adding a team and a channel as a target

Finally, you must give a name to the task and decide whether you want to keep the existing file share permissions (as in Figure 6-9). Click Run.

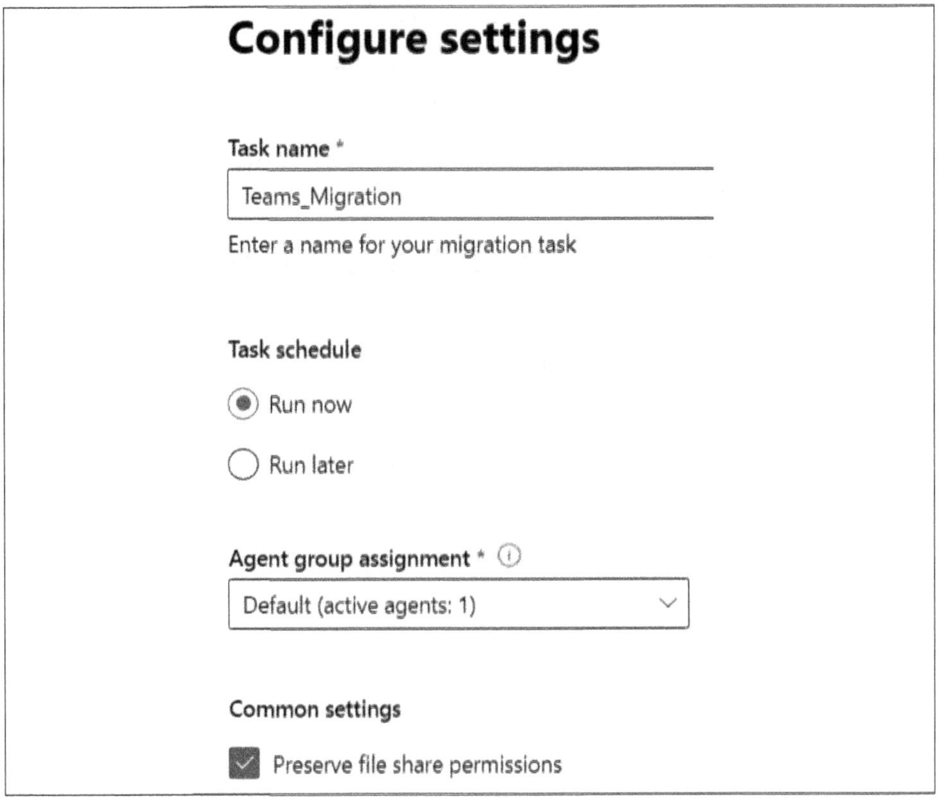

Configure settings

Task name *

Teams_Migration

Enter a name for your migration task

Task schedule

Run now

Run later

Agent group assignment *

Default (active agents: 1)

Common settings

Preserve file share permissions

Figure 6-9. Task parameters

You could just run a scan of the source to detect any issues. The migration creates a copy of the original files, without deleting them, so the whole process has a low level of disruption for the users.

When the task is executed, you will receive a report with the migration results.

When you open the Teams client (as in Figure 6-10), you will see the files stored in the team and channel, with the original folder structure.

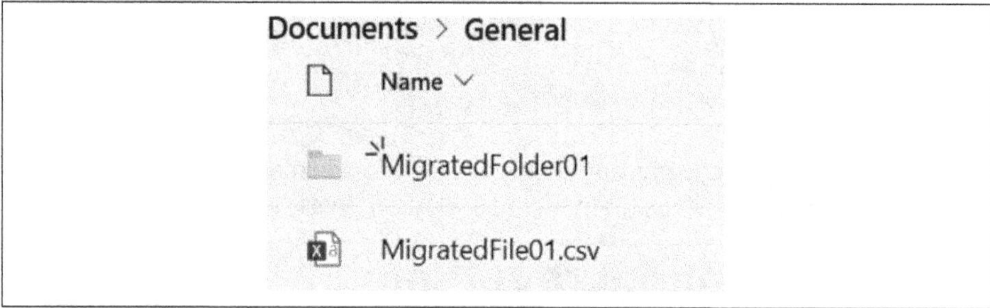

Figure 6-10. Teams client with a view of the migrated files

In a similar way, you can migrate the file share to OneDrive, selecting OneDrive as a destination and inputting an email address or URL (see Figure 6-11).

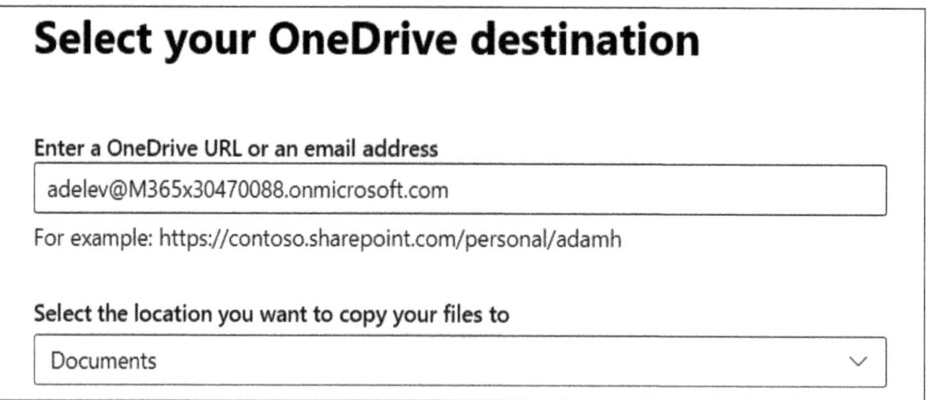

Figure 6-11. Migrating to OneDrive

Upon opening the user's OneDrive, you will see the files and folders that have been migrated (as in Figure 6-12).

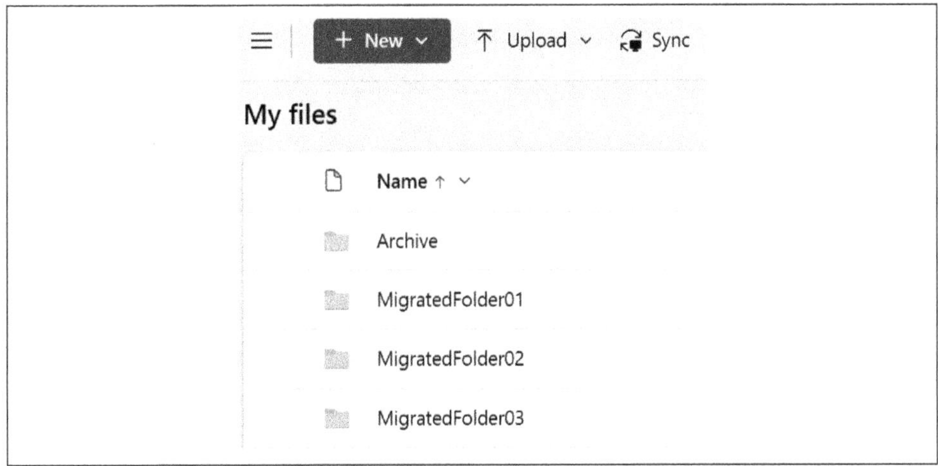

Figure 6-12. Files migrated to OneDrive

Discussion

Using OneDrive, users can store files in a personal drive or in a shared drive (a SharePoint document library, as we will see in Recipe 6.4). Users can share links to files, copy or move files to team drives, or even attach OneDrive files to emails in Outlook.

When you have an existing on-prem file server, the main task is to import your files from the legacy server to OneDrive (or SharePoint, depending on whether the information is personal or shared).

After the migration, permissions to access the data will vary, depending on a series of factors. If the on-prem users with permission to access the files have no license in Microsoft 365, the original permissions will be lost. There are three types of permissions that will be migrated to SharePoint Online: write, read, and full control. Write permission is converted to contribute. Read permissions will be set to read. Full control permissions will be migrated as full control. All other permissions will not be saved. You can see an overview of the resulting permissions in the Microsoft article "File and folder permissions when using the SharePoint Migration Tool" (*https://oreil.ly/Zx3kx*).

Integrating Teams with OneDrive gives you the option to sync the contents of a channel to your OneDrive (see Figure 6-13), which enables you to work on the documents while offline.

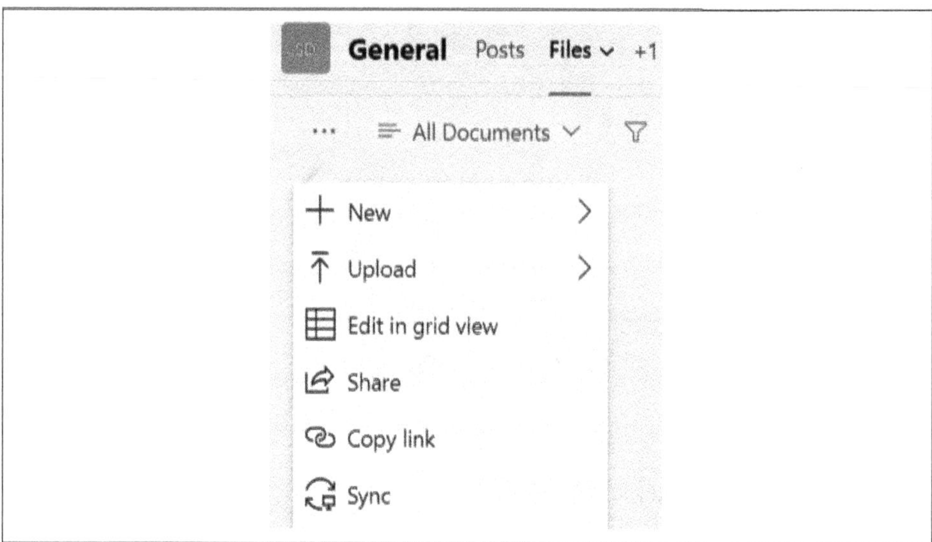

Figure 6-13. Enabling sync from Teams to OneDrive

The folder will be synchronized with your OneDrive (including your mobile device, if you have the app).

6.3 Leveraging Teams and Exchange Online Integration

Problem

You need to generate a notification in Teams when a group mailbox receives an email with a specific word in the subject.

Solution

Teams and Exchange Online work together to provide features like a shared calendar. It is possible to improve the user experience by integrating the two tools and automating certain tasks using Power Automate.

Open the Power Automate home page (*https://oreil.ly/BtwnC*) (Figure 6-14) and click Create.

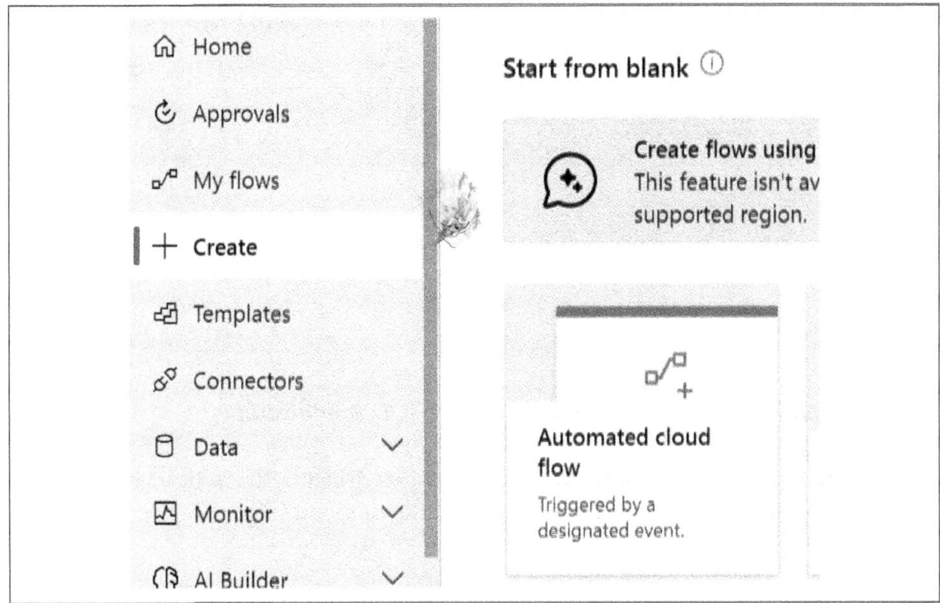

Figure 6-14. The Power Automate home page

For an easier starting point, search in Templates for Teams and select "Post message to Microsoft Teams when an email arrives in Office 365 Outlook." You must connect to Teams and Outlook. Let's look at the default flow and begin to customize it (Figure 6-15). The template looks at the inbox, checks the email body (without any specific parameter, at the moment), and then as an action posts a notification in a team or channel.

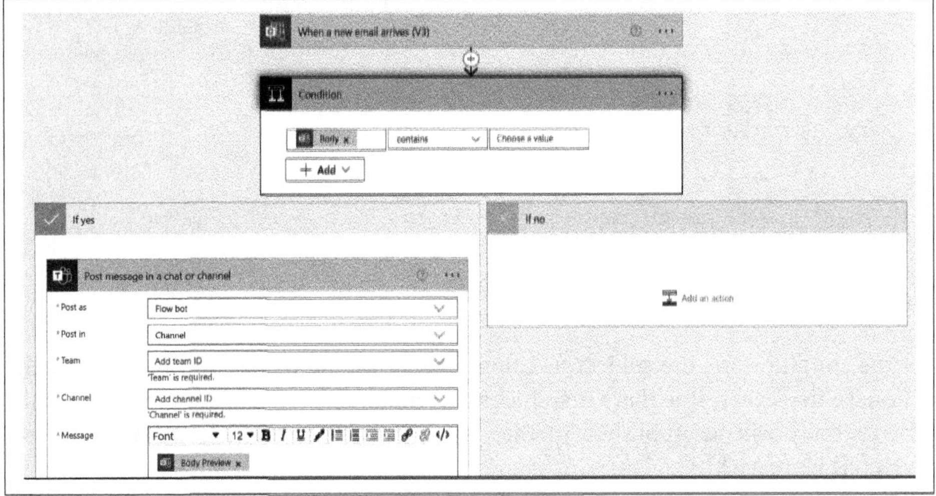

Figure 6-15. The template in Power Automate

The first step will be intercepting only the messages to the MOD Administrator email address (Figure 6-16).

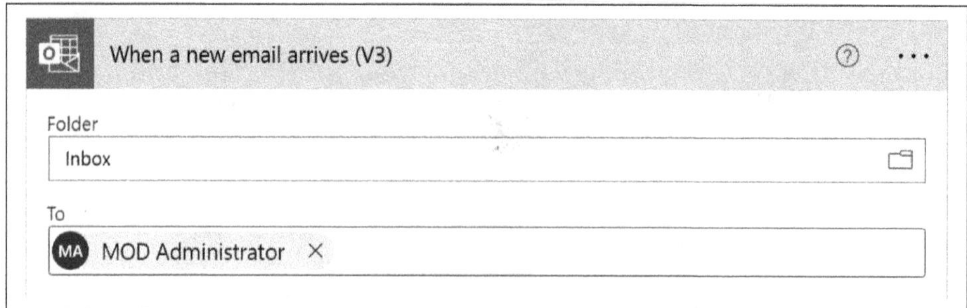

Figure 6-16. Editing the mailbox parameters for MOD Administrator

The second step will be to edit the condition that triggers the action. Remove the existing value and select Subject from the drop-down menu (Figure 6-17).

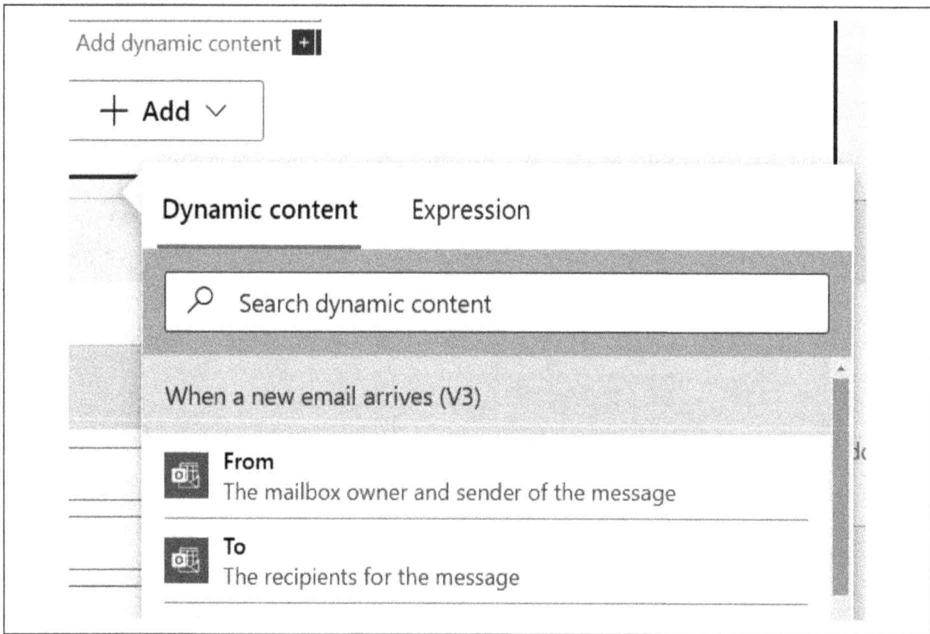

Figure 6-17. Editing the conditions

Set the condition for the subject to contain the word "news." Now you must set the action, so that every time there is an incoming email with the word "news" in the subject, its body will be published in the Retail team, General channel, with subject "News" (Figure 6-18).

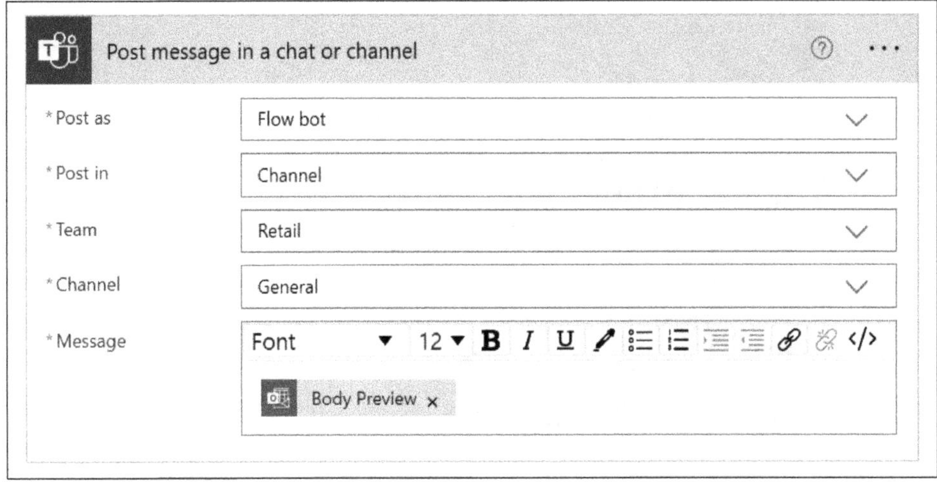

Figure 6-18. Modifying the action if the condition is matched

Click Save. You can use the Flow Checker and Test buttons at the top-right corner to verify that the flow works as expected. Select Test Flow > Manually. A notification will appear on the screen, asking you to send an email to trigger the process.

Write a test email like the one in Figure 6-19 and send it.

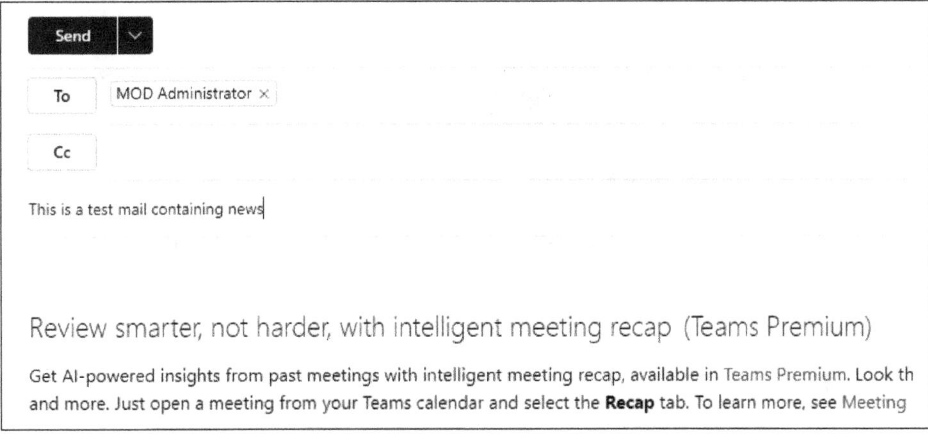

Figure 6-19. Sending a test email

If the message matches the required parameters, the test will give a positive result (Figure 6-20).

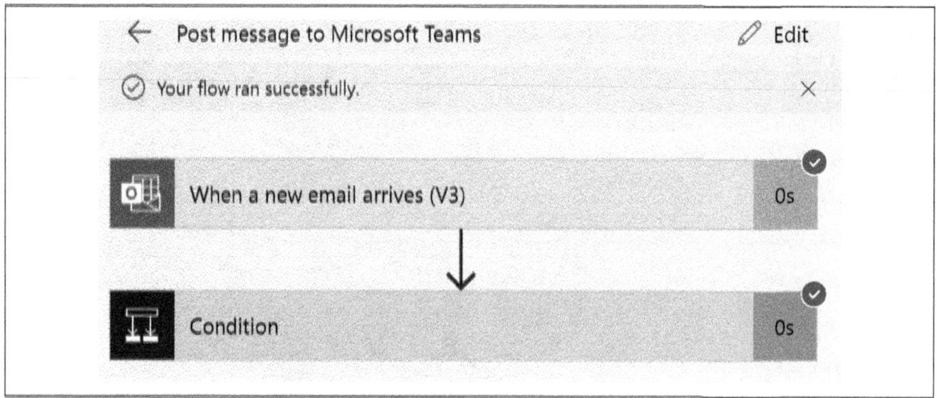

Figure 6-20. Power Automate test returning a positive result

Discussion

There are additional ways to leverage the integration between Outlook and Teams. One is to add an Outlook tab in one of the channels. From the Teams client, add a tab and select Website. Input the Outlook link as a URL (*https://outlook.office365.com/mail/inbox*). The result should look like Figure 6-21.

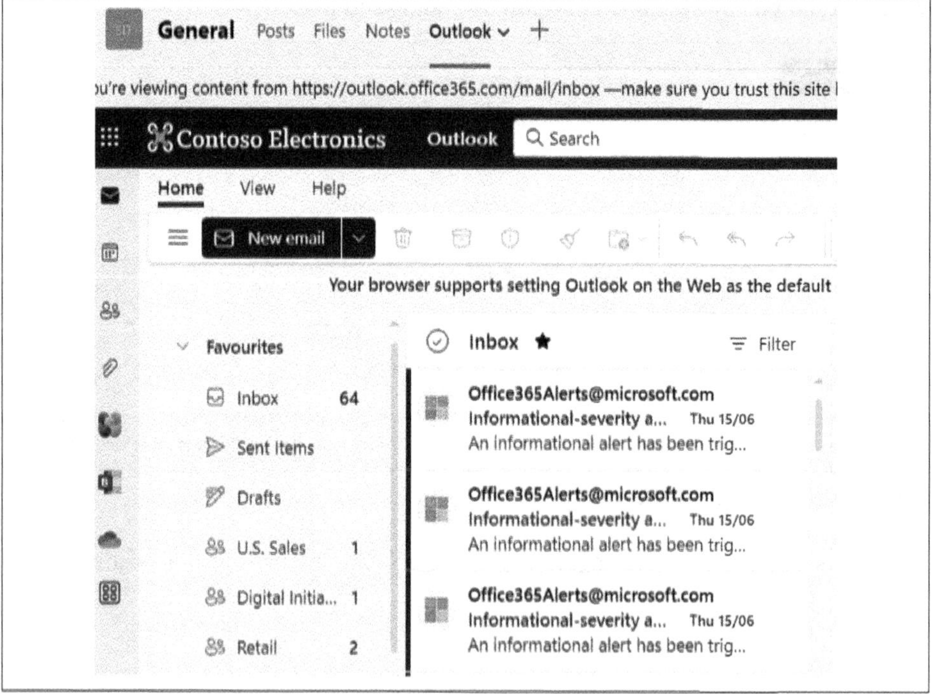

Figure 6-21. Outlook in the Teams client integration

Using the same steps as before, you can add a "Channel calendar." The channel calendar will be open for all channel members, both in Teams and Outlook (using the URL *https://outlook.office365.com/calendar*), as shown in Figure 6-22.

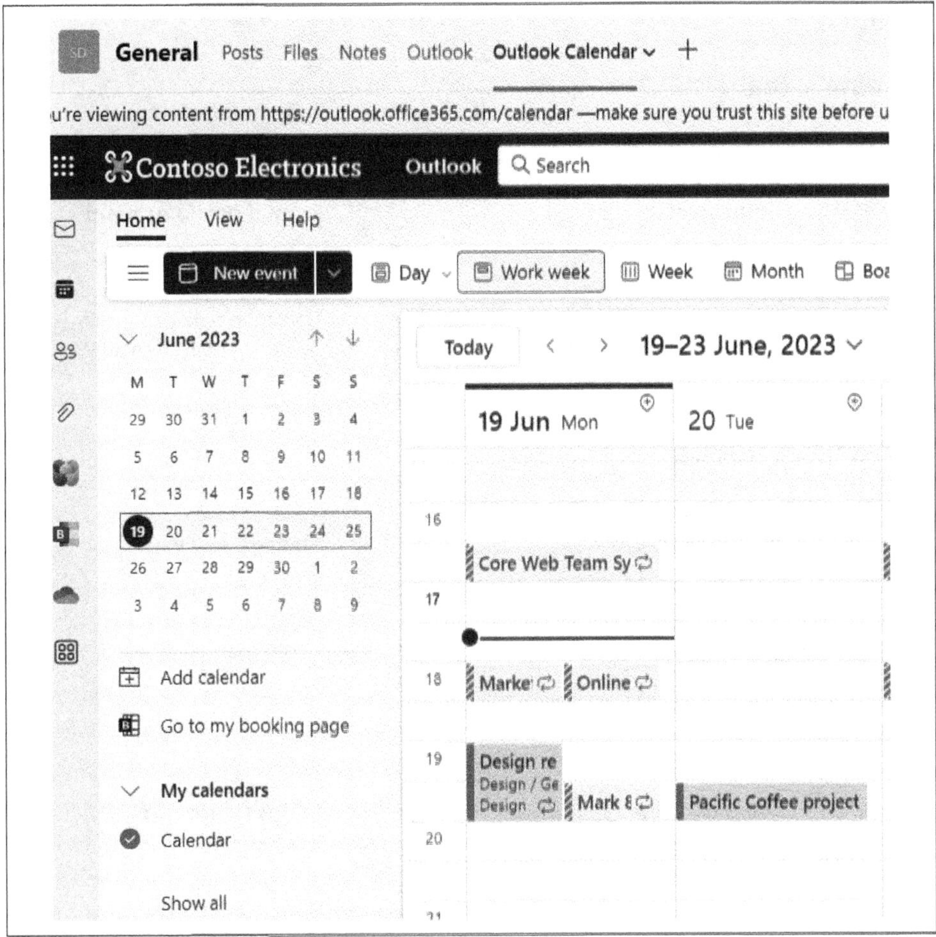

Figure 6-22. Opening a channel calendar from Outlook

6.4 Associating and Customizing SharePoint with Teams

Problem

You need to customize the user experience in Teams, modifying the related SharePoint site.

Solution

You can create a new team from the Teams client (click "Join or create a team" and then "Create a team") by working with one of the available templates or from scratch (Figure 6-23).

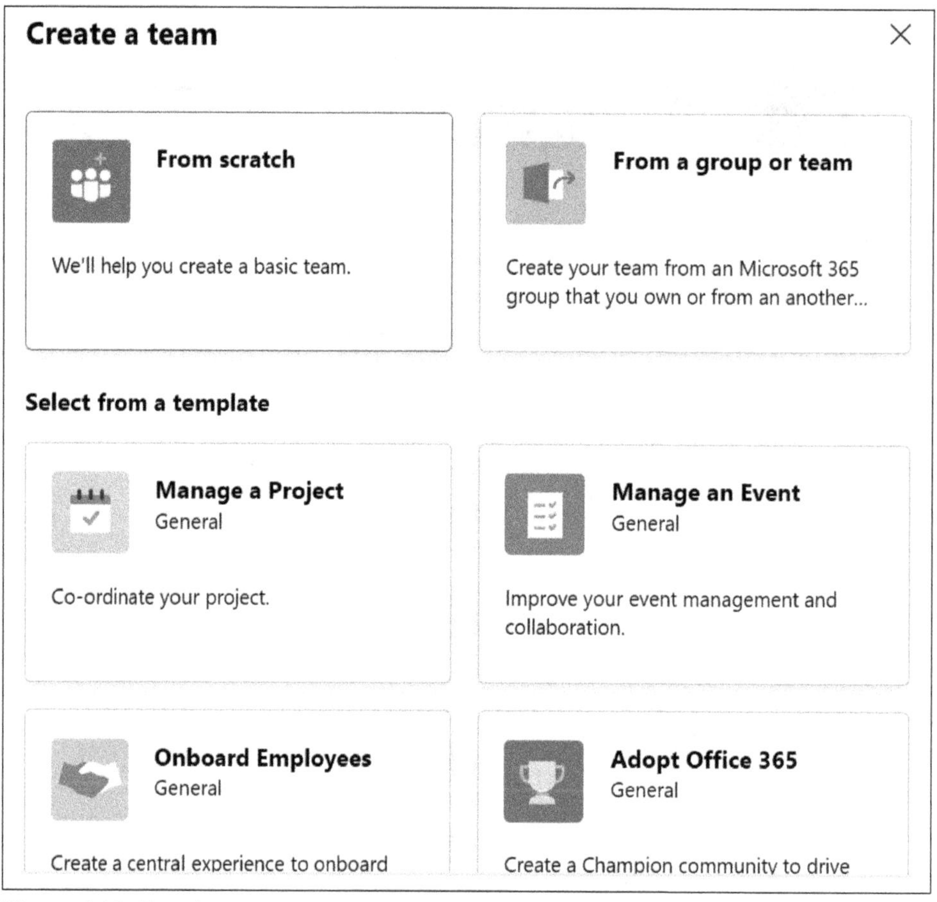

Figure 6-23. Creating a team

For this solution, we'll start from scratch. First, create a public team called "SharePoint Integration." Open the General channel and upload a couple of files. From the menu in the top-right corner, select "Open in SharePoint." The site is presented with the default template. To change the template, select "Get started" under "Apply a site template" (Figure 6-24).

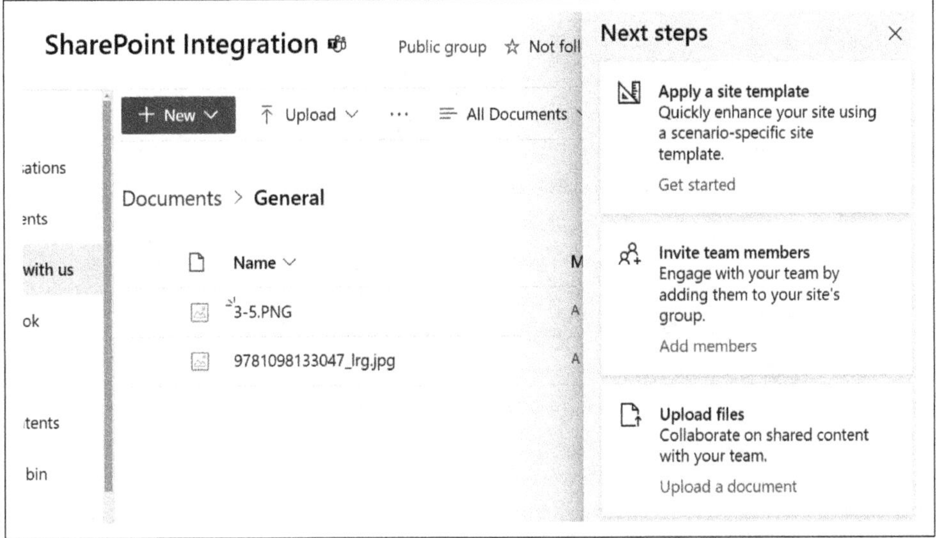

Figure 6-24. Contents in SharePoint

You'll see a few templates to choose from. Select "Training and courses."

The page might present just the gear icon in the top-right corner instead of the menu shown in the figure. In that event, select "Apply a site template" from that menu.

The SharePoint site will now have a different structure and look (without losing your documents and conversation), as shown in Figure 6-25.

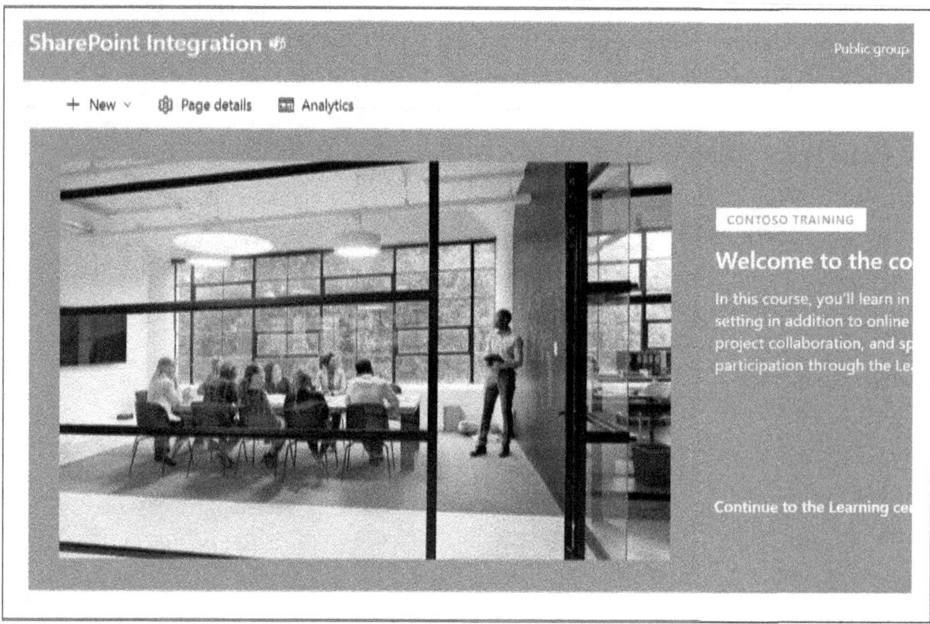

Figure 6-25. Modified look for SharePoint site

More SharePoint templates for your tenant are available in the SharePoint lookbook (*https://oreil.ly/JQexF*). Open the website and select "View the designs" > Team > "Collaboration team site." Click "Add to your tenant." You will receive a permissions request. Click Accept.

An email address, site title, and site alias will be required. Fill in the fields and click Provision, then Confirm. Provisioning will start and a confirmation email will be sent.

You can also do this process in reverse, starting from SharePoint and then linking to Teams. To create a new SharePoint site from the SharePoint administrator center, select "Create a site" and then "Team site" (Figure 6-26).

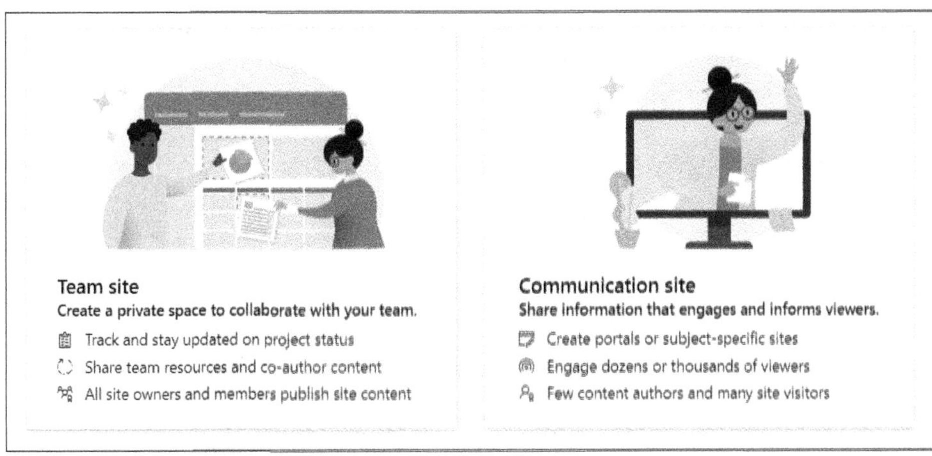

Team site
Create a private space to collaborate with your team.
Track and stay updated on project status
Share team resources and co-author content
All site owners and members publish site content
Communication site
Share information that engages and informs viewers.
Create portals or subject-specific sites
Engage dozens or thousands of viewers
Few content authors and many site visitors

Figure 6-26. Creating a team site in SharePoint

Enter "Unlinked Site" as the name (Figure 6-27). A Microsoft 365 group will be associated to the site. Leave all the remaining settings on the defaults. Click Next, select members from your list of users, and click Finish.

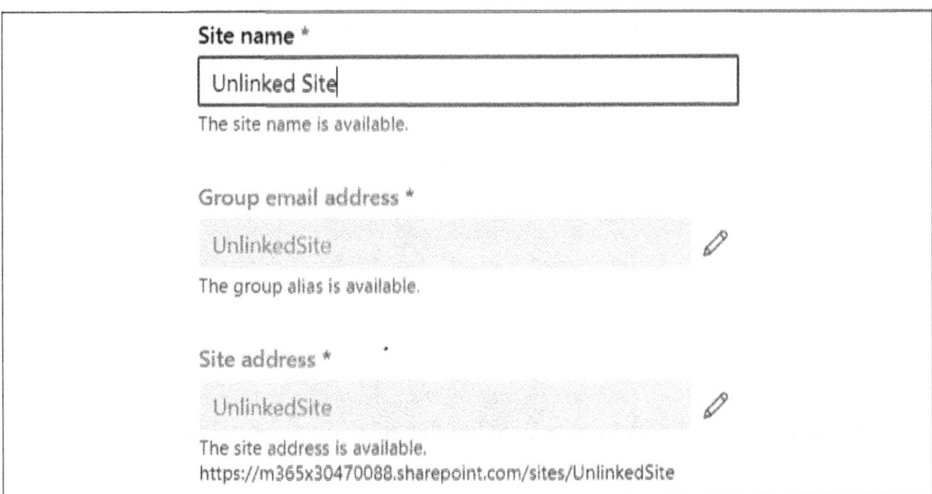

Figure 6-27. Site parameters

Now the team site in SharePoint has been defined with an associated group, but it is not enabled to chat or leverage other Teams features. Navigate to the SharePoint site. In the lower-left corner, you will see a suggestion to "Add real-time chat" (Figure 6-28).

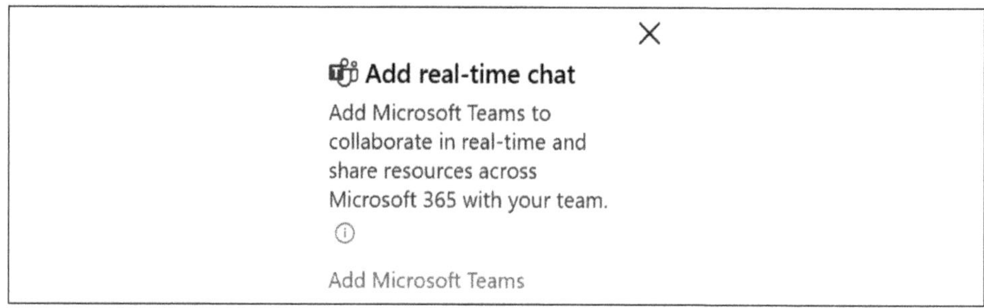

Figure 6-28. Integrating SharePoint site with Teams

Click Add Microsoft Teams and a wizard will guide you through the integration with Teams. Click Add Teams when you have configured the different SharePoint assets to be made available in Teams (Figure 6-29).

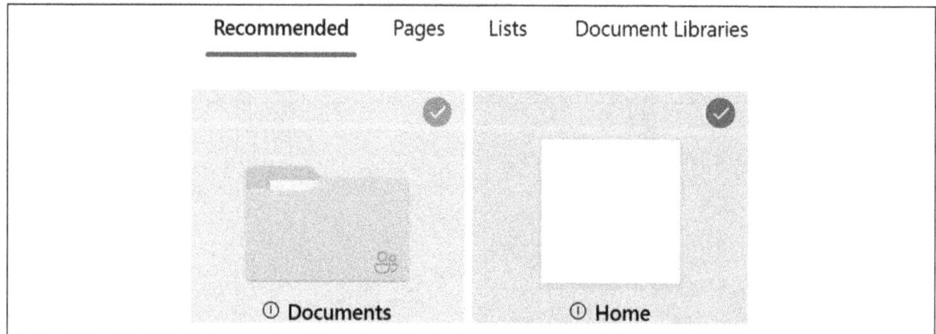

Figure 6-29. The integration wizard

The SharePoint site will now be associated with a team and a channel in Teams.

Discussion

Every time you define a new channel in Teams, a corresponding Microsoft 365 group and a SharePoint Online website are automatically created. This way, each channel's shared Teams documents are associated with a SharePoint document library. The whole process is seamless for the user, leveraging single sign-on. It is also possible to save documents on the user's OneDrive and have them accessible via mobile devices. When you create a team, a standard template is applied to SharePoint.

The solution you have seen is one of the two ways to integrate Teams and SharePoint. Alternatively, from the Teams client, you could click "Join or create a team," "Create a team," and then select "From a group or team."

You are now able to associate a Microsoft 365 group with Teams (Figure 6-30).

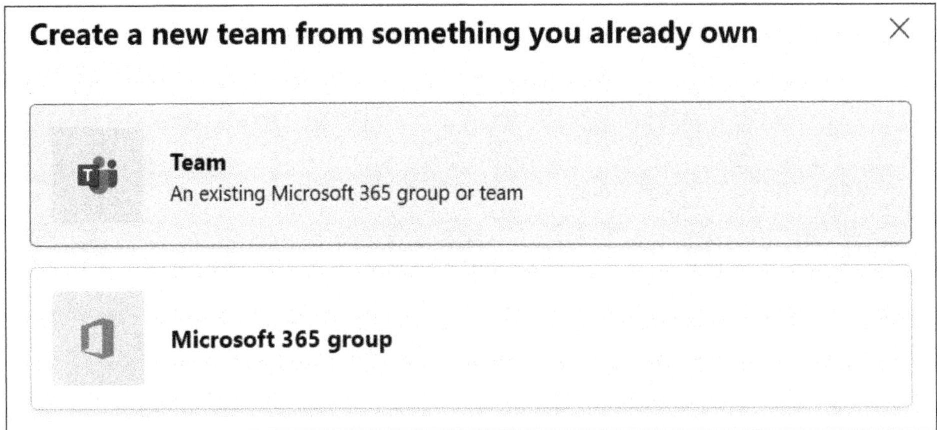

Figure 6-30. Associating a Microsoft 365 group in Teams

In this scenario, Teams will not create the SharePoint site or the Outlook calendar. Instead, the existing assets will be integrated with Teams.

SharePoint sites are customizable in different ways, including using webparts and logos. From the SharePoint site settings, you can "Change the look" to edit the look of SharePoint and make it more aligned with your organization's specifications.

6.5 Summary

In this chapter, you have seen some of the ways that Teams integrates with other third-party and Microsoft 365 apps. Teams remains a preferred tool for working together in files, calls, and meetings, so learning how it integrates with other common tools is essential. OneDrive allows users to store and share files securely, while SharePoint provides a centralized location for team projects and collaboration. Exchange Online provides email and calendaring capabilities, helping teams stay on top of tasks and deadlines.

In the next chapter, we will shift from discussing Teams integration to exploring how to extend Teams with Graph API, bots, and Adaptive Cards.

CHAPTER 7

Extending Microsoft Teams

As an extensible platform, Teams enables you to create add-ons and apps. A Teams app, for example, will already be in the client where users spend a large part of their time, minimizing the need for them to switch to run the app. Working inside Teams, you can leverage the existing collaboration tools and all the different ways that users may consume Teams (desktop, mobile, web, and so on).

Let's say you want to improve the Teams user interface with additional views of the different features; create chatbots that use Teams as a platform for chat, voice, and video; or automate processes. As you'll see in this chapter, there are different ways you can extend Teams, and different tools you can use to do so.

7.1 Building a Chatbot

Problem

You need to create a chatbot to receive return item requests from customers and provide them with the phone number of the return service.

Solution

You will add the Power Virtual Agents app from the Teams app store and create your chatbot directly inside one of your teams.

In the Teams client, click the search bar (in the upper part of the client) and search for Power Virtual Agents. Click the Power Virtual Agents icon and select Add on the next screen (as shown in Figure 7-1).

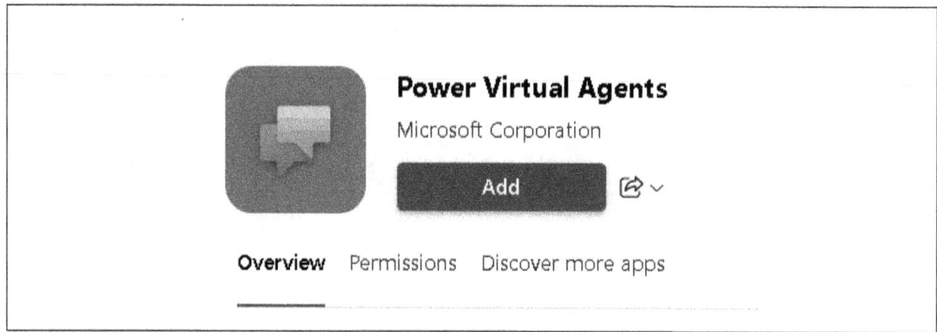

Figure 7-1. Adding the Power Virtual Agents app

Power Virtual Agents will be added to the list on the left side of the client (you may need to click the ellipsis to see the full list of apps). Click the Power Virtual Agents app. It will open to a screen with a "Start now" button. You're ready to create your first chatbot (Figure 7-2).

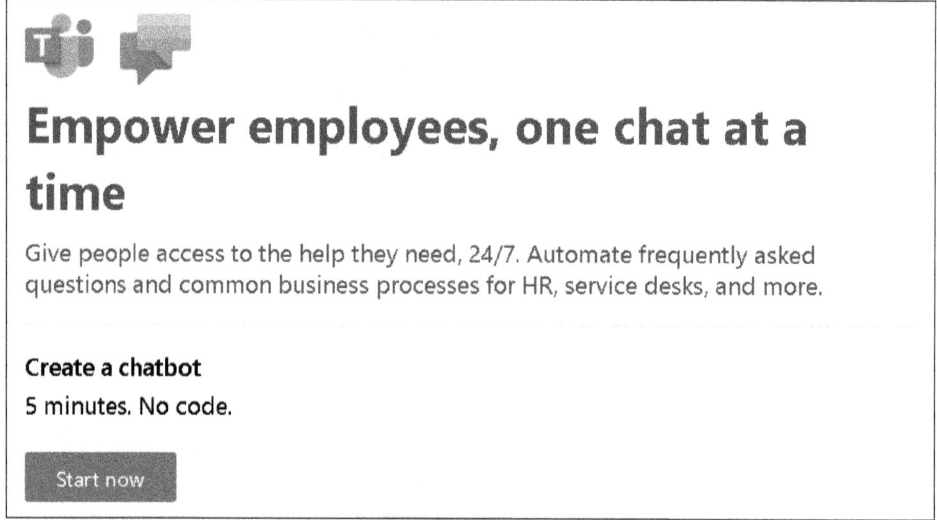

Figure 7-2. Starting the chatbot creation

Choose a team in which the chatbot will be active. For example, you could select the Migration team (see Figure 7-3). Click Continue.

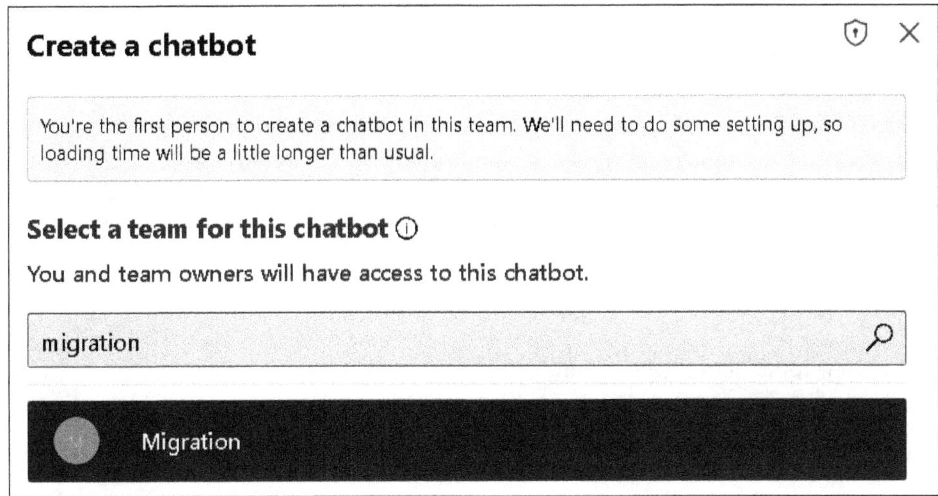

Figure 7-3. Selecting a team in which to enable the chatbot

You must now name the chatbot (for example, Customer Service Bot) and select a language (such as English). Click Create.

The next screen will allow you to modify, test, and deploy the chatbot, as shown in Figure 7-4.

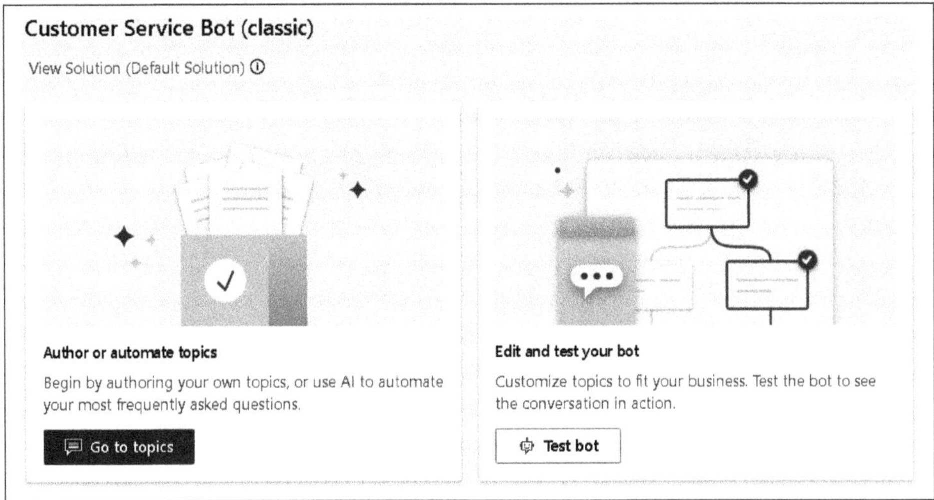

Figure 7-4. Modifying and testing the chatbot

Click "Go to topics." The chatbot will start with a set of user topics and system topics.

In Power Virtual Agents, a *topic* helps a chatbot determine how it responds to a question from a user. All topics have trigger phrases and conversation nodes. *Trigger phrases* are phrases, keywords, or questions that a user is likely to type that are related to a specific issue.

The chatbot can make a guess at what a user means and match it to the right topic, even if you do not have the exact phrase in the list of trigger phrases. This is called *intent*.

Click "New topic" and select "From blank," as shown in Figure 7-5.

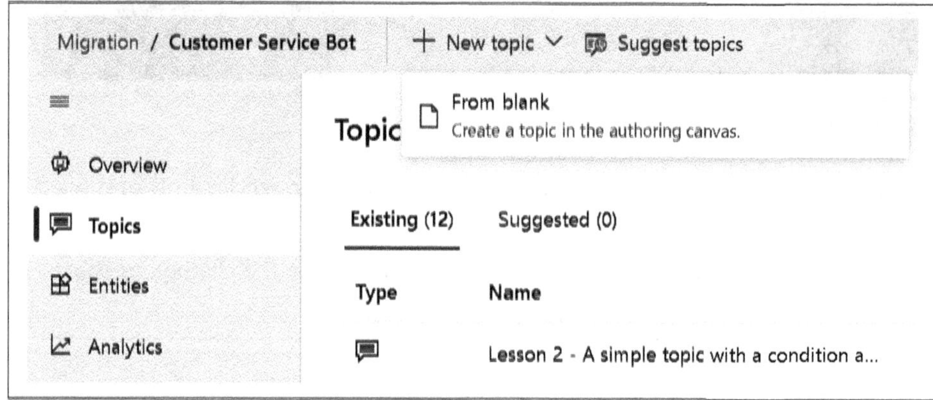

Figure 7-5. Adding a topic to the chatbot's list

On the editing screen, click Settings > Details and select an icon and name for the topic. In our solution, we'll name the topic Item Return Process.

Click "Trigger phrases" and add some phrases in the pane on the right (press Shift + Enter to create multiple lines)—for example, "I want to return my item," "Cancel my order," "Refund for an item," and "I want to return an item," as shown in Figure 7-6. Click the + symbol when you have finished.

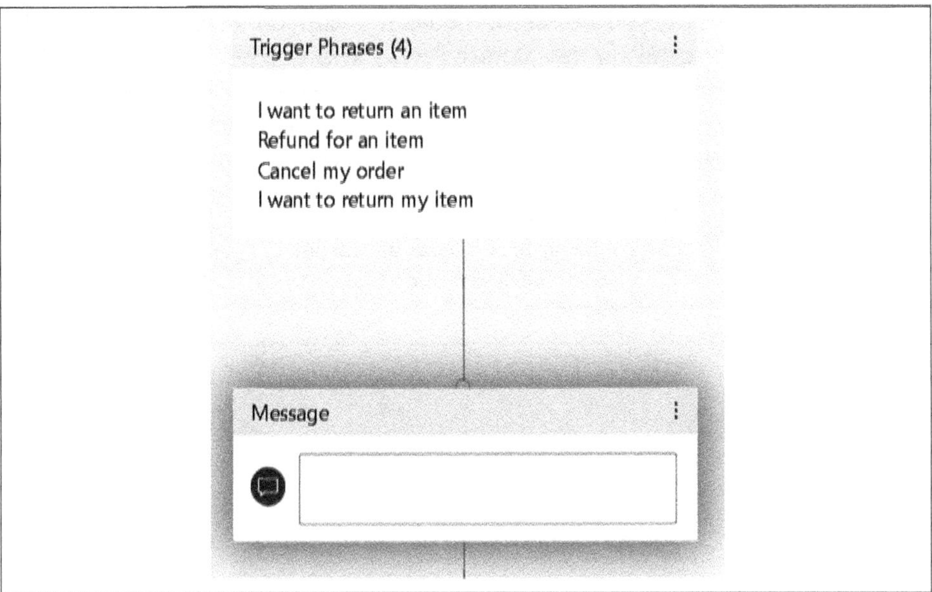

Figure 7-6. Defining trigger phrases for the chatbot

The next step is to edit the *conversation nodes*, or the message the chatbot will respond with when a trigger is matched. In the message box, type something like "We apologize for any inconvenience this may have caused. We will put you in touch with one of our operators."

Under the message box, you can add a node. You can add another message with something like, "Please call our Item Return Service at +xxxxxxxx" (see Figure 7-7).

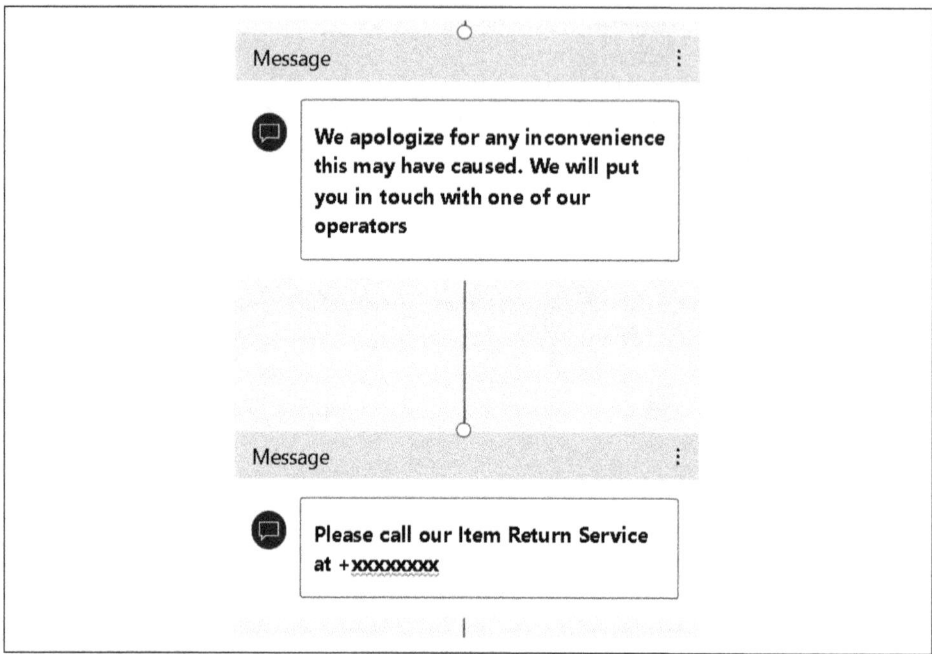

Figure 7-7. Creating conversation nodes

Click Save in the upper-right corner of the screen. Now, you can click "Test bot." If you enable the "Track between topics" option, you can see how the user is moved from one topic to the next. To run the test, type "Good morning" in the message box and then "I want to return an item." The test result should be what is shown in Figure 7-8.

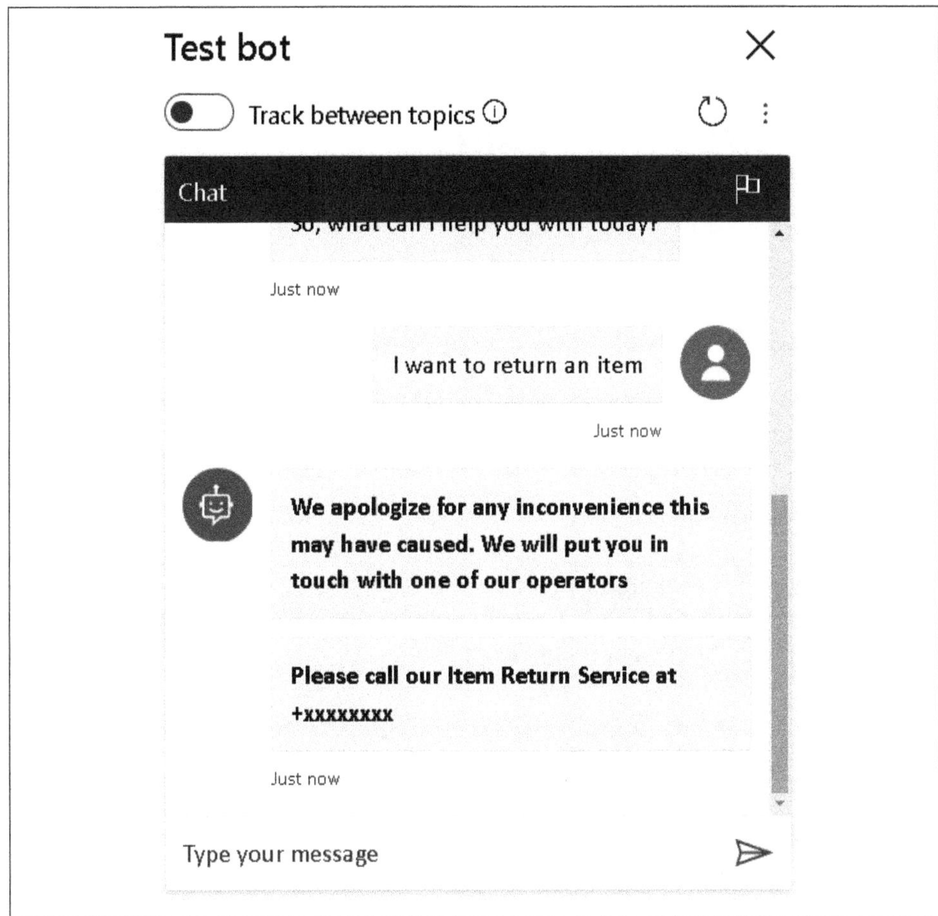

Figure 7-8. Testing the chatbot

During your test, try to write the trigger phrase in different ways (like "Cancel order" or "Item return"). Using intent, the chatbot is usually able to redirect you to the right topic even if the exact trigger phrase isn't used.

Click Overview in the left pane and click "Publish bot" (Figure 7-9).

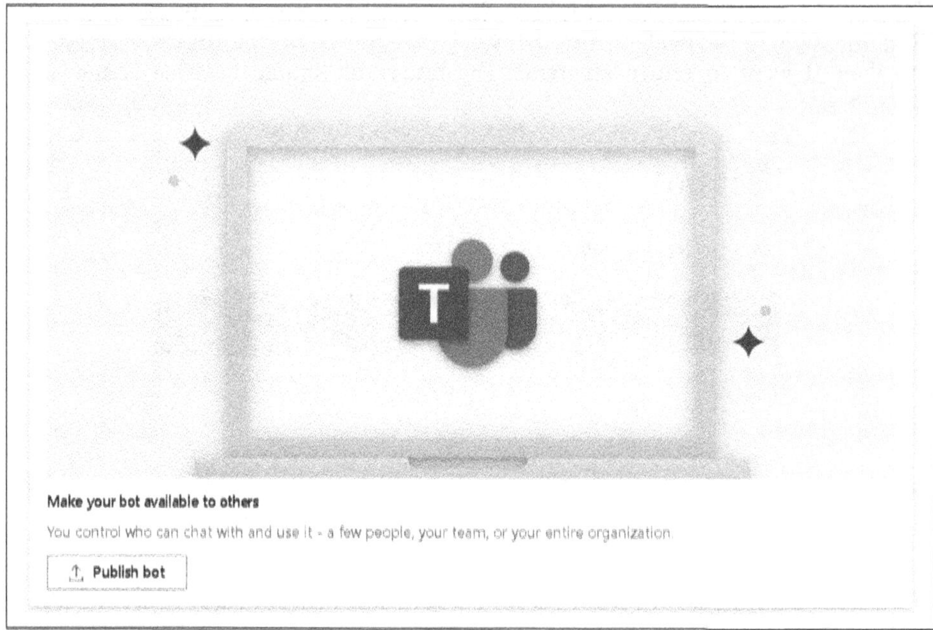

Figure 7-9. Publishing the chatbot

Click Publish and then Publish again on the next screen. Click "Open the bot in Teams" and then click Add. A Customer Service bot icon will appear and a new window will open with the chatbot (as in Figure 7-10).

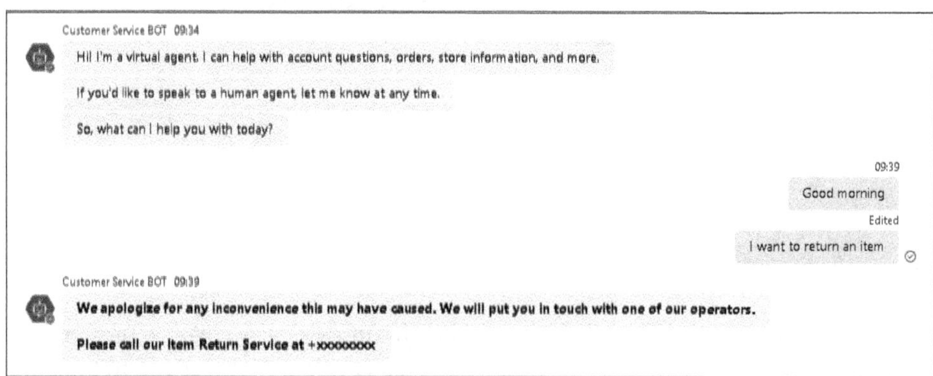

Figure 7-10. Chatbot running on its own app screen

Discussion

Chatbots in Teams enable easy interaction between users and customers. However, most chatbots fail to engage with users in a meaningful way because they are not able to adapt to users' varied input. Power Virtual Agents is a tool that allows you to create AI-powered chatbots for a range of requests. Power Virtual Agents is available as both a standalone web app and an app within Teams. Used in Teams, the chatbots are available internally to your organization and can be deployed quickly.

When a chatbot is created, several system topics called *lessons* are automatically created. Lessons are common topics used in conversations with a chatbot. You cannot delete or disable system topics or edit their trigger phrases.

A common usage scenario for chatbots is Q&A (using a knowledge base). There are different ways to realize a Q&A chatbot—one of them is the FAQ Plus bot (*https://oreil.ly/bsGjk*), available on GitHub. It includes many useful features and a script that allows you to deploy the chatbot using PowerShell.

7.2 Using Adaptive Cards to Improve the Teams User Interface

Problem

You need to integrate a chatbot with Teams to enable automatic scheduling of a conversation with the company's HR department.

Solution

Open Power Virtual Agents and click Chatbots. Select the Customer Service Bot you configured in Recipe 7.1. Click "New topic" and select "From blank." Call it "Company HR bot." Add as triggers "I need to talk with HR," "Human resources," and "People Operations."

In the conversation node message, type "I will connect you to one of our HR Business Partners." Click the + symbol to add a node and select the type "Ask a question" (see Figure 7-11). The prompt will be "Please type your name" and it will be used to identify a person's name. Rename the variable to `PersontoHRname`.

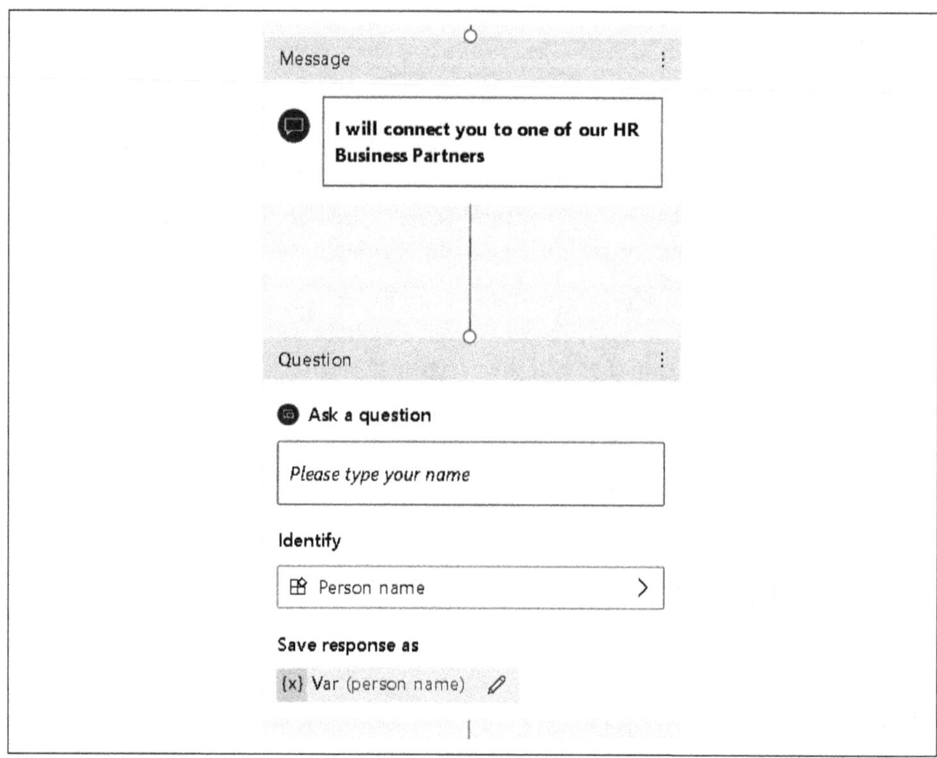

Figure 7-11. Capturing a variable from the chatbot's interaction with the user

Click Save. Click the + symbol to add a node. Select "Call an action," then "Create a flow." Select "Send an adaptive card to a Teams channel." You may be required to authenticate. After the authentication, click Continue. Figure 7-12 shows the whole flow.

Figure 7-12. The flow created from the initial template

In Power Virtual Agents, type a username, a title for the message, and a description (Figure 7-13).

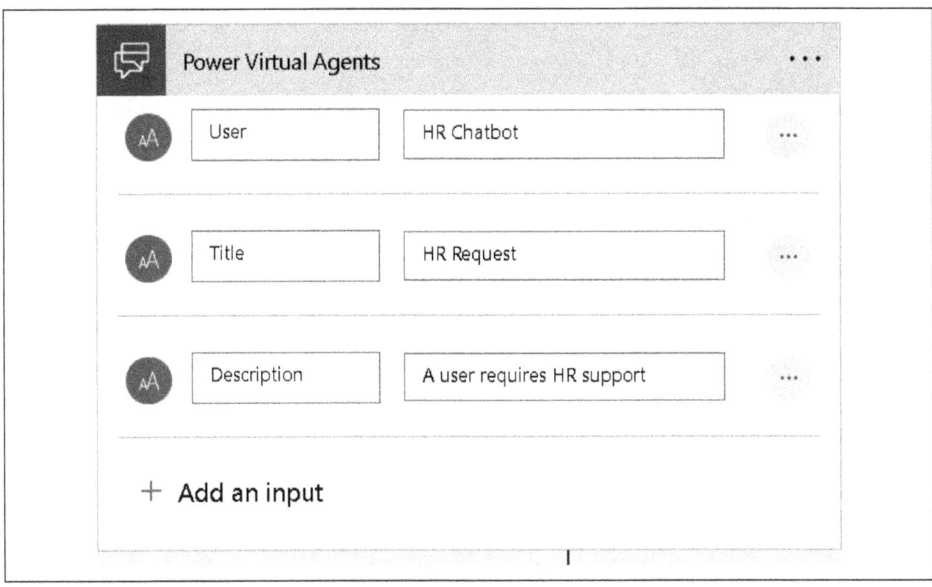

Figure 7-13. Parameters for Power Virtual Agents

In the "Initialize variable" window, enter "Type here" as the initial value, as shown in Figure 7-14.

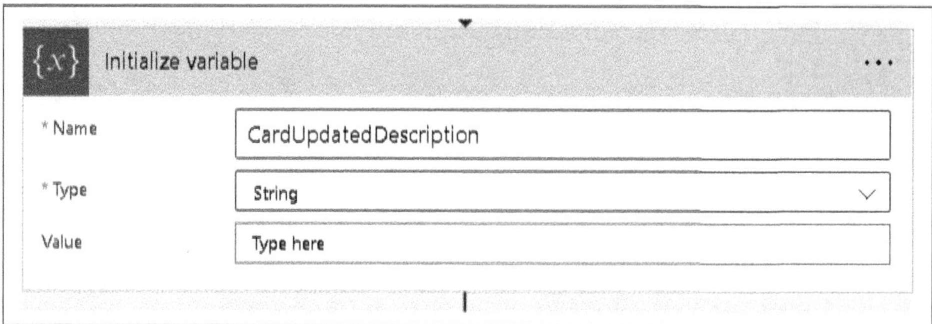

Figure 7-14. Initializing the variable for the Adaptive Card update

In the "Post an Adaptive Card to a Teams channel and wait for a response" window, select a team (for example, Communications) and a channel (for example, General), as shown in Figure 7-15.

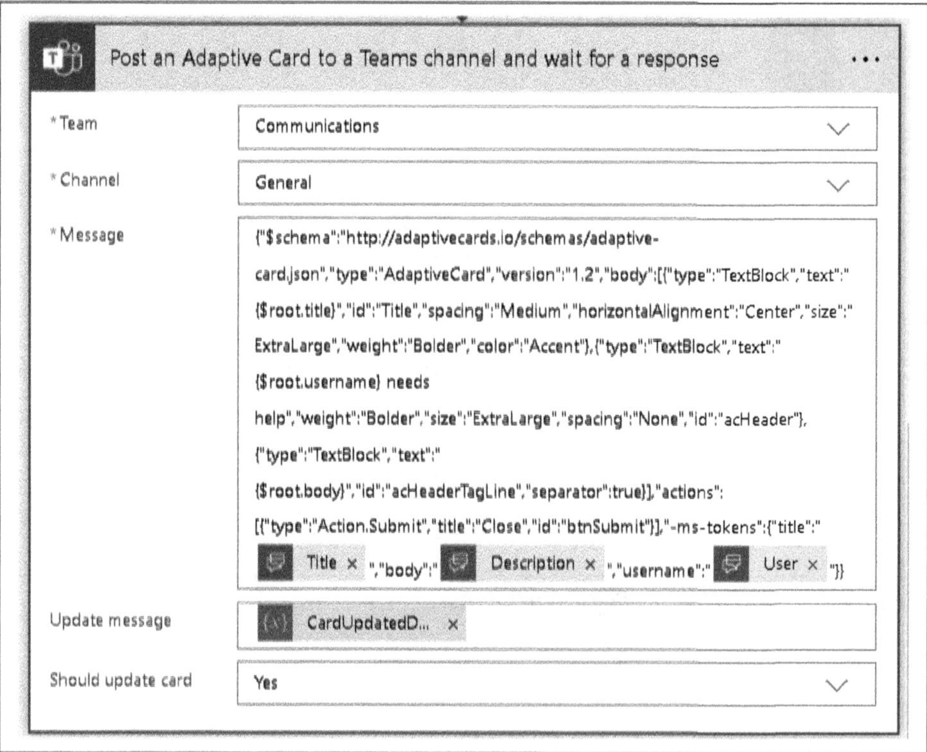

Figure 7-15. Connecting the Adaptive Card to Teams

In the "Return value(s) to Power Virtual Agents" window, type "Thank you. Your request has been recorded."

Click Save, and click Close to return to the Topic screen. If you click "Call an action," you'll have a new possible selection to send an Adaptive Card to a Teams channel. The Action menu will open. Populate the User, Title, and Description fields. You can use text or populate from variables (in our example, the User field will be `bot.UserId` and the Description field will be the `PersontoHRname` variable, as you can see in Figure 7-16).

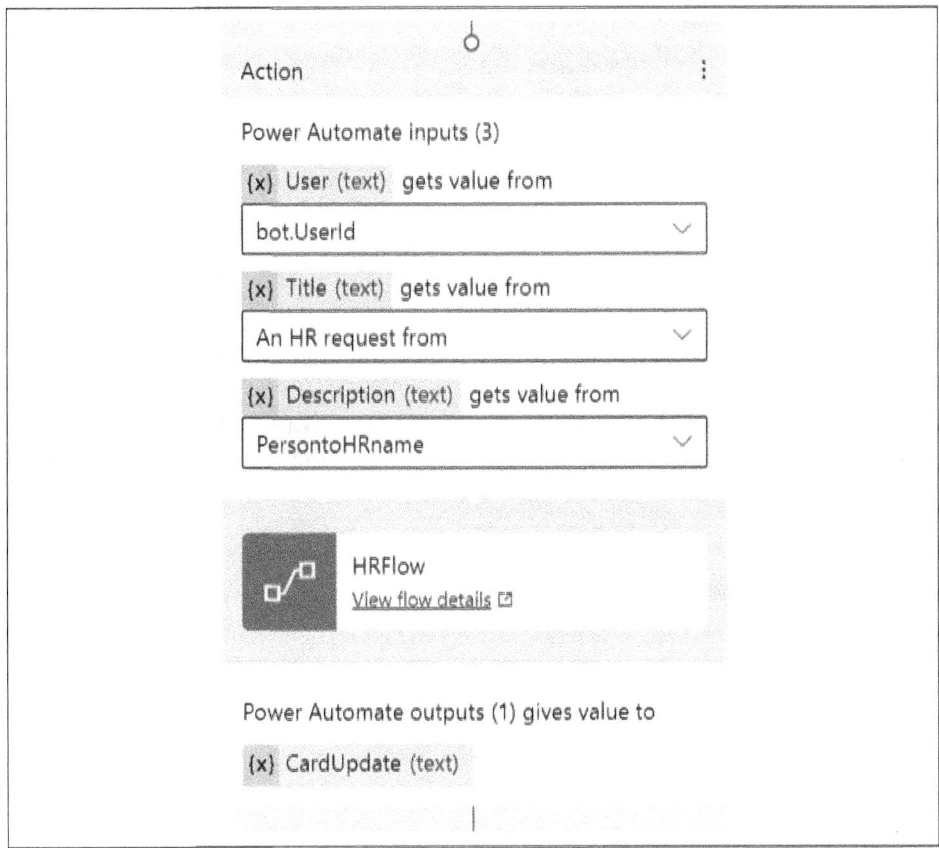

Figure 7-16. Action parameters to send to the flow

Click the + symbol to add a node and select "Show a message." Type "Thank you. Your request has been recorded." Click Save and select "Test bot." Start a conversation with the chatbot, as shown in Figure 7-17.

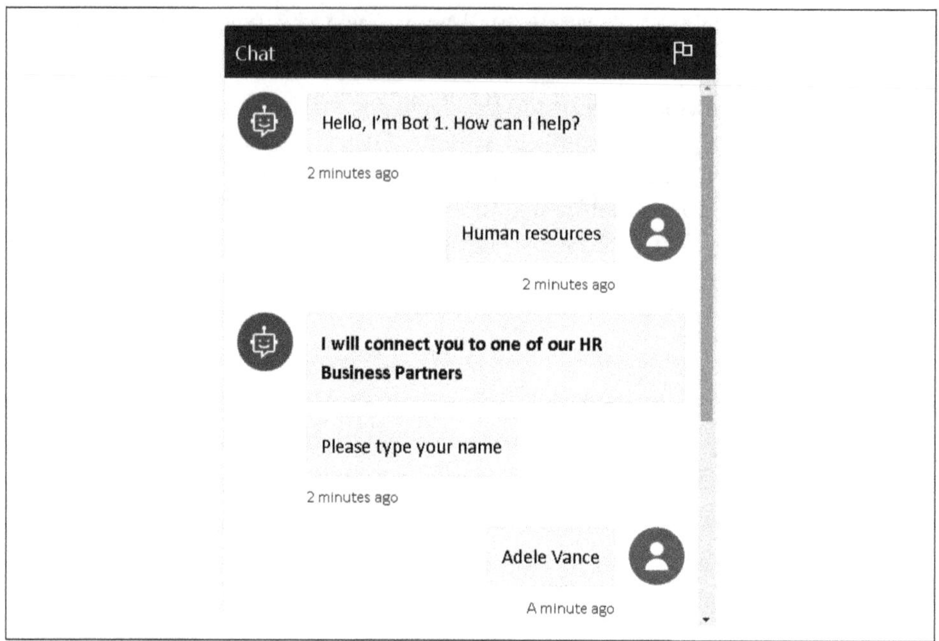

Figure 7-17. Testing the modified chatbot

The chatbot will pause while waiting for an input from Teams. Open a Teams client. In the General channel of the Communications team, you will receive the Adaptive Card (see Figure 7-18).

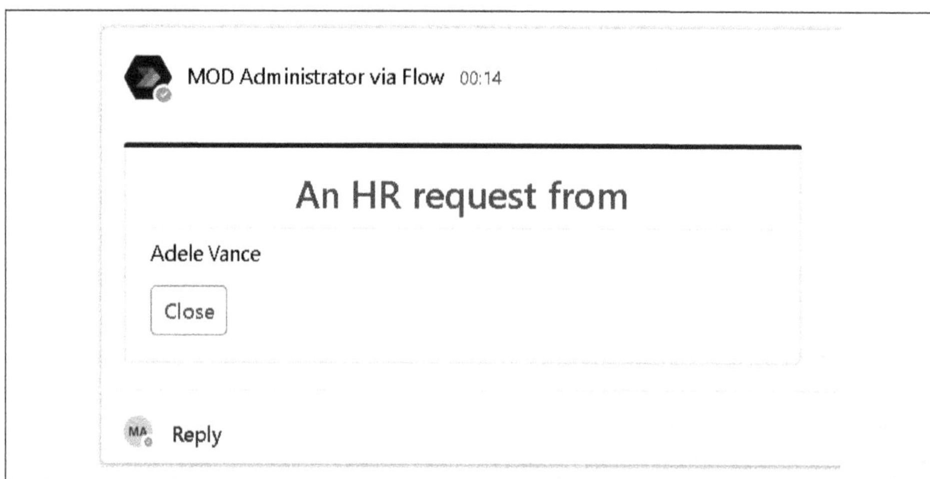

Figure 7-18. Adaptive Card received in the Communication team's General channel

Type a message and click Close. The chatbot will send the final message (Figure 7-19).

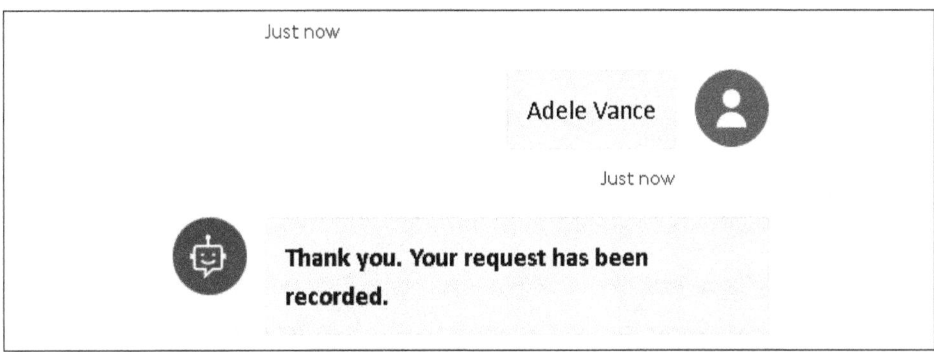

Figure 7-19. The chatbot completes the process

Discussion

Adaptive Cards are an interactive method of displaying information, a cross-platform solution developed to standardize information exchange. The Cards are blocks of the UI that are able to show rich text and graphics and receive input and feedback from users. Their availability across different applications enables a build once, deploy everywhere solution that allows developers to reach a larger audience.

Adaptive Cards are constructed using JavaScript Object Notation (JSON) and can be used to direct content to members in Teams channels or chats. These messaging units will adapt to the interface of the messaging client they are sent to. They will have a consistent look, even when moving from desktop to mobile or web client. The same Card can be used with Outlook and will change its look according to the Outlook interface.

Looking at the same Card used in this recipe from a mobile device (Figure 7-20) gives you an idea of the flexibility of their design.

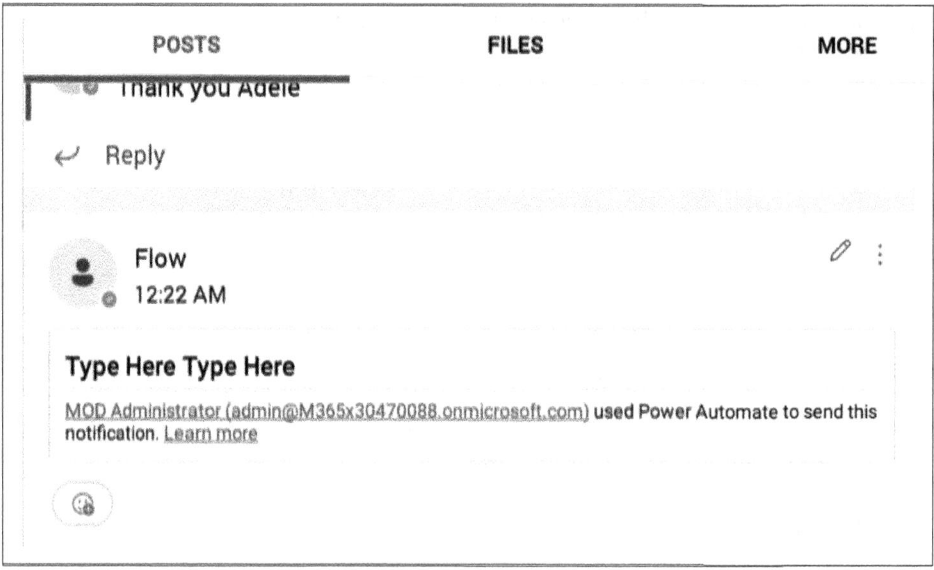

Figure 7-20. Adaptive Card rendered on a mobile phone

It is possible to use templates from the AdaptiveCards.io Samples and Templates page (*https://oreil.ly/mUJTq*). Check out "Weather large sample" (*https://oreil.ly/gw4VO*), and click "Try It Yourself." From the "Select host app" drop-down menu, select Microsoft Teams – Light and then click "Copy card payload" (as shown in Figure 7-21).

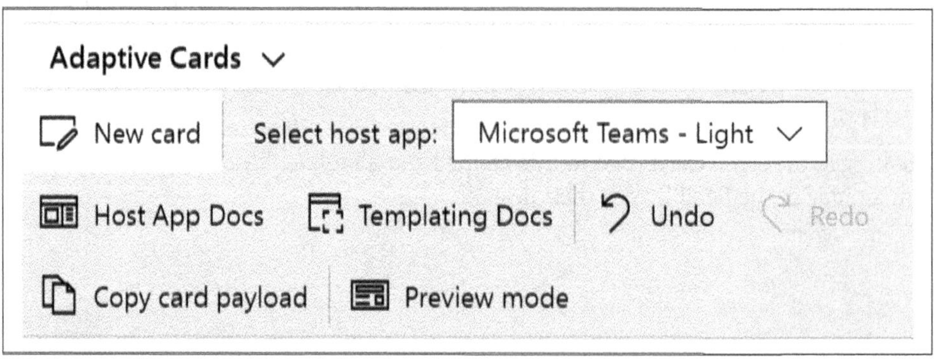

Figure 7-21. Using Adaptive Card samples

From the Teams client, open Power Automate, create a flow with a manual trigger, and post the Adaptive Card in a chat or channel as an action (see Figure 7-22).

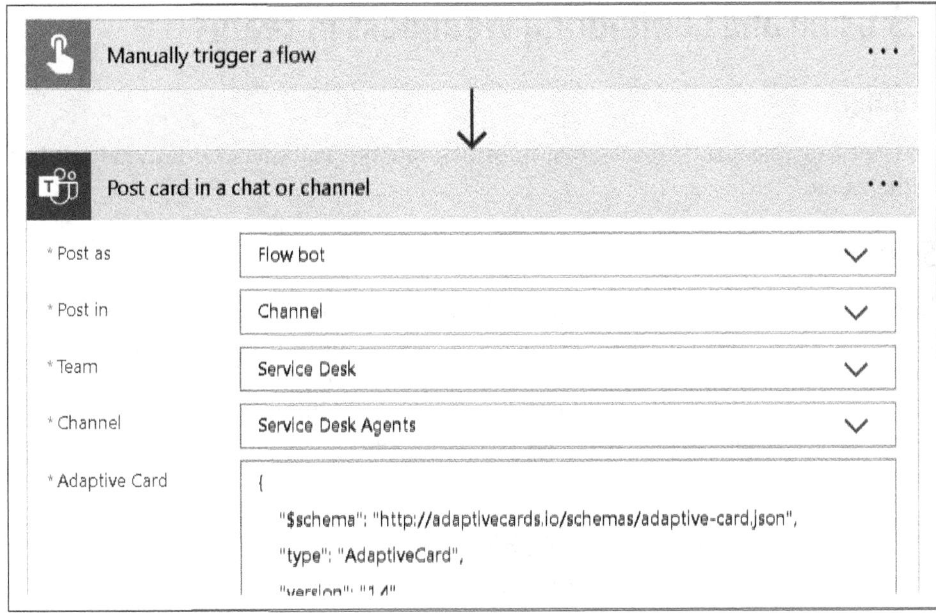

Figure 7-22. Quick test of an Adaptive Card in Power Automate

Select a team and a channel and paste the card payload you copied previously in the Adaptive Card field. Click Save, then click Test. Click Run Flow, then click Done.

If the flow ran correctly, you will have the Adaptive Card with weather in the selected channel (Figure 7-23).

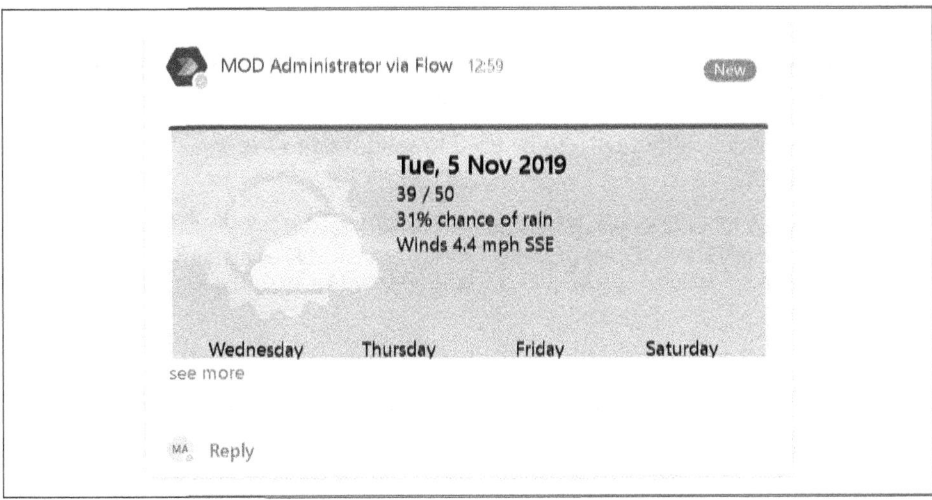

Figure 7-23. The weather Adaptive Card in a channel

7.3 Using and Configuring Webhooks in Teams

Problem

You need to visualize and integrate information from external and internal services with Teams.

Solution

In this recipe, we'll be configuring a webhook in Teams. To create a webhook, you must first select a channel. We will use the General channel in the Service Desk team. Click the + symbol to add a tab. Click "Manage your apps" in the lower-left corner, then click "More apps." In the search bar, type "incoming webhook," then click the Incoming Webhook app and click Add (as in Figure 7-24).

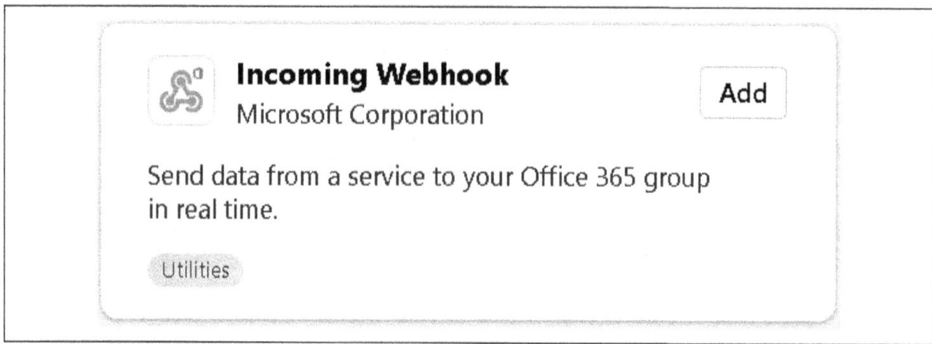

Figure 7-24. Adding incoming webhook

Click "Set up a connector." Give a name to the webhook (for this solution, we'll call it Service Desk Webhook), then click Create (Figure 7-25).

You will be provided with a URL to be used to send data to the webhook. It will look something like this:

> *https://m365x71772990.webhook.office.com/webhookb2/2b58a15f-f295-42e6-b464-480788bbd441@de5773d6-06cc-4b59-b70a-63e906b4c54f/IncomingWebhook/ec234e358d5147c0830db67d83ebca09/ad05f4ed-d044-46a6-b42d-2f5ab085xxxx*

Click Done.

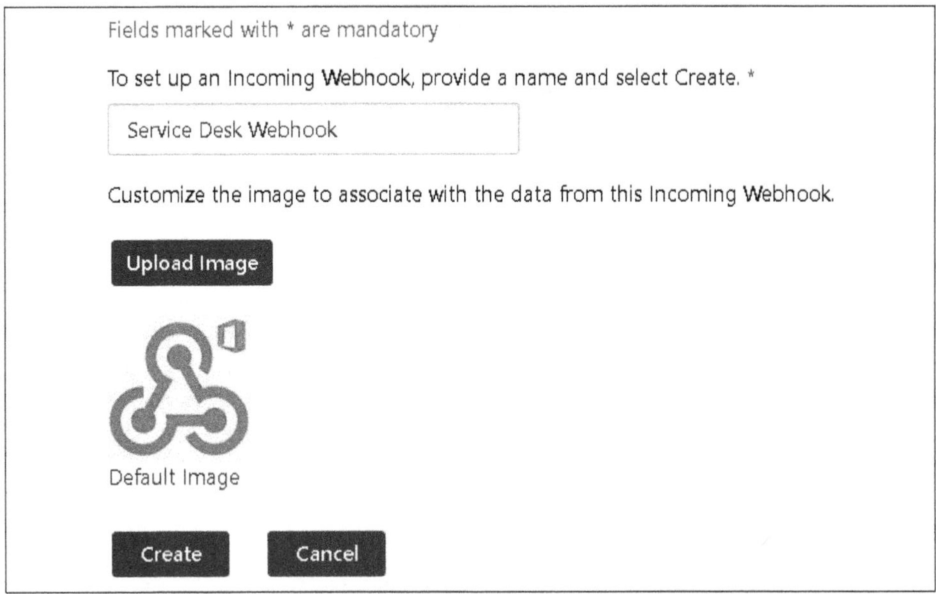

Figure 7-25. Creating the webhook

Every time you need to add a connector (like a webhook), right-click the channel and click Connectors (Figure 7-26).

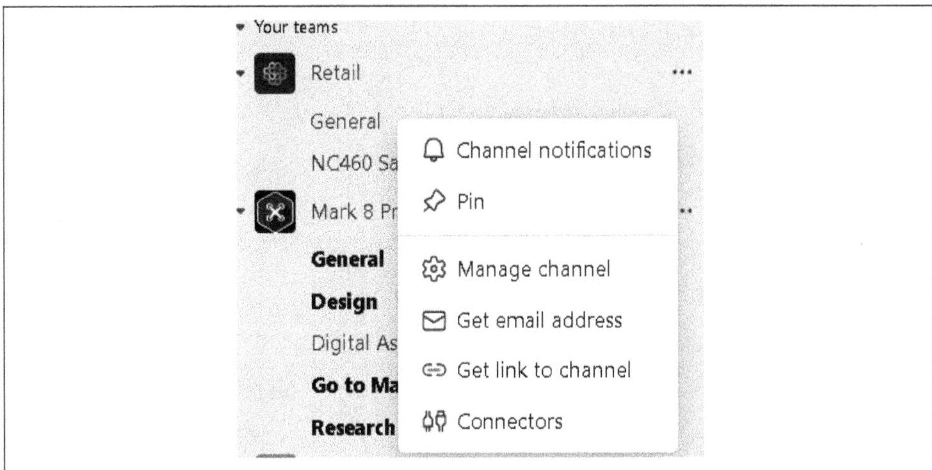

Figure 7-26. Adding connectors

To test the incoming webhook from the Teams client, open Power Automate (you may need to click the ellipsis in the left pane to see it). Click "New flow," select "Create from blank," and select "Manually trigger a flow" as the trigger option. Click "New step," click "Built-in," and click HTTP and then HTTP again.

Select the method POST from the drop-down menu, paste the URL of your incoming webhook into the URL field, and type "Content-type" and "application/json" in the Headers fields. Finally, type the following code in the Body field, as shown in Figure 7-27:

```
{
    "text": "Hello, world."
}
```

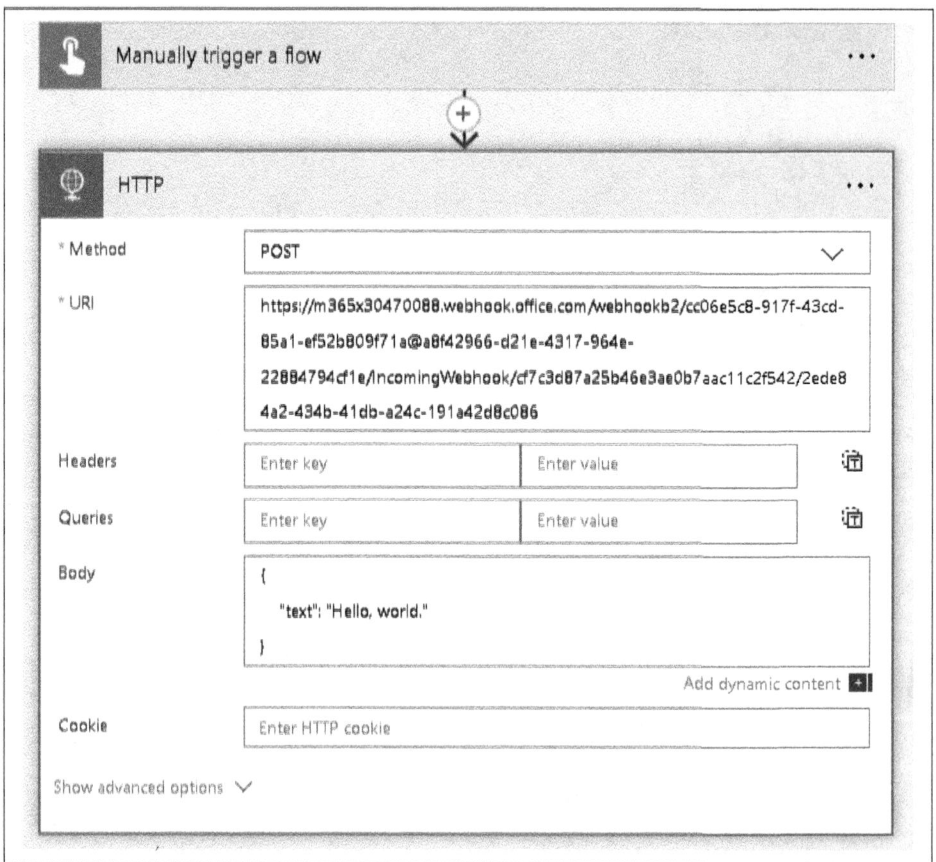

Figure 7-27. HTTP POST ready to communicate with the webhook

Click Save, then click Test in the upper-right corner. Click Test, Run Flow, and Done. You should have an incoming message in the selected channel (as in Figure 7-28).

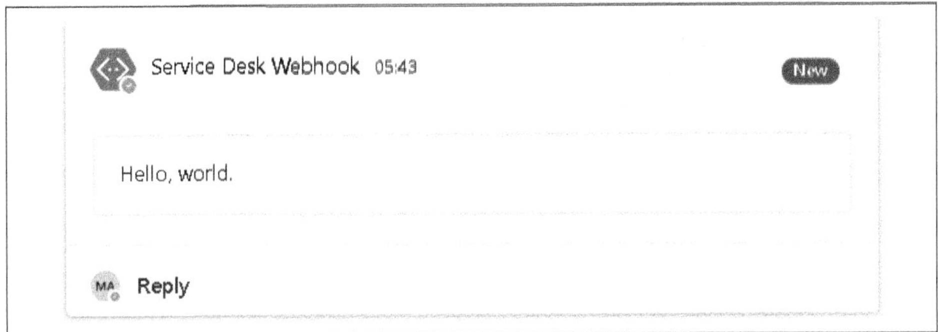

Figure 7-28. Receiving messages in a channel via webhooks

Discussion

You can use outgoing webhooks that call an external web service every time you mention them in Teams. Any web service accessible from the internet can be used in this way. In addition, webhooks allow you to create a solution and access it from Teams if you do not have the permissions to publish inside the tenant. You can also create incoming webhooks so that external applications can share content in Teams channels. Incoming webhooks and notification chatbots offer similar features, though there are some differences to be considered. For example, chatbots require an installation that is not necessary for incoming webhooks. Chatbots are usable in channels, group chats, and personal chats, but webhooks are limited to Teams channels.

You now know how to create incoming webhooks. To create outgoing webhooks, open the Teams client, select a team, click the ellipsis, and select "Manage team." Click Apps and select "Create an outgoing webhook" in the lower-right corner. The "Create an outgoing webhook" wizard will open. For this example, let's use Open Exchange Rates for the Name, *https://openexchangerates.org/api* for the Callback URL, and "Simple JSON API with live and historical foreign exchange" as the Description (Figure 7-29).

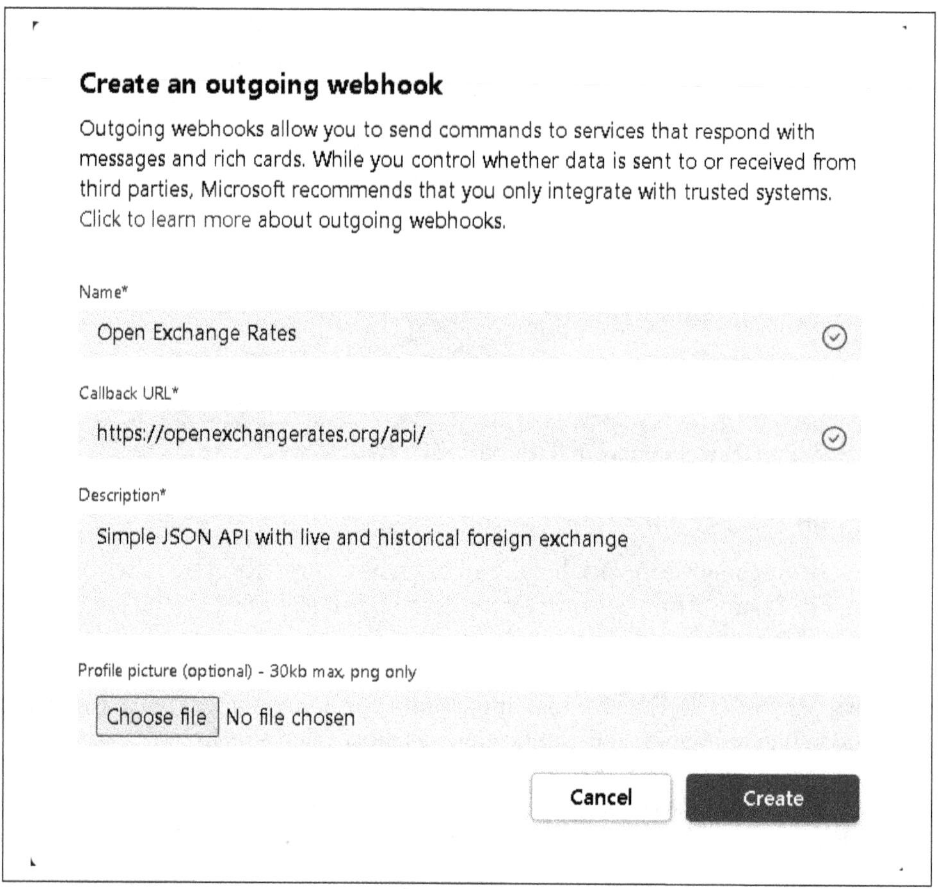

Create an outgoing webhook
Outgoing webhooks allow you to send commands to services that respond with messages and rich cards. While you control whether data is sent to or received from third parties, Microsoft recommends that you only integrate with trusted systems. Click to learn more about outgoing webhooks.
Name*
Open Exchange Rates
Callback URL*
https://openexchangerates.org/api/
Description*
Simple JSON API with live and historical foreign exchange
Profile picture (optional) - 30kb max, png only
Choose file
No file chosen
Cancel
Create

Figure 7-29. Configuring an outgoing webhook

Click Create. A security token will be provided to create a secure communication with Teams (Figure 7-30).

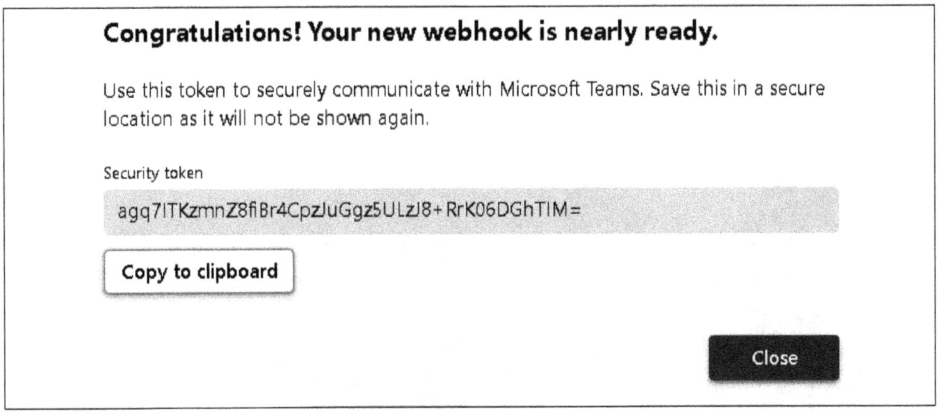

Congratulations! Your new webhook is nearly ready.

Use this token to securely communicate with Microsoft Teams. Save this in a secure location as it will not be shown again.

Security token

agq7ITKzmnZ8fiBr4CpzJuGgz5ULzJ8+RrK06DGhTIM=

Copy to clipboard

Close

Figure 7-30. Security token for the outgoing webhook

7.4 Deploying an App in Teams

Problem

You need to create and deploy an app in Teams.

Solution

Open the Teams Developer Portal (*https://oreil.ly/oCGSd*) and click Apps. Click "New app" and give it a name. In our example, we'll name the app Halloween Haunted House. Click Add, then click "App features" and select Scene from the list in Figure 7-31.

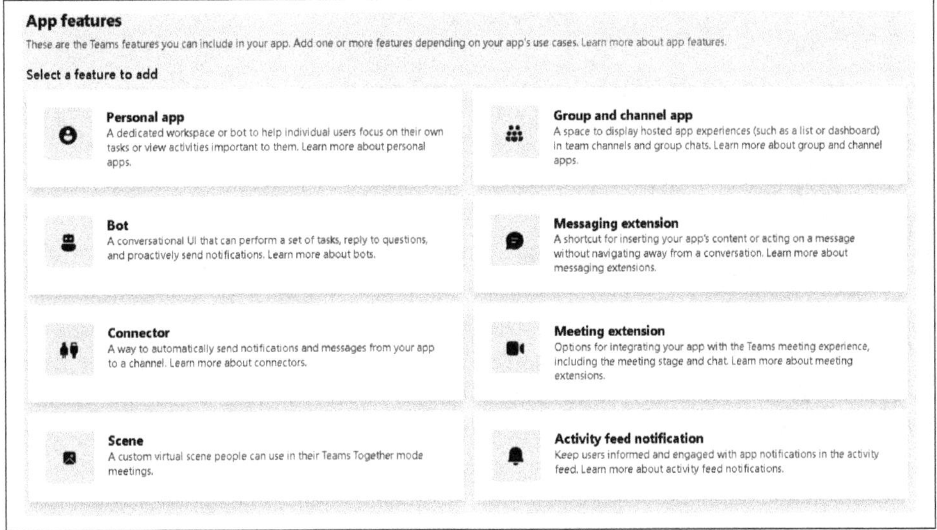

Figure 7-31. Selecting app features from the Teams Developer Portal

Click Add Scene > Scene Studio. Click Halloween Haunted House (as shown in Figure 7-32) and click Save.

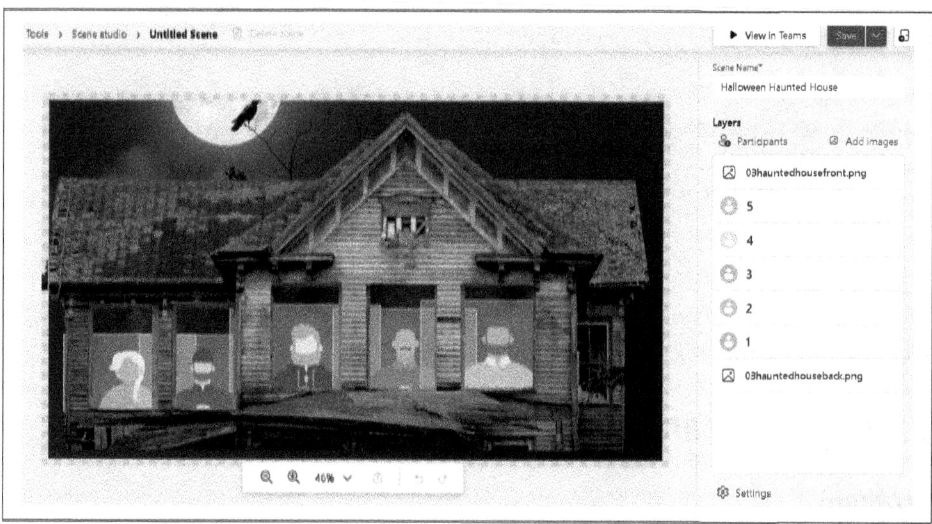

Figure 7-32. Selecting a scene

On the Configure screen, basic information for the mandatory URLs will be prefilled, as in Figure 7-33.

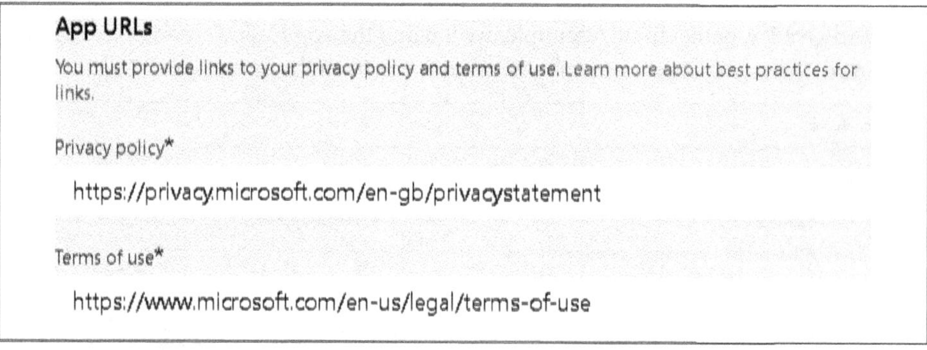

App URLs
You must provide links to your privacy policy and terms of use. Learn more about best practices for links.
Privacy policy*
https://privacy.microsoft.com/en-gb/privacystatement
Terms of use*
https://www.microsoft.com/en-us/legal/terms-of-use

Figure 7-33. Privacy policy and terms of use URLs are mandatory and prefilled

Click Publish and select "Download the app package." The file *Halloween Haunted House.zip* will be downloaded. You can now import your app from the Teams client, by clicking Apps > "Manage your apps." Click "Upload your app" and select *Halloween Haunted House.zip*.

To create and use Custom Together Mode, the Advanced Communications add-on for Microsoft Teams is required.

Discussion

A Teams app can extend the client (for example, adding tabs, message extensions, and so on). You can design and build your Teams app from scratch with basic Fluent UI components. There are different tools on the internet that can help you build your application. These include the Microsoft Graph API, which allows you to add and remove messages and files to and from your channels.

Another good example of a tool to extend the Teams UI is the Microsoft Teams UI Kit (*https://oreil.ly/6ZRd6*), which includes core components, scenario-based templates, best practices, and patterns that are designed specifically for building Teams apps. Microsoft Teams App Templates (*https://oreil.ly/DL0s_*) is another tool that offers a collection of templates for common app use cases and workflows inside Teams. Finally, Fluent UI web (*https://oreil.ly/8-TQu*) is a handy collection of utilities, React components, and web components for building web applications.

All the required parts of an application must be unified in a single entity (a Teams app) to make the installation easier. To define a Teams app, you can use the Teams Developer Portal (*https://oreil.ly/htLIC*). As you have seen in this recipe, a Teams app is a container that puts different parts together using a manifest (a JSON file) that describes the app and its capabilities. The manifest does not include any code.

7.5 Summary

This chapter looked at different tools to extend Teams and add custom features and elements. Some of the methods available require knowledge of development and developer tools. The Teams Development Platform is designed to help users understand their organization's requirements and develop ideas about how to improve their work processes, regardless of their capabilities as a developer. Microsoft is focused on providing no-code and low-code solutions to users with little or no knowledge of software engineering.

In Chapter 8, we'll discuss automating different administrative tasks in Teams using system tools like PowerShell and Power Automate.

CHAPTER 8

Automating Teams Administration

Microsoft Teams administration—and, more generally, Microsoft Office 365 administration—is often time-consuming, and repeating the same task many times can increase the likelihood of administrator errors. However, routine administration tasks can often be automated using one of the many tools and features available in the Microsoft cloud platform. Automation allows the execution of repetitive tasks quickly and with a limited risk of errors. This chapter introduces some new tools for automation, and also discusses how to leverage the tools you have already learned about—for example, Power Automate—to get a desired result.

8.1 Automating New Teams Approvals and Creation

Problem

You need to automate the request, approval, and creation processes for new teams.

Solution

A possible solution to this problem requires integrating Microsoft Forms, Teams Approvals, and Power Automate. Microsoft Forms is a web-based application in Microsoft 365 that allows users to build forms and surveys via a builder. Teams Approvals is an app available within Teams that allows teams to collect, process, and store all project-related requests in one place. For example, a document that requires review or approval from different people in the organization could be routed via Approvals.

As a first step, open the Microsoft Forms page (*https://oreil.ly/I21EG*) and click New Form. For the form title, enter "New Team Creation Request," with the description "Request to create a new team."

Click Next in the top-right corner. On the Form Design screen, select Text (Figure 8-1).

Figure 8-1. Adding a text field to the form

Enter "Team Name" as the name for the field. Repeat this process two more times, entering "Description" and "Office 365 User" as the field names and enabling the "Long answer" option for both of these fields. Then click Preview to see a preview of the form (Figure 8-2).

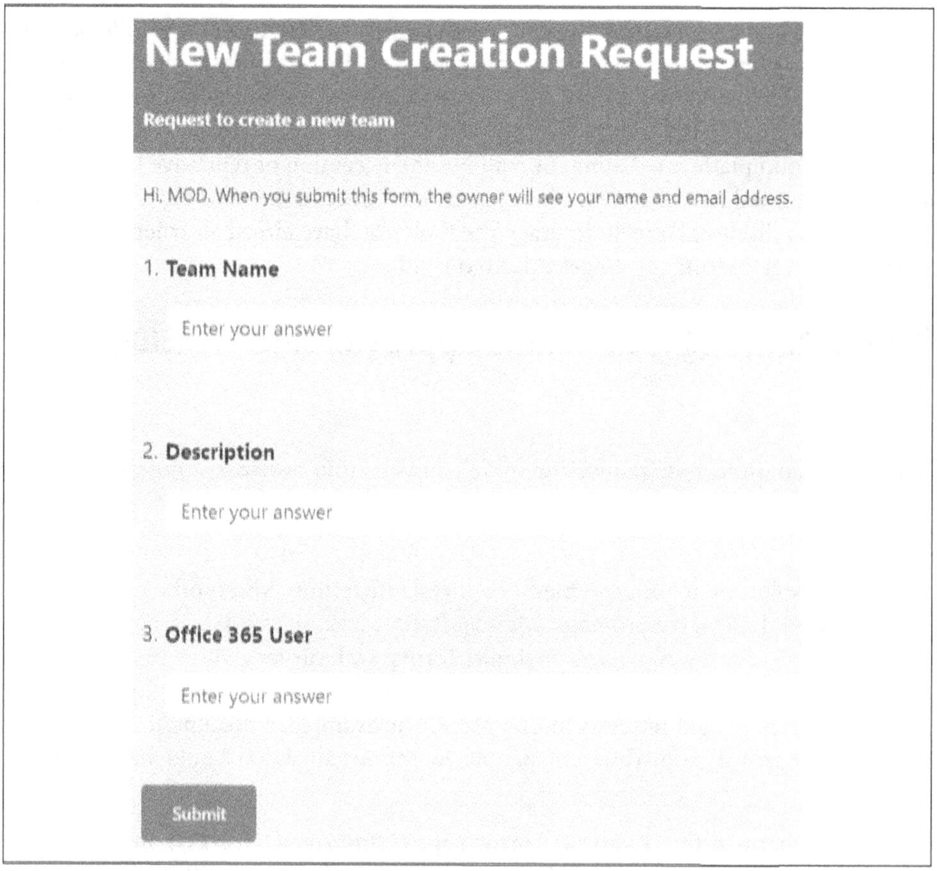

Figure 8-2. A preview of the final form

Click Submit, then open Power Automate from the Teams client. Click "New flow" and select "Create from blank." Select Microsoft Forms as the trigger and click "When a response is submitted" (as shown in Figure 8-3).

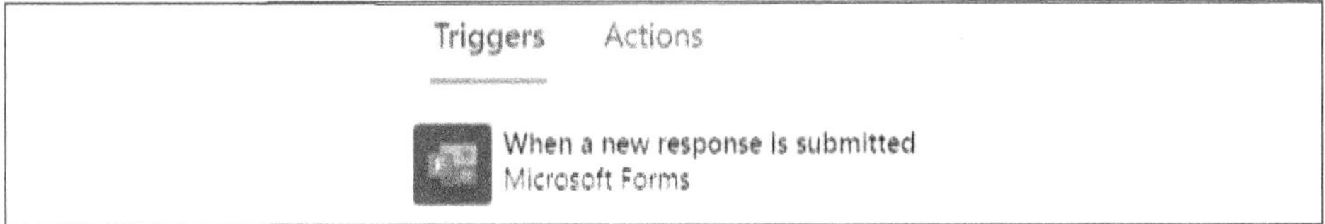

Figure 8-3. Selecting Forms as a trigger

In the Form Id field, select New Team Creation Request from the drop-down menu (see Figure 8-4).

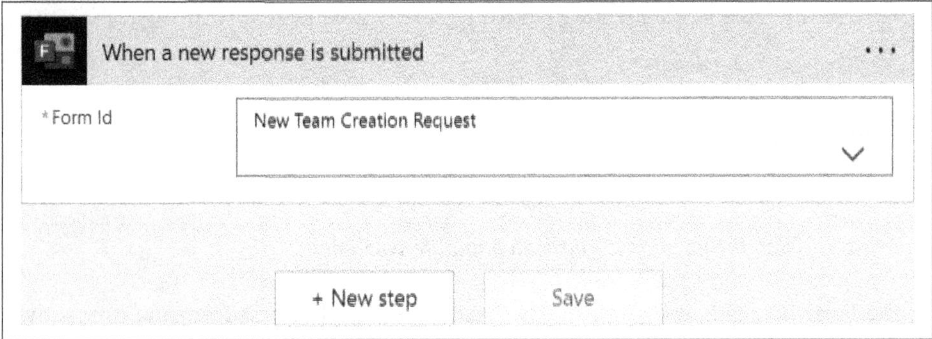

Figure 8-4. Using the form created in the flow

Click "New step." Search for Forms and click "Get response details," as shown in Figure 8-5.

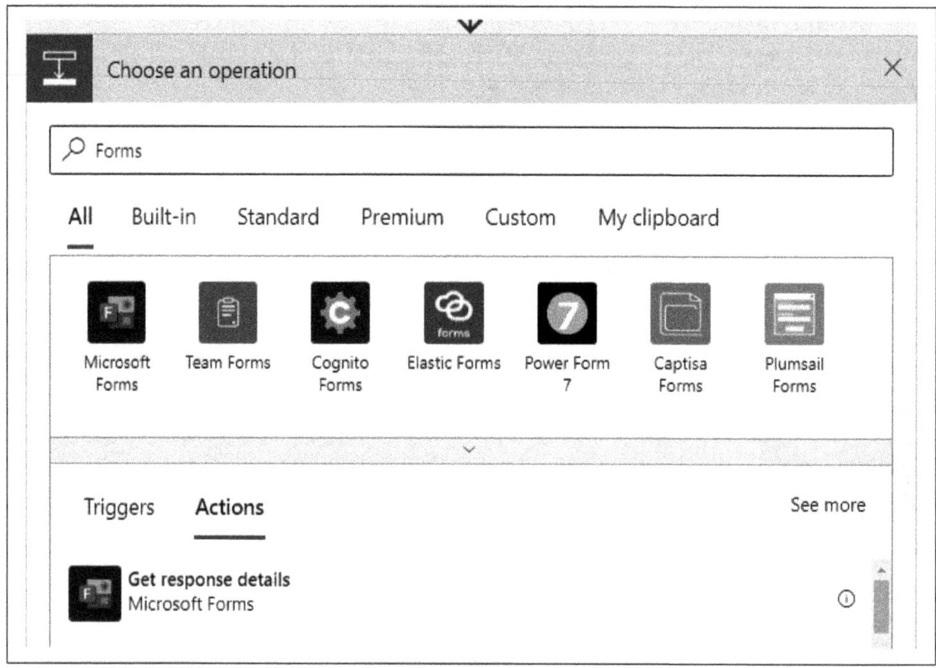

Figure 8-5. Using the form as a source to populate variables

In the Form Id field, again select New Team Creation Request from the drop-down menu. For the Response Id, select Response Id (see Figure 8-6).

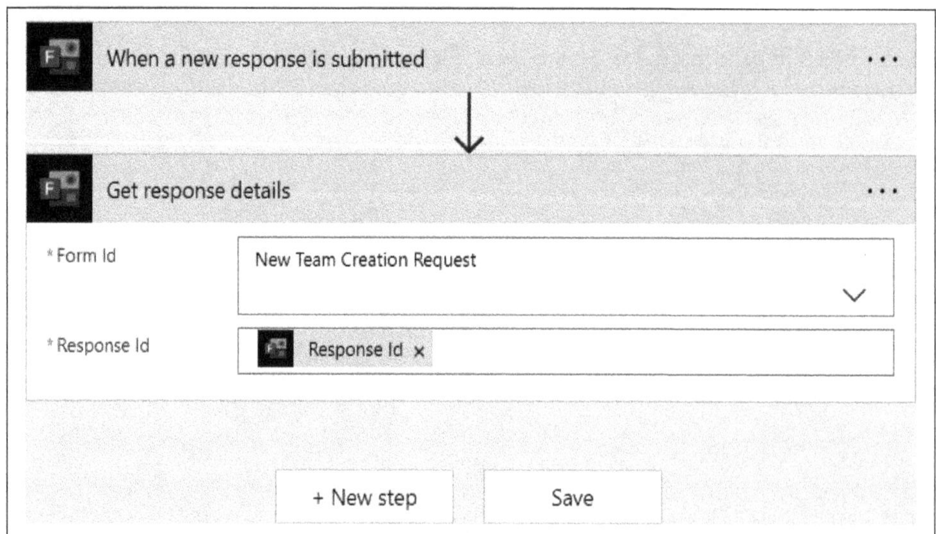

Figure 8-6. Integrating Forms with the flow

Click "New step." In the search field, type "approval," then click "Start and wait for an approval" (shown in Figure 8-7).

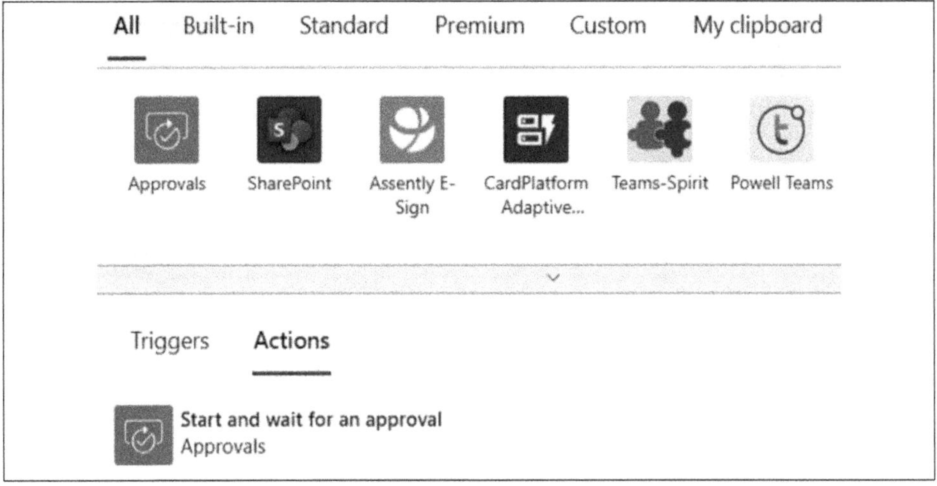

Figure 8-7. Integrating a step based on Teams Approvals

For the Title, use Team Name (the value received from the form). For "Assigned to," select the tenant administrator. In the Details field, choose the Description and Office 365 User values, taken from the form. See Figure 8-8 for the expected configuration.

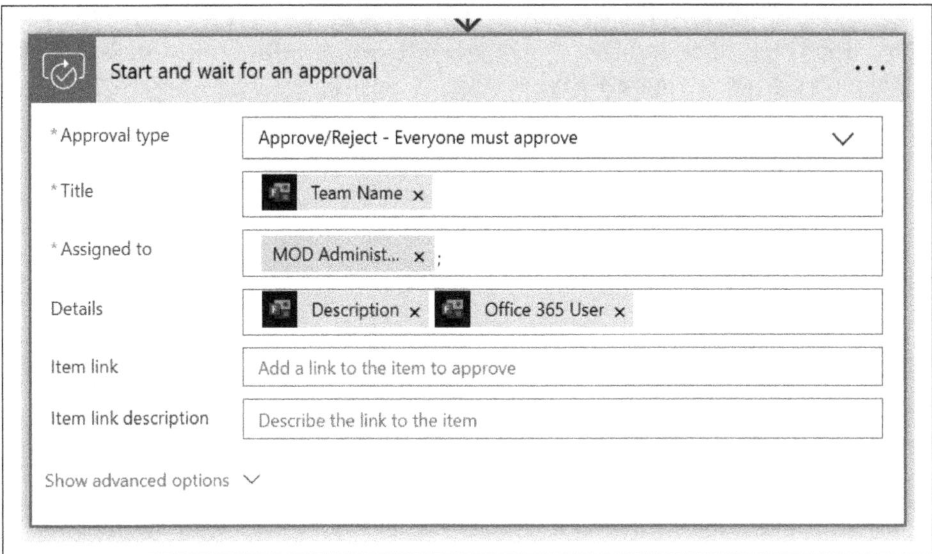

Figure 8-8. Configuring the approval process

Click "New step," click Control, then click Control again. Select the Condition to "Outcome is equal to approve" (see Figure 8-9).

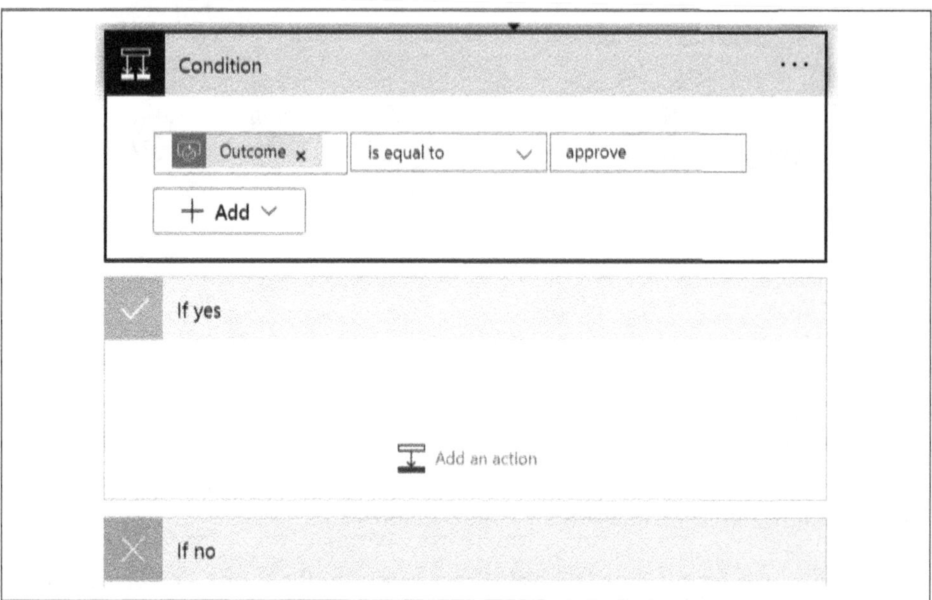

Figure 8-9. The condition has two different actions based on the results of the approval

Under "If yes," click "Add an action" and select Microsoft Teams. Click "Create a team." The Team Name and Description will be taken again from the variables in the initial form (shown in Figure 8-10).

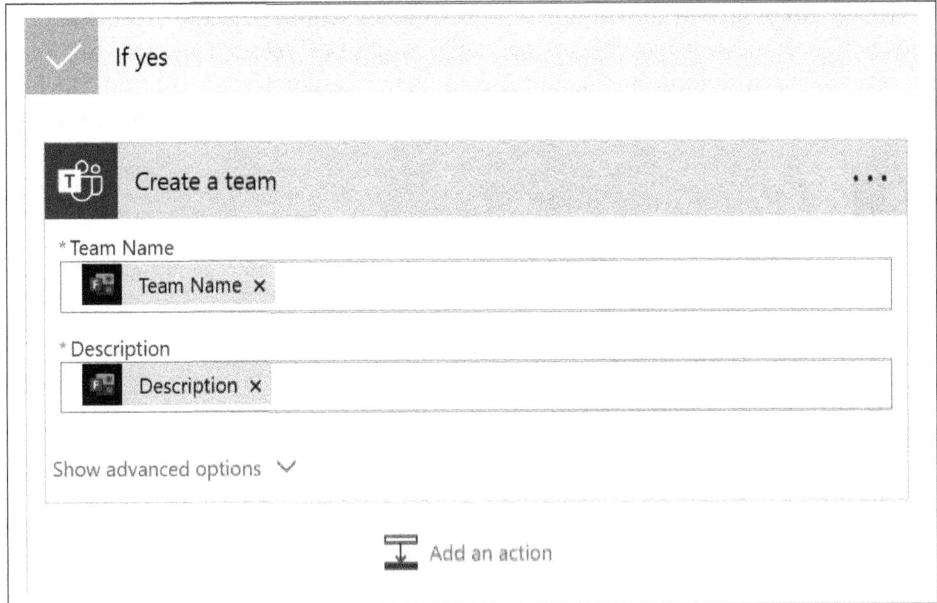

Figure 8-10. Defining the actions in the Yes branch

Click "Add an action," select Microsoft Teams, and click "Add a member to a team." Team is the New Team ID from for the team created in the previous step, and "A user principal name" is the Office 365 User variable from the initial form (see Figure 8-11).

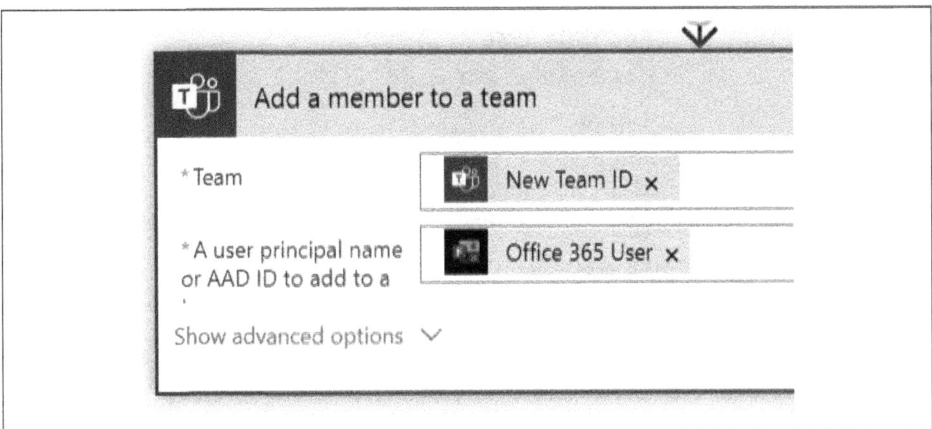

Figure 8-11. Adding a member to a team based on the initial form

Under the No branch of the condition, click "Add an action," select Microsoft Teams, and click "Post message in a chat or channel." For "Post as" select "Flow bot," for "Post in" select "Chat with Flow bot," and Recipient is the Responders' Email from the initial form. For Message, input "New team request refused" (as shown in Figure 8-12).

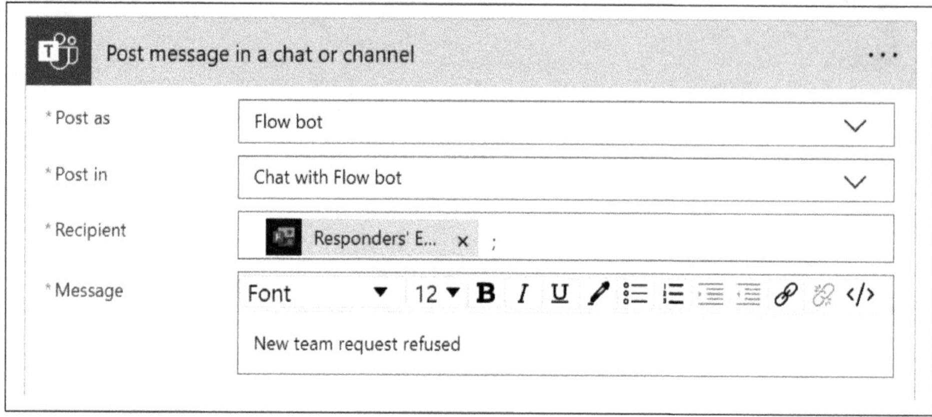

Figure 8-12. Posting a notification for the flow in a chat

Click Save.

A Microsoft Dataverse database is required to run the flow. If you do not have this database, go to the Power Platform admin center (*https://oreil.ly/rUwtj*) and click Environments. Select an existing environment or create a new one, and click Add Dataverse to add the database (see Figure 8-13).

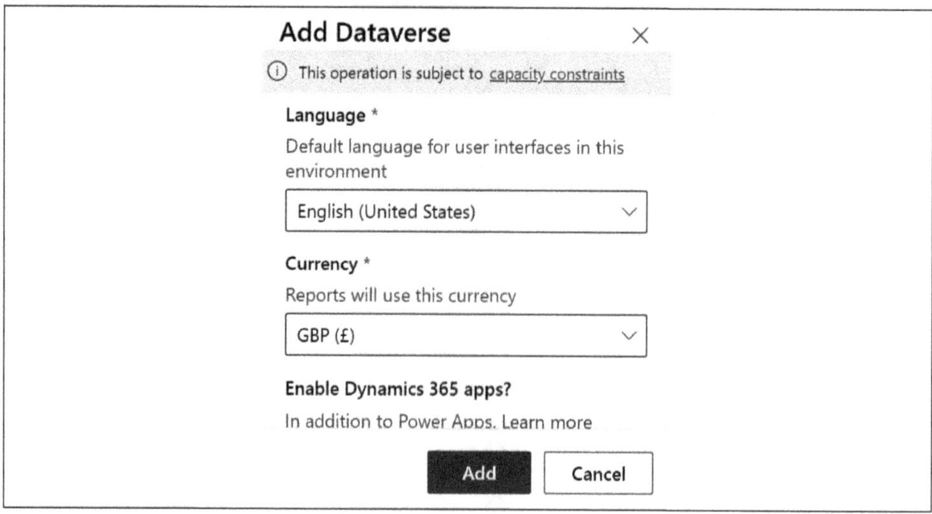

Figure 8-13. Adding a Dataverse database

Select the appropriate Language and Currency from the drop-down menu, then click Add.

When you open the environment again, a database version will be displayed. If you have never used Teams Approvals, you must run at least one approval process to populate the Dataverse database. Install the Approvals app from the Teams client and run a "Basic approval" using "New approval request." It may require a few minutes for the provisioning to be completed.

Open the Microsoft Forms page (*https://oreil.ly/6Jnwy*) and click New Team Creation Request. Click Preview and populate the fields in the form (the preview is shown in Figure 8-14).

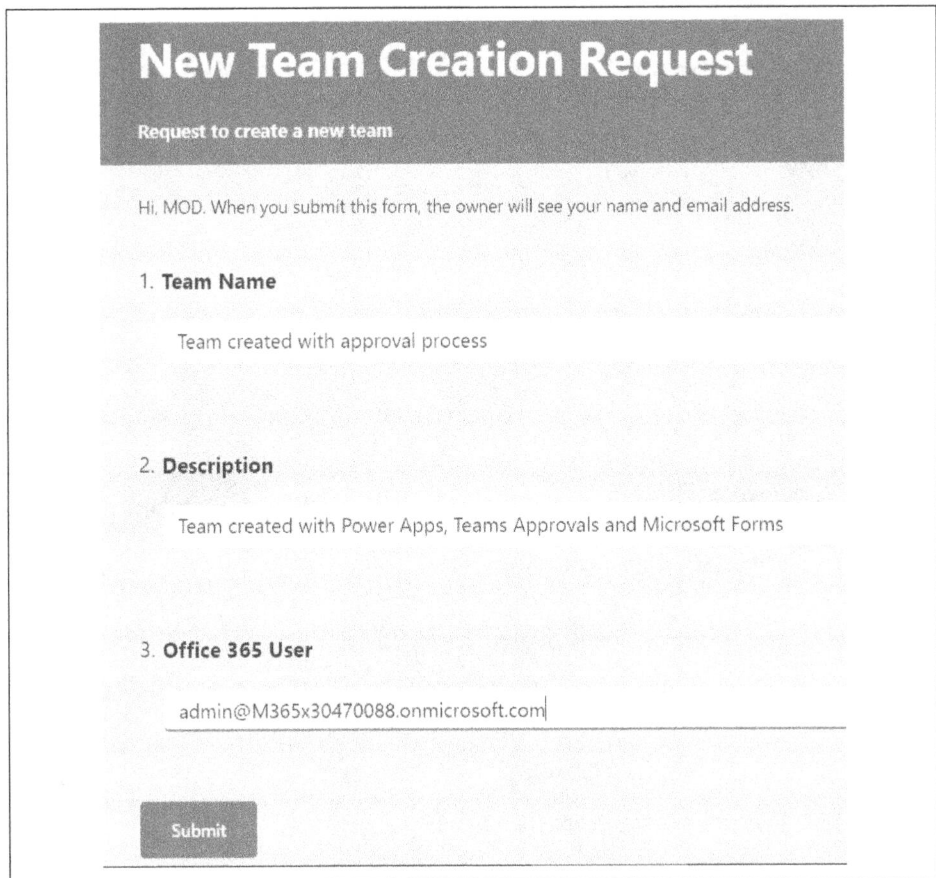

New Team Creation Request
Request to create a new team
Hi, MOD. When you submit this form, the owner will see your name and email address.
1. Team Name
Team created with approval process
2. Description
Team created with Power Apps, Teams Approvals and Microsoft Forms
3. Office 365 User
admin@M365x30470088.onmicrosoft.com
Submit

Figure 8-14. Testing the New Team Creation Request form

Click Submit. A notification will be sent to the user assigned in the approval process. Click Approve (as shown in Figure 8-15).

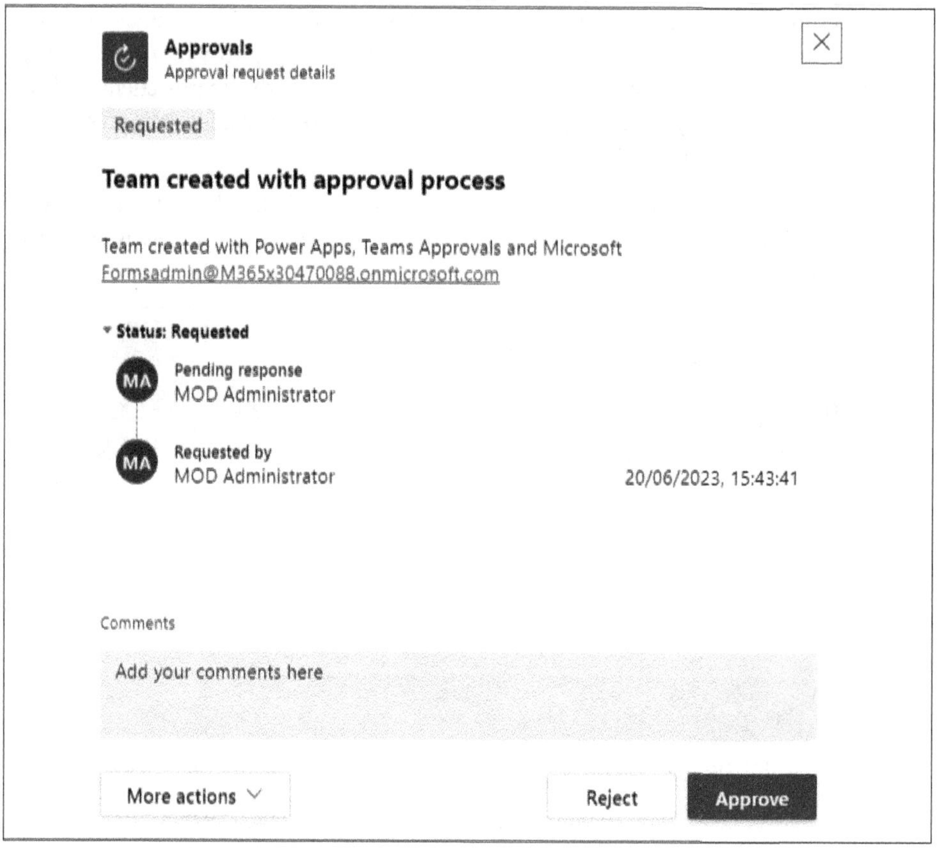

Approvals
Approval request details
Requested
Team created with approval process
Team created with Power Apps, Teams Approvals and Microsoft
Formsadmin@M365x30470088.onmicrosoft.com
Status: Requested
MA
Pending response
MOD Administrator
MA
Requested by
MOD Administrator
20/06/2023, 15:43:41
Comments
Add your comments here
More actions
Reject
Approve

Figure 8-15. Notification from Teams Approvals

A new team will be visible in the Teams client, as expected (see Figure 8-16).

TC
Team created with a...
General

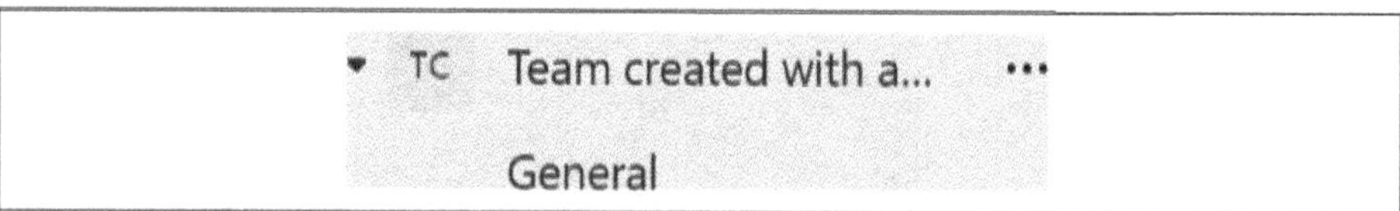

Figure 8-16. The new team was correctly created

The output of the approval process is case-sensitive, and a string with the wrong case will generate an error. It is useful, in case of a failure, to open the flow in Power Automate, open the specific test from the 28-day run history, and check the results of the different steps. For example, the body of the approval step is relevant should you need to debug an issue (as in Figure 8-17).

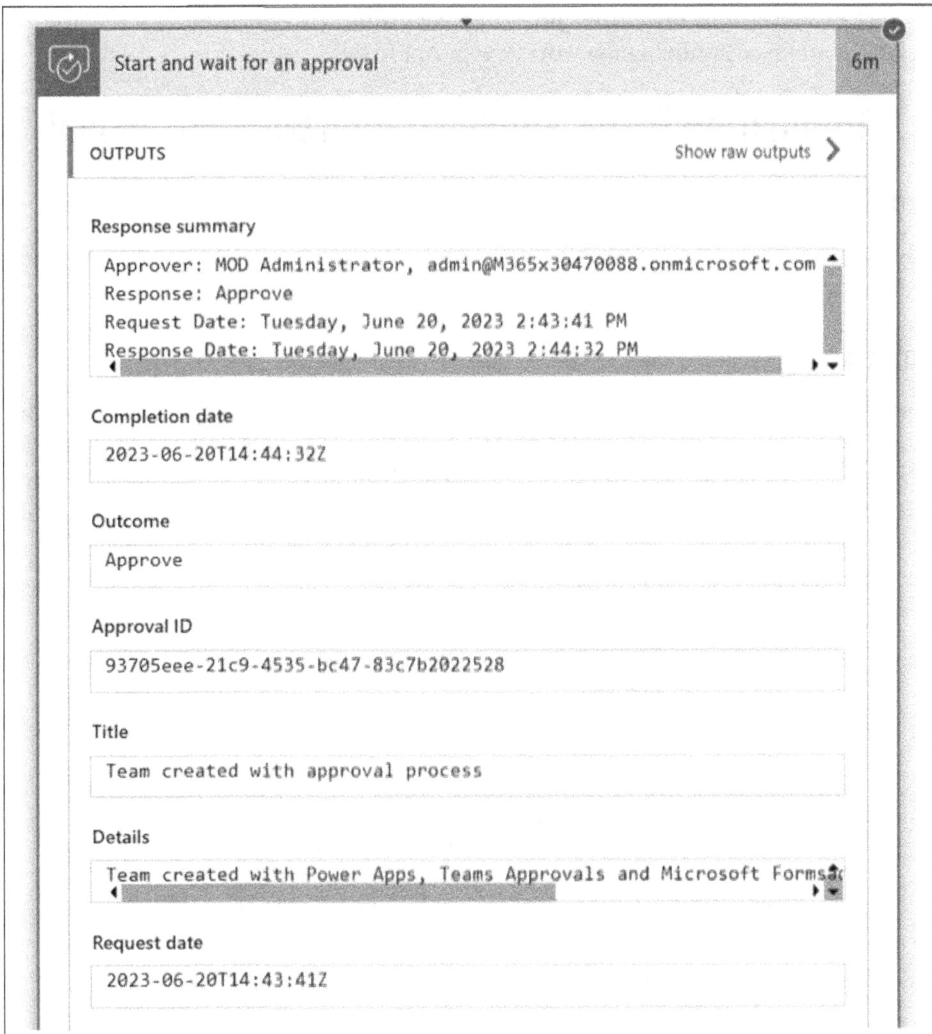

Figure 8-17. Reading debug information from the flow test

Discussion

Approvals have three different scopes that will determine who is able to see and use them: team owners, organization, and specific people. All team owners are authorized to create a template for Approvals available at the team level. The other scopes (organization and specific people) require a Teams administrator to create a template for Approvals. In the Forms web page, it is possible for all users to see how many forms are available to each group in which they are member.

Approvals uses Microsoft Forms, not Adaptive Cards. This means that you have less flexibility when customizing the workflow in Approvals.

8.2 Automating Teams Administration with PowerShell

Problem

You want to use preexisting PowerShell scripts to make your Teams administration tasks easier and quicker.

Solution

You can audit Teams meetings with the *AuditTeamsMeetings.ps1* script available from Office 365 Reports (*https://oreil.ly/vEwMW*). The script exports a CSV file with the following information: Meeting ID, Created By, Meeting Type, Meeting Link/Meeting URL, Start Time, and End Time. Using the following script (from DailySysAdmin (*https://oreil.ly/kxCVn*)), you can dump into a CSV file a list of all the members of all the Teams groups and their owners:

```
Connect-MicrosoftTeams

$AllTeams = (Get-Team).GroupID
$TeamList = @()

Foreach ($Team in $AllTeams)
{
        $TeamGUID = $Team.ToString()
        $TeamName = (Get-Team | ?{$_.GroupID -eq $Team}).DisplayName
        $TeamOwner = (Get-TeamUser -GroupId $Team | ?{$_.Role -eq 'Owner'}).Name
        $TeamMember = (Get-TeamUser -GroupId $Team | ?{$_.Role -eq `
            'Member'}).Name

        $TeamList = $TeamList + [PSCustomObject]@{TeamName = $TeamName; `
            TeamObjectID = $TeamGUID; TeamOwners = $TeamOwner -join ', '; `
            TeamMembers = $TeamMember -join ', '}
}

$TeamList | export-csv c:\temp\TeamsData.csv -NoTypeInformation
```

You can gather the Office 365 users' last activity details using a script from GitHub (*https://oreil.ly/FdBik*). This script returns the Microsoft Graph API reports on users' last activities with Office 365 services like Exchange Online, SharePoint Online, and OneDrive for Business.

You can also search GitHub for specific contributions to Microsoft Teams based on PowerShell (*https://oreil.ly/qF_sx*).

Discussion

GUI-based management tools are limited in cases where bulk edits and tasks are required. In these scenarios, using PowerShell is a better option. The Teams PowerShell module enables management of all aspects of Teams administration, including users, teams, policies, and configuration—in a single module. This module implements two different types of authentication: credentials-based and token-based. OAuth is an alternative to the more traditional (and less secure) credential-based authentication using a username and password. OAuth can use different identity providers (such as Microsoft, Google, and Facebook) to manage your credentials.

When an application wants to identify you, it can defer the job to an identity provider that will take care of your credentials. In exchange, the application gets tokens from the identity provider that act as a kind of virtual key to allow the application to act on your behalf.

8.3 Automating Teams Phone Number Management

Problem

You want to automate management of phone numbers in Teams.

Solution

When organizations deploy Teams as a voice platform connected to the PSTN, they often have to deploy and manage Direct Inward Dialing (DID), where a local phone company provides a block of telephone numbers that allow for calling into a company's PBX system.

The first step is to generate a list of all the available PSTN numbers in the organization. Download the *Get-TeamsNumbers.ps1* script from GitHub (*https://oreil.ly/eb0bP*) (thank you Ståle Hansen) and run it. PowerShell finds the next available numbers in a number range and gives you a list of the numbers you have left. You can see an example of the script's output in Figure 8-18.

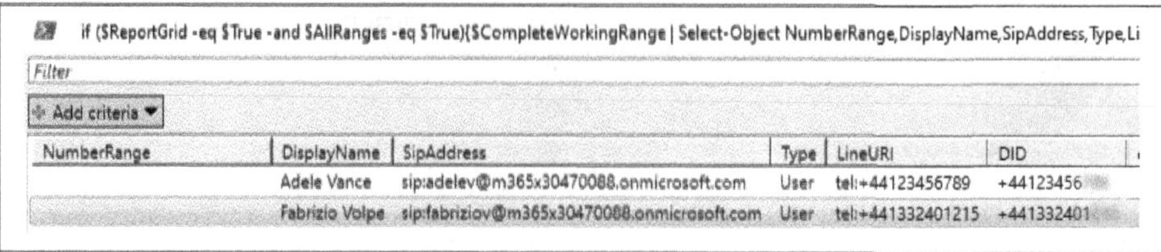

Figure 8-18. Output of the Get-Team Numbers.ps1 script

The start of the script allows you to add your phone ranges. Don't forget to remove the ones that are in the script just as examples:

```
$CRs = @()
$CRs += ,@("NorwayOperatorConnect4050","+4764974050", `
    "+4764974059")
$CRs += ,@("SwedenCallingPlan4050","+46850241520", `
    "+46850241540")
$CRs += ,@("NorwayDirectRouting8050","+4764978050", `
    "+4764979999")
```

By default, the script reserves phone numbers that are defined as *gold* and *silver.* These numbers are so defined because they are easy to remember—for example, because they have four of the same digit in a row—with gold easier than silver). You may prefer to allocate gold and silver numbers manually to specific users and services, considering their value in making it easier for the caller to remember the phone number. You can also reserve phone numbers that have a specific value for your organization, called *vanity numbers.*

Chapter 3 discussed how to bulk assign phone numbers in Teams. The unallocated numbers from the script can be used as a source of information for a PowerShell script for the phone number enabling process.

Discussion

Currently, the Teams Communications Administrator role assigns a Teams number in the TAC. In Chapter 2, we discussed how to mitigate the risks related to assigning an administrative role using Privileged Identity Management (PIM) to allow just-in-time access to the required role. In the scenario we just discussed, running a PowerShell script assigns a Teams number and location without logging in to the TAC.

8.4 Automating Administrative Tasks with Azure Automation

Problem

You want to automatically create a list of the phone numbers activated in Teams (including activation state and number type) and post them into a Teams channel.

Solution

Azure Automation will use an incoming webhook to send the results of the script to the Service Desk Agents Group team channel. Add a webhook, which you learned how to do in Chapter 7, and configure it to be called *Phonelist* (see Figure 8-19).

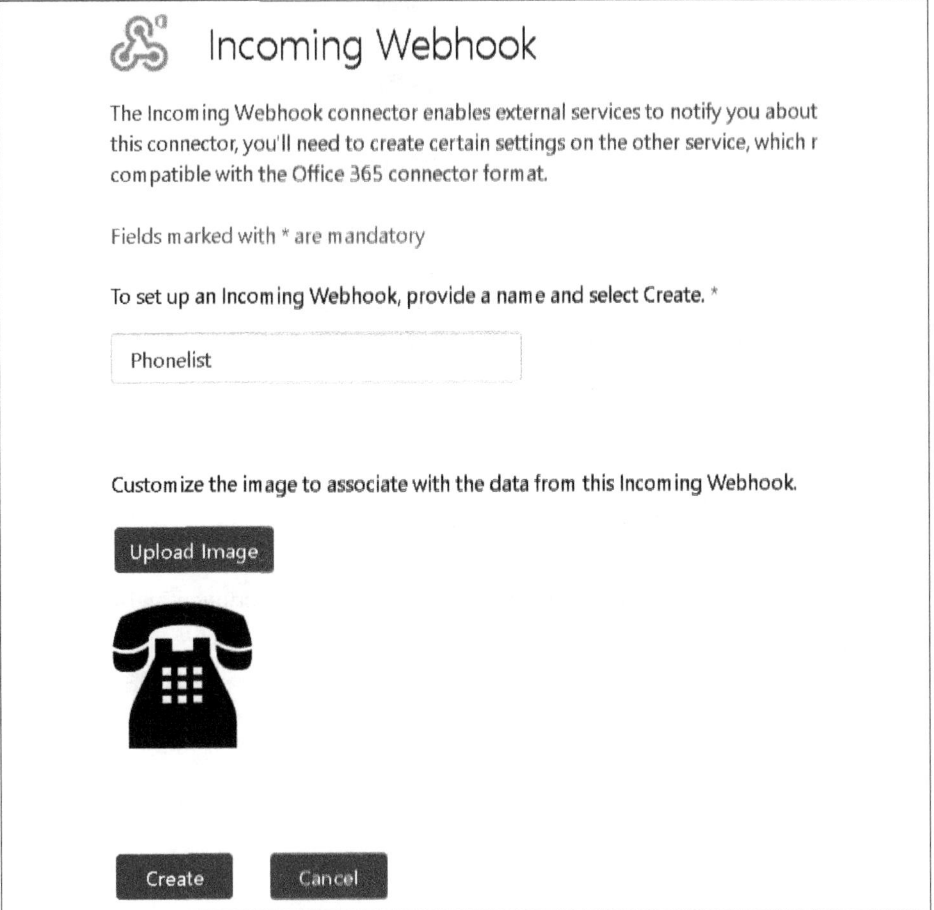

Figure 8-19. Configuring the incoming webhook

The URL for the webhook in this example will be:

https://m365x71772990.webhook.office.com/webhookb2/50a81e77-a6e7-48cb-a10e-90789640aeb6@de5773d6-06cc-4b59-b70a-63e906b4c54f/IncomingWebhook/9fe4ea422e2c4d0093ecbee24b87e9e9/ad05f4ed-d044-46a6-b42d-2f5ab00000b3

When you start Azure Automation, you must create at least one Automation account. Open the Azure portal (*https://oreil.ly/ek7_i*) and click "Create a resource." In the search box, type "Azure Automation" (it should be located under Categories > IT & Management Tools), click Create, and then click Automation (as in Figure 8-20).

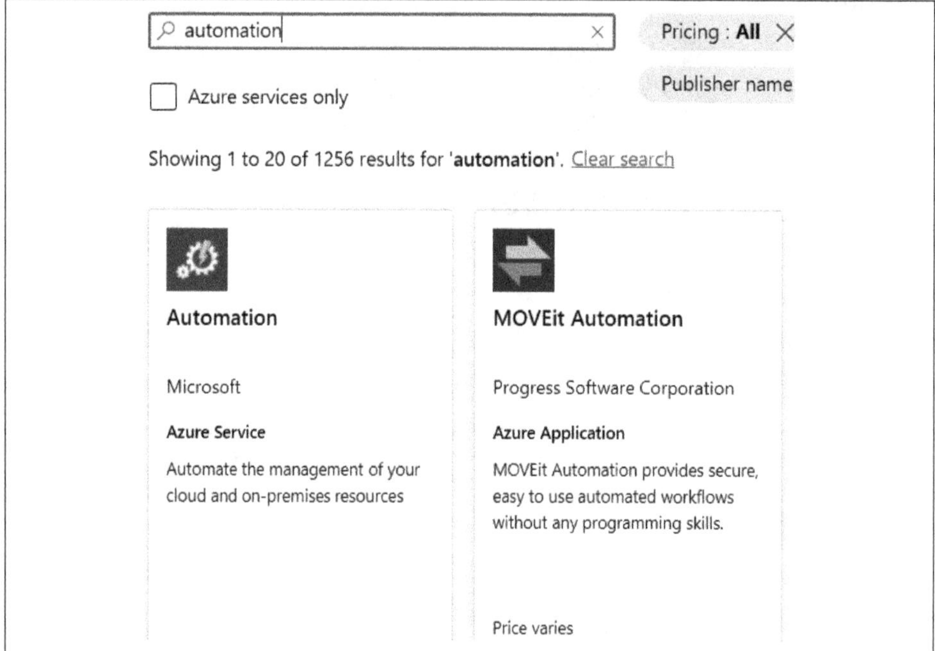

Figure 8-20. Creating an Automation resource

The Automation account requires an Azure subscription and an Azure resource group.

Select a basic account, allocate it to a resource group, and type a name. We'll use "AzureAutomate," as shown in Figure 8-21.

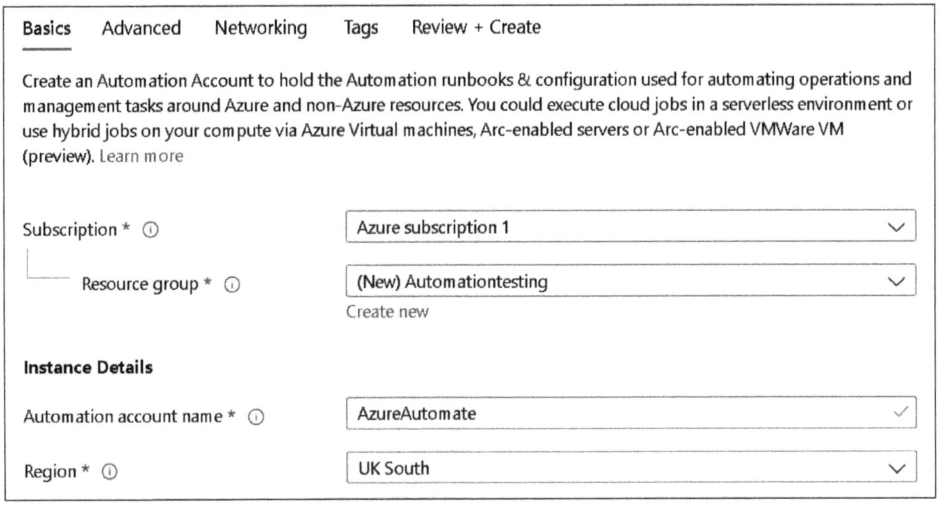

Basics Advanced Networking Tags Review + Create

Create an Automation Account to hold the Automation runbooks & configuration used for automating operations and management tasks around Azure and non-Azure resources. You could execute cloud jobs in a serverless environment or use hybrid jobs on your compute via Azure Virtual machines, Arc-enabled servers or Arc-enabled VMWare VM (preview). Learn more

Subscription * — Azure subscription 1

Resource group * — (New) Automationtesting

Create new

Instance Details

Automation account name * — AzureAutomate

Region * — UK South

Figure 8-21. Setting the parameters for the Automation resource

Click Next. On the Managed Identities screen, select "System assigned." Click Review + Create and then click Create. Click "Go to resource," click Modules in the left pane, then select "Browse gallery." Enter "Microsoft Teams" in the search box, and select the MicrosoftTeams module, as shown in Figure 8-22.

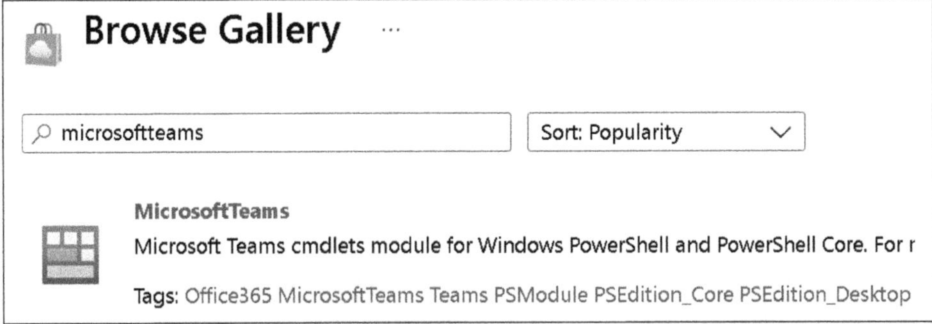

Figure 8-22. Importing the MicrosoftTeams module

On the next screen, click Select. Then, select "Runtime version 7.2 (preview)" and click Import. The MicrosoftTeams module will be in the importing state. Wait for the status to change to "available." Then, click Credentials (under Shared Resources in the left pane) and select "Add a credential." On the New Credential page, enter a name (we'll use AzureCredentials). The username and password will be those of the tenant administrator (shown in Figure 8-23).

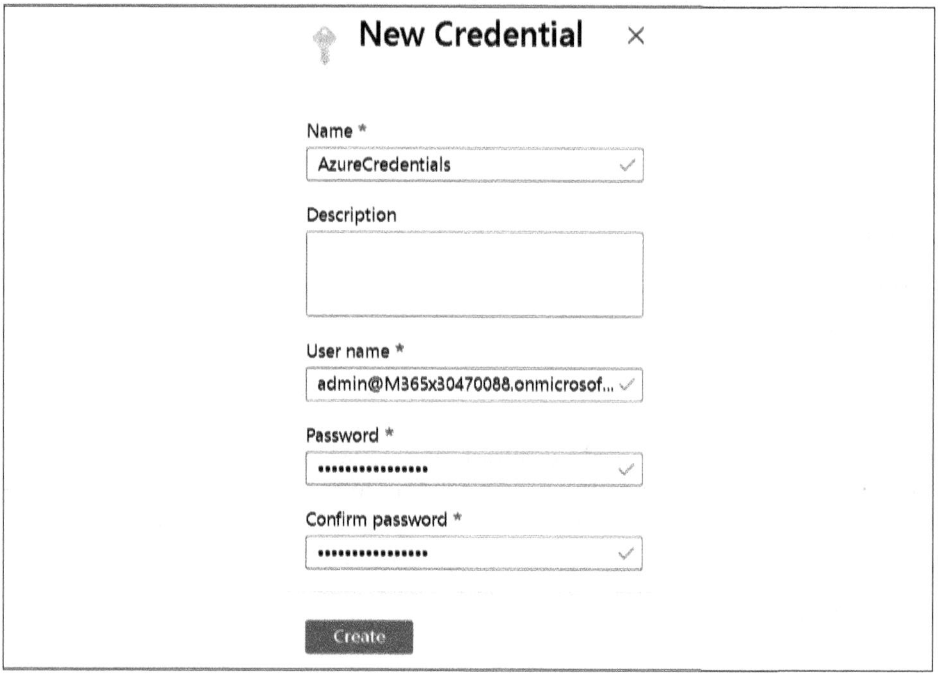

Figure 8-23. Adding Azure credentials

Azure Automation supports several types of runbooks. For this solution, you will create a PowerShell runbook. Click Runbooks in the left pane and select "Create a runbook."

Enter a name for the runbook (we'll use "TeamsAutomationRunBook"). Select PowerShell Workflow as the runbook type and 5.1 as the runtime version, as shown in Figure 8-24.

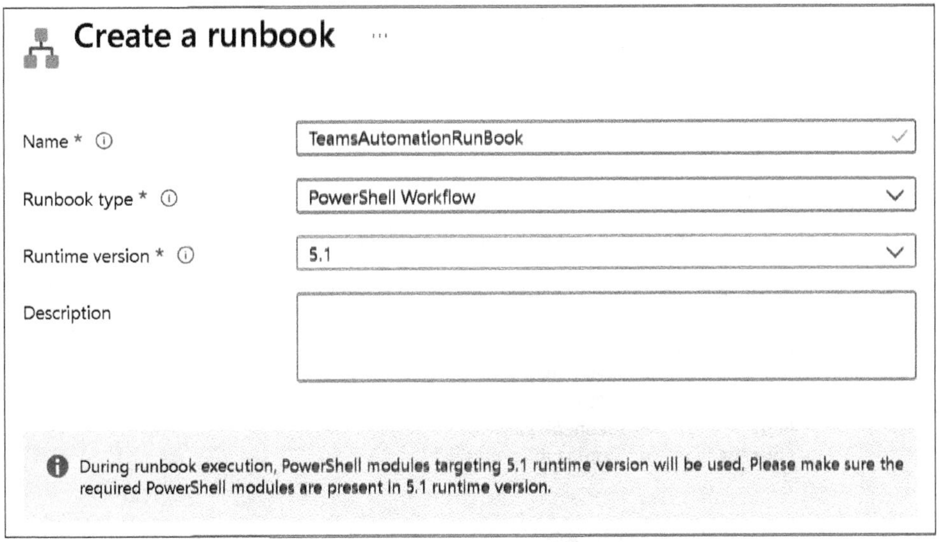

Create a runbook ...

Name * ⓘ TeamsAutomationRunBook

Runbook type * ⓘ PowerShell Workflow

Runtime version * ⓘ 5.1

Description

During runbook execution, PowerShell modules targeting 5.1 runtime version will be used. Please make sure the required PowerShell modules are present in 5.1 runtime version.

Figure 8-24. Defining the basic parameters of the runbook

Click Create. Paste the following PowerShell code in the edit box:

```
# Get the credential from Automation
$credential = Get-AutomationPSCredential -Name 'AzureCredentials'
$userName = $credential.UserName
$securePassword = $credential.Password

$psCredential = New-Object -TypeName System.Management.Automation.PSCredential `
    -ArgumentList $userName, $securePassword

# Connect to Microsoft Teams
Connect-MicrosoftTeams -Credential $psCredential

# Webhook Settings

$webhookUrl = "https://m365x71772990.webhook.office.com/webhookb2/ `
    50a81e77-a6e7-48cb-a10e-90789640aeb6@de5773d6-06cc-4b59-b70a-63e906b4c54f/ `
    IncomingWebhook/9fe4ea422e2c4d0093ecbee24b87e9e9/ `
    ad05f4ed-d044-46a6-b42d-2f5ab00000b3"

# Get Phone Numbers from Teams and convert them to text strings

$text=Get-CsPhoneNumberAssignment | fl `
TelephoneNumber,ActivationState,NumberType | Out-String -Stream

# Prepare the message body

    $webhookMessage = [PSCustomObject][Ordered]@{
        "@type"      = "MessageCard"
        "@context"   = "http://schema.org/extensions"
```

```
            "summary"    = "Assigned Phone Numbers"
            "themeColor" = '700015'
            "title"      = "Assigned Phone Numbers"
            "text"       = "$text"
        }

    # Convert the message body to JSON

        $webhookJSON = convertto-json $webhookMessage -Depth 50

    # Send the message to Teams channel

        $webhookCall = @{
            "URI"          = $webhookUrl
            "Method"       = 'POST'
            "Body"         = $webhookJSON
            "ContentType" = 'application/json'
        }

        Invoke-RestMethod @webhookCall

    # Disconnect from Microsoft Teams
    Disconnect-MicrosoftTeams
```

Click Save. Click "Test pane," and then click Start.

Open the Teams client, and a new message will be shown in the selected channel (as shown in Figure 8-25).

Assigned Phone Numbers

TelephoneNumber : +13436445958 ActivationState : Activated NumberType : CallingPlan
TelephoneNumber : +441218285917 ActivationState : Activated NumberType : CallingPlan
TelephoneNumber : +44123456789 ActivationState : Activated NumberType : DirectRouting
TelephoneNumber : +441246927577 ActivationState : Activated NumberType : CallingPlan
TelephoneNumber : +441332401215 ActivationState : Activated NumberType : CallingPlan

Figure 8-25. Notification received in Teams

Close this window, go back to the editing window, and click Publish.

You can now use the runbook in different ways. For example, you could use it as part of a schedule. Click Schedules, then click "Add a schedule" and "Create a schedule" (this example, shown in Figure 8-26, publishes the telephone numbers every hour for the next day). Click Create.

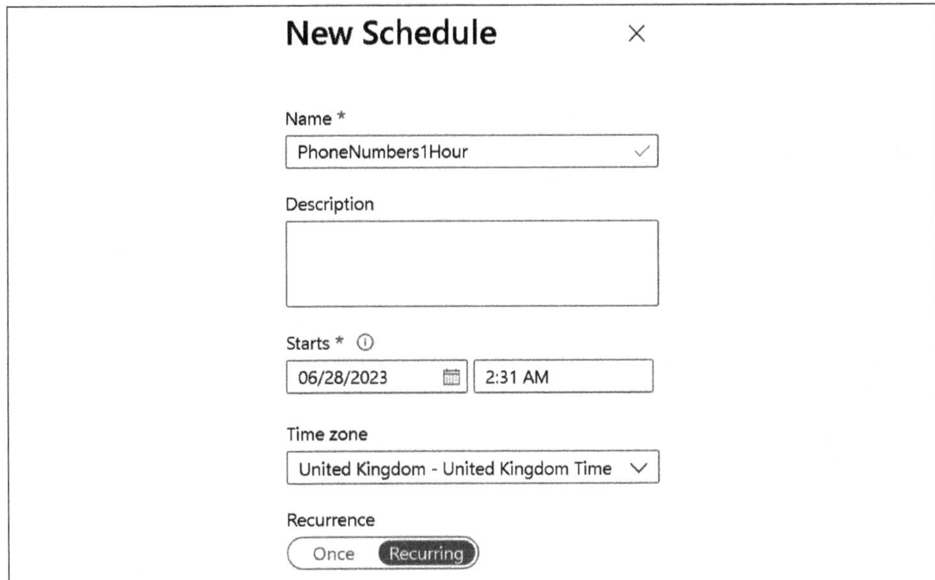

Figure 8-26. Scheduling the runbook

Discussion

Azure Automation is a group of features and tools that can be extremely useful when automating Teams administration tasks. Power Automate, which we have worked with in earlier chapters, is one of the available tools. In this recipe, however, you use runbook execution in Azure Automation. You can use runbooks to automate your tasks, or a Hybrid Runbook Worker if you have business or operational processes to manage outside of Azure.

When you create an Azure Automation Run As account, the following objects are created:

- An Azure AD application with a self-signed certificate
- A service principal account for the application in Azure AD, with the Contributor role for the account in your current subscription
- An Automation certificate asset named AzureRunAsCertificate in the specified Automation account
- An Automation connection asset named AzureRunAsConnection in the specified Automation account

You can see the information in app registrations from Azure AD. Automation accounts isolate the Automation resources, runbooks, assets, and configurations, and can be used to create different logical environments or to delegate responsibilities.

8.5 Summary

In this chapter, we have discussed some ways to automate administrative tasks in Teams. The same tools can also be used to automate some aspects of monitoring in Teams, as you will see in an Chapter 10. A few of the tools you have used can also be used to automate administrator tasks for other products in the Microsoft 365 cloud (such as Exchange Online) and could be extended to interact with other cloud solutions, such as Azure Automation. The recipes we've described in this chapter allow Teams administrators to take a low-code or no-code approach to automation, empowering a larger number of users to work with more efficiency. Some of the resulting automations support exporting and importing the flows or runbooks into a template.

The next chapter focuses on using Microsoft Teams Rooms (MTR), including planning, deploying, and troubleshooting.

CHAPTER 9

Microsoft Teams Rooms

By Randy Chapman

Now that you're using Teams for collaboration, chat, and telephony, it's time to start using it for meetings. Teams meetings are completely integrated with Microsoft 365 and can include attendees who are internal or external to your organization. Scheduling a Teams meeting is no different from sending a standard meeting invite—you simply need to designate it as an *online meeting* and book the room.

A Teams Room is a meeting room with dedicated hardware that is used to conduct or attend Teams meetings and that includes features to enhance the audio, video, and content of a meeting. Meeting attendees can be both in-person and remote. Users can attend meetings using the Teams desktop, browser, or mobile client.

This chapter introduces Teams Rooms, discusses how to successfully set up a room, and details how to manage a room once it is installed.

9.1 Mixing In-Room and Remote Attendees

Problem

Users in your organization need to be able to schedule Teams meetings that include both in-person and remote attendees. You need to allow users to join the meeting and also enable high-quality, two-way audio and video between those in the room and those attending remotely.

Solution

One way to achieve the desired functionality and quality is to equip the physical meeting room with Microsoft Teams Rooms (MTR), an A/V solution designed for Teams Meetings.

MTR is an evolution of similar solutions designed for Lync and Skype for Business—Lync Room Systems (LRS) and Skype Room Systems (SRS), respectively. MTR consists of some common components, including:

- A computing device running a version of the Teams Rooms application
- A touch-based controller
- Front-of-room display(s)
- A camera designed for rooms
- Microphones
- Speakers
- A way to share content in the meeting

These components come in many shapes and sizes to cater to different room types.

Microsoft Teams Rooms on Windows

With this setup, the Teams Rooms application is installed on a Windows computer and runs across three displays. One is the touch controller, which includes a list of meetings, each with a Join button, and the controls for starting a new meeting, placing a call, and sharing content (see Figure 9-1).

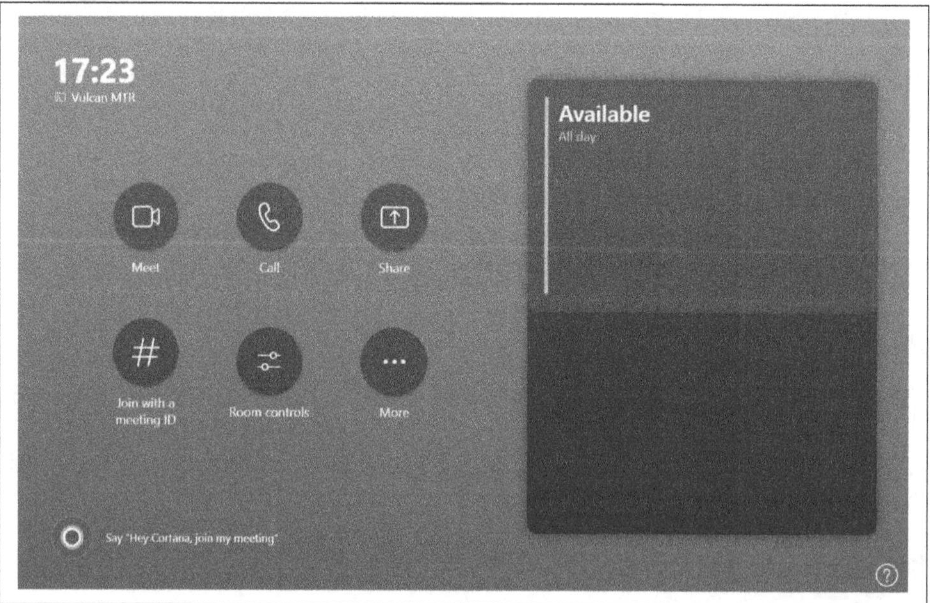

Figure 9-1. MTR touch display

Figure 9-2 shows the meeting settings, where users can configure everything from the account to be used, meeting support, features, and the theme to use on the front-of-room displays.

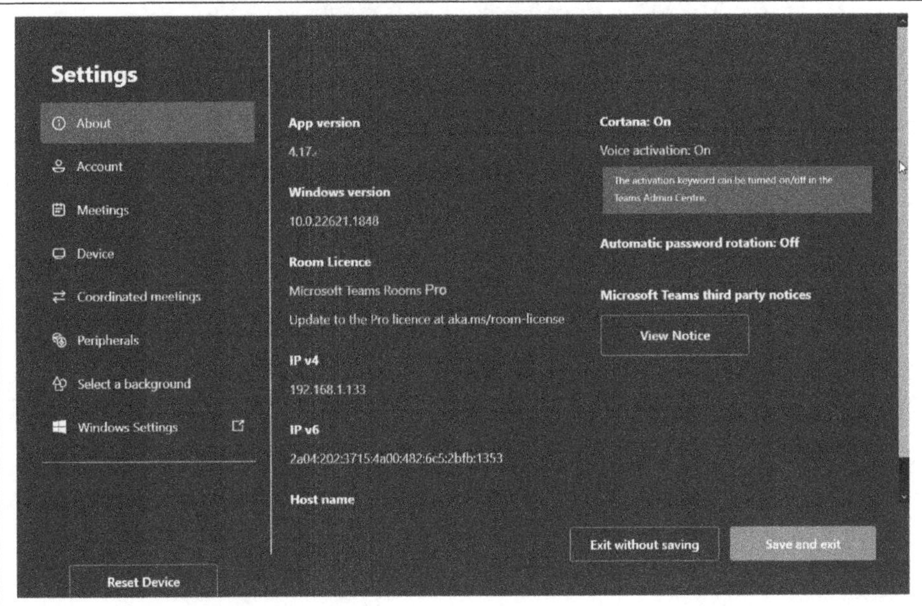

Figure 9-2. MTR Settings page

The other two screens are for the front-of-room displays. MTR can have one or two displays, depending on your room. The two front-of-room displays shown in Figure 9-3 share a single background image that spans the two displays. The right screen has a clock, and some additional text that alternates between "Add this room to a meeting with your personal device" and "Tap Cortana on the console and say, Join my meeting."

Figure 9-3. MTR front-of-room displays

Teams Rooms are built with specific hardware from original equipment manufacturers (OEMs), which must meet or exceed the specifications set out by Microsoft. They are also made to work with vendor-specific touch controllers and other components. These computers and the images they run undergo countless hours of testing by each vendor, as well as Microsoft, to become MTR certified. Running a do-it-yourself MTR setup is completely unsupported by Microsoft.

Microsoft Teams Rooms on Android

Originally called *collaboration bars*, Microsoft Teams Rooms on Android (like the one shown in Figure 9-4) use the Android operating system and a version of the MTR app developed on Android.

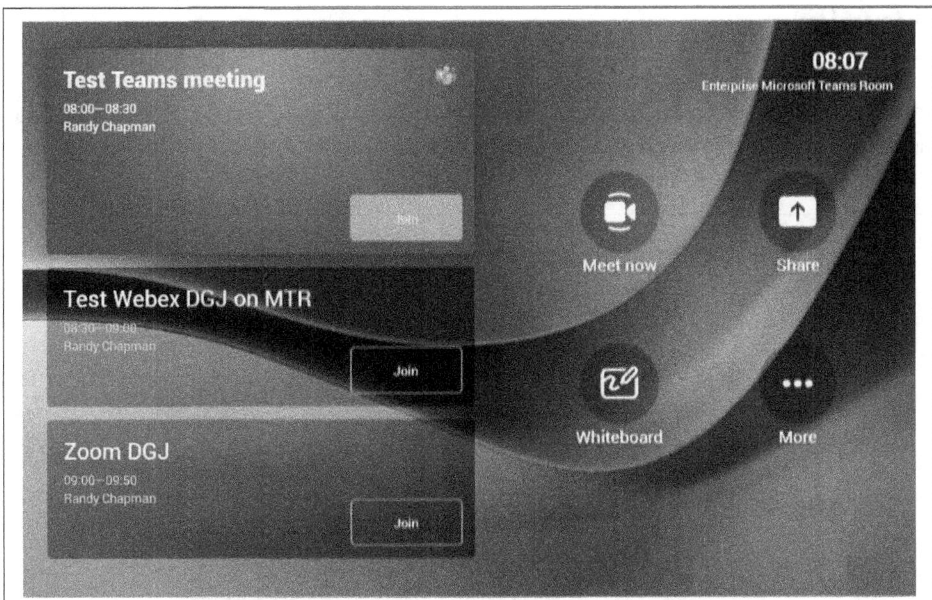

Figure 9-4. MTR on Android

MTR on Android (and all other Android-based Teams devices) a management framework known as Device Administrator (DA), which was specifically designed for devices and appliances, and runs on Android Enterprise.

Discussion

The original MTR solutions were based on a Windows computer with a built-in touch controller. Known by the codename Project Rigel, version 1 of MTR was deployed using a Microsoft Surface Pro computing tablet housed in a docking station that sat on a table (see Figure 9-5).

Figure 9-5. Logitech SmartDock MTR solution at Microsoft Edinburgh

Later versions moved away from the Surface Pro in favor of small form factor Windows 10 PCs, such as the Intel NUC, as well as small form factor PCs from Lenovo, HP, Dell, and Asus, and even PCs built by OEMs. The computer itself is nothing special, but there are some minimum specifications, including a fast processor, 8 to 16 GB of RAM or more, and some specific hardware components like dual HDMI and plenty of USB ports for peripherals. The standard operating system is Windows 10 Enterprise and the PC itself is licensed by IoT, which embeds the license on the hardware layer. (In this context, an IoT device OEM licenses the device to the user with the software attached to the device as a complete product.) It isn't Windows 10 IoT though, which is an important distinction; it's full Windows, not Windows designed for lightweight hardware like ATMs.

From the start, MTR devices could join both Skype for Business and Teams meetings. Later, Microsoft added the ability to join meetings from third-party platforms such as Zoom and Webex. Known as Direct Guest Join (DGJ), this was a way to use your MTR solution even when you were invited to non-Teams meetings.

MTRs were also required to enable connection to a laptop using HDMI, in order to share content to the front-of-room display and to the Teams meeting itself. This HDMI ingest port was usually built into the touch controller. The MTR app now has built-in security to check whether the vendor's HDMI ingest solution is present. If it isn't detected, Microsoft prevents the MTR app from signing in. This is to prevent people (and counterfeiters) from taking any PC and imaging it with the MTR app and calling it a Teams Room.

Initially, MTR on Android had limited features compared to MTR on Windows. The form factor and the built-in resources also limited their use to simpler and smaller spaces. Over the next few years, however, MTR on Android caught up with MTR on Windows in terms of features.

Android Enterprise can be controlled and locked down using Mobile Device Management (MDM). MDM allows organizations to manage and control mobile devices, such as smartphones and tablets, remotely. It provides a range of features and functionalities to ensure the security and proper use of these devices within an enterprise environment.

When you "lock down" an Android device using MDM, you are implementing various security policies and restrictions to control the device's functionality and access. This helps to enforce compliance with the organization's IT policies and safeguards sensitive data on the device.

That said, Android is designed to be used on user devices. DA, which MTR on Android uses, is barely an operating system at all. There is no app store and no widgets. In fact, there are no Google services. DA is an architecture, or scaffolding, designed to allow OEMs to layer on their own operating system to make their solution an appliance. So, don't be scared to add Android-based Teams devices to your standards.

At the time of writing, there is a healthy ecosystem of 16 vendors who make MTR solutions (*https://oreil.ly/M_vS8*). Some make solutions for Android only. Some only make Windows solutions. A handful make solutions for both. Android devices are simpler to install and operate, but Windows devices still have more features (some of which you might never miss). Consider both and weigh the options, but don't get bogged down with the hardware. There is a lot more to consider when designing a solution for your rooms.

MTR devices change from month to month, and there is a very long list of things in development. Check the Microsoft documentation (*https://oreil.ly/vfpAW*) for up-to-date information on MTR.

9.2 Preparing to Install the Equipment

Problem

You want to use MTR equipment in your room, but you need to make sure it works when it is installed, remains operational, and is secure.

Solution

You'll need the following:

- A room Resource Account and a mailbox with an MTR license
- Internet access that allows for connection to Microsoft 365 and Teams
- Some tools to ensure the security of your MTR

A room Resource Account needs an identity or name as well as a mailbox to be able to accept and list meetings that have been booked against it. The mailbox also needs an email address, which will be used in meeting invitations. Depending on how your Microsoft 365 account is set up, you may need to use a slightly different method for setting up the Resource Account.

For hybrid Active Directory, you might need to set up the account in your on-prem AD before synchronizing the account to Azure AD, then adding a mailbox and all the other attributes and settings.

Hybrid AD setups can be complicated. When possible, I recommend setting everything up in the cloud and creating your Resource Account using Exchange Online and Azure AD.

Using a strictly cloud-based approach, Teams meeting room accounts are shared accounts and mailboxes are used for resources such as meeting rooms.

Microsoft provides two ways to create a Resource Account. If you enjoy a click-through user interface, you can use the Microsoft 365 and Exchange admin centers. If you want a quicker, easier experience, you can use PowerShell. In this solution, we'll walk through creating a Resource Account using the admin centers.

First, sign in to the Microsoft 365 admin center using your administrator credentials. Click Resources in the left panel, then select "Rooms & equipment." Select "Add resource" to create a new Resource Account (as shown in Figure 9-6).

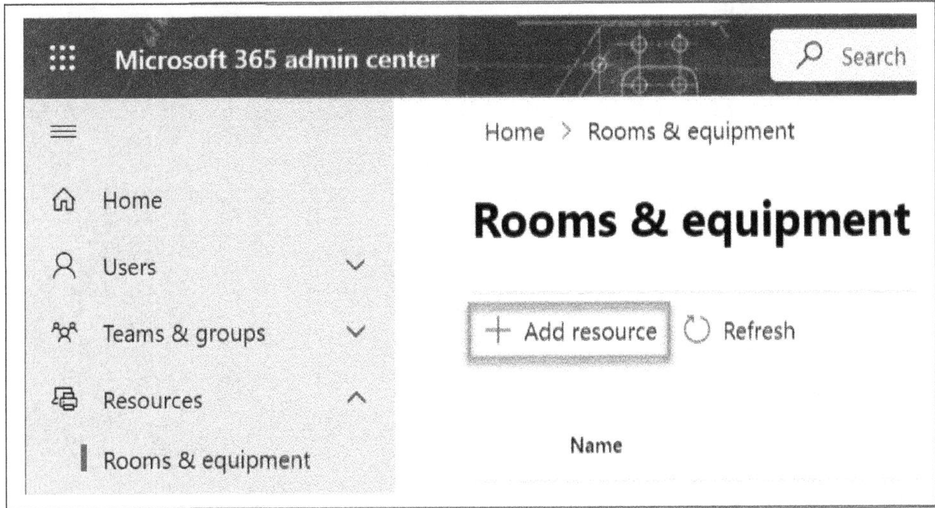

Figure 9-6. Adding a Resource Account

Choose Room as the resource type. Enter a display name and email address for the account. Optionally, you can add a capacity and location. Click Save (Figure 9-7).

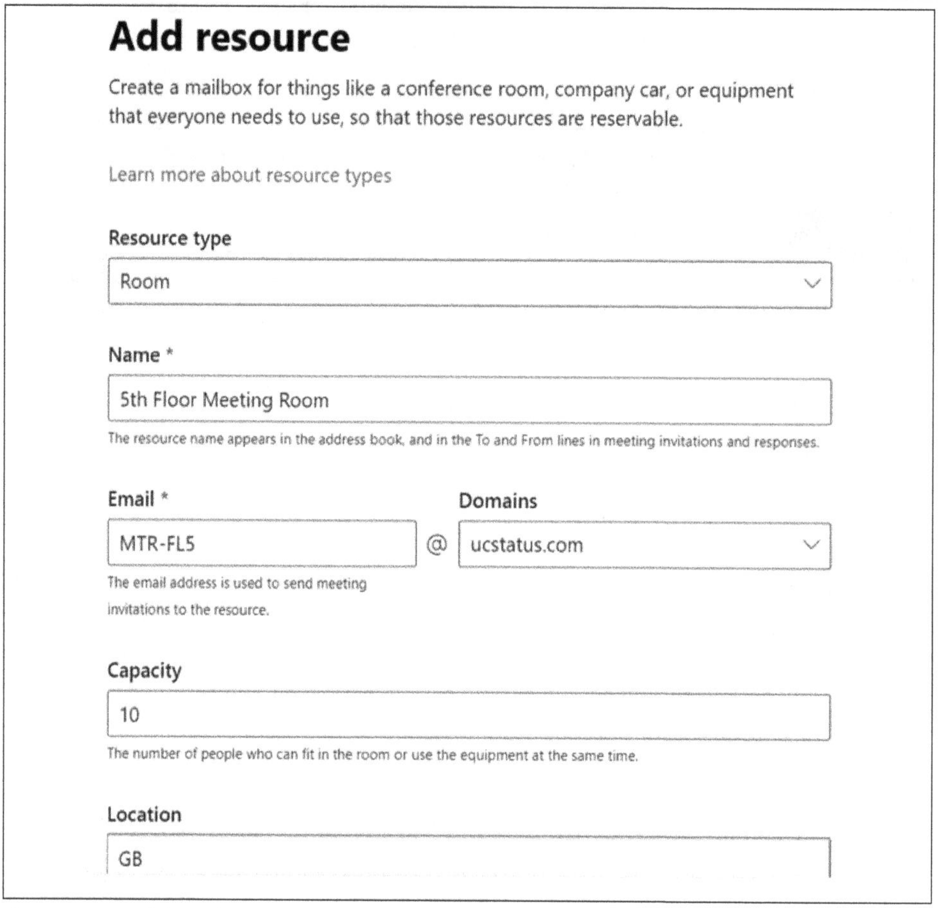

Add resource

Create a mailbox for things like a conference room, company car, or equipment that everyone needs to use, so that those resources are reservable.

Learn more about resource types

Resource type

Room

Name *

5th Floor Meeting Room

The resource name appears in the address book, and in the To and From lines in meeting invitations and responses.

Email * @ **Domains**

MTR-FL5 @ ucstatus.com

The email address is used to send meeting invitations to the resource.

Capacity

10

The number of people who can fit in the room or use the equipment at the same time.

Location

GB

Figure 9-7. Adding the room resource

You will need one or more of the roles shown in Table 9-1 to create Resource Accounts.

Table 9-1. Roles required for the creation of Resource Accounts

Environment	Required roles and permissions
Azure Active Directory	Global Administrator or User Administrator
Active Directory	Member of the Active Directory Enterprise Admins or Domain Admins group, or have delegated rights to create users; also must have Azure AD Connect Sync rights
Exchange Online	Global Administrator or Exchange Administrator
Exchange Server	Exchange Organization Management or Recipient Management

When creating a Resource Account to use for MTRs, the user principal name (UPN) and SMTP address must match.

For example, the UPN and the SMTP address could be *MTR01@m365x02128008.onmicrosoft.com*.

The resource mailbox (room and equipment) does not need an Exchange license to work. The account will also be used to log in to MTR equipment (more on that later).

By default, Resource Accounts are configured with the following settings:

- Allow repeating meetings
- Automatically decline meetings outside of the following limits:
  — Booking window (days): 180
  — Maximum duration (hours): 24
- Automatically accept meeting requests

If you want to change these settings, click "Edit booking options" (as in Figure 9-8) before clicking Close.

5th Floor Meeting Room is ready
You've created a new mailbox for your Room and can now use the email address to book the resource.
Default booking options have been applied, such as allowing repeating meetings and automatically accepting meeting invites. You can change these at any time.
Next Steps
Edit booking options

Figure 9-8. Editing booking options

Next, within the Microsoft 365 admin center, go to Users > "Active users." Select your meeting's room and open the properties panel. Next, assign a password to the Resource Account (in the panel, click "Reset password," as shown in Figure 9-9).

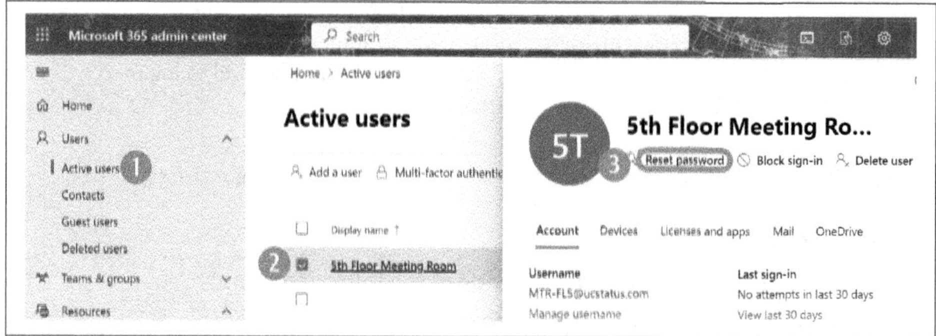

Figure 9-9. Resetting the meeting room account password

Requiring users to change a meeting room account password on a shared device will cause sign-in problems. Uncheck "Require this user to change their password when they first sign in" and click "Reset password" (as in Figure 9-10).

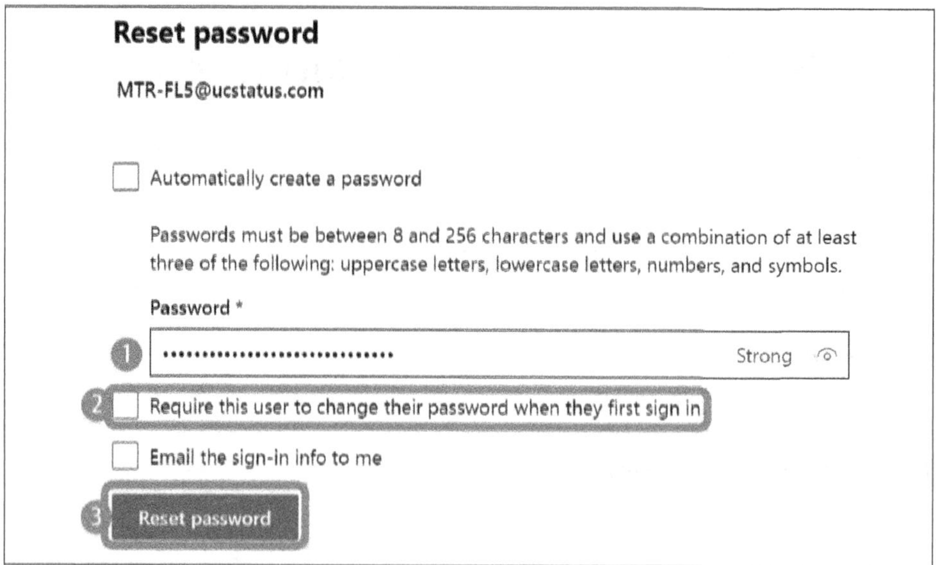

Figure 9-10. Setting a meeting room account password

Go to "Licenses and apps," select your usage location, and then select your license (see Figure 9-11).

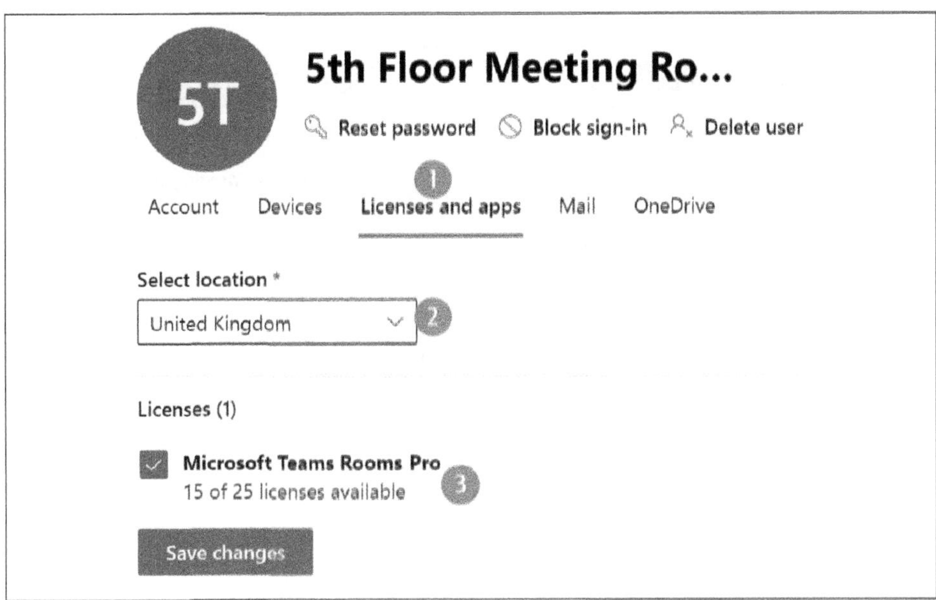

Figure 9-11. Adding a location and license

Next, you need to change some Exchange properties to customize how the Resource Account responds to and processes meeting invitations. To do this, you need to manage the *mail tip*—this is what a user sees in Outlook or Outlook Online when they add the room account to the invitation.

To manage the mail tip, open the Exchange admin center, expand Recipients, and click Resources. Click on the room resource to open the side panel, click the Others tab, and select "Manage mail tip" (as in Figure 9-12).

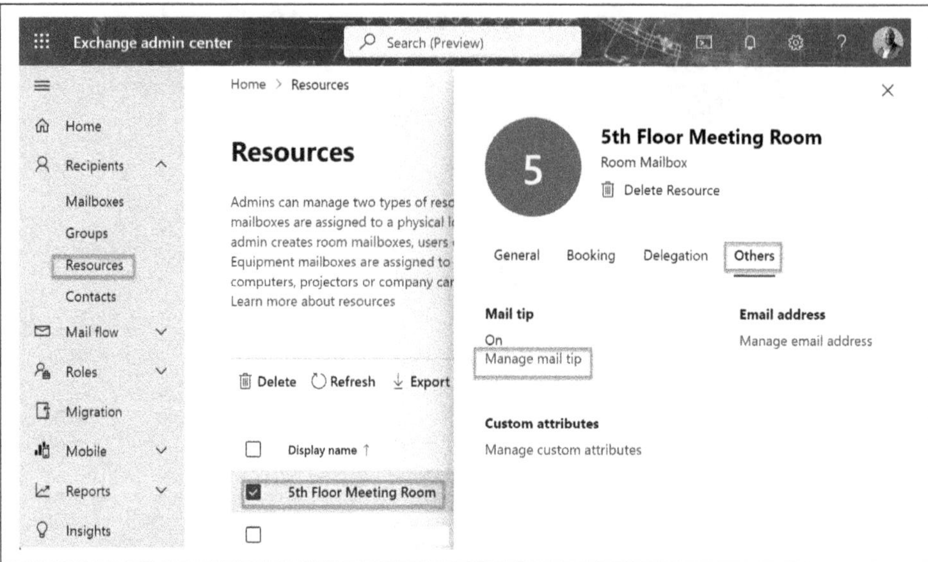

Figure 9-12. Managing mail tip

In this case, I recommend reminding the user to make the meeting a Teams Meeting (as in Figure 9-13).

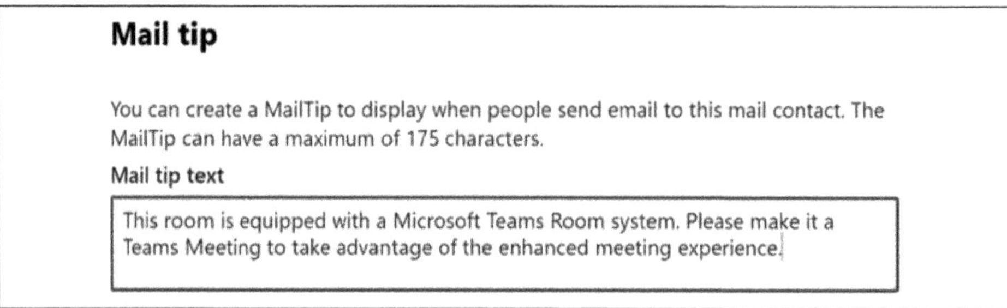

Figure 9-13. Adding a mail tip

Next, you will use the Exchange Online PowerShell module to set the following Resource Account properties:

- When you created the account, `AutomateProcessing` was already set to `AutoAccept`. This means that meetings will be processed and accepted automatically if there are no conflicts. If you would prefer that meetings are not automatically accepted...think again. If you really don't want automatic acceptance of meetings, set it to `False`.
- Set `AddOrganizerToSubject` to `False` to ensure that the original subject is preserved and not replaced by the organizer's name.
- Set `RemovePrivateProperty` to `False` to ensure that the private flag for meeting requests is preserved (private meetings stay private).
- Setting `DeleteComments` and `DeleteSubject` to `False` is critical and ensures that your meeting invitation has a Join button.
- The `AdditionalResponse` parameters are there to send useful information in the message back to the requester:
  - Set `AddAdditionalResponse` to `True`.
  - Use the `AdditionalResponse` parameter to add text to the acceptance response. For this recipe, set `AdditionalResponse` to "Your meeting has been scheduled in a room which has been equipped as a Microsoft Teams Room. If your meeting was scheduled as a Teams meeting, simply tap the Join button on the in-room touch console to start your meeting. If you haven't scheduled it as a Teams meeting, consider changing this so you can take advantage of the enhanced meeting experience."

These parameters are used for both external meeting invitations and meetings on third-party platforms, such as Webex and Zoom. These parameters also enable Direct Guest Join.

- Setting `ProcessExternalMeetingMessages` to `True` enables processing and acceptance of external meeting requests from outside your Exchange organization. This is useful if you want to receive meeting invitations from third-party services such as Webex and Zoom for Direct Guest Join.
- Set `PasswordNeverExpires` to `True`. Now that the room Resource Account has been created, you must set the account to use a *static* password—one that does not expire. The reason for this is simple: the account will be used by a resource, not a user. A resource will never be warned that the password will expire and will not have the ability to reset the password using a command like:

```
Set-MsolUser -UserPrincipalName "<account name>" -PasswordNeverExpires `
$true
```

If your Resource Account password does expire, it will be logged out of your MTR equipment and additional support will be required later.

Finally, you need to exclude the Resource Account from MFA requests, because MTR does not support MFA. This can also be done in PowerShell, using the Azure AD PowerShell module.

Discussion

In this recipe, we used a combination of Microsoft 365 admin center, Exchange admin center, and PowerShell. Since you already need to use PowerShell for some of the solution, you might as well use it for the entire solution. Why make it hard on yourself? You will need to install the Azure AD and Exchange Online PowerShell modules, if you haven't already done so.

I use one script to authenticate and connect to Exchange Online, Azure AD, and Teams. Just replace `your.adminuser@domain.com` with your admin username and change the location of your password file as needed.

Run the following code first, to save your password as an encrypted file to use in the connection script:

```
Read-Host "Enter Password" -AsSecureString | ConvertFrom-SecureString | `
Out-File "C:\Scripts\Password.txt"
```

Then, run the following script to connect to the modules:

```
# Save the Variables
$Username = "your.adminuser@domain.com"
$Password = cat "c:\Scripts\password.txt" | ConvertTo-SecureString
$Creds = New-Object -TypeName System.Management.Automation.PSCredential `
  -ArgumentList $Username, $Password
# Authenticate and connect to a new Exchange Online PowerShell session
Connect-ExchangeOnline -Credential $Creds -ShowProgress $true
# Authenticate and connect to a new Azure AD PowerShell session
Connect-MsolService -Credential $Creds
# Authenticate and connect to Azure AD using the Azure Active Directory `
# PowerShell for Graph module
Connect-AzureAD -Credential $Creds
# Authenticate and connect to a new Microsoft Teams PowerShell session
Connect-MicrosoftTeams -Credential $Creds
```

Now that you have connected to the required and optional modules, you can begin to create the Resource Account. You can do it line-for-line and step-by-step.

Create the resource mailbox and the Azure AD account:

```
New-Mailbox -MicrosoftOnlineServicesID MTR-FL5@domain.com -Name "5th Floor `
Meeting Room" -Alias MTR-FL5 -Room -EnableRoomMailboxAccount $true  `
-RoomMailboxPassword (ConvertTo-SecureString -String 'Password' `
-AsPlainText -Force)
```

The `Name` is a description for the room, and you can be as descriptive as you want. This helps users find the room they need at first glance. The email address will be used as both the UPN and SMTP address for sending invitations. For consistency, settle beforehand on a naming convention.

Set the password to never expire and specify a usage location:

```
Set-MsolUser -UserPrincipalName MTR-FL5@domain.com -PasswordNeverExpires $true `
-UsageLocation GB
```

Change the usage location as needed. For a complete list of country codes, check out *https://oreil.ly/LL7Oi*.

Configure the mail tip:

```
Set-Mailbox -Identity MTR-FL5@domain.com -MailTip "This room is equipped with `
a Microsoft Teams Room system. Please make it a Teams Meeting to take advantage `
of the enhanced meeting experience."
```

Set the calendar processing:

```
Set-CalendarProcessing -Identity MTR-FL5@domain.com -AutomateProcessing `
AutoAccept -AddOrganizerToSubject $false -RemovePrivateProperty $false `
-DeleteSubject $false -DeleteComments $false -AddAdditionalResponse $true `
-AdditionalResponse "Your meeting has been scheduled in a Room which has `
been equipped as a Microsoft Teams Room. If your meeting was scheduled as a `
Teams meeting, simply tap the Join button on the in-room touch panel to start `
your meeting. If you haven't scheduled it as a Teams meeting, consider `
changing this so you can take advantage of the enhanced meeting experience."
```

Assign the license:

```
$licence = (Get-MsolAccountSku).AccountSkuId | where {$_ `
  -like "*:Microsoft_Teams_Room_Pro"}
Set-MsolUserlicence -UserPrincipalName MTR-FL5@domain.com -Addlicences $licence
```

Use the `Set-Place` cmdlet to update room mailboxes with additional metadata, which provides a better search and room suggestion experience (see the Microsoft 365 documentation (*https://oreil.ly/typok*) for more information):

```
Set-Place -Identity MTR-FL5@domain.com -Capacity 10 -IsWheelChairAccessible `
$true -AudioDeviceName "Table Mics and Wall Speakers" -VideoDeviceName `
"Auto Tracking Camera" -Floor 5 -Building "HQ" -City "London" -Street `
"Vanilla Street"
```

In this example, the room is on the fifth floor in a building called HQ on Vanilla Street in London. The room has a capacity of 10 people, is wheelchair accessible, and has wall speakers, table mics, and a tracking camera.

You will need either a Teams Room Basic or Teams Rooms Pro license that you can assign to a Resource Account in a later step. I will assume that you have the required license. For a comparison between the Teams Rooms Basic and Teams Rooms Pro licenses, see the Microsoft documentation (*https://oreil.ly/mkA4u*). I recommend using the Teams Rooms Pro license because it provides everything you need to log in to and manage Teams Rooms devices.

9.3 Dealing with Internet Access and Security

Problem

You need to connect the MTR to the internet to reach the Teams cloud-based service.

Solution

First, make sure the MTR can connect to Teams, can sign in to Entra ID and get its mailbox from Exchange, and can be managed by Intune, the TAC, and the MTR Pro Management portal.

You'll need a high-quality network connection with enough bandwidth to give users a great meeting experience. Teams tries to be conservative on bandwidth usage, where possible, and can deliver HD-quality video at under 1.5 Mbps. The actual bandwidth used depends on several factors, such as video layout, resolution, and frames per second. Microsoft recommends 4 Mbps per room endpoint to provide the best performance for high-fidelity audio, video, and content sharing for larger meetings. For full guidance on how to prepare the network connection, see the Microsoft Teams documentation (*https://oreil.ly/BjpLK*).

You need to allow the right fully qualified domain names (FQDNs), IP ranges, ports, and protocols on the network that your MTRs use. For the full list of IPs and URLs required for MTRs, check out the following documentation:

- Microsoft Teams Office 365 URLs and IP address ranges (*https://oreil.ly/JSKo5*)
- Windows Server Update Services configuration (*https://oreil.ly/NHAuh*)
- Prerequisites for Microsoft Store for Business and Education (*https://oreil.ly/t3SN*)
- Network endpoints for Microsoft Intune (*https://oreil.ly/_IoeX*)

If you use Teams Rooms Pro to manage your rooms, you need to make sure that MTRs can access the following URLs:

- *agent.rooms.microsoft.com*
- *global.azure-devices-provisioning.net*
- *gj3ftstorage.blob.core.windows.net*
- *mmrstgnoamiot.azure-devices.net*
- *mmrstgnoamstor.blob.core.windows.net*
- *mmrprodapaciot.azure-devices.net*
- *mmrprodapacstor.blob.core.windows.net*
- *mmrprodemeaiot.azure-devices.net*
- *mmrprodemeastor.blob.core.windows.net*
- *mmrprodnoamiot.azure-devices.net*
- *mmrprodnoamstor.blob.core.windows.net*

Discussion

MTRs are inherently secure by design, so they don't need a lot of specialist help. InfoSec teams do like to enforce additional security on MTR devices, though, to limit what they perceive as risk. Here are a few considerations and recommendations related to security:

- Consider an A/V VLAN for your MTRs. MTRs don't need to communicate with the LAN. Traffic always traverses the internet, even when you make internal calls between rooms and users. Separate them in a more controllable network and let it communicate with the internet as needed. You can use the A/V VLAN for all your MTRs and related equipment.
- Don't use a proxy if you can help it, and keep in mind that MTRs don't support authenticated proxies. MTRs aren't devices that users log in to and abuse. They are designed for one purpose, so all the traffic will be predictable. You've also configured the firewall to only allow traffic to and from Microsoft 365. Media must bypass the proxy in any case, so do yourself a favor and give yourself one less thing to configure.
- Don't install any third-party stuff like antivirus or monitoring software that can affect performance. Again, users aren't logging in and playing with MTRs. Leave it to Windows Security and Defender. Plus, Microsoft might ask you to uninstall all of it if you need support.
- Use a strong password, and ideally one that is unique for each MTR. You only need to know it when you log in for the first time. If you forget it, you can always set a new one and log in to that MTR again.

- If you want more security, you can use Endpoint Manager and Conditional Access. You can limit accounts to log in only when in a specific location or on specific equipment, filtering by vendor and model, or even by specific MAC addresses. You can be quite creative with your desired level of security.

Though it's possible to enforce all kinds of security and obstacles to protect your business from attack, remember that MTR devices are pre-hardened and secured by design. The fact that they're built on Windows shouldn't mean that you treat them like a Windows computer or laptop for a standard user. Users don't log in to these devices to surf the internet and download viruses. Treat them as appliances; try to get out of their way and let them work as they are designed to.

9.4 MTR Commissioning

Problem

You need to plan for a deployment of a large number of MTRs.

Solution

Teams Rooms on Android can be preprovisioned in the TAC by adding the MAC addresses to the portal (as in Figure 9-14).

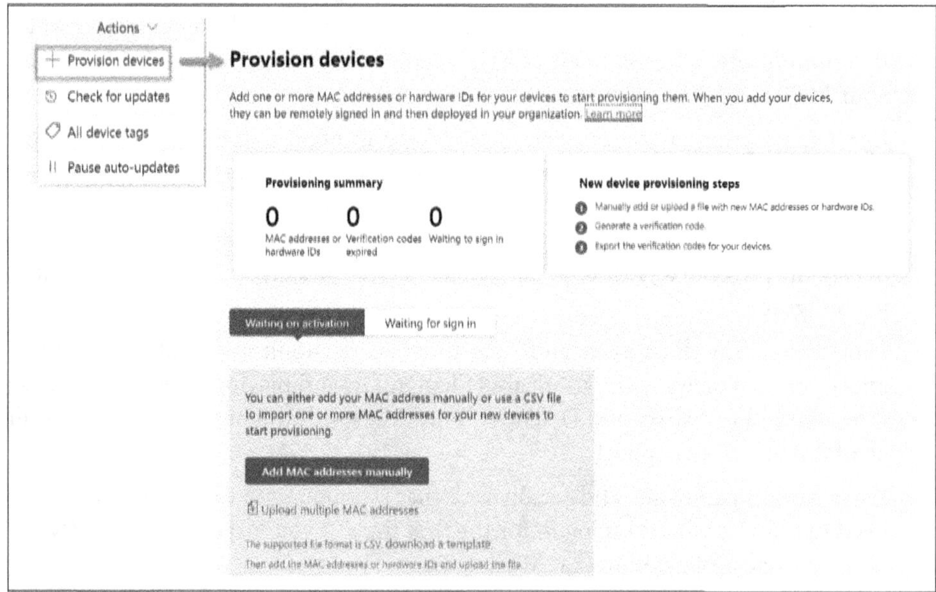

Figure 9-14. Provisioning Teams devices

MTR on Windows needs the credentials to be entered into the MTR app. This can be done through the out-of-the-box experience or applied using an XML file, which is used to push settings to the computer. If you are provisioning MTRs at scale, I suggest the XML method. The device will get some settings from the TAC, but others need to be applied when it's up and running—at least for now. As the MTR Pro Management portal develops, this will hopefully change.

For MTRs on Windows, the settings need to be applied as part of the build process. Again, you can do this with the out-of-the-box experience or with XML (I suggest the latter). With a bit of planning and organization, you can make provisioning MTRs on Windows a seamless process.

There are only a few ways to change settings on MTR on Windows. One way is through the Settings page on the device. Make a change, save and exit, and go back to the MTR interface. Another way is through the TAC or Pro Management portal. Once you change a setting in the TAC or the portal, an XML file is saved and placed in the correct folder.

The last option is via XML. Microsoft allows all settings for an MTR to be changed or set using parameters in an XML file. Covering all the available settings is beyond the scope of this recipe, but just know that you can completely provision an MTR device using only the XML file. This approach is like zero-touch provisioning (ZTP). ZTP automatically and seamlessly configures and sets up a meeting room device, such as a conferencing system or video endpoint, to work with Teams without requiring any manual intervention. It aims to simplify the deployment and management of MTRs by minimizing the need for on-site IT support or extensive configuration steps.

How you shape the XML is up to you. I have seen people store the parameters in a database or spreadsheet, then run a macro or other such script to go line by line, pull the parameters, and create the XML with the correct formatting for each deployed MTR.

The only thing left is to push the XML file, which must be named *SkypeSettings.xml*, to the correct location on the device:

> *C:\Users\Skype\AppData\Local\Packages*
> *\Microsoft.SkypeRoomSystem_8wekyb3d8bbwe\LocalState*

Then, when the device starts or is restarted, it will find the XML file in that folder and apply the settings. Once it is done, it will delete the XML file.

Here is a short example of an XML file that will sign in to the MTR with your Resource Account:

```
<SkypeSettings>
  <UserAccount>
    <SkypeSignInAddress>MTR-FL5@domain.com</SkypeSignInAddress>
    <ExchangeAddress>MTR-FL5@domain.com</ExchangeAddress>
```

```
        <Password>Password!</Password>
        <ModernAuthEnabled>true</ModernAuthEnabled>
    </UserAccount>
</SkypeSettings>
```

Even if that's all you do with the XML, that's a great start. You can now copy the file to each MTR, and the installers won't need to do this. Other settings can be added to the XML or enabled as part of the on-site commissioning prior to the test plan. For a full list of available XML attributes for MTRs, see the Microsoft documentation (*https://oreil.ly/R_rTo*).

Discussion

There are a few approaches to commissioning an MTR, or any meeting room solution for that matter. One is to install it first and then worry about making it work.

The problem with this method is twofold. First, what if part of the solution is faulty? You might have to take it all down to return it or swap it out. Second, all hardware devices are shipped with a point-in-time software release and are almost never up-to-date. So, you'll need to update it. You also can't do a full systems test until the device is at least partially up-to-date. And if you are going to partly update a system, you might as well completely update it. So, it's a bit of a chicken-and-egg situation.

One further consideration is whether you have everything you need. MTR solutions are boxed and should include all necessary components. The computer, camera, mics, and speakers should be accompanied by brackets, cables, cable ties, and even Velcro. You really want to make sure everything is there before you start to install it. You'd do the same thing for a piece of flat-packed furniture; an MTR is no different.

An MTR also needs to be logged in to the Resource Account and enrolled in your Microsoft 365 environment. It is possible to complete the setup after installation, but if you are doing a large rollout of hundreds or thousands of devices you must carefully consider how this will be done. A project like that needs planning. So, plan to make it easy.

Here are a few things to consider during the planning phase:

- Who will log the device in, and where do you store the credentials?
- What policies and settings need to be applied to your devices?
- Who can apply these settings?
- How can they be applied to the device?
- Who will do the testing and sign off the room as complete?

My recommendation is to *bench build* the solution before install. This means taking everything out of the box and doing an inventory to make sure everything is there.

Connect it all and do a basic test. Then, install all available updates. Finally, do a complete systems check to make sure it all works as it should.

9.5 Managing Your Microsoft Teams Room

Problem

You have deployed MTRs and you need to manage them.

Solution

First, a bit of (possibly) frustrating news: there is no single-app way to manage Teams Rooms. Sorry to be the bearer of bad news, but you should be prepared. To manage MTRs, you need the following tools (introduced in earlier chapters):

Teams admin center (TAC)
: Used to manage some of the settings on an MTR, get in-room health and usage stats, and install updates (see Figure 9-15). You can also use it for troubleshooting, including remote restarts, log collection, alerts, and real-time analytics of ongoing meetings.

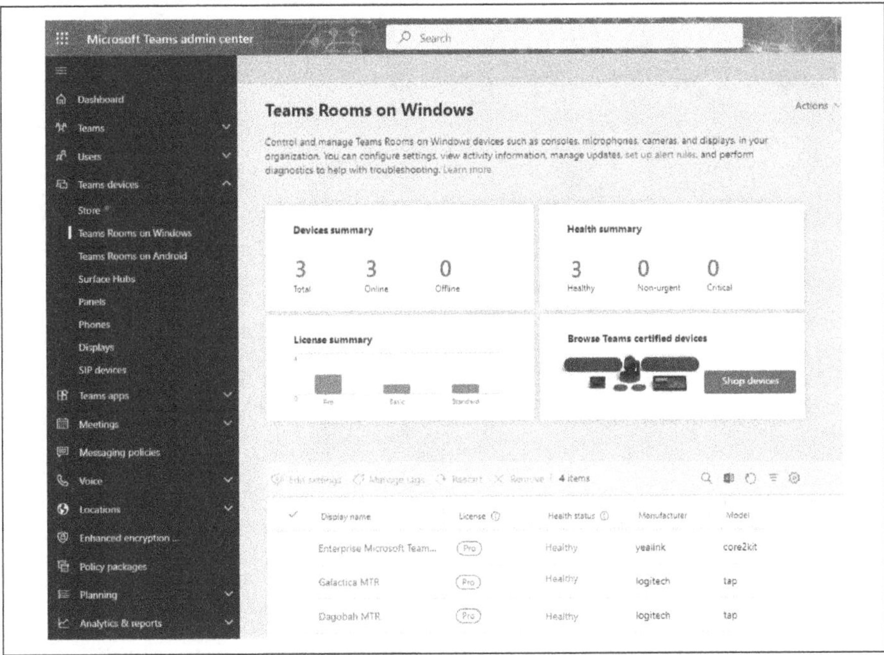

Figure 9-15. The TAC

Pro Management portal

Like the TAC, but focused exclusively on your room estate. One big advantage of the Pro portal is that it offers some very good usage and health reporting (see Figure 9-16). Use these to measure the effectiveness of your adoption plan. Over time, everything for managing MTRs will be moved to the Pro portal.

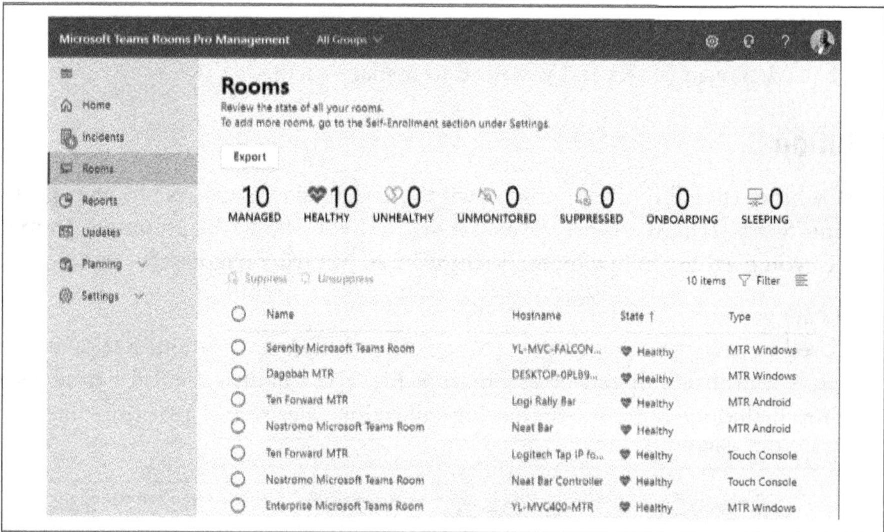

Figure 9-16. MTR Pro Management portal

Vendor management portal(s)

Some may say that a vendor portal (see Figure 9-17) is optional, but in my opinion it is a vital part of MTR management.

Why? First, the TAC and Pro portal can only be used to manage Teams-specific settings and configuration. They can't be used to make vendor-specific changes to the device itself. Vendor portals surface everything from audio and video configuration to networking. None of this can be managed from Microsoft portals. And, because I know you'll ask, no, you can't manage Microsoft settings from a vendor portal. Microsoft hasn't made this possible. Maybe in the future…

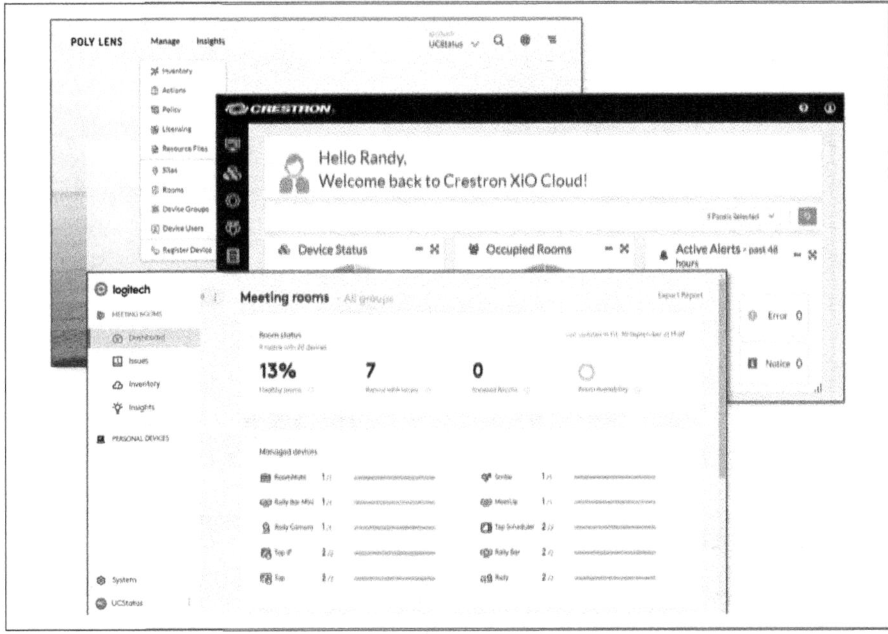

Figure 9-17. Various vendor management portals

Microsoft Endpoint Manager (Intune)

Used to manage device security, compliance, and Conditional Access (see Figure 9-18). For a full list of best practices for Conditional Access and Intune compliance for MTRs, see the Microsoft documentation (*https://oreil.ly/0PQ13*).

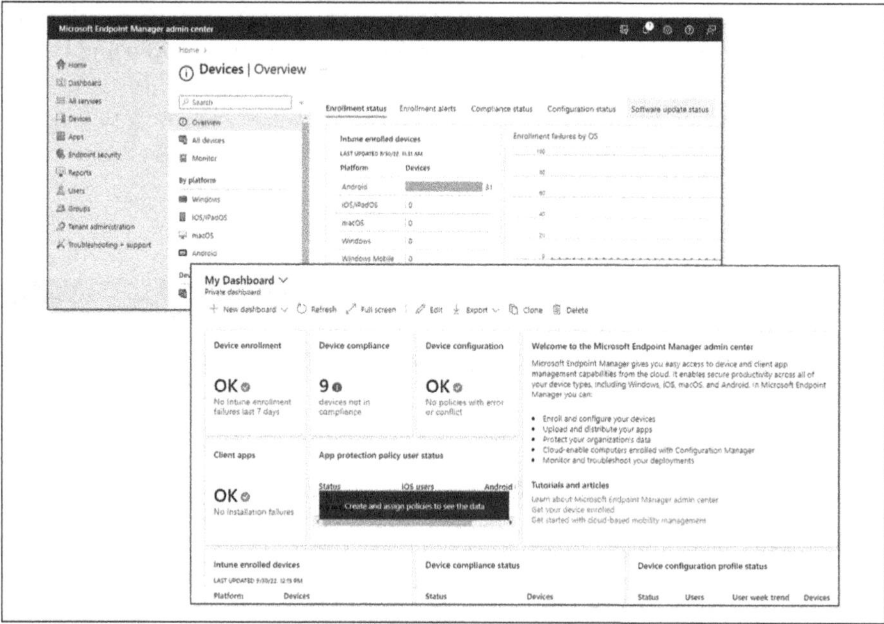

Figure 9-18. Endpoint Manager admin center

9.6 Summary

Meeting rooms aren't just for conducting face-to-face meetings. You can have simple, high-quality Teams meetings with people in other rooms or locations.

In this chapter, you learned how to select the right equipment for your meeting room based on a defined use case and other physical characteristics. We discussed how to provision, install, and commission your equipment, and how to ensure the equipment will operate efficiently and securely. You learned how to set up a Resource Account that you can invite to Teams meetings. You got a sense of just how simple and easy MTRs are to use, and you learned how to ensure your rooms are used effectively by staff. You now know, at a very high level, what tools you need to manage MTRs. The next chapter is dedicated to monitoring availability and quality in Teams.

About the Author

Randy Chapman, Office Apps and Services MVP focused on Microsoft Teams, is the author of this chapter. Randy is a video collaboration solutions engineer at Logitech. He helps clients all over the world understand and realize the benefits of Microsoft UC solutions, audio and video devices, and Microsoft Teams Rooms. He is a blogger and podcaster at *UCStatus.com* and *NoJitter.com*. Randy is also a public speaker, YouTuber (*YouTube.com/UCStatus*), conference co-organizer for *Commsverse.com*, and all-around evangelist for Microsoft Teams.

CHAPTER 10

Monitoring Availability and Quality in Microsoft Teams

As you have seen in the previous chapters, Teams includes different tools that allow you to connect and work with people inside and outside your organization. Because of the multifaceted nature of Teams, different tools are required for assessing the quality of your network, monitoring and controlling the quality of communications, and troubleshooting the platform. Organizations use Teams to share, collaborate, and meet—just ensuring that the service is available is not enough. Your objective as a Teams administrator is to identify Teams performance issues and isolate the cause of service degradations or disruptions.

This chapter examines monitoring and measuring the quality of the Teams service.

10.1 Checking Microsoft 365 Service Health

Problem

You need to quickly check the health of Microsoft 365 to determine whether there are any issues with the services.

Solution

The first place you must visit in the case of an outage in your tenant's services, or anomalies in Microsoft 365 services that have been running for some time, is the "Service health" page in the Microsoft 365 admin center.

From the Microsoft 365 admin center (*https://oreil.ly/IWxG3*), click Health > "Service health." The upper part of the page lists advisories or incidents that are ongoing (as shown in Figure 10-1).

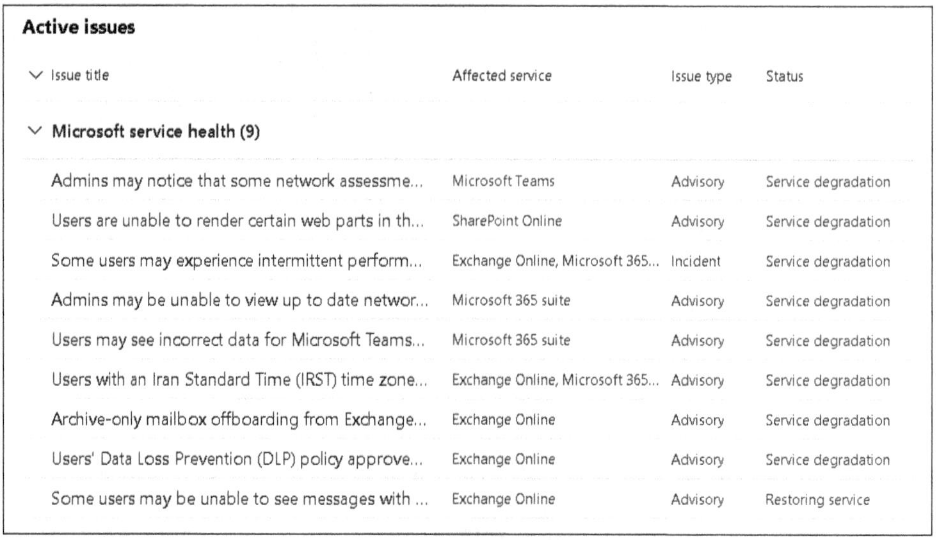

Active issues

Issue title	Affected service	Issue type	Status
Microsoft service health (9)			
Admins may notice that some network assessme...	Microsoft Teams	Advisory	Service degradation
Users are unable to render certain web parts in th...	SharePoint Online	Advisory	Service degradation
Some users may experience intermittent perform...	Exchange Online, Microsoft 365...	Incident	Service degradation
Admins may be unable to view up to date networ...	Microsoft 365 suite	Advisory	Service degradation
Users may see incorrect data for Microsoft Teams...	Microsoft 365 suite	Advisory	Service degradation
Users with an Iran Standard Time (IRST) time zone...	Exchange Online, Microsoft 365...	Advisory	Service degradation
Archive-only mailbox offboarding from Exchange...	Exchange Online	Advisory	Service degradation
Users' Data Loss Prevention (DLP) policy approve...	Exchange Online	Advisory	Service degradation
Some users may be unable to see messages with ...	Exchange Online	Advisory	Restoring service

Figure 10-1. Active issues on the "Service health" page

Click the gear icon (Customize) to do the following:

- Filter the services that you want to monitor in the "Service health" page (via the "Page view" tab, shown in Figure 10-2).
- Receive an email notification for a specific set of issues in services you want to monitor (via the Email tab).

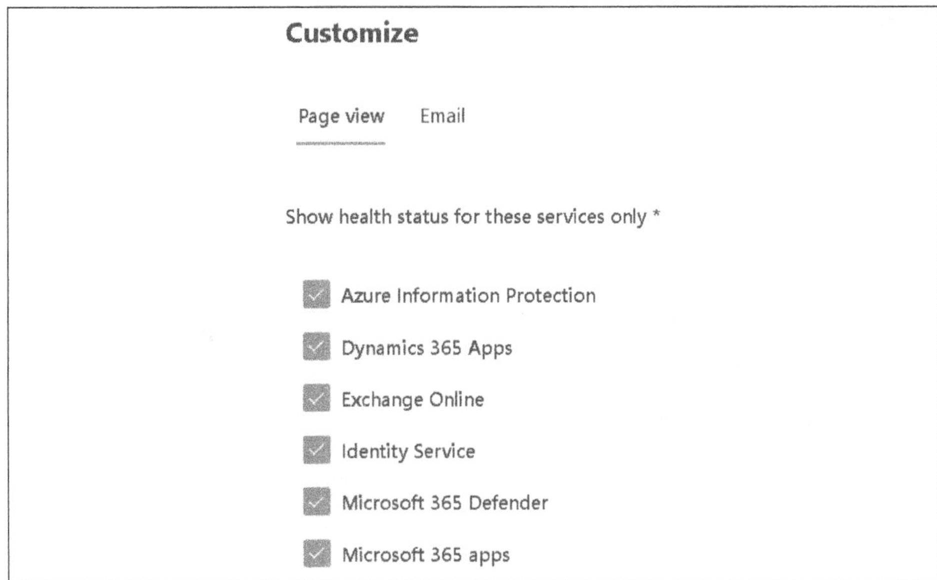

Figure 10-2. Customizing the list of services to monitor

On the "Issue history" tab, you can see a list of the issues that have already been resolved (see Figure 10-3).

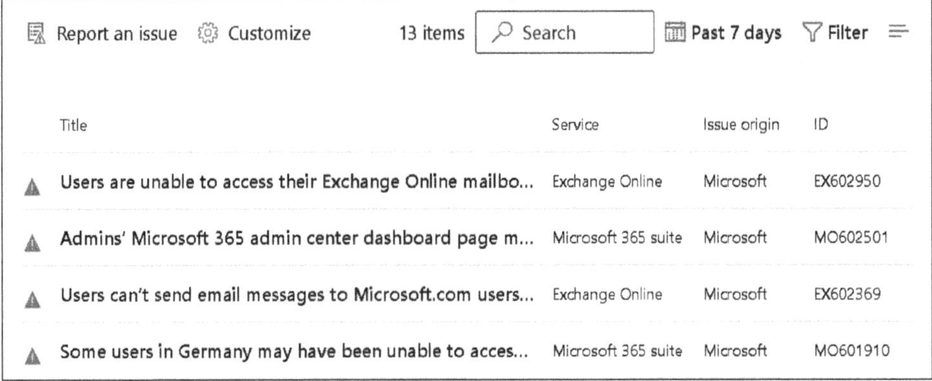

Figure 10-3. Issue history in "Service health"

Clicking on any issue will show you a description of the problem and a list of all related updates.

Discussion

If you are not able to access the admin center, then *@MSFT365Status* on Twitter is an alternative source of information about the health of Microsoft services (see Figure 10-4).

Figure 10-4. Service health notification via Twitter

You can also use the Microsoft 365 Admin app on your mobile phone (opening Health from the icon in the lower-right corner and then tapping "Service health," as shown in Figure 10-5).

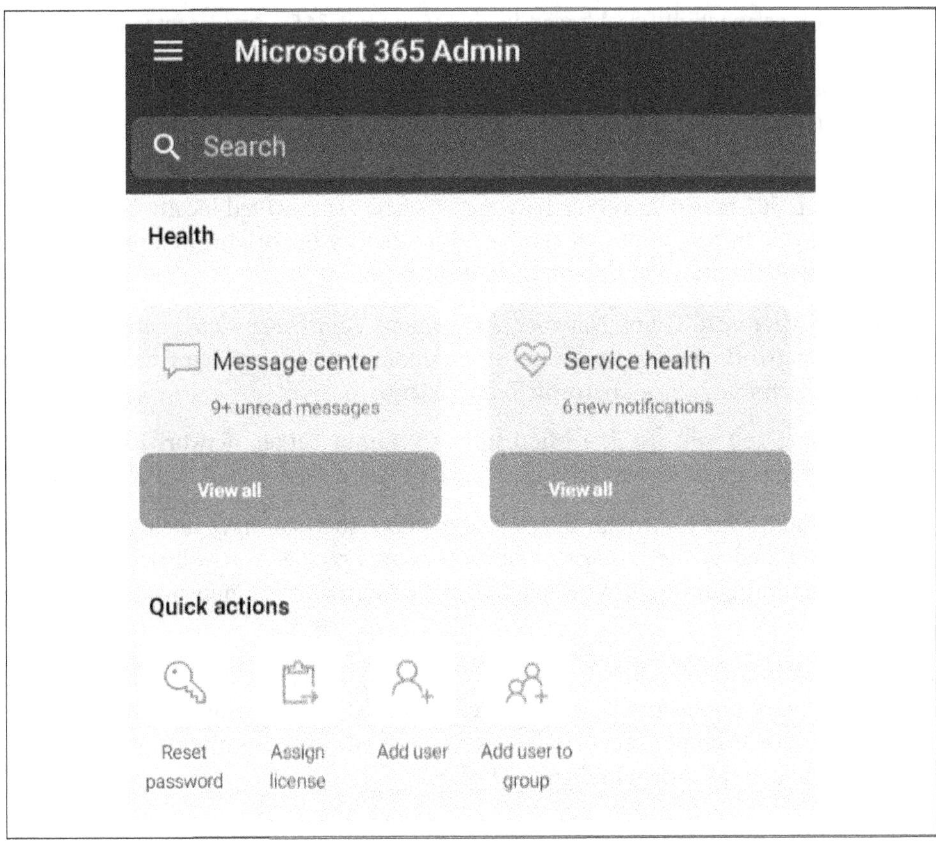

Figure 10-5. The Microsoft 365 Admin app

10.2 Monitoring Network Quality with Microsoft 365 Network Assessment Tools

Problem

You need to verify whether your network is optimized to consume Microsoft 365 services.

Solution

In the past, many enterprise networks were designed to avoid security threats. The Internet was considered an external network, so the level of trust in it was low. This dated network configuration is potentially not optimized for Microsoft 365, and could deliver a low-quality user experience and poor performance.

The network connectivity dashboard in the Microsoft 365 admin center offers both insights and assessments about an organization's network, to help predict issues with and fix the network design to provide the best experience when using Microsoft cloud services.

In addition to the Microsoft 365 admin center, you can gain network insights from the Microsoft 365 network connectivity test. This test is executed locally on the client and can provide information that can help you identify the origins of a problem in a specific network location or at a specific user location.

Finally, the Microsoft Teams Network Assessment Tool (*https://oreil.ly/oydUo*) enables simple network performance and network connectivity tests using the same real-time media technology as a Microsoft Teams client.

In this recipe, you will use the Microsoft 365 admin center network connectivity dashboard, the network connectivity test, and the Teams Network Assessment Tool.

Before starting to work through this solution, check that you have deployed the prerequisites outlined in the Discussion section of this recipe. You will need to create some specific configurations to be able to use the Microsoft 365 network connectivity dashboard.

From the Microsoft 365 admin center (*https://oreil.ly/Z97k5*), click Health > "Microsoft 365 network connectivity" (*https://oreil.ly/18Bds*). Click on one of the locations on the map (for example, Auckland in New Zealand). The Summary page for that location will open (as shown in Figure 10-6).

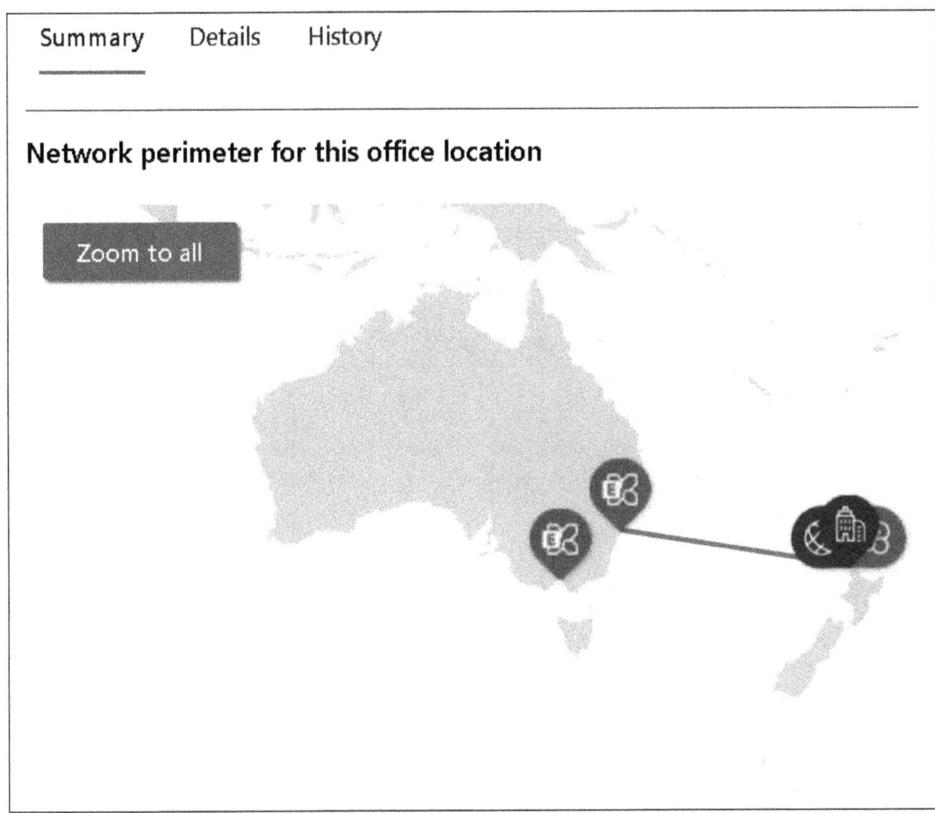

Figure 10-6. Checking the network connectivity in a specific location

On the right, you will see two different scores. For the location assessment, the lower the score, the lower the quality of the user experience when using Microsoft 365. See Table 10-1 for a breakdown of network location assessment to expected user experience. Eighty percent represents a healthy baseline.

Table 10-1. Network assessment scores and expected user experience

Network assessment	Expected user experience
100	Best
80	Meets recommendations
60	Acceptable
40	Users may experience issues
20	Users may complain
0	Network problems a common topic of discussion

Click Details to view information about the quality of the connectivity to the different services (see Figure 10-7).

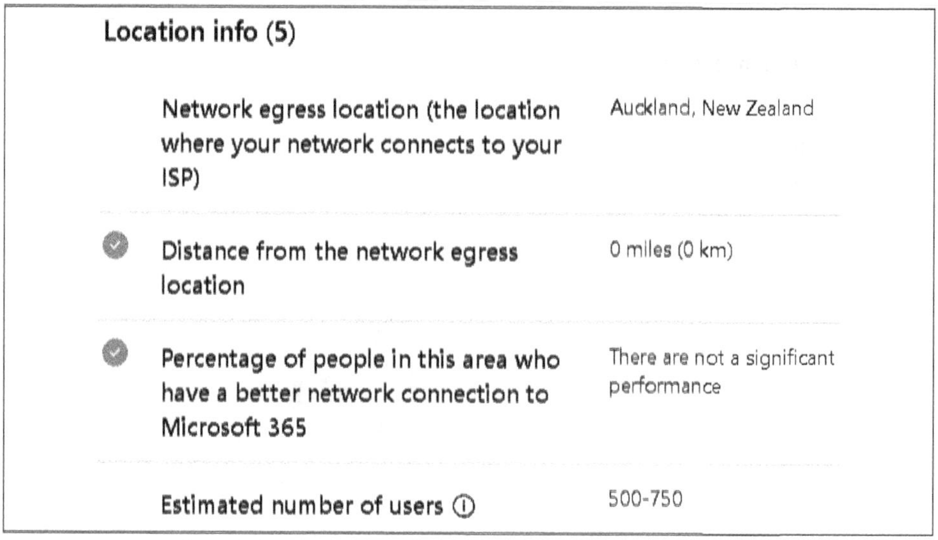

Location info (5)

	Network egress location (the location where your network connects to your ISP)	Auckland, New Zealand
✓	Distance from the network egress location	0 miles (0 km)
✓	Percentage of people in this area who have a better network connection to Microsoft 365	There are not a significant performance
	Estimated number of users ⓘ	500-750

Figure 10-7. Quality of the connection to different Microsoft 365 services

The information here contributes to the Exchange Online, SharePoint, and Teams dedicated scores you see on the Summary page.

See the Microsoft article "Microsoft 365 network assessment" (*https://oreil.ly/f7YPX*) for details regarding each score.

If you open a different location from the "Network connectivity" page, you can compare the location assessment scores between the two locations. For example, the connectivity results in Figure 10-8 are for Olympia, WA.

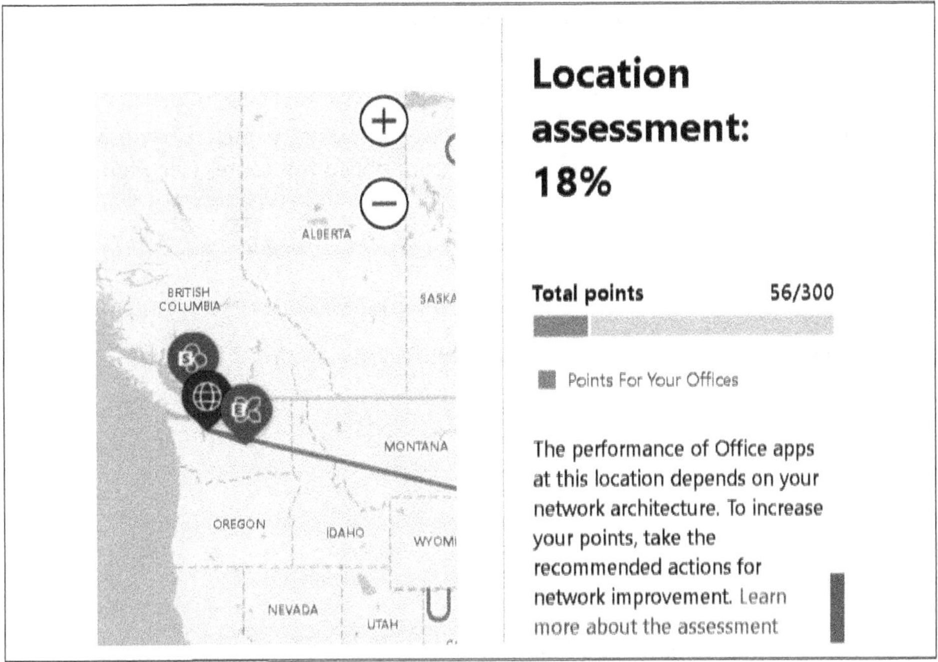

ALBERTA
BRITISH COLUMBIA
SASKA
MONTANA
OREGON
IDAHO
WYOMI
NEVADA
UTAH
Location assessment: 18%
Total points
56/300
Points For Your Offices
The performance of Office apps at this location depends on your network architecture. To increase your points, take the recommended actions for network improvement. Learn more about the assessment

Figure 10-8. A different location with a nonoptimized connectivity

In this case, the location scores lower due to the network sending the traffic to the wrong Microsoft 365 front doors.

From the network client you want to test, go to the Microsoft 365 network connectivity dashboard (*https://oreil.ly/iE3Cf*). In the upper-right corner, click "Network connectivity test."

The "Microsoft 365 network connectivity test" page will open. Select "Automatically detect location" if the client location is already registered in Microsoft 365; otherwise, type it in the "Add your location" box. Click "Run test."

A new page will open, with a summary and details of your client connection. A connectivity test file application (named *Connectivity.<guid>.exe*) will be downloaded to your client. This is required to provide detailed test results.

.NET 6.0 Runtime is required to execute the connectivity test file. If it is not installed in your client, a download of the required runtime will be offered.

Open the application file (don't close your browser, because the results will be available there). In the left pane, click Reports, open the "Reports run by me" menu, and click "View report."

The report will contain additional details about your client connectivity to Microsoft 365, compared to the previous one executed from the admin center (see Figure 10-9).

No one in nearby locations have better network connectivity to Microsoft 365 than your location.

This chart shows the network connection quality for Microsoft 365 customers in your area.

Score	Share
80-100 (best) (you)	48%
60-80	7%
40-60	5%
20-40	21%
0-20 (worst)	19%

Figure 10-9. Network connectivity test results

As a last step, download the Microsoft Teams Network Assessment Tool (*https://oreil.ly/EF-PK*) and install it. Open a command prompt (*cmd.exe*) and execute the *NetworkAssessmentTool.exe* file (the default path is *C:\Program Files (x86)\Microsoft Teams Network Assessment Tool*).

The relay connectivity checker verifies network connectivity to Microsoft's load-balancer relays Virtual IPs (VIPs). It also checks the connection to the one-relay instance Data IPs (DIPs) where the communication is forwarded by the load-balancer relay. The checker tests connectivity via UDP, TCP, and HTTPS transport protocols.

Discussion

To enable the network connectivity assessments, you need to create locations in Microsoft 365. You have three options:

- Adjust your location opt-in setting to automatically collect data from devices using Windows Location Services (in Windows Settings > Privacy > Location). At least two devices for each network location, with location on, are required.
- Go to Locations in the Microsoft 365 network connectivity dashboard and manually add a location by clicking "Add location" (as in Figure 10-10).
- Run the Microsoft 365 network connectivity test from your office locations.

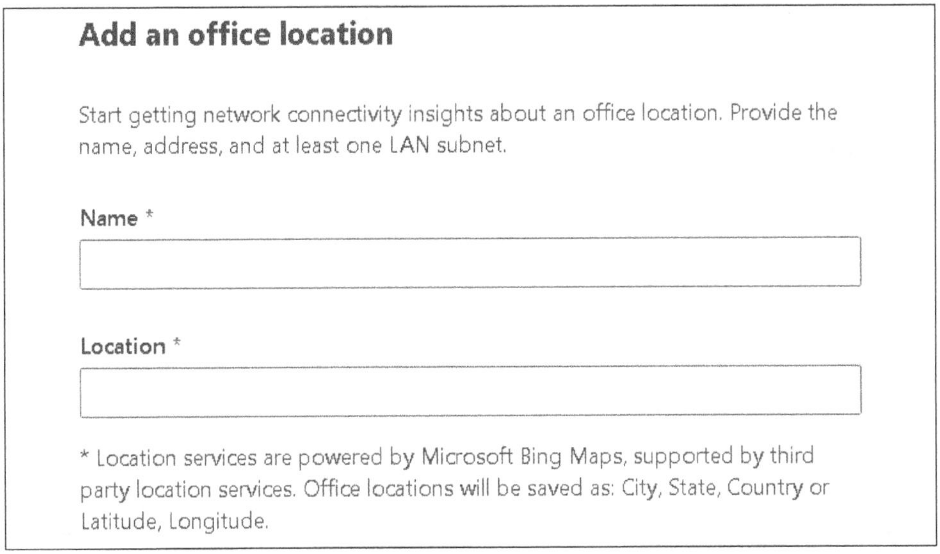

Add an office location

Start getting network connectivity insights about an office location. Provide the name, address, and at least one LAN subnet.

Name *

Location *

* Location services are powered by Microsoft Bing Maps, supported by third party location services. Office locations will be saved as: City, State, Country or Latitude, Longitude.

Figure 10-10. Adding locations manually

10.3 Monitoring User Experience with Teams Analytics and Reports

Problem

You need to gather information about Teams usage and adoption.

Solution

To monitor the usage of Teams, you have two different tools:

- Teams usage reports
- Microsoft Adoption Score

The Teams usage report provides an overview of user activity in Teams. You can view information including the number of active users and channels, guests, and messages in each team. The Adoption Score is a numeric value, on a scale from 0 to 800 (with 800 being the maximum score), that is automatically calculated for your organization based on the digital behavior of your employees (for example, how many participants in meetings have their video enabled) and the quality of your infrastructure. Your Adoption Score is converted into a percentage, between 0 and 100%. The Adoption Score includes data from Exchange Online, SharePoint, OneDrive, Teams, Word, Excel, PowerPoint, OneNote, Outlook, and Yammer.

To open the Teams usage reports, from the TAC click "Analytics & reports" > "Usage reports" and select "Apps usage" from the Report drop-down menu. Click "Run report" (the result is shown in Figure 10-11).

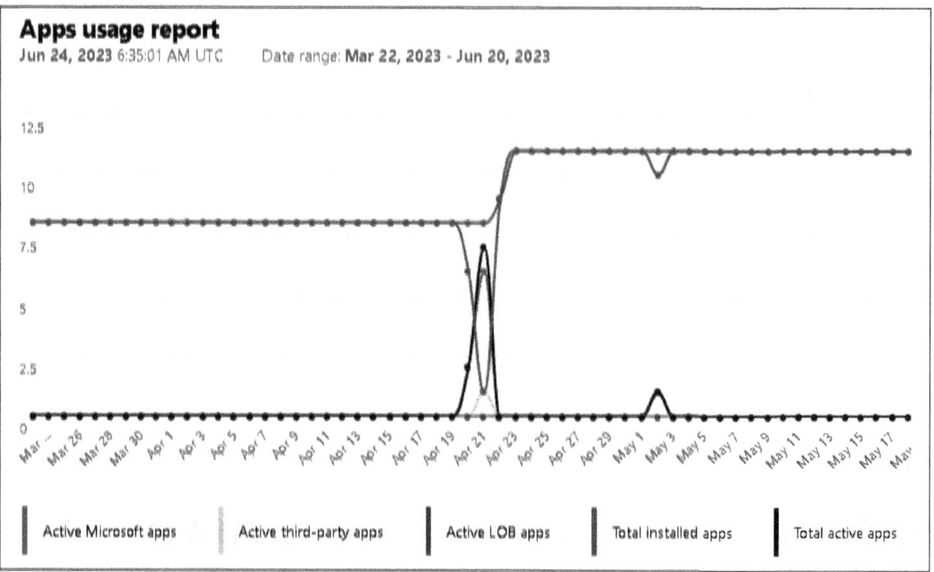

Figure 10-11. Apps usage report

The report will show information about the apps in use, including the source of the activity and the kind of app used. The menu in the upper-right corner allows you to export to a CSV file and to customize the columns used in the table (via the gear icon).

Select "PSTN usage" from the Report drop-down menu, and click "Run report." The report is divided between Calling Plans and Direct Routing, as well as between incoming and outgoing calls. It also includes information about the type of license used, shown in the Capability column (for example, MCOEV_VIRTUALUSER for Resource Accounts). An example of the PSTN usage report is shown in Figure 10-12.

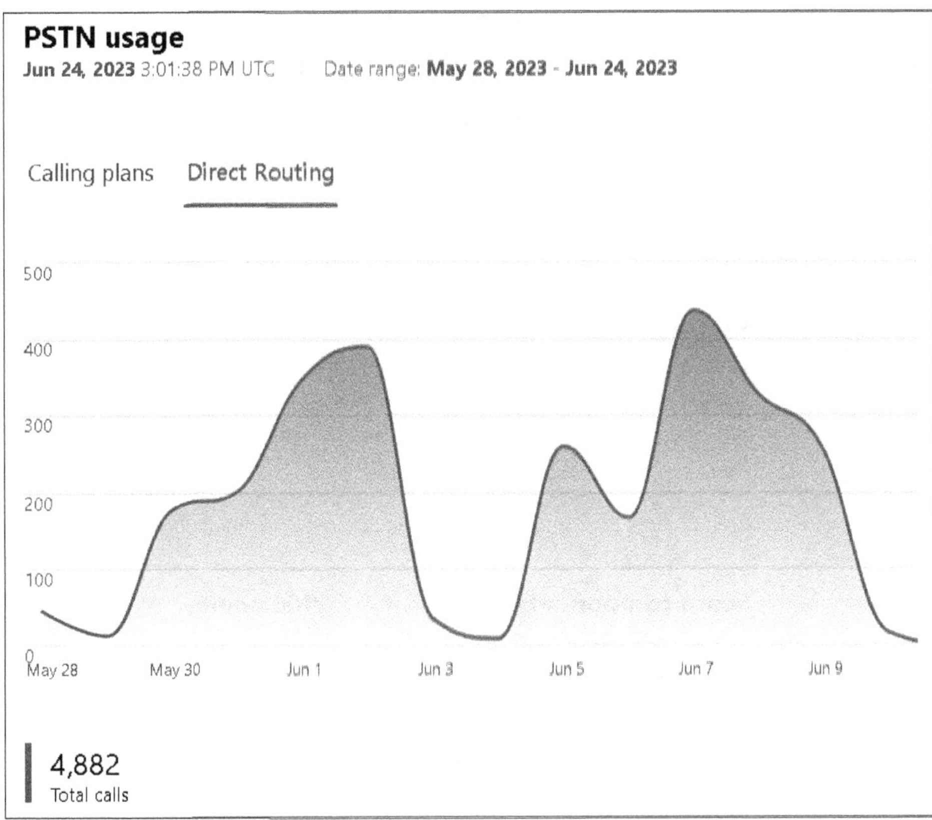

Figure 10-12. PSTN usage report

Now, select "Teams usage report" from the Report drop-down menu. The Teams usage report gives you a view of the number of active users and channels. The metrics are focused on user activity in the different channels, including activity by guest users.

The "Teams user activity report" gives you a view of Teams usage by user. This report includes messages (channel, chat, and so on), meetings (both as an organizer and as a participant), and calls (video, audio, and 1:1).

To access the Adoption Score, from the Microsoft 365 admin center (*https://oreil.ly/Q78tu*), click "Reports" > Adoption Score (see Figure 10-13).

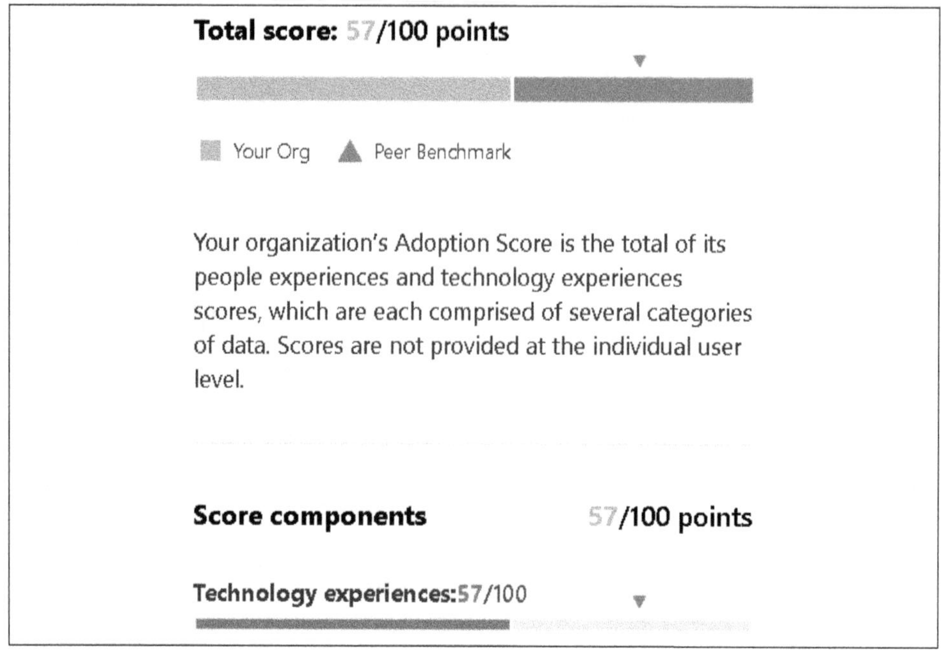

Figure 10-13. Adoption Score for an organization

You may need to enable the Adoption Score. From the Microsoft 365 admin center, go to Reports and select Enable Adoption Score. It can take up to 24 hours for insights to become available.

Discussion

The Adoption Score is an evolution of a similar monitoring tool, the Productivity Score. One issue with the Productivity Score, when it was launched, was the ability to drill down to an individual user level. The data was soon anonymized to avoid any infringement of privacy (as with other Microsoft monitoring tools), but some resistance remained around the usage of the tool and about who had access to personal information.

A part of the Adoption Score is based on how much the organization has embraced best practices around digital work and collaboration ("People experiences"), and a part of it is based on how reliable the service was and how its apps are used ("Technology experiences"). The components of the Adoption Score are shown in Figure 10-14.

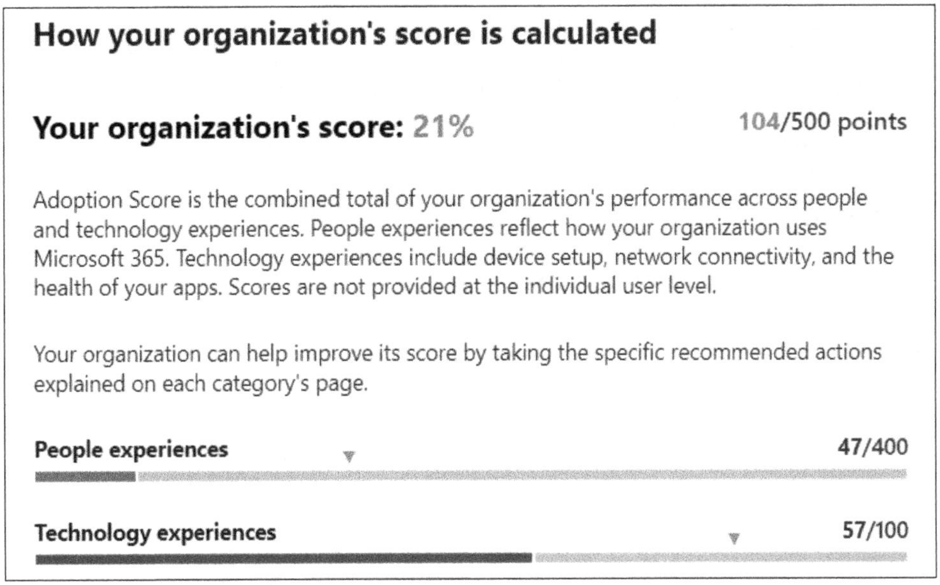

How your organization's score is calculated

Your organization's score: 21% 104/500 points

Adoption Score is the combined total of your organization's performance across people and technology experiences. People experiences reflect how your organization uses Microsoft 365. Technology experiences include device setup, network connectivity, and the health of your apps. Scores are not provided at the individual user level.

Your organization can help improve its score by taking the specific recommended actions explained on each category's page.

People experiences 47/400

Technology experiences 57/100

Figure 10-14. Components of an Adoption Score

You can further examine each of the categories that contribute to the Adoption Score. In the dedicated dashboard, you will find more detailed information and guidance to improve that specific area.

10.4 Analyzing Call and Meeting Quality with the Call Quality Dashboard

Problem

You need to monitor the quality of Teams calls and meetings.

Solution

The Microsoft Call Quality Dashboard (CQD) shows information about quality for calls and meetings, at an organization-wide level. It includes Teams, Skype for Business Online, and Skype for Business Server 2019. CQD is not meant to examine a single user call (which is the objective of a different tool, call analytics). Instead, CQD gives a view of trends and patterns that have an impact on many users, providing different reports about call quality.

It is possible to use the data in the CQD via Power BI. Microsoft offers a set of templates that you can use as a starting point for querying and reporting on call quality in Teams. The Quality of Experience Report (QER) template is a reporting template that is meant to replace the original CQD Power BI query templates (you can download CQD Power BI query templates from the official Microsoft download center (*https://oreil.ly/pmlJq*)). You will install and use the QER in this recipe.

Unzip the *CQD-Power-BI-query-templates.zip* file in the *C:\temp* folder. For the next step, you need to have Power BI Desktop installed (available from the Power BI download page (*https://oreil.ly/J5FOy*)). Using QER requires the Power BI Connector for Microsoft Advanced CQD.

To enable the Connector, first check to see whether your computer already has the following folder: *%username%\Documents\Power BI Desktop\Custom Connectors*. If not, create this folder. Then copy the *MicrosoftCallQuality.pqx* file from *C:\temp* into the *%username%\Documents\Power BI Desktop\Custom Connectors* folder, as shown in Figure 10-15.

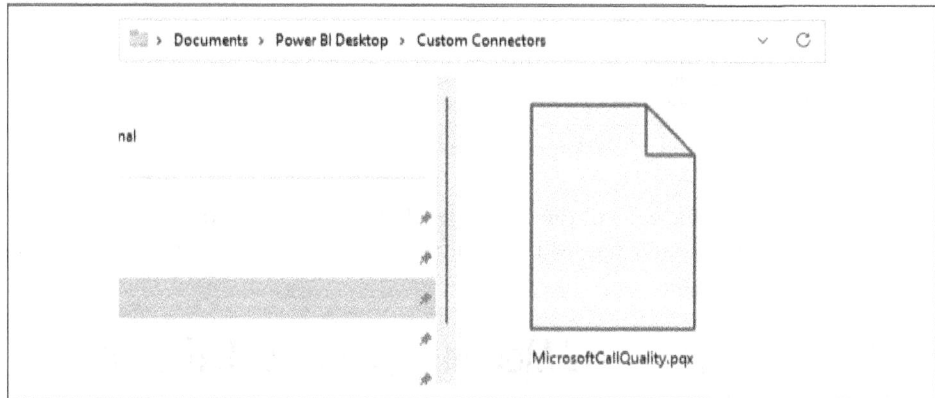

Figure 10-15. Adding the required folder and the custom Connector file

Open Power BI Desktop and select File > "Options and settings" > Options > Security. Under Data Extensions, select "(Not Recommended) Allow any extension to load without validation or warning."

Click OK and restart Power BI Desktop. Select File > "Open report" > "Browse reports," and navigate to *QER v4.7.pbit* from *C:\temp*.

The current version (4.8) is saved in the *C:\temp\QER* folder. The default behavior is to show PBIT files when the Explorer window opens, so you may need to select ".pbit" to see the QER you want.

Sign in with your Teams admin credentials. The template will open, and you will be connected to the CQD (you can verify that you are connected to the CQD if you see a list of dimensions and measures in the Fields pane).

Now you can navigate between the different tabs. For example, see the Media Usage tab to examine the information related to the quality of media for the calls and meetings in your tenant (as in Figure 10-16).

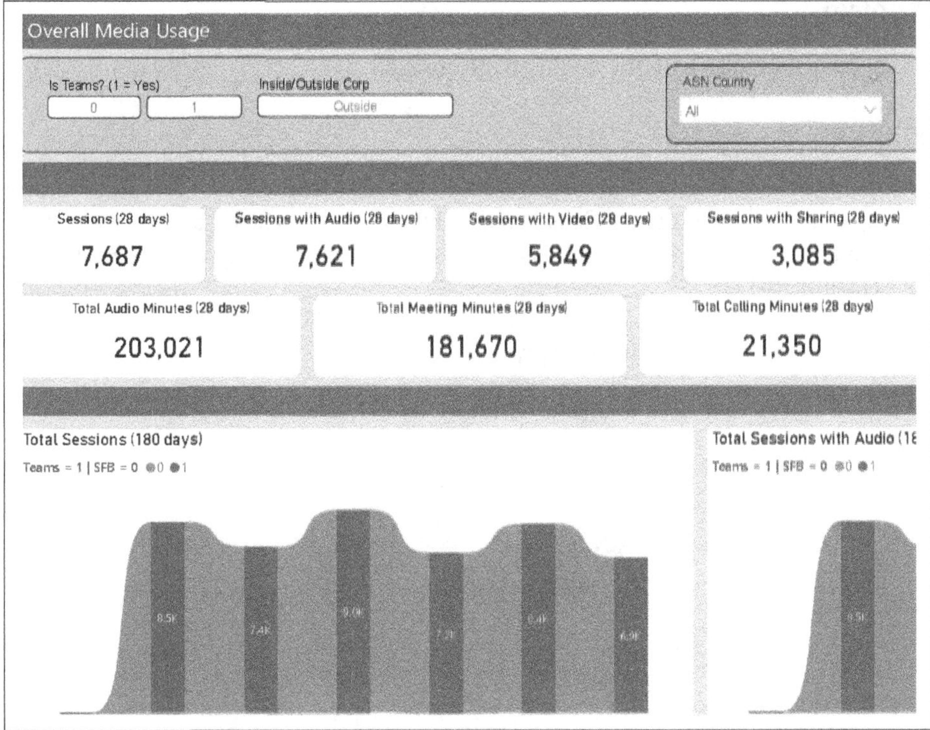

Figure 10-16. Opening a QER in Power BI Desktop

Discussion

The QER template provides a variety of reports, listed in the Microsoft documentation (*https://oreil.ly/MFQ-k*).

The following roles enable users to read the CQD information: Global Administrator, Teams Administrator, Teams Communications Administrator, Teams Communications Support Engineer, Teams Communications Support Specialist, Skype for Business Administrator, Global Reader, and Reports Reader.

10.5 Using Call Analytics to Identify Call Quality Issues

Problem

You need to fix issues with the quality of Teams calls.

Solution

In the TAC, click Users > "Manage users." Select the desired user (we'll use Adele Vance), then click Meetings & Calls. On the right side, you will see an overview of the call quality and numeric values related to the calls and meetings in the past seven days (Figure 10-17).

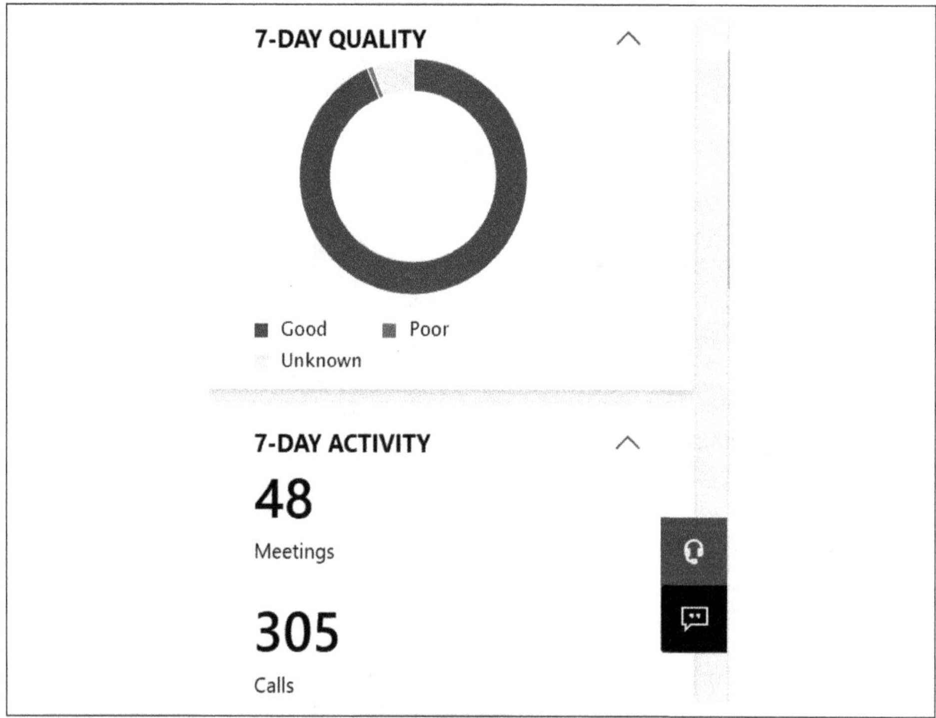

Figure 10-17. An overview of the quality of calls and meetings for the past seven days

A list of the past meetings will be shown. Calls that involved only Teams clients as participants will show Microsoft Teams in the Client column. Otherwise, Multiple will be shown. By clicking an entry in the "Meeting or call ID" column, you can open a single call. In the Overview tab, a summary of the call will be shown. If any error was encountered, the overview will show it (see Figure 10-18).

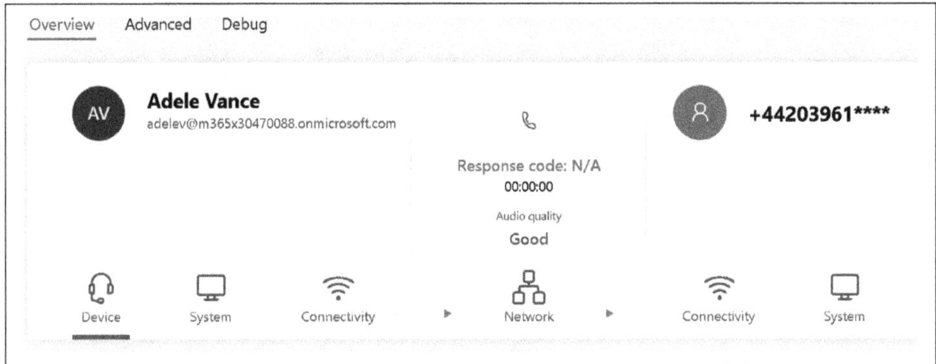

Figure 10-18. A call with an error in Call Analytics

The Overview tab will also show the call rating that users provided as feedback at the end of the call.

Inside Call Analytics, click the Advanced tab to see more details about the users' devices during the call as well as audio stream, connectivity, and network information (see Figure 10-19).

Inbound network

Average jitter	8 ms
Maximum jitter	27 ms
Average round-trip time	103 ms
Maximum round-trip time	438 ms
Average packet loss rate	0.00%
Maximum packet loss rate	0.00%
Maximum compressed samples	0
Compressed sample ratio	0.67%

Figure 10-19. Looking at details in the Call Analytics tool

In a call with multiple users, you'll see the Timeline tab, which provides a high-level view of when each user joined and left the call. Figure 10-20 shows a multi-user call.

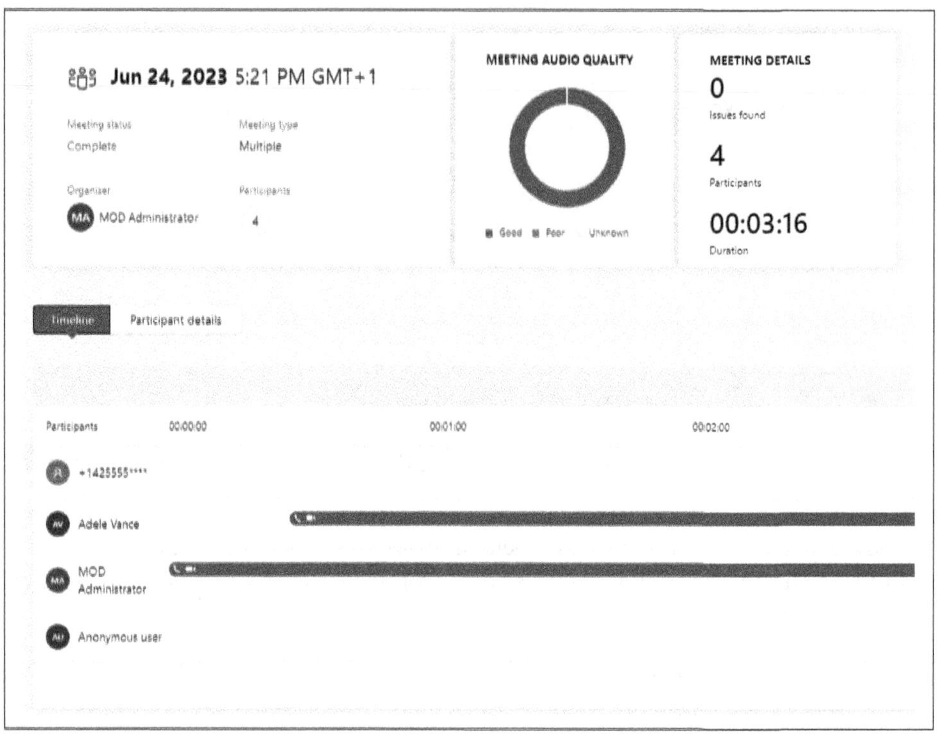

Figure 10-20. Multi-user meeting overview

On the "Participant details" tab, you will find similar information in a table.

When the call is upgraded from a peer-to-peer call to a multi-person meeting, all the connections from the clients are redirected to the Teams service, even if the original call was a direct communication between the two clients (the connection from the client to the Teams service is shown in Figure 10-21).

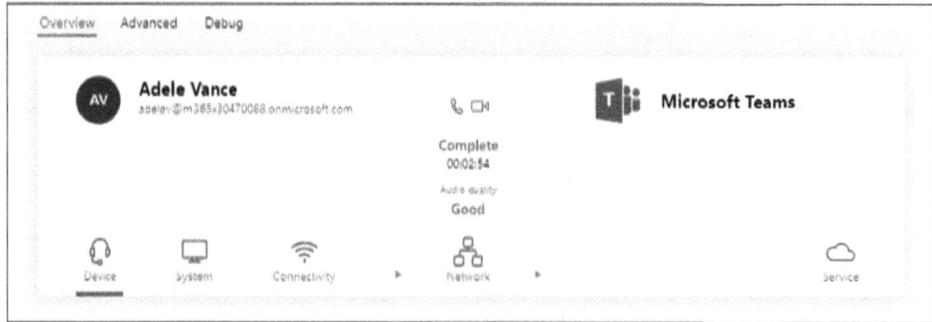

Figure 10-21. A leg of a meeting call

Discussion

Call Analytics shows Teams calls and meetings at a user level, in your Microsoft 365 account, including information about all the participants in a meeting or call. Call Analytics helps to identify the cause of poor-quality calls and communication issues.

For an audio call, there are three parameters that need to be monitored. If any of the following parameters exceed the values in the list, that is a signal of poor call quality:

Jitter >30 ms
: Audio packets are sent at regular intervals on the network, but they could have a delay due to network latency (jitter). Jitter is mitigated by Teams using buffering. The buffer waits for all the packets before reconstructing them in the correct order.

Packet loss rate >10% or 0.1
: When encountering low levels of packet loss, the Teams SILK codec implements specialized techniques, including forward error correction (where extra packets are transmitted as a precautionary measure against potential losses) and concealing lost packets. These strategies effectively minimize the impact caused by the issue. The limit is reached when there is not enough information to reconstruct the stream. Teams also supports an audio codec called Satin, designed for challenging network conditions such as mobile data networks or busy WiFi. Satin can replace, in an even more effective way, the lost packets (more information can be found in the article "Satin: Microsoft's latest AI-powered audio codec for real-time communications" (*https://oreil.ly/jVtiz*)).

Round-trip time >500 ms
: Round-trip time measures the time taken to send a data packet from point A to point B, and back.

10.6 Summary

This chapter covered some of the Teams monitoring and analysis tools that you can use to improve and analyze call and meeting quality. Some of the tools take a high-level approach (like the CQD and the Adoption Score), while others are more useful to troubleshoot the issues of a single user. The next chapter is about collaborating with external users via shared channels, Azure Communication Services, and other communication platforms.

CHAPTER 11

Collaborating with External Users

Teams enables collaboration with users inside and outside your organization. Collaboration with external users—leveraging a common set of features, as well as chats and documents—minimizes the effort required to work with customers and partners who aren't part of your Microsoft 365 tenant. There are three types of external access in Teams:

- Guest access
- External access
- Shared channels

The three access modalities are technically different and each has a unique impact on the user experience, compliance, and security of the platform.

Another way to communicate with external users while in Teams is with Azure Communication Services (ACS). ACS is a set of cloud-based services with REST APIs and client library SDKs that integrate communication (voice and video calling, rich text chat, SMS, and email) with your custom applications.

11.1 Activating External Identities

Problem

You need to enable and secure External Identities.

Solution

The default settings in Entra ID are not restrictive, allowing you to facilitate the external collaboration. However, in many scenarios it is advisable to limit who can invite guest users and bar some domains from the collaboration.

In the recipe, you will:

- Verify that your Entra ID tenant is linked to a subscription.
- Check the cross-tenant access settings.
- Restrict some of the default settings for external collaboration.
- Delegate guest invites to the tenant to the desired user.

First, open the Microsoft Entra admin center (*https://oreil.ly/RTs7M*) and select Billing in the left pane, then click "Linked subscriptions." If no subscription is linked, as shown in Figure 11-1, check the box next to the tenant's name and then click "Link subscription."

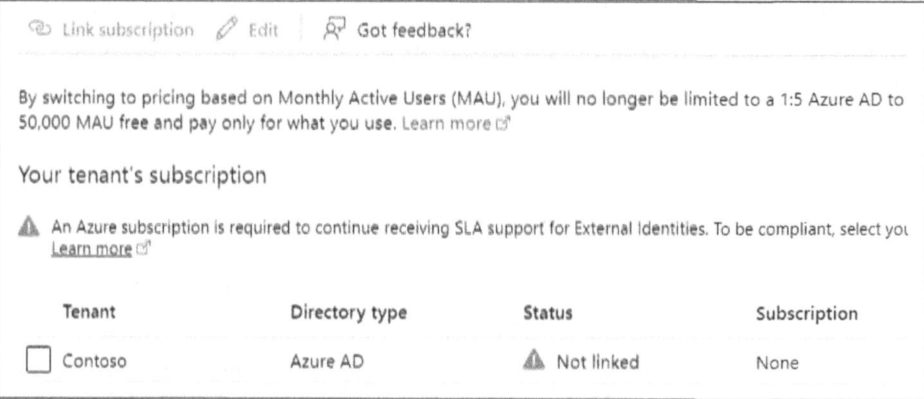

Figure 11-1. Linking a subscription in Azure

The "Link a subscription" screen will open. You can select a subscription and an existing resource group from the drop-down menus, or create new ones (as Figure 11-2 shows). Click Apply.

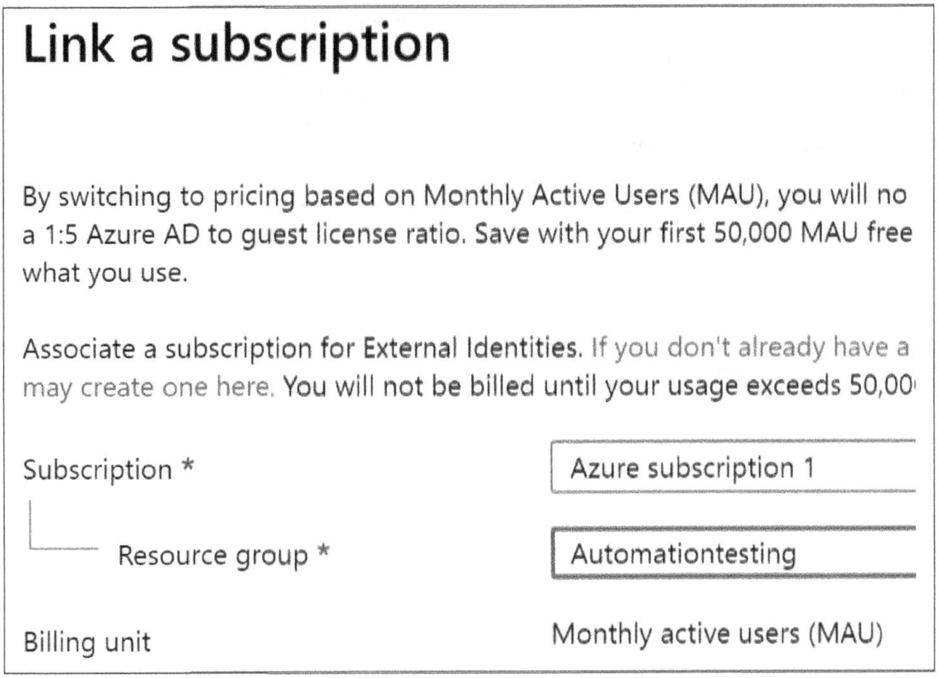

Link a subscription
By switching to pricing based on Monthly Active Users (MAU), you will no
a 1:5 Azure AD to guest license ratio. Save with your first 50,000 MAU free
what you use.
Associate a subscription for External Identities. If you don't already have a
may create one here. You will not be billed until your usage exceeds 50,00
Subscription *
Azure subscription 1
Resource group *
Automationtesting
Billing unit
Monthly active users (MAU)

Figure 11-2. Completing the subscription linking

If you receive the error message "Subscription is not registered to use namespace *Microsoft.AzureActiveDirectory*," go to Subscriptions (*https://oreil.ly/HESRB*) in the Azure portal, click on your subscription, select "Resource providers," select *Microsoft.AzureActiveDirectory*, and click Register in the upper part of the screen (see Figure 11-3).

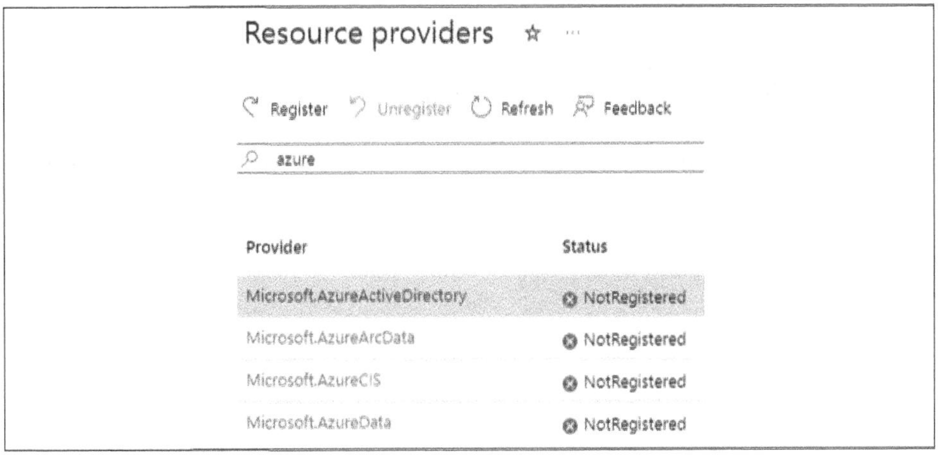

Figure 11-3. Activating the resource provider

Back in the Microsoft Entra admin center, select External Identities, then click "Cross-tenant access settings." Here, you can check what kind of collaboration is enabled or disabled in your tenant (the default settings are shown in Figure 11-4).

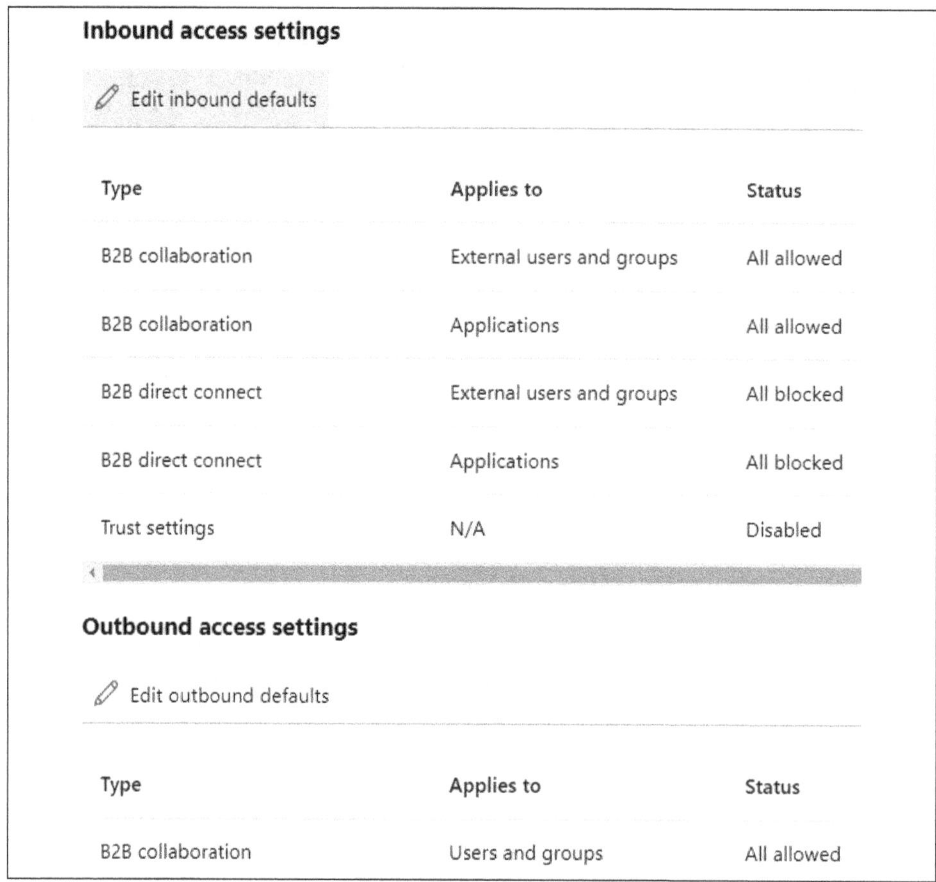

Figure 11-4. Inbound and outbound access settings

Click "External collaboration settings" to modify the settings, as shown in Figure 11-5.

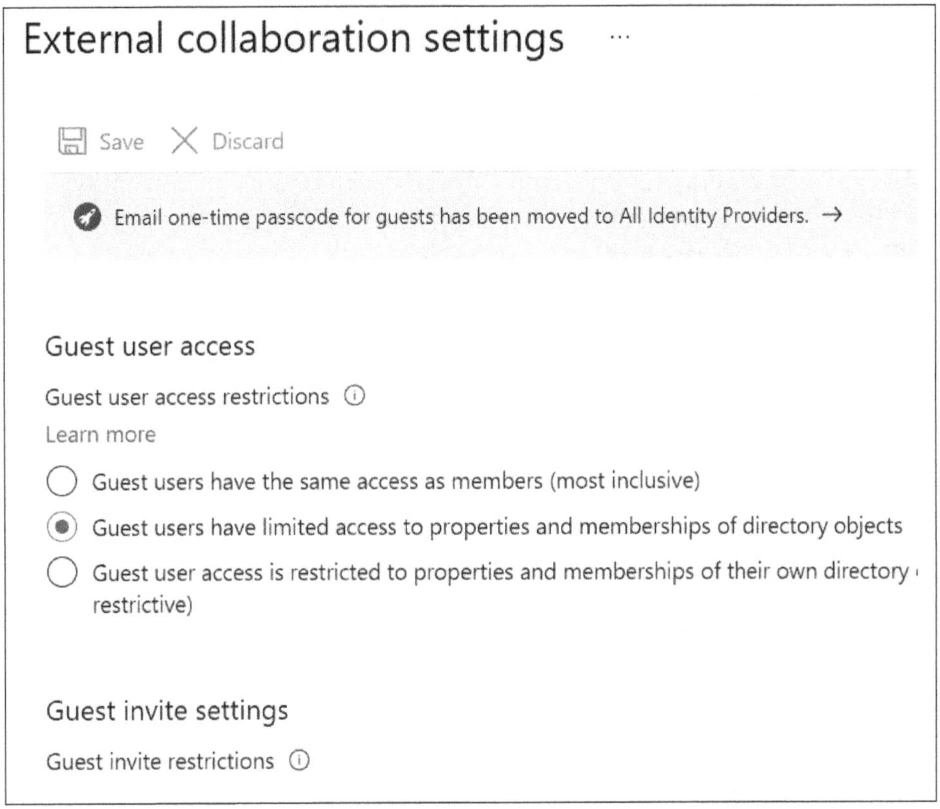

External collaboration settings ...

Save Discard

Email one-time passcode for guests has been moved to All Identity Providers. →

Guest user access

Guest user access restrictions ⓘ

Learn more

- Guest users have the same access as members (most inclusive)
- Guest users have limited access to properties and memberships of directory objects
- Guest user access is restricted to properties and memberships of their own directory (most restrictive)

Guest invite settings

Guest invite restrictions ⓘ

Figure 11-5. External collaboration settings

The default settings are as follows:

- Guest users have restricted access to directory objects' properties and memberships. This configuration prevents guests from performing certain directory tasks, such as listing users, groups, or other directory resources. However, guests can view the membership of all non-hidden groups.
- Any individual within the organization, regardless of their status as a guest or non-administrator, can invite guest users. Setting the parameter this way enables guests within the organization to invite other guests, even if they are not members of the organization.
- You can activate the option for guest sign-up through user flows. By default, this option is set to No. However, if you wish to create user flows that allow users to register for applications, you can select Yes.
- Regarding external user leave settings, the default choice is no. You have the option to enable external users to remove themselves from the organization by selecting yes.

- You can provide a list of domains from which users can (or cannot) be invited for collaboration purposes. The default is to allow collaboration invitations to be sent to users from any domain.

Change the "Guest invite settings" option to "Only users assigned to specific admin roles can invite guest users." Change the "Collaboration restrictions" option to "Deny invitations to the specified domains" and type **.blockeddomain.com* in the "Target domains" box. Click Save in the upper part of the screen.

The external collaboration settings in Entra ID override the other settings available in Microsoft 365 (like the ones you will see for Teams).

In the Entra admin center, select Users. Click a user (I've selected Christie Cline), then click "Assigned roles." Click "Add assignments" and search the role "guest." Select the Guest Inviter role, as shown in shown in Figure 11-6, and click Add.

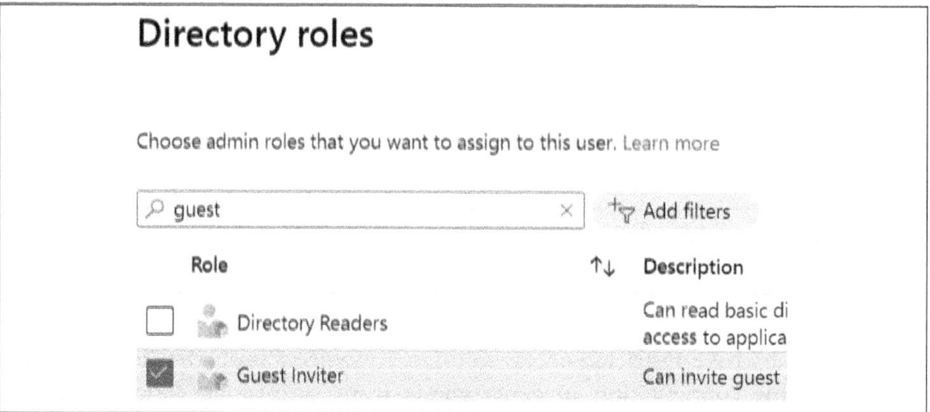

Figure 11-6. Assigning the required role

The roles of Global Administrator and User Administrator also have permission to create guest user accounts.

Discussion

The core technology enabling guest access and shared channels in Teams is External Identities. External Identities, part of Microsoft Entra, incorporates all possible usage modalities to securely interact with users outside of your organization. The external users' identity providers manage their identities, and you manage access to your apps with Entra ID to keep your resources protected. Organizations have two options for collaboration with external users:

- Create locally managed credentials for external users.
- Establish federations with partner identity providers.

External Identities can be enabled in different ways:

B2B collaboration
: Invite guest users to collaborate with your organization. With B2B collaboration, you maintain control over your own corporate data.

B2B direct connect
: Establish mutual, two-way trust with another Entra ID organization. B2B direct connect supports Teams shared channels. B2B direct connect users aren't represented in your directory.

Azure AD B2C
: Publish SaaS apps or custom-developed apps to consumers and customers.

External Identities pricing is based on Monthly Active Users (MAU), which counts the unique users with authentication activity within a calendar month. The first 50,000 MAU per month are free for both Premium P1 and Premium P2 features (like Conditional Access).

11.2 Collaborating with External Access and Guest Access

Problem

You need to manage external access and guest access to Teams.

Solution

In this recipe, you will use two different tenants and domains. You will act as an administrator in the *M365x01033383.onmicrosoft.com* host domain and manage external access and guest access for incoming users from the *M365x71772990.onmicrosoft.com* external domain.

In the TAC, click Users and then click "External access" (using the host domain). In the "Choose which external domains your users have access to" drop-down menu, change the default "Allow all external domains" to "Allow only specific external domains" (as in Figure 11-7).

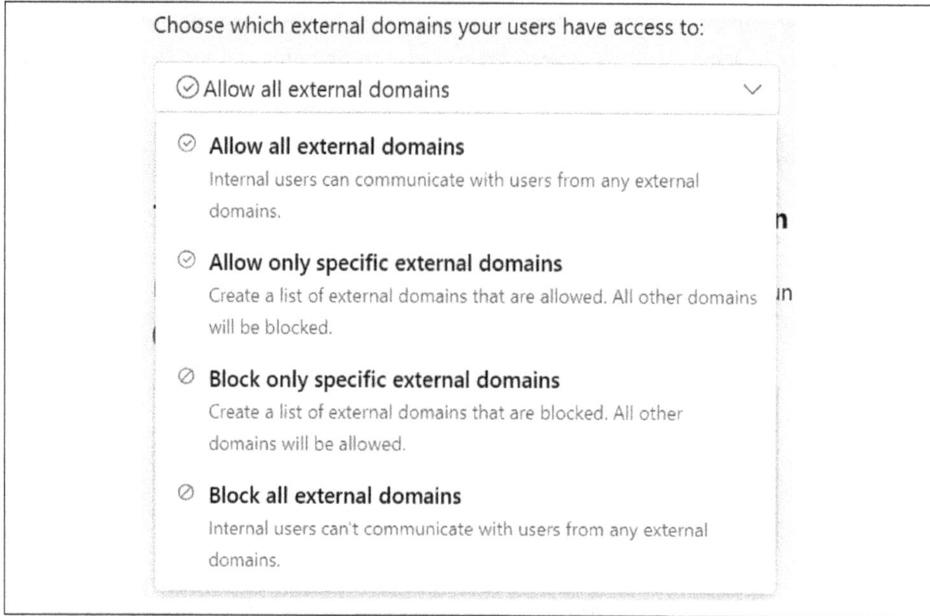

Figure 11-7. Managing external access from the TAC

Click "Allow domains" and add an external domain (we'll use *M365x71772990.onmicrosoft.com*). Disable unmanaged users (external Teams accounts not managed by an organization) by turning off the option "People in my organization can communicate with Teams users whose accounts aren't managed by an organization" (see Figure 11-8).

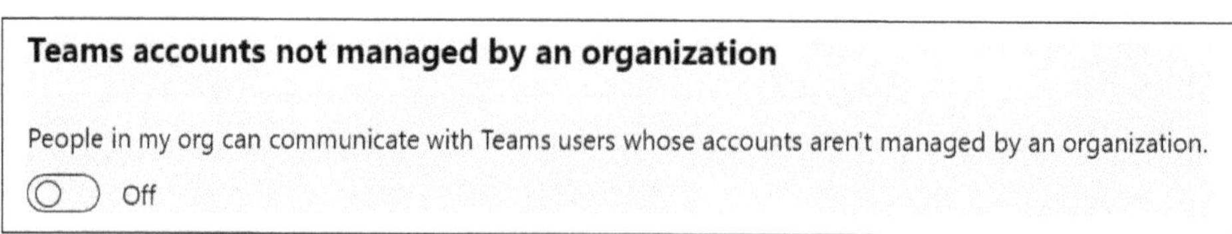

Figure 11-8. Blocking unmanaged external accounts

With these settings, you can test the external access by opening a Teams client with a user in the external domain (we'll use Lidia Holloway). Search for Adele Vance in the host domain. The external user can see Adele's status, start a chat, and so on, as shown in Figure 11-9.

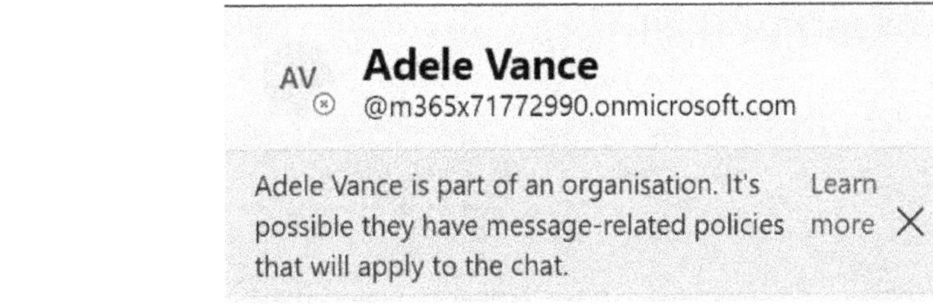

Figure 11-9. Interaction between users in different domains

The collaboration with an external user does not include joining teams in a different tenant. With the "Guest access" feature, you have the ability to include individual users from external sources, who are not affiliated with your company, into your Teams and channels on the Teams platform.

To configure guest access in the TAC, click Users and then click "Guest access." The default policy is to allow guest access in Teams. Other policies dictate meeting and messaging for the guest user.

Guest Access Versus Regular Teams Membership

There are some limitations to guest access, compared to regular Teams membership. For example, guests in Teams don't have access to features like the following:

- OneDrive for Business
- People search outside of Teams
- The calendar, scheduled meetings, or meeting details
- PSTN calling
- The organization chart
- Uploading files to a person-to-person chat

A full comparison is available in the article "Use guest access and external access to collaborate with people outside your organization" (*https://oreil.ly/o6AUX*).

To create a guest account, open the Microsoft Entra admin center (*https://oreil.ly/DVsqk*) in the host domain. Select Users. Click "New user" and select "Invite external user" from the menu. Add the guest user's information (including the external email address). You can add a personal message for the invite and add the guest user to groups or Azure roles. Click "Review + invite" when you're finished to review the invitation, as in Figure 11-10, then click Invite.

Figure 11-10. Sending the invite to a guest user

The user account is automatically added to Entra ID as a guest.

Next, sign in as the external user (here, Lidia Holloway). In Outlook, open the invitation message and click "Accept invitation," as shown in Figure 11-11.

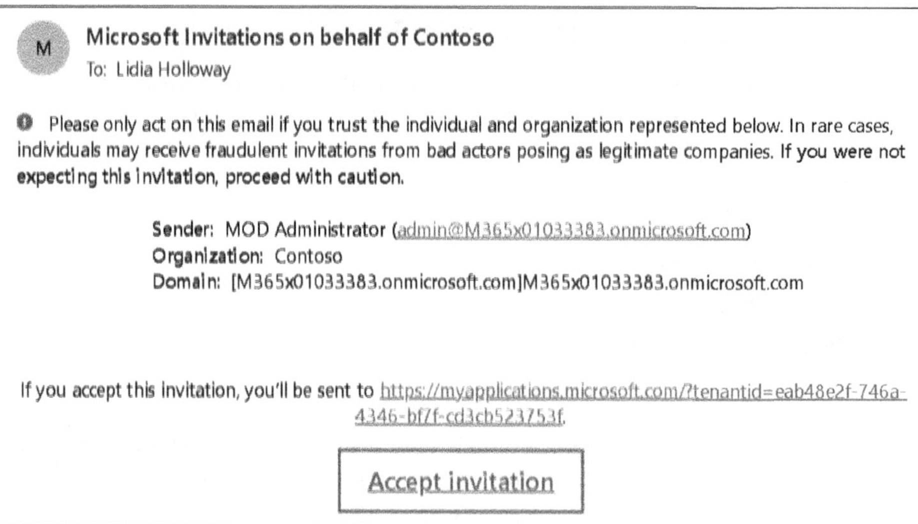

Figure 11-11. Guest account invitation within Outlook

A "Permission request" page will open in the browser. Now the users in the host domain can add the guest user Lidia Holloway to teams and channels (see Figure 11-12).

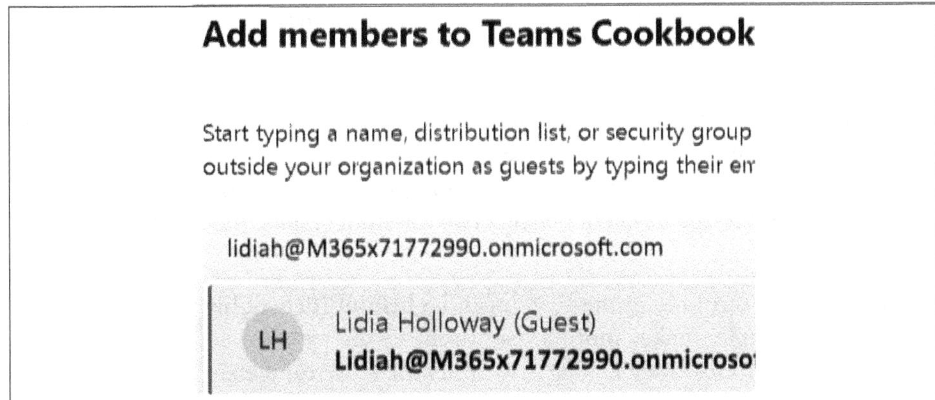

Figure 11-12. Adding guest users to a team

The guest user will receive an invitation (there may be a waiting time before the invite is sent). That user, from a Teams client in the external domain, has a choice between their domain account and the guest account in the host domain. If they select the guest account, they will have access to the teams and channels shared with them (the choices are shown in Figure 11-13).

Figure 11-13. Switching between domain and guest accounts

Discussion

Teams has two external sharing options. The first (external access) lets users in other domains find, call, and chat with your users. The second (guest access) lets you add individuals to your teams, as guests, using their email address. Invited people get a guest account in Entra ID and must switch between their standard domain account and the guest user account to access external tenants.

External access to Teams is a good solution to collaborate with users outside your organization who do not require working on the same documents as internal users. Guest access to Teams is a better solution in scenarios where people outside your organization require access to teams, channels, chats, documents, and applications. Guests will not be able to create meetings, add apps, or share chat files.

Using guest access has an impact on the user experience. For the users in the external domain, using the guest account means that they must switch between their standard domain account and the external guest account. The usage of Teams gets more complex with the requirement to switch tenants, especially when the user is a guest in more than one domain. Also, from the point of view of a user in the host domain, there is some additional complexity. For example, searching for the external user email address in the Teams client delivers two different results: the guest user and the external account.

Having both the accounts in the search can be helpful (depending on the scenario). An IM, for example, makes more sense if sent to the external account that will be used more often. However, having two different and completely separate ways to communicate with the same person is also a potential cause of misunderstandings and errors.

The latest version of the Teams client (sometimes referred to as 2.0) includes different improvements. The most relevant to this recipe is the Multi-Tenant Multi-Account (MTMA), which allows users to quickly switch between the different accounts and tenants they have.

The latest Teams client also has an additional notification area called "Activity in your other accounts and orgs" that allows the user to be aware of the activities of all the accounts they have in the different tenants (as you can see in Figure 11-14).

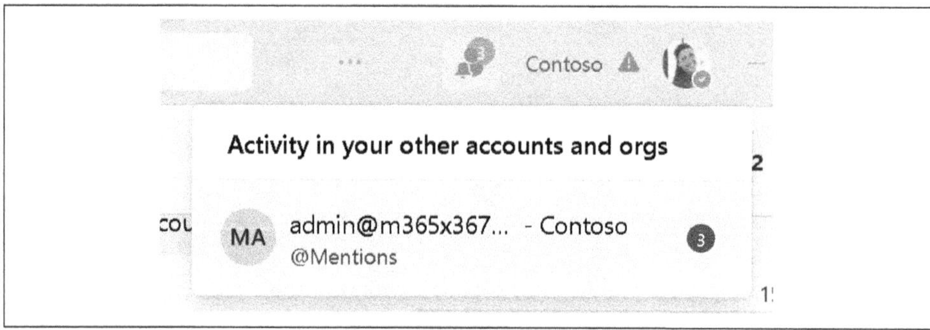

Figure 11-14. Tenant switching with the latest Teams client

11.3 Accepting External Users in Your Organization: Shared Channels

Problem

You need to create shared channels and invite external users.

Solution

In this recipe, you will again use two different tenants and domains. You will act as an administrator in the *M365x01033383.onmicrosoft.com* host domain and grant access to a shared channel for incoming users from the *M365x71772990.onmicrosoft.com* external domain. You will also have to configure the external domain so that shared channels are reachable in an external tenant.

In the Microsoft Entra admin center (*https://oreil.ly/tMIaG*), select External Identities and then "Cross-tenant access settings." Click "Default settings," then, in the "Inbound access settings" section, click "Edit inbound defaults." Change the "B2B direct connect" setting for "External users and groups" to "Allow access."

Click Applications and change the setting to "Allow access." Change the "Applies to" setting to "Select applications," then click "Add Microsoft applications" and select Office 365. Click Save and click Yes in the warning message.

Now for the external domain. In the Microsoft Entra admin center (*https://oreil.ly/BQLdi*), click Entra ID in the left pane. Click External Identities and then "Cross-tenant access settings." In the "Outbound access settings" section, click "Edit outbound defaults." Change the "B2B direct connect" settings for "Users and groups" to "Allow access."

You can use the Select option to limit the access to external shared channels to specific users and groups. This action makes sense for security, compliance, or licensing motivations, depending on your requirements.

Click "External applications." Select "Allow access" and "Select external applications." Click "Add Microsoft applications" and select Office 365. Click Save and click Yes in the warning message.

With a user from the host domain, open the Teams client, select a team (for example, Service Desk), and click "More options" (the ellipsis). Click "Add channel." Type a channel name (for example, Service Desk Shared Channel) and, from the Privacy drop-down menu, select Shared. Then click Create, as shown in Figure 11-15.

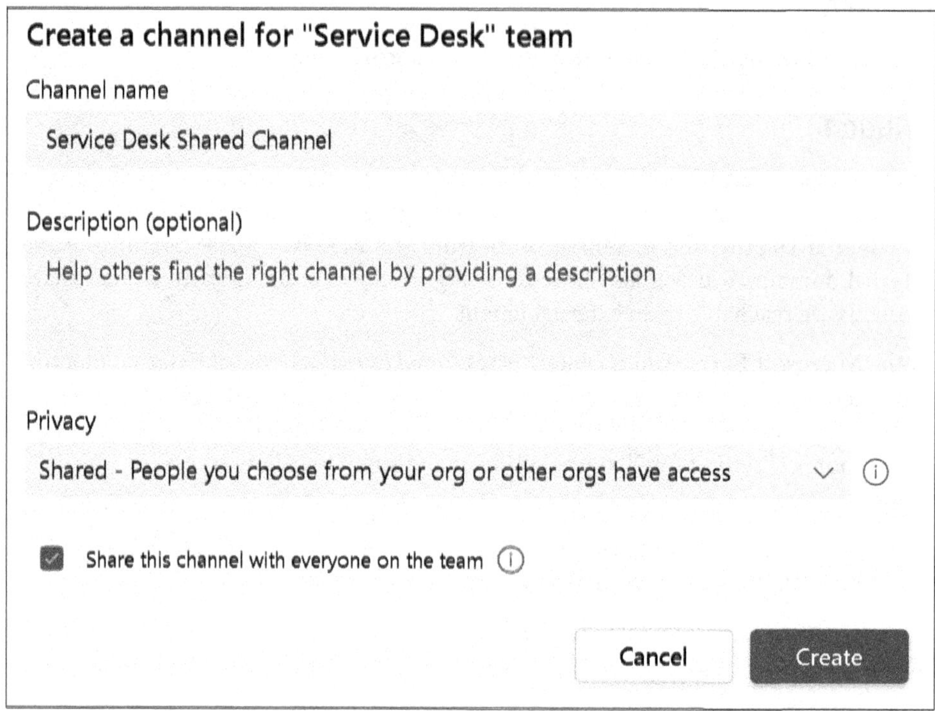

Figure 11-15. Creating a shared channel

Now, you can add users from the external domain to the shared channel (an example is shown in Figure 11-16).

Figure 11-16. Adding an external user as a member of the shared channel

Open the Teams client as the external user (here, Alex Wilber). You will see a notification regarding a new channel shared with you. Upon accepting the invitation, the user will receive a permission request from the host domain.

The user is now able to start collaborating in a channel in the host domain without having to switch accounts.

Discussion

Shared channels use Azure B2B direct connect to grant access to users from an external authentication to your tenant. This direct connection allows external users to work with your users in a Teams channel without having to switch their account (as happens with guest access). The capability to use a B2B direct connect is regulated by the settings for External Identities in Entra ID. The user must be allowed to connect outside their tenant (outbound access settings), but the tenant where the shared channel is located must also allow B2B direct connect for external users (inbound access settings). Figure 11-17 shows the trust mechanism.

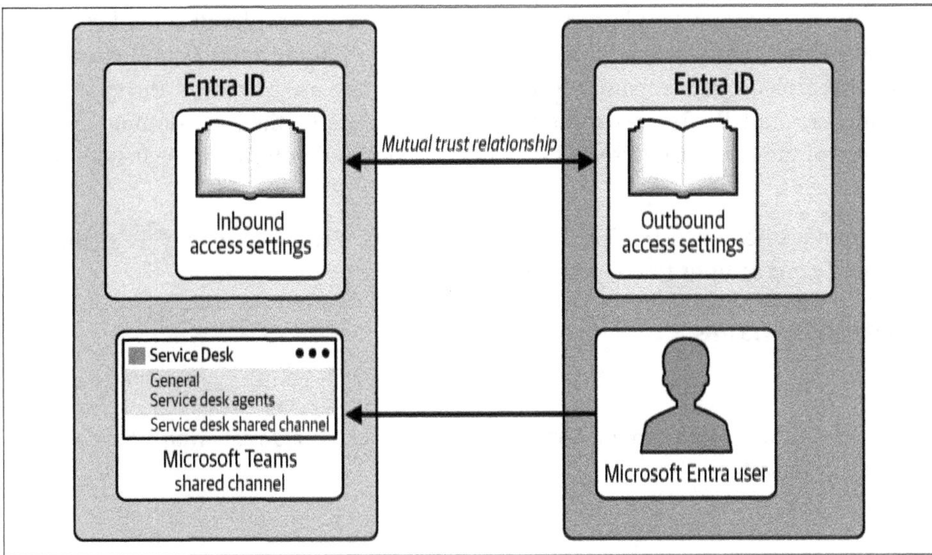

Figure 11-17. Entra ID direct connect diagram

Shared channels are a seamless way to collaborate with external users, but there are some compliance and security considerations that have made the adoption of this solution less widespread than it could be. One of the most relevant points is that the host tenant, where the shared channel is created, owns the channel's data, and so the host's compliance policies will apply. The implication is that administrators must plan how to manage the activities of their users in other tenants that are hosting shared channels.

This kind of planning requires the administrators in the two collaborating domains to agree on the security and compliance policies to be used.

Considering that shared channels integrate with Exchange Online and SharePoint, the agreed compliance and security policies must also involve products outside Teams, making the process more complicated.

11.4 Controlling Communication with Information Barriers

Problem

You need to separate external and internal user communications, creating different segments.

Solution

In the previous recipe, you learned about some of the downsides of shared channels. To mitigate the risk of sharing information with users (both internal and external) in a way that violates your organization's policies, you can use Microsoft Purview Information Barriers (IB). In this solution, you want users of the host domain that are members of the group *Contoso@M365x01033383.onmicrosoft.com* to be inside a dedicated segment.

As a prerequisite, go to the TAC and confirm that "Search by name" is enabled in Teams > Teams settings (see Figure 11-18).

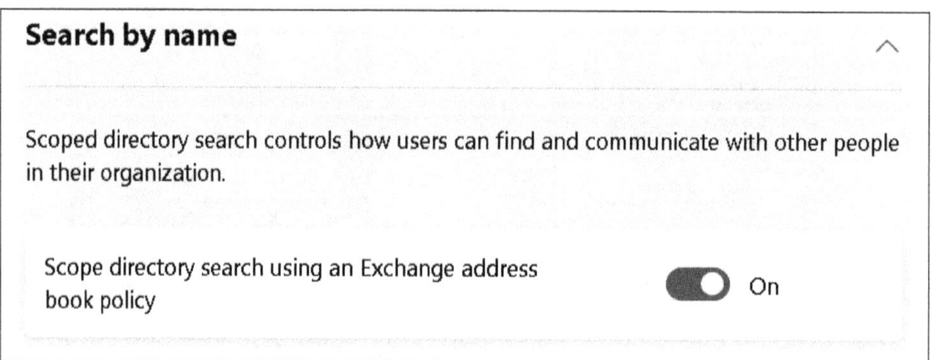

Figure 11-18. Enabling search by name in the TAC

Run the following PowerShell script for the host domain (in the example, *M365x01033383.onmicrosoft.com*):

```
Connect-AzureAD -Tenant "M365x01033383.onmicrosoft.com"
$appId="bcf62038-e005-436d-b970-2a472f8c1982"
$sp=Get-AzureADServicePrincipal -Filter "appid eq '$($appid)'"
if ($sp -eq $null) { New-AzureADServicePrincipal -AppId $appId }
Start-Process  https://login.microsoftonline.com/common/ `
    adminconsent?client_id=$appId
```

After the authentication, a "Permissions requested" screen will be shown. Click Accept.

Open the Purview compliance portal (*https://oreil.ly/wrS3w*) and click "Information barriers," then click "New segment." In the Name field, type *Internal users*. Click Next, then click Add. Select "Member of" from the drop-down menu, then Equal, and type *Contoso@M365x01033383.onmicrosoft.com* (as in Figure 11-19).

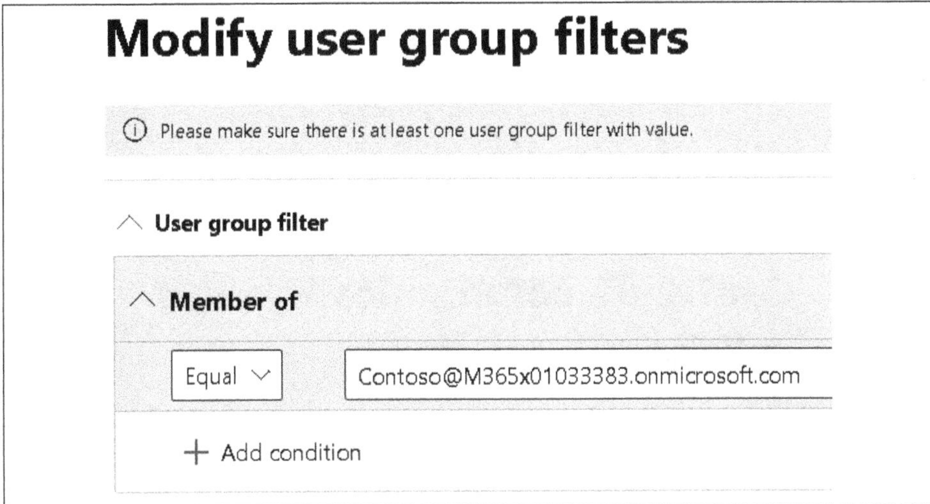

Figure 11-19. Adding a filter for segmentation

Click Next, then click Submit. Click "New segment." In the Name field, type *External users*. Click Next, then Add. Select "Member of" from the drop-down menu, then "Not equal," and type *Contoso@M365x01033383.onmicrosoft.com*.

Click Next, then Submit. Under "Information barriers," select Policies and click "Create policy." For the policy name, type *Teams external segmentation*. Click Next, then click "Choose segment" and select "External users" (see Figure 11-20).

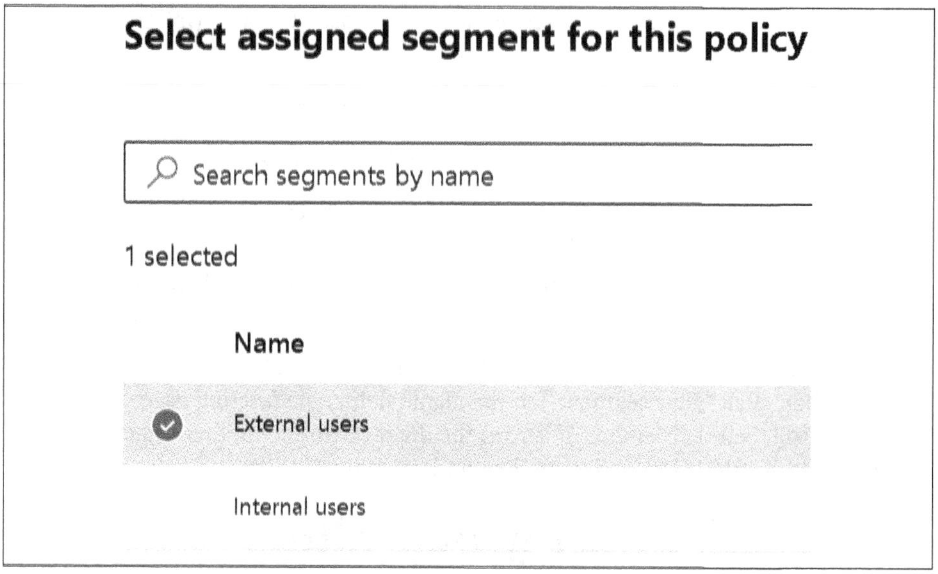

Select assigned segment for this policy

Search segments by name

1 selected

Name

External users

Internal users

Figure 11-20. Assigning the policy to a segment

Click Add, then Next. On the "Configure communication and collaboration details" page, from the "Communication and collaboration" drop-down menu, select Blocked (see Figure 11-21). Click "Choose segment" and select "Internal users."

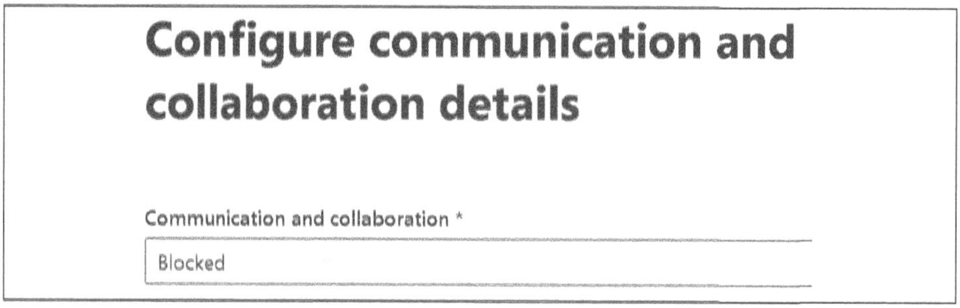

Configure communication and collaboration details

Communication and collaboration *

Blocked

Figure 11-21. Blocking communication between segments

Click Next. On the "Configure policy status" page, select On, click Next, then click Submit. Under "Information barriers," select Policies and click "Create policy." As the policy name, type *Teams internal segmentation*. Click Next, then click "Chose segment." Select "Internal users" and click Add.

Click Next. On the "Configure communication and collaboration details" page, from the "Communication and collaboration" drop-down menu, select Blocked. Click "Choose segment" and select "External users," as in Figure 11-22.

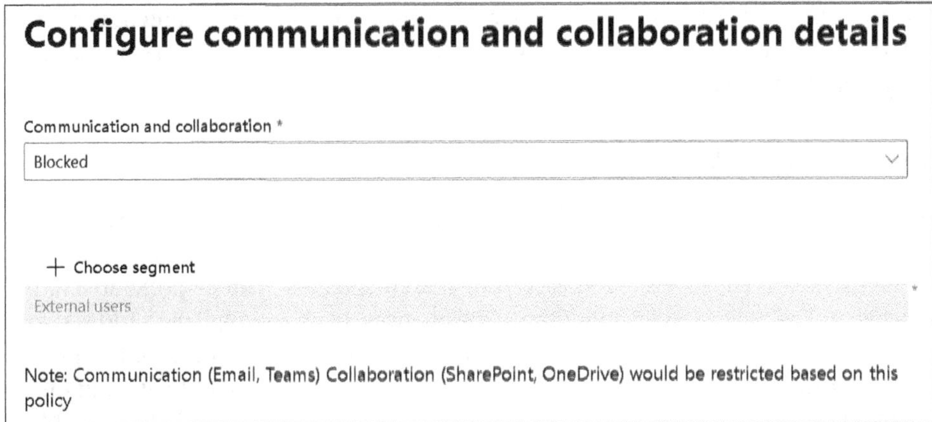

Figure 11-22. Applying the policy to the required segment

Click Next. On the "Configure policy status" page, select On, click Next, then click Submit.

A user can only be in one segment, and each segment can have only one IB policy applied. Policies must be defined in both directions, or they will not be applied. That is why you must create two policies: one to block communication from the external users' segment to the internal one, and one to block communication from the internal users' segment to the external one.

Now click "Policy application" and select "Apply all policies." When the process is complete, progress will be set to 100. The policy will limit the communication from the external users to the users in the host domain.

Discussion

Applying IB in Teams, where two users are in different segments and there is a block policy applied between them, will block the following features:

- Adding a user to a team or channel
- User access to team or channel content
- User access to 1:1 and group chats
- User access to meetings
- Lookups and discovery (users won't be visible in the people picker)

If a user's IB policy changes and their access to chats, activities, and content is restricted, the previously accessible content will be locked, or the user will be removed from the groups that violate the policy.

11.5 Summary

In this chapter, you have learned about the three different ways to interact with external users in Teams. Depending on the scenario, one of the available communication modalities (external access, guest access, or shared channels) will be preferable to the other two. You have learned about the consequences, from a compliance and security point of view, of interacting with external users in Teams. A balanced approach between ease of use and controlled access is required. Planning and agreeing on an approach to compliance between different tenants is mandatory before enabling external access.

In the next chapter, we'll cover improving user productivity in Teams and automating apps and bots to make information and features more accessible.

CHAPTER 12

Productivity in Microsoft Teams

Teams is built in a way that makes integration of apps and bots with the client easy and straightforward. The *App* directory offers hundreds of apps, both from Microsoft and from third parties, to improve user experience and productivity. There are many examples of small bots (like Who (*https://oreil.ly/p2ySI*)) and apps (like Employee Ideas (*https://oreil.ly/edMTF*)) that aim to reduce the effort required for users to execute tasks and collaborate. Some additional examples are available on the "App templates for Microsoft Teams" page (*https://oreil.ly/u2m4S*).

This chapter focuses on some features, apps, and bots that have an impact on the way information is gathered, catalogued, and made available in Teams. It is important to understand that some of the recipes here leverage the progress made in the field of AI to execute repetitive tasks in a smarter way.

12.1 Improving Microsoft Teams with Microsoft Syntex

Problem

You want to automatically label information in Teams using AI.

Solution

Microsoft Syntex is an AI solution that discovers, assembles, classifies, and reproduces content by integrating Microsoft 365 apps like Teams and SharePoint. As soon as documents and images are uploaded to its library, Syntex extracts, analyzes, and categorizes the data. Syntex can also automatically apply retention and compliance to document labels.

In this recipe, you will train a Syntex model and apply it to a Microsoft 365 tenant. For this solution, I have uploaded a few documents found online that contain laundry prices. These are listed in the Communications team, General channel, and are meant to be used as training material for Syntex.

First, in the Microsoft 365 admin center (*https://oreil.ly/auFoe*), select Setup, then view "Files and content."

Select "Use content AI with Microsoft Syntex," then Manage Microsoft Syntex (as you can see in Figure 12-1).

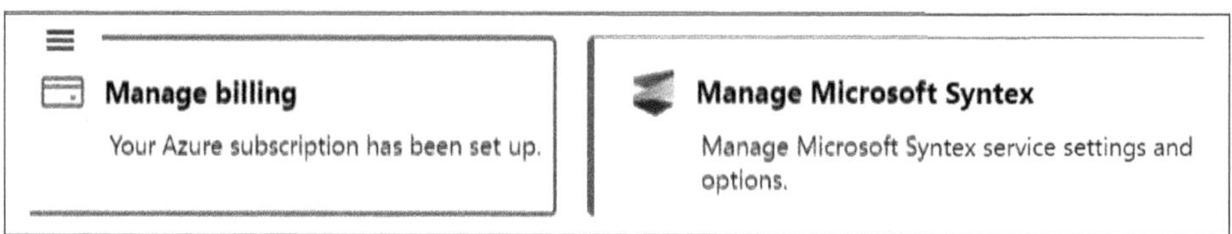

Figure 12-1. Setting up Syntex

Syntex requires a dedicated license and billing configuration. On the "Use content AI with Microsoft Syntex" screen, you'll be required to set up the billing using an Azure subscription. The subscription must also include a resource group.

On the "Create content center" page, type *Syntex Content Center* and click Next (see Figure 12-2).

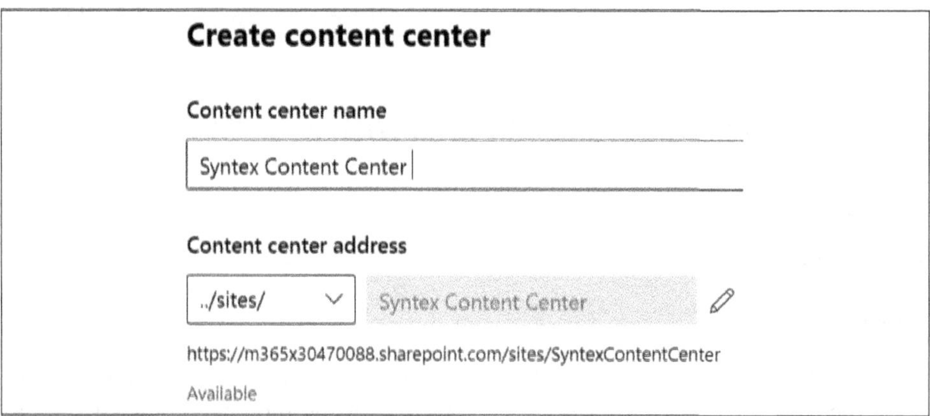

Figure 12-2. Creating the content center in SharePoint

The SharePoint site you have just defined is the default content center for your organization. Administrators can view analytics about the form processing and document analyzing models they have deployed in the tenant. Members of the site can build SharePoint Syntex models, as well. Additional content center sites can be created from the SharePoint admin center.

On the "Review and finish" page, click Activate. Click Done when the setup is complete, then click Manage Microsoft Syntex. From the "Content center" page, open the Syntex Content Center by clicking the link at the bottom of the page (see Figure 12-3).

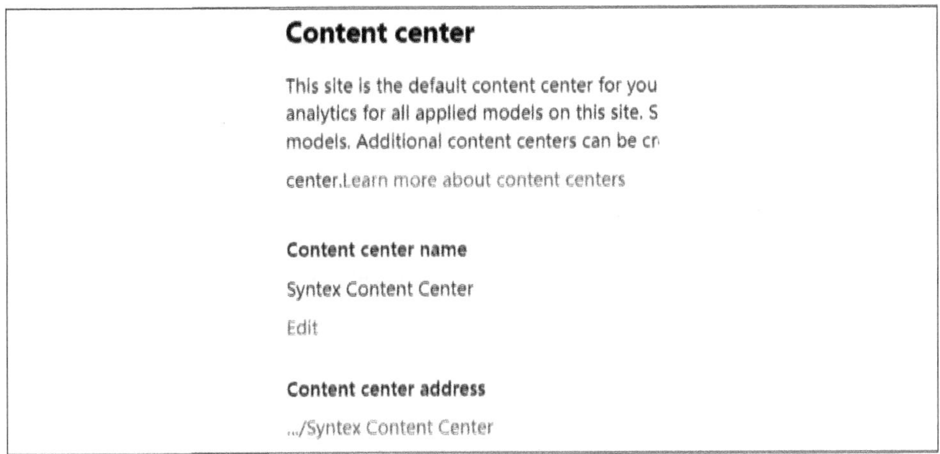

Content center
This site is the default content center for you
analytics for all applied models on this site. S
models. Additional content centers can be cr
center.Learn more about content centers
Content center name
Syntex Content Center
Edit
Content center address
.../Syntex Content Center

Figure 12-3. Opening the Syntex Content Center

Syntex offers three prebuilt models: contracts, invoices, and receipt. In our recipe, the documents we are going to use do not match any of the existing categories, so we must create a custom model. Open the Syntex Content Center and click Models > "Create a model" (as in Figure 12-4).

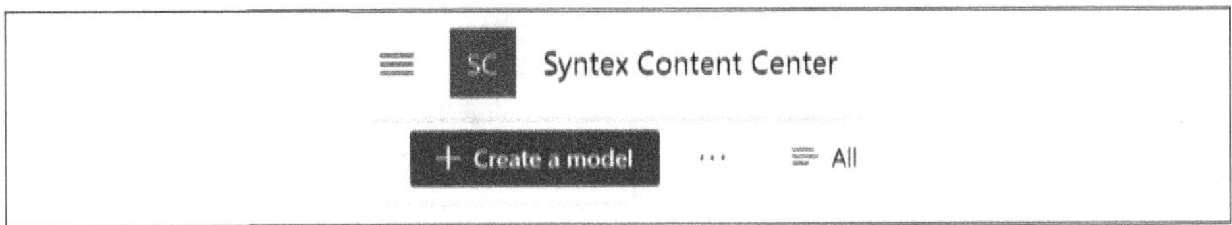

Figure 12-4. Creating a model in Syntex

Select "Train a custom model." On the next page, "Teaching method: Details," click Next. Type a name for the model (in our solution, we'll name the model *Laundry Prices*) and click Create (see Figure 12-5).

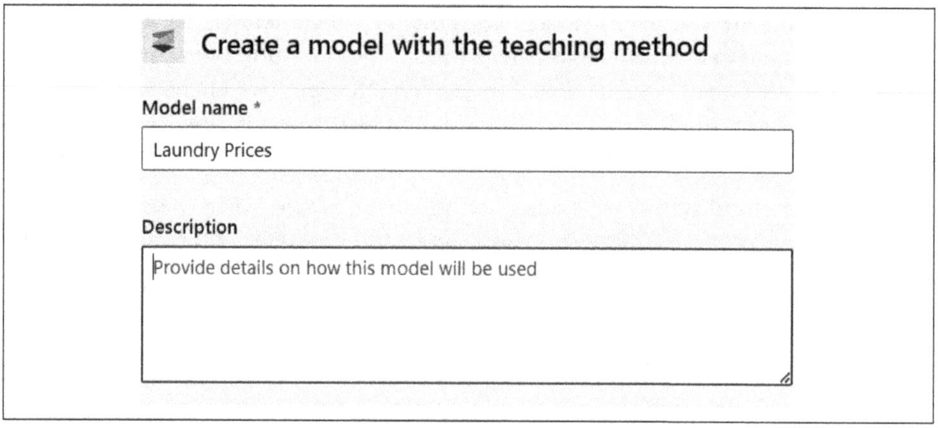

Create a model with the teaching method

Model name *

Laundry Prices

Description

Provide details on how this model will be used

Figure 12-5. Naming the new model in Syntex

All the required steps are shown on the Models > Laundry Prices page (Figure 12-6). Start with the "Add example files" box and click "Add files."

Figure 12-6. First actions for the new model

On the "Select example files for your model" page, select at least five files to train your model on, and click Add. Back on the Laundry Prices model page, click "Train classifier." The first step, Label, will require you to confirm, for each training file, "Is this file an example of Laundry Prices?" (see Figure 12-7). You must also provide at least one file that is a negative example.

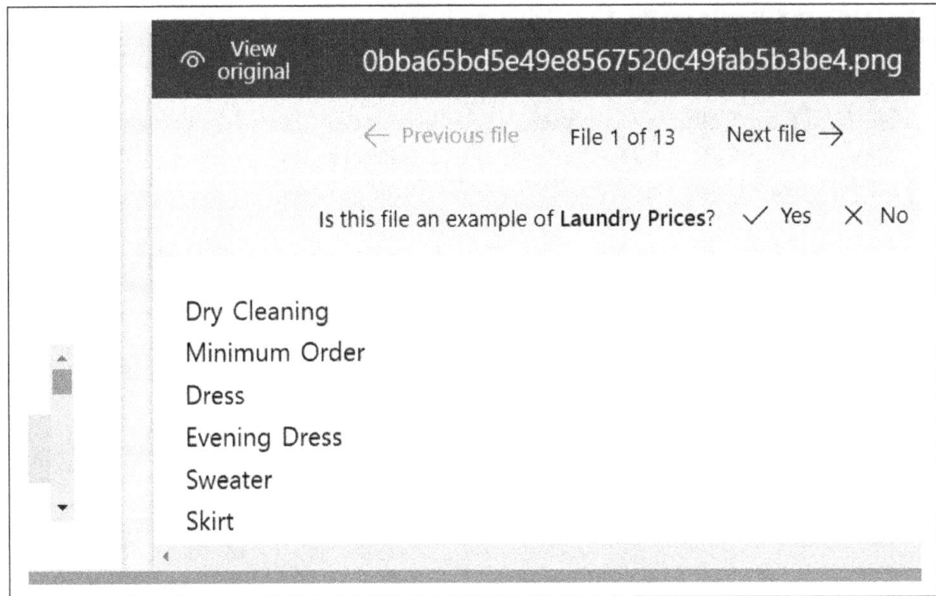

Figure 12-7. Selecting example files for model training

When the selection is complete, click Train.

You must now configure explanations (ways for the model to categorize the information). Click New and select Blank or "From a template." Start with Blank. On the "Create an explanation" page, enter a name for the explanation (for example, *Shirt*). Select "Phrase list" from the drop-down menu and add all the words that could indicate a shirt in the laundry prices list (for example, *Shirt*, *Shirt-Hanging*, *T-shirt*, *Shirts—Silk*, *Shirts-Folded*, and *Dress Shirt*). See Figure 12-8 for an example. Click Save when you're done.

Create an explanation
Explanations help identify the type of document extract.
Name *
Shirt
Explanation type
Phrase list

Figure 12-8. Creating an explanation

Click New and Blank again. Add a new explanation named *Suit*. Select "Phrase list" from the drop-down menu and add all the words and phrases that could be a positive match (for example, *2 Piece Suit, 3 Piece Suit*). Click "Save and train," then click "Train model." When the training is complete, click Test. Under "Test files," click "Add example files." Based on the model, the files will be categorized as positive or negative. If the model is working as expected, click Exit Training (Figure 12-9).

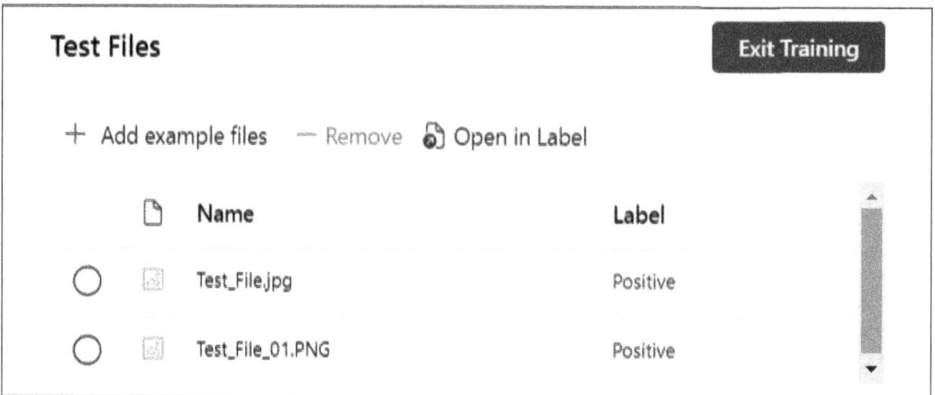

Figure 12-9. Testing the model

Now, click "Create extractor" in the "Create and train extractors" box. On the "New entity extractor" page, type a name in the "New name" box (in this recipe, we'll use the name *LaundryPricesExtractor*, as shown in Figure 12-10) and click Create.

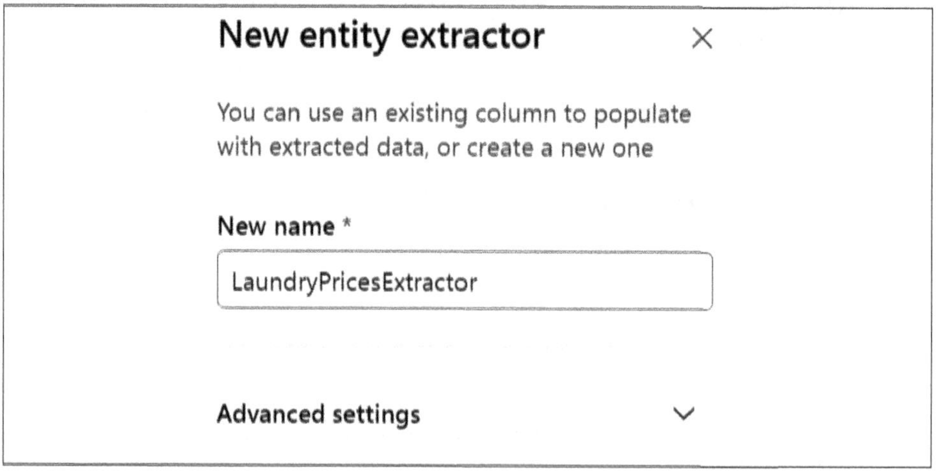

Figure 12-10. Creating an extractor

For each document, select the text that matches the model, as shown in Figure 12-11, or check the "No label" box.

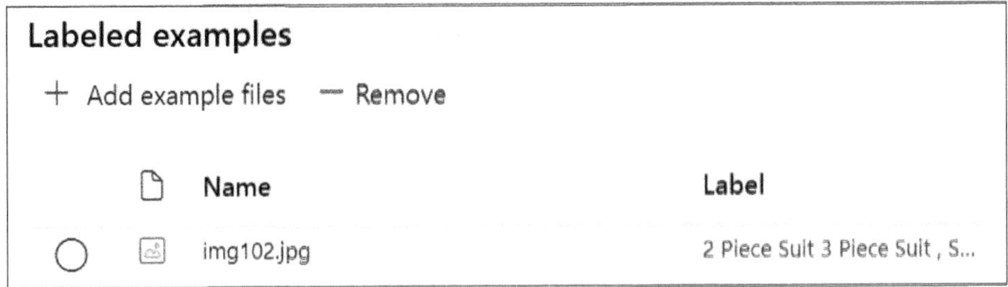

Figure 12-11. Selecting text in the files

Click Train and create explanations as before. Click "Train model." Click Test, then click "Exit training." Finally, click "Apply model." Select a SharePoint library in which to apply the model (for example, Migration > Documents, as in Figure 12-12, and click Apply.

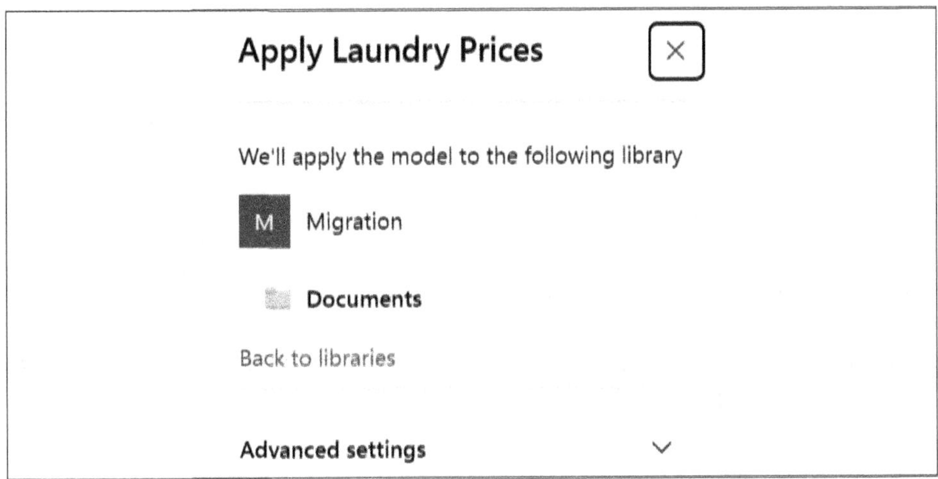

Figure 12-12. Applying the Syntex model to a library

When this step is complete, click "Go to library." Any new document uploaded in the selected team (Communication) will be classified and tags will be added. Back in the Syntex Content Center, you can see how your models are performing when applied to your document libraries (as shown in Figure 12-13).

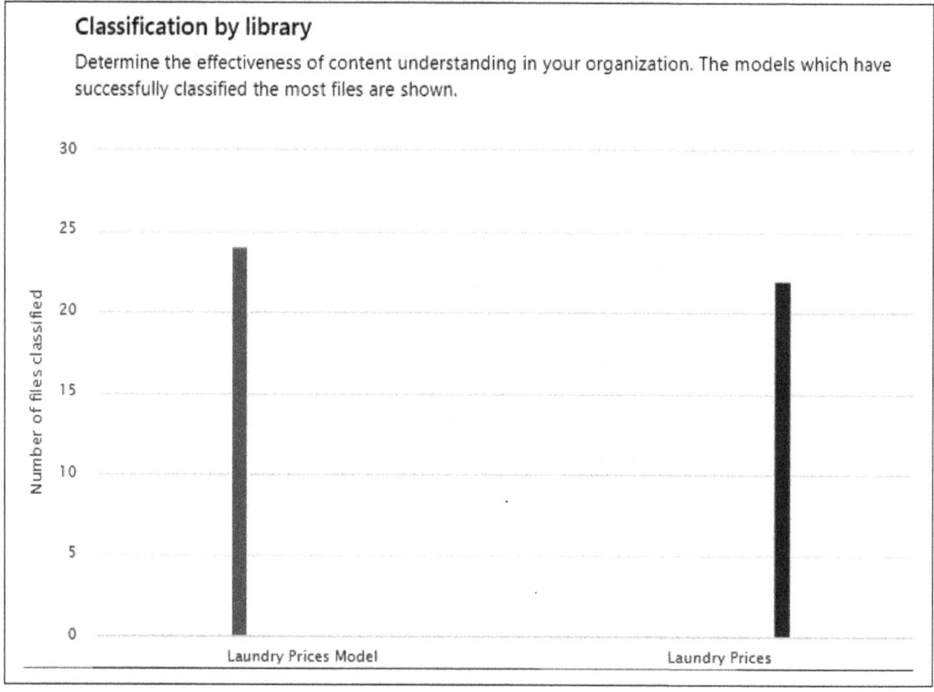

Figure 12-13. Analyzing model performance in Syntex

In the Teams client, upon opening the library where the model is applied, we have new tabs that help identify and manage the documents (as you can see in Figure 12-14).

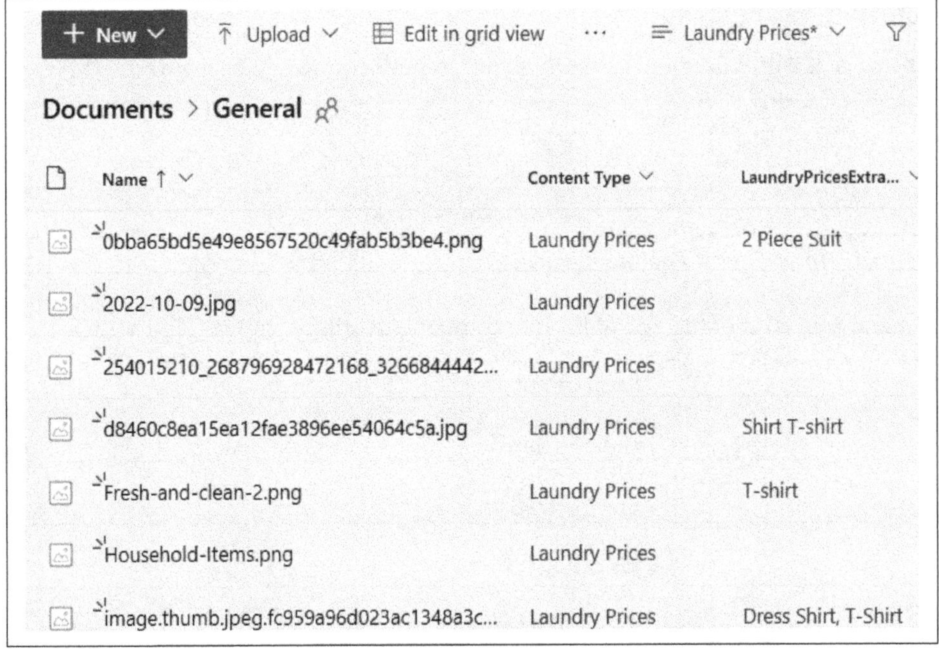

Figure 12-14. Documents classified by the Syntex model

Discussion

Microsoft Syntex helps reduce the amount of time spent examining documents, removing the need to open them and check whether the information you require is there. Organizations often keep relevant information about their business on their own intranet, so using an AI solution to extract and catalogue information (creating metadata) has value.

Syntex can be used in different ways. It can use a classifier to automatically tag documents with a specific format and contents (and then apply policies based on the tags). Its extractor capabilities are used to pull out information from documents and store them in SharePoint columns (which is what we did in this solution).

12.2 Integrating Loop with Microsoft Teams

Problem

You want to add features in the Teams client using Microsoft's collaboration tool Loop.

Solution

Open a chat with a user and select the Loop components icon (see Figure 12-15).

Figure 12-15. Adding a Loop component

A menu with a list of the available Loop components will be shown (Figure 12-16).

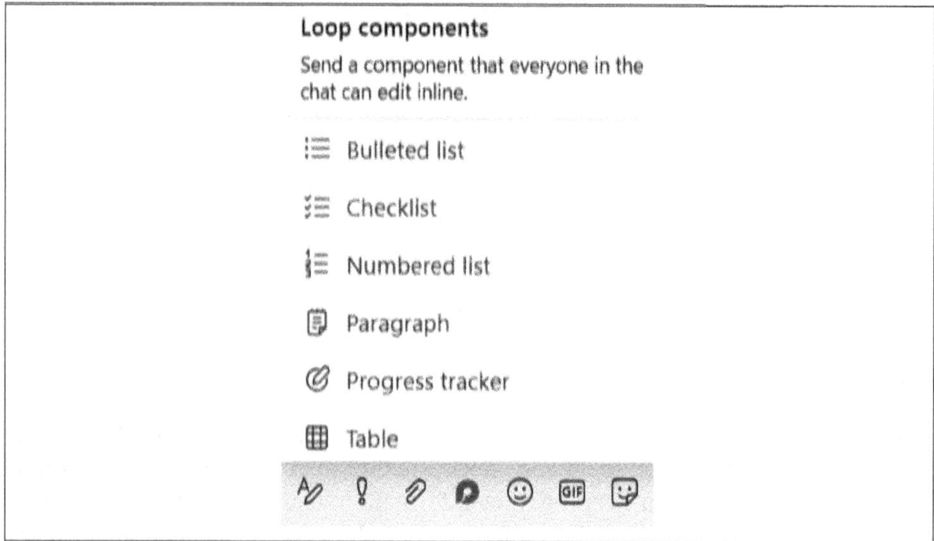

Figure 12-16. Available Loop components

Select Table from the "Loop components" menu. Edit the table to have a row of headers and some text in each cell (as in Figure 12-17). You can simply drag the columns to resize them.

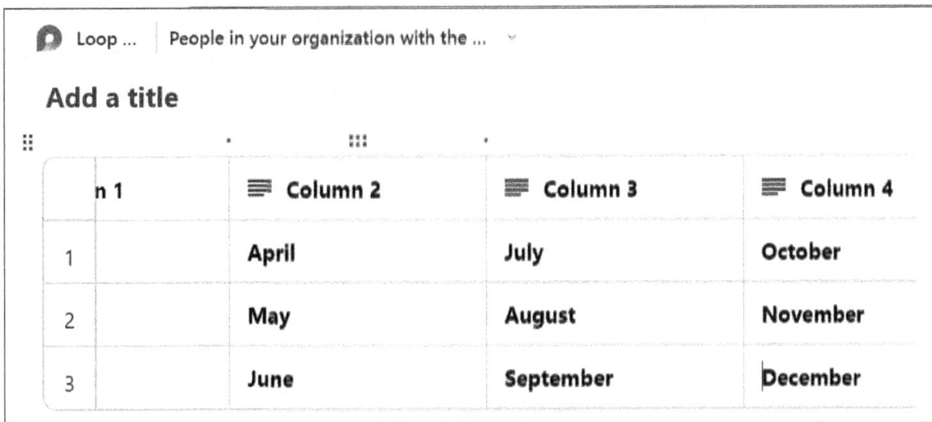

Figure 12-17. Customizing a Loop table

The menu on top allows you to set sharing permissions for the Loop component (an example is shown in Figure 12-18).

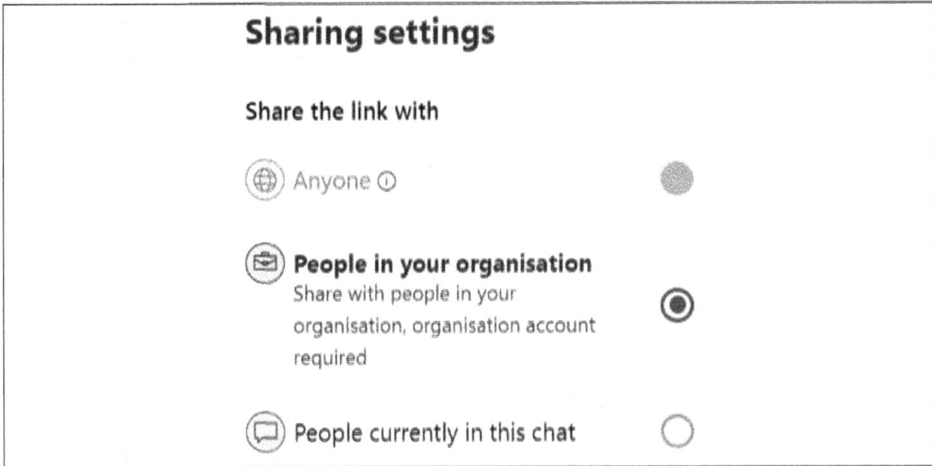

Figure 12-18. Setting permissions for the Loop component

When the component is correctly set up, you can publish it by clicking the "Send Loop component" icon in the lower-right corner.

It is possible to nest Loop components within one another. Type a forward slash (/), and a pop-out menu will appear to allow you to choose a Loop component to insert. Add a / in one of the cells and select Image (see Figure 12-19).

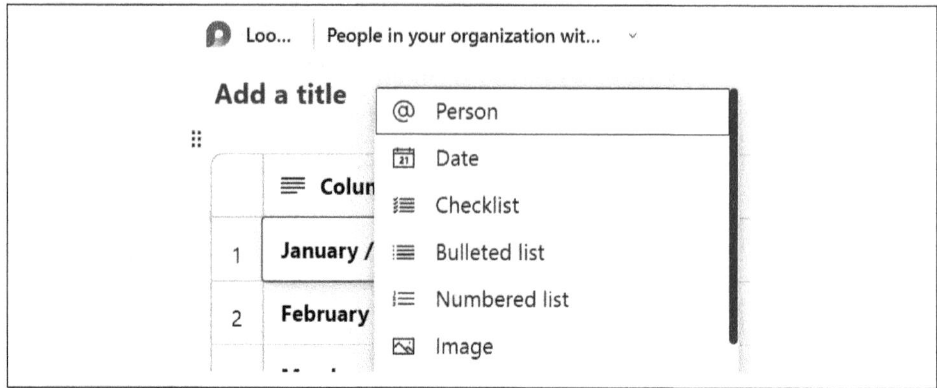

Figure 12-19. Nesting Loop components

By clicking the name of the Loop component (in the top-left corner), you can open it in the browser. Working in the browser gives you a better view of the components (Figure 12-20 shows the browser interface).

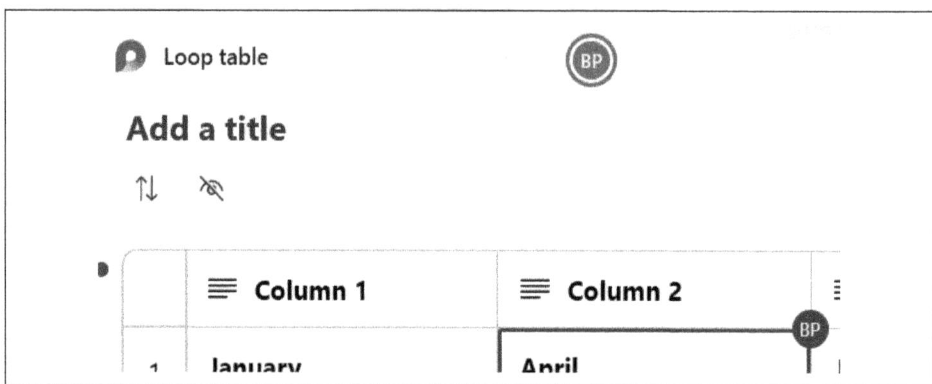

Figure 12-20. Working in the browser at the same time as other users

You can see what actions the other users are performing on the Loop component in real time.

Discussion

Loop components are little collaboration objects that you can add to Microsoft 365 apps. Loop allows you to see the same object (for example, an agenda) across various Microsoft apps, such as Outlook, Teams, OneNote, Excel, and Word. The process is based on the Fluid development framework (live components). Fluid is a collection of client libraries that allow multiple clients to simultaneously create and operate on shared data. Loop can be used both as a standalone app and inside other apps in the form of embeddable components.

Loop is made up of three elements:

Loop components
: Interactive canvases that move freely between apps and provide more flexibility when collaborating on and sharing different types of content across Microsoft 365 apps. Microsoft has developed ready-to-use Loop components such as the ones that you used in the previous recipe.

Loop pages
: Flexible canvases where users can organize various components and pull in elements like links, files, or data.

Loop workspaces
: Shared areas or spaces. Workspaces make it easy for users to catch up on what everyone is working on.

12.3 Creating Power Automate Flows with AI Builder

Problem

You want to add automation in Teams using AI.

Solution

AI Builder is a Microsoft Power Platform capability that allows you to add AI to Power Apps and Power Automate. You can train both prebuilt AI models (like the language detection model) and custom AI models (like the object detection model).

At the time of writing, AI Builder is available only for environments created in the United States.

First, go to the Power Platform admin center (*https://oreil.ly/8cmSr*), click Environments, and select New (see Figure 12-21).

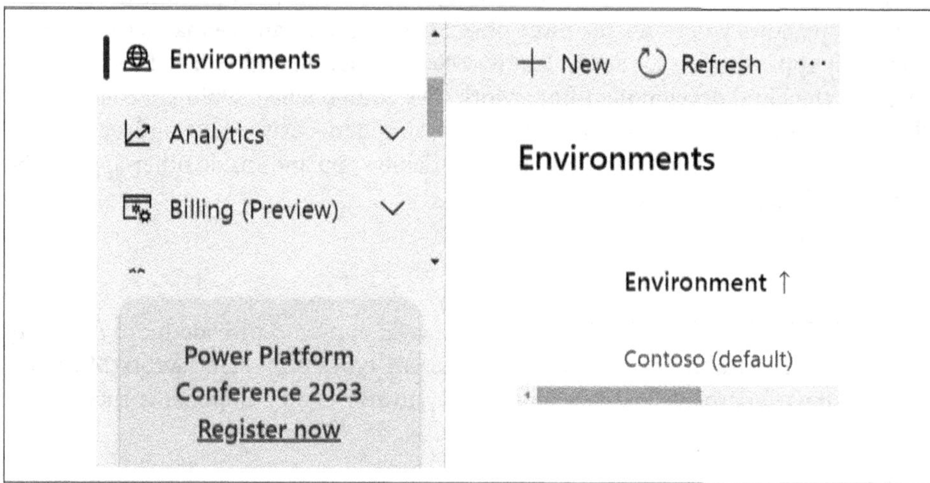

Figure 12-21. Defining the new environment

Type *PreviewEnvironment* in the Name field, select United States from the Region drop-down menu, and select Trial from the Type drop-down menu, as shown in Figure 12-22. Activate the "Add a Dataverse data store" option, and click Next.

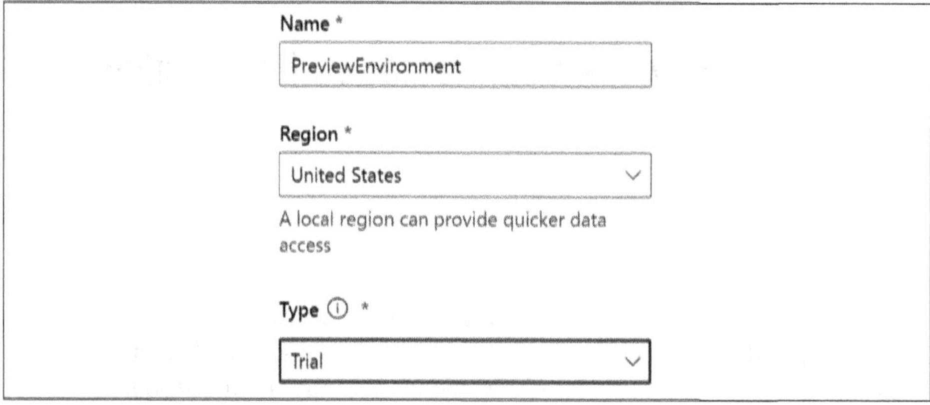

Figure 12-22. Setting up the new environment

On the "Add Dataverse" page, select a security group (for example, Contoso, as in Figure 12-23) and click Save.

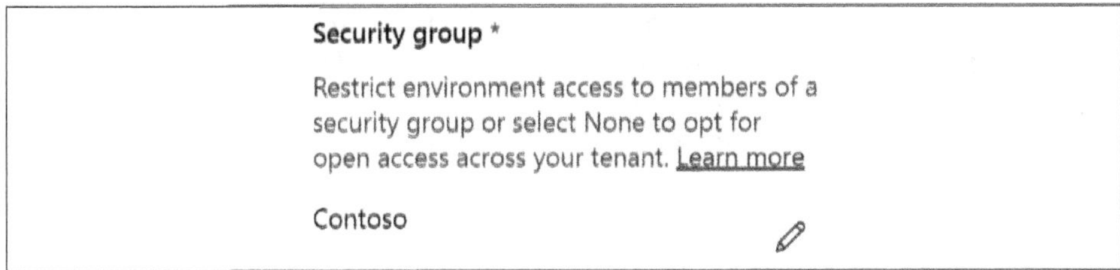

Figure 12-23. Adding the security group

On the "Add database" screen, click Add. When the PreviewEnvironment is ready, open the Power Automate page (*https://oreil.ly/MrAGI*) and select it as the environment in the top-right corner (Figure 12-24).

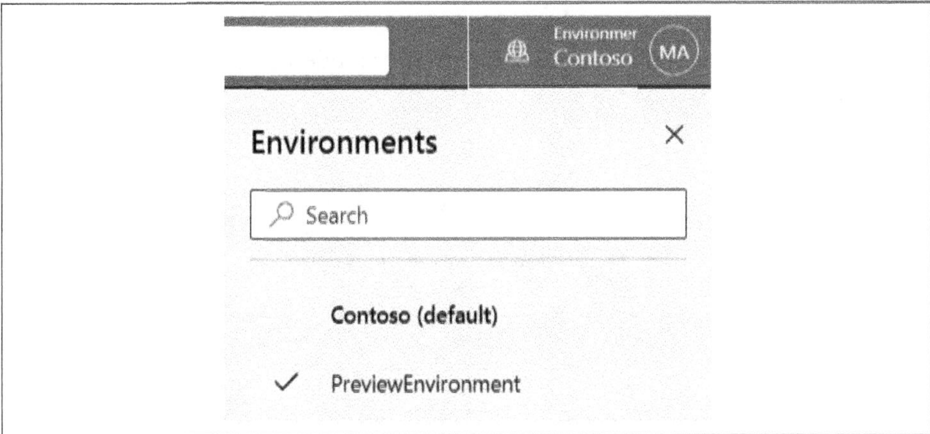

Figure 12-24. Accessing the new environment

Click Create and select "Describe it to design it" (as in Figure 12-25).

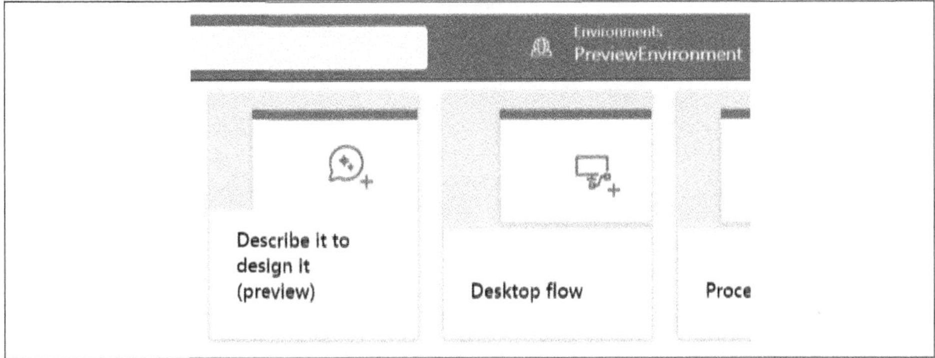

Figure 12-25. Creating the flow with AI Builder

In the "Describe your flow in everyday words" field, type *Create a new team in Teams when an email with the subject "New team request" is received* (see Figure 12-26).

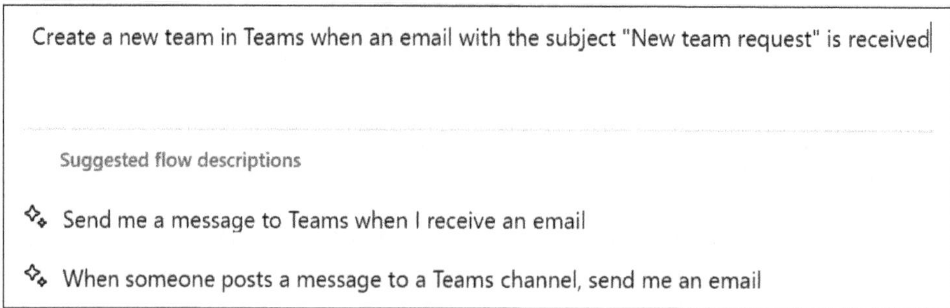

Figure 12-26. Describing the flow to AI Builder

AI Builder will suggest a flow compatible with your request (the result will be like the one in Figure 12-27).

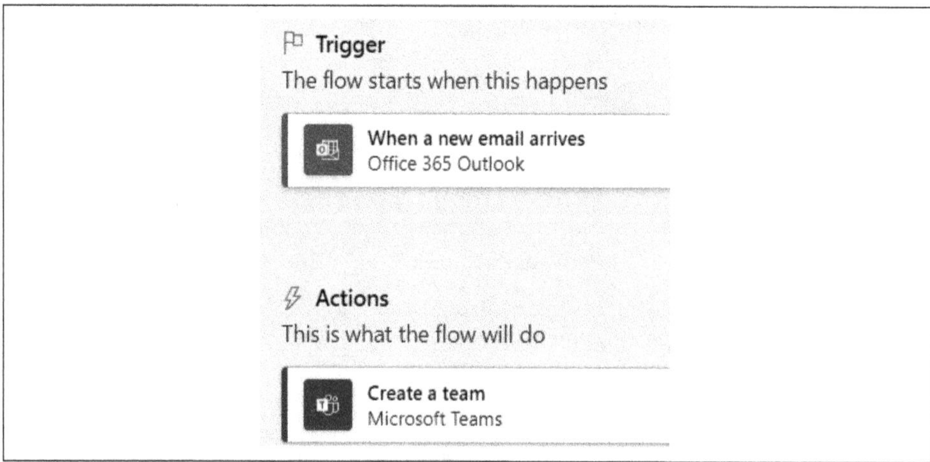

Figure 12-27. AI Builder suggestion for flow

Click the suggested flow and select Next. After the permissions check (shown in Figure 12-28), click Next again.

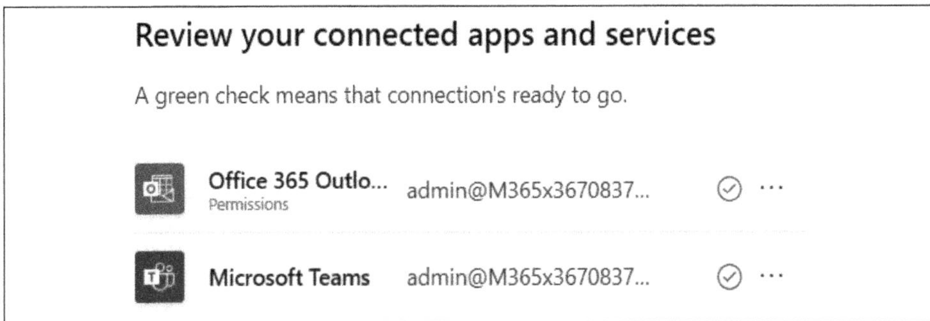

Figure 12-28. Checking the required permissions

In the Microsoft Teams Description field, type *New Team Defined with Power Automate*. Click Create Flow and fill in the required fields for the "Create a team" step (see Figure 12-29).

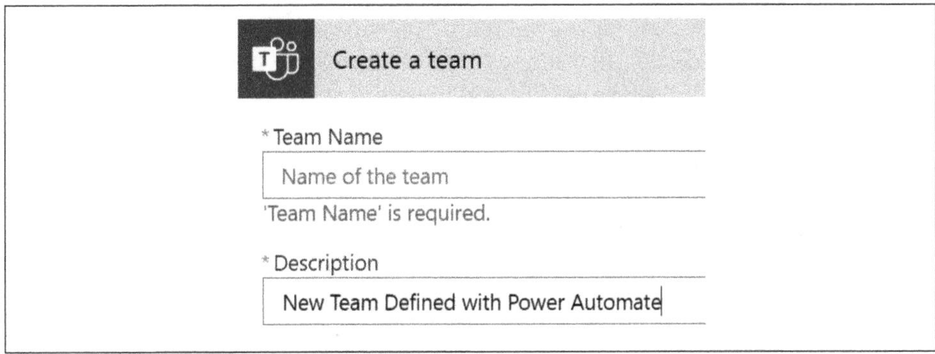

Figure 12-29. Creating the new flow

Now you can customize the flow as required and integrate it with your Teams processes (like in Figure 12-30).

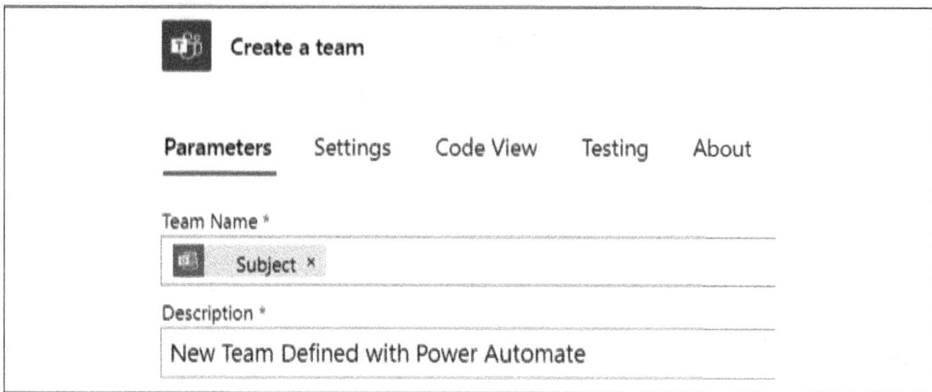

Figure 12-30. Customizing the flow using the suggested template

Discussion

AI Builder in Power Automate is powered by OpenAI's Codex, the code-generating machine learning system underpinning GitHub Copilot. The original purpose of Codex was to suggest new lines of code and functions, starting with a few snippets of existing code. Codex is the system used to generate suggestions for the flow creation in AI Builder. The flow recommendations from Codex, after the appropriate connectors are deployed, can be customized within the flow designer. AI Builder can also train AI systems so that Power Automate can pull data from documents.

12.4 Adding Personal Apps to Microsoft Teams

Problem

You want to deploy personalized contents inside the Teams client tabs using a personal app.

Solution

Open the Microsoft Teams Developer Portal (*https://oreil.ly/wvSDG*) in your browser. Click Apps, then "New app" (see Figure 12-31).

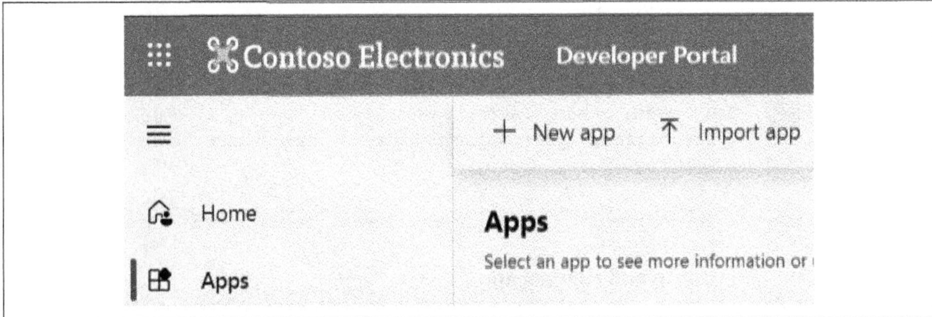

Figure 12-31. New app in the Teams Developer Portal

In the Name field, type *Personal App 1.1* (as in Figure 12-32).

Figure 12-32. Naming the new app

Complete all the mandatory (starred) fields in the "Basic information" tab with text or URLs. Click "App features" and select "Personal app" (see Figure 12-33).

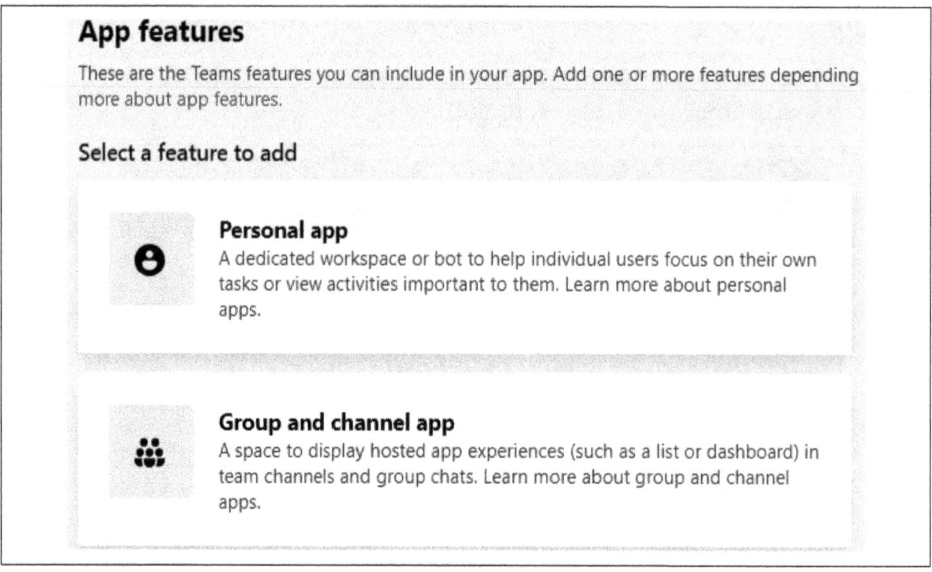

App features
These are the Teams features you can include in your app. Add one or more features depending
more about app features.
Select a feature to add
Personal app
A dedicated workspace or bot to help individual users focus on their own tasks or view activities important to them. Learn more about personal apps.
Group and channel app
A space to display hosted app experiences (such as a list or dashboard) in team channels and group chats. Learn more about group and channel apps.

Figure 12-33. Creating a personal app

Click the "Create your first personal app" tab. In this solution, the first personal app tab will be named UNESCO. The Content URL will be *https://www.unesco.org/en*. An Entity ID is automatically generated, as seen in Figure 12-34. Click Confirm.

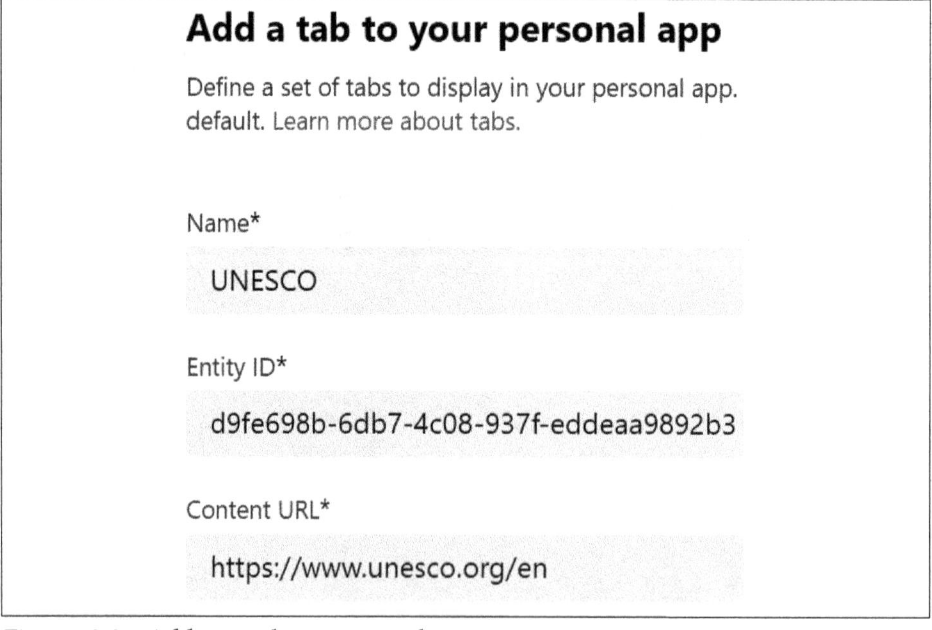

Figure 12-34. Adding a tab to a personal app

Click Save, then "Add a personal app" (as in Figure 12-35).

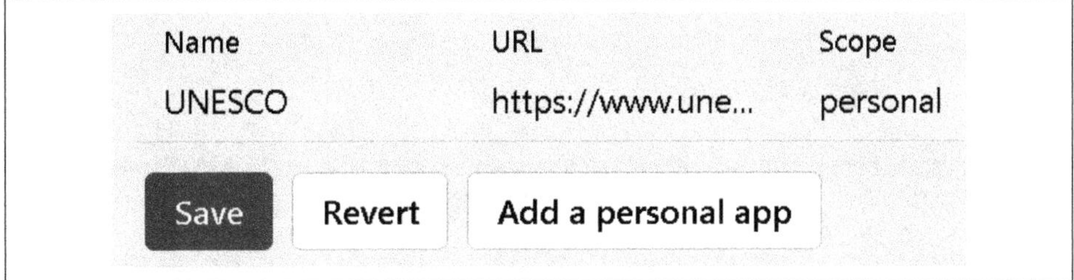

Figure 12-35. Saving the tab and adding an additional one

Repeat the previous process for Defence Blog (*https://defence-blog.com*) and Unicef (*https://www.unicef.org.uk*). The personal app will now present three different tabs (as in Figure 12-36).

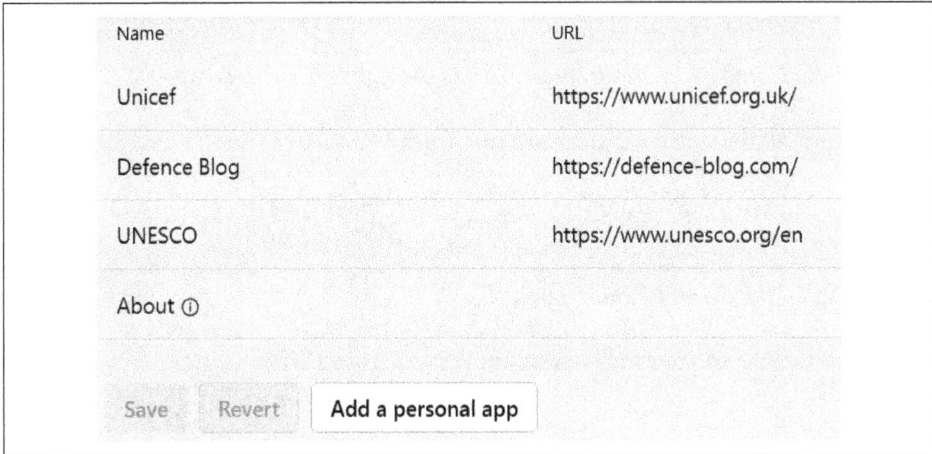

Figure 12-36. Customized personal app

The Domains tab will be automatically populated with the domains used in your personal app tabs (as shown in Figure 12-37).

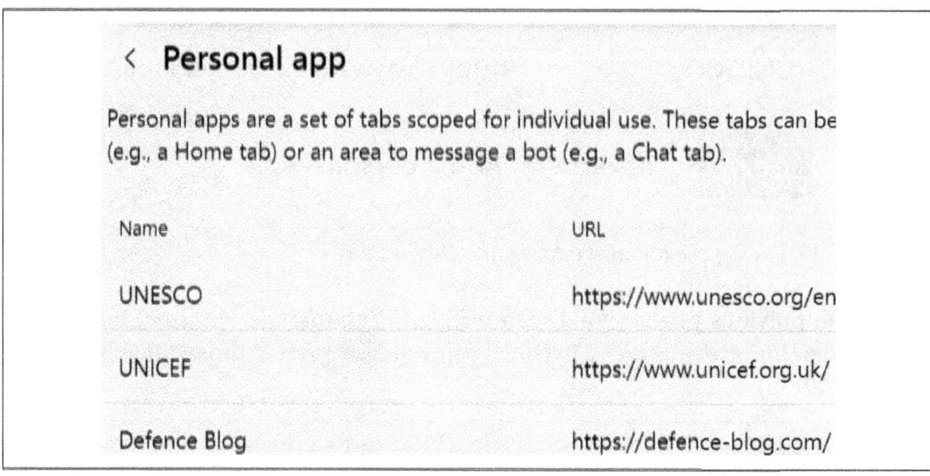

Figure 12-37. Domains needed from the Teams client for the personal app

Click Publish in the upper-right corner (see Figure 12-38).

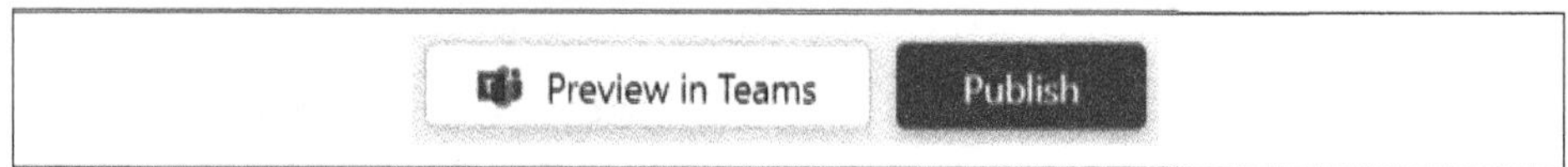

Figure 12-38. Preview and Publish options

Select the "Publish to your org" option shown in Figure 12-39.

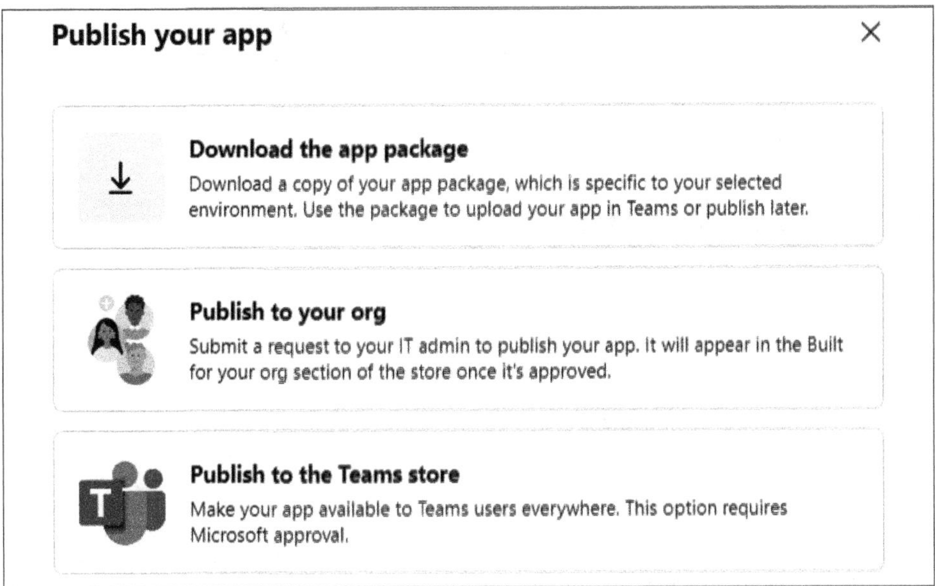

Figure 12-39. The publishing options for the app

Click "Publish your app." The app will be shown as Submitted (see Figure 12-40).

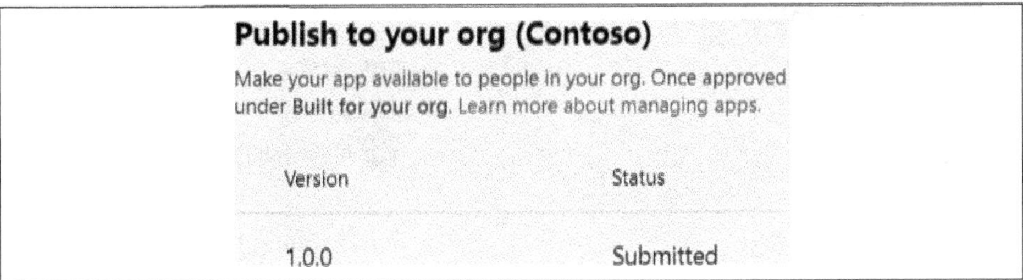

Figure 12-40. App submitted

Go to the TAC and open "Teams apps," then click "Manage apps." In the "Search by name" field, type *Personal App*, then select the app (shown in Figure 12-41).

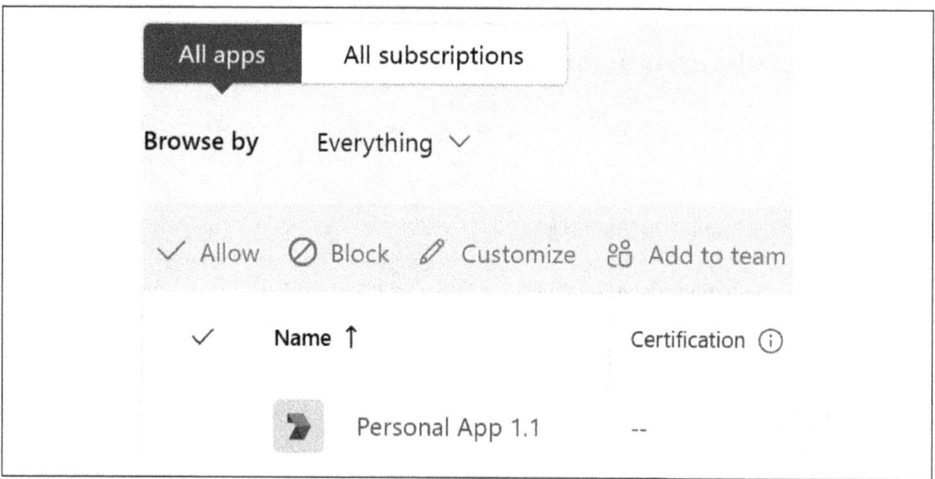

Figure 12-41. Pending approval of a personal Teams app

Open Personal App 1.1 and click Publish, then Publish again (as in Figure 12-42).

Figure 12-42. Publishing the personal app

Now, from the Teams client, click Apps and in the Search field (shown in Figure 12-43), type *Personal App*.

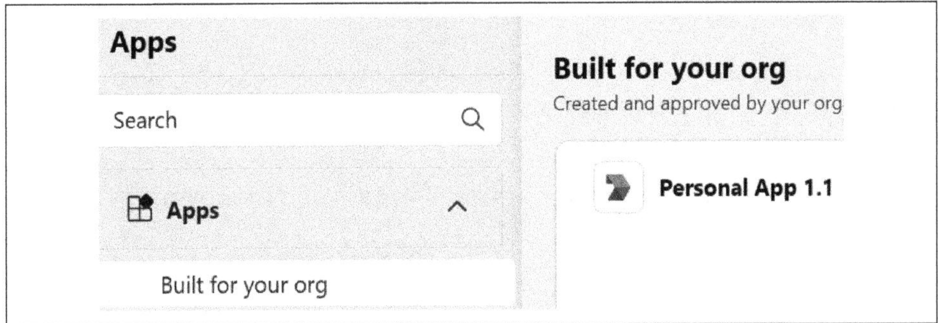

Figure 12-43. Locating the app in the Teams client

Install the app and open it. The tabs connected to the different websites will show the contents (as shown in Figure 12-44).

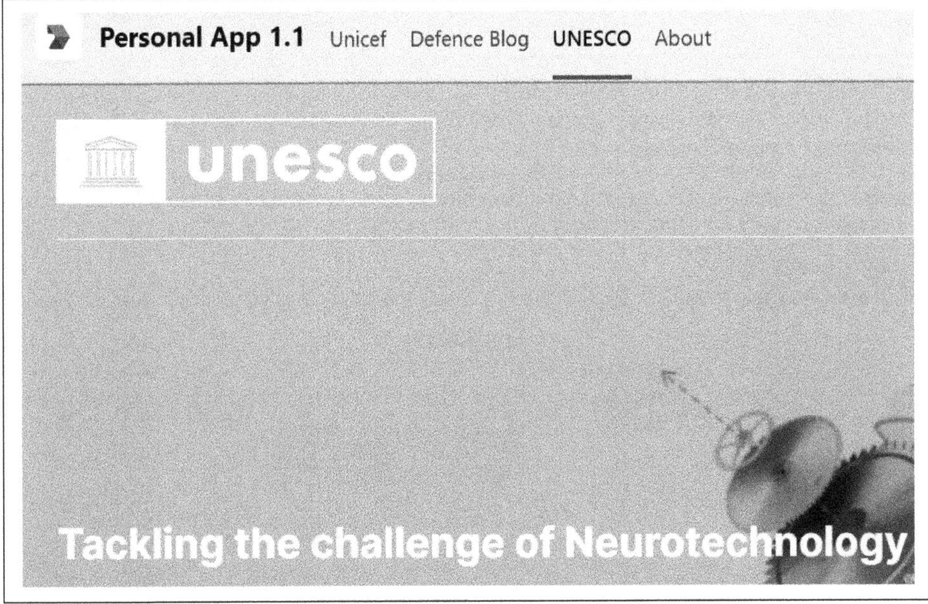

Figure 12-44. Active tabs connected to the selected websites

Discussion

Some apps, such as OneNote in the Teams client, can give you a private workspace, outside the team or channel (see Figure 12-45).

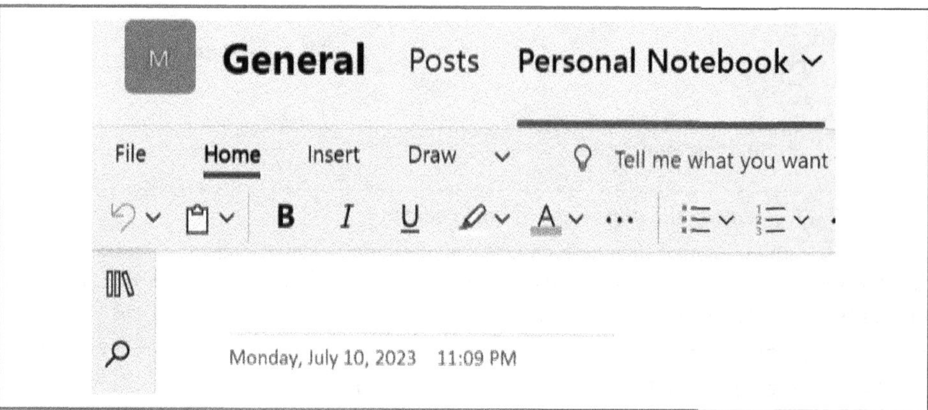

Figure 12-45. Private workspace in Teams

A personal app can also be a bot.

Some of the shared apps can support a personal apps view. This capability is listed in the "App features" paragraph when you install them (Figure 12-46 shows the app features for OneNote).

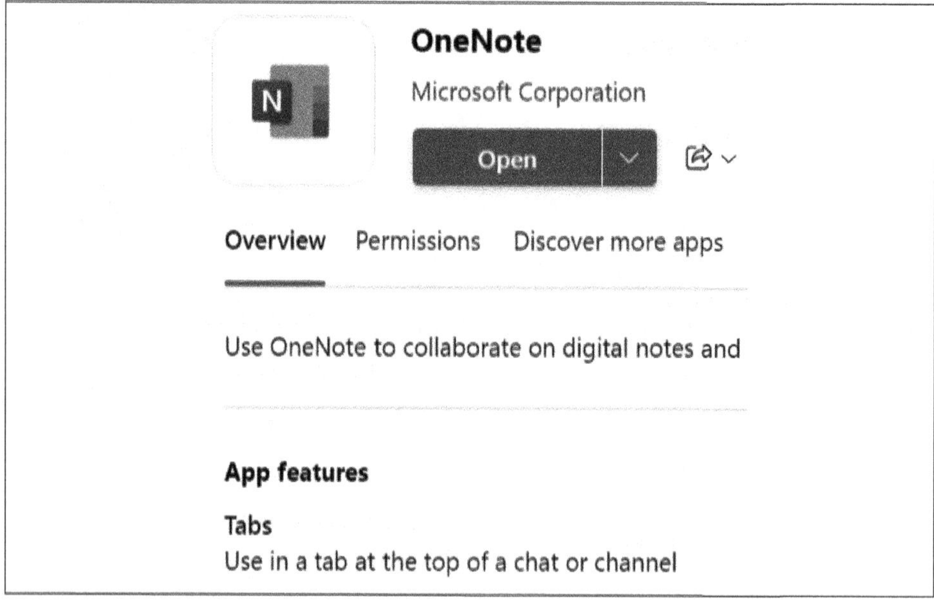

Figure 12-46. OneNote app features

The Teams Developer Portal allows you to create your own personal apps and tabs. Potential users for these include people who have no developer experience and who want to create a solution with little or no code. To create personal apps and tabs, Teams supports Teams Toolkit and other SDKs, such as C#, Blazor, Node.js, and more. Node.js must be installed to support an application called SharePoint Online SPFx Yeoman Generator (see Figure 12-47), which creates base SharePoint Framework (SPFx) solutions. SPFx is used to deploy personal apps in Teams.

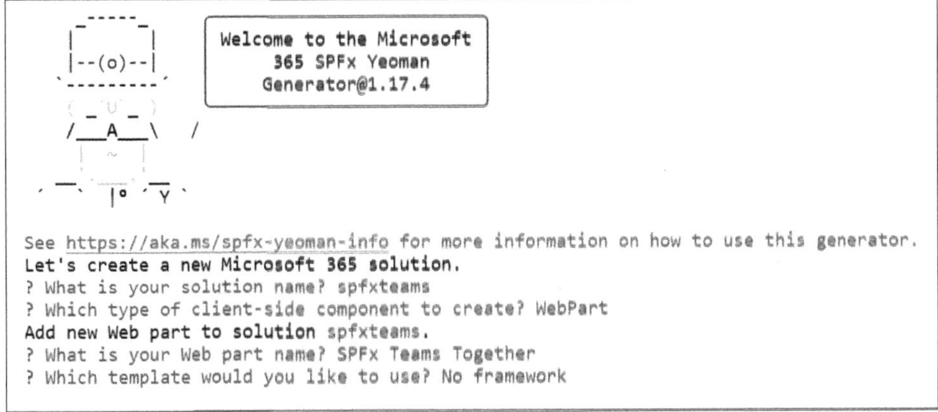

Figure 12-47. Running the SPFx Yeoman Generator

12.5 Summary

This chapter discussed different tools that help improve user productivity in Teams. AI solutions like Syntex and AI Builder work side by side with low- and no-code tools to empower all Teams users to realize apps and solutions that match their needs. For the recipes in this chapter, an additional consideration may need to be made before adoption—one that is related to the cost of licensing (and cost weighs into the business decision). The next chapter focuses on Teams and the employee experience platform Microsoft Viva.

CHAPTER 13

Teams and Virtual Machines

A *virtual desktop* (VD) is a computer operating system that is hosted on a remote server and accessed over a network connection. It is a software-based version of a traditional desktop computer, where the OS, applications, and data are hosted on a remote server and delivered to the user's device (such as a laptop, tablet, or smartphone) via the internet. The user interacts with the virtual desktop infrastructure (VDI) as if it were running on their own device, but all processing and storage are handled by the remote server. This allows users to access their desktop environment and applications from anywhere, using any device with an internet connection.

The recipes in this chapter focus on the concept of media optimization. Teams media optimization plays a crucial role in offloading from the VDI workloads such as device redirection of the camera and microphone to the client, encoding and encrypting media within Teams, and handling all communication with the Teams service.

With media optimization enabled, the VDI environment no longer needs to manage all the intricate processes involved in Teams usage. Instead, specialized optimization techniques are implemented to streamline media handling, encoding, and encryption.

There are a few factors that can make using Teams on a VDI more complex, including network latency, limited local resources, and limited control of the user over the virtual environment.

However, some of these limitations can be mitigated by using a robust and reliable network infrastructure, as well as proper configuration and management of the VDI environment. Additionally, Teams has been optimized for VDI use, and some of the issues we'll cover in this chapter can be addressed via Teams settings and configurations.

Enabling Teams media optimizations shifts the resource-intensive tasks from the VD to the VD client, resulting in improved performance and efficiency. With media optimizations activated, Teams retrieves data from the Teams service and directs it to WebRTC, which then delivers the data to the VD client.

The VD client, leveraging local media optimization capabilities, tries to establish a direct connection with the remote Teams user. This direct connection enables more efficient transmission of audio and video data, reducing latency and enhancing the overall user experience during Teams interactions.

The two processes—with and without media optimization—are shown in Figure 13-1.

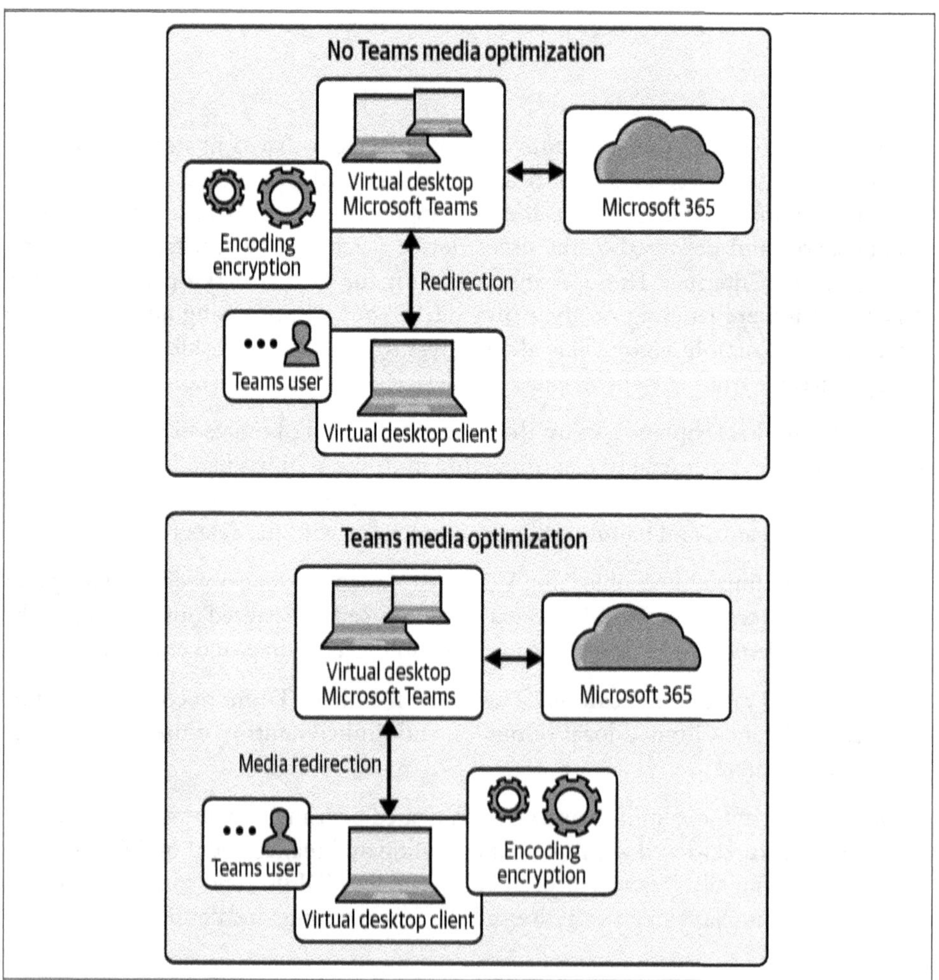

Figure 13-1. A VD user connecting to Teams with and without media optimization

13.1 Managing Teams on Virtual Desktops

Problem

You need to manage Teams on VD technology.

Solution

How you install Teams on a VD depends on the setup you have for your virtual desktops, which can be one of the following:

Persistent
: A persistent VD is configured to save any changes made by the user during a session. This means that any installed software, files, or system settings will be retained for subsequent sessions. The desktop is effectively customized and personalized to the user's preferences and requirements.

Non-persistent
: A non-persistent VD is configured to discard any changes made by the user during a session. This means that the desktop reverts to a standard, preconfigured state at the start of each new session. Any installed software, files, or system settings are deleted, and the desktop is reset to its original state.

To deploy the Teams desktop app for VDs, you can choose between a per-machine or per-user installation using the Microsoft Software Installer (MSI) package, depending on whether you have a persistent or non-persistent setup.

- For a persistent setup, either a per-machine and per-user installation can be used.
- For a non-persistent setup, a per-machine installation is required.

With a per-machine installation, automatic updates are disabled, so the current version must be uninstalled to install a newer version.

To install Teams in a per-machine configuration, download the Teams installer (*https://oreil.ly/_UFCJ*).

The following key must be added to the registry (letting the Teams installer know it is a VDI instance) using the command shown here:

```
reg add "HKLM\SOFTWARE\Microsoft\Teams" /v IsWVDEnvironment /t REG_DWORD /d 1 /f
```

Then, run this command with the appropriate path to the installer and logfile name:

```
msiexec /i <path_to_msi> /l*v <install_logfile_name> ALLUSER=1 ALLUSERS=1
```

The Teams MSI installer is stored in different directories depending on the Windows architecture. On 32-bit Windows, it is located in *%SystemDrive%\Program Files\Teams Installer*, while on 64-bit Windows it can be found in *%SystemDrive%\Program Files (x86)\Teams Installer.*

When a user signs in to a new Windows user profile, the Teams installer is automatically triggered, and a fresh copy of the Teams app is installed in the respective user's *%LocalAppData%\Microsoft\Teams* folder. This ensures that each user has their own independent installation of Teams.

However, if a user already has the Teams app installed in their *%LocalAppData%\Microsoft\Teams* folder, the MSI installer recognizes this and skips the installation process for that particular user. This allows for efficient management of the Teams app across multiple user profiles and prevents unnecessary duplication of the application.

I recommend using a profile-caching manager to sync two folders:

- *C:\Users\<username>\AppData\Local\Microsoft\IdentityCache* (*%LocalAppData%\Microsoft\IdentityCache*)
- *C:\Users\username\AppData\Roaming\Microsoft\Teams* (*%AppData%\Microsoft\Teams*)

Depending on your infrastructure, you may prefer to disable the Teams calling and meeting features for the VD users (for example, if you are unable to deploy Teams optimization). You can assign the DisallowCalling calling policy and the AllOff meeting policy using the TAC or PowerShell, with the following commands:

```
Grant-CsTeamsCallingPolicy -PolicyName DisallowCalling -Identity "user email id"

Grant-CsTeamsMeetingPolicy -PolicyName AllOff -Identity "user email id"
```

Teams has a fallback mode on a VD that allows the Teams app to continue functioning even if the VDI environment doesn't meet the minimum hardware requirements for audio and video calls. In fallback mode AV isn't optimized.

To control the behavior of fallback mode in Teams, you have the option to enable or disable it by adjusting specific registry `DWORD` values. Here are the corresponding registry paths:

To disable fallback mode

Set the `DWORD` value `DisableFallback` to `1` in the registry key *HKEY_LOCAL_MACHINE\SOFTWARE\Microsoft\Teams*.

Set the `DWORD` value `DisableFallback` to `1` in the registry key *HKEY_CURRENT_USER\SOFTWARE\Microsoft\Office\Teams*.

To enable audio-only mode

Set the `DWORD` value `DisableFallback` to `2` in the registry key *HKEY_LOCAL_MACHINE\SOFTWARE\Microsoft\Teams*.

Set the `DWORD` value `DisableFallback` to `2` in the registry key *HKEY_CURRENT_USER\SOFTWARE\Microsoft\Office\Teams*.

If the `DWORD` value is not present or set to `0` (zero), this indicates that fallback mode is enabled.

Discussion

When using a VDI to connect to Teams, there are also network requirements to be satisfied. Several firewall ports need to be opened between the client device and the VD to ensure a successful connection. These might include the following:

TCP port 3389

This is the default port used for Remote Desktop Protocol (RDP), which is used to establish a connection between the client device and the VD.

UDP port 3478

This port is used for Real-time Transport Protocol (RTP) traffic for audio and video communication. (UDP ports 3478–3481 are used by the WebRTC media engine for establishing and maintaining the media connection for audio and video communication.)

UDP ports 50,000–59,999

These ports are used for RTP traffic for audio and video communication.

TCP port 443

This port is for HTTPS traffic, to connect to the Teams service.

TCP port 80

This port is also used for HTTP traffic, to connect to the Teams service.

It's important to ensure that these firewall ports are opened and accessible to establish a successful connection between the client device and the VD. You could also use tools like the Microsoft Teams Network Assessment Tool (*https://oreil.ly/Ot_4n*) to check that your connectivity is configured correctly for Teams.

13.2 Using Windows 365 Cloud PCs with Microsoft Teams

Problem

You need to configure Azure Virtual Desktop (AVD) for Teams.

Solution

This recipe uses a Business Cloud PC.

First, connect to *https://windows365.microsoft.com/#/*. There are different ways to connect to the Cloud PC, including web browsers and different clients. All of them connect to the virtual machine using a subscription URL. Both the clients and the URL are available on the "Download an app to use Windows 365 from your device" page (see Figure 13-2).

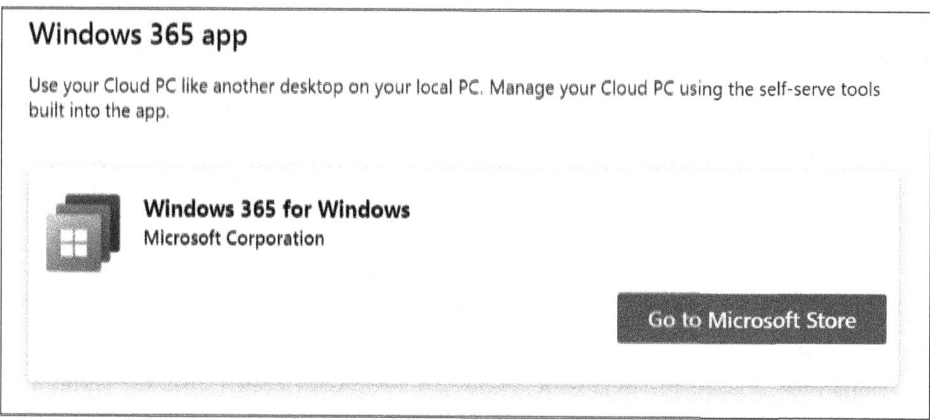

Figure 13-2. Opening the "Download an app" page

On the home page you can see all the deployed Cloud PCs (as in Figure 13-3).

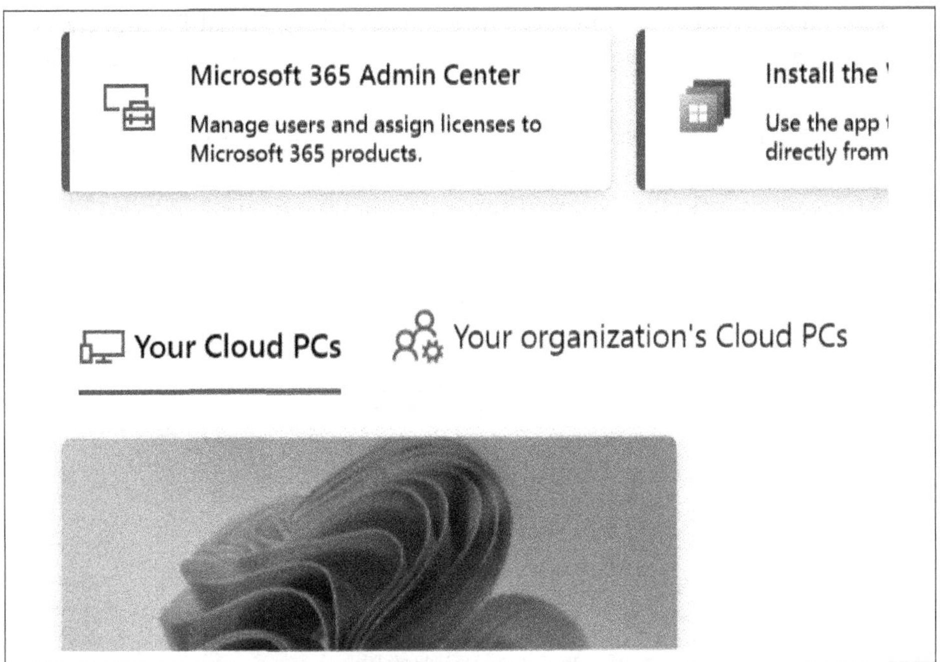

Figure 13-3. The home page with the connection apps

Install and open the Remote Desktop app. Access a Workspace by copying the subscription URL and logging in with your username and password (as in Figure 13-4).

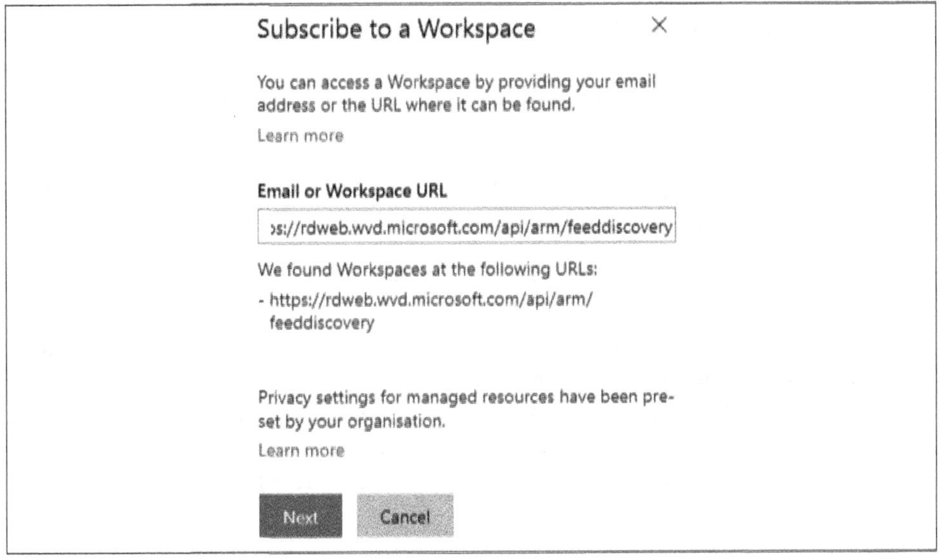

Figure 13-4. Subscribing to a Workspace

If the Remote Desktop app is installed, you can launch the Cloud PC directly from the home page by selecting "Open in Remote Desktop app" from the drop-down menu.

From the Cloud PC, open the Start menu and search for "Add or remove programs." In the Apps > "Installed apps" menu, you should see that the Remote Desktop WebRTC Redirector Service is already installed (as in the example in Figure 13-5).

Figure 13-5. Confirming installation of the Remote Desktop WebRTC Redirector Service

You can also check whether the media optimization for Teams is enabled by checking the following registry key:

```
HKLM\SOFTWARE\Microsoft\Teams\IsWVDEnvironment
```

If the registry key is missing, you can add it using this command:

```
reg add "HKLM\SOFTWARE\Microsoft\Teams" /v IsWVDEnvironment /t REG_DWORD /d 1 `
/f /reg:64
```

The Teams Machine-Wide Installer is in the list of installed apps, but the Teams client will be installed the first time you click the "Microsoft Teams (work or school)" icon. To verify that the AVD media optimization is running, open the Teams client, click the ellipsis icon and select About, then Version. If the banner shows AVD Media Not Connected, the optimization is not running (as in Figure 13-6).

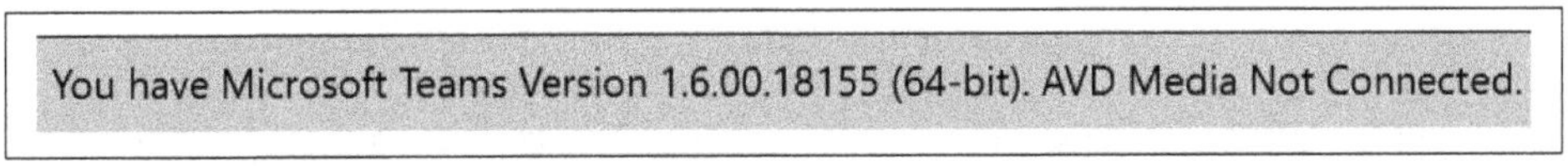

You have Microsoft Teams Version 1.6.00.18155 (64-bit). AVD Media Not Connected.

Figure 13-6. AVD media optimization not running correctly

Also, if you open the Teams client settings and go to Devices, you should see the microphones, headsets, and cameras connected to the local PC. Otherwise, Remote Audio means that AVD media is not activated (as in Figure 13-7).

Audio devices
Custom Setup
Speaker
Remote Audio
Microphone
Remote Audio

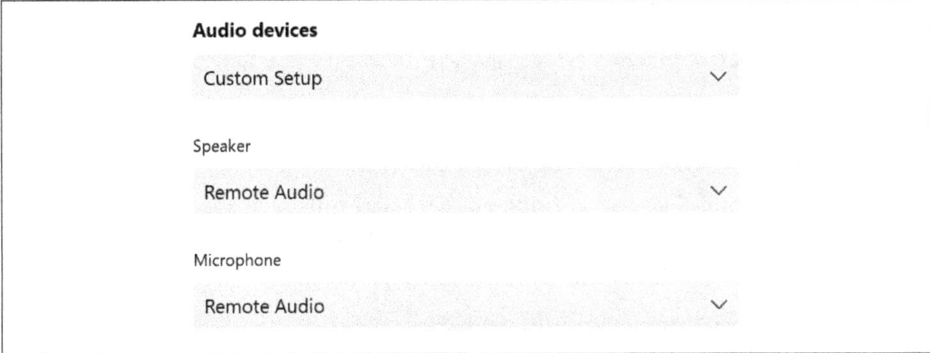

Figure 13-7. The client devices are not redirected as expected

You may need to quit the Teams client and try again. The banner should show AVD Media Optimized (as in Figure 13-8).

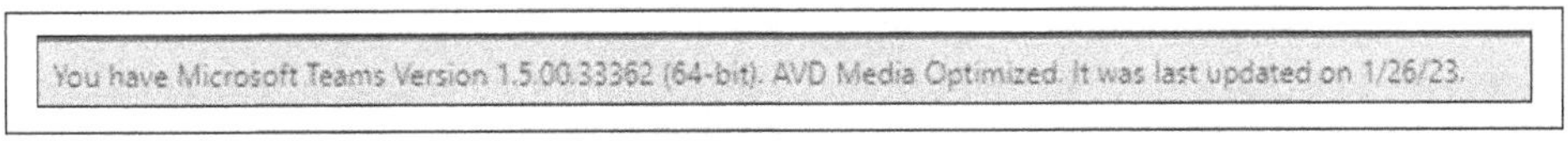

You have Microsoft Teams Version 1.5.00.33362 (64-bit). AVD Media Optimized. It was last updated on 1/26/23.

Figure 13-8. AVD media-optimized client

Also, upon opening Devices from the Teams client you should see the devices connected to your local computer. If the devices still don't appear in the menu, go to the Settings menu in Windows, open "Privacy & security," and check the microphone settings in "App permissions." "Allow apps to access your microphone" must be enabled. To join calls and meetings with video, you must also grant permission for apps to access your camera.

There are two options to enable additional features.

The first option is to enable hardware encoding, which allows you to increase video quality for the outgoing camera during Teams calls. To enable this feature, open a command prompt with administrative privileges in the Cloud PC and run the following command:

```
reg add "HKCU\SOFTWARE\Microsoft\Terminal Server Client\Default\AddIns\ `
WebRTC Redirector" /v UseHardwareEncoding /t REG_DWORD /d 1 /f /reg:64
```

The second option is to enable content sharing for Teams for the Remote Desktop app:

1. Open the Registry Editor on your session host VM by launching it from the Start menu with administrator privileges.
2. Navigate to the following registry path: *HKLM\SYSTEM\CurrentControlSet\Control\Terminal Server\AddIns\WebRTC Redirector\Policy*.
3. Create a new `DWORD` value named `ShareClientDesktop`.
4. Set the value of the newly created `DWORD` to `1` in order to enable the feature:

```
reg add "HKLM\SYSTEM\CurrentControlSet\Control\Terminal Server\AddIns\ `
WebRTC Redirector\Policy" /v ShareClientDesktop /t REG_DWORD /d 1 /f `
/reg:64
```

Discussion

Windows 365 Cloud PC service, offered by Microsoft, is a Desktop-as-a-Service (DaaS) solution. It provides two distinct versions of Cloud PCs: Enterprise and Business, catering to different user requirements.

Enterprise Cloud PCs are specifically designed for organizations that have adopted Microsoft Endpoint Manager. To assign a Cloud PC M365 SKU to a user, that user must possess an Intune license. These Enterprise Cloud PCs rely on Azure and AD. An Azure subscription with a properly configured network is essential, along with access to AD featuring Azure AD Hybrid Join. It's important to note that Azure AD Domain Services is currently not supported, and Azure AD Join is also not supported. The VM itself operates within a Microsoft-managed Azure subscription, which means administrators do not have direct access to it and are not responsible for the associated costs within their own Azure subscriptions.

Business Cloud PCs target individual users and small businesses. Unlike Enterprise Cloud PCs, Business Cloud PCs do not require an Intune license. These VMs run entirely within Microsoft's Azure subscription, including the network interface cards. Customers are not obligated to provide their own Azure subscriptions. Business Cloud PCs natively join Azure AD, eliminating the dependency on AD. Additionally, there is no requirement for Intune licensing. Business Cloud PCs are solely managed by the user, similar to managing a standalone physical Windows device. In Windows 365, different Cloud PC sizes are available. If you plan to use Teams, the minimum recommended values are as follows:

- CPUs: 2vCPU
- RAM: 4 GB
- Storage: 256, 128, or 64 GB
- Microsoft Teams (audio only)

If you want to also use video conferencing, the hardware specifics should be higher. More details are available in the Microsoft article "Cloud PC size recommendations" (*https://oreil.ly/H4q6_*).

The steps in this recipe also apply if you want to deploy a VDI in Azure and optimize it for Teams. If you're using a VDI with Teams without media optimization, you must edit the following RDP file properties to enable microphone and camera redirection:

- `audiocapturemode:i:1` (enables audio capture from the local device and redirects audio applications in the remote session)
- `audiomode:i:0` (plays audio on the local computer)
- `camerastoredirect:s:*` (redirects all cameras)

13.3 Applying the Citrix HDX Optimization for Microsoft Teams

Problem

You need to apply settings and configurations to enable the Citrix HDX optimization for Teams.

Solution

Citrix Virtual Apps and Desktops, previously known as XenApp and XenDesktop, offers the Citrix HDX optimization for Teams, a set of features and tools that improve the performance and user experience of Teams when it is delivered via Citrix Virtual Apps and Desktops.

Before deploying the HDX RealTime Media Engine to a Windows client device, you must install the Citrix Workspace app for Windows (*https://oreil.ly/73aBG*) on the user device. Ensure that it can connect through Citrix Virtual Desktops or to Citrix Virtual Apps.

You must also download the installation files for the RealTime Optimization Pack (*https://oreil.ly/JVV4x*). For a new installation, close the Citrix Workspace app if it is running and then install the RealTime Media Engine on your user devices (the file for a Windows client is *HDX_RealTime_Media_Engine_<z.x.yyy>_for_Windows.msi*). Now you must install the RealTime Connector on your Citrix Virtual Desktops and Citrix Virtual Apps servers.

The RealTime Connector for Teams still uses the Skype for Business product name. On the virtual desktop, run the installation file *HDX_RealTime_Connector_<x.y>_for_Skype_For_Business.msi* or *HDX_RealTime_Connector_<x.y>_for_Skype_For_Business_32.msi* and follow the instructions.

There is a Citrix policy that you must enable to allow Teams redirection, as shown in Figure 13-9 (it should be enabled by default).

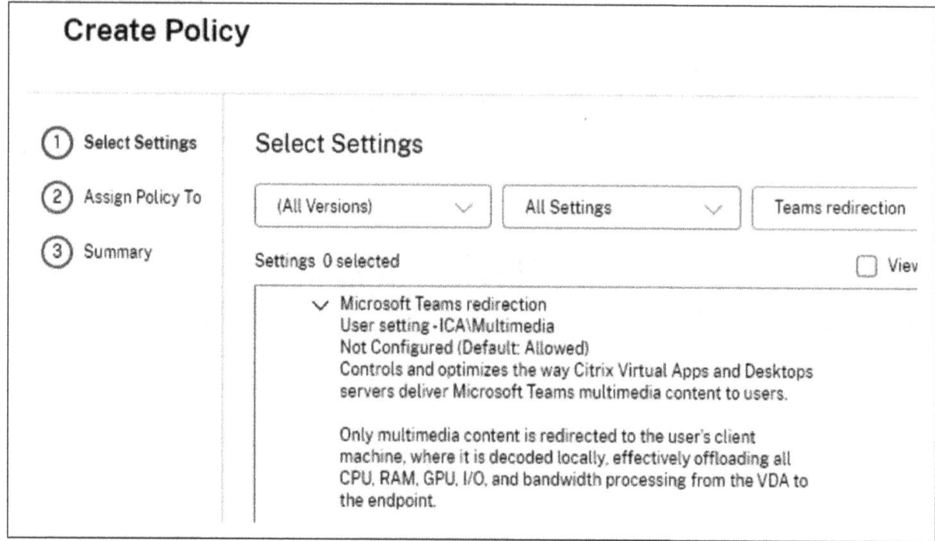

Figure 13-9. Policy settings to enable Teams redirection for Citrix VDs

Enabling this configuration allows the optimization of Microsoft Teams using the HDX technology. When this policy is enabled and you are using a compatible version of the Citrix Workspace app, a specific registry key is automatically set to `1` on the Virtual Delivery Agent (VDA). The Microsoft Teams application references this registry key to load in VDI mode. The registry key is located in *HKEY_CURRENT_USER\Software\Citrix\HDXMediaStream* and is named *MSTeamsRedirSupport*.

Now you can install the Teams client. To verify that the media optimization is running, open the Teams client, click the ellipsis, and select About, then Version. If you see the Citrix HDX Not Connected banner (Figure 13-10), the Citrix API is loaded in Teams—loading the API is the first step toward redirection—but there's an error in a later part of the stack. The error is most likely in the VDA services or the Citrix Workspace app.

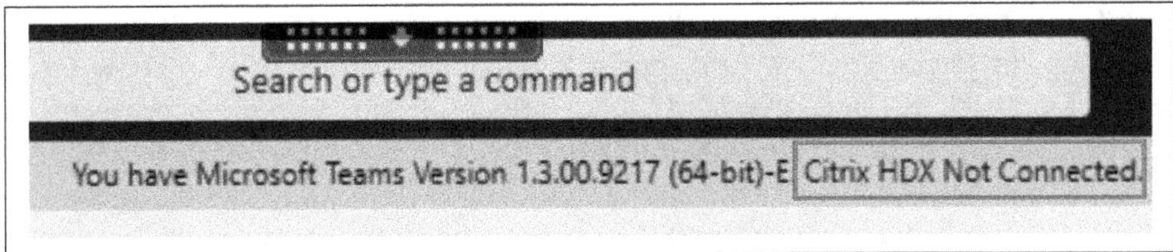

Figure 13-10. Teams' optimization on Citrix HDX not running correctly

If you don't see anything in the banner, Teams failed to load the Citrix API. Exit Teams by right-clicking the notification area icon and restarting. Make sure that the policy isn't set to Prohibited and that the Citrix Workspace app version is supported. If the optimization is running correctly, the banner will display Citrix HDX Optimized (Figure 13-11).

Figure 13-11. Citrix VD optimized for Teams

Relaunch Teams to get an HDX-optimized session when your connectivity changes (for example, if you are roaming from an unsupported endpoint to a supported one or vice versa).

Discussion

Citrix VDs can be deployed in several ways and on different platforms:

On-prem deployment
: This deployment option involves setting up the Citrix Virtual Desktop infrastructure on the customer's own physical or virtual servers within their own data center.

Cloud deployment
: This deployment option involves hosting the Citrix Virtual Desktop infrastructure on a public cloud platform, such as AWS or Azure.

Hybrid deployment
: This deployment option combines on-prem and cloud deployment, allowing customers to use both on-prem and cloud resources as needed.

Citrix Cloud Services
: This deployment option involves using the Citrix Cloud Services platform to manage the deployment, configuration, and delivery of Citrix Virtual Desktops.

The Citrix VD Agent is used in all types of Citrix Virtual Desktop deployments, including on-prem, cloud, hybrid, and Citrix Cloud Services. The VD Agent is installed on each VD and is responsible for providing communication between the VD and the Citrix Virtual Desktop infrastructure. This communication enables features such as policy enforcement, user profile management, and printing. If the VD Agent is installed, it already contains the Teams optimization components. The optimization includes features such as multimedia redirection, which offloads the processing of video and audio to the user's device, and adaptive transport, which improves the performance of Teams over poor network connections.

More details about the Citrix HDX optimization for Teams are available in the Citrix article "PoC Guide: Microsoft Teams optimization in Citrix Virtual Apps and Desktops environments" (*https://oreil.ly/4IbEx*).

13.4 Deploying Media Optimization for Microsoft Teams in VMware Horizon

Problem

You need to deploy Teams and the related optimization in VMware Horizon.

Solution

VMware Horizon is a VDI and remote desktop solution developed by VMware. With VMware Horizon, IT administrators can create and manage VDs, as well as configure access and security policies for different groups of users. End users can access their VDs and applications from any device with a compatible client, including laptops, smartphones, and tablets.

The Media Optimization for Microsoft Teams feature is installed by default with Horizon Client for Windows (see Figure 13-12).

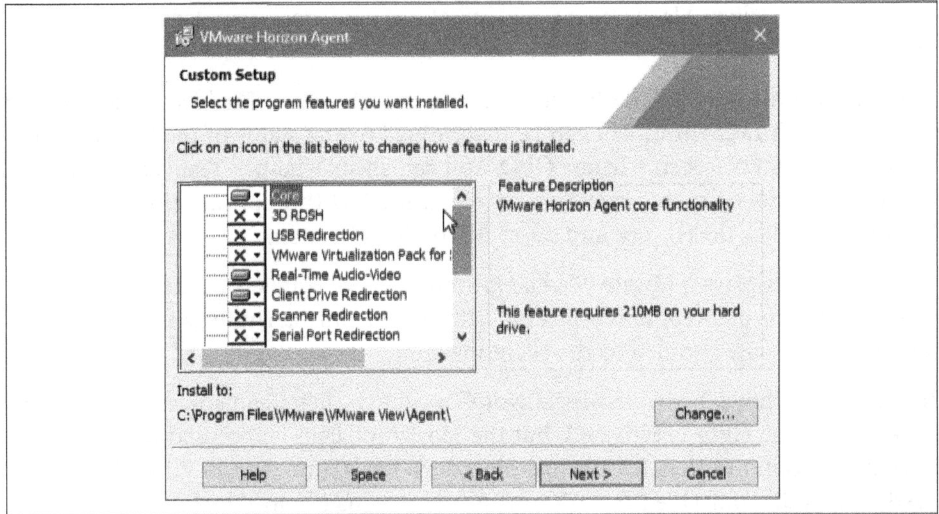

Figure 13-12. Real-Time Audio-Video feature installed as part of the VMware Horizon Agent

The Horizon Agent must be installed before you install Teams. If you installed Teams before installing Horizon Agent, delete the *%APPDATA%\Microsoft\Teams* folder and relaunch Teams. The Media Optimization for Microsoft Teams Group Policy Object (GPO) settings must be used to activate this feature with Horizon Client for Chrome or the HTML Access Web client (the "Enable WebRTC Redirection" option must be activated in the client settings).

The Horizon ADMX template files provide GPO settings that allow you to control and optimize Horizon components. The ADMX files are available in a bundle (in a file named *VMware-Horizon-Extras-Bundle-<YYMM-x.x.x-yyyyyyyy>.zip*) that you can download from the VMware Downloads site (*https://oreil.ly/oN1TP*). Go to the Desktop & End-User Computing category, locate VMware Horizon Apps, and click Download Product. In the list, select the one that is relevant for you (for example, VMware Horizon Apps 8 2306 Standard) and click "Go to Downloads."

In the list of available files, you will see Horizon GPO Bundle. Download the file and extract the contents. Copy the ADMX files into the *C:\Windows\PolicyDefinitions* folder of a Domain Controller (the relevant one for this recipe is *vdm_agent.admx*, which contains the Horizon Agent policy settings).

The contents in the VMware Downloads site are available only to VMware customers and partners.

Open Group Policy Management and create a new policy under Group Policy Objects.

The Enable VMware HTML5 Features setting must be set to Enabled. The behavior of Teams in a VD environment can be determined by the status of the Enable Media Optimization for Microsoft Teams GPO. You can check whether Teams is running in optimized mode, fallback mode, or natively in the VD (no optimization). Open the Teams client, click the ellipsis, and select About, then Version.

If the banner displays VMware Media Optimized, then Teams is running in the optimized mode. In this mode, the GPO is activated, Teams is running in the VD, and audio and video are handled by the client machine.

If the banner shows VMware Media Not Connected, then Teams is running in fallback mode. The GPO is activated, but the Horizon Client being used does not support media optimization for Teams. Horizon's Real-Time Audio-Video (RTAV) is used, and audio and video from Teams are not offloaded to the client machine. In fallback mode, the same limitations apply as in the optimized mode, and users may receive a warning during calls.

If the banner does not show any text related to VMware, then the GPO is not activated. In this case, RTAV is used and audio and video from Teams is not offloaded to the client machine.

Discussion

VMware Horizon supports a variety of use cases, including VDs for knowledge workers, call center agents, and graphic designers. It can be used to deliver remote desktop sessions and applications to remote users, as well as to provide secure access to virtualized desktops and applications from public and private clouds.

VMware Horizon also includes features such as user profile management, application delivery, and real-time monitoring and reporting. These features help IT administrators ensure the smooth and secure operation of their VD environment, while also providing end users with a high-quality and consistent experience.

Media Optimization for Microsoft Teams has the following limitations for all supported client platforms:

- Outgoing application window sharing is not supported.
- The camera light stays on if the user puts the video call on hold (but video is not sent).
- When a Teams video call window is minimized, the small Teams window in the lower-right corner will not show an active video.

- Teams running in fallback mode on a Remote Desktop Service Host (RDSH) machine cannot access the remote machine's microphone and speaker. See VMware Knowledge Base article 84205 (*https://oreil.ly/H3e7Q*) for a workaround.
- VDI participants cannot create breakout rooms; they can only join them.
- VDI users can attend Live Events, but the media stream is not optimized. Producer and presenter roles are not supported for VDI users. As a workaround, use the Teams Live Events (web) client with Horizon Browser Content Redirection. See VMware Knowledge Base article 88274 (*https://oreil.ly/TNLV4*) for details.
- Media bypass for direct routing is not supported.
- 1080p video is not supported.
- Zoom in and out functionality in Teams is not supported.
- Microsoft starts meetings with a lower resolution and gradually increases the resolution based on network conditions, such as the bandwidth of meeting participants and video window size.
- Quality of Service (QoS) in Teams is not supported.
- The test Call button is not available.
- The 3 × 3 video gallery is not supported.
- Giving control while screen sharing is not supported if Teams is an RDSH application.
- When screen sharing is being controlled by a peer, the cursor sometimes moves to the last location of the controller.
- In the sharing toolbar, the Give Control toolbar only shows two participants at a time. To scroll to other participants, use the up/down arrow keys.
- When screen sharing, the sharing toolbar might be hidden under the Horizon Client toolbar when Horizon Client is in full-screen mode. To access the Teams sharing toolbar, do one of the following:
  - — Hide the Horizon Client toolbar.
  - — Exit Horizon Client Fullscreen (use Horizon Client in window mode).
  - — Drag the floating Horizon Client toolbar to another location.
- Shared system audio/computer sound is not supported while screen sharing.

13.5 Summary

As you have seen in this chapter, Teams can be optimized for use in VD environments such as Citrix Virtual Apps and Desktops, VMware Horizon, and Windows Virtual Desktop. The optimization process involves configuring the virtualization platform and the client machine to handle audio and video content in the most efficient manner, improving the overall user experience.

The exact optimization process varies depending on the virtualization platform being used but typically involves the use of media optimization technologies, such as VMware Media Optimization or RTAV, and activating relevant GPOs. The optimization process can result in improved audio and video quality, reduced latency, and a more seamless user experience.

However, the optimization process is complex and can vary depending on the specific virtualization platform and client setup. I recommend consulting with the virtualization platform vendor and your IT administrator for more information on optimizing Teams in a VD environment.

Teams is one digital tool that has recognized the importance of accessibility and inclusivity. The platform has introduced several features that make it more accessible and inclusive for everyone. The next chapter discusses some of these features and how they can benefit users with disabilities.

CHAPTER 14

Accessibility and Inclusivity Features in Teams

The University of Leeds in the UK estimates that approximately 70% of disabilities are hidden, meaning they cannot be physically observed. People with disabilities can often find a way to work around them, but remote work technologies, including video calling and meetings, are requiring some workers to disclose their disabilities. This may cause concern about how an individual's disability may be perceived in the workplace.

Employers must recognize how they can be more digitally inclusive for their workforce. The topic of disability can be complex, because one person's characteristics might be incredibly disabling in one scenario and not disabling in another. Disability is also something that can be acquired gradually or suddenly. This chapter focuses on tools you can use with Teams (and Microsoft 365) that support some scenarios involving disabilities related to hearing, vision, mobility, and dexterity.

14.1 Checking Accessibility in Microsoft 365 Apps

Problem

You need to check that Microsoft 365 contents are easy to read and edit for people with disabilities.

Solution

Open a Word document stored in SharePoint (like the one in Figure 14-1).

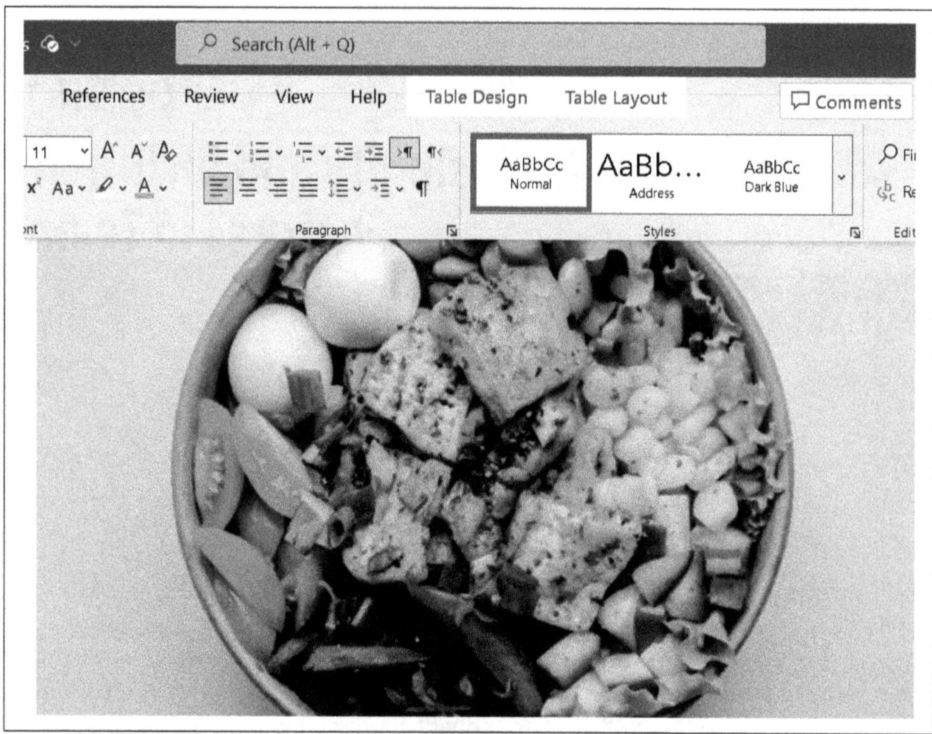

Figure 14-1. Opening a Word document in Teams

From Word, open the Review tab and click Check Accessibility (see Figure 14-2).

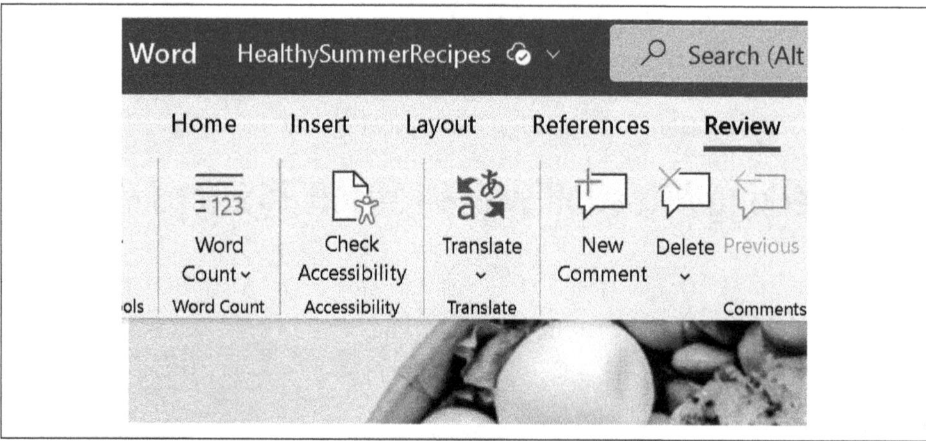

Figure 14-2. The Check Accessibility tool in Word

The Accessibility pane will open. The accessibility check might show some findings (as in the example in Figure 14-3).

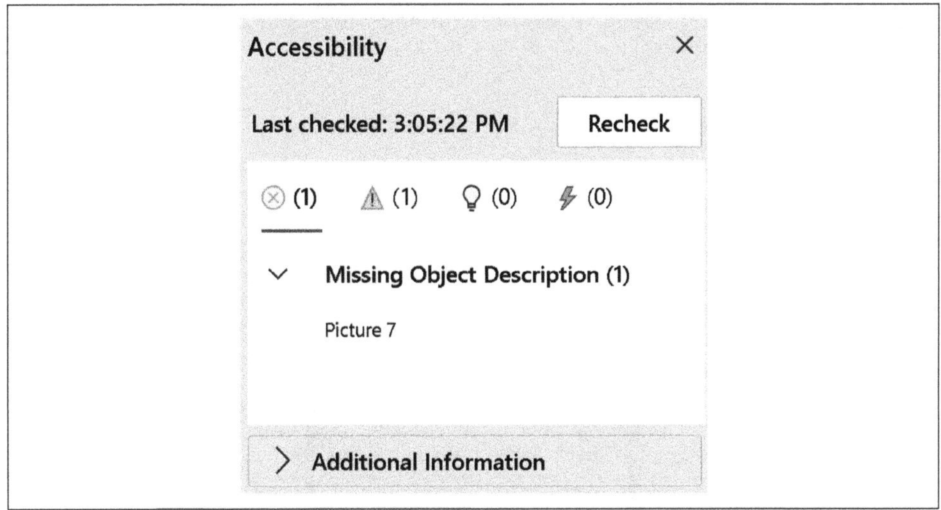

Figure 14-3. Accessibility issues in the sample document

If you click "Additional information," you'll be advised to fix the issues using the desktop version of the app. Click the Editing button and select "Open in Desktop App," as shown in Figure 14-4.

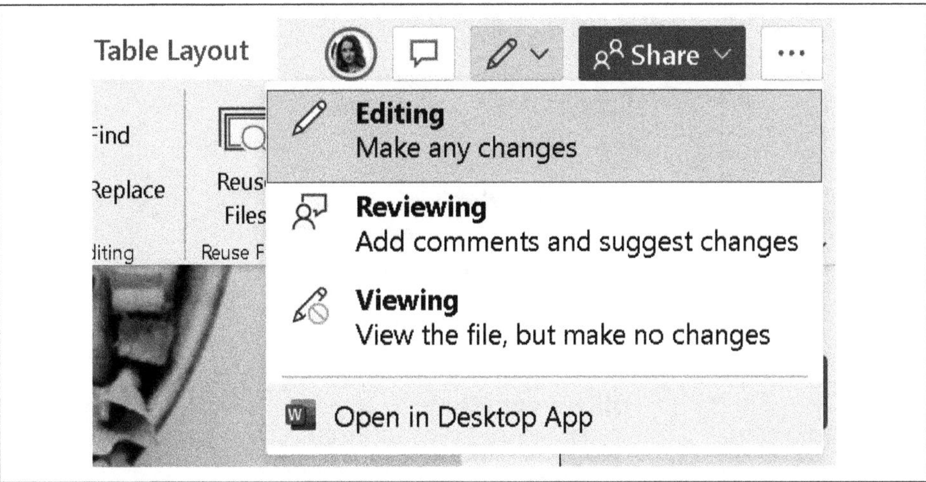

Figure 14-4. Opening the Editing tool in the desktop app

The Check Accessibility menu in the desktop app offers additional options, as you can see in Figure 14-5.

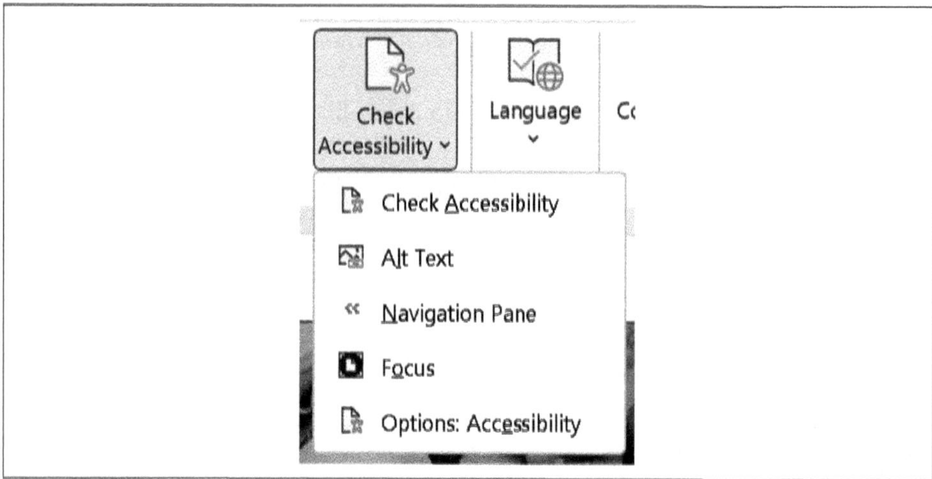

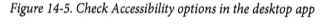

Figure 14-5. Check Accessibility options in the desktop app

Click Check Accessibility. The Accessibility pane will offer a set of Recommended Actions, as in Figure 14-6. Selecting the "Mark as decorative" action will fix both of the accessibility issues pointed out in Figure 14-3.

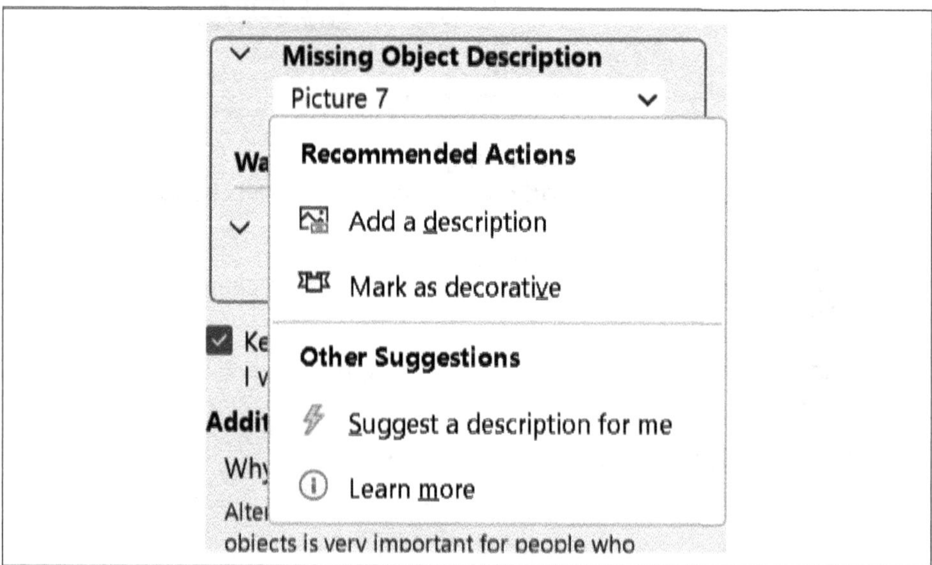

Figure 14-6. Recommended Actions to fix the accessibility issues in the sample document

You can use the same tool in other Microsoft 365 apps.

Discussion

The Accessibility Checker verifies that your Microsoft 365 contents are easy for people with disabilities to read and edit.

You can use the Accessibility Checker in Excel, Word, PowerPoint, and Outlook for Microsoft 365 to check for accessibility issues while you work on your email messages, documents, slides, and spreadsheets.

The issues identified by the tool are categorized by severity level into four classifications:

Error
: This classification applies to content that renders the document challenging or impossible to comprehend for individuals with disabilities.

Warning
: Content falling under this category generally makes the document difficult for people with disabilities to understand, although there may be exceptional cases where it does not pose a barrier.

Tip
: This classification encompasses content that can be understood by individuals with disabilities but presents an opportunity for improvement by altering its presentation or format, thereby enhancing the user experience.

Intelligent Services
: Content classified under Intelligent Services is automatically made accessible using AI. However, it is advisable to review such content for accuracy and contextual appropriateness.

Details about the rules that are applied and the classifications are available in the post "Rules for the Accessibility Checker" (*https://oreil.ly/rb3oh*).

14.2 Improving Accessibility of Teams Meetings

Problem

You want to enable accessibility tools in Teams meetings.

Solution

Live captions can be enabled during a meeting by clicking More > "Language and speech" > "Turn on live captions" (see Figure 14-7).

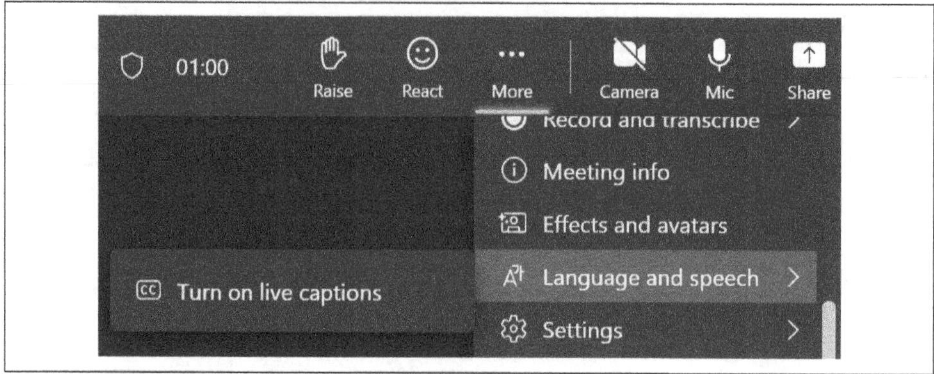

Figure 14-7. Turning on live captions in Teams

The "What language is everyone speaking" menu will appear, allowing you to select from among more than 25 languages. The live captions will start in the bottom part of the screen (an example is shown in Figure 14-8).

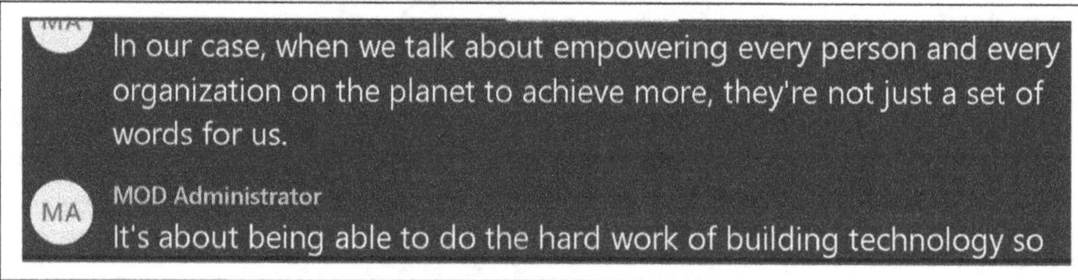

Figure 14-8. Live captions active during a Teams meeting

Live captions are enabled on a per-user basis, so they are not visible to the other meeting participants if they do not enable them. Live captions are also not included in the meeting recording; they appear on the screen and then disappear. Live captions have speaker attribution so that understanding the flow of the conversation is easier.

If you need to be able to translate the transcription of a meeting, you must enable the Transcription feature in your tenant by modifying or creating a dedicated meeting policy. From the TAC, go to Meetings and then click "Meeting policies." In Figure 14-9, we're modifying the "Global (Org-wide default)" policy to enable transcription.

Enabling this option generates a duplicate of the transcript associated with the meeting recording. This duplicate transcript is stored alongside the recording itself, providing several functionalities. These include the ability to search through the transcript, enable closed captioning (CC), and access the transcript directly within the meeting recording.

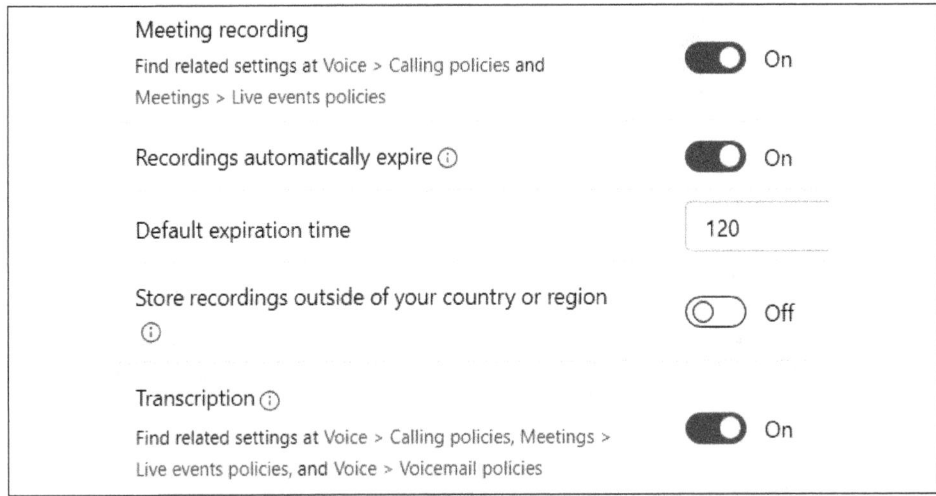

Figure 14-9. Enabling transcriptions in the meeting policy

The change we have made to the settings still allows the meeting organizer to enable or disable transcripts.

The transcript will be made available, together with the recording, at the end of the meeting, as shown in Figure 14-10. Supported formats are DOCX and VTT.

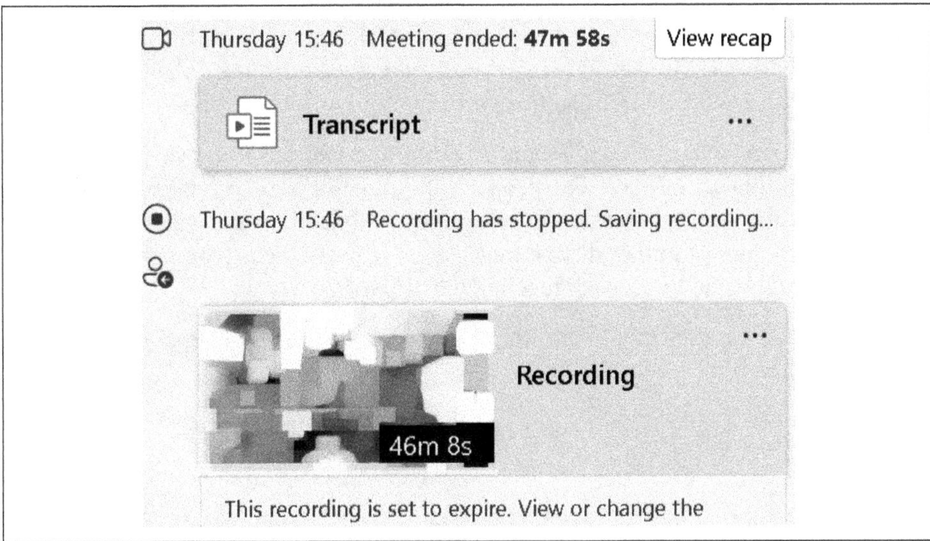

Figure 14-10. Transcripts are available after the Teams meeting

Transcripts, like live captions, have speaker attribution.

The live transcription feature is only available for scheduled meetings, not for channel meetings or Meet Now meetings.

During the meeting, there is also support for Communication Access Realtime Translation (CART), where the captioning is realized by a certified third-party provider instead of the AI. To provide CART support, you must select it from Meeting Options when organizing the meeting in Outlook. Select Provide CART Captions (as shown in Figure 14-11) and then click Save.

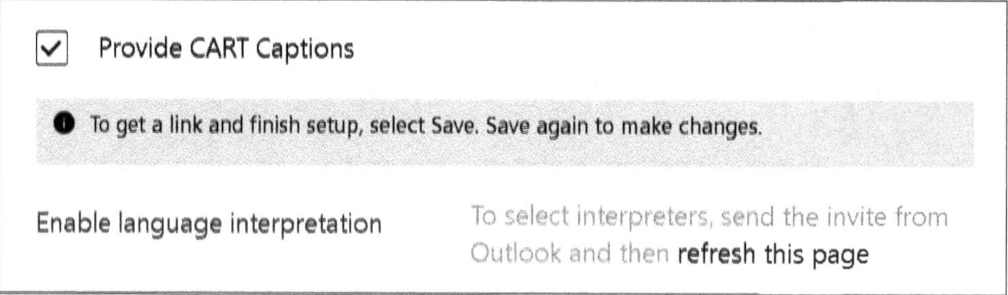
Provide CART Captions
To get a link and finish setup, select Save. Save again to make changes.
Enable language interpretation
To select interpreters, send the invite from Outlook and then refresh this page

Figure 14-11. CART options

A link (starting with *https://api.captions.office.microsoft.com/cartcaption?meetingid*) will be generated. This link must be sent to the CART captioner and allows the CART software to connect to the Meeting apps APIs. It is also possible, during a meeting, to enable and disable CART by opening the More menu, selecting "Meeting options," and altering the Provide CART Captions setting.

Another tool available during a Teams meeting that can have a positive impact for accessibility is Together Mode. For people with attention deficit hyperactivity disorder (ADHD) and similar attention deficits, Teams' Together Mode allows removal of all the backgrounds and other distractions, allowing more focus (compared to a lot of small, changing windows for each meeting participant).

Together Mode is available from the "..." menu during a Teams meeting (see Figure 14-12).

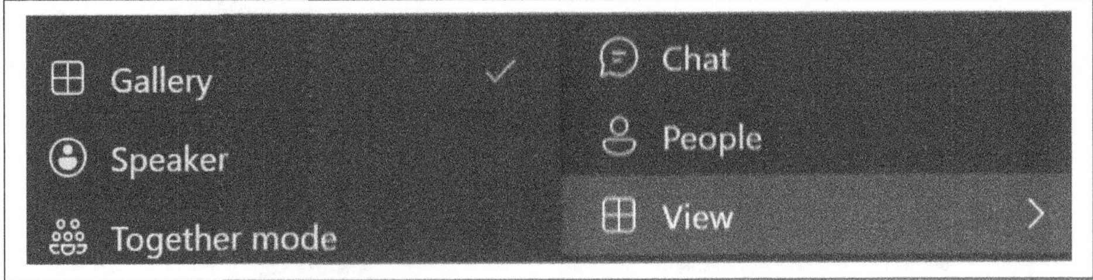

Figure 14-12. Activating Together Mode

Click "Change scene" to open the "Select a scene" screen (Figure 14-13), which offers a selection of backgrounds for the meeting (including the maximum number of participants that can be displayed in a specific background).

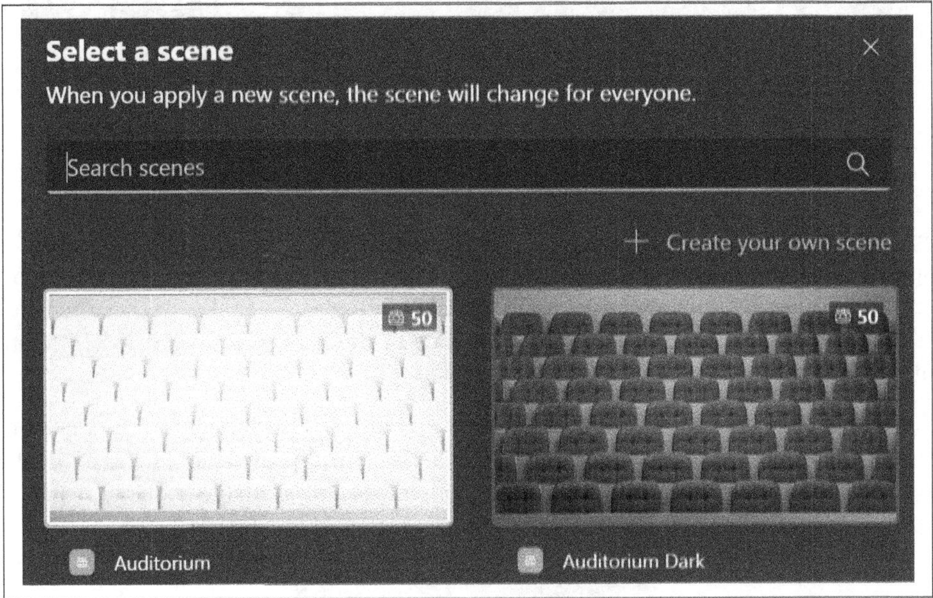

Figure 14-13. Scene selection menu showing the maximum number of participants in the upper-right corner

From the "Select a scene" screen, it is also possible to position the participants in the different spots available. An example is shown in Figure 14-14.

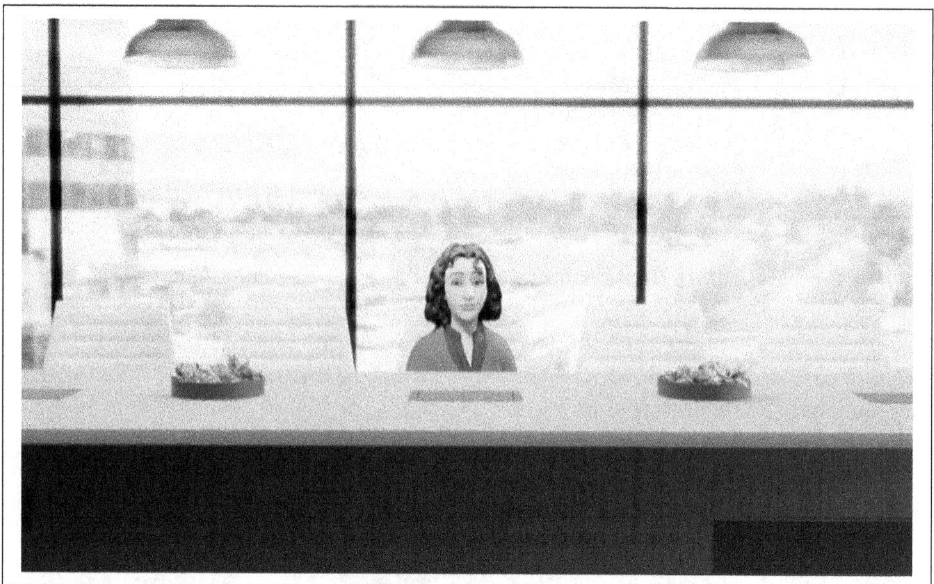

Figure 14-14. A Teams meeting with Together Mode enabled

In a similar way, it is possible to help the participants in a meeting focus on a single speaker or a single person in the meeting using the Spotlight feature. The Spotlight feature is generally only available to the meeting presenter. To enable it, click the People icon, select the "..." menu on the right side of the person you want to spotlight, and choose "Spotlight for everyone."

A notification in the lower-left corner of the screen will show an icon for the person in the spotlight. The "..." menu in the same message will provide an "Exit spotlight" option (as shown in Figure 14-15). "Exit spotlight" is also available in the top part of the meeting window.

Figure 14-15. A spotlighted user status

To reduce the number of distractions during a meeting where there is a shared document, it is also possible to use "Focus on content" and "Full screen" (available from the "..." menu). The "Full screen" option is shown in Figure 14-16.

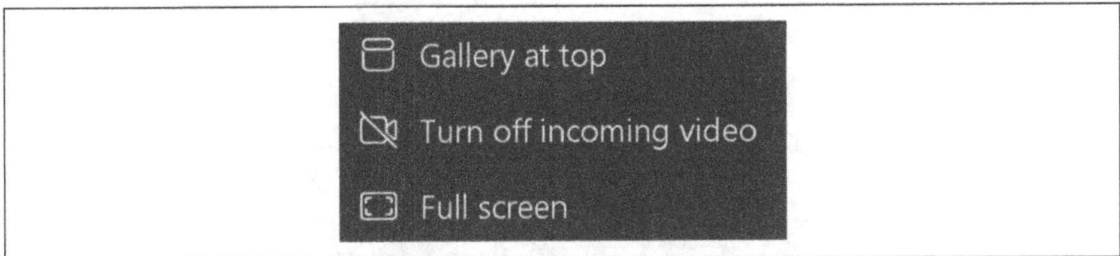

Figure 14-16. Focus on content and Full screen options

"Focus on content" puts the shared content at the center of the screen and removes the gallery. "Full screen" sets the shared content in full screen mode.

Teams meetings provide support for sign language through the Sign Language View feature. Sign Language View is meant to give prominence to interpreters and other signers in one consistent location. With Sign Language View, users can prioritize up to two other signers' video streams. When enabled, the prioritized signers' video streams are presented with the correct aspect ratio and the best possible video quality.

You have the flexibility to enable Sign Language View dynamically during a meeting or as a persistent setting that remains active for all your calls. This feature ensures that sign language interpreters and participants using sign language can be prominently featured and easily viewed by all meeting attendees.

This unique functionality prioritizes the visibility of signers, including individuals who are deaf or hard of hearing, sign language interpreters, and others who rely on sign language. By consistently maintaining their on-screen presence, Sign Language View ensures a consistent and inclusive experience for all meeting participants.

DTo enable this feature during a meeting, open the "..." menu and select Settings, then Accessibility. Under Hearing, enable "Sign language" (as shown in Figure 14-17).

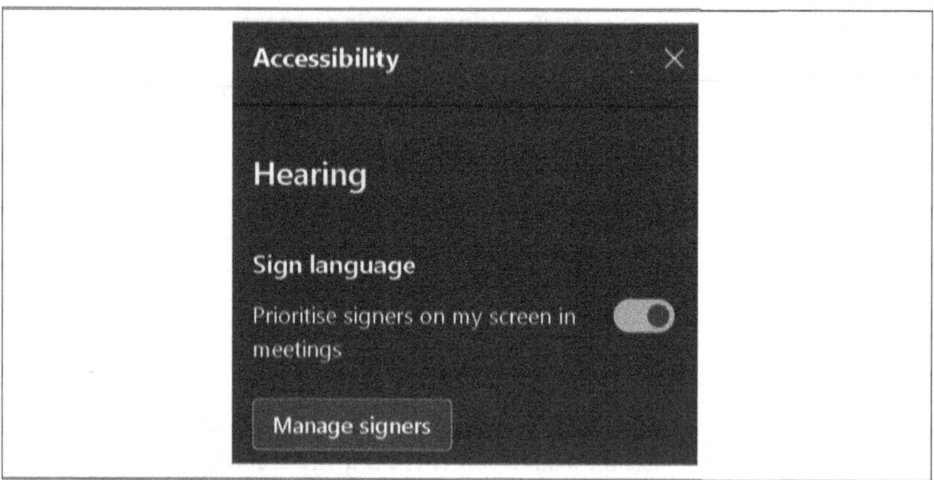

Figure 14-17. Enabling Sign Language View

It is possible to manage more than one signer, depending on the required languages (see Figure 14-18).

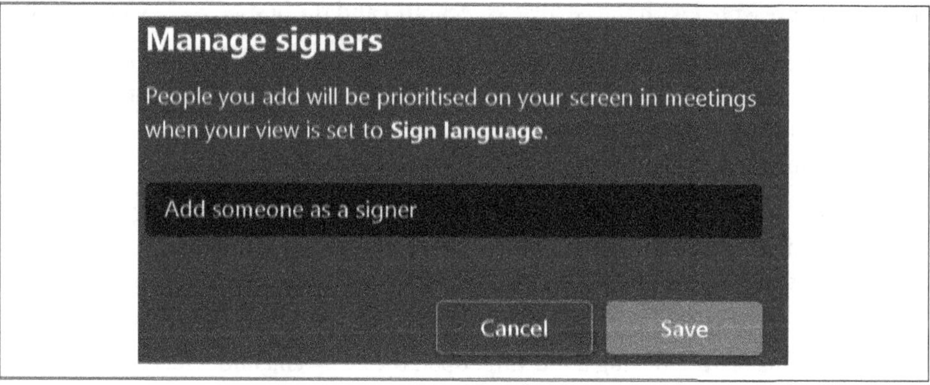

Figure 14-18. Managing signers

Teams also supports translation for inline messages. The feature must be enabled from the TAC by creating or modifying a messaging policy. Then, in Teams, you can activate it by opening the "..." menu in a chat and clicking Translate. The language you can translate to is determined by the language you select in the Teams client settings.

Discussion

CART can provide assistance in situations where speech recognition software faces difficulties, such as in environments with specialized terminology or diverse accents among participants. CART offers an alternative solution by having real-time captioners connected simultaneously, ensuring accurate and effective transcription.

Having multiple CART captioners available also gives participants the option to choose their preferred captioner during the meeting. This flexibility allows individuals to select the captioner who best meets their needs, ensuring clear and accessible communication throughout the session.

There are some minor adjustments that neurodiverse users can perform on the client side that could be helpful to improve their focus. For example, users can configure their activity feed notifications by right-clicking an individual item in the feed, mute notifications during meetings (for all meetings or on a per-meeting basis), or use Viva Insights (if available) to enroll in a focus plan.

14.3 Using Accessibility Features in the Teams Client

Problem

You want to make text in Teams more readable and accessible.

Solution

Teams offers different tools to improve text readability, like the "High contrast" theme (in the Settings menu) and the zoom tool. It is also possible to zoom in and out during a Teams meeting by holding the Ctrl key and rotating the mouse wheel (or using Command instead of Control on a Mac). The Teams client also offers Immersive Reader, which can read aloud posts, chat messages, and assignments. It is available in every chat, via the "..." menu.

Click Play to hear your document read aloud and to see the text highlighted simultaneously (the highlighted text feature is shown in Figure 14-19).

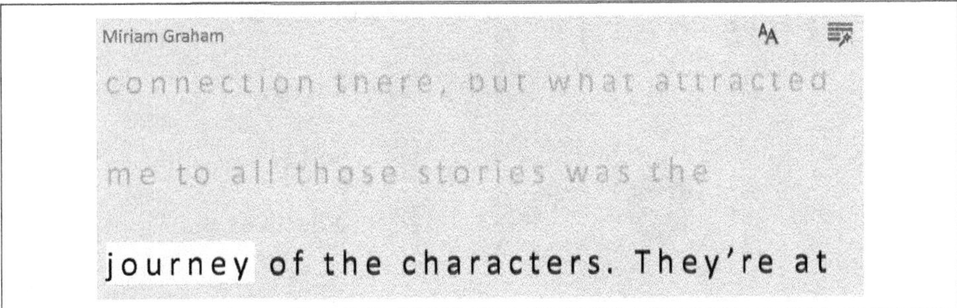

Miriam Graham
connection there, but what attracted
me to all those stories was the
journey of the characters. They're at

Figure 14-19. Immersive Reader reads a document aloud with highlighted text

Select Voice Settings on the right of the Play button to change the speed of narration and the voice selection (as shown in Figure 14-20).

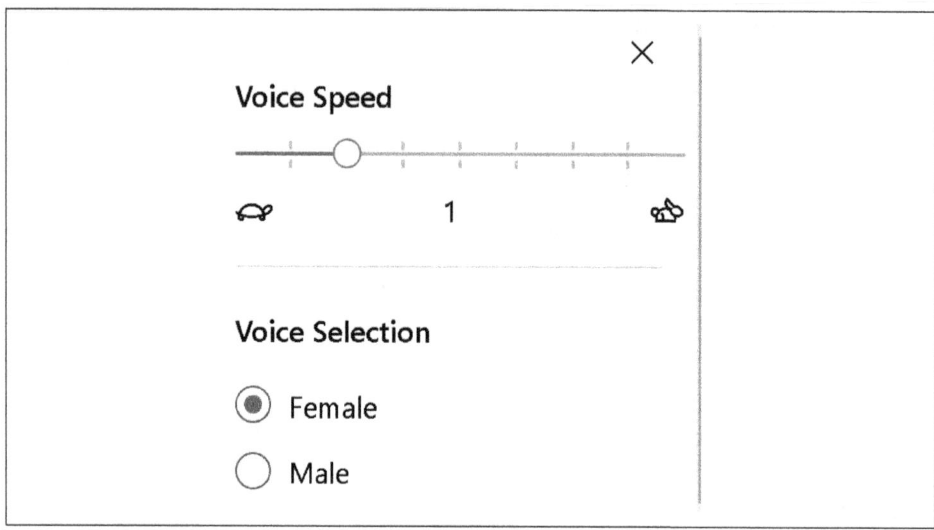

Figure 14-20. Narration speed and voice selection

You can change the format of the text and use the "Parts of Speech" settings under Grammar Options to highlight verbs, nouns, and so on (as shown in Figure 14-21).

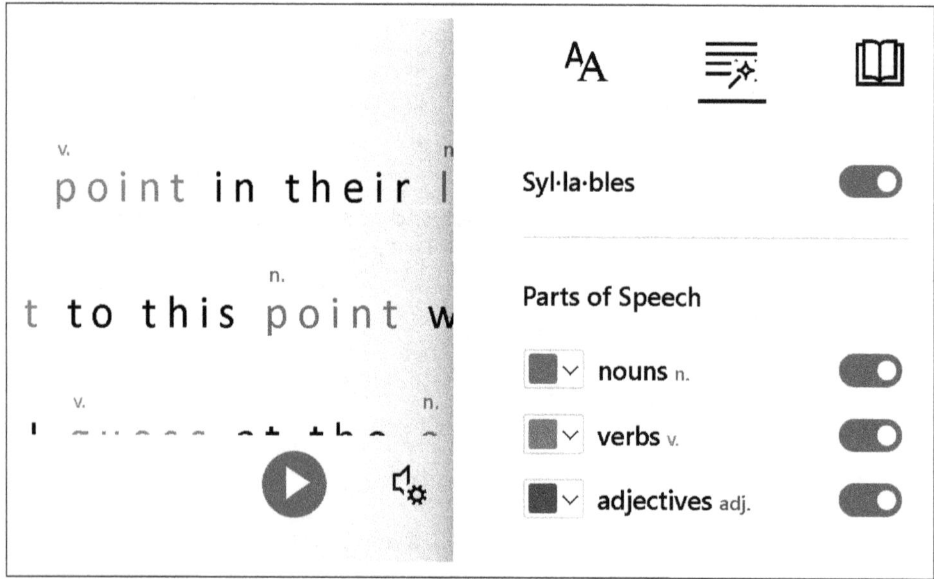

Figure 14-21. Highlighting parts of speech

In Teams, all documents created with Microsoft 365 apps support the Dictate feature, which allows the user to perform speech-to-text actions in different languages. For example, to try it out you can open a PowerPoint presentation in Teams and, from the Home tab, click Dictate.

Discussion

All the tools discussed in this recipe are useful to reduce the impact of learning differences like dyslexia and difficulty with fluent reading and writing. It is estimated that dyslexia affects approximately 1 in 10 people, with 1 in 25 classified as severely dyslexic.

The text prediction feature (available in Teams) serves as an excellent example of embedded features that can be helpful for individuals with dyslexia. Text prediction functionality assists in simplifying the typing process and reducing the occurrence of errors. By offering word suggestions or completing phrases based on context, it enables individuals with dyslexia to benefit from increased typing speed and accuracy.

Microsoft also offers additional tools specifically designed to support individuals in the education field. These tools, available through Digital Learning Tools from Microsoft Education (*https://oreil.ly/kBklm*), provide further assistance and accommodations. By leveraging these resources, educators and students can access a range of supportive features, such as immersive reading experiences, dictation tools, and customizable learning environments. These tools aim to enhance accessibility, promote independent learning, and empower individuals to overcome challenges commonly associated with reading and writing tasks.

14.4 Using Microsoft Teams with the JAWS Virtual Cursor

Problem

You want to use Job Access with Speech (JAWS) as a screen reader with Teams and other Microsoft 365 products.

Solution

JAWS, developed by the Blind and Low Vision Group of Freedom Scientific and available via the JAWS Downloads page (*https://oreil.ly/fztEW*) on the organization's website, is software that enables individuals who are blind or visually impaired to effectively use a Windows computer. Offering a range of essential features, JAWS supports Braille integration, multilingual speech synthesis, and multi-screen functionality. Users can configure JAWS to launch automatically upon logging in to Windows or initiate it manually through the desktop icon or the Start menu entry dedicated to JAWS.

Within JAWS, there are three distinct cursors available, with the virtual cursor being specifically designed for navigating HTML, web, and similar environments. Like when navigating a text document or a Word file, the virtual cursor empowers users to explore and read web pages seamlessly.

The virtual cursor in JAWS allows free movement through various units of text. While navigating web pages or similar content, the virtual cursor does not display a visible indicator of its position, ensuring users can freely move beyond the currently visible screen content. Figure 14-22 shows a comprehensive view of the Virtual PC cursor options.

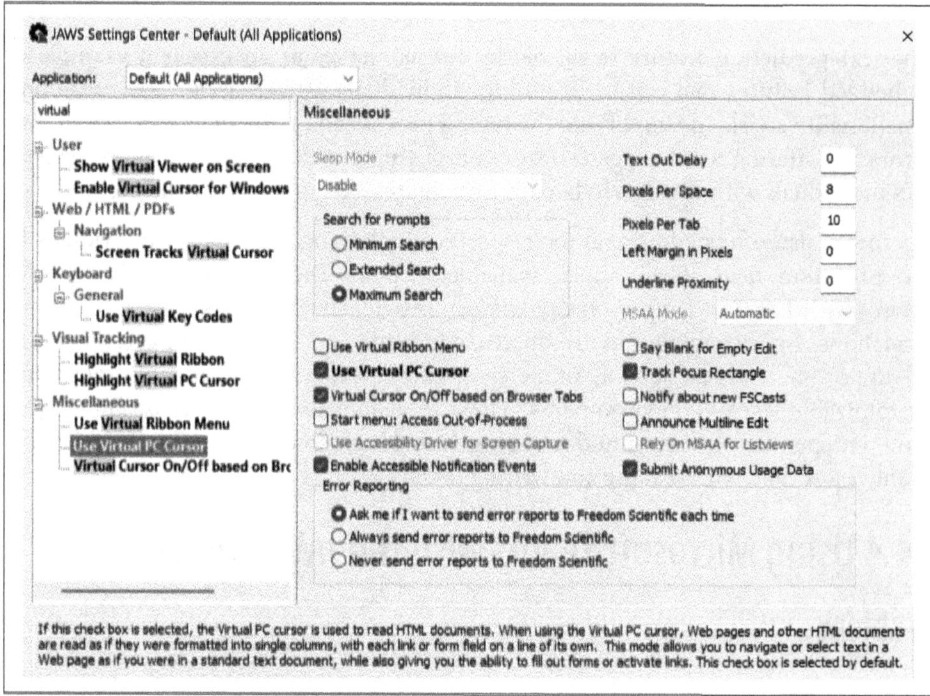

Figure 14-22. Enabling the Virtual PC cursor

While JAWS is active, launch Microsoft Teams and utilize the keyboard shortcut JAWS key + 6 to access the JAWS Settings Center window. (The default JAWS key in Windows is the Insert key.) This window serves as a central hub for configuring various JAWS settings related to Teams.

Within the JAWS Settings Center, you will find different views, each presenting a main content area positioned at the center of the screen. This content area is further divided into two sections: the list pane and the content pane. The specific contents displayed in each pane depend on the currently selected view.

When you navigate and select a particular view from the JAWS Settings Center, the focus automatically shifts to either the list pane or the content pane, allowing you to interact with the corresponding elements and adjust settings accordingly.

To navigate between the list and content panes, either press the Tab key, or Shift + Tab, or Ctrl + F6.

There is no cursor shown on the screen; the selected content in view is pointed out by the JAWS voice comment.

The list pane, situated on the left side of the main content area, facilitates browsing and selection of items, which are then displayed in detail within the content pane on the right.

To access a list, simply press the Tab key or the down arrow key until you hear the first item within the list. Once inside the list, you can navigate through the available items using the up and down arrow keys. As you move through the list, the screen reader will audibly announce the details or buttons associated with each item.

To select a specific item from the list and view its comprehensive details in the content pane, press the Enter key.

When managing a chat using JAWS, navigate to the Chat menu located in the left pane of the Teams client. From there, select the "Type a new message" field and begin typing your message. Throughout this process, JAWS will audibly articulate the different selections and menus.

Discussion

More details about the interaction between a screen reader and Microsoft Teams are available in the support article: "Use a screen reader to explore and navigate Microsoft Teams" (*https://oreil.ly/Tsd2I*).

JAWS supports both Windows 10 and Windows 11, as well as all versions of Windows Server released since Windows Server 2016. It offers two editions: the Home edition designed for noncommercial usage and the Professional edition tailored for commercial environments.

One notable feature of JAWS is its Scripting Language, which empowers users to interact with programs lacking standard Windows controls or programs that were not originally designed for accessibility.

With JAWS, users can control various essential functions of the Microsoft Windows operating system using keyboard shortcuts and receive spoken feedback. These shortcuts strive to maintain consistency across most programs. However, due to the extensive range of functions required to effectively navigate modern computer software, users are encouraged to memorize specific keystrokes to fluidly utilize the software.

A list of the default hotkeys is available at JAWS Hotkeys (*https://oreil.ly/K2YME*).

Virtually every aspect of JAWS can be customized by the user, including all keystrokes and factors such as reading speed, granularity used when reading punctuation, and hints.

14.5 Summary

This chapter covered different tools and settings that allow you to improve and offer better accessibility for users. With more than 1 billion people worldwide living with a disability (*https://oreil.ly/Jcoaw*), you need to ensure everyone is included. All tools used in these recipes are part of Teams and the other Microsoft 365 apps, with no need for customization and no additional costs.

In the next chapter, we'll change our focus to Teams governance, including retention policies and guest access controls.

CHAPTER 15

Microsoft Teams Governance

The previous chapters have highlighted how Teams brings value to a business by making the digital transformation easier, adding communication tools, and improving automation and accessibility. These positive changes aside, organizations that adopt Teams must also think about IT governance—managing IT risks and ensuring that the technology usage is aligned with business objectives.

Some of the potential Teams governance issues that organizations may encounter include:

- Difficulty finding information in the different teams and channels
- Accidental exposure of sensitive data
- Users creating duplicate teams, or teams without clear purpose

Good governance helps ensure that the platform is used appropriately, securely, and efficiently. This includes setting up rules and guidelines for users, managing access to data, and defining roles and responsibilities. Governing Teams also has a positive impact on user adoption—if the user experience is negative because one of the issues listed previously isn't managed correctly, then adoption will suffer.

15.1 Planning Governance in Teams

Problem

You need to define governance rules for Teams based on your organization's requirements.

Solution

To define the IT governance for Teams, you must first gather the organization's requirements. Then, create clear guidelines from that. The process must involve both IT staff and staff representing the different parts of the business, like HR and Marketing. In this recipe, you will see some of the topics that are usually part of Teams governance planning.

The first phase in governance planning includes deciding:

- Who is allowed to create groups and teams
- What is the naming convention (if any)
- What is the classification
- What kind of external access will be permitted (if any)
- Who is allowed to grant guest access
- When to have public teams, and when to have private teams

By default, all users can create Microsoft 365 groups; if you don't want that to be the case, then you'll have to make that change. (You will learn about limiting the creation of groups and teams in Recipe 15.3.) Once you've made these first-phase decisions, be sure to document everything clearly.

The second phase in governance planning includes:

- Establishing a third-party app availability policy
- Defining an expiration, retention, and archiving policy for groups and teams

Third-party apps are apps used from Teams (or even inside Teams) that users can enable without the need of admin or IT approval. Some third-party apps may be not compliant with your organization's policy regulations and licensing. You can manage which applications are available in your Teams tenant by using custom App Permissions policies. In this planning phase, it is important to make a list of which apps are already used in the organization. In Microsoft 365, there are policies dedicated to expiration, retention, and archiving. Some of them have a default behavior that could require modification to match with the organization's requirements.

Discussion

The main objective of many of the governance aspects listed in this recipe is protecting sensitive organizational data. Teams is based on information sharing and exchange, but this carries with it a risk of leaks and misusage. A governance with rules that are too strict, however, may drive users outside the corporate framework to shadow IT solutions for obtaining the tools they need. It's important to find the right balance.

15.2 Enforcing a Naming Convention

Problem

You need to create a consistent naming convention for Microsoft 365 groups.

Solution

Group naming policies support:

- Prefix/suffix naming
- Custom blocked words

As a first step, open the Microsoft Entra admin center (*https://oreil.ly/JJUFp*) and click Azure Active Directory > Identity > Groups. Select "Naming policy" under Settings (as shown in Figure 15-1).

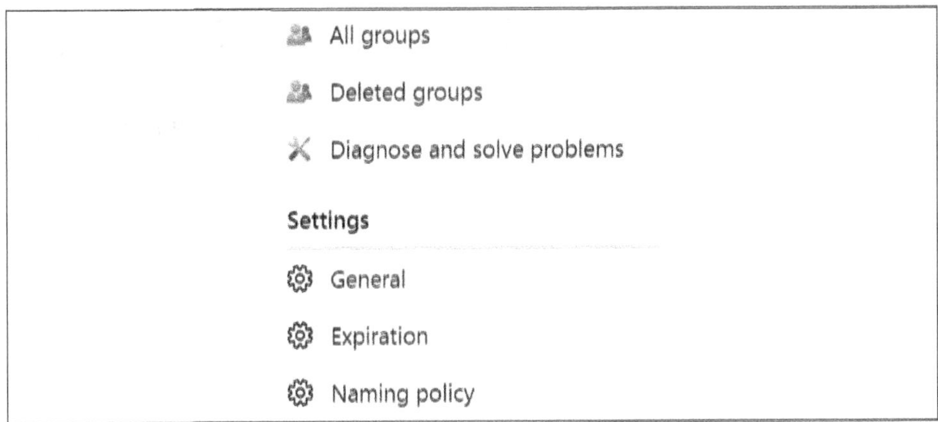

Figure 15-1. Setting the naming policy in Entra

On the "Group naming policy" tab, you can add one or more prefixes and one or more suffixes. Both prefixes and suffixes can use strings or AD attributes). In this example, the prefix is a string (O365) and the suffixes are the Department and Office attributes taken from AD (see Figure 15-2).

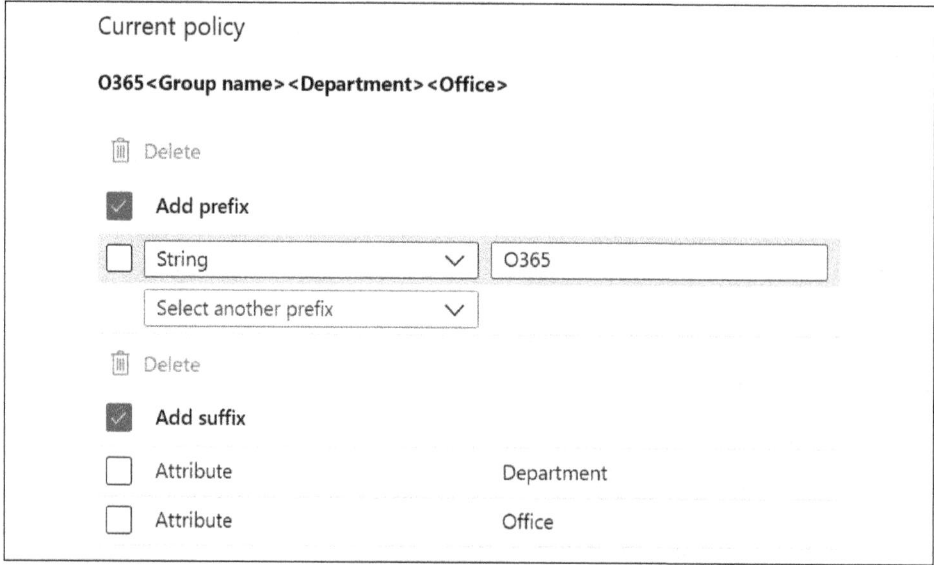

Figure 15-2. Creating a naming policy with strings and AD attributes

When you're done, click Save. With the policy applied, every time a user tries to create a new team, the team's name will be automatically modified to include the required prefixes and suffixes.

Now, to add words that are not allowed when naming a group, click "Blocked words" and then Download (as shown in Figure 15-3).

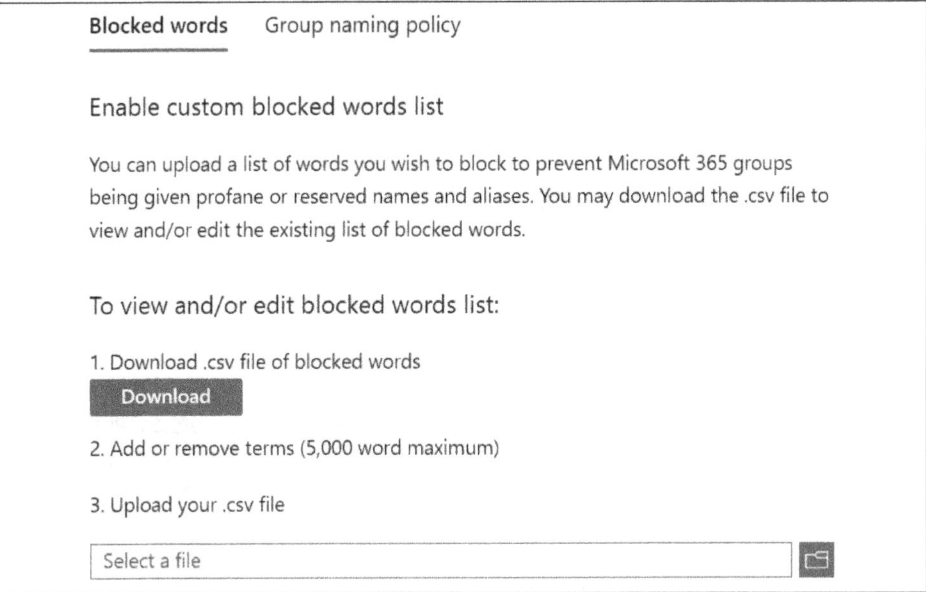

Blocked words
Group naming policy
Enable custom blocked words list
You can upload a list of words you wish to block to prevent Microsoft 365 groups being given profane or reserved names and aliases. You may download the .csv file to view and/or edit the existing list of blocked words.
To view and/or edit blocked words list:
1. Download .csv file of blocked words
Download
2. Add or remove terms (5,000 word maximum)
3. Upload your .csv file
Select a file

Figure 15-3. Adding blocked words to the naming policy

Populate the CSV file with a list of the words to block, as shown in Figure 15-4, and then upload it by clicking on the small folder icon.

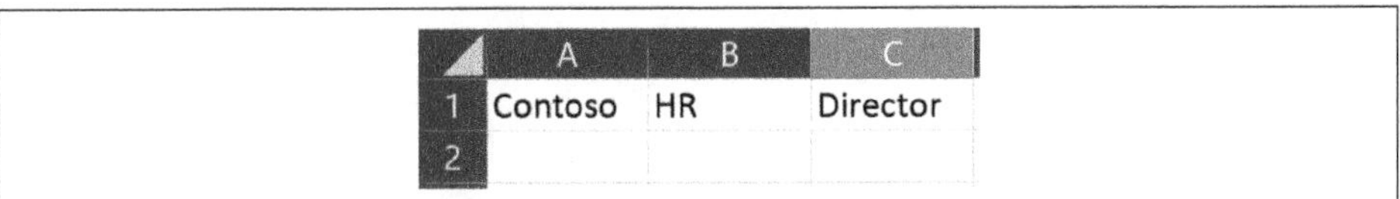

Figure 15-4. Editing the blocked words in the CSV file

A notification of "Upload completed" will be displayed in the upper-right corner of the screen. You can test the policy by opening the Teams client and creating a new team. You'll be able to see the prefixes and suffixes applied (see the Teams client behavior in Figure 15-5).

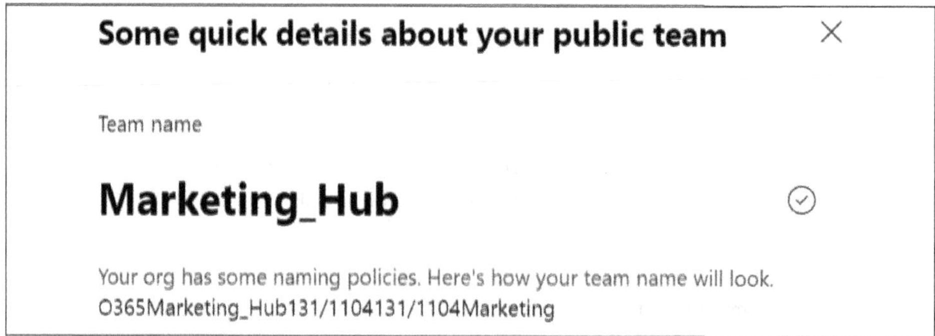

Some quick details about your public team
Team name
Marketing_Hub
Your org has some naming policies. Here's how your team name will look.
O365Marketing_Hub131/1104131/1104Marketing

Figure 15-5. Creating a new team with the naming policy applied

Figure 15-6 shows the error message you'll get if you try to use a blocked word.

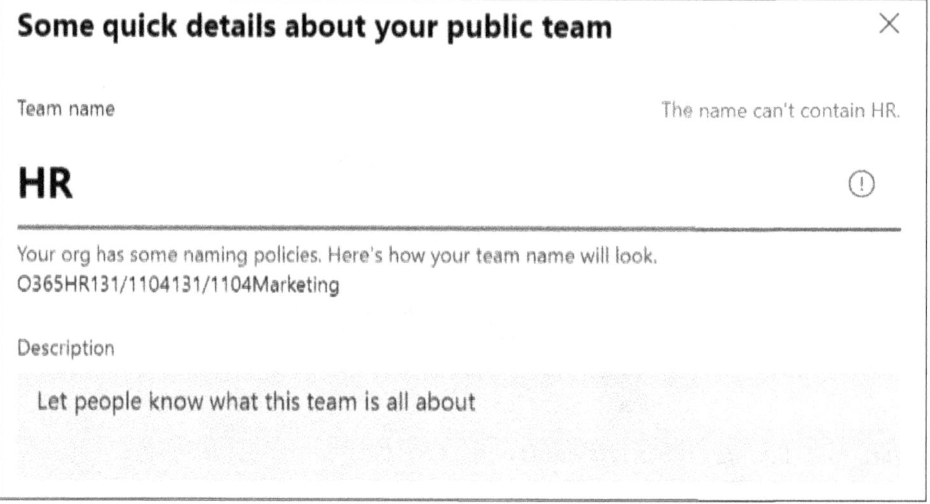

Figure 15-6. Blocked words user error

Discussion

A naming convention is a set of rules that are used to apply consistent and systematic names to items like files, folders, and teams. A naming convention for Teams might include rules for how long names can be, what characters can be used, and whether names should be structured in a particular way (such as using a specific prefix and/or suffix). For example, a naming convention for Teams might specify that team names should be no longer than 20 characters and should start with the name of the department or project, followed by a hyphen and a short description of the team's purpose. Using a naming convention can help to make it easier for users to find and access teams and can also help to maintain consistency and organization within the platform.

The naming policy will be applied to all the workloads in the tenant for new Microsoft 365 groups created by end users. Members of the Global Administrator and User Administrator groups are exempted from the policy.

For existing Microsoft 365 groups, the policy will not immediately apply. Once the group owner edits the group name, the naming policy will be enforced, even if no changes are made.

In Chapter 8, you learned how to use Microsoft Forms and Power Automate to manage the creation of new teams. When using automation in that way (or with a similar method), you can enforce naming conventions as part of the process.

15.3 Controlling Which Users Can Create Microsoft 365 Groups

Problem

You want to limit the ability of users to create groups in all Microsoft 365 services, including Outlook, SharePoint, and Teams.

Solution

First, open the Microsoft 365 admin center (*https://oreil.ly/dc3or*), go to "Teams & groups," and click "Active teams and groups." Select "Add a group" (see Figure 15-7).

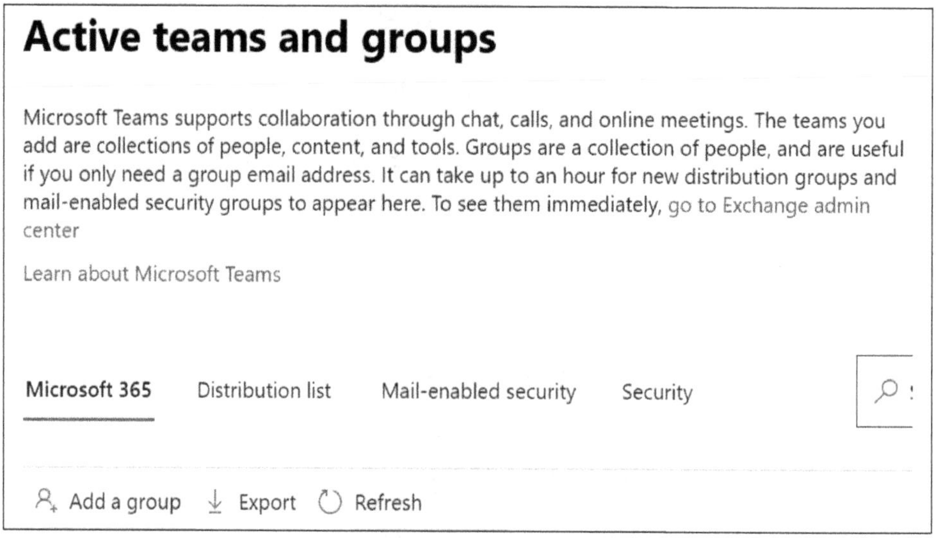

Active teams and groups

Microsoft Teams supports collaboration through chat, calls, and online meetings. The teams you add are collections of people, content, and tools. Groups are a collection of people, and are useful if you only need a group email address. It can take up to an hour for new distribution groups and mail-enabled security groups to appear here. To see them immediately, go to Exchange admin center

Learn about Microsoft Teams

Microsoft 365 | Distribution list | Mail-enabled security | Security

Add a group | Export | Refresh

Figure 15-7. Adding the group in Microsoft 365

On the "Choose a group type" page, select Security (as in Figure 15-8), then click Next.

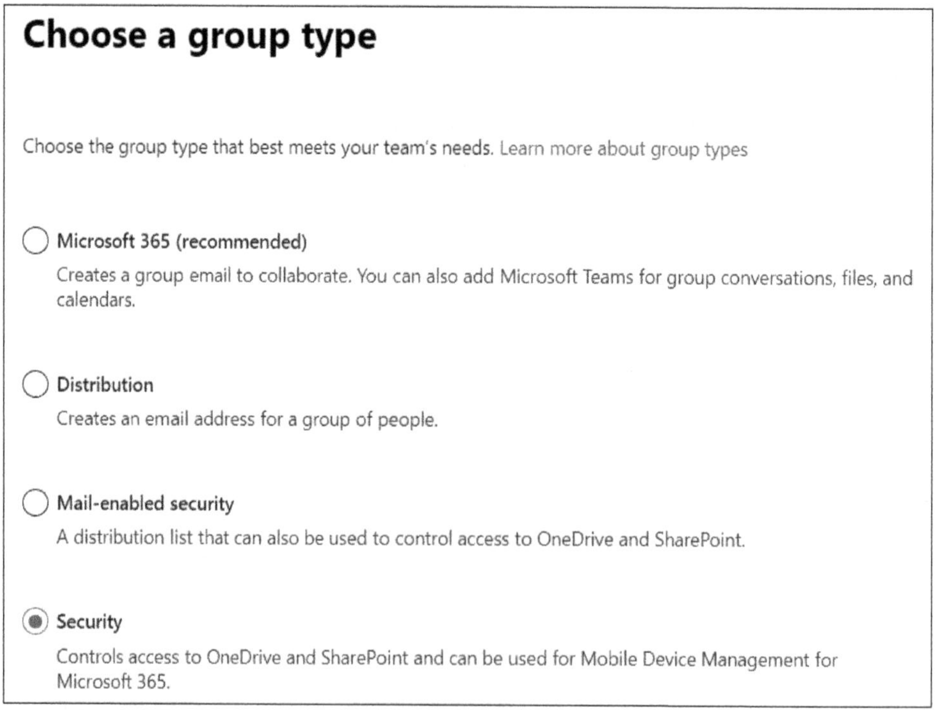

Choose a group type

Choose the group type that best meets your team's needs. Learn more about group types

( ) **Microsoft 365 (recommended)**
Creates a group email to collaborate. You can also add Microsoft Teams for group conversations, files, and calendars.

( ) **Distribution**
Creates an email address for a group of people.

( ) **Mail-enabled security**
A distribution list that can also be used to control access to OneDrive and SharePoint.

(•) **Security**
Controls access to OneDrive and SharePoint and can be used for Mobile Device Management for Microsoft 365.

Figure 15-8. Select Security for the group type

Specify a name for the group by typing *GroupCreationAllowed*, as shown in Figure 15-9, then click Next.

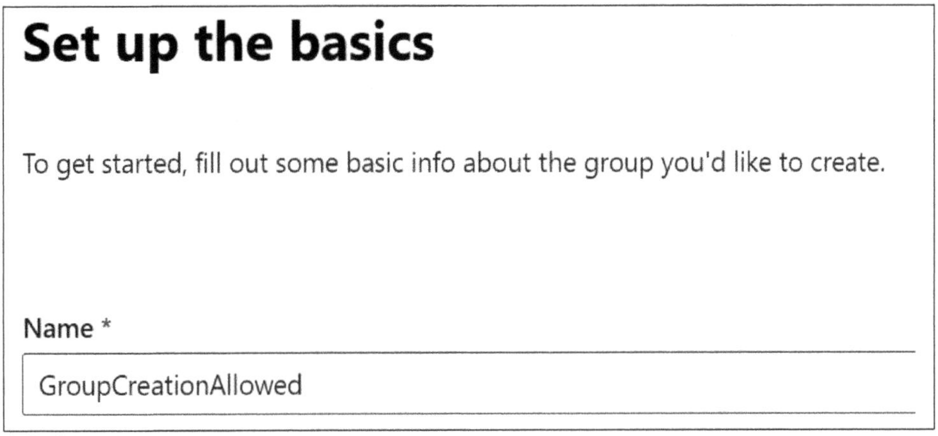

Set up the basics

To get started, fill out some basic info about the group you'd like to create.

Name *

GroupCreationAllowed

Figure 15-9. Naming the group

Click Next again, then click "Create group." At the end of the process, click Close. Select the Security tab, then click on the GroupCreationAllowed group (see Figure 15-10).

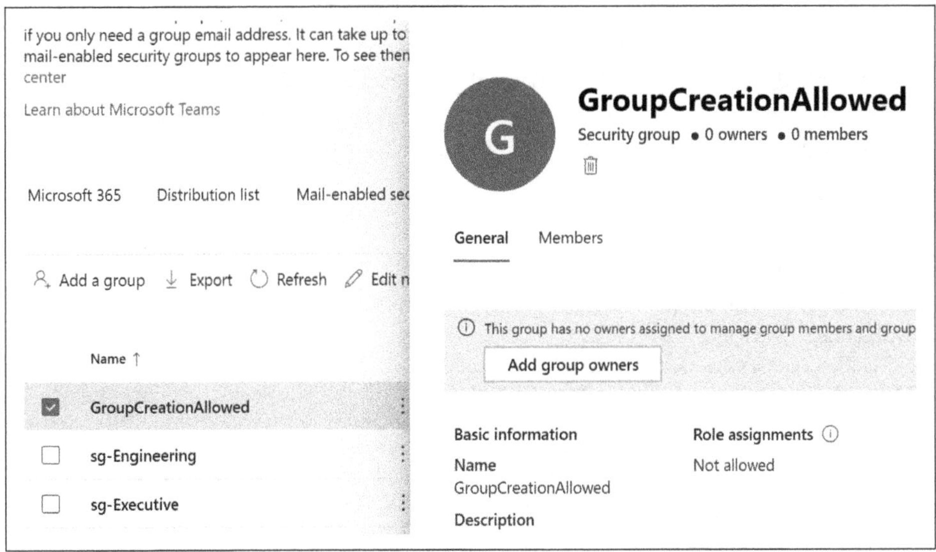

Figure 15-10. Managing the group membership

Select the Members tab, then click "View all and manage members." Click "Add members" and add all the users who will be allowed to create groups (as shown in Figure 15-11).

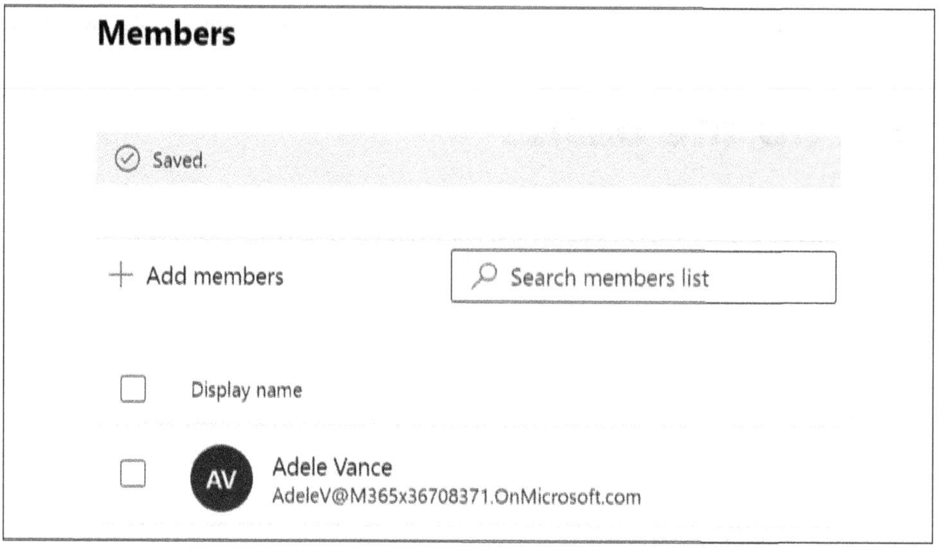

Members

Saved.

\+ Add members

Search members list

Display name

AV Adele Vance
AdeleV@M365x36708371.OnMicrosoft.com

Figure 15-11. Adding members to the group

Finish setting up the group by adding the people or other security groups that you want to have the ability to create groups in your tenant.

The next step requires you to run a PowerShell script based on Azure Active Directory PowerShell for Graph. If you have the General Availability (GA) module AzureAD installed, you will need to remove it and install the AzureADPreview module. To verify the installed version, use the `Get-InstalledModule` command. To remove the GA module and to install the preview, run the following two commands:

```
Uninstall-Module AzureAD
Install-Module AzureADPreview
```

Figure 15-12 shows that the installed module has been verified, the GA version of AzureAD has been uninstalled, the preview version has been installed, and the version has been verified.

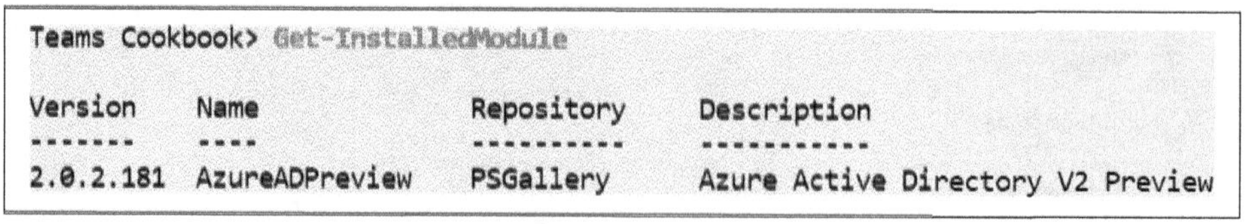

```
Teams Cookbook> Get-InstalledModule

Version     Name            Repository    Description
-------     ----            ----------    -----------
2.0.2.181   AzureADPreview  PSGallery     Azure Active Directory V2 Preview
```

Figure 15-12. Preparing the AzureADPreview module

Save the following script in a PS1 file (for example, *groupcreation.ps1*). In the script, replace the value in `$GroupName` with your group name:

```
$GroupName = "GroupCreationAllowed"
$AllowGroupCreation = $False

Connect-AzureAD

$settingsObjectID = (Get-AzureADDirectorySetting | Where-object -Property `
  DisplayName -Value "Group.Unified" -EQ).id
if(!$settingsObjectID)
{
    $template = Get-AzureADDirectorySettingTemplate | Where-object `
      {$_.displayname -eq "group.unified"}
    $settingsCopy = $template.CreateDirectorySetting()
    New-AzureADDirectorySetting -DirectorySetting $settingsCopy
    $settingsObjectID = (Get-AzureADDirectorySetting | Where-object -Property `
      DisplayName -Value "Group.Unified" -EQ).id
}

$settingsCopy = Get-AzureADDirectorySetting -Id $settingsObjectID
$settingsCopy["EnableGroupCreation"] = $AllowGroupCreation

if($GroupName)
{
  $settingsCopy["GroupCreationAllowedGroupId"] = (Get-AzureADGroup `
    -SearchString $GroupName).objectid
} else {
$settingsCopy["GroupCreationAllowedGroupId"] = $GroupName
}
Set-AzureADDirectorySetting -Id $settingsObjectID -DirectorySetting `
    $settingsCopy

(Get-AzureADDirectorySetting -Id $settingsObjectID).Values
```

The output of the script will show the ID of the GroupCreationAllowed group under `GroupCreationAllowedGroupId` and `False` under `EnableGroupCreation` (as in the example in Figure 15-13).

```
Name  : GroupCreationAllowedGroupId
Value : b72371b4-4c1e-4a67-8904-14a6c0bff5a3


Name  : AllowToAddGuests
Value : true


Name  : UsageGuidelinesUrl
Value :


Name  : ClassificationList
Value :


Name  : EnableGroupCreation
Value : False
```

Figure 15-13. Checking the settings in PowerShell

Now, if you log in to the Teams client as a user who is not a member of the administrative groups or the GroupCreationAllowed group and click the "Join or create a team" button, only the "Join a team" option will be offered (as shown in Figure 15-14).

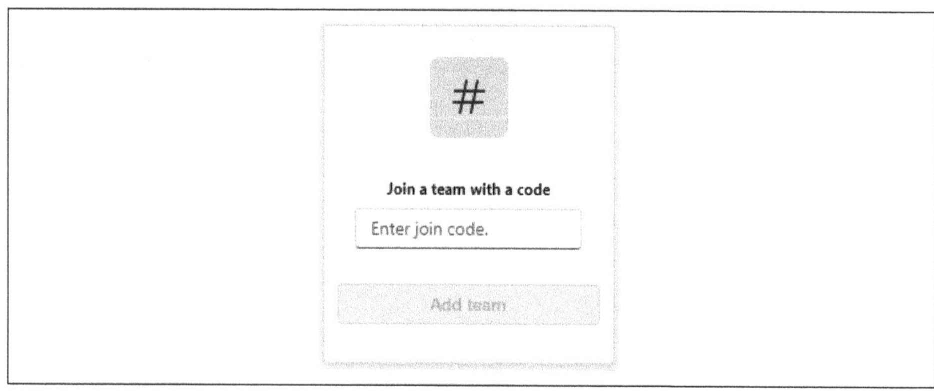

Figure 15-14. The "Create a new team" option is not available for certain users

Discussion

The default settings allow every user in your tenant to create their own teams at will with no restrictions. Every team created generates a Microsoft 365 group on the back-end, which in turn creates other Microsoft 365 services (as you saw in Chapter 6, a SharePoint Online site and document library, an Exchange Online shared mailbox and calendar, and a OneNote notebook).

Administrator roles will still be able to create groups even after the changes in this recipe have been applied (using the admin interfaces of the different services). The list of groups unaffected by the limitation includes Microsoft 365 global administrators, Exchange administrators, SharePoint administrators, and Teams Service administrators.

The security group created in this recipe had no owner. A group without owners can be managed only by administrators of the tenant. If you are not sure who the owner of a group should be, you can ask the group members (using the "Ask members" button, as shown in Figure 15-15).

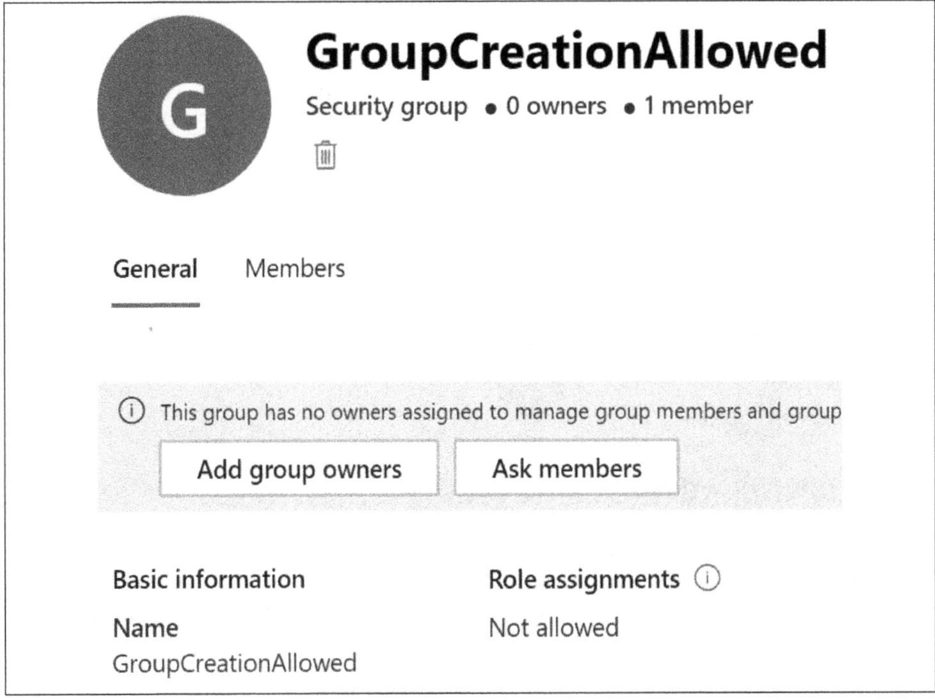

Figure 15-15. Managing the owner of the group

An email (that you can customize) will be sent to all members of the group requiring their assistance. The default email format is shown in Figure 15-16.

Enter up to 90 members to send this email to. If this group has more than 90 members, 90 recipients will be selected by default.

Bcc

Adele Vance

Edit email recipients

Subject *

Need your help with GroupCreationAllowed group

Message *

Hi there,

You're in the Security group GroupCreationAllowed which doesn't have a group owner right now. Owners manage group settings, members, and a few other things. If this group and its content are important to you, please 'reply' to let me know who the new group owner should be or to delete the group.

If I don't hear from anyone soon, I'll assume the group should be deleted.

Figure 15-16. Default email format for contacting group members to propose a group owner

To revert the changes and enable all users to create Microsoft 365 groups again, modify the second line of the script to:

```
$AllowGroupCreation = $True
```

15.4 Controlling Microsoft Teams Guest Access

Problem

You want to protect the information in Teams that is exposed to external users in a granular way.

Solution

Sensitivity labels can be used to protect content in Teams. Since they can be applied at the individual team level, sensitivity labels remove the need for a complete "on" or "off" switch for guest access.

Guest access in Teams relies on settings that are distributed in different Microsoft 365 services:

- Entra ID (to define whether external collaborators can be invited into your tenant as guests)
- Teams (to control the guest experience in Teams)
- Microsoft 365 groups
- SharePoint Online and OneDrive for Business

From a governance point of view, external collaboration settings in Entra ID are particularly relevant. Open the Microsoft Entra admin portal (*https://oreil.ly/dVYZ8*) and click External Identities in the left pane. Then select "External collaboration settings" (see Figure 15-17).

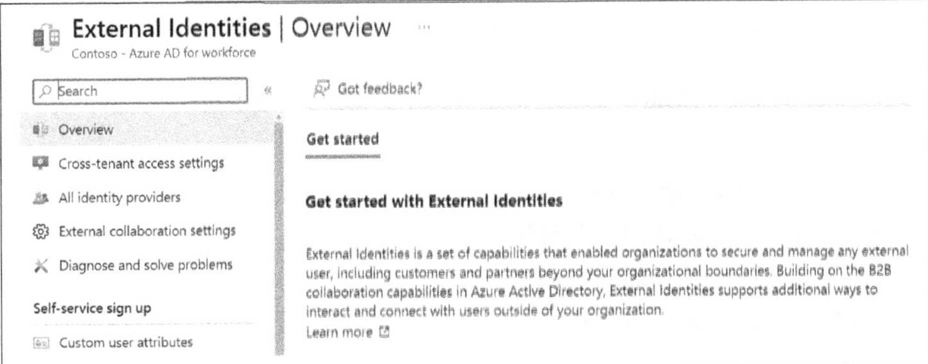

Figure 15-17. External Identities in Entra ID

The "Guest invite settings" section defines who can invite external users as guests (an example is shown in Figure 15-18).

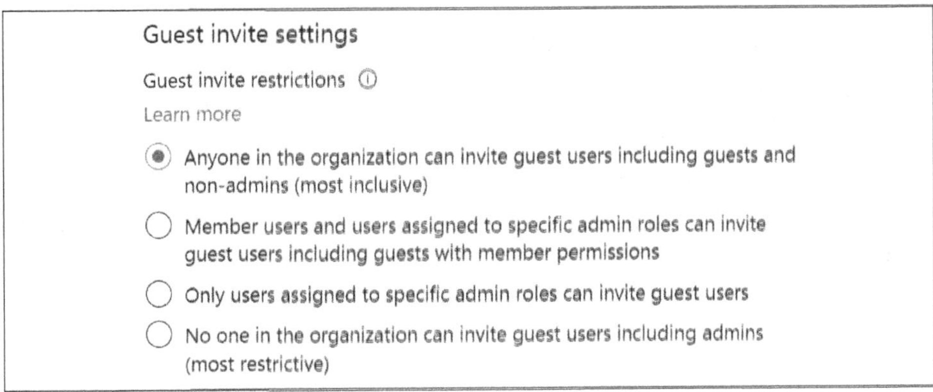

Figure 15-18. Guest invite settings

From the TAC, on the "Guest access" page under Users, you can allow guest access in Teams and define which actions a guest is allowed to perform (see Figure 15-19).

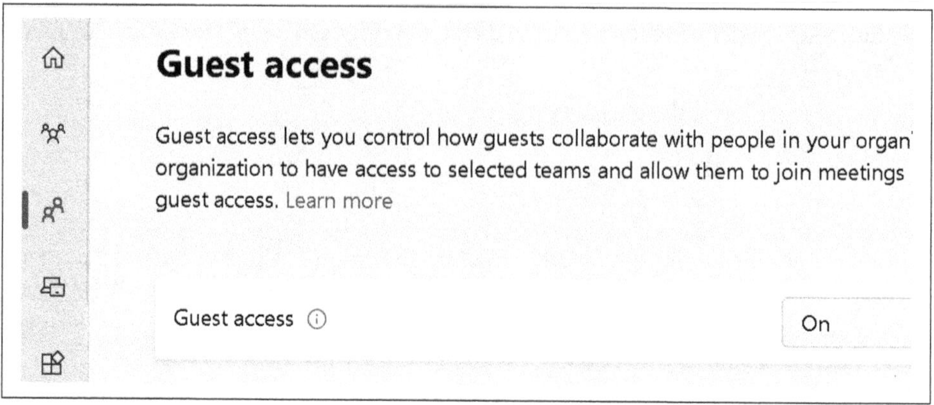

Figure 15-19. Guest access management in the TAC

After you have allowed guest access, the following steps are required to enable sensitivity labels in Teams:

- Enable sensitivity labels for containers (you must enable the feature in Entra ID).
- Synchronize sensitivity labels to Entra ID.
- Configure "Groups & sites" settings in the sensitivity labeling wizard.
- Publish sensitivity labels that are configured for sites and groups.

To enable sensitivity labels, you must work with the AzureADPreview module, as we discussed in Recipe 15.3. Run the following commands:

```
Uninstall-Module AzureAD
Install-Module AzureADPreview
Connect-AzureAD
```

Then, retrieve the existing settings with the following commands:

```
$grpUnifiedSetting = (Get-AzureADDirectorySetting | where -Property `
  DisplayName -Value "Group.Unified" -EQ)
$Setting = $grpUnifiedSetting
$grpUnifiedSetting.Values
```

If `EnableMIPLabels` is set to `False`, sensitivity labels are not enabled (as in Figure 15-20).

```
Name                               Value
----                               -----
NewUnifiedGroupWritebackDefault true
EnableMIPLabels                    false
CustomBlockedWordsList             Contoso,HR,Director
EnableMSStandardBlockedWords       false
ClassificationDescriptions
DefaultClassification
PrefixSuffixNamingRequirement      O365[GroupName][Department][Office]
AllowGuestsToBeGroupOwner          false
AllowGuestsToAccessGroups          true
GuestUsageGuidelinesUrl
GroupCreationAllowedGroupId
AllowToAddGuests                   true
UsageGuidelinesUrl
ClassificationList
EnableGroupCreation                True
```

Figure 15-20. Checking sensitivity labels enablement

To enable sensitivity labels, use the following commands:

```
$Setting["EnableMIPLabels"] = "True"
Set-AzureADDirectorySetting -Id $Setting.Id -DirectorySetting $Setting
```

To activate the labels, you need to run commands using the ExchangeOnlineManagement module.

You may need to install the module and alter the script execution policy to enable the module to run. If this is the case, use the following commands:

```
Install-Module ExchangeOnlineManagement
Set-ExecutionPolicy Unrestricted
```

Now you need to synchronize your sensitivity labels to Entra ID using the following commands:

```
Import-Module ExchangeOnlineManagement
Connect-IPPSSession
Execute-AzureAdLabelSync
```

The final step is executed by opening the Purview portal (*https://oreil.ly/GcKLg*) and clicking "Information protection" (see Figure 15-21).

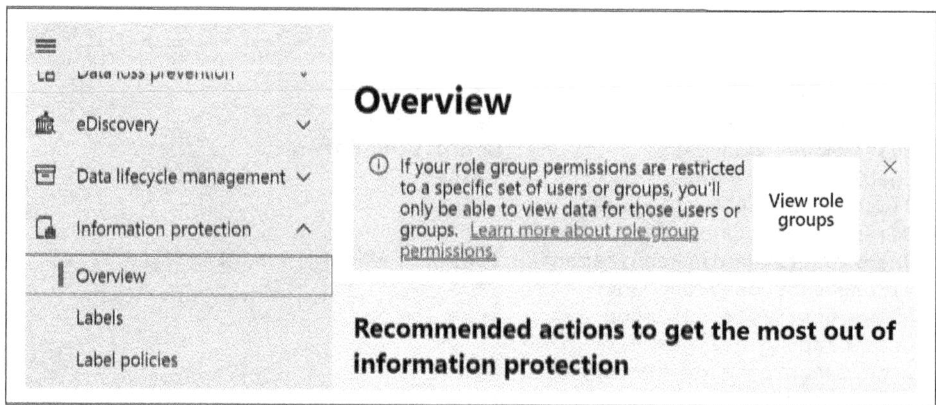

Figure 15-21. Working in the Purview portal

Click Labels > "Create a label," then click the + sign (shown in Figure 15-22) to add a label.

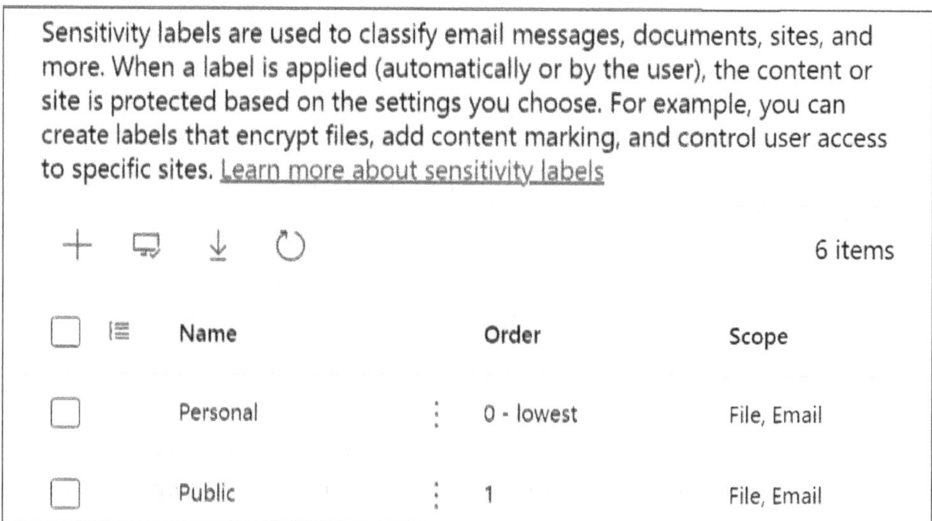

Sensitivity labels are used to classify email messages, documents, sites, and more. When a label is applied (automatically or by the user), the content or site is protected based on the settings you choose. For example, you can create labels that encrypt files, add content marking, and control user access to specific sites. Learn more about sensitivity labels
6 items
Name
Order
Scope
Personal
0 - lowest
File, Email
Public
1
File, Email

Figure 15-22. Starting the label creation process

You'll need to provide a name, a display name, and a description. As shown in Figure 15-23, type *Limiting Guest Access* for the name and display name and *Label used to limit Guest Access* for the description. Click Next.

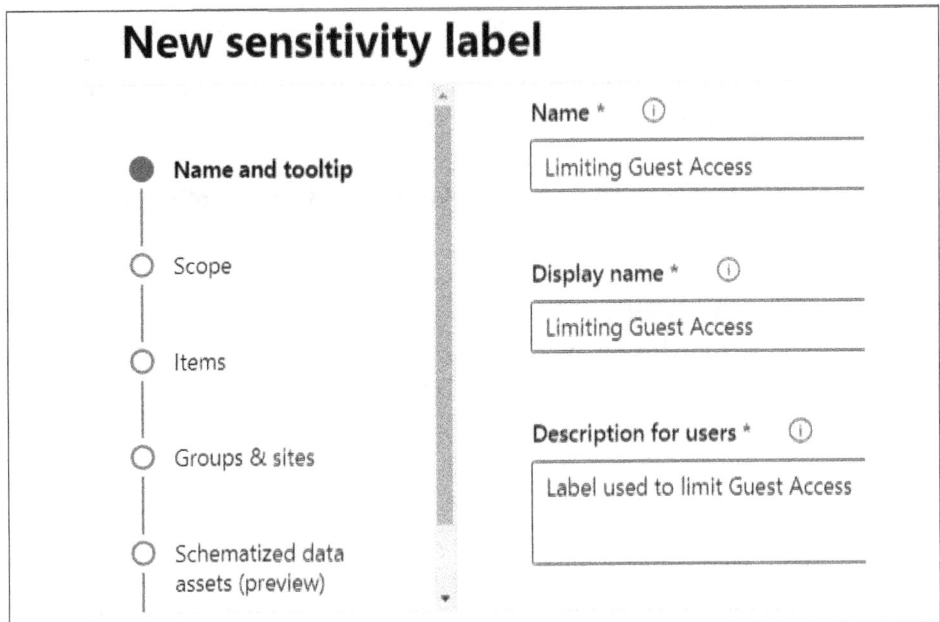

Figure 15-23. Naming the new label

Select "Groups & sites" as the defined scope (see Figure 15-24), and click Next.

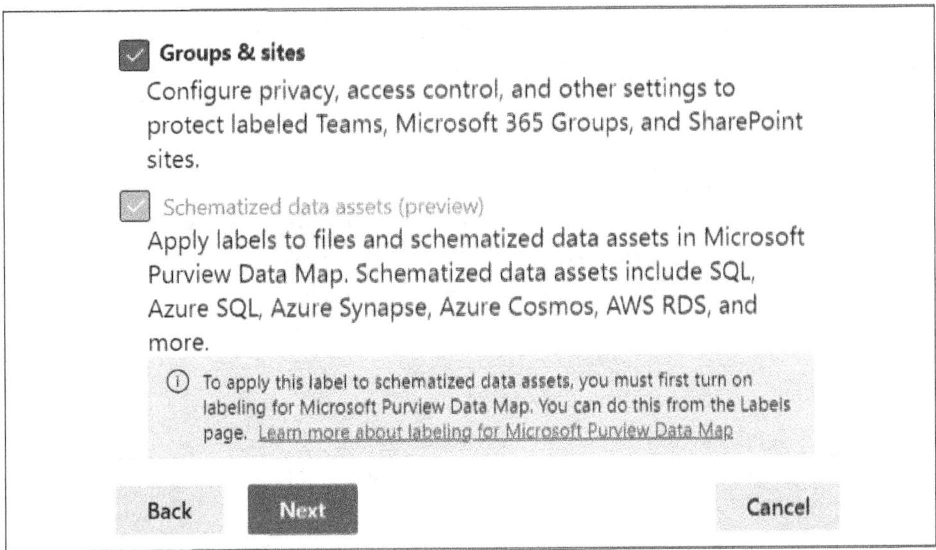

Figure 15-24. Setting the scope of the label

On the "Choose protection settings for labeled items" page, click Next. On the "Define protection settings for groups and sites" page, select "Privacy and external user access settings" and "External sharing and Conditional Access settings," as in Figure 15-25. Click Next.

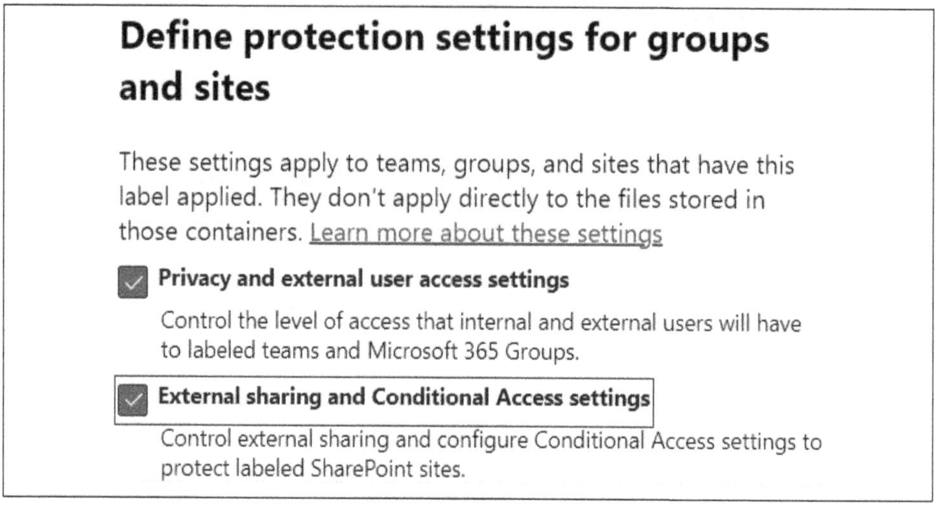

Figure 15-25. Defining the protection settings

On the "Define privacy and external user access settings" page, select the privacy settings you want to apply to the team (for example, Public inside the organization, as shown in Figure 15-26, with the "External user access" option disabled).

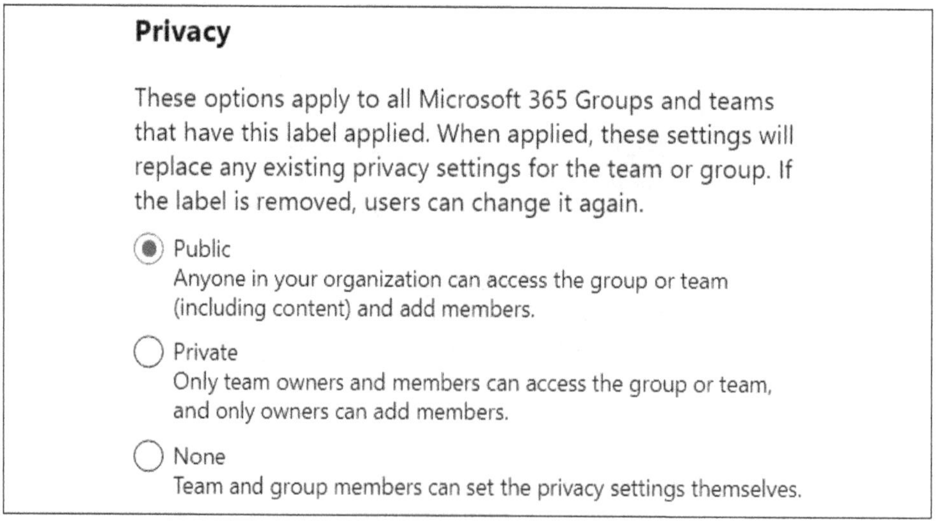

Privacy
These options apply to all Microsoft 365 Groups and teams that have this label applied. When applied, these settings will replace any existing privacy settings for the team or group. If the label is removed, users can change it again.
Public
Anyone in your organization can access the group or team (including content) and add members.
Private
Only team owners and members can access the group or team, and only owners can add members.
None
Team and group members can set the privacy settings themselves.

Figure 15-26. Privacy related to the sensitivity label

If you select Public or Private, the label will be usable only with teams that have the same level of privacy.

On the "Define external sharing and Conditional Access settings" page, decide who can access the SharePoint site (for example, only users from your organization) and what kind of access is allowed (the settings are shown in Figure 15-27). Then, click Next.

Control external sharing from labeled SharePoint sites

When this label is applied to a SharePoint site, these settings will replace existing ‹

Content can be shared with

Anyone

Users can share files and folders using links that don't require sign-in.

New and existing guests

Guests must sign in or provide a verification code.

Existing guests

Only guests in your organization's directory.

Only people in your organization

No external sharing allowed.

Use Azure AD Conditional Access to protect labeled SharePoint sites

You can either control the level of access users have from unmanaged devices or s

Determine whether users can access SharePoint sites from unmanaged de Intune).

For this setting to work, you must also configure the SharePoint feature that blc

Allow full access from desktop apps, mobile apps, and the web

Allow limited, web-only access

Block access

Figure 15-27. External sharing and Conditional Access settings

Click Next on the "Auto-labeling for schematized data assets (preview)" page, and click "Create label" on the final screen. Back on the "Information protection" page, select the sensitivity label you have created and click "Publish label" (see Figure 15-28).

+ Create sublabel Publish label Edit label

Name	Order
Personal	0 - lowest
Public	1
> General	2
> Confidential	5
> Highly Confidential	9
Confidential - Finance	13
Limiting Guest Access	14 - highest

Figure 15-28. Publishing the label

Click Next on the "Choose sensitivity labels to publish" page. On the "Publish to users and groups" page, leave the default settings (shown in Figure 15-29) and click Next.

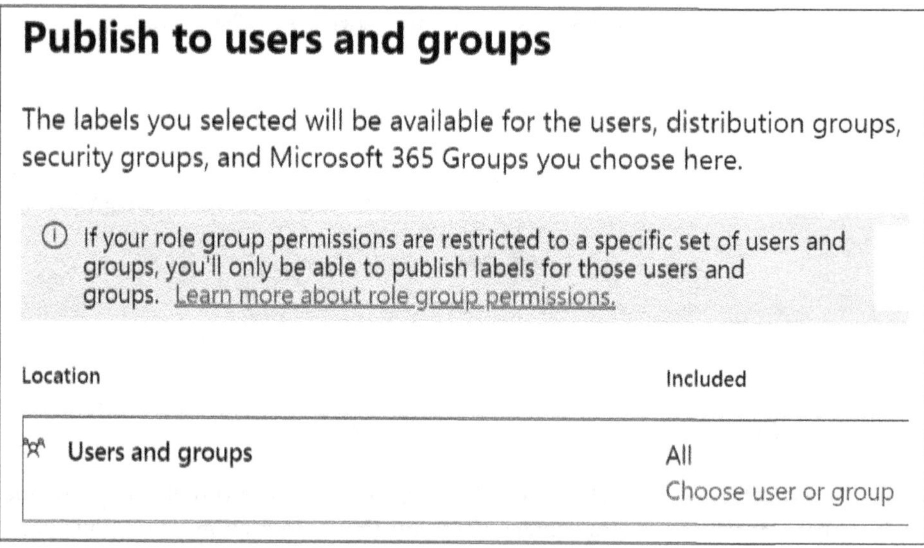

Publish to users and groups
The labels you selected will be available for the users, distribution groups, security groups, and Microsoft 365 Groups you choose here.
If your role group permissions are restricted to a specific set of users and groups, you'll only be able to publish labels for those users and groups. Learn more about role group permissions.
Location
Included
Users and groups
All
Choose user or group

Figure 15-29. "Publish to users and groups" default settings

On the "Policy settings" page, leave the default options (shown in Figure 15-30) and click Next.

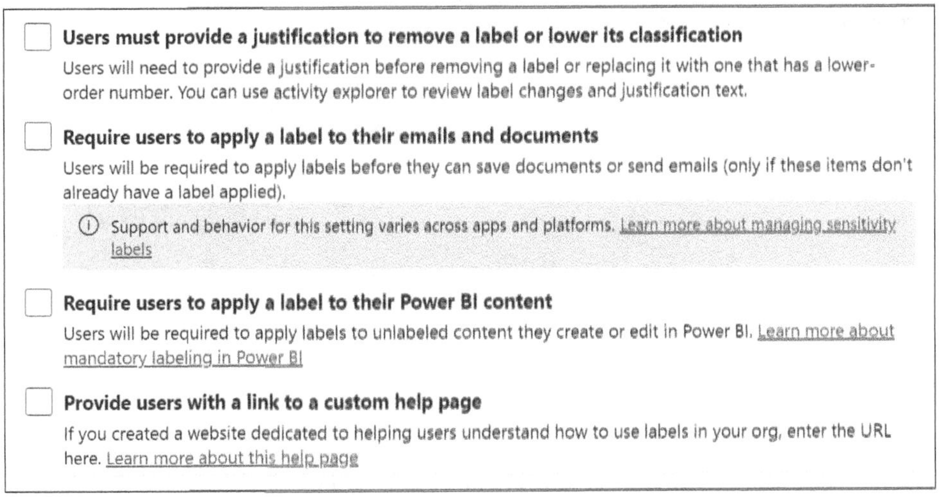

Users must provide a justification to remove a label or lower its classification
Users will need to provide a justification before removing a label or replacing it with one that has a lower-order number. You can use activity explorer to review label changes and justification text.
Require users to apply a label to their emails and documents
Users will be required to apply labels before they can save documents or send emails (only if these items don't already have a label applied).
Support and behavior for this setting varies across apps and platforms. Learn more about managing sensitivity labels
Require users to apply a label to their Power BI content
Users will be required to apply labels to unlabeled content they create or edit in Power BI. Learn more about mandatory labeling in Power BI
Provide users with a link to a custom help page
If you created a website dedicated to helping users understand how to use labels in your org, enter the URL here. Learn more about this help page

Figure 15-30. "Policy settings" default settings

On the "Default settings for sites and groups" page, click Next. On the "Name your policy" page, type a name for your policy (for example, *Limiting Access*, as shown in Figure 15-31) and then click Next.

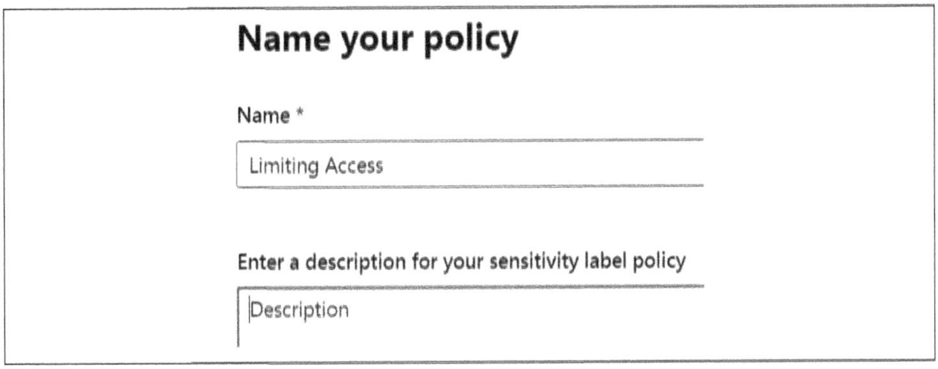

Name your policy
Name *
Limiting Access
Enter a description for your sensitivity label policy
Description

Figure 15-31. Naming the policy

On the final page, click Submit.

It can take some time for the label to be published. When the process is complete, log in to the Teams client as one of the users that has access to the label. Select an existing team and click Edit. In the Sensitivity field, you can select the labels you have published (as shown in Figure 15-32).

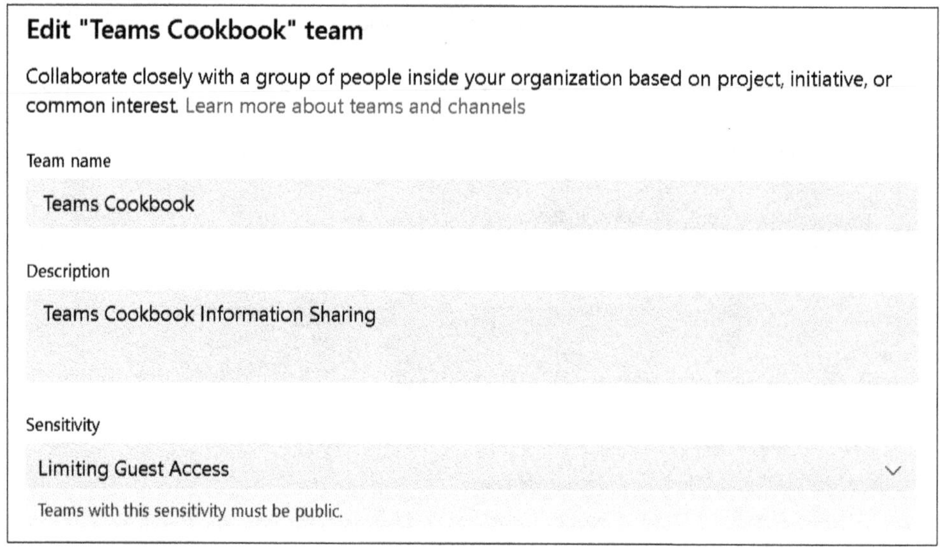

Figure 15-32. Applying sensitivity labels to an existing team

The labels will also be available when you create a new team (see Figure 15-33).

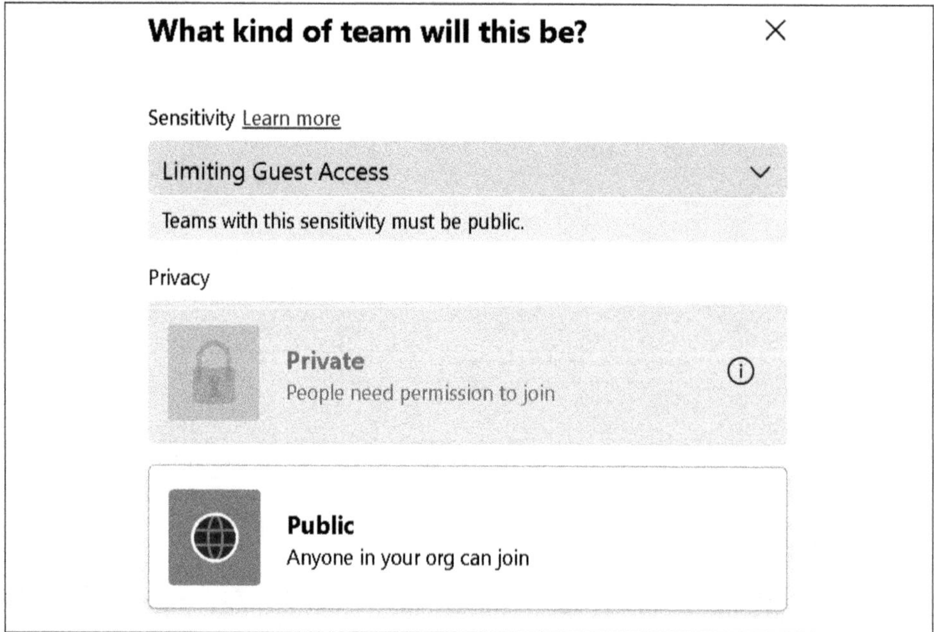

Figure 15-33. Applying sensitivity labels to a new team

Depending on the settings in the selected label, certain privacy settings may not be available (in this example, only Public and Org-wide users can access the team).

Discussion

In Chapter 11 we talked about how to manage external user access to Teams. When planning and deploying a Teams governance policy, it is important to clarify how the external access (for example, guest access) is implemented and what rules prevent data leaking and similar issues. The guest access policy (at a tenant level) is meant to allow or disallow access. If you select "allow," then the only way to limit guest access is to block specific groups for guest users.

Sensitivity labels in Teams are part of the broader Microsoft 365 security and compliance features. They allow administrators to create and apply labels to messages and files in order to classify and protect sensitive information. These labels can be configured to apply specific restrictions, such as preventing messages from being forwarded or shared outside the organization or requiring that messages be encrypted when they are sent.

When a sensitivity label is applied to a message or file in Teams, it will be indicated by a visual marker, such as a colored banner or icon. This allows users to easily identify sensitive content and take appropriate action, such as not forwarding the message or handling the file with care.

In addition to applying sensitivity labels manually, administrators can also configure automatic labeling rules that will apply labels to messages and files based on specific criteria, such as the presence of sensitive keywords or phrases. This can help ensure that sensitive information is consistently labeled and protected. Overall, sensitivity labels in Teams can help organizations protect sensitive information and maintain compliance with various regulations and standards.

In Purview, sensitivity labels can be applied to specific items or containers to classify and protect sensitive data. When a sensitivity label is applied to a specific item, such as a file or a database table, it indicates that the item contains sensitive data and specifies the type of data and the level of sensitivity. This helps to ensure that the item is properly classified, and that access to it is restricted to authorized users or groups. When a sensitivity label is applied to a container, such as a folder or a database schema, it indicates that *all* the items within that container are sensitive and should be treated accordingly. This can be useful when there are many items within a container, and it is more efficient to apply the sensitivity label to the container rather than to each individual item.

15.5 Summary

Teams data access controls are used to ensure that only authorized users have access to the information stored in Teams. This includes setting up user roles and permissions, defining who can view or edit certain files, and setting up restrictions on who can share files with external users. Additionally, these controls help ensure that data is protected from unauthorized access and misuse.

The next chapter focuses on Teams compliance and the related features, including Data Loss Prevention (DLP) policies and the Purview compliance portal.

CHAPTER 16

Microsoft Teams Compliance

Compliance for Teams (and more generally in Microsoft 365) refers to the platform's ability to meet the legal and regulatory requirements that apply to an organization's data and activities. This can include requirements related to data privacy, security, and retention, as well as industry-specific regulations. Microsoft 365 includes a range of features and tools to help organizations comply with these requirements, such as data encryption, access controls, and auditing capabilities.

It is important to clarify the differences between compliance and governance. *Compliance* means adhering to specific rules and regulations. *Governance* means making decisions and setting policies to ensure that an organization operates in a responsible and sustainable manner.

As a collaboration platform, Teams includes many features that can help organizations meet various compliance requirements. For example, Teams offers data encryption, which can help protect sensitive information from unauthorized access. It also includes tools for managing access controls, which allow organizations to specify who can access specific resources within Teams (as you learned in Chapter 15).

Additionally, Teams includes features for managing user activity and tracking changes to files and documents. This can be helpful for meeting certain compliance requirements related to auditing and record keeping. Furthermore, Teams integrates with other Microsoft products that have their own compliance features, like eDiscovery.

16.1 Applying Data Loss Prevention in Microsoft Teams

Problem

You need to create rules to block chat messages based on certain content.

Solution

Microsoft Purview Data Loss Prevention (DLP) is a tool that helps organizations prevent the accidental or intentional sharing of sensitive information (such as financial information, customer data, or intellectual property) in different services, including Teams. This tool monitors and blocks the sharing of data classified as sensitive and provides detailed reports that allow administrators to review and investigate any potential data leakage. Additionally, DLP in Teams can be used to enforce organizational policies and ensure compliance with applicable regulations or standards.

The creation of a DLP policy starts with an intent statement that identifies what you need to monitor, where you need to monitor, the conditions that must be met for the policy to be applied, and the action to be performed when the conditions are matched. DLP policies use AND and OR statements (so all the conditions must be met, or at least one of the conditions must be met). In this recipe, the intent statement is to block all chat messages that contain physical address or password, excluding chats with recipients that are only inside your organization's tenant. The intent must be translated into a content rule that is applied to all the messages that contain physical addresses OR passwords with an additional AND statement to require that the content is shared with external users.

As a first step, open the Microsoft Purview compliance portal (*https://oreil.ly/CXOCT*) and go to "Data loss prevention." Click Policies, then click "Create policy" (as in Figure 16-1).

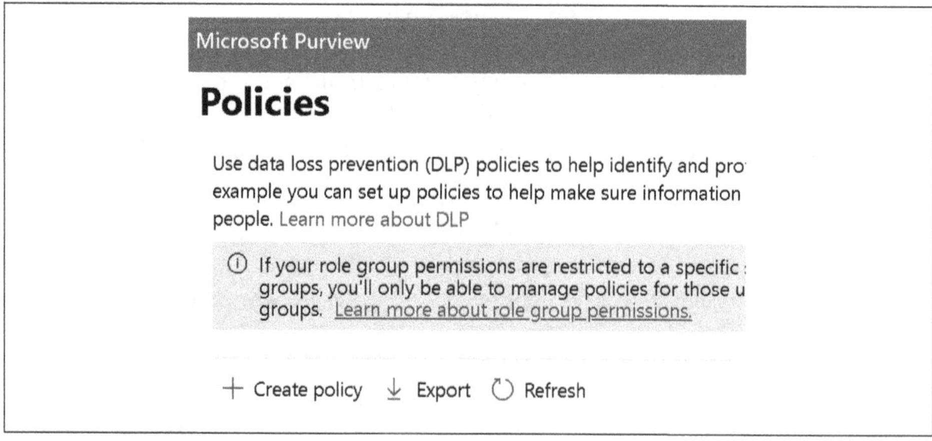

Figure 16-1. Creating a new DLP policy

In the Categories list, click Custom, and then click "Custom policy" in the Templates list (as shown in Figure 16-2). Click Next.

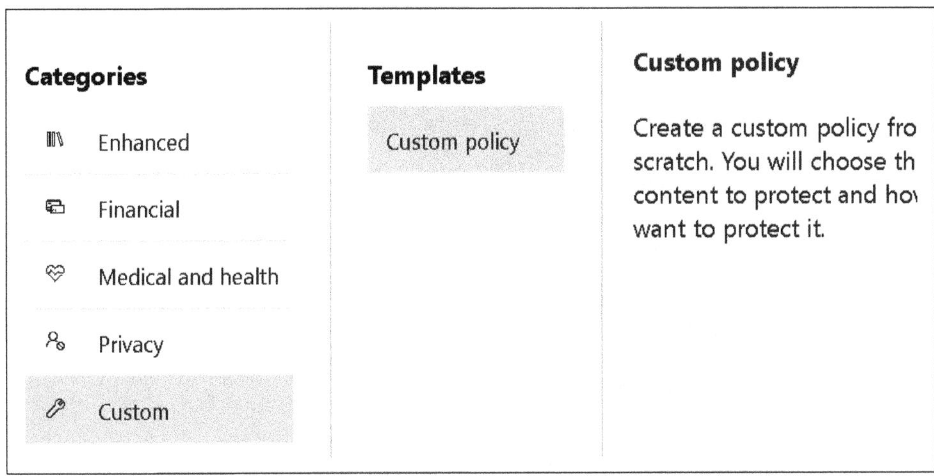

Figure 16-2. Defining a custom policy

Type a name for your policy (in this example, *DLP policy for Teams*) and click Next. On the "Assign admin units (preview)" page, leave the default value ("Admin units" set to "Full directory") and click Next. On the "Choose locations to apply the policy" page, select "Teams chat and channel messages" (see Figure 16-3), then click Next.

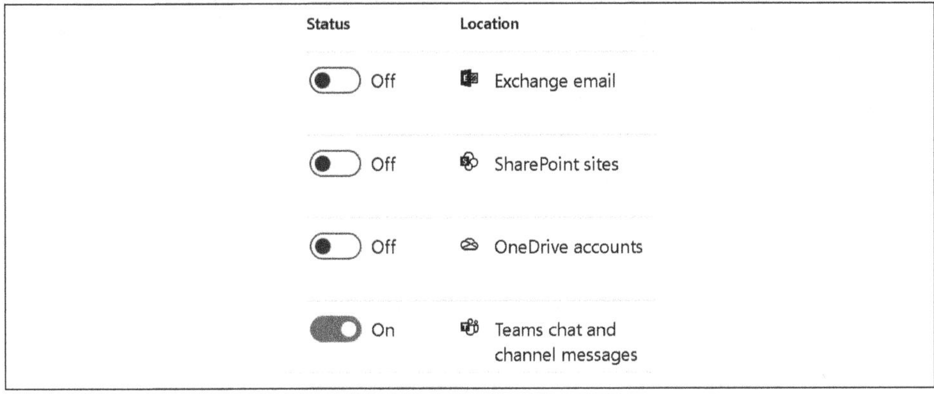

Figure 16-3. Selecting a location for the policy

Click Next on the "Define policy settings" page. On the "Customize advanced DLP rules" page, click "Create rule." Type a name for the rule (in this example, *Data Protection in Teams*), then click "Add condition" and select "Content contains" (the list of available conditions is shown in Figure 16-4).

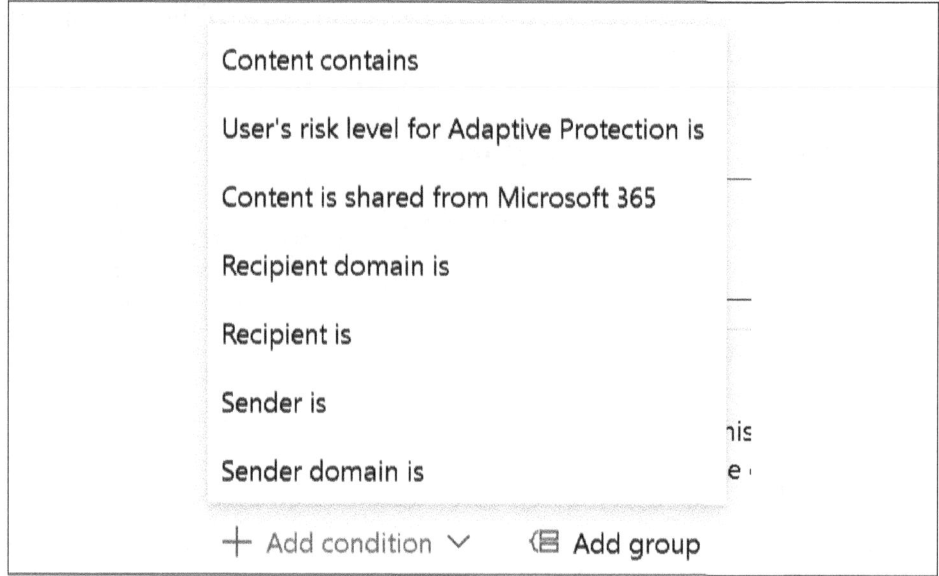

Figure 16-4. Adding conditions to the policy

On the "Create rule" page, you have two different "Group operator" choices: "Any of these" (equivalent to an OR operator) or "All of these" (equivalent to an AND operator). Your intent statement indicates that any of the two conditions is enough to apply the rule, so select "Any of these." Under "Sensitive info types," click Add and select "Sensitive info types" (the other option is "Trainable classifiers," as shown in Figure 16-5).

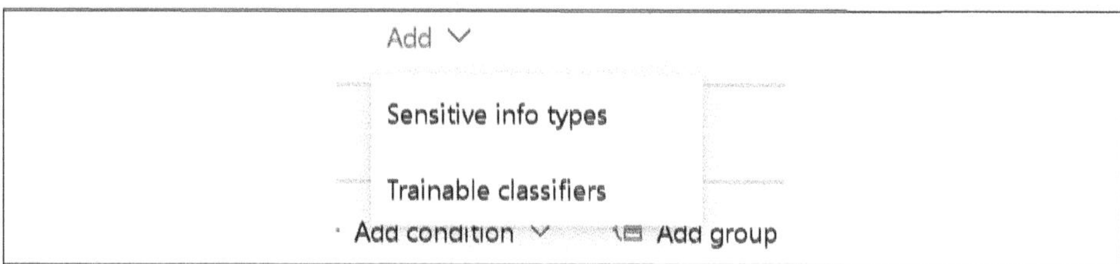

Figure 16-5. Selecting the info type

On the "Sensitive info types" page, select "All Physical Addresses" and "General Password" and click Add. You will be taken back to the "Create rule" page. The "Instance count" is a counter that specifies the minimum number of occurrences of a certain type of information in the message before the rule is matched. In this recipe, we will consider one occurrence enough for a match. The result is shown in Figure 16-6.

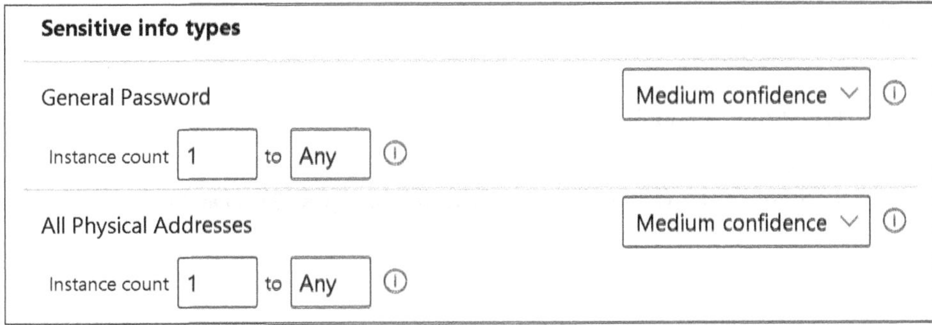

Figure 16-6. The policy with the information and the number of instances considered

Now click "Add condition" again, and select "Content is shared from Microsoft 365" and "with people outside my organization." The condition must be set to AND so that if the conversation is only among people within your organization there is no match (the AND statement is shown in Figure 16-7).

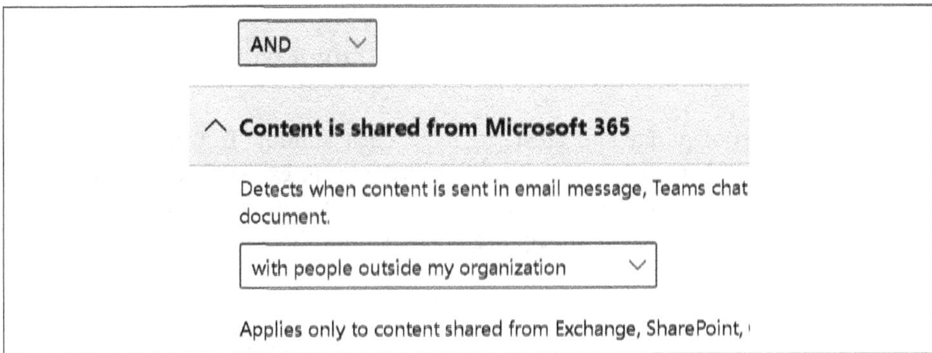

Figure 16-7. Adding an AND statement

Under Actions, select "Restrict access or encrypt the content in Microsoft 365 locations," then select "Block only people outside my organization." Enable "User notifications." Click Save. A summary of your rule will be shown (as in Figure 16-8). Click Next.

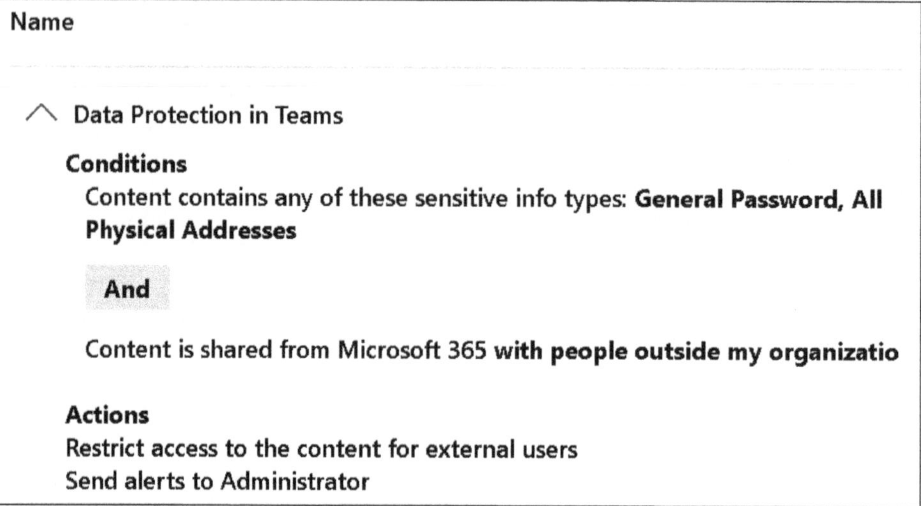

Figure 16-8. Summary of the policy rules

On the "Test or turn on the policy" page, select "Turn it on right away" and click Next.

On the "Review your policy and create it" page, click Submit. To test the rule, open the Teams client and try to send a physical address to an external contact in a chat. The message will be blocked with an error. The "What can I do?" tip will open the Microsoft documentation page to help users understand the policy (a test is shown in Figure 16-9).

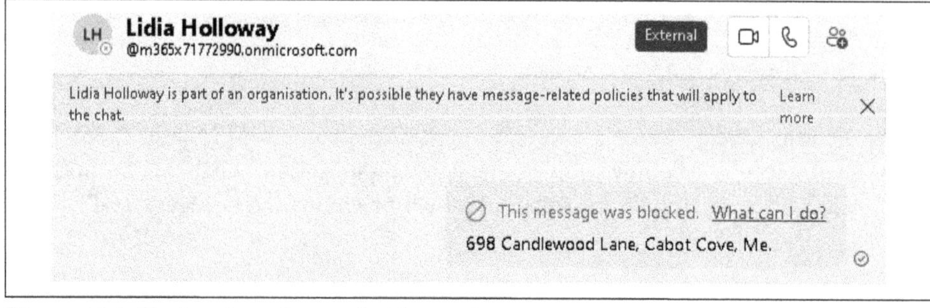

Figure 16-9. Testing the policy in the Teams client

The same content will not be filtered for users within your organization (as shown in Figure 16-10).

Figure 16-10. Internal users are unaffected

Discussion

The easiest way to generate a summary of all the events related to DLP is via the Microsoft Purview compliance portal home page. All the messages and actions that matched the DLP rules will generate an alert (as shown in Figure 16-11). By clicking "Show more" in the portal, you can see details about a single alert and implement some actions, including "Notify users."

Figure 16-11. Viewing alerts in the compliance portal

16.2 Enforcing Communication Compliance in Microsoft Teams

Problem

You need to define a communication compliance policy that blocks targeted harassment, threats, and discrimination in Teams.

Solution

First, open the Microsoft Purview compliance portal (*https://oreil.ly/bGVJq*) and go to "Communication compliance." Click Policies, then click "Create policy" (see Figure 16-12).

Figure 16-12. Policies in "Communication compliance"

From the drop-down menu, select "Detect inappropriate text" (the list of available policies is shown in Figure 16-13).

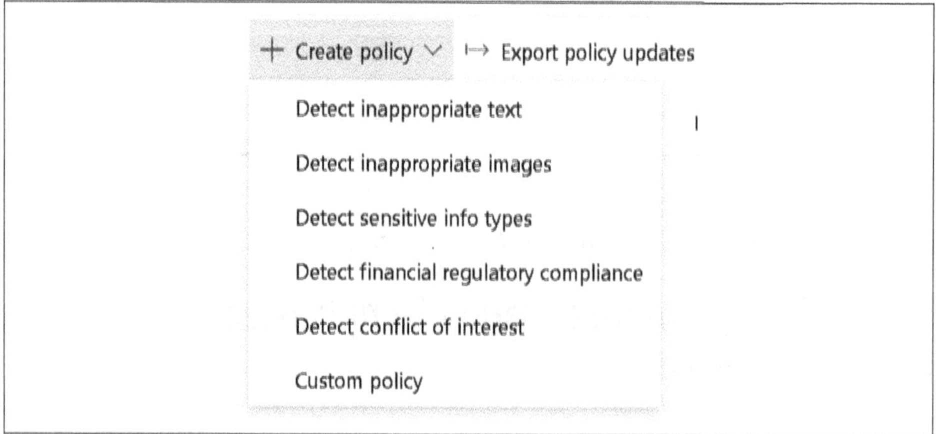

Figure 16-13. Creating a new policy

Click "Customize policy." Click Next in the "Name and describe your policy" section. On the "Choose supervised users and reviewers" page, add the users who will act as reviewers in the Reviewers box, and add the same names in the "Excluded users and groups" box, as shown in Figure 16-14. Then, click Next.

All users

Select users

Select adaptive scopes

Start typing to find users or groups

Excluded users and groups

Specify the group members to be excluded from the policy

AV Adele Vance × BP Bianca Pisani × Start typing

Reviewers *

Choose users to review the communications that are returne

AV Adele Vance × BP Bianca Pisani × Start typing

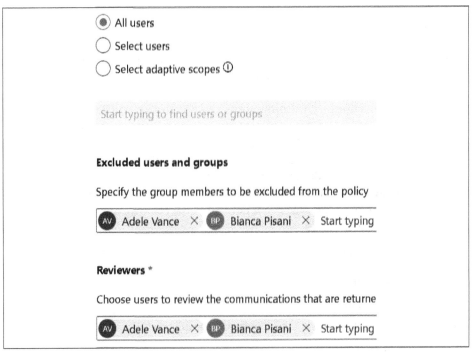

Figure 16-14. Adding exclusions and reviewers

Unselect Exchange and Yammer, and click Next. On the "Choose conditions and review percentage" page, click Next. Then, on the "Review and finish" page, click "Create policy." All the events that break the compliance policy will be shown in the Alerts and Reports tabs (as shown in Figure 16-15).

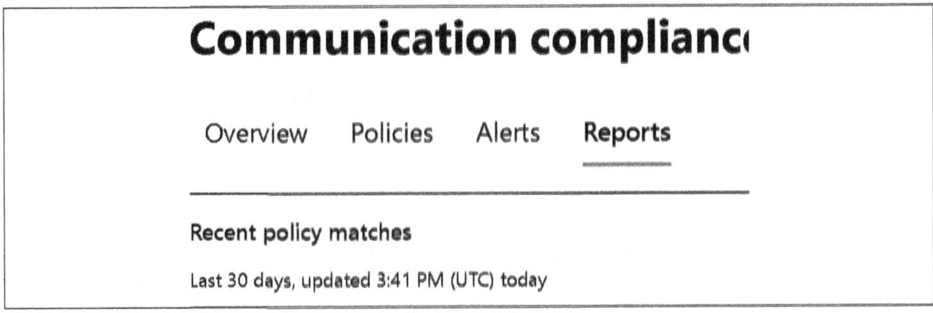

Figure 16-15. Reporting on compliance events

Discussion

Communication compliance policies help you detect, capture, and act on inappropriate messages. Reviewers can investigate scanned email, Teams, or third-party communications, and take appropriate actions to ensure they comply with the organization's message guidelines. After communication compliance policies are configured, reviewers can investigate alerts and remove messages flagged as inappropriate in Teams. Removed messages and content are replaced by notifications explaining that the message was removed and providing details about the specific policy that triggered the removal. The sender of the removed message is also notified of the deletion status and provided with the message's content, for context related to its removal. The recipient of the removed message is not notified of the removal unless the recipient is also the sender of the message.

Communication compliance in Teams includes additional monitoring for:

- Inappropriate images
- Sensitive information
- Information related to financial regulatory compliance
- Conflicts of interest

The default sensitive information types are financial, medical, health, and privacy.

16.3 Managing the Information Lifecycle in Teams with Retention Policies

Problem

You need to define a data retention policy for Teams chat messages and then recover selected messages based on a custom filter.

Solution

From the Microsoft Purview compliance portal (*https://oreil.ly/rvQwr*), select "Data lifecycle management," then click "Microsoft 365" and select "Retention policies." Click "New retention policy," as shown in Figure 16-16.

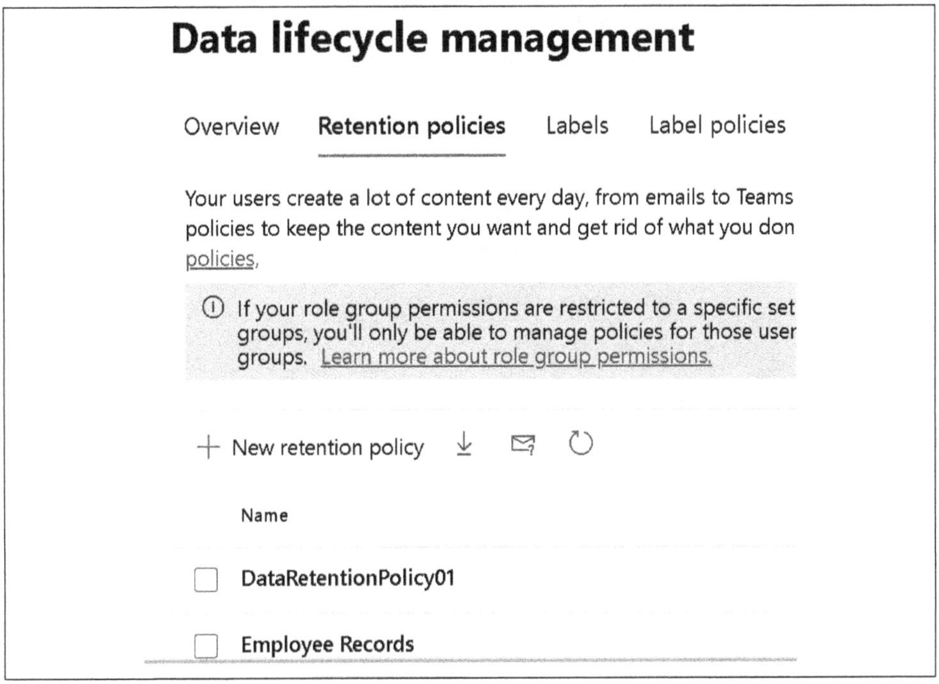

Employee Records

Figure 16-16. Creating a new retention policy

On the "Name your retention policy" page, enter a name for the new policy (in this example, we'll use *Teams Retention Policy).* Click Next. On the "Choose the type of retention policy to create " page, select "Static" (the two options are shown in Figure 16-17), and click Next.

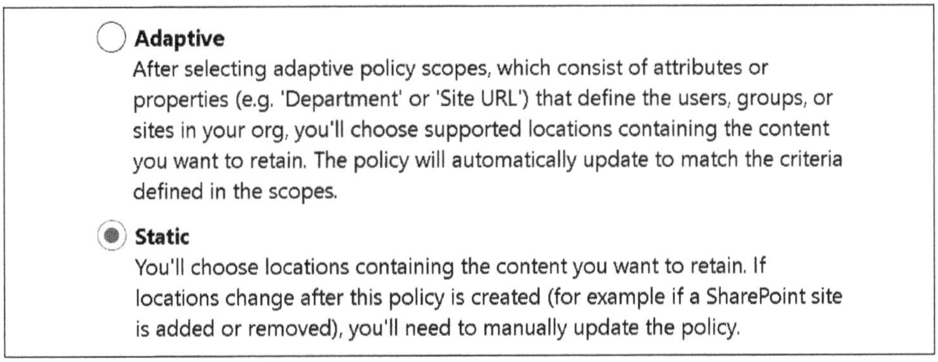

Adaptive
After selecting adaptive policy scopes, which consist of attributes or properties (e.g. 'Department' or 'Site URL') that define the users, groups, or sites in your org, you'll choose supported locations containing the content you want to retain. The policy will automatically update to match the criteria defined in the scopes.
Static
You'll choose locations containing the content you want to retain. If locations change after this policy is created (for example if a SharePoint site is added or removed), you'll need to manually update the policy.

Your users create a lot of content every day, from emails to Teams

Figure 16-17. Selecting an adaptive or static policy

Select "Teams channel messages," then "Teams chats," and click Next. On the next page ("Decide if you want to retain content, delete it, or both"), opt to retain items for a specific period (in this example, five years) from the drop-down menu. Select "Delete items automatically" as the action to take at the end of the retention period (see Figure 16-18). Click Next and then click Submit on the "Review and finish" page.

Figure 16-18. Setting the retention policy

A final report will be shown. Click Done.

Static policies do not adapt to the content when it changes (for example, when a OneDrive URL is created). To manage a more complex or dynamic environment, you must use dynamic policies. To define a dynamic policy, you must define adaptive scopes. Click the "Adaptive scopes" tab and then click "Create scope" (see Figure 16-19).

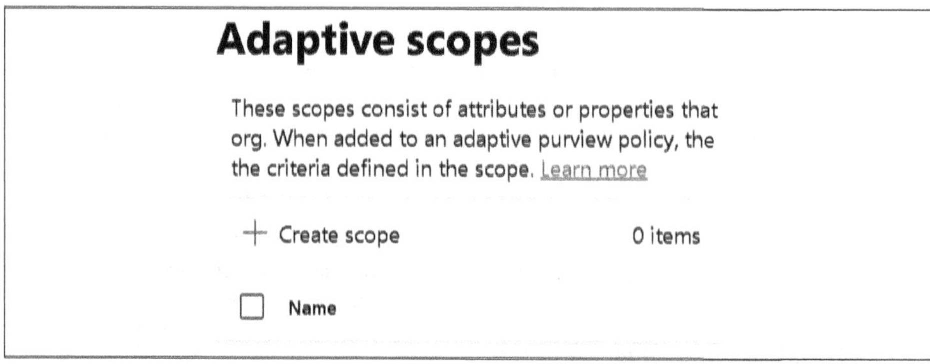

Adaptive scopes
These scopes consist of attributes or properties that
org. When added to an adaptive purview policy, the
the criteria defined in the scope. Learn more
Create scope
0 items
Name

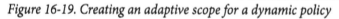

Figure 16-19. Creating an adaptive scope for a dynamic policy

On the "Name your adaptive policy scope" page, type a name for the policy (in this example, we'll use *Teams Adaptive Scope*). Click Next. On the following screen, select Microsoft 365 Groups as the scope, and click Next.

The system supports a selection based on different attributes. In this recipe, we are going to include in the scope all the Microsoft 365 groups whose names start with "M365" (as shown in Figure 16-20). Click Next, then click Submit on the "Review and finish" page.

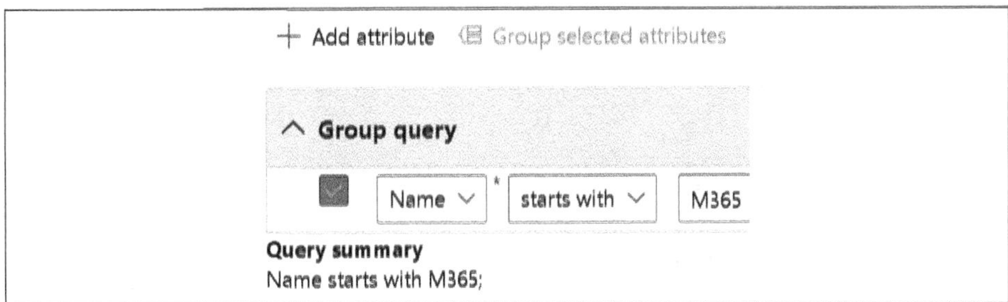

Figure 16-20. Adding a query for the adaptive scope

To recover a deleted chat message from the Microsoft Purview compliance portal (*https://oreil.ly/E-hLA*), click "Content search," then click "New search." Type a name for the search (in this example, we'll use *Chat Message Recovery*). Click Next. Select "Exchange mailboxes" as the location (Teams messages are stored in Exchange Online), as shown in Figure 16-21, and click Next.

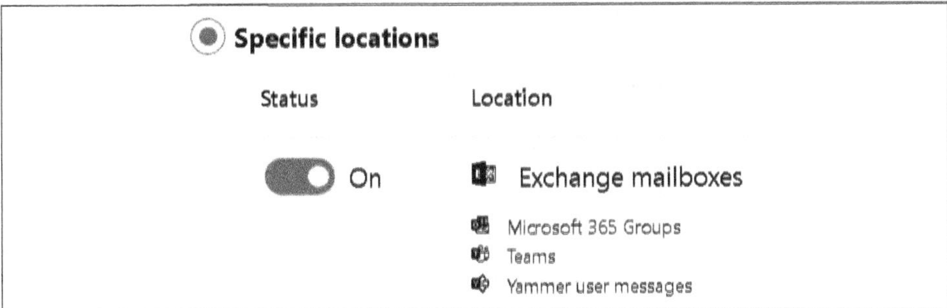

Figure 16-21. Using Exchange as a search location for Teams chats

Using the "Condition card builder," click "Add condition" and select only the messages sent in the past year. Click "Add condition" again, select Type, and then select "Instant messages" (the query builder is shown in Figure 16-22). Click Next.

^ Date

Between

2023-06-07

2023-07-07

AND

^ Type

Equals any of

E-mail messages

Documents

Instant messages

Figure 16-22. Using the query builder

On the "Review your search and create it" page, click Submit. Back on the "Content search" page, click Chat Message Recovery. The search will return all the chat messages (including the deleted ones that have been stored by the retention policy), as in the example shown in Figure 16-23.

Chat Message Recovery
2023-07-07T15:53:08.52Z
Searched by
MOD Administrator
Search conditions
(c:c)(date=2023-06-07..2023-07-07)(Item
(ItemClass=IPM.Note.Microsoft.Convers
Status
The search is completed
562 item(s) (14.82 MB)
4 unindexed items, 1.92 MB
79 mailbox(es)

Figure 16-23. Summary of the content search results

Click Actions in the lower-left corner and select "Export results." Select your export format from the "Export results" page (for example, a single PST file containing all the messages), and click Export.

Discussion

Retention policies in Teams are used to control how long messages and other types of content, such as files and conversations, are kept in the system. When a retention policy is applied to a team or channel, it determines how long content is kept before it is automatically deleted. For example, a retention policy might specify that all messages in a particular channel are kept for 90 days, after which they are automatically deleted.

In addition to specifying how long content is retained, retention policies can also be used to specify how content is deleted. A retention policy might specify that deleted content is permanently erased from the system, or that it is moved to a long-term storage location for later review. Retention policies in Teams can be applied at the organization level, or they can be customized for specific teams and channels. This allows organizations to set different retention periods for different types of content, depending on their specific needs and requirements.

The search query we used in this recipe uses Kusto Query Language (KQL), a query language that allows users to perform complex searches for content in a variety of data sources, including SharePoint, Exchange, and Azure. Some common uses of KQL in Microsoft content search include finding specific items or files based on their properties or metadata, searching for specific words or phrases within the content of a document, and filtering search results based on specific criteria. KQL queries can also be used to combine multiple search criteria using logical operators, such as AND, OR, and NOT. To learn more about KQL, visit the Microsoft documentation "Write your first query with Kusto Query Language" (*https://oreil.ly/AzA2k*).

If a user is covered by an active retention policy that retains Teams messages, and the mailbox is deleted, the user's mailbox will be converted to an inactive mailbox and Teams data will be preserved. If you don't want to retain this Teams data for the user, you can exclude the account from the retention policy and wait for the changes to take effect before deleting the mailbox.

16.4 Assessing Compliance with Compliance Manager

Problem

You need to identify actions to improve your organization's compliance and plan (or apply) them.

Solution

From the Microsoft Purview compliance portal (*https://oreil.ly/bBtFK*), select Compliance Manager. On the Overview page, you can view your organization's compliance score, which is based on the Microsoft 365 data protection baseline. This score is expressed as a percentage and as points achieved out of the total attainable points (see Figure 16-24).

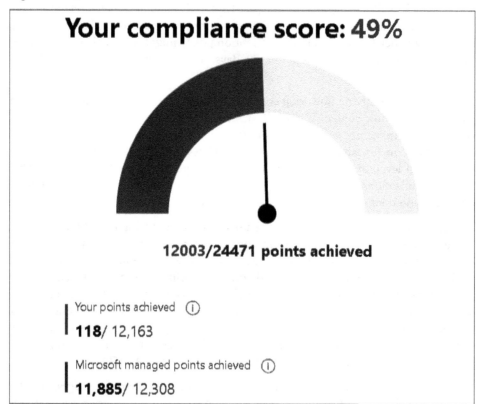

Figure 16-24. Compliance score in Compliance Manager

Locate the "Key improvement actions" section on the Compliance Manager Overview page, and click "View all improvement actions."

Depending on the status of your tenant, you may be required to run an assessment before you can see any data in "Key improvement actions."

Clicking on any of the "Improvement actions" gives you more details. The actions with the higher number of points achieved will more greatly improve your compliance. In this example, click "Enable self-service password reset."

The next page provides information about how to implement the improvement, how to perform the testing, and what standards and regulations are involved (some of the tabs are shown in Figure 16-25).

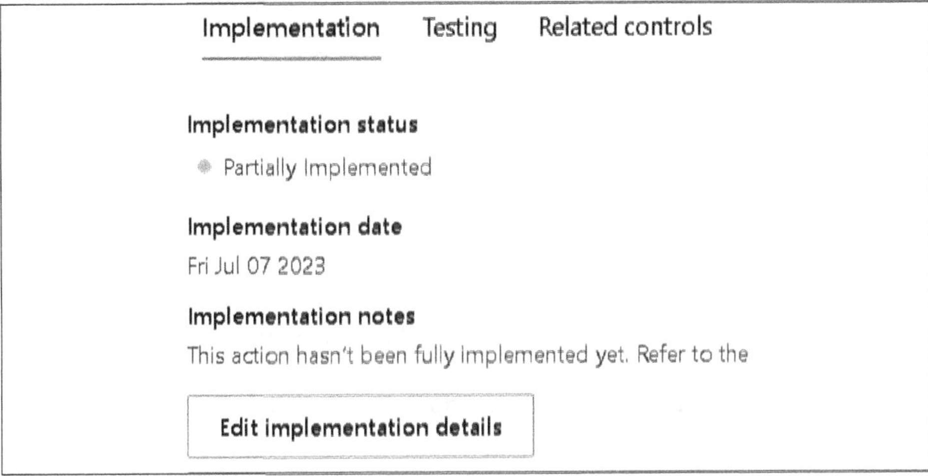

Figure 16-25. Implementation details for the selected action

Going back to the "Improvement actions" page in Compliance Manager, you can select one or more actions, export or import actions, or assign actions to a user. Click "Export actions."

The export will create an XLSX document that contains the required steps and allows you to update the status of the improvement action by making changes, then uploading it to Compliance Manager (an example is shown in Figure 16-26).

The action update functionality allows users to update data for existing improvement actions, including their implementation and test status and date, testing source, and data source.
Ensure that any actions you wish to update already exist in your assessments. If you want to create a new action, use the "Create new template" function in the Assessment templates page of
To update actions, make all of your changes on the "Action Update" tab of this spreadsheet. Refer to the instructions below to ensure that your updates are valid.

Column Header Key

	Action Identifier Field - Required but can't be edited. Changing this field will result in validation errors.
	Validated Field - This field can be edited, but must conform to specific rules as described below. Note that changes to this field will overwrite existing data.
	Free Text Field - This field can be edited, and you may enter any value. Note that changes to this field will overwrite existing data.

Validated Field Requirements

Field Name	Field Validation Rules
ImplementationStatus	Allows the following values: Implemented, AlternativeImplementation, NotImplemented, Planned, NotInScope
ImplementationDate	Allows any date in format MM/DD/YYYY HH:MM:SS
Test Status	Allowable values are based on the current ImplementationStatus value. See below for allowable combinations of ImplementationStatus and Test Status
Test Date	Allows a date in format MM/DD/YYYY HH:MM:SS that is equal to or after the specified ImplementationDate for this action
	Format as {name of first document}::{URL of document};;{name of second document}::{URL of second document}
Documents	Note that you must append additional files you wish to link to this action - replacing existing file references will remove those references from the updated acti
Assigned To	Use email address of the intended user
Testing Source	Allows Manual, Automatic, or Parent. When choosing Parent, provide the Action Parent Title and Action Parent Product as well. Only actions that support auto
Action Parent Title	Only necessary when Testing Source = Parent. Use full action title
Action Parent Product	Only necessary when Testing Source = Parent. Use action's Product dimension - can be found on action drilldown page, default is Microsoft 365

ImplementationStatus	TestStatus
Implemented	Passed, FailedLowRisk, FailedMediumRisk, FailedHighRisk, InProgress, NotInScope
AlternativeImplementation	Passed, FailedLowRisk, FailedMediumRisk, FailedHighRisk, InProgress, NotInScope

Figure 16-26. The export document

Discussion

Compliance Manager is a feature within the Microsoft Purview compliance portal that offers a comprehensive solution for managing compliance requirements. It is a cross-platform tool that helps organizations meet their complex compliance obligations.

Compliance Manager includes tools for tracking and assessing data protection risks, monitoring changes in regulations or certifications, and providing reports to auditors. The centralized dashboard reports on compliance and offers prebuilt assessments for common standards, custom assessments for specific needs, suggested improvements, and a risk-based score for understanding the organization's compliance posture.

Compliance Manager uses several data elements, including controls, assessments, templates, and remediation actions.

Controls are the requirements of regulations, standards, or policies. They define how to evaluate and manage system configurations, organizational processes, and those responsible for meeting specific requirements. Compliance Manager tracks the progress of different types of controls, including those implemented by Microsoft, those shared between the organization and Microsoft, and those that are only partially implemented.

Assessments are groupings of controls from a particular regulation, standard, or policy. Completing the actions within an assessment helps organizations meet these requirements. Compliance Manager provides templates to create assessments quickly and easily, and they can be customized as needed.

Templates help organizations create assessments quickly and easily. You can modify the templates to fit the organization's specific needs, or you can create custom assessments by adding controls and actions.

Improvement actions provide recommendations and guidance to help organizations comply with privacy laws and standards. They can be assigned to users in the organization to perform implementation and testing work, and you can save documents, notes, and updates within the actions. These actions help centralize compliance workflows and affect the organization's compliance score.

16.5 Summary

Teams offers a range of features to help organizations with compliance, including communication compliance for channels, chats, and attachments; retention policies; DLP policies; eDiscovery and legal hold for channels, chats, and files; and audit log search. Compliance can be managed through the Microsoft Purview compliance portal, which includes tools such as Information Barriers and Communication Compliance. Teams also offers sensitivity labels and customer key encryption to further protect sensitive data and meet compliance requirements.

These tools need to be tailored to an organization's specific requirements and needs, which can take time. Because Teams integrates with different services, additional effort is required to ensure that all data is retained and checked, including controls in SharePoint, Exchange, and OneDrive.

The next chapter is dedicated to free and open source tools for Teams, including tools created by the Microsoft community and by third parties.

CHAPTER 17

Free and Open Source Tools for Microsoft Teams

The recipes in this chapter will explore some of the open source tools released by the Microsoft community, as well as by third parties, that enhance the administrative experience and the management of Teams.

The Microsoft community is a group of people who are interested in Microsoft products and technologies, and who often share their knowledge and expertise to help others. Many members of the community are experts in specific Microsoft technologies, who are active on forums, blogs, and other online channels.

Some of the people involved with the Microsoft community have received, over the years, the Microsoft MVP (Most Valuable Professional) award. This distinction is given to individuals who have demonstrated exceptional expertise and knowledge in Microsoft products and technologies. MVPs are chosen based on their contributions to the technical community.

17.1 Rendering Call Flows for Auto Attendants and Call Queues Automatically

Problem

You need to quickly and automatically generate a diagram of the call flows for Auto Attendants and Call Queues.

Solution

The tool we'll use in this solution was created by Microsoft MVP Martin Heusser (*https://oreil.ly/DiV06*). It is a script for the Microsoft 365 Phone System that allows you to visualize the call flow (including a PNG format image version created with *mermaid-js*). The script can be run with various parameters, such as specifying the name and type of the voice app and configuring whether to save the output to a file or copy it to the clipboard.

The script can also be used to export the call flow as a PNG file and preview the call flow in an HTML file. Overall, this tool provides a convenient way to visualize and understand the call flow for Microsoft 365 Phone System Auto Attendants and Call Queues.

The Graph permissions required to use the tool include the following:

- `User.Read.All`: Read all users' full profiles.
- `Group.Read.All`: Read all groups.
- `offline_access`: Allow the app to read and update user data, even when the users are not currently using the app.

The permissions must be granted by an administrator of the tenant if the users do not have the right level of privilege to assign them by themselves.

The tool requires the Teams PowerShell module and the Microsoft Graph PowerShell module. If you do not have the Microsoft Graph PowerShell module, then install and import it using the following commands:

```
Install-Module Microsoft.Graph
Import-Module Microsoft.Graph
```

You might be required to change the script execution policy on your workstation to install the `Microsoft.Graph` module. Also, if you receive the error "Function Add-MgApplicationKey cannot be created because function capacity 4096 has been exceeded for this scope" when importing the module, use the following command:

```
$maximumfunctioncount = 32768
```

If you want to export to PNG export, you'll need two additional components: Node.js and the *@mermaid-js/mermaid-cli* npm package. Node.js can be downloaded and installed from the tool's Downloads page (*https://oreil.ly/TjZMA*).

After installation, to be able to use Node.js you must close PowerShell (if it was open).

To check your Node.js installation, use the following command:

```
npm --version
```

The *@mermaid-js/mermaid-cli* npm package can be installed using the following command:

```
npm install -g @mermaid-js/mermaid-cli
```

You can check the installation of the package using this command:

```
mmdc -version
```

The following actions are now required:

- Copy all the scripts from the Functions page of the M365CallFlowVisualizer repository (*https://oreil.ly/loyia*) into a subfolder called *Functions* (for example, if you are executing the script in *C:\Scripts*, copy them into *C:\Scripts\Functions*).
- Create a file *HtmlTemplate.html* in the *C:\scripts* folder with the content in the HtmlTemplate.html page (*https://oreil.ly/m1snJ*).
- Copy the script in the *C:\Scripts* folder, saving the latest version of the M365CallFlowVisualizer (*https://oreil.ly/WLV2o*) in the *M365CallFlowVisualizerV2.ps1* file.

Run the tool with the following command to save the output in *C:\Scripts*:

```
.\M365CallFlowVisualizerV2.ps1 -CustomFilePath "C:\Scripts"
```

You will receive a permissions request (see Figure 17-1) for Microsoft Graph PowerShell. Click Accept.

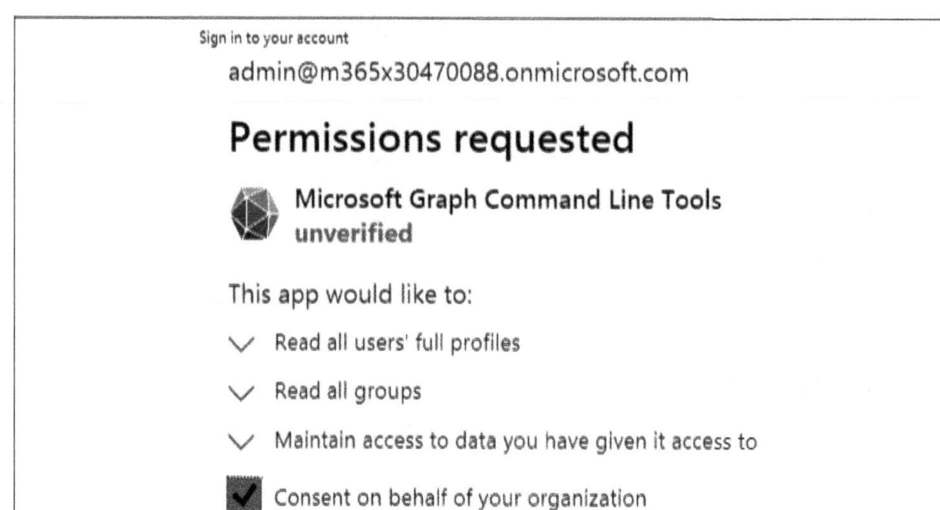

Figure 17-1. Graph permissions request

Running the script without specifying a Call Queue or an Auto Attendant will show a screen with a list of all the queues and attendants in the tenant. Select the one you want to map (as in Figure 17-2) and click OK.

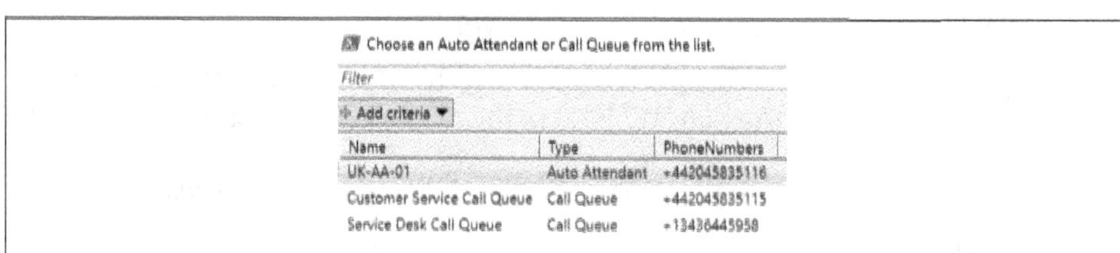

Figure 17-2. Selecting the attendant or queue for the script execution

The output will be an HTML (*.htm*) file with the name of the attendant or queue (in this example, *UK_Test_AA_01_CallFlow.htm*, as shown in Figure 17-3) and a Markdown file (*.md*).

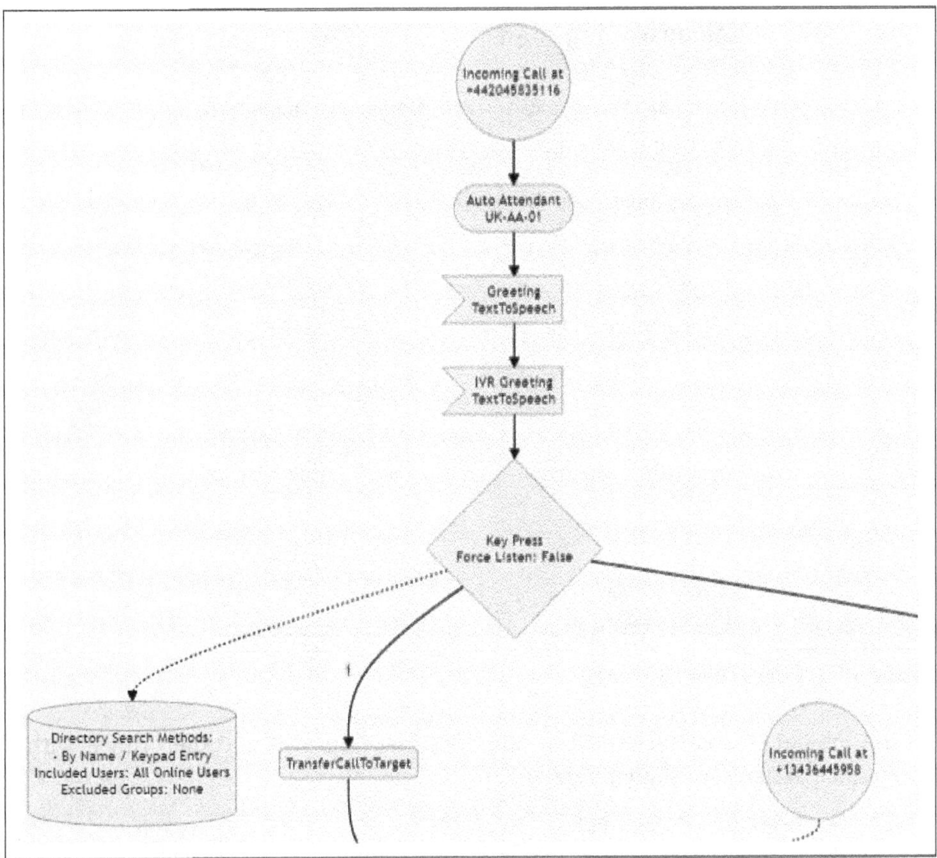

Figure 17-3. HTML preview of the call flow mapping

Discussion

Similar to the tool used in this recipe, Render Teams User Calling Settings (*https://oreil.ly/_3ciq*) from the same Microsoft MVP is dedicated to mapping the user's call answering rules (an example of a user's settings is shown in Figure 17-4).

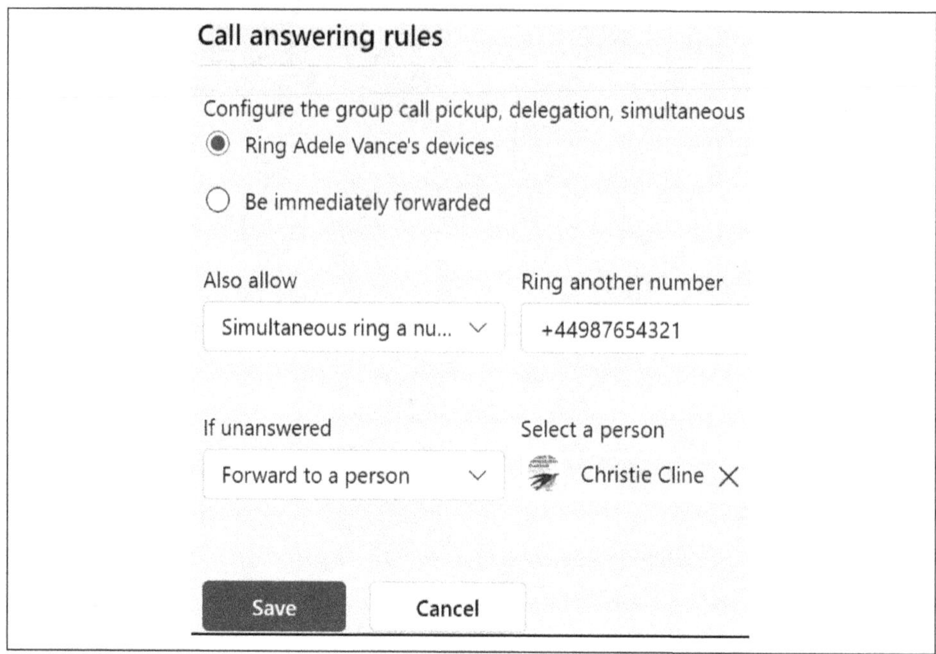

Figure 17-4. User's call answering rules

To use the `Get-TeamsUserCallFlow` function, first import it and then run it with a user principal name, as shown here:

```
. .\Get-TeamsUserCallFlow.ps1
Get-TeamsUserCallFlow -UserId "Adele Vance" -CustomFilePath c:\scripts
```

The `-CustomFilePath` parameter can be used to create an SVG file containing the call-answering rules in a destination folder of your choice.

17.2 Creating a Global Address Book for Teams

Problem

You need to search for contacts and users that have a phone number but no Teams license assigned (similar to a global address book).

Solution

In Teams, you can search for your personal contacts and for colleagues in your organization who are also enabled for Teams. However, the search does not include contacts or users in Active Directory who have a phone number with no Teams license assigned. Stefano Ceruti, cloud solution architect for Microsoft, created a PowerApp—explained in his post "Create a Global Address Book for Teams" (*https://oreil.ly/Z8bHw*)—to handle this use case.

Two versions of the PowerApp are available: one that reads from Entra ID (user objects, not contacts) and another that uses the Contacts application in SharePoint. This recipe uses the first version, PowerApp for the Global Address Book in Entra ID.

First, download the app (*https://oreil.ly/tNkUo*). The file we are going to use is *PowerApps-Template-GlobalAddressBook-AD.bin*.

The app file is downloaded as a BIN file. Rename the downloaded file to have a *.zip* extension before importing it into PowerApps.

After you download the app, you can import it in your tenant by going to the PowerApps portal (*https://oreil.ly/eS1KA*), selecting Apps from the left menu (as in Figure 17-5), and then clicking "Import canvas app."

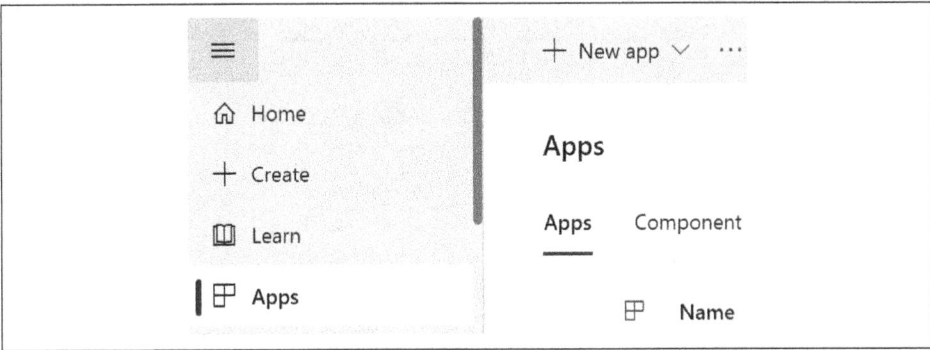

Figure 17-5. Importing the PowerApp

When the ZIP file is uploaded, click Import. You should see the screen shown in Figure 17-6.

Figure 17-6. Importing the app in ZIP format

After the import operation, you can test the app by clicking "Open app" (testing and sharing options are shown in Figure 17-7).

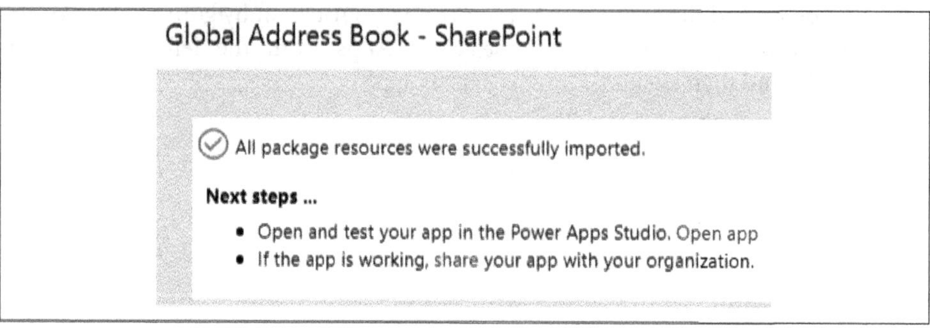

Global Address Book - SharePoint
All package resources were successfully imported.
Next steps ...
Open and test your app in the Power Apps Studio. Open app
If the app is working, share your app with your organization.

Figure 17-7. Testing the app

The app will require permissions to read your full profile and the full profiles of all the users. Click Allow. The Global Address Book app will be shown. Click F5 to run a test of the app (as shown in Figure 17-8).

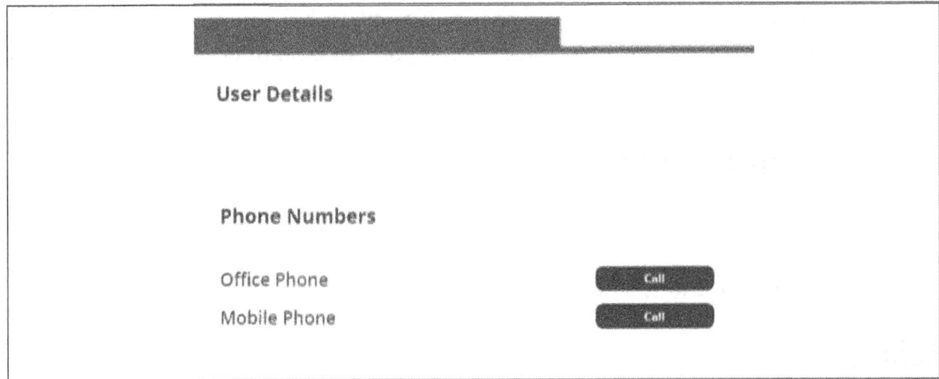

Figure 17-8. Testing the app on the tenant

Back in the PowerApps portal (*https://oreil.ly/xLbcQ*), click Apps. Select the Global Address Book app and click "Add to Teams" in the upper part of the page (as shown in Figure 17-9).

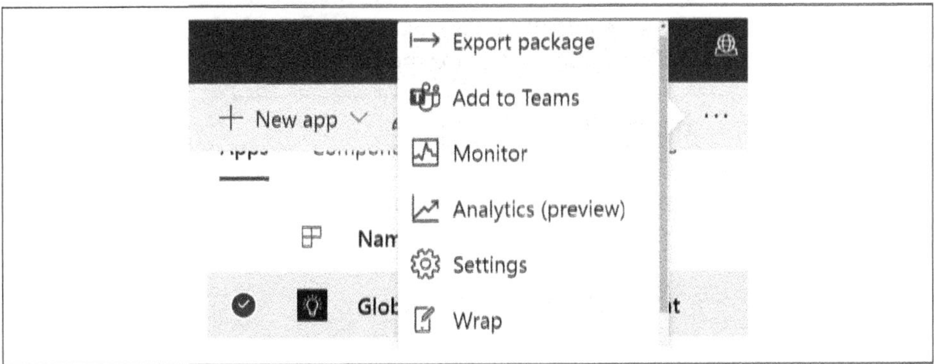

Figure 17-9. PowerApps portal with the Global Address Book app added

Click "Add to Teams" again when asked for confirmation.

Discussion

The SharePoint version requires some additional steps that are described here and on Stefano's Blog (*https://oreil.ly/lOX4Z*):

1. Create a contacts application in a SharePoint site that is accessible to the users who will be using the application.
2. After you create the SharePoint list that includes the contacts in it, modify the PowerApp pointing to this new list.

3. If you have contacts in Entra ID that you want to bulk import to the Address Book, there is a script (available in the blog post) to bulk import the contact from Entra ID to SharePoint.

17.3 Merging Teams and SharePoint Activity Reports

Problem

You need to generate a unified usage report for Teams and SharePoint.

Solution

A script by Microsoft MVP Alexander Holmeset (*https://oreil.ly/1F0Js*) combines data from the usage reports for Teams and SharePoint. The objective (as you will see in this recipe) is to report on all your teams with SharePoint data, excluding SharePoint sites without a team.

First, download the reports from the Teams and SharePoint admin portals. To do this, open the SharePoint admin center and click "Active sites." Click the Export button to get a CSV file with SharePoint activity data for the last 180 days (see Figure 17-10).

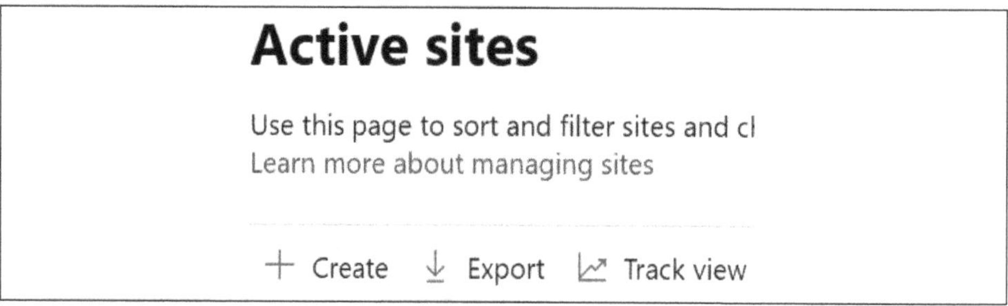

Figure 17-10. Gathering the SharePoint reports

In the TAC, click "Analytics and reports" and select "Usage reports." From the Report drop-down menu, select "Teams usage," and from the "Data range" drop-down menu, select "Last 180 days." Click "Run report" (as in Figure 17-11).

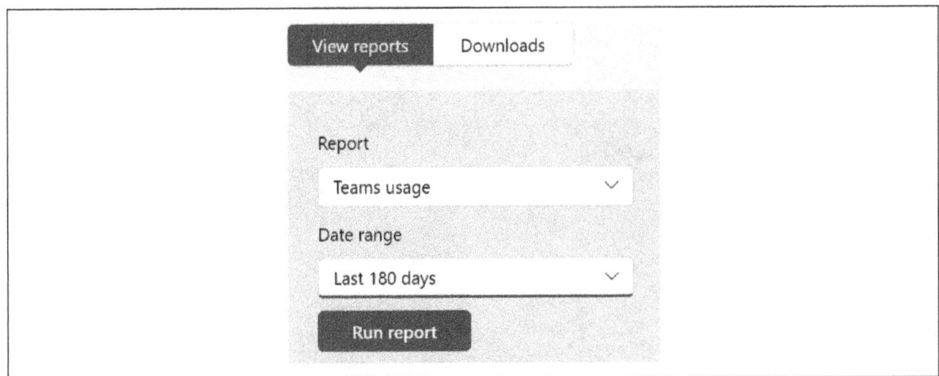

Figure 17-11. Compiling the Teams usage report

When the report is ready, click "Export to Excel" (the export feature is shown in Figure 17-12).

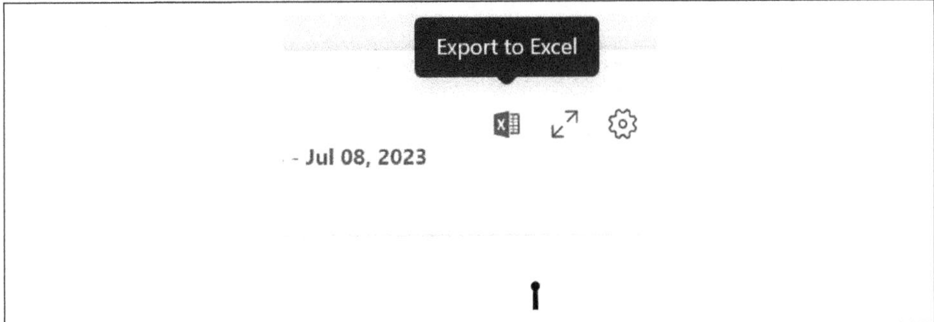

Figure 17-12. Exporting the Teams usage report

The script uses an Azure app. You will need to have an Azure application to authenticate through when doing Graph API requests. Open the Azure portal (*https://oreil.ly/ItSKQ*) and search for and select the "App registrations" service, as shown in Figure 17-13.

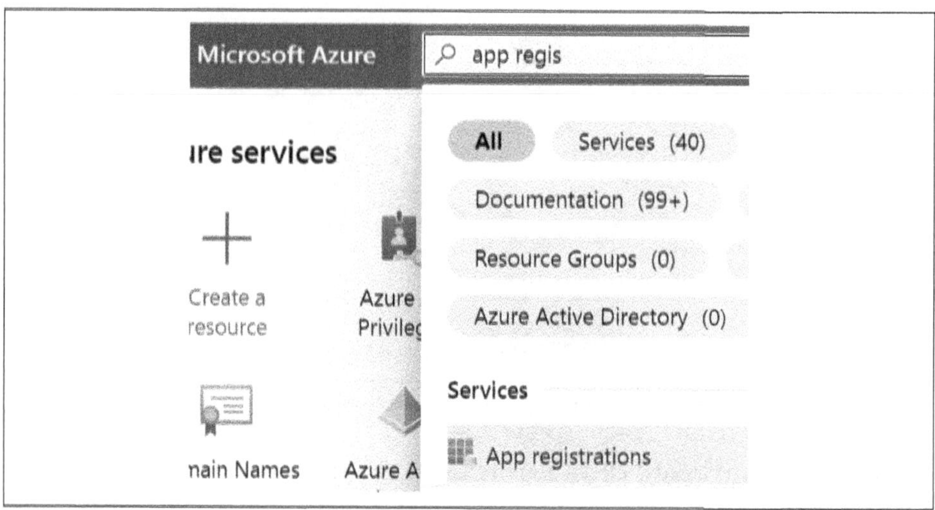

Figure 17-13. App registration in the Azure portal

Click "New registration" (as shown in Figure 17-14).

Figure 17-14. Registering an app in Azure

On the "Register an application" page, type a name in the Name box (in our example, we'll use *Teams_SharePoint_Usage_Report*). Select "Accounts in any organizational directory (Any Azure AD directory - Multitenant) and personal Microsoft accounts (e.g. Skype, Xbox)" (as shown in Figure 17-15) and from the "Redirect URI" drop-down menu, select Web. Click Register in the bottom part of the screen.

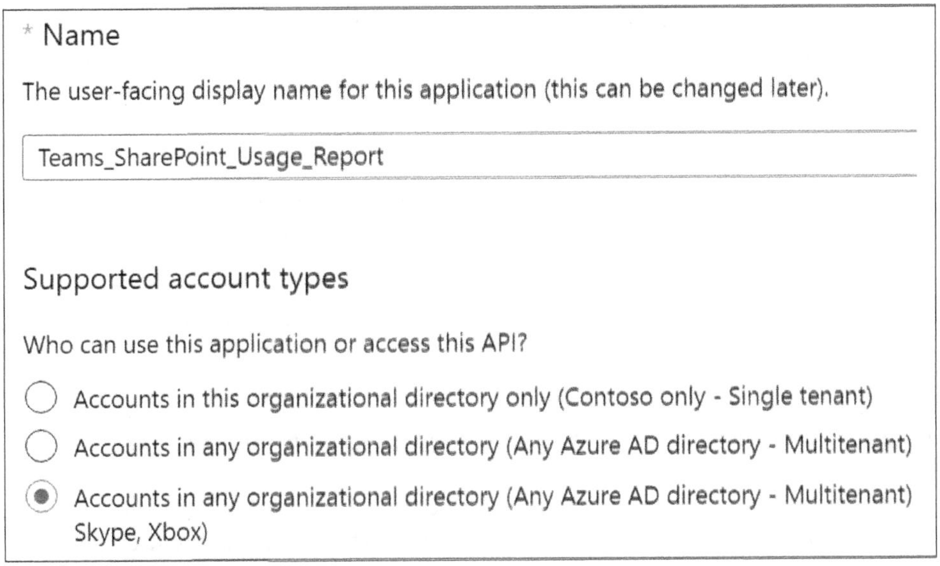

* Name

The user-facing display name for this application (this can be changed later).

Teams_SharePoint_Usage_Report

Supported account types

Who can use this application or access this API?

Accounts in this organizational directory only (Contoso only - Single tenant)

Accounts in any organizational directory (Any Azure AD directory - Multitenant)

Accounts in any organizational directory (Any Azure AD directory - Multitenant) Skype, Xbox)

Figure 17-15. Configuring the basic settings of the app

On the next page, note the "Application (client) ID" (in our example, *face3150-4092-4f5a-9b1d-bd1d02232e61*) and the "Directory (tenant) ID" (in our example, *eab48e2f-746a-4346-bf7f-cd3cb523753f*), as you can see in Figure 17-16.

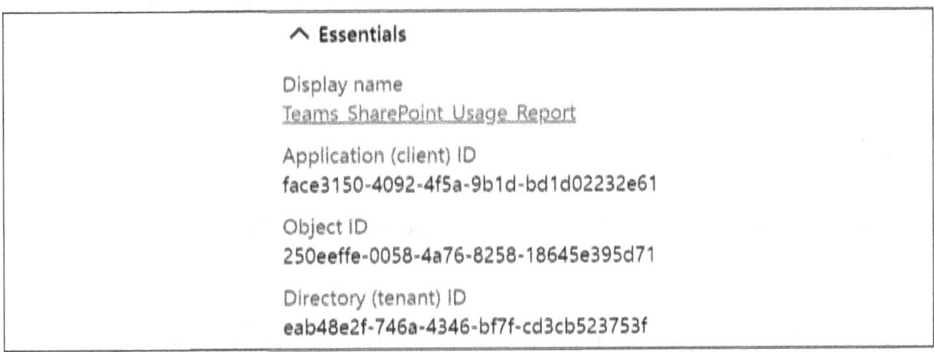

Figure 17-16. Client ID and tenant ID to be used in the script

Click "Add a Redirect URI" (as in Figure 17-17).

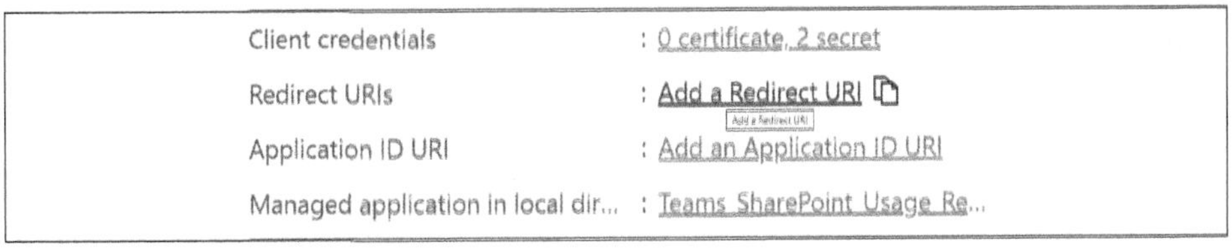

Client credentials : 0 certificate, 2 secret

Redirect URIs : Add a Redirect URI

Application ID URI : Add an Application ID URI

Managed application in local dir... : Teams_SharePoint_Usage_Re...

Figure 17-17. Adding a redirect URI

Click "Add a platform" and select "Mobile and desktop applications" (as shown in Figure 17-18).

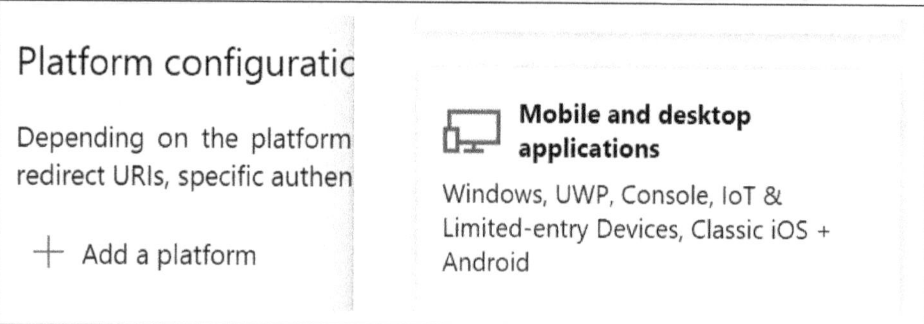

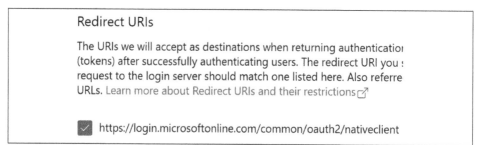

Figure 17-18. Configuring the authentication and platforms for the app

Select the URL ending with */nativeclient*. Take note of the URL (in our example, *https://login.microsoftonline.com/common/oauth2/nativeclient*) and click Configure (see Figure 17-19).

Redirect URIs

The URIs we will accept as destinations when returning authenticatio
(tokens) after successfully authenticating users. The redirect URI you
request to the login server should match one listed here. Also referre
URLs. Learn more about Redirect URIs and their restrictions

https://login.microsoftonline.com/common/oauth2/nativeclient

Figure 17-19. Configuring the app for desktops and devices

Back on the previous screen, click "API permissions" (Figure 17-20).

Figure 17-20. Opening the API permissions screen

Click "Add permission" and then click Microsoft Graph (as shown in Figure 17-21).

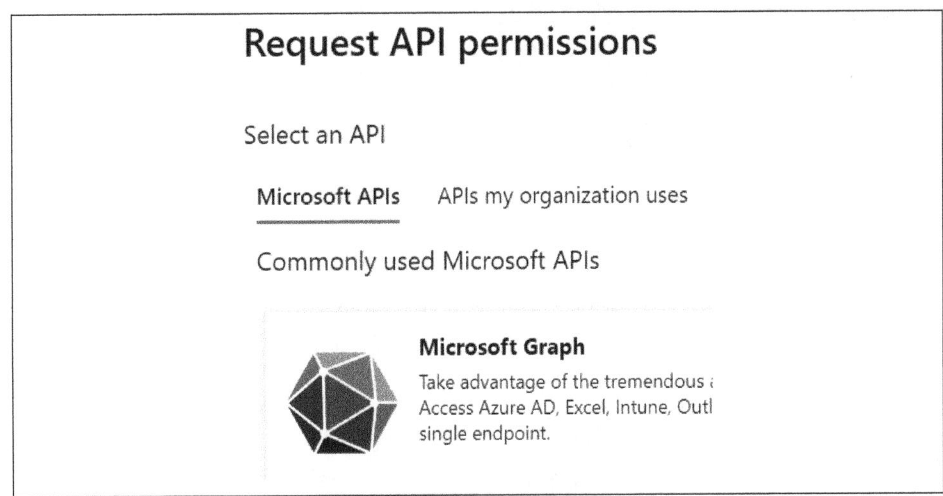

Figure 17-21. Selecting Microsoft Graph permissions

Click "Application permissions" (the option on the right in Figure 17-22).

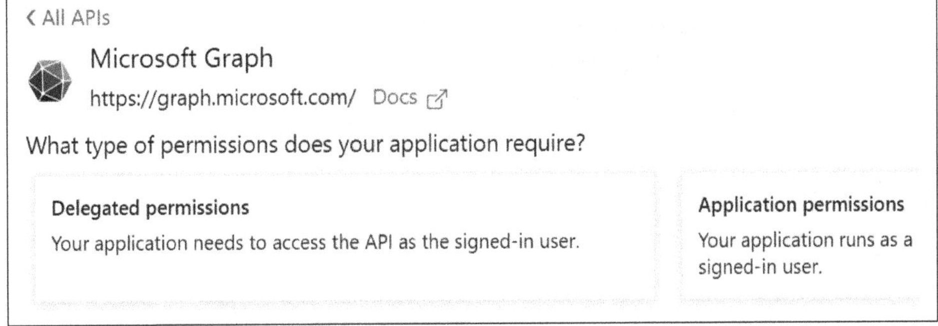

Figure 17-22. Adding application permissions

Select the `Group.Read.All` permission, as in Figure 17-23, and click "Add permissions." Repeat the same process to add `User.Read.All` and `Directory.Read.All`.

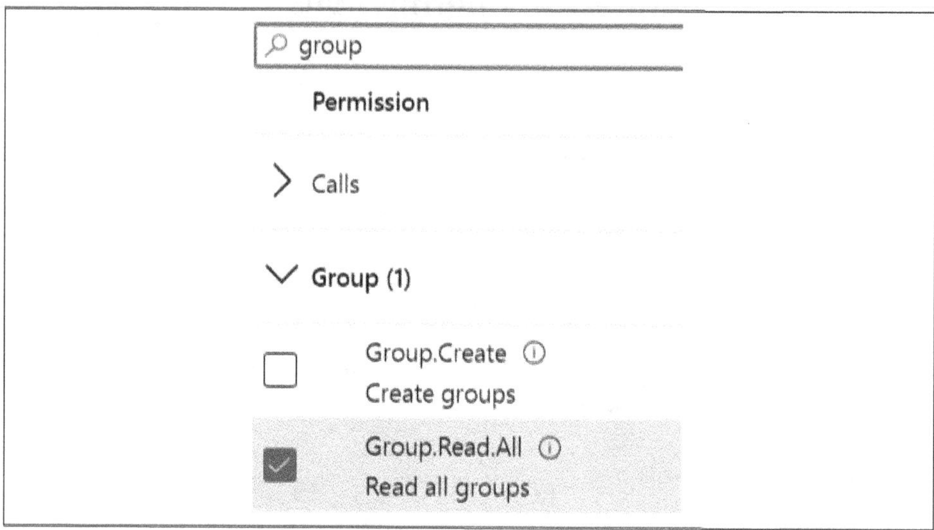

Figure 17-23. Adding the required permissions

At the bottom of the permissions list, click "Grant admin consent" and click Yes in the confirmation pop-up (see Figure 17-24).

+ Add a permission ✓ Grant admin consent for Contoso

API / Permissions n...	Type	Description	Admin consent req...
Microsoft Graph (4)			
Directory.Read.All	Application	Read directory data	Yes
Group.Read.All	Application	Read all groups	Yes
User.Read	Delegated	Sign in and read user ...	No
User.Read.All	Application	Read all users' full pro...	Yes

Figure 17-24. Granting the permissions

Click Overview and then click "Add a certificate or secret" (Figure 17-25).

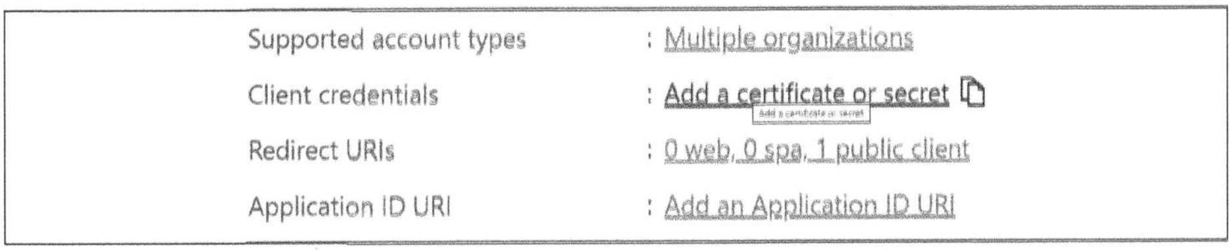

Supported account types	: Multiple organizations
Client credentials	: Add a certificate or secret
Redirect URIs	: 0 web, 0 spa, 1 public client
Application ID URI	: Add an Application ID URI

Figure 17-25. Adding a secret as a credential

Click "New client secret." Add a Description (in this example, we'll use *App Secret*) and select an expiration (in this example, the expiration will be six months), as in Figure 17-26. Click Add.

Add a client secret

Description: App Secret

Expires: Recommended: 180 days (6 months)

Add | Cancel

Figure 17-26. Configuring the client secret for the app

Take note of the Secret ID (in our example, *e8918b83-da02-4a51-bca3-3cf7c748fa16*). Copy the *TeamsSharePointUsageReport.ps1* script from GitHub (*https://oreil.ly/SyUyZ*) and save it in a PS1 file (in our example, *Teams_SharePoint_Usage_Report.ps1*).

Add your details (client ID, tenant ID, client secret) in the script before you run it (see Figure 17-27 for the settings in our example).

```
param (
    [parameter(Mandatory = $true, HelpMessage = "eab48e2f-746a-4346-bf7f-cd3cb52375xx")]
    [ValidateNotNullOrEmpty()]
    [string]$TenantID,
    [parameter(Mandatory = $true, HelpMessage = "face3150-4092-4f5a-9b1d-bd1d02232exx")]
    [ValidateNotNullOrEmpty()]
    [string]$ClientID,
    [parameter(Mandatory = $true, HelpMessage = "7Tk8Q~VvaaqaDBD_31TFhR1k5Q.7~Wi2Oqna~dxx.")]
    [ValidateNotNullOrEmpty()]
    [string]$ClientSecret
```

Figure 17-27. Populating the values required in the script

Also update the `$sites` and `$teamsactivity` variables to point to the path of the reports you created previously from SharePoint and Teams (see Figure 17-28).

```
#Import the SharePoint Active Sites report from the SharePoint Admin Portal.
$sites = Import-Csv C:\temp\Sites_20230710153848885.csv


#Import the Teams Usage report from the Teams Admin Portal.
$teamsactivity = Import-Csv C:\temp\TeamsTeamActivityDetail7_10_2023 3_41_14 PM.csv
```

Figure 17-28. Updating the paths and report filenames

The script uses the Microsoft Graph PowerShell module. If you do not have this module, install it and import it using the following commands:

```
Install-Module Microsoft.Graph
Import-Module Microsoft.Graph
```

Discussion

Alexander has also created a tool for automatically uploading a CSV file with location information to the Teams Network Planner. The Teams Network Planner uses the same data that's in the CSV file provided for uploading building information to the Teams Call Quality Dashboard (CQD), with a few additional pieces of information. However, unlike the CQD, the Network Planner does not have a button for uploading a CSV file, so users must manually enter each site's information. This can be a tedious and time-consuming process, especially for organizations with many sites.

To use Alexander's solution, first copy the script from the blog post "Teams Network Planner Automated!" (*https://oreil.ly/bvspF*) into a PS1 file (for example, *Teams_Network_Planner_CSV_uploader.ps1*)

Next, download the CSV template (*https://oreil.ly/ShTKR*).

To change the path to the location of the CSV file, modify the `$sites` variable (for example, *C:\scripts\locations1.xlsx*).

You will need an access token for Teams. To get one, you can use the AADInternals tool, which we will discuss in Recipe 17.5.

17.4 Fixing Device Registration Issues

Problem

You need to troubleshoot issues with device registration, including Hybrid Microsoft Entra Joined, Microsoft Entra Joined, and Entra ID Register.

Solution

A free utility not strictly connected to Teams but useful from a Microsoft 365 administrator's point of view is the Device Registration Troubleshooter Tool (DSRegTool). This tool makes it easy to identify and fix common device registration issues in Entra ID. It performs more than 50 different tests to help you quickly troubleshoot issues with all types of device registration, including Hybrid Microsoft Entra Joined, Microsoft Entra Joined, and Entra ID Register.

To use the tool, download the script from GitHub (*https://oreil.ly/AvO0e*), save it as *DSRegTool.ps1*, and run it using one of the offered Entra ID Join or troubleshooting options.

Using option 1, for example, you can test Entra ID registration of a device. The script verifies whether the device is already registered and then asks the user to type a test code and authenticate to grant the permissions. You will get a report about the test results (an example is shown in Figure 17-29).

```
Please make a selection, and press Enter: 1

Troubleshoot Azure AD Register option has been chosen

DSRegTool 3.7 has started
Device Name : A877815A-3174-4
User Account: a877815a-3174-4\wdagutilityaccount, UPN:

Testing OS version...
Test passed: device has current OS version (10.0.19041.0)

Testing if the device is Azure AD Registered...
Test failed: a877815a-3174-4937-a669-56f68846e23a device is NOT connected to Azure AD

Testing Internet Connectivity...
Connection to login.microsoftonline.com .............. Succeeded.
Connection to device.login.microsoftonline.com ......  Succeeded.
Connection to enterpriseregistration.windows.net ..... Succeeded.

Test passed: User is able to communicate with MS endpoints successfully
```

Figure 17-29. Results from testing Entra ID registration of a device

Option 7—collect the logs—lets you gather a log when reproducing an issue, starting and stopping the log gathering as required (see Figure 17-30).

```
Please make a selection, and press Enter: 7

Collect the logs option has been chosen

DSRegTool 3.7 has started
Device Name : A877815A-3174-4
User Account: a877815a-3174-4\wdagutilityaccount, UPN:

Testing if script running with elevated privileges...
PowerShell is running with elevated privileges

Creating DSRegToolLogs folder under C:\Temp
Checking PreTrace folder under C:\Temp\DSRegToolLogs
Collecting PreTrace logs...

Please press ENTER to start log collection...
```

Figure 17-30. Using option 7 to gather logs during troubleshooting

Discussion

This solution helps in troubleshooting Workplace Join, a feature that allows users to register their personal devices with the organization's Entra ID tenant. This allows the devices to be used for accessing certain corporate resources, such as email and file-sharing services, that are protected by Entra ID. As well as being registered in the organization's Entra ID tenant, the devices are also joined to the organization's Active Directory domain. This allows them to be managed and controlled by the organization's IT administrators.

17.5 Gathering Additional Information from Microsoft 365

Problem

You need a tool that provides additional information for troubleshooting in Microsoft 365 services.

Solution

Although Microsoft 365 offers various modules and portals for management, a lot of information is still not accessible using the default tools. To address this, you can use AADInternals (*https://oreil.ly/94_jp*), an open source PowerShell module by *@DrAzureAD* (Nestori Syynimaa) that provides a range of tools and resources related to Entra ID and Microsoft 365. This module is intended to assist administrators in reverse-engineering and troubleshooting Microsoft tools such as PowerShell modules, directory synchronization, and admin portals.

To install and import the AADInternals module, run the following commands in PowerShell (successfully importing the module will show the prompt in Figure 17-31):

```
Install-Module AADInternals
Import-Module AADInternals
```

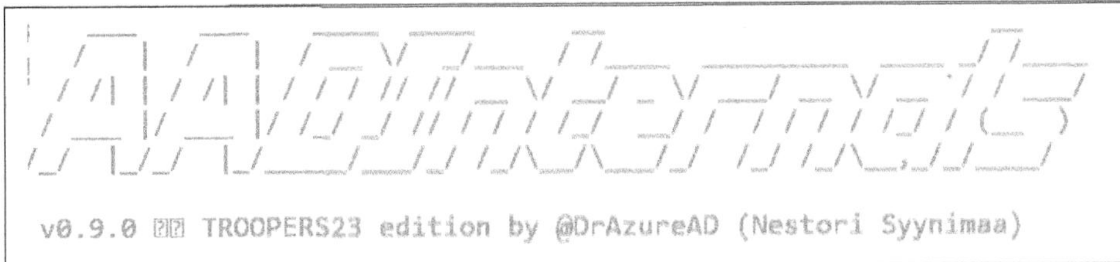

v0.9.0 TROOPERS23 edition by @DrAzureAD (Nestori Syynimaa)

Figure 17-31. AADInternals imported correctly

To execute the import, you may have to change the script security using the following command:

```
Set-ExecutionPolicy Unrestricted
```

Some tools allow Teams users to set their availability status (via PowerShell) to Available, Busy, DoNotDisturb, BeRightBack, or Away. To set the status to Busy, use the following commands:

```
Get-AADIntAccessTokenForTeams -SaveToCache

Set-AADIntTeamsAvailability -Status Busy
```

The first execution of the `Get-AADIntAccessTokenForTeams` command may require saving registry keys and relaunching PowerShell.

The `Get-AADIntAccessTokenForTeams` command will prompt you for permissions to create and enable the WebBrowser control emulation registry key. Run the script a second time, and your credentials will be required.

`Get-AADIntAccessTokenForTeams` is used to get an access token for Teams and save it to the cache. When the access token is stored, you can also display the chat messages for the user (including deleted ones), as shown in Figure 17-32, using the following command:

```
Get-AADIntTeamsMessages | fl id,content,deletiontime,*type*,DisplayName
```

```
Id          : 1687377295355
Content     : <div>Yes! Stop by my office when you have a moment. If I'm not here,
              <div style="display:inline"><span itemtype="http://schema.skype.com/Mention"
              itemscope="" itemid="0">Alex Wilber</span></div> can show you what we have.</div>
              <div></div>
DeletionTime :
MessageType  : RichText/Html
Type         : Message
DisplayName  : Megan Bowen

Id          : 1687377291585
Content     : <div>Hi
              <div style="display:inline"><span itemtype="http://schema.skype.com/Mention"
              itemscope="" itemid="0">Sales and Marketing</span></div> - I'm attending a conference
              next month. Do you have any Contoso swag for me to hand out?</div>
              <div></div>
```

Figure 17-32. Displaying the user's Teams messages

You can search for an external Teams user with a command like the following:

```
Find-AADIntTeamsExternalUser -UserPrincipalName external.user@company.com
```

The following command sets the Teams status message:

```
Set-AADIntTeamsStatusMessage -Message "Out of office til noon"
```

The next command gets an access token for Teams (here, to Outlook) and saves it to the cache:

```
Get-AADIntAccessTokenForTeams -Resource https://outlook.com -SaveToCache
```

Finally, you can search for all the users with the following command (example results are shown in Figure 17-33):

```
Search-AADIntTeamsUser | Format-Table UserPrincipalName,DisplayName
```

```
UserPrincipalName                                     DisplayName
-----------------                                     -----------
LeeG@M365x36708371.OnMicrosoft.com                    Lee Gu
MeganB@M365x36708371.OnMicrosoft.com                  Megan Bowen
AlexW@M365x36708371.OnMicrosoft.com                   Alex Wilber
GradyA@M365x36708371.OnMicrosoft.com                  Grady Archie
MiriamG@M365x36708371.OnMicrosoft.com                 Miriam Graham
AdeleV@M365x36708371.OnMicrosoft.com                  Adele Vance
IsaiahL@M365x36708371.OnMicrosoft.com                 Isaiah Langer
LynneR@M365x36708371.OnMicrosoft.com                  Lynne Robbins
NestorW@M365x36708371.OnMicrosoft.com                 Nestor Wilke
ChristieC@M365x36708371.OnMicrosoft.com               Christie Cline
DebraB@M365x36708371.OnMicrosoft.com                  Debra Berger
IrvinS@M365x36708371.OnMicrosoft.com                  Irvin Sayers
PattiF@M365x36708371.OnMicrosoft.com                  Patti Fernandez
PowerPlat-noreply@microsoft.com                       Microsoft Power Platform
Userriskimprovements@M365x36708371.onmicrosoft.com    User risk improvements
```

Figure 17-33. Gathering the user list

Using the `Search-AADIntTeamsUser -SearchString "<user>"` format for the previous command, you can search for users with a specific string.

Discussion

The AADInternals module uses various types of OAuth access tokens to perform most of its functions, which are accessed through REST APIs, as Table 17-1 shows. If the `-SaveToCache` switch is enabled, all tokens will be saved to the cache. If any of the cached tokens have expired, they will be automatically renewed using the corresponding refresh token.

Table 17-1. OAuth tokens used in the AADInternals module

Token/API	Function	Remarks
AAD Graph	`Get-AADIntAccessTokenForAADGraph`	Functions using AAD Graph access token
MS Graph	`Get-AADIntAccessTokenForMSGraph`	Functions using MS Graph access token
Pass Through Authentication	`Get-AADIntAccessTokenForPTA`	Used when enabling/disabling PTA and Seamless SSO (Desktop SSO)
Azure Admin Portal	`Get-AADIntAccessTokenForAADIAMAPI`	Used when inviting guest users
Exchange Online	`Get-AADIntAccessTokenForEXO`	Used with Exchange Online and ActiveSync functions
Support and Recovery Assistant	`Get-AADIntAccessTokenForSARA`	Used with Support and Recovery Assistant functions
SharePoint Online	`Get-AADIntSPOAuthenticationHeader`	Used with SharePoint Online functions
OneDrive for Business	`New-AADIntOneDriveSettings`	Used with OneDrive for Business functions
Azure Core Management	`Get-AADIntAccessTokenForAzureCoreManagement`	Used with Azure Core Management functions
Entra ID Join	`Get-AADIntAccessTokenForAADJoin`	Used with Entra ID Join functions

Token/API	Function	Remarks
Azure Intune MDM	`Get-AADIntAccessTokenForIntuneMDM`	Used with Intune MDM functions
Azure Cloud Shell	`Get-AADIntAccessTokenForCloudShell`	Used with Azure Cloud Shell functions

17.6 Summary

In this chapter, you learned about some open source tools that can be useful for Teams administrators, and Microsoft 365 administrators in general. These and other community-made tools have numerous advantages. For example:

- Open source tools are a cost-effective option for administrators who are looking to add new features or functionality to their Microsoft 365 environment.
- Many open source tools are designed to be easy to use, making them a great option for administrators who may not have a lot of technical expertise.
- Open source tools often offer a high degree of customizability, allowing administrators to tailor them to their specific needs.
- Many open source tools have a large community of users that can offer support and guidance to administrators.

The next chapter discusses Teams and SharePoint, looking at topics like custom Teams tabs with SharePoint Framework and leveraging SharePoint and Teams integration.

CHAPTER 18
Teams and SharePoint

As we discussed in Chapter 6, there is a strong integration between SharePoint and Teams. You can use Teams to:

- Access and share SharePoint files, libraries, and lists.
- Collaborate on and edit SharePoint documents.
- Access and use SharePoint apps and integrations.

This chapter focuses on a few additional aspects of the integration between Teams and SharePoint. The first recipe examines SharePoint and Teams security and permissions. By aligning the security and compliance settings of both platforms, organizations can ensure that their data is secure and accessible only to authorized users.

You'll also see how to apply Conditional Access to SharePoint sites and Teams. This feature allows organizations to control access to their data based on specific conditions, such as location or device, in a granular way.

The final recipe covers using SharePoint Framework and web parts in Teams. SharePoint web parts can be added to Teams channels, allowing users to personalize their channels with the information that is most relevant to them.

18.1 Matching Teams with the SharePoint Infrastructure

Problem

You need to manage the permissions for the SharePoint sites connected to Teams.

Solution

The first step is to create a new team—we'll call it "Cookbook18." Open the Teams client and create a new team. Then, inside the new team, click the "Add channel" button to create a channel, which we'll call "Paragraph1."

You will notice that a parent site is created in SharePoint for "Cookbook18," and a document library folder is created for "Paragraph1" within that site. To view these resources, open the SharePoint admin center. You will see two libraries within the "Cookbook18" site: a default library called General, and a library called Paragraph1 that corresponds to the "Paragraph1" channel in Teams. The default document library of the SharePoint site contains a folder for each channel. When a new channel is created in Teams, a corresponding folder is created in the document library. However, this does not apply to private channels or shared channels.

To create a new private channel in the "Cookbook18" team called "Cookbook18_Private," use the Teams client. When you open the "Cookbook18" site in the SharePoint admin center, you will notice that a new channel site has been created instead of a library (as shown in Figure 18-1).

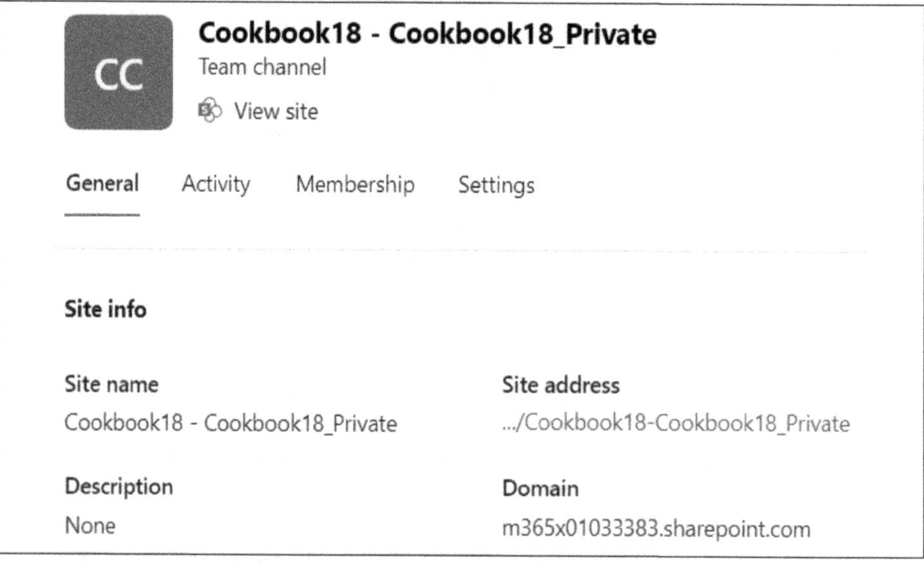

Figure 18-1. A private channel site in SharePoint

If you click "View site," you will see a list of all the sites that have been created to manage private channels. Now, from the Teams client, add a shared channel called "Cookbook18_Shared." Opening the "Cookbook18" site again, you will now see an additional site in the list.

You cannot manage the permissions for sites associated with private and shared Teams channels from the SharePoint admin center. If you open the information page for these sites, you will see a message directing you to the TAC. It is also not possible to hold channel meetings in private channels.

Chapter 6 covered how to add a team to an existing SharePoint site. There are some additional steps if the site is a classic team site (an older version of a team site in SharePoint, based on the classic user interface and functionality that existed before the introduction of modern SharePoint experiences). Open the SharePoint site and click the gear (Settings) icon in the top-right corner. Click "Connect to new Microsoft 365 Group" (the menu for a classic team site is shown in Figure 18-2).

Settings ×

SharePoint

Shared with...
Edit page
Add a page
Add an app
Site contents
Change the look
Site settings
Connect to new Microsoft 365 Group
Getting started

Figure 18-2. Settings for a classic team site

The guided process will start. Click "Let's get started." Some checks will be performed to verify that the site does not overlap with other sites and that the group email is available. Click "Connect group" (see Figure 18-3).

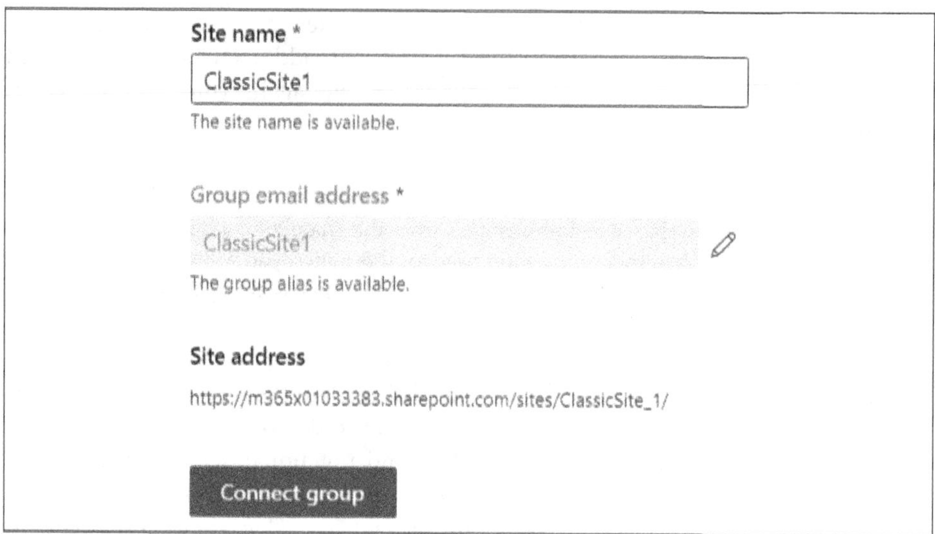

Figure 18-3. Associating the new site with a Microsoft 365 group

Add members to the group, then click Finish.

The site is then converted to a modern site, with the "Add real-time chat" option (to connect the SharePoint site to Teams) available.

Discussion

Chapter 6 introduced the idea that each team has a corresponding site in SharePoint. Teams channels also have correlations to SharePoint sites, pages, libraries, folders, and lists. It is important to understand exactly how the SharePoint logic matches with Teams and the channels. SharePoint sites and libraries have their own security and permission settings, which can be different from those of the teams in which they are used. Understanding how these permissions work can help you ensure that your team has the appropriate access to the resources they need.

Teams and SharePoint manage permissions (which determine the ability of certain users to access, edit, and manage specific resources within the platform) differently. This can be confusing for users who are familiar with one platform but not the other.

In Teams, permissions are managed using Microsoft 365 groups. When a new team is created within Teams, a corresponding Microsoft 365 group is also created. The members of this group are then given access to the team's resources, such as channels, files, and conversations. The permissions for each member of the team are determined by their role within the Microsoft 365 group.

By contrast, SharePoint uses communication sites as a standard, and the permissions for these sites are managed using SharePoint groups. SharePoint groups were originally designed for on-prem SharePoint deployments, but they are now also used for SharePoint Online. SharePoint groups can be used to manage permissions for specific resources within a SharePoint site, such as lists, libraries, and pages.

18.2 Enabling Conditional Access Policies for SharePoint Sites, OneDrive, and Teams

Problem

You need to use Conditional Access in SharePoint to improve security and compliance, ensuring that only authorized users can access sensitive information.

Solution

Solving this problem requires taking the following steps:

1. Add an authentication context in Entra ID.
2. Create a Conditional Access policy that applies to that authentication context.
3. Set a sensitivity label to apply the authentication context to labeled sites.

To create the authentication context, open Microsoft Entra Conditional Access (*https://oreil.ly/27MLz*) in the Entra ID portal and select "Authentication context." Click "New authentication context" (the starting screen for the process is shown in Figure 18-4).

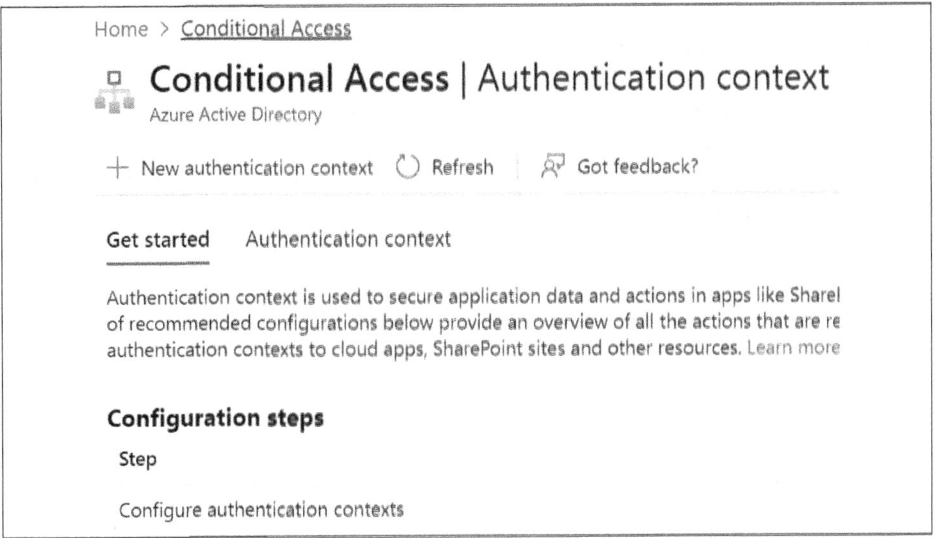

Figure 18-4. Creating an authentication context

In the Name and Description fields, type *Authentication Context SharePoint Sites.* Select "Publish to apps" and select an ID from the drop-down menu (for example, c1). This step is shown in Figure 18-5.

Figure 18-5. Naming and configuring the authentication context

To create the Conditional Access policy, open Microsoft Entra Conditional Access (*https://oreil.ly/_wwvv*) again and click Policies. Click "Create new policy." In the Name field, type *Adding MFA to SharePoint sites.* Under Assignments, in the Users section, click "Users and groups selected." Click "Select users and groups," then "Guest or external users." From the drop-down menu, select all the B2B users and "Other external users" (the options to be selected are shown in Figure 18-6).

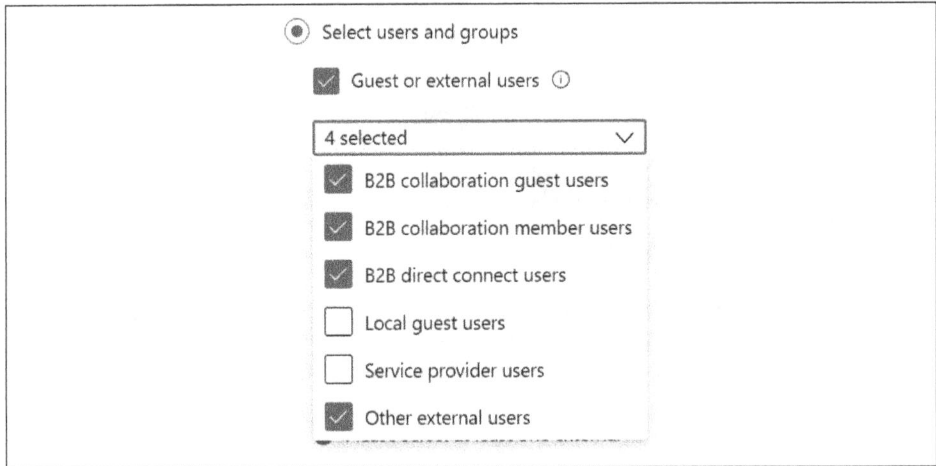

Figure 18-6. Selecting users and groups that will have the policy assigned

Under Assignments, in the "Cloud apps or actions" section, select "Authentication context" from the drop-down menu. Select the authentication context you created previously (the context will be available as an option, as in Figure 18-7).

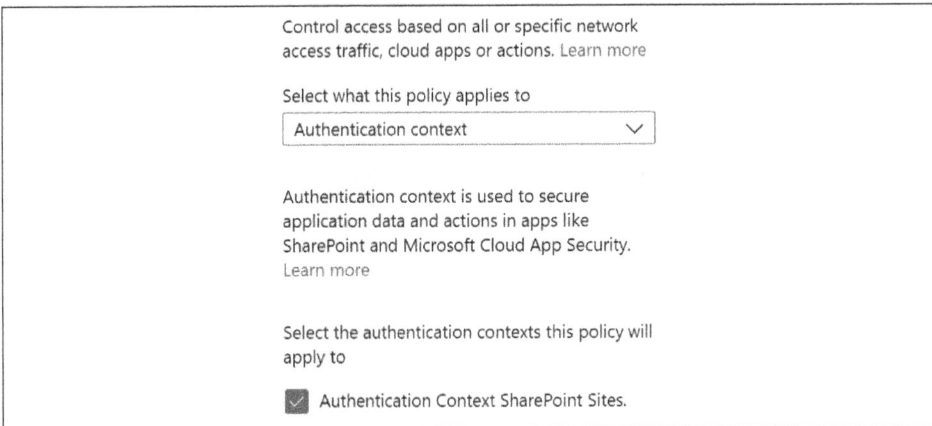

Figure 18-7. Adding the authentication context

Under Access Control, in the Grant section, select "Grant access." Select "Require multifactor authentication." Click Select.

Enable the policy and click Create (as shown in Figure 18-8).

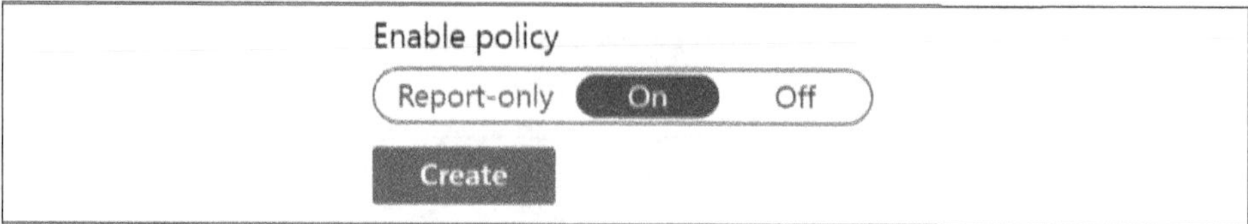

Figure 18-8. Enabling the policy

Now, to create the sensitivity label, from the Microsoft Purview compliance portal (*https://oreil.ly/DGnPT*) click "Information protection," select the Labels tab, and click "Create a label." Type *MFA required* in all the mandatory fields, then click Next (see Figure 18-9).

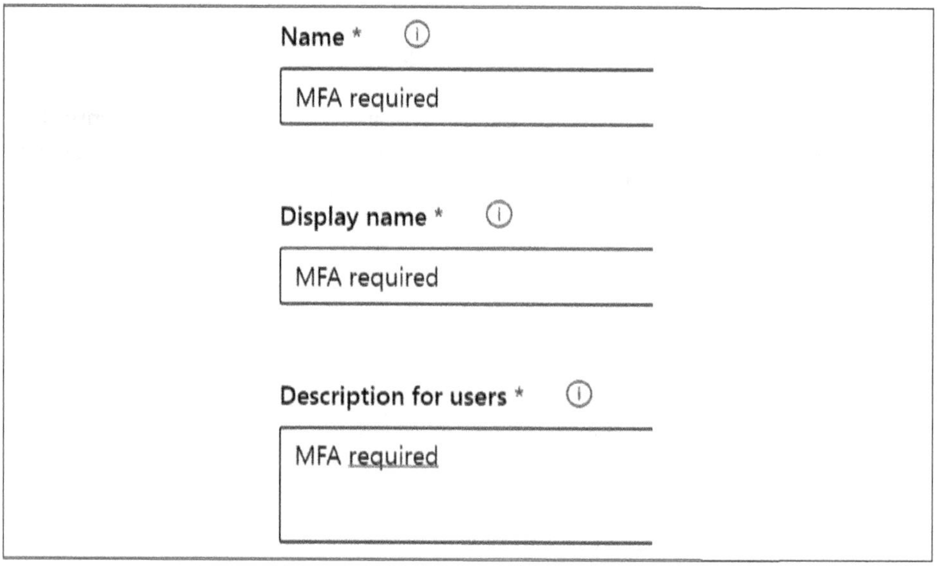

Name *

MFA required

Display name *

MFA required

Description for users *

MFA required

Figure 18-9. Specifying a name, display name, and description for the label

Select "Groups & sites" on the "Define the scope for this label" page and click Next. Click Next on the following page. Then, on the "Define protection settings for groups and sites" page, select "External sharing and Conditional Access settings" and click Next. On the "Define external sharing and device access settings" page, select "Use Azure AD Conditional Access to protect labeled SharePoint sites." Select the "Choose an existing authentication context" option. In the drop-down list, choose the authentication context that you created earlier, then click Next (see Figure 18-10).

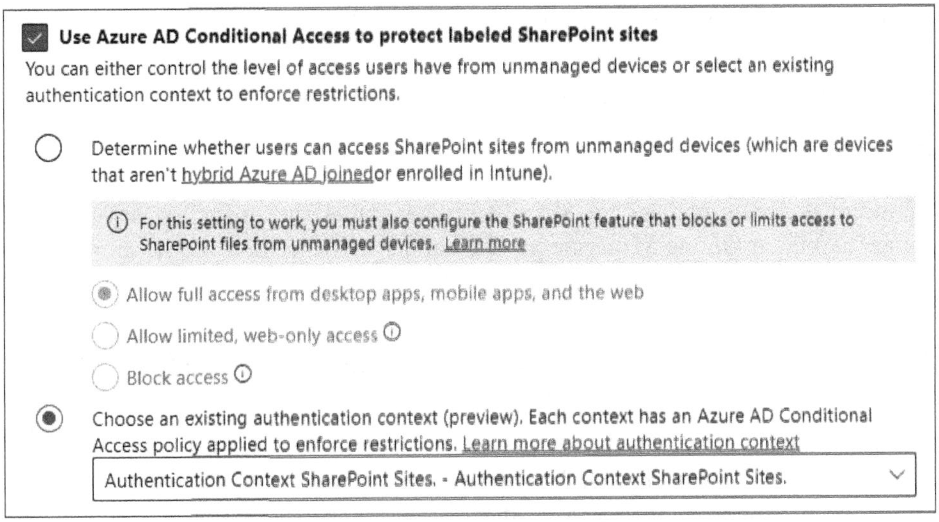

Use Azure AD Conditional Access to protect labeled SharePoint sites

You can either control the level of access users have from unmanaged devices or select an existing authentication context to enforce restrictions.

Determine whether users can access SharePoint sites from unmanaged devices (which are devices that aren't hybrid Azure AD joinedor enrolled in Intune).

For this setting to work, you must also configure the SharePoint feature that blocks or limits access to SharePoint files from unmanaged devices. Learn more

Allow full access from desktop apps, mobile apps, and the web

Allow limited, web-only access

Block access

Choose an existing authentication context (preview). Each context has an Azure AD Conditional Access policy applied to enforce restrictions. Learn more about authentication context

Authentication Context SharePoint Sites. - Authentication Context SharePoint Sites.

Figure 18-10. Applying the Conditional Access policy to the SharePoint sites

Click Next on the next page, then click "Create label." Select "Publish label to users' apps" and click Done. To apply the label to a SharePoint site, you must use the SharePoint Online Management Shell. Check whether the module is already installed with the following command:

```
Get-Module -Name Microsoft.Online.SharePoint.PowerShell -ListAvailable | `
Select Name,Version
```

If the module is not installed, use the following commands to install and import:

```
Install-Module -Name Microsoft.Online.SharePoint.PowerShell
Import-Module Microsoft.Online.SharePoint.PowerShell
```

Connect to SharePoint Online using your tenant URL. For example:

```
Connect-SPOService -Url https://m365x01033383-admin.sharepoint.com/
```

To apply the Conditional Access policy to a site, you need:

- The identity of the site (for example, *https://m365x01033383.sharepoint.com/sites/msteams_4d0288*)
- The name of the authentication context (for example, *Authentication Context SharePoint Sites*)

The command to be used is as follows:

```
Set-SPOSite -Identity https://m365x01033383.sharepoint.com/sites/ `
msteams_4d0288 -ConditionalAccessPolicy AuthenticationContext `
-AuthenticationContextName "Authentication Context SharePoint Sites"
```

You can check the result with the following command:

```
Get-SPOSite -Identity https://m365x01033383.sharepoint.com/sites/msteams_4d0288 `
| fl AuthenticationContextName,ConditionalAccessPolicy
```

Discussion

Conditional Access policies for SharePoint sites, OneDrive, and Teams can be set using SharePoint Online Management Shell and specifying the conditions that must be met to access a particular site. This capability allows users to only go through additional security checks when accessing sites or teams containing sensitive information.

There are several benefits to using Conditional Access in SharePoint, including the following:

Improving security
: Conditional Access allows administrators to set rules that determine who can access specific content, and from where.

Increasing compliance
: Conditional Access can be used to enforce compliance with regulatory requirements, such as HIPAA or GDPR.

Enforcing granular access control
: Conditional Access allows administrators to set different access levels for different users or groups of users.

Improving productivity
: By controlling access to content, Conditional Access can help ensure that only the appropriate users have access to the information they need, when they need it.

Controlling remote user access
: Conditional Access can also be used to set conditions for remote access, ensuring that only authorized users can access SharePoint content from an external location and adding another layer of security.

Be aware of any local or international regulations regarding access control and data privacy, as this can be an important factor when deciding how to implement Conditional Access in SharePoint.

18.3 Using SharePoint Framework to Improve Teams

Problem

You need to deploy a custom app in Teams.

Solution

For this solution, you will use a custom tab and SharePoint Framework (SPFx), as well as Microsoft Graph Toolkit (MGT), to create a web part that works as a Teams tab.

A prerequisite for this recipe is to install the SharePoint Framework development environment and ensure it is already deployed. You saw some of the steps for doing this in Chapter 12. If you need more information, use the instructions outlined in the Microsoft article "Set up your SharePoint Framework development environment" (*https://oreil.ly/7BBP3*).

One of the tools required for the recipe—Gulp—is supported only by specific versions of Node.js (from 12.13.0–13.0.0, from 14.15.0–15.0.0, and from 16.13.0–17.0.0). You can download one of the these versions from nodejs.org (*https://oreil.ly/KEdhI*). This recipe has been tested using Node.js 16.13.1 (*https://oreil.ly/eWhv4*).

The high-level steps for this solution are as follows:

- Create the SharePoint web part.
- Create and deploy the Teams app package.
- Create and deploy the SharePoint package.

Create a folder called *SPFx*. Open a command prompt, go to the *SPFx* folder, and run the following command:

```
yo @microsoft/sharepoint
```

Use the following answers to complete the prompts displayed (as shown in Figure 18-11):

- What is your solution name? *spfxteams*
- Which type of client-side component to create? *WebPart*
- What is your web part name? *SPFx Teams Together*
- Which template would you like to use? *No framework*

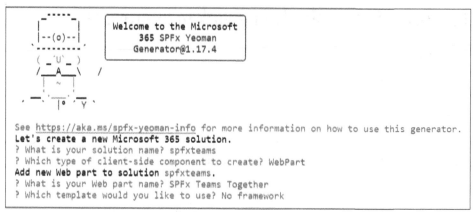

```
     _-----_
    |       |    ╭──────────────────────────╮
    |--(o)--|    │  Welcome to the Microsoft │
   `---------´   │     365 SPFx Yeoman       │
    ( _´U`_ )    │    Generator@1.17.4       │
    /___A___\   /╰──────────────────────────╯
     |  ~  |
   __'.___.'__
 ´   `  |° ´ Y `

See https://aka.ms/spfx-yeoman-info for more information on how to use this generator.
Let's create a new Microsoft 365 solution.
? What is your solution name? spfxteams
? Which type of client-side component to create? WebPart
Add new Web part to solution spfxteams.
? What is your Web part name? SPFx Teams Together
? Which template would you like to use? No framework
```

Figure 18-11. The SharePoint Online Yeoman Generator

The project will be created in the folder. Launch Visual Studio Code and select File > Open Folder. Open the *SPFx* folder, then open the *SpFxTeamsTogetherWebPart.manifest.json* file in *.\SPFx\src\webparts\spFxTeamsTogether* (see Figure 18-12). Check that the `supportedHosts` line includes at least `SharePointWebPart` and `TeamsTab`.

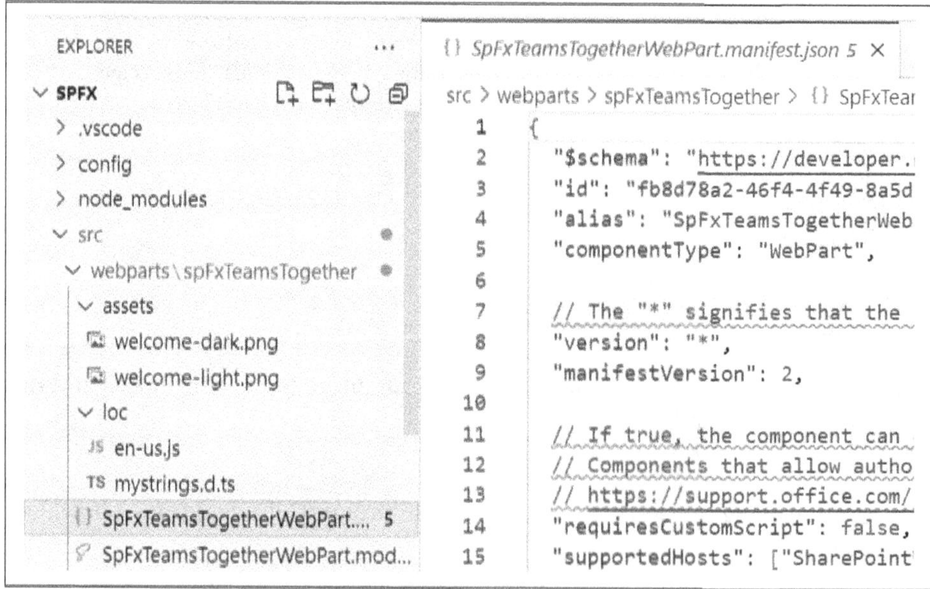

Figure 18-12. Opening the manifest file for SharePoint

The *teams* folder contains two images that will be used to display the custom tab. In this folder, create a *manifest.json* file and save the following code in it:

```json
{
  "$schema": "https://developer.microsoft.com/en-us/json-schemas/teams/v1.10/ `
    MicrosoftTeams.schema.json",
  "manifestVersion": "1.10",
  "packageName": "{{SPFX_COMPONENT_ALIAS}}",
  "id": "{{SPFX_COMPONENT_ID}}",
  "version": "0.1",
  "developer": {
    "name": "Parker Porcupine",
    "websiteUrl": "https://products.office.com/en-us/sharepoint/collaboration",
    "privacyUrl": "https://privacy.microsoft.com/en-us/privacystatement",
    "termsOfUseUrl": "https://www.microsoft.com/en-us/servicesagreement"
  },
  "name": {
    "short": "{{SPFX_COMPONENT_NAME}}"
  },
  "description": {
    "short": "{{SPFX_COMPONENT_SHORT_DESCRIPTION}}",
    "full": "{{SPFX_COMPONENT_LONG_DESCRIPTION}}"
  },
  "icons": {
    "outline": "{{SPFX_COMPONENT_ID}}_outline.png",
    "color": "{{SPFX_COMPONENT_ID}}_color.png"
  },
  "accentColor": "#004578",
  "configurableTabs": [
    {
      "configurationUrl": "https://{teamSiteDomain}{teamSitePath}/_layouts/15/ `
      TeamsLogon.aspx?SPFX=true&dest={teamSitePath}/_layouts/15/ `
      teamshostedapp.aspx%3FopenPropertyPane=true%26teams%26componentId= `
      {{SPFX_COMPONENT_ID}}%26forceLocale={locale}",
      "canUpdateConfiguration": true,
      "scopes": [
        "team"
      ]
    }
  ],
  "validDomains": [
    "*.login.microsoftonline.com",
    "*.sharepoint.com",
    "*.sharepoint-df.com",
    "spoppe-a.akamaihd.net",
    "spoprod-a.akamaihd.net",
    "resourceseng.blob.core.windows.net",
    "msft.spoppe.com"
  ],
  "webApplicationInfo": {
    "resource": "https://{teamSiteDomain}",
    "id": "00000003-0000-0ff1-ce00-000000000000"
  }
}
```

Open the *SpFxTeamsTogetherWebPart.manifest.json* file located in *./src/webparts/spFxTeamsTogether/*.

The values in the *manifest.json* file you just created must match the ones in the *SpFxTeamsTogetherWebPart.manifest.json* file. Replace `{{SPFX_COMPONENT_ID}}` with the correct `id` value (in our example, `a2bd1a0d-3a23-4ffc-a985-a564ae27b919`), as shown in Figure 18-13.

```
teams > {} manifest.json > id
{
    "$schema": "https://developer.microsoft.com/en
    "manifestVersion": "1.10",
    "packageName": "{{SPFX_COMPONENT_ALIAS}}",
    "id": "a2bd1a0d-3a23-4ffc-a985-a564ae27b919",
```

Figure 18-13. Replacing the values in the manifest.json file

You'll also need to replace `{{SPFX_COMPONENT_ALIAS}}` with the `alias` value (in our example, `SpFxTeamsTogetherWebPart`).

The same applies to the following values:

- Replace `{{SPFX_COMPONENT_NAME}}` with `preconfiguredEntries[0].title.default`
- Replace `{{SPFX_COMPONENT_SHORT_DESCRIPTION}}` with `preconfiguredEntries[0].description.default`
- Replace `{{SPFX_COMPONENT_LONG_DESCRIPTION}}` with `preconfiguredEntries[0].description.default`

In our example, the values are:

```
"preconfiguredEntries": [{
  "title": { "default": "SPFx Teams Together" },
  "description": { "default": "SPFx Teams Together description" }
```

Visual Studio Code has a feature that compares two files. To use it:

1. From the left Explorer panel, right-click the first file and choose "Select for Compare."
2. Select a file to compare.
3. Right-click the second file and choose "Compare with Selected."

Create a ZIP file named *app.zip* that contains the files in the *teams* folder. Open *https://dev.teams.microsoft.com*, then click Apps and select "Import app."

You will be required to modify the version to a format like *X.Y.Z*. In our example, we'll modify *0.1* to *0.1.1*.

Click Publish and select "Publish to your org." Now open a command prompt and go to the *SPFx* folder again. Execute the following command (output is shown in Figure 18-14):

```
gulp build
```

```
          _=+#####!
       ###########|        .-------------------------------------.
       ###/    (##|(@)     |            Congratulations!          |
       ###  ######|   \    |   Solution spfxteams is created.     |
       ###/   /###|   (@)  |   Run gulp serve to play with it!    |
       #######  ##|   /    '-------------------------------------'
       ###     /##|(@)
       ###########|
          **=+####!

PS C:\SPFx>
PS C:\SPFx>      build
Build target: DEBUG
[15:53:17] Using gulpfile C:\SPFx\gulpfile.js
[15:53:17] Starting 'build'...
[15:53:17] Starting gulp
[15:53:17] Starting subtask 'pre-copy'...
```

Figure 18-14. Running the Gulp tool

Create a production bundle of the project by running the following command:

```
gulp bundle --ship
```

Create a deployment package of the project by running the following command:

```
gulp package-solution --ship
```

Open your SharePoint administrative portal, select "More features," and click Open under Apps.

The button will take you to the "Manage apps" page (the URL should be similar to *https://<your_SharePoint_page>/sites/appcatalog/_layouts/15/tenantAppCata log.aspx/manageApps?firstCreatedAppCatalog=1*).

Click Upload and browse to the *sharepoint\solution* folder inside the *SPFx* folder. Select the *spfxteams.sppkg* file and click Open.

In the "Enable app" panel, select "Enable this app and add it to all sites." Select the "Add to Teams" option, then click "Enable app," as shown in Figure 18-15. This will make the web part available to all site collections in the tenant, including those that are behind a Teams team.

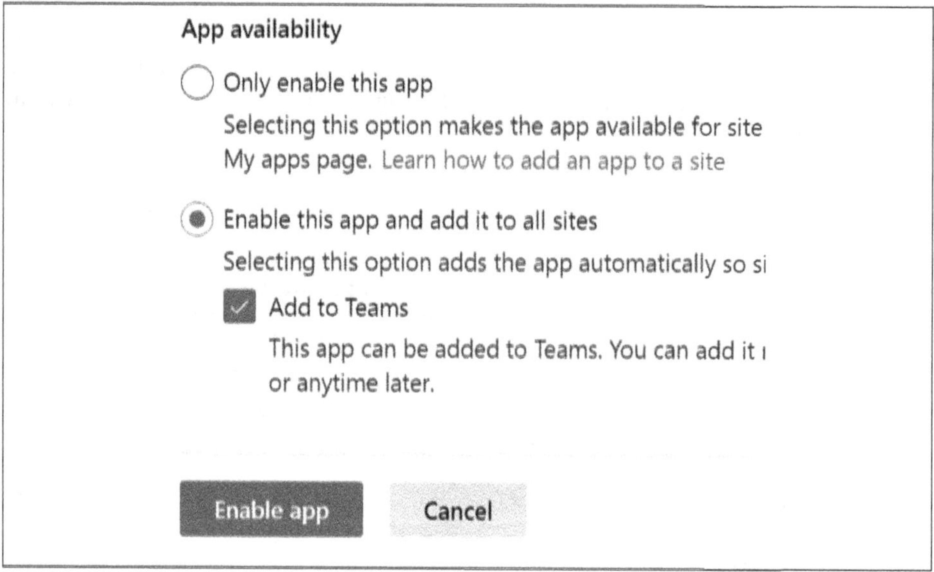

App availability
Only enable this app
Selecting this option makes the app available for site
My apps page. Learn how to add an app to a site
Enable this app and add it to all sites
Selecting this option adds the app automatically so si
Add to Teams
This app can be added to Teams. You can add it
or anytime later.
Enable app
Cancel

Figure 18-15. Enabling the app

Open Teams and create a new team (for example, "WebPartsTest"). Select the + symbol ("Add a tab"). From the list of apps, select SPFx Teams Together (see Figure 18-16).

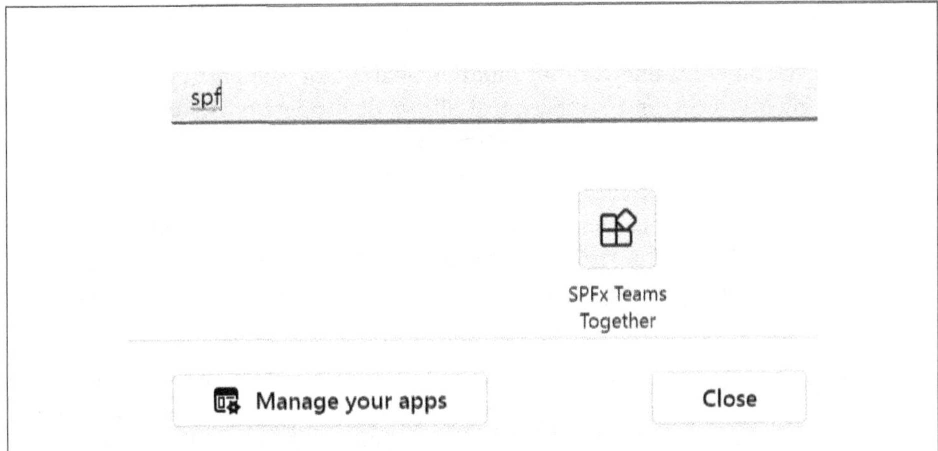

Figure 18-16. Adding the app to a tab in Teams

On the SPFx Teams Together page, click Add. Click Save on the next page. The tab will be populated with the web part you created.

It is possible to add the same web part to a SharePoint site. To do that, open the site, go into editing mode, and select SPFx Teams Together (as shown in Figure 18-17).

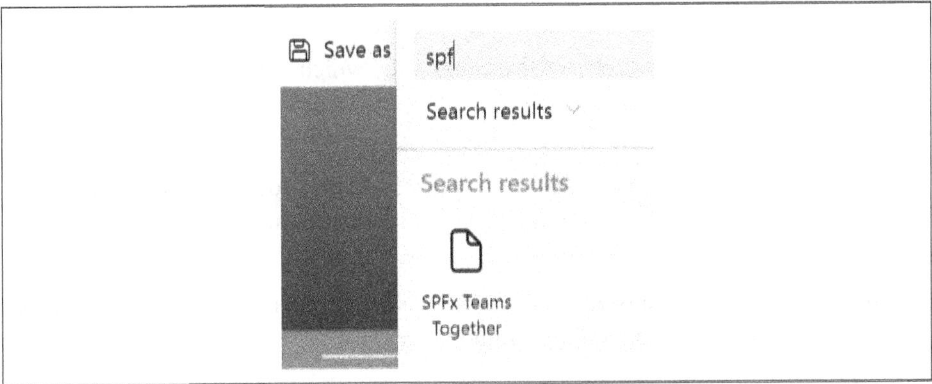

Figure 18-17. Adding the web part to a SharePoint site

A *tab* in Teams is just a web page rendered in an Iframe. Your tab and configuration page will have a URL that's used by Teams to determine the location of the page to load in the Iframe.

Discussion

SPFx is a development framework for building SharePoint web parts, extensions, and apps using HTML, CSS, and JavaScript. It allows developers to build solutions that run entirely on the client side, using modern web development tools and frameworks such as React, Angular, and Vue.js, with no server-side code required.

MGT is a set of web components that can be used to build web applications that interact with the Microsoft Graph API. It is built on top of the Microsoft Graph JavaScript Client Library, which provides a simplified way to interact with Microsoft Graph and various Microsoft services.

MGT includes components for authentication, calendars, email, people, and more. The web applications you build using these components can access and display information from various Microsoft services, such as Office 365, Entra ID, Outlook, and others.

SPFx provides several benefits over the previous development models for SharePoint, including the following:

Improved development experience
: SPFx uses modern web development tools and frameworks, which makes it easier and more efficient for developers to build web parts and solutions.

Improved performance
: SPFx solutions run entirely on the client side, which can improve performance and reduce server load.

Increased flexibility
: SPFx allows for cross-platform development, allowing you to build web parts that run on both SharePoint Online and SharePoint on-prem.

Improved security
: SPFx solutions are deployed to SharePoint as packages, making it easy to manage the security of a solution and its components.

Support for open source libraries
: SPFx allows you to use the latest web technologies and JavaScript libraries, including third-party tools like Webpack, npm, Yeoman, and so on.

18.4 Summary

The SharePoint integration with Teams allows users to access SharePoint content and features directly within the Teams interface. It also enables the use of SharePoint's advanced permissions and governance features within Teams, improving security and compliance. Additionally, the integration allows the use of SharePoint's customization and development capabilities, such as custom forms, workflows, and apps, within the context of Teams. Overall, the SharePoint integration with Teams greatly enhances the collaboration and organizational capabilities of the platform.

APPENDIX

Teams and Viva Adoption Examples

By Lesley Crook

This appendix is dedicated to user adoption, so the content revolves around storytelling and experience sharing instead of technical recipes. You can read more about this guest author at the end of the appendix.

In November 2021, four Microsoft Viva modules were announced through the lens of Microsoft Teams—Viva Connections, Viva Insights, Viva Learning, and Viva Topics—with the not-so-secret ingredients of SharePoint Online, Exchange Online, and what was Workplace Analytics, with a dash of AI. The Viva suite has since been expanded to include Viva Engage, Viva Goals, and Viva Sales (see Figure A-1 for a quick overview).

The Viva suite is a diverse, inclusive, and accessible platform for productivity, collaboration, learning, and well-being, enabling employees to thrive in a hybrid workplace. It comes with features to help staff in HR, internal communications, and marketing to do their best work and support their colleagues. The Viva suite integrations accessed through Teams offer good employee experiences.

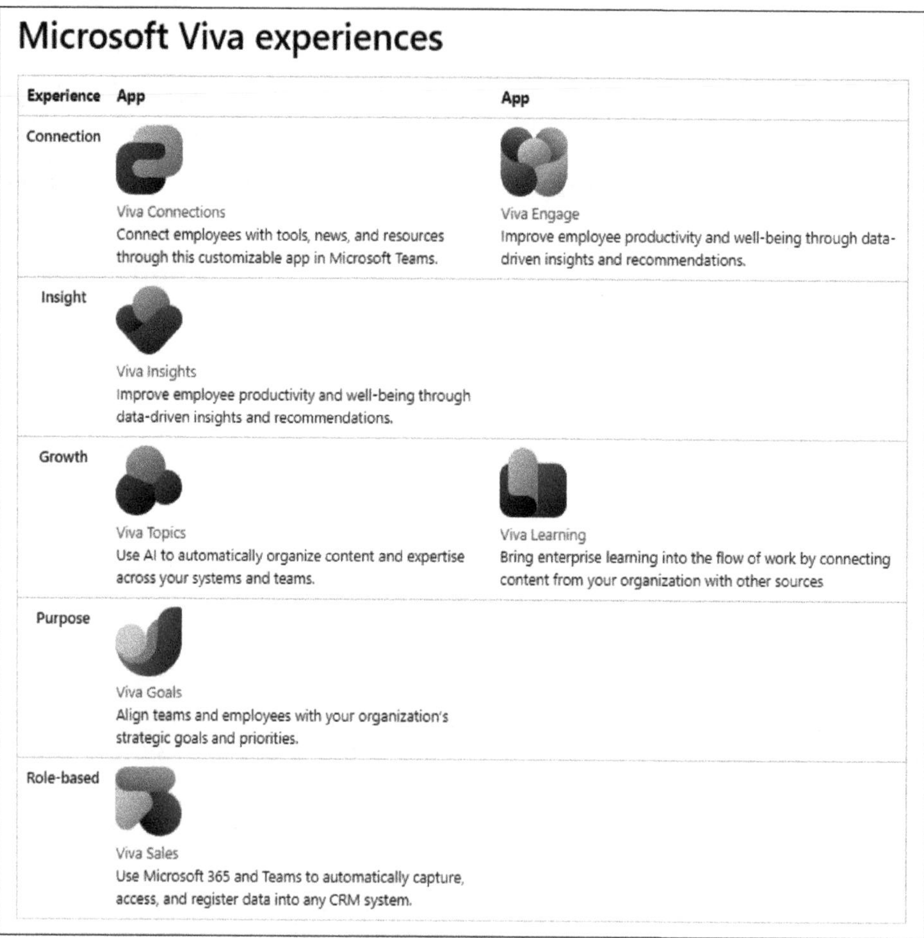

Microsoft Viva experiences

Experience	App	App
Connection	Viva Connections Connect employees with tools, news, and resources through this customizable app in Microsoft Teams.	Viva Engage Improve employee productivity and well-being through data-driven insights and recommendations.
Insight	Viva Insights Improve employee productivity and well-being through data-driven insights and recommendations.	
Growth	Viva Topics Use AI to automatically organize content and expertise across your systems and teams.	Viva Learning Bring enterprise learning into the flow of work by connecting content from your organization with other sources
Purpose	Viva Goals Align teams and employees with your organization's strategic goals and priorities.	
Role-based	Viva Sales Use Microsoft 365 and Teams to automatically capture, access, and register data into any CRM system.	

Figure A-1. The apps in the Microsoft Viva suite

This appendix draws on some of my Yammer (now rebranded Viva Engage) and Teams user adoption good practices that were designed to support some of the Viva suite modules. I do not consider them best practices, as there is always room for improvement. It includes Microsoft 365 Champion success stories from three enterprise customers led by talented chief technology officers (CTOs). Microsoft 365 Champions are experts in using Microsoft 365 to solve business problems and are enthusiastic about sharing their knowledge and experiences with others.

The Viva suite is designed to help organizations enhance employee productivity, engagement, and well-being. It is built on the Teams platform and brings together various Microsoft 365 services and tools that were previously scattered across different applications.

Yammer is a social networking platform for enterprise use, designed to help organizations collaborate and communicate more effectively. Yammer is typically used by organizations as an internal social networking tool, allowing employees to share information, ask questions, and collaborate on projects. Viva Engage is the evolution of Yammer.

There is a difference between having access to technology and using it smartly. Upskilling is needed to understand how Viva drives best practice use and adoption of what you already have alongside Teams and Microsoft 365. Take a leap of faith and consider some of the tried-and-tested approaches I'll discuss in this appendix. Experiment with appropriate modules to match your current or near-term objectives, and see how you can create a thriving employee experience in a hybrid workplace.

Critical to success is establishing a good relationship with a key sponsor who will assign appropriate colleagues around the business to support the effort and clear any blockers. The best sponsors for this business change are senior leaders in HR, internal communications, marketing, or a transformation program.

Even more important is having a CTO or equivalent with a forward-thinking, tenacious growth mindset, and plenty of empathy. They can articulate the art of the modern workplace to leaders and staff. The individuals discussed in the success stories I share here all have these traits, and fantastic leadership skills.

When I work with a customer on a user adoption and change management engagement, I follow the renowned Prosci ADKAR model (*https://oreil.ly/O2utz*). To set yourself up for success, you need to prepare your Teams environment and culture. The projects in my stories fit into the ADKAR model—they were managed by passionate people who received recognition for going above and beyond their day jobs.

ADKAR stands for the following:

Awareness
: Build awareness that change is coming and you need to act. You might want to evaluate current productivity, or ask people to volunteer as Champions if they already have experience with the tools.

Desire
: Get employees excited about making the change.

Knowledge
: Let employees know that training is available (or mandatory), and check in with them about the training experience.

Ability
: Help employees put their new knowledge to use effectively, using surveys and metrics to adjust the process as needed.

Reinforcement
: Capture success stories, and reward and recognize excellent work.

After completing the ADKAR cycle, rinse and repeat six months later to continuously improve employee ability and business productivity.

A.1 Using Viva Insights for Employee Well-Being and Productivity

Viva Insights is an application designed to help organizations improve employee well-being and productivity. It provides insights and analytics based on data collected from various Microsoft 365 services, such as Teams, Exchange, and SharePoint. Viva Insights uses this data to generate personalized recommendations and actionable insights for individuals and teams, allowing them to better understand their work patterns, habits, and behaviors.

Some of the key features of Viva Insights include the ability to track the time spent in meetings, analyze email and chat behavior, monitor work/life balance, and identify opportunities for skill development and training. By providing visibility into these aspects of work, Viva Insights helps organizations foster a culture of well-being and productivity, while also supporting employee growth and development (see Figure A-2).

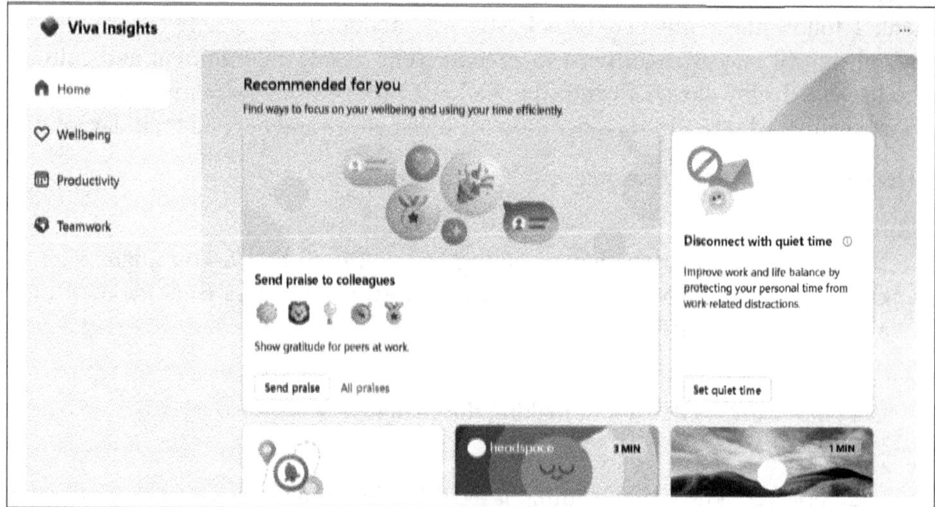

Figure A-2. The Viva Insights app in the Microsoft Teams client

To clarify the value of Viva Insights, Table A-1 compares the potential state of internal communications with the targets we could achieve with Viva Insight.

Table A-1. The current state of internal communication and the results that you can obtain with Viva Insights

Current state	Future state
I suffer from anxiety; this often affects my sleep and can affect my health.	With encouragement from my manager, I use the Headspace meditation app, Virtual Commute, and Quiet Time on my mobile. I now have downtime between work, helping me focus.
I work in HR, and our outsourced annual staff survey takes weeks, if not months, to collate and share and is expensive.	We share corporate-wide plans to improve well-being using tools that quickly support complex staff challenges and map reactions, enabling easy-to-reach shared content.
As leaders, we need mechanisms to regularly and easily measure engagement with our brand, products, vision, or culture.	I now have data-driven visibility into how work patterns affect well-being, productivity, and business performance—quick access to company content!

Research says many people want to work flexibly from home but also want an office culture experience, known as the *hybrid work paradox*. To navigate and effectively handle such complex scenarios, I suggest acquiring the skill of *empathetic leadership*, which is widely recognized as invaluable in fostering a thriving hybrid work environment. This means taking an interest in employees' well-being—spanning mental, physical, emotional, and economic health—across the whole workforce, including undervalued frontline workers, using real-time data.

As Satya Nadella, CEO of Microsoft, puts it: "Employee expectations are changing, and we will need to define productivity much more broadly—inclusive of collaboration, learning, and well-being—to drive career advancement for every worker with flexibility in when, where, and how people work."

That might sound like a substantial expectation, with a company to run, products or services to deliver, and targets to meet, but it can be fulfilled relatively easily. To drive this new leadership style, with an unusual focus on kindness and an appreciation of how employees are coping, there are fantastic AI-enhanced features in Viva Insights, delivered through the lens of Teams.

Viva helps with personal development, learning, collaboration, and knowledge sharing across the enterprise. The importance of digital well-being contributes to individual productivity, collaboration, and an empathetic culture.

The importance of taking breaks and relaxing is also highlighted, and Viva Insights offers various features to support well-being, such as virtual commutes, daily briefing emails, and focus time.

For example, the Productivity Dashboard in Viva Insights provides a view of how users are spending their time in Teams, Outlook, and other Office apps. This dashboard enables individuals and managers to track their productivity over time and provides insights into how they can optimize their work patterns (see Figure A-3).

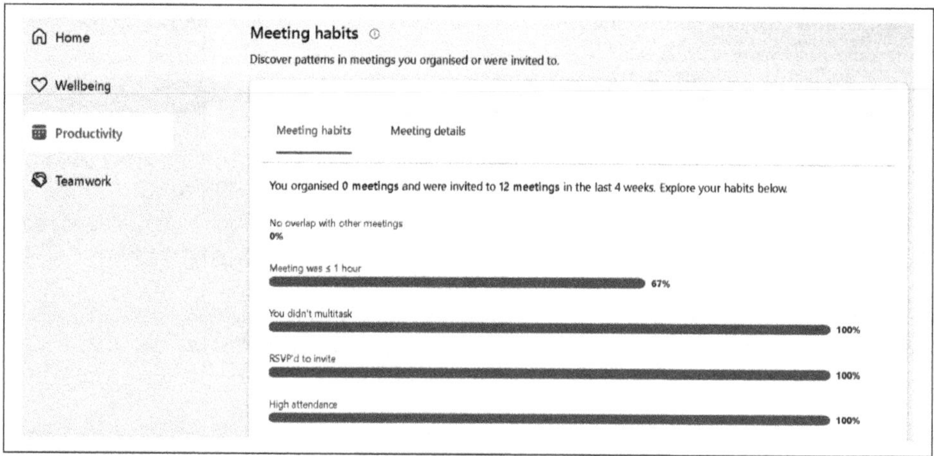

Figure A-3. The Productivity Dashboard in Viva Insights

The dashboard displays data on the number of emails sent and received, the number of meetings attended and organized, and the amount of time spent on focused work, communication, and collaboration tasks. Users can also view the percentage of time spent in meetings and on time spent on tasks performed outside of their regular working hours.

In addition to individual insights, managers can view aggregated data on the productivity of their teams, identify trends, and take actions to optimize team productivity. They can identify common sources of distractions or time-consuming tasks and take steps to address them.

A.2 Managing Viva Learning to Make Personal Development a Natural Part of Your Day

Viva Learning simplifies access to learning resources by providing employees with a centralized hub for all their learning needs. The platform seamlessly integrates with Teams, allowing users to easily discover, share, and track learning from a variety of sources, including LinkedIn Learning, Microsoft Learn, SharePoint libraries, and third-party providers. Viva Learning eliminates the need for employees to switch between different applications to access the learning content they need (Figure A-4 shows how the app works in the Teams client).

One of the standout features of Viva Learning is its ability to provide personalized learning experiences for each employee. By leveraging AI, the platform can suggest learning content based on an employee's role, skills, and past learning experiences. This personalized approach to learning helps employees develop the skills they need to excel in their current roles, while also preparing them for future career growth opportunities.

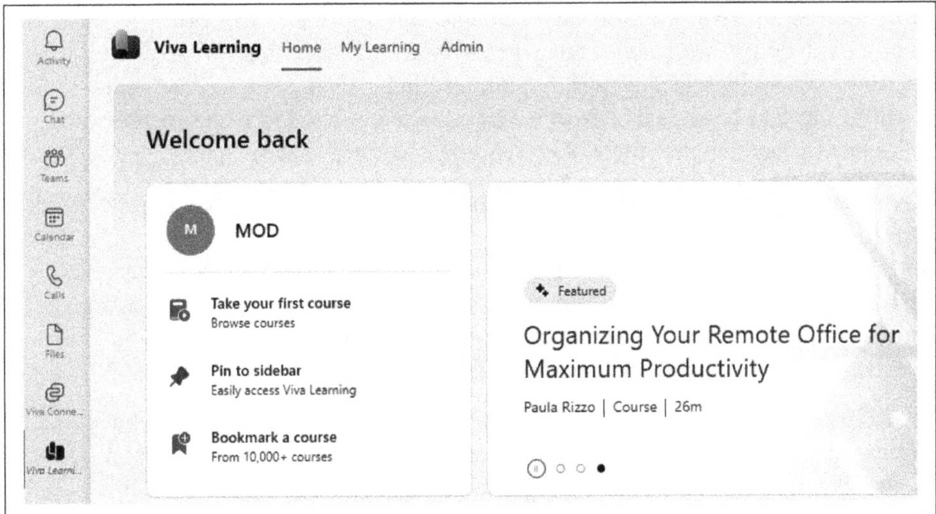

Figure A-4. The Viva Learning app in Teams

It's important to note that Viva Learning is not intended to replace a company's existing Learning Management System (LMS). Instead, Viva Learning is classified as a Learning Experience Platform (LXP) and serves a different purpose. While an LMS is primarily focused on delivering, managing, and tracking formal training programs, an LXP like Viva Learning is designed to provide a more personalized and social learning experience.

An LMS is a crucial tool used by organizations to facilitate employee training and education. It plays a significant role in various sectors, including the public sector, R&D, manufacturing, and healthcare, where audits and mandatory training are common.

The primary purpose of an LMS is to support a learning-oriented business model. It enables companies to operate based on established business rules, deliver formal or scheduled training, and generate revenue through the sale of learning products and services. By leveraging specialized software, an LMS effectively delivers educational experiences to learners, placing a strong emphasis on providing and disseminating content. This content often takes the form of structured online courses meticulously designed by the organization that owns the LMS.

An LMS provides basic testing and generates reports, enabling a manager to enroll learners in courses, and launch and access those courses. It also allows you to track learners' activity, scores, and completion of studies. An LMS enables a company to ensure that employees have completed the required training so that tasks can be performed safely and securely, rather than providing a learning pathway for personal development.

By contrast, an LXP focuses on the learners and is intended to empower them to access the learning resources they need when they want them, based on their preferences. The content found in Viva Learning is on-demand and informal, from videos to blogs and recommendations from peers or managers. Users can check their progress and browse the latest content by selecting tags that interest them. They can bookmark courses they might like to take later, revisit previous training materials, and recommend courses to colleagues by searching for them, then sending a link in a chat or channel.

Viva Learning (*https://oreil.ly/POJMg*) is intended to make building a growth mindset easier in a hybrid workplace. We are all capable of a lot more than we think. Focus time helps users think clearly, without interruptions by email notifications and alerts from other apps. Having scheduled, uninterrupted time to focus on deep work allows employees to complete complex tasks, produce high-quality output, generate innovative ideas, and set time aside for personal development.

Viva Learning is free and enabled by default. SharePoint and supported third-party content provider sources are available to users; the admin configures those sources to ensure the content is available for search and discovery and can be browsed by employees. Creating a Viva Learning hub (*https://oreil.ly/hRDgw*) is helpful for the new-hire process.

A.3 Aligning Objectives and Key Results with Viva Goals

Viva Goals is an employee performance management tool that is designed to help organizations and individuals set, track, and achieve their goals. By providing a single, centralized platform for managing goals and objectives, Viva Goals eliminates the need for multiple tools and systems, which can often lead to confusion and inconsistencies. Viva Goals integrates seamlessly with other Microsoft tools, such as Teams and Outlook, allowing employees to access their goals from the applications they use every day.

The Viva Goals application was created by Ally.io, and it includes features that need to be tuned by leaders. A common challenge for leaders is writing objectives and key results (OKRs). Doing so requires in-depth consideration but is a worthy exercise. Consider a boat where everyone must be rowing in the same direction, or a team of bricklayers who must know where each brick must be laid to create the perfect wall or building. Similarly, Viva Goals connects teams to the business's strategic priorities, mission, and purpose, aligning OKRs in a dashboard. *Objectives* are simply what needs to be accomplished—they define success at an organization, team, and individual level, as they connect work to outcomes. OKRs, created from scratch or with built-in templates, are integrated into the employee experience through the lens of Teams.

Viva Goals requires a dedicated license. You can buy the licenses or start a 60-day free trial for 50 users from the Microsoft 365 admin center (select Billing > "Purchase services").

After you define an organization, Viva Goals will be available in the Teams client, as seen in Figure A-5.

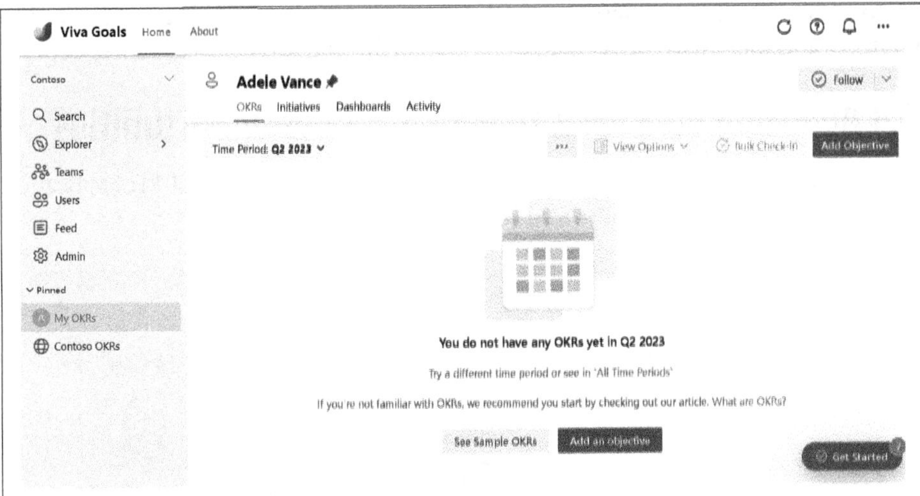

Figure A-5. The Viva Goals app in Teams

In Table A-2, you can see a mapping between the existing state of goals tracking in many companies, using personal development plans with annual or semiannual reviews, compared to what you can achieve by executing the same tasks in Viva Goals.

Table A-2. The current state of internal training and objectives tracking and the goals that you can obtain with Viva Goals

Current state	Future state
We are trying to use spreadsheets to track team objectives manually, and they are not tied to corporate goals or individuals.	Even though I am working from home, it has helped me connect my direct reports to achieve the targets and goals of the organization—this has helped us all focus.
It can often take weeks, if not months, to find out if I am on track with my objectives—and I am still determining how my efforts affect revenues or sales.	We now go straight into conversations at our monthly meeting to track our objectives against business performance in a friendly dashboard—it's a great time-saver, improving our productivity.
I am a new manager and find it challenging to set my direct reports' objectives so that they see how they align with company strategy.	I have OKR examples of how to set goals that are defined and quantified, and these can be used as references for developing our plans—this is easy-to-reach shared content.

Another key feature of Viva Goals is its ability to provide feedback and recognition for employees. Managers can give feedback to employees on their progress and performance, and employees can receive recognition from their peers and colleagues for their achievements. This feedback loop is essential in creating a culture of continuous improvement and growth.

Finally, Viva Goals provides insights and analytics to help organizations measure the effectiveness of their goals and performance-management processes. It allows managers to track their teams' progress toward their goals, identify areas where they need to improve, and make data-driven decisions to improve employee performance.

A.4 Adopting Viva Sales to Manage Sales Opportunities

Viva Sales is a "role-based" Customer Relationship Management (CRM) application with features for managing sales leads more efficiently (Figure A-6).

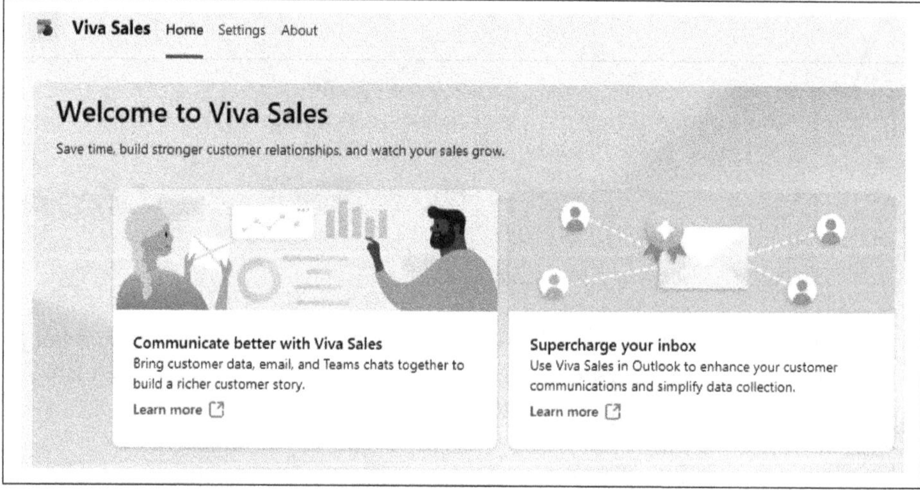

Figure A-6. The Viva Sales app

Viva Sales includes features that deep-dive into Outlook conversations and Teams Meetings. It creates reports and follow-up alerts to monitor and maintain sales opportunities, and it integrates with other CRMs and Microsoft Dynamics. Viva Sales also integrates with your email via an add-on that you can install from the Outlook client (see Figure A-7).

You can view CRM data in Outlook and automatically sync customer engagement data from Outlook with Salesforce and Microsoft Dynamics 365. In the future, Viva Sales may be expanded and could replace the Dynamics 365 App for Teams and Outlook.

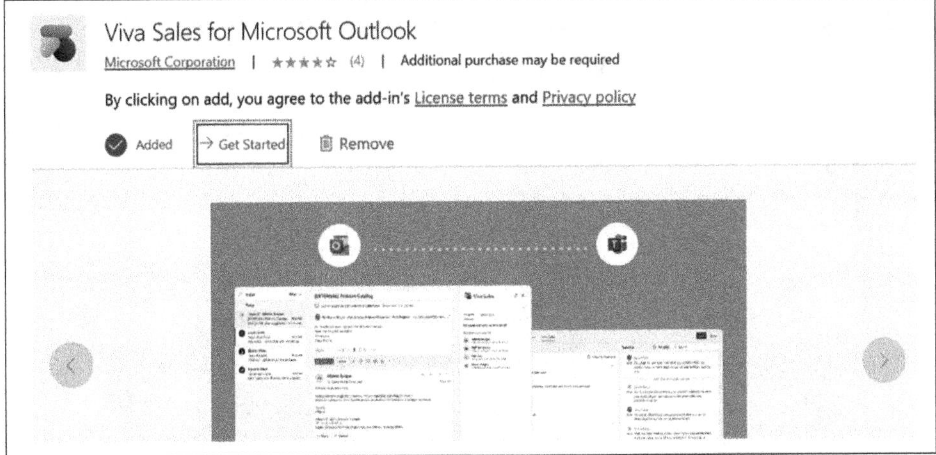

Figure A-7. Integrating Viva Sales with Outlook

The add-on requires sign-in with Salesforce or Microsoft Dynamics (shown in the right part of the Outlook client, as in Figure A-8).

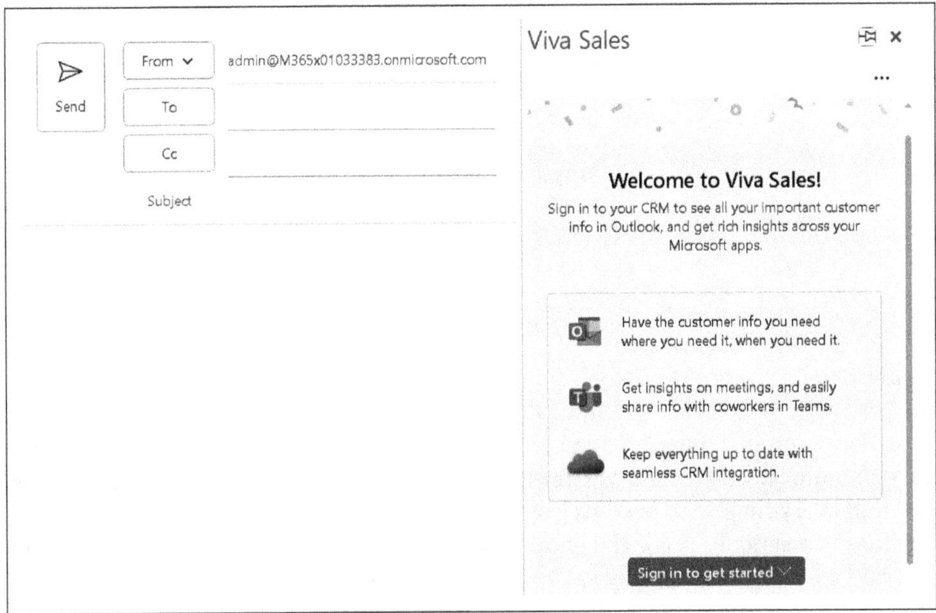

Figure A-8. Connecting the Viva Sales add-on to the CRM

A.5 Deploying Viva Connections and Viva Engage as Frontline Workers' Hybrid Workplace

Viva Connections is a personalized desktop and mobile app accessible via the Teams client (Figure A-9). This app provides leaders and communications teams with various ways to reach all staff quickly.

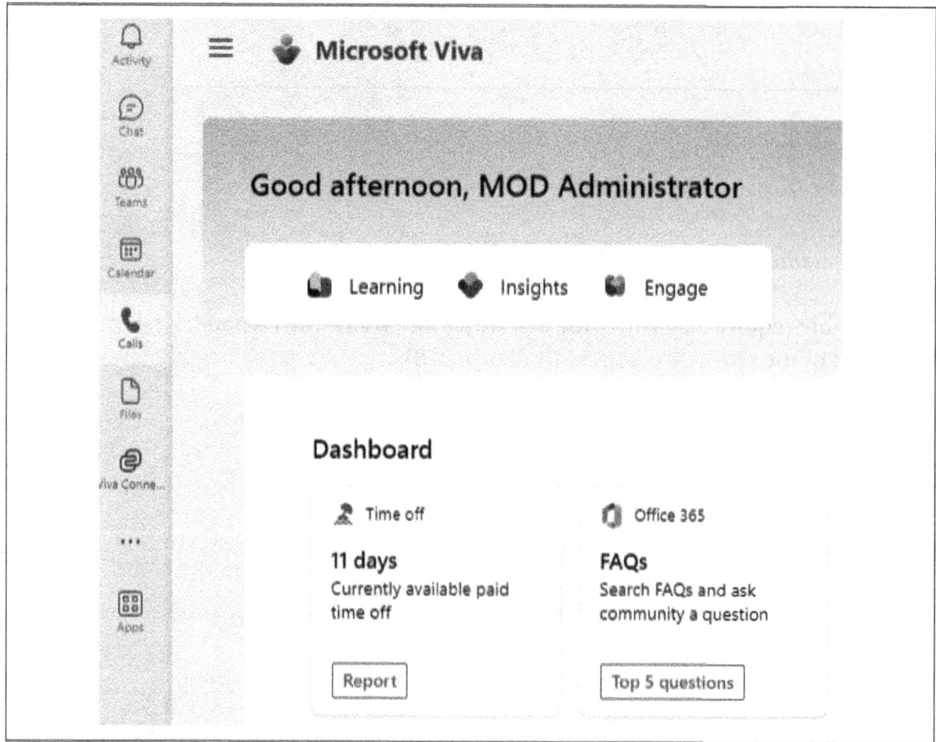

Figure A-9. Accessing Viva Connections from the Teams client

Viva Connections is the gateway to employee engagement, controlled mostly by internal communicators. It offers organizations a branded company app where employees can find everything they need to get their jobs done and stay connected. Viva Connections is positioned to be the "home" for Microsoft Viva. It's a place where people can start their day and quickly catch up and keep up with organizational news, tasks, and resources (an example is shown in Figure A-10).

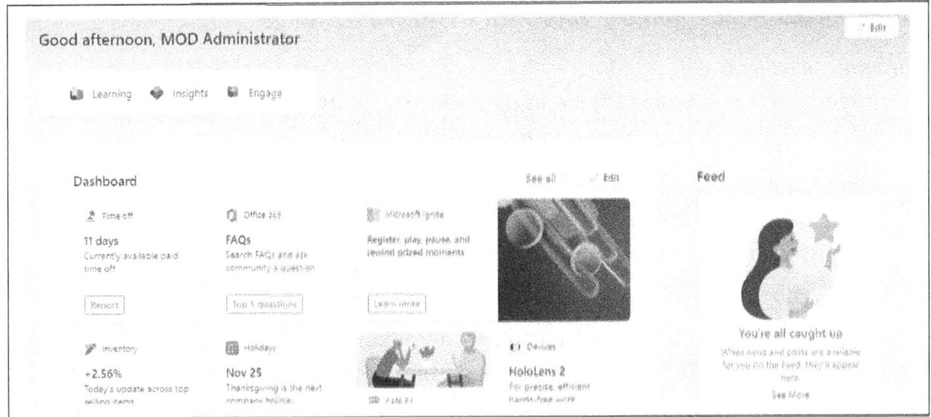

Figure A-10. The Viva Connections dashboard with customized company contents

Viva Engage (shown in Figure A-11) is the social layer of Microsoft Viva and Microsoft 365, and should be owned by empowered employees who are trusted not to post anything that would upset their boss or their mother.

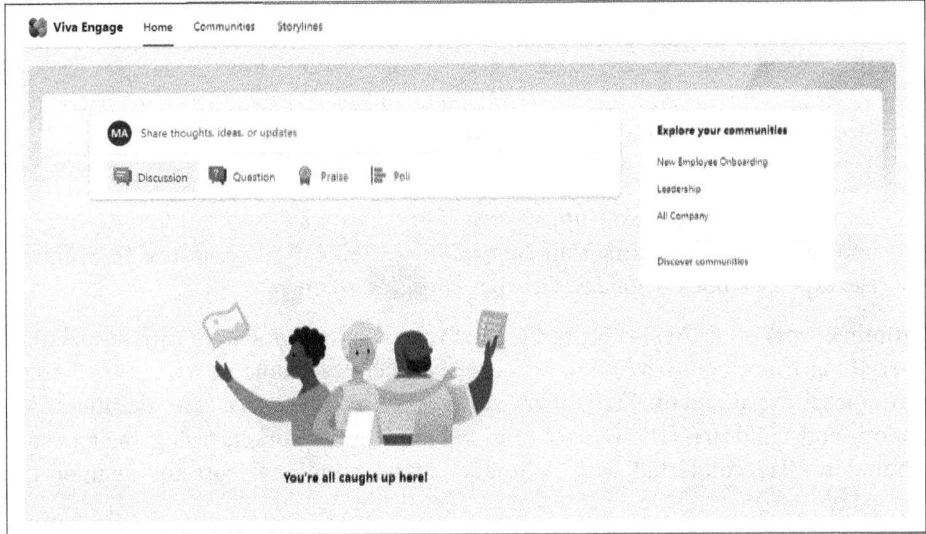

Figure A-11. The Viva Engage app, focused on growing your network at work

The Viva Engage app is "a place to connect and engage with leaders, colleagues, and communities; featuring experiences for serendipitous discovery of conversations happening across the organization, for asking questions and sharing knowledge, for deeper engagement, for virtual events, and for building social capital and extending your network at work," according to a Microsoft article on the topic (*https://oreil.ly/_3Fcp*).

Here are a few things users can access with Viva Connections:

Corporate news feed
: Intended for everyone in the company; ensures staff has access to the latest information that drives the brand on modern SharePoint.

Regional news feed
: News relevant to the region that employees are based in that might impact their daily operations.

Location news feed
: News relevant to staff for the location where they are based, such as a factory or a retail store; might include staff recognitions, health and safety updates, news about local company sports and social clubs, and staff charity events on Viva Engage/Yammer.

Employee resource groups
: Company groups for employees with shared backgrounds or experiences (working parents; LGBTQIA+; military, cultural, or ethnic communities) or shared interests (perhaps around topics like cycling, baking, pets, or photography) on Viva Engage/Yammer.

Events
: Town halls, team celebrations, etc.; If a user misses an event, they can watch it on Stream, Microsoft's YouTube-like service.

Dashboard
: Users can manage tasks (*https://oreil.ly/4FtvV*) or shifts (*https://oreil.ly/btLI5*), book a safe desk, read the staff canteen menu and company address book, manage expenses, book a holiday, view pay slips, and so on.

Frontline workers (FLWs) comprise a massive part of our global industries spanning everything from food, beverages, and entertainment to public safety, national security, transport, gas and oil, IT, financial services, healthcare, social care, charities, education, and childcare. These days, you will find these workers using their smartphones to stay connected with colleagues at no additional cost to them or the company.

You can now easily onboard FLWs using only their phone number and give them full access to Teams channels, shifts, and Viva Connections with Yammer/Viva Engage to share news and views. You can invite them to Teams calls and share documents with them using Microsoft 365 F1 licenses. However, they should *not* use unapproved apps to manage what are often confidential conversations about your business.

This Microsoft article "Use audience targeting in Viva Connections to personalize the experience" (*https://oreil.ly/RvnTQ*) explains how audience targeting and segmentation can ensure that the right audiences see the right content in Viva Connections and

Viva Engage. Audience targeting can be applied to the tool's three primary components: Dashboard, Feed, and Resources.

A.6 Harvesting and Curating Knowledge with Viva Topics

Viva Topics is a knowledge management solution that helps organizations identify, capture, and organize knowledge. Topics applies AI to identify expertise inside the organization and then arranges the information into shared topics. The AI system also automatically creates a page for each topic, making it easier for the organization to access and utilize this knowledge.

One of the key features of Viva Topics is its ability to automatically generate knowledge cards. These cards provide a summary of information on a particular topic, along with links to related resources such as documents, videos, and experts within the organization. The knowledge cards are curated using AI techniques, including natural language processing, entity recognition, and knowledge graph construction. This ensures that the knowledge cards are highly accurate, relevant, and up-to-date.

Another feature of Viva Topics is its ability to create topic pages. These pages serve as a centralized location for all information related to a particular topic. They can be created manually or automatically, and can include information from multiple sources, such as documents, emails, and conversations. Topic pages also provide a way to collaborate and offer improvements, allowing employees to contribute, comment, and rate the information.

In addition to these features, Viva Topics also provides analytics and insights into knowledge usage. This information can help organizations identify knowledge gaps and areas where knowledge is not being effectively used. It can also enable them to identify experts within the organization who can be relied upon to provide valuable insights and information.

A realistic example of the current state of knowledge management at a company and the transformation that you can effect with Viva Topics are illustrated in Table A-3.

Table A-3. Knowledge management as it is and the results you can obtain with Viva Topics

Current state	Future state
I just joined the company and need to know who has the correct information or how to find it quickly.	As I work, I can hover over unusual words like acronyms and find helpful content and experts immediately. This helps me focus.
I know my expertise and knowledge will be lost when I leave after 15 years—that is demoralizing.	I am a subject matter expert, and my company knowledge will remain when I leave—allowing quick access to company content for others.
I am not encouraged to share my knowledge, as this is regarded as showing off.	I love "working out loud" to share my knowledge in a way others might find helpful, and others might help me improve my work.

Viva Topics is like Wikipedia for your enterprise, where AI creates the first draft. The topic pages surface as topic cards right in your workflow. You hover over an acronym or unusual word, and the right pane is automatically populated with helpful and appropriate content associated with the phrase.

A.7 Persona Profiling and Modern Workplace Storyboards

Persona profiling is a useful tool for understanding specific training needs in a business when implementing user adoption programs. I'll share a case study.

As part of the adoption process for Company A, focus groups and interviews were conducted to create persona profiles for a healthcare organization in the UK, (referred to as Organization B). These profiles went beyond general demographics and provided a visualization of fictional employees, allowing the company to examine and understand the drivers and barriers to adoption on a personal level.

To further enhance the adoption process, the CTO of Organization B and I created a lighthearted adoption play in a modern workplace storyboard format. It featured seven fictitious staff members and incorporated everyday healthcare pain points and challenges sourced from actual interviews and focus groups with Organization B staff. The aim of the play was to generate excitement around the potential of Office 365 adoption in healthcare. The play ran for less than five minutes and served as a fun and engaging way to showcase the art of the possible with Microsoft 365.

This model blends persona profile feedback into a fun user adoption analogy that matches the business/industry—in this case, healthcare. We visited each surgery and ran Microsoft 365 clinics on adoption. We created an adoption engagement campaign with posters and a SharePoint Adoption Hub and ran Champion training workshops on Teams.

I love creating adoption analogies that complement the sector, service, or product with the customer. Over the next few years, I gained extensive experience in persona profiling and modern workplace storyboards that include the personas as actors to visualize the current challenges and then sequence, in no more than six steps, a roadmap to improve ways of working and focus on a current process or program.

For example, I made a modern workplace storyboard (see Figure A-12) for customers to appreciate how you might use Yammer and Teams together to host a leadership conference. You might add Viva Connections for Comms to announce the conference is coming and then report on how it went. You can use Viva Engage features to support it. I'll return to this later.

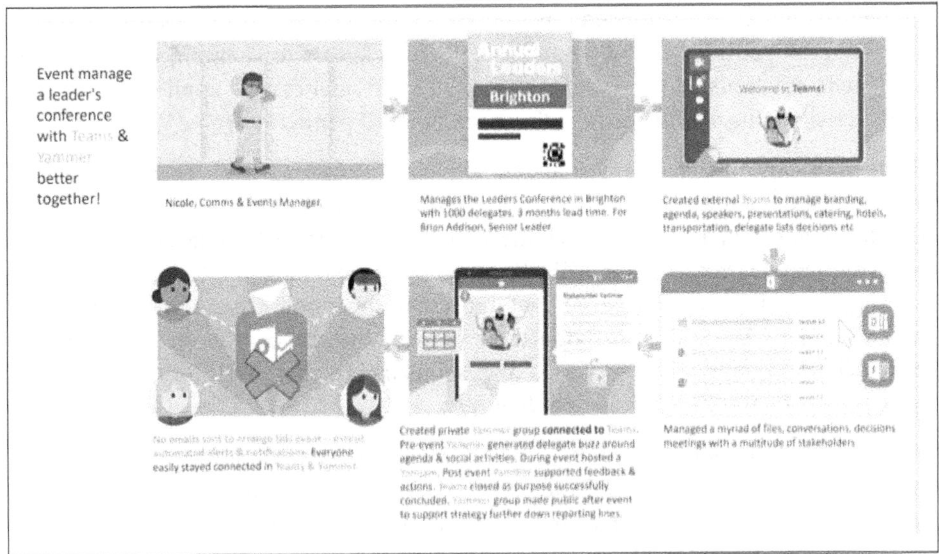

Figure A-12. The modern workplace storyboard

A.8 Identifying Teams Power Users and Creating a Champion Network

Unfortunately, too often the way to crowdsource a Champion network for change management is for the line manager to nominate staff or recruit volunteers for something they know little about, and who only show up for free swag. One of my colleagues involved in our company's adoption team used a different approach and identified the "power users" within functional areas that were already advocates of Teams, using the Microsoft Productivity Score assessment. As discussed in Recipe 10.3, the Microsoft Productivity Score assessment has since been replaced by the Adoption Score in the Purview compliance portal, which does not permit drilling down to an individual level.

I facilitated many Champion training workshops to enable a cultural change at pace with the Covid-19 pandemic. When creating a Champion network, I first look at the organization's website and its values or mission statement, and see if I can align them to working in Teams and Microsoft Viva. In most cases, this works well; Teams can make visionary core values a reality by supporting teamwork, trust, goals, responsibility, innovation, ethics, sustainability, diversity, inclusion, and, of course, customers. The first workshop thus goes beyond the usual features training with a narrative to help articulate Teams' business values and focus on a sense of community with empathy.

The purpose of Champion training workshops is to take the "power users" on a journey of discovery. To illustrate, I'll share another case study.

At one workshop, we introduced power users to the Change Curve, based on a model initially developed in the 1960s by Elisabeth Kubler-Ross for helping people understand their reactions to meaningful change. This model can be applied to any dramatic life-changing situation, including the Covid-19 pandemic.

Change resistance often involves anger, spreading rumors, or refusal to participate. You might hear comments like "It won't work," or "It used to be like that," or "We tried this before." When I introduce the Change Curve model, I engage stakeholders in identifying the current state of the business and visualizing the desired future state by marking points on the curve that represent their collective agreement. I also encourage the Champions to name their network, which can be an engaging, fun approach when supported by CTOs and sponsors. In this workshop, the network name chosen by the Champions was *Pioneers*.

We introduced the idea of a *fixed mindset*, which means a tendency to give up on challenging tasks easily or avoid things you have failed at before. People with a fixed mindset believe that being good or bad at a particular activity is a fixed state and is something they cannot control. It's better to have a *growth mindset* (a method developed by psychologist Carol Dweck) and look at problems as opportunities, which enables bouncing back quickly from failure. A growth mindset also makes you more likely to explore and discover how you can get better at doing something. You believe you can improve your abilities by practicing or finding an unusual way to achieve your goal with a curious mind.

A growth mindset is an excellent philosophy for life: you'll only know if you try! We urged staff to experiment with the new features in Teams and learn new ways of working with others. We then focused on those features. People often need clarification about when to use chat or channels, for example, so we introduced the business benefits of using channels to avoid falling back into Teams chat or using Slack or WhatsApp.

We also discussed the importance of empathy at work in challenging conditions, and understanding the feelings of others who might be experiencing anxiety due to the new ways of working. We invited the Pioneers to be "go-to people," demonstrating empathy. Teams training should be made available as part of the onboarding process, with recorded sessions covering the top features. If people are struggling with Teams, you can point them to the Teams Learn site (*https://oreil.ly/3ChOC*), or if they need more training, they can watch recorded webinars.

To instill the idea of a growth mindset, we shared ideas on how to experiment with Teams in the channels and came up with the following:

- Send praise.
- Involve passive users who hesitate to contribute.

- Brainstorm on Whiteboard.
- Try moving your Excel projects to Planner.
- Share documents and newsletters in Teams rather than by email.
- Use analytics to see how your team is being used.
- Create a fun Work/Life Balance channel.

We then ran a five-minute Whiteboard session and asked participants two questions:

1. Using sticky notes, what would you like to try in Teams?
2. For which company processes might Teams enable improvements?

We ended the workshop by telling participants "We hope to see you again at the Pioneers 'Go Beyond' workshop running next Thursday and Friday, where you will receive your Pioneers digital badge and access to the Pioneers SharePoint on Teams. The SharePoint is packed with learning and training and is a place for you to collaborate and share your successes. It's a trusted place, and remember, there is no such thing as a stupid question."

We shared a Microsoft Forms survey immediately after each session. This was how participants registered to join the Pioneers SharePoint site. We asked what they thought of the training they had just received so we could continuously improve the content.

During our second workshop, we invited the power users—those who had been using Teams for about three months and had already attended the first workshop—to take over the session and share their experiences with their peers. This was a successful approach, as almost all (99%) of the attendees returned for the second workshop.

The power users were encouraged to share their stories, frustrations, and challenges, and describe their current and intended future use of Teams. Among the various applications available within Teams, Planner was found to be the most popular among the attendees. Additionally, the use of Whiteboard and OneNote, a shared digital notebook, became popular after the workshops.

At the end of the second workshop, we surveyed attendees again and asked: What are the perceived challenges around reluctance to take up Teams? This helped clarify topics that required further engagement. We responded by facilitating more training for specialist users who might want to know more about OneNote or Planner. The biggest frustration was file management using SharePoint: managing documents at scale, lists, and retention labels. This group had an internal SharePoint and Search team, so we asked them to help their staff directly.

We encouraged them to have fun: create a dedicated Teams Playground, Staffroom, or Fun channel, play Whiteboard Hangman or Pictionary, create polls, use Breakout Rooms for quizzes, and so on. They even had DJ sessions.

During the adoption program, the employees were encouraged to use Teams more frequently and reduce their reliance on email. To promote this shift, they were advised to add a strapline to their email signature, emphasizing the importance of using Teams as the primary communication platform.

A *mail strapline* is a short statement or tagline that is added to the bottom of an email signature. It is used to convey a message or promote a specific idea or action. In the context of promoting the use of Teams over email, a strapline could be used to encourage employees to use Teams as the primary communication platform instead of relying on email.

The adoption program also introduced a "think-Teams-first" culture, which encouraged employees to start their day by reading their Viva Briefing email. This email provided a summary of their schedule for the next 12 hours, pulling data from Exchange in meetings and emails.

To wrap up their day, employees were encouraged to use the Virtual Commute feature on Teams at around 4 p.m. This feature allowed them to review their outstanding tasks and prepare for the next day's meetings.

The Teams Viva Insights app add-in was also made available to the employees as a tool to monitor their usage and adoption of Teams.

The Pioneers' digital badge proved to be immensely popular. In an organization of over 100,000 employees, these people wanted to stand out from the crowd in a highly governed public sector department. In a nutshell, the Pioneers were *not* to be the support for the whole project but would help "bang the drum" for Teams, guided by their modus operandi as described.

The third workshop was a 20-minute train-the-trainer session that included some of the content just discussed but focused on the features, applications, and training specifically for team owner responsibilities, with a deck for participants to take away and make their own.

By the end of the 10-month program, I had facilitated about 60 workshops, including team owners training with friendly and enthusiastic civil servants. Many attendees had worked in the public sector for over ten years and now loved Teams. The internal digital team curated over 30 success stories to inspire others.

A.9 Looking at Bite-Sized Adoption Tips for Teams Features

Before I move on to the adoption of Microsoft Viva, here are some more tasty tips related to what it means to be a Team owner, creating and managing a team, adding channels, creating tags, and general best practices for maintaining a successful team. The following tips were discussed in a training session with the UK government:

- There should be a minimum of three owners responsible for managing a team and its content throughout its lifecycle, as this helps share the responsibilities of managing the team. If an owner leaves, there will still be someone who's accountable.
- The default lifespan for a team is 90 days. If a team is inactive for a sustained period, the owners receive email notifications asking if they would like to renew the team.
- Add new people as you go. When adding people as you go, try to avoid creating situations where the list of members of different teams is the same.
- Upload your documents into the Files tab. Encourage team members to upload their Teams profile photos; otherwise, their profiles will show a colored box with your initials.
- Each channel has an email address, and emails can be forwarded to that channel. By doing this, you stop the "email snail trail" and start a collaborative conversation where others not included in the email are able to take appropriate steps.
- Use the Teams rich text editor (compose box) to format and color text. Include GIFs and emojis. Reserve email for a more formal means of communication.
- Praise colleagues for their work. Select the Lightbulb icon in the text toolbar and select the person you want to praise and why.
- To communicate essential things, use the Announcement feature. Your post will be more prominent in the conversation area, including the header, subheader, and background image.
- *@mention* someone or *@tag* colleagues if you want to get their attention in a conversation. Kevin Hamnett, a top-notch adoption trainer, once put it this way: "Imagine you are in a real room with 200 people in that room. You want to tell 200 people that they've done a great job, but Pradeep has done a fantastic job, so *@mention* Pradeep. Everyone else will be able to see that message when they next visit the team."
- Add Microsoft 365 applications to your channel tabs. Everyone can directly work with the right tools to enable teamwork in one platform: Planner, OneNote, Forms, SharePoint, and Whiteboard.

- Create a Work/Life Balance (or Playground, Social Club, or Noticeboard) channel for fun at work. I once ran Teams training with a company in the marine industry, and since most of the staff were on boats, I suggested they call their fun channel The Galley, which they liked.

There are many more features in Teams, but these are the ones I also tend to point out in training:

- Normalize a conversation on Teams: just *@someone* and remove their last name (*https://oreil.ly/BBqDQ*)
- Run a solo Teams meeting (*https://oreil.ly/ZtNhY*)
- Bring the outside in with LinkedIn Teams Chat (*https://oreil.ly/1Sx6_*)

Topics need to be managed in the Topic Center (*https://oreil.ly/JNuKX*). AI suggests topics, and then knowledge workers/subject matter experts curate the topics. This may become a full-time role for an individual or small team; be aware that you'll need to have insightful people prepared to curate this content.

Microsoft Graph (*https://oreil.ly/_FFzU*) is a valuable resource for gathering insights pertaining to content and knowledge across Microsoft 365. Viva Topics leverages the capabilities of Microsoft Graph to establish and expand your knowledge network. It provides seamless content integration through Search and efficient knowledge sharing via the Topic Center, topic cards, and the Yammer *#hashtags*.

New with Viva Topics and other Viva modules is *cross-solution integration* everywhere in the Microsoft 365 productivity cloud, with end-to-end security that is compliant and governed through the lens of Teams. Most companies have dozens of content management and indexing systems in sales, manufacturing, finance, HR, and other support functions. Viva Topics, with its dynamic search, has the potential to blend this data. It curates the priceless tacit knowledge that we all have in our heads, which can become explicit knowledge once you share it with collaboration features. It then becomes discoverable in the future, via Viva Topics.

Explicit knowledge is expressed and recorded as words, numbers, codes, scientific formulae, and musical notations. It's easy to communicate, store, distribute, and find in books and on the internet. At work, explicit knowledge is the tip of the knowledge iceberg found in emails and file shares. Also, the intranet is primarily a one-way push of company information. *Tacit* knowledge is an unwritten, unspoken, vast remote database of knowledge held by humans based on emotions, experiences, and observations. It's acquired through collaboration with other people and shared activities.

To get started with Viva Topics, launch the Topics admin center (*https://oreil.ly/BTr5E*). Find subject matter experts from Microsoft 365 usage reports for your users and run some experiments. Microsoft documentation provides information on how to run a trial of Viva Topics (*https://oreil.ly/yz-Ci*) and on understanding Viva Topics (*https://oreil.ly/6Bcnt*).

Microsoft is reimagining robust but underconsumed products and features and fully integrating them through the lens of Teams, making them easily accessible on mobile devices—eradicating myriad confusing standalone apps—and enabling connected collaboration across the enterprise. The goal is to improve productivity with features the customer is paying for but not consuming.

Viva is meant to improve the employee experience from when staff are hired to when they leave. Everyone is expected to create formal documentation at work from time to time. This is explicit knowledge, but we also need to spend time nurturing collaboration networks, sharing, supporting each other, and innovating.

Teams features with the SharePoint backend are the place to store our explicit knowledge. With Viva, there are now many more quick ways to share priceless tacit knowledge so that it becomes discoverable explicit knowledge.

Summary

In this appendix, I discussed the Viva suite and its cross-solution integrations with tools and services you are already paying for but might not be consuming. The Viva modules can be swiftly hooked up by IT partnering with HR, communications, marketing, or the project management office.

You only need to prepare to deploy one or two of the Viva modules at a time. With the support of a Microsoft Partner, you should assess your current business frustrations and challenges. For example, perhaps you need a new intranet or learning hub. Commission a proof of concept with a report of recommendations and next steps with costs, including setup and licenses.

I shared in this appendix the importance of a good business sponsor, the usefulness of persona profiles, modern workplace storyboards, building a small but perfectly formed Champion network using productivity scores, and capturing success stories written by the Champions, endorsed by their leaders.

Highly recommended is end user training and train-the-trainer sessions by a Microsoft Partner who offers Microsoft Cloud Incentives (MCI). These workshops are free to eligible customers and are part of the Microsoft Jumpstart Program.

Work out loud and share on Teams, Yammer, or Viva Engage and publish on Viva Connections or SharePoint News. Use whatever means appropriate to get the message out that the new tools and application features are doing a fantastic job, and employees are thriving from wherever they are working.

You should only consider Microsoft Viva if you have experience with Teams channels and appreciate that Teams is far more than a Skype for Business replacement. Implementing Viva requires thoughtful timing; it must be appropriate to the company culture and strategy and must be securely managed with compliance and governance.

Once Champions are comfortable and confident with the tools, let them have some fun. I shared examples in this appendix that helped drive a tremendous modern company culture.

This involves devoting a small budget to training and enabling cloud consumption on Teams and Microsoft 365 to the best of your ability for greater productivity and a thriving culture. Short user adoption training sessions can change the culture of your business in a matter of weeks. Sessions can be recorded and used as part of your new hire process, supported by your local Champions on Viva Learning.

Email is not dead, as it is still needed for third-party communication, Microsoft 365 alerts, and notifications. But you can start and end your day on collaborative Teams.

About the Author

Lesley Crook, a Viva Visionary and MVP on Microsoft 365 Apps & Services for seven years, is the author of this appendix. She is focused on the employee experience, employee engagement, hybrid work, adoption and change management, and Champions programs on Yammer, Teams, and now Viva. You can find Lesley on different social networks, including her blog, Viva Visionary (*https://oreil.ly/mBlOg*), and Twitter, *@Lesley_wolan*.

Index

B

C

D

E

F

G

H

I

J

K

L

M

N

O

T

U

V

W

X

Y

Z

About the Author

Fabrizio Volpe has more than 20 years of experience with Microsoft technologies (plus years with Cisco, Fortinet, and VMware, depending on the role). All those years have been spent working with real customers and real organizations that he helped succeed and develop. When he started administering IT systems, the latest Microsoft product was Windows NT 4 server. The NT4 server back then was not usually the main OS in the organization but just a small piece of a bigger and more complex infrastructure, including solutions like IBM host systems and Novell NetWare solutions.

Fabrizio has also been a proud member of the MVP community for many years and has experience with many different technologies, including Active Directory, Lync, Skype for Business, and Office Servers and Services. As Tom Stoppard has said, "Every exit is an entry somewhere else," and after his experience as an MVP, he even had an opportunity to work with Microsoft.

After 15 years working in the ICCREA banking group in Italy, he moved to the United Kingdom where he now works with large, global organizations in the unified communications/modern workplace field.

Fabrizio has never been shy about sharing his expertise with other members of the Microsoft community. He is an author, online trainer, and conference speaker. You can find his published work on Microsoft solutions at *modern-workplace.uk*.

Colophon

The animal on the cover of *Microsoft Teams Administration Cookbook* is the collared pratincole (*Glareola pratincola*), which is also known by the names common pratincole and red-winged pratincole.

Collared pratincoles are small birds with short legs, long pointed wings, and a long forked tail. They have a short bill with a red base, and their tail streamers are longer than their wing tips. Adults are mostly gray-brown, with darker brown on their wings and white on their bellies. Their preferred habitat is open country, such as grasslands and wetlands. During the evening, they gravitate toward water, sweeping back and forth to catch and eat insects. While they mostly hunt during flight, they occasionally feed on the ground. They can be found in warmer parts of Europe, southwest Asia, and Africa.

The conservation status (IUCN) of the collared pratincole is "Least Concern." Many of the animals on O'Reilly covers are endangered; all of them are important to the world.

The cover illustration is by Karen Montgomery, based on an antique line engraving from *Shaw's Zoology*. The cover fonts are Gilroy Semibold and Guardian Sans. The text font is Adobe Minion Pro; the heading font is Adobe Myriad Condensed; and the code font is Dalton Maag's Ubuntu Mono.

Printed in the USA
CPSIA information can be obtained
at www.ICGtesting.com
JSHW051652201123
52414JS00010B/76